the *illustrated* Bible

New Testament

With Selected Psalms & Proverbs

New International Reader's Version®

BiblesPlus
1-866-9BIBLES
www.biblesplus.com

CONTRIBUTORS

Bob Edwards, Project Director
CKA, Project Editor
Chip Johnson, Master Artist - Durango, Colorado
Ron Wheeler, Contributing Artist - Kansas City, Kansas
Jennifer Johnson, Contributing Artist - Silverado, California
Lyndsey Barrett, Graphic Designer/Layout
Trey Johnson, Graphic Design/Layout
Dr. Merilyn Copeland, Contirbuting Editor
Dr. Jeff Hargis, Contirbuting Editor

Published by: BiblesPlus - 1(866)924-2537 - www.biblesplus.com

Printed in the United States.   Twelth Edition October 2015

Steps to Peace with God

Step 1   God's Purpose: Peace and Life

God loves you and wants you to experience peace and life–abundant and eternal.

The Bible Says . . .

"We have peace with God through our Lord Jesus Christ." Romans 5:1, NKJV

"For God so loved the world that He gave His only begotten Son, that whoever believes in Him should not perish but have everlasting life." John 3:16, NKJV

"I have come that they may have life, and that they may have it more abundantly." John 10:10, NKJV

Since God planned for us to have peace and the abundant life right now, why are most people not having this experience?

Step 2   Our Problem: Separation

God created us in His own image to have an abundant life. He did not make us as robots to automatically love and obey Him, but gave us a will and freedom of choice.

We chose to disobey God and go our own willful way. We still make this choice today. This results in separation from God.

Our choice results in separation from God.

The Bible Says . . .

"For all have sinned and fall short of the glory of God." Romans 3:23, NKJV

"For the wages of sin is death, but the gift of God is eternal life in Christ Jesus our Lord." Romans 6:23, NKJV

Our Attempts

There is only one remedy for this problem of separation.

Through the ages, individuals have tried in many ways to bridge this gap . . . without success . . .

The Bible Says . . .

"There is a way that seems right to a man, but in the end it leads to death." Proverbs 14:12, NIV

"But your iniquities have separated you from your God; and your sins have hidden His face from you, so that He will not hear." Isaiah 59:2, NKJV

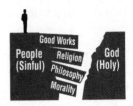

Step 3 God's Remedy: The Cross

Jesus Christ is the only answer to this problem. He died on the Cross and rose from the grave, paying the penalty for our sin and bridging the gap between God and people.

The Bible Says . . .

"For there is one God and one mediator between God and men, the man Christ Jesus." 1 Timothy 2:5, NIV

"For Christ also suffered once for sins, the just for the unjust, that He might bring us to God." 1 Peter 3:18, NKJV

"But God demonstrates his own love for us in this: While we were still sinners, Christ died for us." Romans 5:8, NIV

God has provided the only way . . . we must make the choice . . .

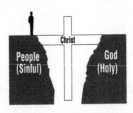

Step 4 | Our Response:
Receive Christ

We must trust Jesus Christ and receive Him by personal invitation.

The Bible Says . . .

"Behold, I stand at the door and knock. If anyone hears My voice and opens the door, I will come in to him and dine with him, and he with Me." Revelation 3:20, NKJV

Are you here . . . or here?

"But as many as received Him, to them He gave the right to become children of God, to those who believe in His name." John 1:12, NKJV

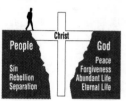

"If you confess with your mouth the Lord Jesus and believe in your heart that God has raised Him from the dead, you will be saved." Romans 10:9, NKJV

Is there any good reason why you cannot receive Jesus Christ right now?

How to receive Christ:

1. Admit your need (I am a sinner).
2. Be willing to turn from your sins (repent).
3. Believe that Jesus Christ died for you on the Cross and rose from the grave.
4. Through prayer, invite Jesus Christ to come in and control your life through the Holy Spirit. (Receive Him as Lord and Savior.)

What to Pray:

Dear Lord Jesus,
I know that I am a sinner and need Your forgiveness. I believe that You died for my sins. I want to turn from my sins. I now invite You to come into my heart and life. I want to trust and follow You as Lord and Savior.

In Jesus' name. Amen

_____   _____
Date   Signature

God's Assurance:
His Word

If you prayed this prayer,

The Bible Says . . .

"For 'whoever will call upon the name of the Lord will be saved.' " Romans 10:13, NASB

Did you sincerely ask Jesus Christ to come into your life? Where is He right now? What has He given you?

"For it is by grace you have been saved, through faith–and this not from yourselves, it is the gift of God–not by works, so that no one can boast." Ephesians 2:8,9, NIV

The
Bible Says . . .

"He who has the Son has life; he who does not have the Son of God does not have life. These things I have written to you who believe in the name of the Son of God, that you may know that you have eternal life, and that you may continue to believe in the name of the Son of God." 1 John 5:12-13, NKJV

Receiving Christ, we are born into God's family through the supernatural work of the Holy Spirit who indwells every believer . . . this is called regeneration or the "new birth."

This is just the beginning of a wonderful new life in Christ. To deepen this relationship you should:

1. Read your Bible every day to know Christ better.
2. Talk to God in prayer every day.
3. Tell others about Christ.
4. Worship, fellowship, and serve with other Christians in a church where Christ is preached.
5. As Christ's representative in a needy world, demonstrate your new life by your love and concern for others.

God bless you as you do.

Billy Graham

If you want further help in the decision you have made, write to:
Billy Graham Evangelistic Association,
1 Billy Graham Parkway, Charlotte, North Carolina 28201-0001

Contents...

New Testament

Selected Psalms & Proverbs

Answers to Tough Issues

Jesus said

"I AM ..."

"The Good Shepherd"

"The True Vine"

"I Am He"   "The Light of the World"

"The Door to the Sheepfold"

"The Resurrection and the Life"

"Before Abraham"

"The Bread of Life"

"The Way, the Truth and the Life"

MATTHEW

- *Links Old Testament prophecies with Jesus as the Messiah*
- *Written by Matthew, formally a despised tax collector*
- *Matthew was one of the 12 Apostles chosen by Jesus*
- *Written to the Jews*
- *Focuses on the "Kingdom of Heaven"*
- *Theme: "Jesus as King"*

The Family Line of Jesus

1 This is a record of the family line of Jesus Christ. He is the son of David. He is also the son of Abraham.

² Abraham was the father of Isaac.
Isaac was the father of Jacob.
Jacob was the father of Judah and his brothers.
³ Judah was the father of Perez and Zerah. Tamar was their mother.
Perez was the father of Hezron.
Hezron was the father of Ram.
⁴ Ram was the father of Amminadab.
Amminadab was the father of Nahshon.
Nahshon was the father of Salmon.
⁵ Salmon was the father of Boaz. Rahab was Boaz's mother.
Boaz was the father of Obed. Ruth was Obed's mother.
Obed was the father of Jesse.
⁶ And Jesse was the father of King David.

David was the father of Solomon. Solomon's mother had been Uriah's wife.
⁷ Solomon was the father of Rehoboam.
Rehoboam was the father of Abijah.
Abijah was the father of Asa.
⁸ Asa was the father of Jehoshaphat.
Jehoshaphat was the father of Jehoram.
Jehoram was the father of Uzziah.
⁹ Uzziah was the father of Jotham.
Jotham was the father of Ahaz.
Ahaz was the father of Hezekiah.
¹⁰ Hezekiah was the father of Manasseh.
Manasseh was the father of Amon.
Amon was the father of Josiah.
¹¹ And Josiah was the father of Jeconiah and his brothers. At that time, the Jewish people were forced to go away to Babylon.
¹² After this, the family line continued.
Jeconiah was the father of Shealtiel.
Shealtiel was the father of Zerubbabel.
¹³ Zerubbabel was the father of Abiud.
Abiud was the father of Eliakim.
Eliakim was the father of Azor.
¹⁴ Azor was the father of Zadok.
Zadok was the father of Akim.
Akim was the father of Eliud.
¹⁵ Eliud was the father of Eleazar.
Eleazar was the father of Matthan.
Matthan was the father of Jacob.
¹⁶ Jacob was the father of Joseph. Joseph was the husband of Mary. And Mary gave birth to Jesus, who is called Christ.

¹⁷ So there were 14 generations from Abraham to David. There were 14 from David until the Jewish people were forced to go away to Babylon. And there were 14 from that time to the Christ.

Jesus Christ Is Born

¹⁸ This is how the birth of Jesus Christ came about. His mother Mary and Joseph had promised to get married. But before they started to live together, it became clear that she was going to have a baby. She became pregnant by the power of the

Holy Spirit. [19]Her husband Joseph was a godly man. He did not want to put her to shame in public. So he planned to divorce her quietly.

[20]But as Joseph was thinking about this, an angel of the Lord appeared to him in a dream. The angel said, "Joseph, son of David, don't be afraid to take Mary home as your wife. The baby inside her is from the Holy Spirit. [21]She is going to have a son. You must give him the name Jesus. That is because he will save his people from their sins."

[22]All of this took place to bring about what the Lord had said would happen. He had said through the prophet, [23]"The virgin is going to have a baby. She will give birth to a son. And he will be called Immanuel." *(Isaiah 7:14)* The name Immanuel means "God with us."

[24]Joseph woke up. He did what the angel of the Lord commanded him to do. He took Mary home as his wife. [25]But he did not make love to her until after she gave birth to a son. And Joseph gave him the name Jesus.

The Wise Men Visit Jesus

2 Jesus was born in Bethlehem in Judea. This happened while Herod was king of Judea.

After Jesus' birth, Wise Men from the east came to Jerusalem. [2]They asked, "Where is the child who has been born to be king of the Jews? When we were in the east, we saw his star. Now we have come to worship him."

[3]When King Herod heard about it, he was very upset. Everyone in Jerusalem was troubled too. [4]So Herod called together all the chief priests of the people. He also called the teachers of the law. He asked them where the Christ was going to be born.

[5]"In Bethlehem in Judea," they replied. "This is what the prophet has written. He said,

[6]" 'But you, Bethlehem, in the land of Judah,

are certainly not the least important among the towns of Judah.

A ruler will come out of you.

He will be the shepherd of my people Israel.' " *(Micah 5:2)*

[7]Then Herod called for the Wise Men secretly. He found out from them exactly when the star had appeared. [8]He sent them to Bethlehem. He said, "Go! Make a careful search for the child. As soon as you find him, bring me a report. Then I can go and worship him too."

[9]After the Wise Men had listened to the king, they went on their way. The star they had seen when they were in the east went ahead of them. It finally stopped over the place where the child was. [10]When they saw the star, they were filled with joy.

[11]The Wise Men went to the house. There they saw the child with his mother Mary. They bowed down and worshiped him. Then they opened their treasures. They gave him gold, incense and myrrh.

[12]But God warned them in a dream not to go back to Herod. So they returned to their country on a different road.

Jesus' Family Escapes to Egypt

[13]When the Wise Men had left, Joseph had a dream. In the dream an angel of the Lord appeared to him. "Get up!" the angel said. "Take the child and his mother and escape to Egypt. Stay there until I tell you to come back. Herod is going to search for the child. He wants to kill him."

[14]Joseph got up. During the night, he left for Egypt with the child and his mother Mary. [15]They stayed there until King Herod died. So the words the Lord had spoken through the prophet came true. He had said, "I chose to bring my son out of Egypt." *(Hosea 11:1)*

[16]Herod realized that the Wise Men had tricked him. So he became very angry. He gave orders concerning Bethlehem and the area around it. All the boys two years old and under were to be killed. This agreed with the time when the Wise Men had seen the star.

[17]In this way, the words the prophet Jeremiah spoke came true. He had said,

[18] "A voice is heard in Ramah.

It's the sound of crying and deep
sadness.
Rachel is crying over her children.
She refuses to be comforted,
because they are gone."   *(Jeremiah 31:15)*

Jesus' Family Returns to Nazareth

[19] After Herod died, Joseph had a dream while he was still in Egypt. In the dream an angel of the Lord appeared to him. [20] The angel said, "Get up! Take the child and his mother. Go to the land of Israel. Those who were trying to kill the child are dead."

[21] So Joseph got up. He took the child and his mother Mary back to the land of Israel. [22] But then he heard that Archelaus was king of Judea. Archelaus was ruling in place of his father Herod. This made Joseph afraid to go there.

Warned in a dream, Joseph went back to the land of Galilee instead. [23] There he lived in a town called Nazareth. So what the prophets had said about Jesus came true. They had said, "He will be called a Nazarene."

John the Baptist Prepares the Way

3 In those days John the Baptist came and preached in the Desert of Judea. [2] He said, "Turn away from your sins! The kingdom of heaven is near."

[3] John is the one the prophet Isaiah had spoken about. He had said,

"A messenger is calling out in the desert,
'Prepare the way for the Lord.
Make straight paths for him.' "
(Isaiah 40:3)

[4] John's clothes were made out of camel's hair. He had a leather belt around his waist. His food was locusts and wild honey. [5] People went out to him from Jerusalem and all of Judea. They also came from the whole area around the Jordan River. [6] When they admitted they had sinned, John baptized them in the Jordan.

[7] John saw many Pharisees and Sadducees coming to where he was baptizing. He said to them, "You are like a nest of poisonous snakes! Who warned you to escape the

By The Numbers

300+
prophecies in the Old Testament regarding the coming of Christ which have been fulfilled

Over **60** quotes from Isaiah in the New Testament

20 of the 27 New Testament books have direct quotes from Isaiah

REPENT!

coming of God's anger? [8] Produce fruit that shows you have turned away from your sins. [9] Don't think you can say to yourselves, 'Abraham is our father.' I tell you, God can raise up children for Abraham even from these stones. [10] The ax is already lying at the roots of the trees. All the trees that don't produce good fruit will be cut down. They will be thrown into the fire.

[11]"I baptize you with water, calling you to turn away from your sins. But after me, one will come who is more powerful than I am. And I'm not fit to carry his sandals. He will baptize you with the Holy Spirit and with fire. [12]His pitchfork is in his hand to clear the straw from his threshing floor. He will gather his wheat into the storeroom. But he will burn up the husks with fire that can't be put out."

Jesus Is Baptized

[13]Jesus came from Galilee to the Jordan River. He wanted to be baptized by John. [14]But John tried to stop him. He told Jesus, "I need to be baptized by you. So why do you come to me?"

[15]Jesus replied, "Let it be this way for now. It is right for us to do this. It carries out God's holy plan." Then John agreed.

[16]As soon as Jesus was baptized, he came up out of the water. At that moment heaven was opened. Jesus saw the Spirit of God coming down on him like a dove.

[17]A voice from heaven said, "This is my Son, and I love him. I am very pleased with him."

Jesus Is Tempted

4 The Holy Spirit led Jesus into the desert. There the devil tempted him. [2]After 40 days and 40 nights of going without eating, Jesus was hungry.

[3]The tempter came to him. He said, "If you are the Son of God, tell these stones to become bread."

[4]Jesus answered, "It is written, 'Man doesn't live only on bread. He also lives on every word that comes from the mouth of God.' " *(Deuteronomy 8:3)*

[5]Then the devil took Jesus to the holy city. He had him stand on the highest point of the temple. [6]"If you are the Son of God," he said, "throw yourself down. It is written,

" 'The Lord will command his angels to take good care of you.
They will lift you up in their hands.

Then you won't trip over a stone.' "
(Psalm 91:11,12)

[7]Jesus answered him, "It is also written, 'Do not put the Lord your God to the test.' " *(Deuteronomy 6:16)*

[8]Finally, the devil took Jesus to a very high mountain. He showed him all the kingdoms of the world and their glory. [9]"If you bow down and worship me," he said, "I will give you all of this."

[10]Jesus said to him, "Get away from me, Satan! It is written, 'Worship the Lord your God. He is the only one you should serve.' " *(Deuteronomy 6:13)*

[11]Then the devil left Jesus. Angels came and took care of him.

Jesus Begins to Preach

[12]John had been put in prison. When Jesus heard about this, he returned to Galilee.

[13]Jesus left Nazareth. He went to live in the city of Capernaum. It was by the lake in the area of Zebulun and Naphtali. [14]In that way, what the prophet Isaiah had said came true. He had said,

[15] "Land of Zebulun! Land of Naphtali!
     Galilee, where non-Jewish people live!
     Land along the Mediterranean Sea!
          Territory east of the Jordan River!
[16] The people who are now living in
          darkness
     will see a great light.
     They are now living in a very dark land.
     But a light will shine on them."
(Isaiah 9:1,2)

[17]From that time on Jesus began to preach. "Turn away from your sins!" he said. "The kingdom of heaven is near."

Jesus Chooses the First Disciples

[18]One day Jesus was walking beside the Sea of Galilee. There he saw two brothers. They were Simon Peter and his brother Andrew. They were throwing a net into the lake. They were fishermen. [19]"Come. Follow me," Jesus said. "I will make you fishers of people."

[20]At once they left their nets and followed him.

A Bible Reading Plan

Through the New Testament in 30 days

	DAY	PASSAGE
☐	1	Matthew 1-9
☐	2	Matthew 10-15
☐	3	Matthew 16-22
☐	4	Matthew 23-28
☐	5	Mark 1-8
☐	6	Mark 9-16
☐	7	Luke 1-6
☐	8	Luke 7-11
☐	9	Luke 12-18
☐	10	Luke 19-24
☐	11	John 1-7
☐	12	John 8-13
☐	13	John 14-21
☐	14	Acts 1-7
☐	15	Acts 8-14
☐	16	Acts 15-21
☐	17	Acts 22-28
☐	18	Romans 1-8
☐	19	Romans 9-16
☐	20	1 Corinthians 1-9
☐	21	1 Corinthians 10-16
☐	22	2 Corinthians
☐	23	Galatians-Ephesians
☐	24	Philippians-2 Thessalonians
☐	25	1 Timothy-Philemon
☐	26	Hebrews
☐	27	James-2 Peter
☐	28	1 John-Jude
☐	29	Revelation 1-11
☐	30	Revelation 12-22

²¹Going on from there, he saw two other brothers. They were James, son of Zebedee, and his brother John. They were in a boat with their father Zebedee. As they were preparing their nets, Jesus called out to them.

²²Right away they left the boat and their father and followed Jesus.

Jesus Heals Sick People

²³Jesus went all over Galilee. There he taught in the synagogues. He preached the good news of God's kingdom. He healed every illness and sickness the people had.

²⁴News about him spread all over Syria. People brought to him all who were ill with different kinds of sicknesses. Some were suffering great pain. Others were controlled by demons. Some were shaking wildly. Others couldn't move at all. And Jesus healed all of them.

²⁵Large crowds followed him. Some people came from Galilee, from the area known as the Ten Cities, and from Jerusalem and Judea. Others came from the area across the Jordan River.

Jesus Gives Blessings

5 Jesus saw the crowds. So he went up on a mountainside and sat down. His disciples came to him. ²Then he began to teach them.

He said,

³ "Blessed are those who are spiritually needy.
   The kingdom of heaven belongs to them.
⁴ Blessed are those who are sad.
   They will be comforted.
⁵ Blessed are those who are free of pride.
   They will be given the earth.
⁶ Blessed are those who are hungry and thirsty for what is right.
   They will be filled.
⁷ Blessed are those who show mercy.
   They will be shown mercy.
⁸ Blessed are those whose hearts are pure.
   They will see God.
⁹ Blessed are those who make peace.
   They will be called sons of God.
¹⁰ Blessed are those who suffer for doing what is right.
   The kingdom of heaven belongs to them.

¹¹"Blessed are you when people make fun of you and hurt you because of me. You are also blessed when they tell all kinds of evil lies about you because of me. ¹²Be joyful and glad. Your reward in heaven is great. In the same way, people hurt the prophets who lived long ago.

Salt and Light

¹³"You are the salt of the earth. But suppose the salt loses its saltiness. How can it be made salty again? It is no longer good for anything. It will be thrown out. People will walk all over it.

¹⁴"You are the light of the world. A city

God **Blesses** Those Who Seek Him

hearts are pure

hunger and thirst for justice

seek peace

merciful

persecuted for following Christ

realize need for God

Matthew 5

The Beatitudes

on a hill can't be hidden. ¹⁵Also, people do not light a lamp and put it under a bowl. Instead, they put it on its stand. Then it gives light to everyone in the house.

¹⁶"In the same way, let your light shine in front of others. Then they will see the good things you do. And they will praise your Father who is in heaven.

Jesus Gives Full Meaning to the Law

¹⁷"Do not think I have come to get rid of what is written in the Law or in the Prophets. I have not come to do that. Instead, I have come to give full meaning to what is written. ¹⁸What I'm about to tell you is true. Heaven and earth will disappear before the smallest letter disappears from the Law. Not even the smallest stroke of a pen will disappear from the Law until everything is completed.

¹⁹"Do not break even one of the least important commandments. And do not teach others to break them. If you do, you will be called the least important person in the kingdom of heaven. Instead, practice and teach these commands. Then you will be called important in the kingdom of heaven.

²⁰"Here is what I tell you. You must be more godly than the Pharisees and the teachers of the law. If you are not, you will certainly not enter the kingdom of heaven.

Murder

²¹"You have heard what was said to people who lived long ago. They were told, 'Do not commit murder. *(Exodus 20:13)* Anyone who murders will be judged for it.' ²²But here is what I tell you. Do not be angry with your brother. Anyone who is angry with his brother will be judged. Again, anyone who says to his brother, 'Raca,' must stand trial in the Sanhedrin. But anyone who says, 'You fool!' will be in danger of the fire in hell.

²³"Suppose you are offering your gift at the altar. And you remember that your brother has something against you. ²⁴Leave your gift in front of the altar. First go and make peace with your brother. Then come back and offer your gift.

²⁵"Suppose someone has a claim against you and is taking you to court. Settle the matter quickly. Do it while you are still with him on your way. If you don't, he may hand you over to the judge. The judge may hand you over to the officer. And you may be thrown into prison. ²⁶What I'm about to tell you is true. You will not get out until you have paid the very last penny!

Adultery

²⁷"You have heard that it was said, 'Do not commit adultery.' *(Exodus 20:14)* ²⁸But here is what I tell you. Do not even look at a woman in the wrong way. Anyone who does has already committed adultery with her in her heart.

²⁹"If your right eye causes you to sin, poke it out and throw it away. Your eye is only one part of your body. It is better to lose it than for your whole body to be thrown into hell.

God Rewards Those Who Are Faithful

inherit the earth — called children of God — will see God — receive justice — receive Kingdom of Heaven — comforted by God

The Beatitudes

Matthew 5

30"If your right hand causes you to sin, cut it off and throw it away. Your hand is only one part of your body. It is better to lose it than for your whole body to go into hell.

Divorce

31"It has been said, 'Suppose a man divorces his wife. If he does, he must give her a letter of divorce.' *(Deuteronomy 24:1)* 32But here is what I tell you. Anyone who divorces his wife causes her to commit adultery. And anyone who gets married to the divorced woman commits adultery. A man may divorce his wife only if she has not been faithful to him.

Oaths

33"Again, you have heard what was said to your people long ago. They were told, 'Do not break the promises you make to the Lord. Keep the oaths you have made to him.' 34But here is what I tell you. Do not make any promises like that at all. Do not make them in the name of heaven. That is God's throne. 35Do not make them in the name of the earth. That is the stool for God's feet. Do not make them in the name of Jerusalem. That is the city of the Great King. 36And do not take an oath in the name of your head. You can't make even one hair white or black.

37"Just let your 'Yes' mean 'Yes.' Let your 'No' mean 'No.' Anything more than this comes from the evil one.

Be Kind to Others

38"You have heard that it was said, 'An eye must be put out for an eye. A tooth must be knocked out for a tooth.' *(Exodus 21:24; Leviticus 24:20; Deuteronomy 19:21)* 39But here is what I tell you. Do not fight against an evil person.

"Suppose someone hits you on your right cheek. Turn your other cheek to him also. 40Suppose someone takes you to court to get your shirt. Let him have your coat also. 41Suppose someone forces you to go one mile. Go two miles with him.

42"Give to the one who asks you for something. Don't turn away from the one who wants to borrow something from you.

Love Your Enemies

43"You have heard that it was said, 'Love your neighbor. *(Leviticus 19:18)* Hate your enemy.' 44But here is what I tell you. Love your enemies. Pray for those who hurt you. 45Then you will be sons of your Father who is in heaven.

"He causes his sun to shine on evil people and good people. He sends rain on those who do right and those who don't.

46"If you love those who love you, what reward will you get? Even the tax collectors do that. 47If you greet only your own people, what more are you doing than others? Even people who are ungodly do that. 48So be perfect, just as your Father in heaven is perfect.

Giving to Needy People

6 "Be careful not to do 'good works' in front of others. Don't do them to be seen by others. If you do, your Father in heaven will not reward you.

2"When you give to needy people, do not announce it by having trumpets blown. Do not be like those who only pretend to be holy. They announce what they do in the synagogues and on the streets. They want to be honored by others. What I'm about to tell you is true. They have received their complete reward.

3"When you give to the needy, don't let your left hand know what your right hand is doing. 4Then your giving will be done secretly. Your Father will reward you. He sees what you do secretly.

Prayer

5"When you pray, do not be like those who only pretend to be holy. They love to stand and pray in the synagogues and on the street corners. They want to be seen by others. What I'm about to tell you is true. They have received their complete reward.

6"When you pray, go into your room. Close the door and pray to your Father, who can't be seen. He will reward you. Your Father sees what is done secretly.

7"When you pray, do not keep talking on and on the way ungodly people do. They think they will be heard because they talk

You are Salt • You are Light

Salt - inward character - "Being"
Light - outward action - "Doing"

"You are the salt of the earth."
Matthew 5:13

Salt is Being

Protects against decay, corruption and sin.

"Have salt in yourselves."
Mark 9:50

Stimulates spiritual appetite of joy, zeal, and to know God

"You are the light of the world."
Matthew 5:14

Light is Doing

Illuminates, shines, shows the way - as a lighthouse

"Let your light shine in front of others ..."
Matthew 5:16

Warmth from flame welcomes wanderers in from the cold, harsh world

Why Salt?   Why Light?

Praise   Worship   Love   Honor

Extol   Exalt

Reverence   **Glory of God**   Adore

Respect   Devotion

a lot. [8]Do not be like them. Your Father knows what you need even before you ask him.

[9]"This is how you should pray.

" 'Our Father in heaven,
may your name be honored.
[10]May your kingdom come.
May what you want to happen be done
on earth as it is done in heaven.
[11]Give us today our daily bread.
[12]Forgive us our sins,
just as we also have forgiven those who
sin against us.
[13]Keep us from falling into sin when we are
tempted.
Save us from the evil one.'

[14]"Forgive people when they sin against you. If you do, your Father who is in heaven will also forgive you. [15]But if you do not forgive people their sins, your Father will not forgive your sins.

Fasting

[16]"When you go without eating, do not look gloomy like those who only pretend to be holy. They make their faces very sad. They want to show people they are fasting. What I'm about to tell you is true. They have received their complete reward.

[17]"But when you go without eating, put olive oil on your head. Wash your face. [18]Then others will not know that you are fasting. Only your Father, who can't be seen, will know it. He will reward you. Your Father sees what is done secretly.

Put Away Riches in Heaven

[19]"Do not put away riches for yourselves on earth. Moths and rust can destroy them. Thieves can break in and steal them. [20]Instead, put away riches for yourselves in heaven. There, moths and rust do not destroy them. There, thieves do not break in and steal them. [21]Your heart will be where your riches are.

[22]"The eye is like a lamp for the body. Suppose your eyes are good. Then your whole body will be full of light. [23]But suppose your eyes are bad. Then your whole body will be full of darkness. If the light inside you is darkness, then it is very dark!

[24]"No one can serve two masters at the same time. He will hate one of them and love the other. Or he will be faithful to one and dislike the other. You can't serve God and Money at the same time.

Do Not Worry

[25]"I tell you, do not worry. Don't worry about your life and what you will eat or drink. And don't worry about your body and what you will wear. Isn't there more to life than eating? Aren't there more important things for the body than clothes?

[26]"Look at the birds of the air. They don't plant or gather crops. They don't put away crops in storerooms. But your Father who is in heaven feeds them. Aren't you worth much more than they are?

[27]"Can you add even one hour to your life by worrying?

[28]"And why do you worry about clothes?

See how the wild flowers grow. They don't work or make clothing. [29]But here is what I tell you. Not even Solomon in all of his glory was dressed like one of those flowers.

[30]"If that is how God dresses the wild grass, won't he dress you even better? After all, the grass is here only today. Tomorrow it is thrown into the fire. Your faith is so small!

[31]"So don't worry. Don't say, 'What will we eat?' Or, 'What will we drink?' Or, 'What will we wear?' [32]People who are ungodly run after all of those things. Your Father who is in heaven knows that you need them.

[33]"But put God's kingdom first. Do what he wants you to do. Then all of those things will also be given to you.

[34]"So don't worry about tomorrow. Tomorrow will worry about itself. Each day has enough trouble of its own.

Be Fair When You Judge Others

7 "Do not judge others. Then you will not be judged. [2]You will be judged in the same way you judge others. You will be measured in the same way you measure others.

[3]"You look at the bit of sawdust in your friend's eye. But you pay no attention to the piece of wood in your own eye. [4]How can you say to your friend, 'Let me take the bit of sawdust out of your eye'? How can you say this while there is a piece of wood in your own eye?

[5]"You pretender! First take the piece of wood out of your own eye. Then you will be able to see clearly to take the bit of sawdust out of your friend's eye.

[6]"Do not give holy things to dogs. Do not throw your pearls to pigs. If you do, they might walk all over them. Then they might turn around and tear you to pieces.

Ask, Search, Knock

[7]"Ask, and it will be given to you. Search, and you will find. Knock, and the door will be opened to you. [8]Everyone who asks will receive. He who searches will find. The door will be opened to the one who knocks.

[9]"Suppose your son asks for bread. Which of you will give him a stone? [10]Or suppose he asks for a fish. Which of you will give him a snake? [11]Even though you are evil, you know how to give good gifts to your children. How much more will your Father who is in heaven give good gifts to those who ask him!

[12]"In everything, do to others what you would want them to do to you. This is what is written in the Law and in the Prophets.

The Large and Small Gates

[13]"Enter God's kingdom through the narrow gate. The gate is large and the road is wide that lead to death and hell. Many people go that way. [14]But the gate is small and the road is narrow that lead to life. Only a few people find it.

A Tree and Its Fruit

[15]"Watch out for false prophets. They come to you pretending to be sheep. But on the inside they are hungry wolves. [16]You can

tell what they really are by what they do.

"Do people pick grapes from bushes? Do they pick figs from thorns? [17]In the same way, every good tree bears good fruit. But a bad tree bears bad fruit. [18]A good tree can't bear bad fruit. And a bad tree can't bear good fruit. [19]Every tree that does not bear good fruit is cut down. It is thrown into the fire. [20]You can tell each tree by its fruit.

[21]"Not everyone who says to me, 'Lord, Lord,' will enter the kingdom of heaven. Only those who do what my Father in heaven wants will enter.

[22]"Many will say to me on that day, 'Lord! Lord! Didn't we prophesy in your name? Didn't we drive out demons in your name? Didn't we do many miracles in your name?' [23]Then I will tell them clearly, 'I never knew you. Get away from me, you who do evil!'

The Wise and Foolish Builders

[24]"So then, everyone who hears my words and puts them into practice is like a wise man. He builds his house on the rock. [25]The rain comes down. The water rises. The winds blow and beat against that house. But it does not fall. It is built on the rock.

[26]"But everyone who hears my words and does not put them into practice is like a foolish man. He builds his house on sand. [27]The rain comes down. The water rises. The winds blow and beat against that house. And it falls with a loud crash."

[28]Jesus finished saying all these things. The crowds were amazed at his teaching. [29]He taught like one who had authority. He did not speak like their teachers of the law.

Jesus Heals a Man Who Had a Skin Disease

8 Jesus came down from the mountainside. Large crowds followed him. [2]A man who had a skin disease came and got down on his knees in front of Jesus. He said, "Lord, if you are willing to make me 'clean,' you can do it."

[3]Jesus reached out his hand and touched the man. "I am willing to do it," he said. "Be 'clean'!"

Right away the man was healed of his skin disease.

[4]Then Jesus said to him, "Don't tell anyone. Go and show yourself to the priest. Offer the gift Moses commanded. It will be a witness to them."

A Roman Commander Has Faith

[5]When Jesus entered Capernaum, a Roman commander came to him. He asked Jesus for help. [6]"Lord," he said, "my servant lies at home and can't move. He is suffering terribly."

[7]Jesus said, "I will go and heal him."

[8]The commander replied, "Lord, I am not good enough to have you come into my house. But just say the word, and my servant will be healed. [9]I myself am a man under authority. And I have soldiers who obey my orders. I tell this one, 'Go,' and he goes. I tell that one, 'Come,' and he comes. I say to my servant, 'Do this,' and he does it."

[10]When Jesus heard this, he was amazed. He said to those following him, "What I'm about to tell you is true. In Israel I have not found anyone whose faith is so strong.

[11]"I say to you that many will come from the east and the west. They will take their places at the feast in the kingdom of heaven. They will sit with Abraham, Isaac and Jacob. [12]But those who think they belong to the kingdom will be thrown outside, into the darkness. There they will sob and grind their teeth."

[13]Then Jesus said to the Roman commander, "Go! It will be done just as you believed it would."

And his servant was healed at that very hour.

Jesus Heals Many People

[14]When Jesus came into Peter's house, he saw Peter's mother-in-law. She was lying in bed. She had a fever.

[15]Jesus touched her hand, and the fever left her. She got up and began to wait on him.

[16]When evening came, many people controlled by demons were brought to Jesus. He drove out the spirits with a word. He healed all who were sick.

Hidden Message Puzzle

Find the hidden words on the tape below that make up the complete message

SECRET, KEEP OUT!

```
WLT D O D B R N O T L K R
B E P D L A M S B C A R B O N J F L P M S K C O P Y Q R S T
P O F L F M W P B S K L S O M E O N E F H I J K E L S E Q S
B K L W M S I J K L M A K E W P Y Z S G D F G H I J K R V N
M G Z P Q Y O U R V W X B Z R P H L G M X O W N K L P L Q Z
P D M G H I M P R E S S I O N C D T S P L M S R M T B P S T
```

Circle each hidden word on the tape and place in the space below. Check your decoding skills with the answer at the bottom of page 303 in the Illustrated New Testament.

1. _ _   2. _ _ _   3. _ _   4. _

5. _ _ _ _ _ _   6. _ _ _ _   7. _ _

8. _ _ _ _ _ _ _   9. _ _ _ _ ...

10. _ _ _ _   11. _ _ _ _ _   12. _ _ _

13. _ _ _ _ _ _ _ _ _ _ .

[17]He did it to make what the prophet Isaiah had said come true. He had said,

"He suffered the things we should have suffered.
He took on himself the sicknesses that should have been ours."

(*Isaiah 53:4*)

It Costs to Follow Jesus

[18]Jesus saw the crowd around him. So he gave his disciples orders to go to the other side of the Sea of Galilee.

[19]Then a teacher of the law came to him. He said, "Teacher, I will follow you no matter where you go."

[20]Jesus replied, "Foxes have holes. Birds of the air have nests. But the Son of Man has no place to lay his head."

[21]Another follower said to him, "Lord, first let me go and bury my father."

[22]But Jesus told him, "Follow me. Let the dead bury their own dead."

Jesus Calms the Storm

[23]Jesus got into a boat. His disciples followed him. [24]Suddenly a terrible storm came up on the lake. The waves crashed over the boat. But Jesus was sleeping.

[25]The disciples went and woke him up. They said, "Lord! Save us! We're going to drown!"

[26]He replied, "Your faith is so small! Why are you so afraid?"

Then Jesus got up and ordered the winds and the waves to stop. It became completely calm.

[27]The disciples were amazed. They asked, "What kind of man is this? Even the winds and the waves obey him!"

Jesus Heals Two Men Controlled by Demons

[28]Jesus arrived at the other side of the lake in the area of the Gadarenes. Two men controlled by demons met him. They came from the tombs. The men were so wild that no one could pass that way.

[29]"Son of God, what do you want with us?" they shouted. "Have you come here to punish us before the time for us to be judged?"

[30]Not very far away, a large herd of pigs was feeding. [31]The demons begged Jesus, "If you drive us out, send us into the herd of pigs."

[32]Jesus said to them, "Go!"

So the demons came out of the men and went into the pigs. The whole herd rushed down the steep bank. They ran into the lake and drowned in the water.

[33]Those who were tending the pigs ran off. They went into the town and reported all this. They told the people what had happened to the men who had been controlled by demons.

[34]Then the whole town went out to meet Jesus. When they saw him, they begged him to leave their area.

Jesus Heals a Man Who Could Not Walk

9 Jesus stepped into a boat. He went over to the other side of the lake and came to his own town. [2]Some men brought to him a man who could not walk. He was lying on a mat. Jesus saw that they had faith. So he said to the man, "Don't lose hope, son. Your sins are forgiven."

[3]Then some teachers of the law said to themselves, "This fellow is saying a very evil thing!"

[4]Jesus knew what they were thinking. So he said, "Why do you have evil thoughts in your hearts? [5]Is it easier to say, 'Your sins are forgiven'? Or to say, 'Get up and walk'? [6]I want you to know that the Son of Man has authority on earth to forgive sins."

Then he spoke to the man who could not walk. "Get up," he said. "Take your mat and go home." [7]The man got up and went home.

[8]When the crowd saw this, they were filled with wonder. They praised God for giving that kind of authority to men.

Jesus Chooses Matthew

[9]As Jesus went on from there, he saw a man named Matthew. He was sitting at the tax collector's booth.

"Follow me," Jesus told him. Matthew got up and followed him.

[10]Later Jesus was having dinner at Mat-

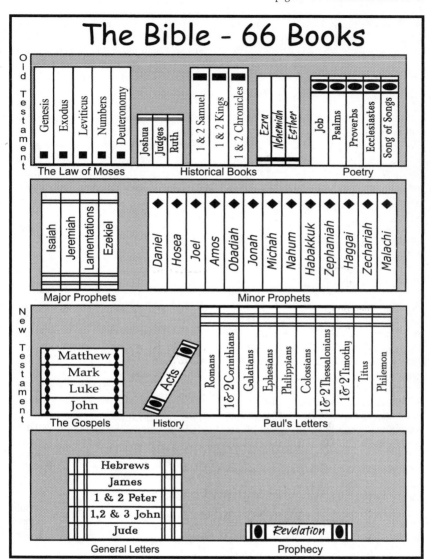

The Bible - 66 Books

Old Testament

The Law of Moses	Historical Books	Poetry
Genesis, Exodus, Leviticus, Numbers, Deuteronomy	Joshua, Judges, Ruth; 1 & 2 Samuel, 1 & 2 Kings, 1 & 2 Chronicles; Ezra, Nehemiah, Esther	Job, Psalms, Proverbs, Ecclesiastes, Song of Songs

Major Prophets	Minor Prophets
Isaiah, Jeremiah, Lamentations, Ezekiel	Daniel, Hosea, Joel, Amos, Obadiah, Jonah, Micah, Nahum, Habakkuk, Zephaniah, Haggai, Zechariah, Malachi

New Testament

The Gospels	History	Paul's Letters
Matthew, Mark, Luke, John	Acts	Romans, 1 & 2 Corinthians, Galatians, Ephesians, Philippians, Colossians, 1 & 2 Thessalonians, 1 & 2 Timothy, Titus, Philemon

General Letters	Prophecy
Hebrews, James, 1 & 2 Peter, 1,2 & 3 John, Jude	Revelation

thew's house. Many tax collectors and "sinners" came. They ate with Jesus and his disciples.

[11]The Pharisees saw this. So they asked the disciples, "Why does your teacher eat with tax collectors and 'sinners'?"

[12]Jesus heard that. So he said, "Those who are healthy don't need a doctor. Sick people do. [13]Go and learn what this means, 'I want mercy and not sacrifice.' *(Hosea 6:6)* I have

not come to get those who think they are right with God to follow me. I have come to get sinners to follow me."

Jesus Is Asked About Fasting

[14]One day John's disciples came. They said to Jesus, "We and the Pharisees go without eating. Why don't your disciples go without eating?"

[15]Jesus answered, "How can the guests

of the groom be sad while he is with them? The time will come when the groom will be taken away from them. Then they will fast.

[16]"People don't sew a patch of new cloth on old clothes. The new piece will pull away from the old. That will make the tear worse.

[17]"People don't pour new wine into old wineskins. If they do, the skins will burst. The wine will run out, and the wineskins will be destroyed. No, everyone pours new wine into new wineskins. Then both are saved."

A Dead Girl and a Suffering Woman

[18]While Jesus was saying this, a ruler came. He got down on his knees in front of Jesus. He said, "My daughter has just died. But come and place your hand on her. Then she will live again."

[19]Jesus got up and went with him. So did his disciples.

[20]Just then a woman came up behind Jesus. She had a sickness that made her bleed. It had lasted for 12 years. She touched the edge of his clothes. [21]She thought, "I only need to touch his clothes. Then I will be healed."

[22]Jesus turned and saw her. "Dear woman, don't give up hope," he said. "Your faith has healed you." The woman was healed at that very moment.

[23]When Jesus entered the ruler's house, he saw the flute players there. And he saw the noisy crowd. [24]He said, "Go away. The girl is not dead. She is sleeping." But they laughed at him.

[25]After the crowd had been sent outside, Jesus went in. He took the girl by the hand, and she got up. [26]News about what Jesus had done spread all over that area.

Jesus Heals Two Blind Men

[27]As Jesus went on from there, two blind men followed him. They called out, "Have mercy on us, Son of David!"

[28]When Jesus went indoors, the blind men came to him. He asked them, "Do you believe that I can do this?"

"Yes, Lord," they replied.

[29]Then he touched their eyes. He said, "It will happen to you just as you believed." [30]They could now see again. Jesus strongly warned them, "Be sure that no one knows about this." [31]But they went out and spread the news. They talked about him all over that area.

[32]While they were going out, another man was brought to Jesus. A demon controlled him, and he could not speak. [33]When the demon was driven out, the man spoke.

The crowd was amazed. They said, "Nothing like this has ever been seen in Israel." [34]But the Pharisees said, "He drives out demons by the power of the prince of demons."

There Are Only a Few Workers

[35]Jesus went through all the towns and villages. He taught in their synagogues. He preached the good news of the kingdom. And he healed every illness and sickness. [36]When he saw the crowds, he felt deep concern for them. They were beaten down and helpless, like sheep without a shepherd.

[37]Then Jesus said to his disciples, "The harvest is huge. But there are only a few workers. [38]So ask the Lord of the harvest to send workers out into his harvest field."

Jesus Sends Out the Twelve Disciples

10 Jesus called for his 12 disciples to come to him. He gave them authority to drive out evil spirits and to heal every illness and sickness.

[2]Here are the names of the 12 apostles. First are Simon Peter and his brother Andrew. Then come James, son of Zebedee, and his brother John. [3]Next are Philip and Bartholomew, and also Thomas and Matthew the tax collector. Two more are James, son of Alphaeus, and Thaddaeus. [4]The last are Simon the Zealot and Judas Iscariot. Judas is the one who was later going to hand Jesus over to his enemies.

[5]Jesus sent these 12 out with the following orders. "Do not go among those who aren't Jews," he said. "Do not enter any town of the Samaritans. [6]Instead, go to the people of Israel. They are like sheep that have become

"I'm not a Christian because ..."

"There are too many hypocrites in the Church."

Jesus' original group of 12 disciples had them too!

One betrayed Him – Judas
One denied Him – Peter
One doubted Him – Thomas

The Church is not a retail store where everything is "perfect." Rather, the Church is a repair shop for broken and wounded people. Jesus said:

"I have come to call sinners, not those who think they are already good enough."

Matthew 9:13 NLT

---

lost. [7]As you go, preach this message, 'The kingdom of heaven is near.' [8]Heal those who are sick. Bring those who are dead back to life. Make those who have skin diseases 'clean' again. Drive out demons. You have received freely, so give freely.

[9]"Do not take along any gold, silver or copper in your belts. [10]Do not take a bag for the journey. Do not take extra clothes or sandals or walking sticks. A worker should be given what he needs.

[11]"When you enter a town or village, look for someone who is willing to welcome you. Stay at that person's house until you leave. [12]As you enter the home, greet those who live there. [13]If that home welcomes you, give it your blessing of peace. If it does not, don't bless it.

[14]"Some people may not welcome you or listen to your words. If they don't, shake the dust off your feet when you leave that home or town. [15]What I'm about to tell you is true. On judgment day it will be easier for Sodom and Gomorrah than for that town.

[16]"I am sending you out like sheep among wolves. So be as wise as snakes and as harmless as doves.

[17]"Watch out! Men will hand you over to the local courts. They will whip you in their synagogues. [18]You will be brought to governors and kings because of me. You will be witnesses to them and to those who aren't Jews.

[19]"But when they arrest you, don't worry about what you will say or how you will say it. At that time you will be given the right words to say. [20]It will not be you speaking. The Spirit of your Father will be speaking through you.

[21]"Brothers will hand over brothers to be killed. Fathers will hand over their children. Children will rise up against their parents and have them put to death. [22]Everyone will hate you because of me. But anyone who stands firm to the end will be saved.

[23]"When people attack you in one place, escape to another. What I'm about to tell you is true. You will not finish going through the cities of Israel before the Son of Man comes.

[24]"A student is not better than his teacher. A servant is not better than his master. [25]It is enough for the student to be like his teacher. And it is enough for the ser-

vant to be like his master. If the head of the house has been called Beelzebub, what can the others who live there expect?

26"So don't be afraid of your enemies. Everything that is secret will be brought out into the open. Everything that is hidden will be uncovered. 27What I tell you in the dark, speak in the daylight. What is whispered in your ear, shout from the rooftops. 28Do not be afraid of those who kill the body but can't kill the soul. Instead, be afraid of the One who can destroy both soul and body in hell.

29"Aren't two sparrows sold for only a penny? But not one of them falls to the ground without your Father knowing it. 30He even counts every hair on your head! 31So don't be afraid. You are worth more than many sparrows.

32"What about someone who says in front of others that he knows me? I will also say in front of my Father who is in heaven that I know him. 33But what about someone who says in front of others that he doesn't know me? I will say in front of my Father who is in heaven that I don't know him.

34"Do not think that I came to bring peace to the earth. I didn't come to bring peace. I came to bring a sword. 35I have come to turn

" 'sons against their fathers.
    Daughters will refuse to obey their
        mothers.
Daughters-in-law will be against their
    mothers-in-law.
36 A man's enemies will be the members
        of his own family.'   (Micah 7:6)

37"Anyone who loves his father or mother more than me is not worthy of me. Anyone who loves his son or daughter more than me is not worthy of me. 38And anyone who does not pick up his cross and follow me is not worthy of me. 39If anyone finds his life, he will lose it. If anyone loses his life because of me, he will find it.

40"Anyone who welcomes you welcomes me. And anyone who welcomes me welcomes the One who sent me. 41Suppose someone welcomes a prophet as a prophet. That one will receive a prophet's reward.

And suppose someone welcomes a godly person as a godly person. That one will receive a godly person's reward. 42Suppose someone gives even a cup of cold water to a little one who follows me. What I'm about to tell you is true. That one will certainly be rewarded."

Jesus and John the Baptist

11 Jesus finished teaching his 12 disciples. Then he went on to teach and preach in the towns of Galilee.

2John was in prison. When he heard what Christ was doing, he sent his disciples to him. 3They asked Jesus, "Are you the one who was supposed to come? Or should we look for someone else?"

4Jesus replied, "Go back to John. Report to him what you hear and see. 5Blind people receive sight. Disabled people walk. Those who have skin diseases are healed. Deaf people hear. Those who are dead are raised to life. And the good news is preached to those who are poor. 6Blessed are those who do not give up their faith because of me."

7As John's disciples were leaving, Jesus began to speak to the crowd about John. He said, "What did you go out into the desert to see? Tall grass waving in the wind? 8If not, what did you go out to see? A man dressed in fine clothes? No. People who wear fine clothes are in kings' palaces. 9Then what did you go out to see? A prophet? Yes, I tell you, and more than a prophet. 10He is the one written about in Scripture. It says,

" 'I will send my messenger ahead of you.
    He will prepare your way for you.'
                            (Malachi 3:1)

11"What I'm about to tell you is true. No one more important than John the Baptist has ever been born. But the least important person in the kingdom of heaven is more important than he is. 12Since the days of John the Baptist, the kingdom of heaven has been advancing with force. And forceful people are taking hold of it. 13All the Prophets and the Law prophesied until John came. 14If you are willing to accept it, John is the Elijah who was supposed to come. 15Those who have ears should listen.

[16]"What can I compare today's people to? They are like children sitting in the market places and calling out to others. They say,

[17]" 'We played the flute for you.
  But you didn't dance.
We sang a funeral song.
  But you didn't become sad.'

[18]When John came, he didn't eat or drink as you do. And people say, 'He has a demon.' [19]But when the Son of Man came, he ate and drank as you do. And people say, 'This fellow is always eating and drinking far too much. He's a friend of tax collectors and "sinners." ' Those who act wisely prove that wisdom is right."

Cities That Do Not Turn Away From Sin

[20]Jesus began to speak against the cities where he had done most of his miracles. The people there had not turned away from their sins. So he said, [21]"How terrible it will be for you, Korazin! How terrible for you, Bethsaida! Suppose the miracles done in you had been done in Tyre and Sidon. They would have turned away from their sins long ago. They would have put on black clothes. They would have sat down in ashes. [22]But I tell you this. On judgment day it will be easier for Tyre and Sidon than for you.

[23]"And what about you, Capernaum? Will you be lifted up to heaven? No! You will go down to the place of the dead. Suppose the miracles done in you had been done in Sodom. It would still be here today. [24]But I tell you this. On judgment day it will be easier for Sodom than for you."

Rest for All Who Are Tired

[25]At that time Jesus said, "I praise you, Father. You are Lord of heaven and earth. You have hidden these things from the wise and educated. But you have shown them to little children. [26]Yes, Father. This is what you wanted.

[27]"My Father has given all things to me. The Father is the only one who knows the Son. And the only ones who know the Father are the Son and those to whom the Son chooses to make him known.

Jesus Heals

"He makes even the deaf to hear!"

"Stand up...you are healed!"

"Lord, you can make me well!"

"I can see!"

"Agh ... its a ghost!"

and walks on water!

[28]"Come to me, all of you who are tired and are carrying heavy loads. I will give you rest. [29]Become my servants and learn from me. I am gentle and free of pride. You will find rest for your souls. [30]Serving me is easy, and my load is light."

Jesus Is Lord of the Sabbath Day

12 One Sabbath day Jesus walked through the grainfields. His disciples were hungry. So they began to break off some heads of grain and eat them. [2]The Pharisees saw this. They said to Jesus, "Look! It is against the Law to do this on the Sabbath. But your disciples are doing it anyway!"

[3]Jesus answered, "Haven't you read about what David did? He and his men were hungry. [4]So he entered the house of God. He and his men ate the holy bread. Only priests were allowed to eat it. [5]Haven't you read the Law? It tells how every Sabbath day the priests in the temple have to do their work on that day. But they are not considered guilty.

[6]"I tell you that one who is more important than the temple is here. [7]Scripture says, 'I want mercy and not sacrifice.' *(Hosea 6:6)* You don't know what those words mean. If you did, you would not bring charges against those who are not guilty. [8]The Son of Man is Lord of the Sabbath day."

[9]Going on from that place, Jesus went into their synagogue. [10]A man with a weak and twisted hand was there. The Pharisees were trying to find fault with Jesus. So they asked him, "Does the Law allow us to heal on the Sabbath day?"

[11]He said to them, "What if one of your sheep falls into a pit on the Sabbath? Won't you take hold of it and lift it out? [12]A man is worth more than sheep! So the Law allows us to do good on the Sabbath day."

[13]Then Jesus said to the man, "Stretch out your hand." So he stretched it out. It was as good as new, just as good as the other hand. [14]But the Pharisees went out and planned how to kill Jesus.

God's Chosen Servant

[15]Jesus knew all about the Pharisees' plans. So he left that place. Many followed him, and he healed all their sick people. [16]But he warned them not to tell who he was. [17]This was to make what was spoken through the prophet Isaiah come true. It says,

[18] "Here is my servant. I have chosen him.
  He is the one I love. I am very pleased with him.
I will put my Spirit on him.
  He will announce to the nations that everything will be made right.
[19] He will not argue or cry out.
  No one will hear his voice in the streets.
[20] He will not break a bent twig.
  He will not put out a dimly burning flame.
He will make everything right.
[21]   The nations will put their hope in him."   *(Isaiah 42:1–4)*

Jesus and Beelzebub

[22]A man controlled by demons was brought to Jesus. The man was blind and could not speak. Jesus healed him. Then the man could speak and see. [23]All the people were amazed. They said, "Could this be the Son of David?"

[24]The Pharisees heard this. So they said, "This fellow drives out demons by the power of Beelzebub, the prince of demons."

[25]Jesus knew what they were thinking. So he said to them, "Every kingdom that fights against itself will be destroyed. Every city or family that is divided against itself will not stand. [26]If Satan drives out Satan, he fights against himself. Then how can his kingdom stand? [27]You say I drive out demons by the power of Beelzebub. Then by whose power do your people drive them out? So then, they will be your judges. [28]But suppose I drive out demons by the Spirit of God. Then God's kingdom has come to you.

[29]"Or think about this. How can you enter a strong man's house and just take what the man owns? You must first tie him up. Then you can rob his house.

[30]"Anyone who is not with me is against me. Anyone who does not gather sheep with me scatters them. [31]So here is what I tell you. Every sin and every evil word spoken against God will be forgiven. But speaking evil things against the Holy Spirit will not be forgiven. [32]Anyone who speaks a word against the Son of Man will be forgiven. But anyone who speaks against the Holy Spirit will not be forgiven. A person like that won't be forgiven either now or in days to come.

[33]"If you make a tree good, its fruit will be good. If you make a tree bad, its fruit will be bad. You can tell a tree by its fruit.

[34]"You nest of poisonous snakes! How can you who are evil say anything good? Your mouths say everything that is in your hearts. [35]A good man says good things. These come from the good that is put away inside him. An evil man says evil things. These come from the evil that is put away inside him. [36]But here is what I tell you. On judgment day, people will have to account for every careless word they have spoken. [37]By your words you will be found guilty or not guilty."

The Miraculous Sign of Jonah

[38]Some of the Pharisees and the teachers of the law came to Jesus. They said, "Teacher, we want to see a miraculous sign from you."

[39]He answered, "Evil and unfaithful people ask for a miraculous sign! But none will be given except the sign of the prophet Jonah. [40]Jonah was in the stomach of a huge fish for three days and three nights. Something like that will happen to the Son of Man. He will spend three days and three nights in the grave.

[41]"The men of Nineveh will stand up on judgment day with the people now living. And the Ninevites will prove that those people are guilty. The men of Nineveh turned away from their sins when Jonah preached to them. And now one who is more important than Jonah is here.

[42]"The Queen of the South will stand up on judgment day with the people now living. And she will prove that they are guilty. She came from very far away to listen to Solomon's wisdom. And now one who is more important than Solomon is here.

[43]"What happens when an evil spirit comes out of a man? It goes through dry areas looking for a place to rest. But it doesn't find it. [44]Then it says, 'I will return to the house I left.' When it arrives there, it finds the house empty. The house has been swept clean and put in order. [45]Then the evil spirit goes and takes with it seven other spirits more evil than itself. They go in and live there. That man is worse off than before. That is how it will be with the evil people of today."

Jesus' Mother and Brothers

[46]While Jesus was still talking to the crowd, his mother and brothers stood outside. They wanted to speak to him. [47]Someone told him, "Your mother and brothers are standing outside. They want to speak to you."

[48]Jesus replied to him, "Who is my mother? And who are my brothers?" [49]Jesus pointed to his disciples. He said, "Here is my mother! Here are my brothers! [50]Anyone who does what my Father in heaven wants is my brother or sister or mother."

The Story of the Farmer

13 That same day Jesus left the house and sat by the Sea of Galilee. [2]Large crowds gathered around him. So he got into a boat. He sat down in it. All the people stood on the shore. [3]Then he told them many things by using stories.

He said, "A farmer went out to plant his seed. [4]He scattered the seed on the ground. Some fell on a path. Birds came and ate it up. [5]Some seed fell on rocky places, where

God is looking for ordinary people, empowered by Him, to do extraordinary things.

there wasn't much soil. The plants came up quickly, because the soil wasn't deep. [6]When the sun came up, it burned the plants. They dried up because they had no roots. [7]Other seed fell among thorns. The thorns grew up and crowded out the plants. [8]Still other seed fell on good soil. It produced a crop 100, 60 or 30 times more than what was planted. [9]Those who have ears should listen."

[10]The disciples came to him. They asked, "Why do you use stories when you speak to the people?"

[11]He replied, "You have been given the chance to understand the secrets of the kingdom of heaven. It has not been given to outsiders. [12]Everyone who has that kind of knowledge will be given more. In fact, they will have very much. If anyone doesn't have that kind of knowledge, even what little he has will be taken away from him. [13]Here is why I use stories when I speak to the people. I say,

"They look, but they don't really see.
    They listen, but they don't really hear
        or understand.

[14]"In them the words of the prophet Isaiah come true. He said,

" 'You will hear but never understand.
    You will see but never know what you
        are seeing.
[15]The hearts of these people have become
        stubborn.
    They can barely hear with their ears.
    They have closed their eyes.
Otherwise they might see with their
        eyes.
    They might hear with their ears.
    They might understand with their
        hearts.
They might turn to the Lord, and then he
        would heal them.'   *(Isaiah 6:9,10)*

[16]"But blessed are your eyes because they see. And blessed are your ears because they hear. [17]What I'm about to tell you is true. Many prophets and godly people wanted to see what you see. But they didn't see it. They wanted to hear what you hear. But they didn't hear it.

[18]"Listen! Here is the meaning of the story of the farmer. [19]People hear the message about the kingdom but do not understand it. Then the evil one comes. He steals what was planted in their hearts. Those people are like the seed planted on a path. [20]Others received the seed that fell on rocky places. They are those who hear the message and at once receive it with joy. [21]But they have no roots. So they last only a short time. They quickly fall away from the faith when trouble or suffering comes because of the message. [22]Others received the seed that fell among the thorns. They are those who hear the message. But then the worries of this life and the false promises of wealth crowd it out. They keep it from producing fruit. [23]But still others received the seed that fell on good soil. They are those who hear the message and understand it. They produce a crop 100, 60 or 30 times more than the farmer planted."

The Story of the Weeds

[24]Jesus told the crowd another story. "Here is what the kingdom of heaven is like," he said. "A man planted good seed in his field. [25]But while everyone was sleeping, his enemy came. The enemy planted weeds among the wheat and then went away. [26]The wheat began to grow and form grain. At the same time, weeds appeared.

[27]"The owner's servants came to him. They said, 'Sir, didn't you plant good seed in your field? Then where did the weeds come from?'

[28]" 'An enemy did this,' he replied.

"The servants asked him, 'Do you want us to go and pull the weeds up?'

[29]" 'No,' the owner answered. 'While you are pulling up the weeds, you might pull up the wheat with them. [30]Let both grow together until the harvest. At that time I will tell the workers what to do. Here is what I will say to them. First collect the weeds. Tie them in bundles to be burned. Then gather the wheat. Bring it into my storeroom.' "

The Stories of the Mustard Seed and the Yeast

[31]Jesus told the crowd another story. He said, "The kingdom of heaven is like a

mustard seed. Someone took the seed and planted it in a field. ³²It is the smallest of all your seeds. But when it grows, it is the largest of all garden plants. It becomes a tree. Birds come and rest in its branches."

³³Jesus told them still another story. "The kingdom of heaven is like yeast," he said. "A woman mixed it into a large amount of flour. The yeast worked its way all through the dough."

³⁴Jesus spoke all these things to the crowd by using stories. He did not say anything to them without telling a story. ³⁵So the words spoken by the prophet came true. He had said,

"I will open my mouth and tell stories.
I will speak about things that were
    hidden since the world was
    made."   *(Psalm 78:2)*

Jesus Explains the Story of the Weeds

³⁶Then Jesus left the crowd and went into the house. His disciples came to him. They said, "Explain to us the story of the weeds in the field."

³⁷He answered, "The one who planted the good seed is the Son of Man. ³⁸The field is the world. The good seed stands for the people who belong to the kingdom. The weeds are the people who belong to the evil one. ³⁹The enemy who plants them is the devil. The harvest is judgment day. And the workers are angels.

⁴⁰"The weeds are pulled up and burned in the fire. That is how it will be on judgment day. ⁴¹The Son of Man will send out his angels. They will weed out of his kingdom everything that causes sin. They will also get rid of all who do evil. ⁴²They will throw them into the blazing furnace. There people will sob and grind their teeth. ⁴³Then God's people will shine like the sun in their Father's kingdom. Those who have ears should listen.

The Stories of the Hidden Treasure and the Pearl

⁴⁴"The kingdom of heaven is like treasure that was hidden in a field. When a man found it, he hid it again. He was very happy.

So he went and sold everything he had. And he bought that field.

⁴⁵"Again, the kingdom of heaven is like a trader who was looking for fine pearls. ⁴⁶He found one that was very valuable. So he went away and sold everything he had. And he bought that pearl.

The Story of the Net

⁴⁷"Again, the kingdom of heaven is like a net. It was let down into the lake. It caught all kinds of fish. ⁴⁸When it was full, the fishermen pulled it up on the shore. Then they sat down and gathered the good fish into baskets. But they threw the bad fish away. ⁴⁹This is how it will be on judgment day.

Famous Quotes

"You ... nest of poisonous snakes!"
John the Baptist
Matthew 3:7

●

"Throw yourself down."
Satan
Matthew 4:6

●

"Have you come here to punish us?"
Demons
Matthew 8:29

●

"What reward will be given us?"
Peter
Matthew 19:27

●

"Blind guides!"
Jesus
Matthew 23:16

●

"Why this waste?"
Disciples
Matthew 26:8

nace. There the evil ones will sob and grind their teeth.

⁵¹"Do you understand all these things?" Jesus asked.

"Yes," they replied.

⁵²He said to them, "Every teacher of the law who has been taught about the kingdom of heaven is like the owner of a house. He brings new treasures out of his storeroom as well as old ones."

A Prophet Without Honor

⁵³Jesus finished telling these stories. Then he moved on from there. ⁵⁴He came to his hometown of Nazareth. There he began teaching the people in their synagogue. They were amazed.

"Where did this man get this wisdom? Where did he get this power to do miracles?" they asked. ⁵⁵"Isn't this the carpenter's son? Isn't his mother's name Mary? Aren't his brothers James, Joseph, Simon and Judas? ⁵⁶Aren't all his sisters with us? Then where did this man get all these things?" ⁵⁷They were not pleased with him at all.

But Jesus said to them, "A prophet is not honored in his hometown. He doesn't receive any honor in his own home."

⁵⁸He did only a few miracles there because they had no faith.

John the Baptist's Head Is Cut Off

14 At that time Herod, the ruler of Galilee and Perea, heard reports about Jesus. ²He said to his attendants, "This is John the Baptist. He has risen from the dead! That is why he has the power to do miracles."

³Herod had arrested John. He had tied him up and put him in prison because of Herodias. She was the wife of Herod's brother Philip. ⁴John had been saying to Herod, "It is against the Law for you to have her." ⁵Herod wanted to kill John. But he was afraid of the people, because they thought John was a prophet.

⁶On Herod's birthday the daughter of Herodias danced for Herod and his guests. She pleased Herod very much. ⁷So he promised with an oath to give her anything she

The angels will come. They will separate the people who did what is wrong from those who did what is right. ⁵⁰They will throw the evil people into the blazing fur-

asked for. [8]Her mother told her what to say. So the girl said to Herod, "Give me the head of John the Baptist on a big plate."

[9]The king was very upset. But he thought of his promise and his dinner guests. So he told one of his men to give her what she asked for. [10]Herod had John's head cut off in the prison. [11]His head was brought in on a big plate and given to the girl. She then carried it to her mother.

[12]John's disciples came and took his body and buried it. Then they went and told Jesus.

Jesus Feeds the Five Thousand

[13]Jesus heard what had happened to John. He wanted to be alone. So he went in a boat to a quiet place. The crowds heard about this. They followed him on foot from the towns. [14]When Jesus came ashore, he saw a large crowd. He felt deep concern for them. He healed their sick people.

[15]When it was almost evening, the disciples came to him. "There is nothing here," they said. "It's already getting late. Send the crowds away. They can go and buy some food in the villages."

[16]Jesus replied, "They don't need to go away. You give them something to eat."

[17]"We have only five loaves of bread and two fish," they answered.

[18]"Bring them here to me," he said. [19]Then Jesus directed the people to sit down on the grass. He took the five loaves and the two fish. He looked up to heaven and gave thanks. He broke the loaves into pieces. Then he gave them to the disciples. And the disciples gave them to the people.

[20]All of them ate and were satisfied. The disciples picked up 12 baskets of leftover pieces. [21]The number of men who ate was about 5,000. Women and children also ate.

Jesus Walks on the Water

[22]Right away Jesus made the disciples get into the boat. He had them go on ahead of him to the other side of the Sea of Galilee. Then he sent the crowd away. [23]After he had sent them away, he went up on a mountainside by himself to pray. When evening came, he was there alone. [24]The boat was already a long way from land. It was being pounded by the waves because the wind was blowing against it.

[25]Early in the morning, Jesus went out to the disciples. He walked on the lake. [26]They saw him walking on the lake and were terrified. "It's a ghost!" they said. And they cried out in fear.

[27]Right away Jesus called out to them, "Be brave! It is I. Don't be afraid."

[28]"Lord, is it you?" Peter asked. "If it is, tell me to come to you on the water."

[29]"Come," Jesus said.

So Peter got out of the boat. He walked on the water toward Jesus. [30]But when Peter saw the wind, he was afraid. He began to sink. He cried out, "Lord! Save me!"

[31]Right away Jesus reached out his hand and caught him. "Your faith is so small!" he said. "Why did you doubt me?"

[32]When they climbed into the boat, the wind died down. [33]Then those in the boat worshiped Jesus. They said, "You really are the Son of God!"

[34]They crossed over the lake and landed at Gennesaret. [35]The men who lived there recognized Jesus. So they sent a message all over the nearby countryside. People brought all their sick to Jesus. [36]They begged him to let those who were sick just touch the edge of his clothes. And all who touched him were healed.

What Makes People "Unclean"?

15 Some Pharisees and some teachers of the law came from Jerusalem to see Jesus. They asked, [2]"Why don't your disciples obey what the elders teach? Your disciples don't wash their hands before they eat!"

[3]Jesus replied, "And why don't you obey God's command? You would rather follow your own teachings! [4]God said, 'Honor your father and mother.' *(Exodus 20:12; Deuteronomy 5:16)* He also said, 'If anyone calls down a curse on his father or mother, he will be put to death.' *(Exodus 21:17; Leviticus 20:9)* [5]But you allow people to say to their parents, 'Any help you might have received from us is a gift set apart for God.' [6]So they do not need to honor their parents with

their gift. You make the word of God useless in order to follow your own teachings.

[7] "You pretenders! Isaiah was right when he prophesied about you. He said,

[8] " 'These people honor me by what they
say.
But their hearts are far away from me.
[9] Their worship doesn't mean anything
to me.
They teach nothing but human rules.' "
(Isaiah 29:13)

[10] Jesus called the crowd to him. He said, "Listen and understand. [11] What goes into your mouth does not make you 'unclean.' It's what comes out of your mouth that makes you 'unclean.' "

[12] Then the disciples came to him. They asked, "Do you know that the Pharisees were angry when they heard this?"

[13] Jesus replied, "There are plants that my Father in heaven has not planted. They will be pulled up by the roots. [14] Leave them. The Pharisees are blind guides. If a blind person leads another who is blind, both of them will fall into a pit."

[15] Peter said, "Explain this to us."

[16] "Don't you understand yet?" Jesus asked them. [17] "Don't you see? Everything that enters the mouth goes into the stomach. Then it goes out of the body. [18] But the things that come out of the mouth come from the heart. Those are the things that make you 'unclean.' [19] Evil thoughts come out of the heart. So do murder, adultery, and other sexual sins. And so do stealing, false witness, and telling lies about others. [20] Those are the things that make you 'unclean.' But

eating without washing your hands does not make you 'unclean.' "

The Faith of a Woman From Canaan

[21] Jesus left Galilee and went to the area of Tyre and Sidon. [22] A woman from Canaan lived near Tyre and Sidon. She came to him and cried out, "Lord! Son of David! Have mercy on me! A demon controls my daughter. She is suffering terribly."

[23] Jesus did not say a word. So his disciples came to him. They begged him, "Send her away. She keeps crying out after us."

[24] Jesus answered, "I was sent only to the people of Israel. They are like lost sheep."

[25] Then the woman fell to her knees in front of him. "Lord! Help me!" she said.

[26] He replied, "It is not right to take the children's bread and throw it to their dogs."

[27] "Yes, Lord," she said. "But even the dogs eat the crumbs that fall from their owners' table."

[28] Then Jesus answered, "Woman, you have great faith! You will be given what you are asking for." And her daughter was healed at that very moment.

Jesus Feeds the Four Thousand

[29] Jesus left there. He walked along the Sea of Galilee. Then he went up on a mountainside and sat down. [30] Large crowds came to him. They brought blind people and those who could not walk. They also brought disabled people, those who could not speak, and many others. They laid them at his feet,

and he healed them.

[31]The people were amazed. Those who could not speak were speaking. The disabled were made well. Those not able to walk were walking. Those who were blind could see. So the people praised the God of Israel.

[32]Then Jesus called for his disciples to come to him. He said, "I feel deep concern for these people. They have already been with me three days. They don't have anything to eat. I don't want to send them away hungry. If I do, they will become too weak on their way home."

[33]His disciples answered him. "There is nothing here," they said. "Where could we get enough bread to feed this large crowd?"

[34]"How many loaves do you have?" Jesus asked.

"Seven," they replied, "and a few small fish."

[35]Jesus told the crowd to sit down on the ground. [36]He took the seven loaves and the fish and gave thanks. Then he broke them and gave them to the disciples. And the disciples passed them out to the people. [37]All of them ate and were satisfied. After that, the disciples picked up seven baskets of leftover pieces. [38]The number of men who ate was 4,000. Women and children also ate.

[39]After Jesus had sent the crowd away, he got into the boat. He went to the area near Magadan.

Jesus Is Asked for a Miraculous Sign

16 The Pharisees and Sadducees came to put Jesus to the test. They asked him to show them a miraculous sign from heaven.

[2]He replied, "In the evening you look at the sky. You say, 'It will be good weather. The sky is red.' [3]And in the morning you say, 'Today it will be stormy. The sky is red and cloudy.' You know the meaning of what you see in the sky. But you can't understand the signs of what is happening right now. [4]An evil and unfaithful people look for a miraculous sign. But none will be given to them except the sign of Jonah."

Then Jesus left them and went away.

The Yeast of the Pharisees and Sadducees

[5]The disciples crossed over to the other side of the lake. They had forgotten to take bread. [6]"Be careful," Jesus said to them. "Watch out for the yeast of the Pharisees and Sadducees."

[7]The disciples talked about this among themselves. They said, "He must be saying this because we didn't bring any bread."

[8]Jesus knew what they were saying. So he said, "Your faith is so small! Why are you talking to each other about having no bread? [9]Don't you understand yet? Don't you remember the five loaves for the 5,000? Don't you remember how many baskets of pieces you gathered? [10]Don't you remember the seven loaves for the 4,000? Don't you remember how many baskets of pieces you gathered? [11]How can you possibly not understand? I wasn't talking to you about bread. But watch out for the yeast of the Pharisees and Sadducees."

[12]Then the disciples understood that Jesus was not telling them to watch out for the yeast used in bread. He was warning them against what the Pharisees and Sadducees taught.

Peter Says That Jesus Is the Christ

[13]Jesus went to the area of Caesarea Philippi. There he asked his disciples, "Who do people say the Son of Man is?"

[14]They replied, "Some say John the Baptist. Others say Elijah. Still others say Jeremiah, or one of the prophets."

[15]"But what about you?" he asked. "Who do you say I am?"

[16]Simon Peter answered, "You are the Christ. You are the Son of the living God."

[17]Jesus replied, "Blessed are you, Simon, son of Jonah! No mere man showed this to you. My Father in heaven showed it to you. [18]Here is what I tell you. You are Peter. On this rock I will build my church. The gates of hell will not be strong enough to destroy it. [19]I will give you the keys to the kingdom of heaven. What you lock on earth will be locked in heaven. What you unlock on earth will be unlocked in heaven."

[20]Then Jesus warned his disciples not to

Disciples Trivia

Considered momma's boys
Matthew 20:20

Profited by gambling
Acts 1:26

Winners of a
"sleep-a-thon"
Matthew 26:37

Told to fish for money
Matthew 17:27

shortest walk on water
Matthew 14:29

I'll believe it when
I see it and feel it
John 20:25

Had "foot-in-mouth" disease
Matthew 16:23

First disciple to be killed
Acts 12:2

What's in it for me?
Matthew 19:27

tell anyone that he was the Christ.

Jesus Tells About His Coming Death

21From that time on Jesus began to explain to his disciples what would happen to him. He told them he must go to Jerusalem. There he must suffer many things from the elders, the chief priests and the teachers of the law. He must be killed and on the third day rise to life again.

22Peter took Jesus to one side and began to scold him. "Never, Lord!" he said. "This will never happen to you!"

23Jesus turned and said to Peter, "Get behind me, Satan! You are standing in my way. You do not have in mind the things of God. Instead, you are thinking about human things."

24Then Jesus spoke to his disciples. He said, "If anyone wants to follow me, he must say no to himself. He must pick up his cross and follow me. 25If he wants to save his life, he will lose it. But if he loses his life for me, he will find it.

26"What good is it if someone gains the whole world but loses his soul? Or what can anyone trade for his soul? 27The Son of Man is going to come in his Father's glory. His angels will come with him. And he will reward everyone in keeping with what they have done.

28"What I'm about to tell you is true. Some who are standing here will not die before they see the Son of Man coming in his kingdom."

Jesus' Appearance Is Changed

17 After six days Jesus took Peter, James, and John the brother of James with him. He led them up a high mountain. They were all alone. [2]There in front of them his appearance was changed. His face shone like the sun. His clothes became as white as the light. [3]Just then Moses and Elijah appeared in front of them. Moses and Elijah were talking with Jesus.

[4]Peter said to Jesus, "Lord, it is good for us to be here. If you wish, I will put up three shelters. One will be for you, one for Moses, and one for Elijah."

[5]While Peter was still speaking, a bright cloud surrounded them. A voice from the cloud said, "This is my Son, and I love him. I am very pleased with him. Listen to him!"

[6]When the disciples heard this, they were terrified. They fell with their faces to the ground. [7]But Jesus came and touched them. "Get up," he said. "Don't be afraid." [8]When they looked up, they saw no one except Jesus.

[9]They came down the mountain. On the way down, Jesus told them what to do. "Don't tell anyone what you have seen," he said. "Wait until the Son of Man has been raised from the dead."

[10]The disciples asked him, "Why do the teachers of the law say that Elijah has to come first?"

[11]Jesus replied, "That's right. Elijah is supposed to come and make all things new again. [12]But I tell you, Elijah has already come. People didn't recognize him. They have done to him everything they wanted to do. In the same way, they are going to make the Son of Man suffer."

[13]Then the disciples understood that Jesus was talking to them about John the Baptist.

Jesus Heals a Boy Who Had a Demon

[14]When they came near the crowd, a man approached Jesus. He got on his knees in front of him. [15]"Lord," he said, "have mercy on my son. He shakes wildly and suffers a great deal. He often falls into the fire or into the water. [16]I brought him to your disciples. But they couldn't heal him."

[17]"You unbelieving and evil people!" Jesus replied. "How long do I have to stay with you? How long do I have to put up with you? Bring the boy here to me."

[18]Jesus ordered the demon to leave the boy, and it came out of him. He was healed at that very moment.

[19]Then the disciples came to Jesus in private. They asked, "Why couldn't we drive out the demon?"

[20/21]He replied, "Because your faith is much too small. What I'm about to tell you is true. If you have faith as small as a mustard seed, it is enough. You can say to this mountain, 'Move from here to there.' And it will move. Nothing will be impossible for you."

[22]They came together in Galilee. Then Jesus said to them, "The Son of Man is going to be handed over to men. [23]They will kill him. On the third day he will rise from the dead."

Then the disciples were filled with deep sadness.

Jesus Pays the Temple Tax

[24]Jesus and his disciples arrived in Capernaum. There the tax collectors came to Peter. They asked him, "Doesn't your teacher pay the temple tax?"

[25]"Yes, he does," he replied.

When Peter came into the house, Jesus spoke first. "What do you think, Simon?" he asked. "Who do the kings of the earth collect taxes and fees from? Do they collect from their own sons or from others?"

[26]"From others," Peter answered.

"Then the sons don't have to pay," Jesus said to him. [27]"But we don't want to make them angry. So go to the lake and throw out your fishing line. Take the first fish you catch. Open its mouth. There you will find the exact coin you need. Take it and give it to them for my tax and yours."

Who Is the Most Important Person in the Kingdom?

18 At that time the disciples came to Jesus. They asked him, "Who is the most important person in the kingdom of heaven?"

²Jesus called a little child over to him. He had the child stand among them. ³Jesus said, "What I'm about to tell you is true. You need to change and become like little children. If you don't, you will never enter the kingdom of heaven. ⁴Anyone who becomes as free of pride as this child is the most important in the kingdom of heaven.

⁵"Anyone who welcomes a little child like this in my name welcomes me.

⁶"But what if someone leads one of these little ones who believe in me to sin? If he does, it would be better for him to have a large millstone hung around his neck and be drowned at the bottom of the sea.

⁷"How terrible it will be for the world because of the things that lead people to sin! Things like that must come. But how terrible for those who cause them!

⁸"If your hand or foot causes you to sin, cut it off and throw it away. It would be better for you to enter the kingdom of heaven with only one hand or one foot than to go into hell with two hands and two feet. In hell the fire burns forever. ⁹If your eye causes you to sin, poke it out and throw it away. It would be better for you to enter the kingdom of heaven with one eye than to have two eyes and be thrown into the fire of hell.

The Story of the Lost Sheep

¹⁰/¹¹"See that you don't look down on one of these little ones. Here is what I tell you. Their angels in heaven can go at any time to see my Father who is in heaven.

¹²"What do you think? Suppose a man owns 100 sheep and one of them wanders away. Won't he leave the 99 sheep on the hills? Won't he go and look for the one that wandered off? ¹³What I'm about to tell you is true. If he finds that sheep, he is happier about the one than about the 99 that didn't wander off. ¹⁴It is the same with your Father in heaven. He does not want any of these little ones to be lost.

When Someone Sins Against You

¹⁵"If your brother sins against you, go to him. Tell him what he did wrong. Keep it between the two of you. If he listens to you, you have won him back.

¹⁶"But what if he won't listen to you? Then take one or two others with you. Scripture says, 'Every matter must be proved by the words of two or three witnesses.' *(Deuteronomy 19:15)* ¹⁷But what if he also refuses to listen to the witnesses? Then tell it to the church. And what if he refuses to listen even to the church? Then don't treat him as your brother. Treat him as you would treat an ungodly person or a tax collector.

¹⁸"What I'm about to tell you is true. What you lock on earth will be locked in heaven. What you unlock on earth will be unlocked in heaven.

¹⁹"Again, here is what I tell you. Suppose two of you on earth agree about anything you ask for. My Father in heaven will do it for you. ²⁰Where two or three people meet together in my name, I am there with them."

The Servant Who Had No Mercy

²¹Peter came to Jesus. He asked, "Lord, how many times should I forgive my brother when he sins against me? Up to seven times?"

²²Jesus answered, "I tell you, not seven times, but 77 times.

²³"The kingdom of heaven is like a king who wanted to collect all the money his servants owed him. ²⁴As the king began to do it, a man who owed him millions of dollars was brought to him. ²⁵The man was not able to pay. So his master gave an order. The man, his wife, his children, and all he owned had to be sold to pay back what he owed.

²⁶"The servant fell on his knees in front of him. 'Give me time,' he begged. 'I'll pay everything back.'

²⁷"His master felt sorry for him. He forgave him what he owed and let him go.

²⁸"But then that servant went out and found one of the other servants who owed him a few dollars. He grabbed him and

began to choke him. 'Pay back what you owe me!' he said.

²⁹"The other servant fell on his knees. 'Give me time,' he begged him. 'I'll pay you back.'

³⁰"But the first servant refused. Instead, he went and had the man thrown into prison. The man would be held there until he could pay back what he owed. ³¹The other servants saw what had happened. It troubled them greatly. They went and told their master everything that had happened.

³²"Then the master called the first servant in. 'You evil servant,' he said. 'I forgave all that you owed me because you begged me to. ³³Shouldn't you have had mercy on the other servant just as I had mercy on you?' ³⁴In anger his master turned him over to the jailers. He would be punished until he paid back everything he owed.

³⁵"This is how my Father in heaven will treat each of you unless you forgive your brother from your heart."

Jesus Teaches About Divorce

19 When Jesus finished saying these things, he left Galilee. He went into the area of Judea on the other side of the Jordan River. ²Large crowds followed him. He healed them there.

³Some Pharisees came to put him to the test. They asked, "Does the Law allow a man to divorce his wife for any reason at all?"

⁴Jesus replied, "Haven't you read that in the beginning the Creator 'made them male and female'? *(Genesis 1:27)* ⁵He said, 'That's why a man will leave his father and mother and be joined to his wife. The two will become one.' *(Genesis 2:24)* ⁶They are no longer two, but one. So a man must not separate what God has joined together."

⁷They asked, "Then why did Moses command that a man can give his wife a letter of divorce and send her away?"

⁸Jesus replied, "Moses let you divorce your wives because you were stubborn. But it was not this way from the beginning. ⁹Here is what I tell you. Anyone who divorces his wife and gets married to another woman commits adultery. A man may divorce his wife only if she has not been faithful to him."

¹⁰The disciples said to him, "If that's the way it is between a husband and wife, it is better not to get married."

¹¹Jesus replied, "Not everyone can accept the idea of staying single. Only those who have been helped to live without getting married can accept it. ¹²Some men are not able to have children because they were born that way. Some have been made that way by other people. Others have made themselves that way in order to serve the kingdom of heaven. The one who can accept living that way should do it."

Little Children Are Brought to Jesus

¹³Some people brought little children to Jesus. They wanted him to place his hands on the children and pray for them. But the disciples told the people to stop.

¹⁴Jesus said, "Let the little children come to me. Don't keep them away. The kingdom of heaven belongs to people like them." ¹⁵Jesus placed his hands on them. Then he went on from there.

Jesus and the Rich Young Man

¹⁶A man came up to Jesus. He asked, "Teacher, what good thing must I do to receive eternal life?"

¹⁷"Why do you ask me about what is good?" Jesus replied. "There is only One who is good. If you want to enter the kingdom, obey the commandments."

¹⁸"Which ones?" the man asked.

Jesus said, " 'Do not commit murder. Do not commit adultery. Do not steal. Do not give false witness. ¹⁹Honor your father and mother.' *(Exodus 20:12–16; Deuteronomy 5:16–20)* And 'love your neighbor as you love yourself.' " *(Leviticus 19:18)*

Everything we have belongs to God. What you think you own is really on loan.

²⁰"I have obeyed all those commandments," the young man said. "What else do I need to do?"

²¹Jesus answered, "If you want to be perfect, go and sell everything you have. Give the money to those who are poor. You will have treasure in heaven. Then come and follow me."

²²When the young man heard this, he went away sad. He was very rich.

²³Then Jesus said to his disciples, "What I'm about to tell you is true. It is hard for rich people to enter the kingdom of heaven. ²⁴Again I tell you, it is hard for a camel to go through the eye of a needle. But it is even harder for the rich to enter God's kingdom."

²⁵When the disciples heard this, they were really amazed. They asked, "Then who can be saved?"

²⁶Jesus looked at them and said, "With man, that is impossible. But with God, all things are possible."

²⁷Peter answered him, "We have left everything to follow you! What reward will be given to us?"

²⁸"What I'm about to tell you is true," Jesus said to them. "When all things are made new, the Son of Man will sit on his glorious throne. Then you who have followed me will also sit on 12 thrones. You will judge the 12 tribes of Israel. ²⁹Everyone who has left houses or families or fields because of me will receive 100 times as much. They will also receive eternal life. ³⁰But many who are first will be last. And many who are last will be first.

The Story of the Workers in the Vineyard

20 "The kingdom of heaven is like a man who owned land. He went out early in the morning to hire people to work in his vineyard. ²He agreed to give them the usual pay for a day's work. Then he sent them into his vineyard.

³"About nine o'clock in the morning he went out again. He saw others standing in the market place doing nothing. ⁴He told them, 'You also go and work in my vineyard. I'll pay you what is right.' ⁵So they went.

"He went out again about noon and at three o'clock and did the same thing. ⁶About five o'clock he went out and found still others standing around. He asked them, 'Why have you been standing here all day long doing nothing?'

⁷"'Because no one has hired us,' they answered.

"He said to them, 'You also go and work in my vineyard.'

⁸"When evening came, the owner of the vineyard spoke to the person who was in charge of the workers. He said, 'Call the workers and give them their pay. Begin with the last ones I hired. Then go on to the first ones.'

⁹"The workers who were hired about five o'clock came. Each received the usual day's pay. ¹⁰So when those who were hired first came, they expected to receive more. But each of them also received the usual day's pay.

¹¹"When they received it, they began to complain about the owner. ¹²'These people who were hired last worked only one hour,' they said. 'You have paid them the same as us. We have done most of the work and have been in the hot sun all day.'

¹³"The owner answered one of them. 'Friend,' he said, 'I'm being fair to you. Didn't you agree to work for the usual day's pay? ¹⁴Take your money and go. I want to give the ones I hired last the same pay I gave you. ¹⁵Don't I have the right to do what I want with my own money? Do you feel cheated because I gave so freely to the others?'

¹⁶"So those who are last will be first. And those who are first will be last."

Jesus Again Tells About His Coming Death

¹⁷Jesus was going up to Jerusalem. On the way, he took the 12 disciples to one side to talk to them.

¹⁸"We are going up to Jerusalem," he said. "The Son of Man will be handed over to the chief priests and the teachers of the law. They will sentence him to death. ¹⁹Then they will turn him over to people who are not Jews. The people will make fun of him and whip him. They will nail him to a cross. On the third day, he will rise from the dead!"

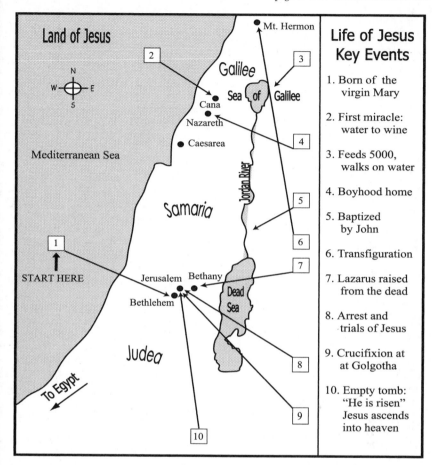

Land of Jesus

N
W ⊕ E
S

Mediterranean Sea

Mt. Hermon

Galilee

2

3

Sea of Galilee

Cana

Nazareth

Caesarea

4

Jordan River

Samaria

5

6

1

7

START HERE

Jerusalem   Bethany

Bethlehem

Dead Sea

Judea

8

To Egypt

9

10

Life of Jesus Key Events

1. Born of the virgin Mary

2. First miracle: water to wine

3. Feeds 5000, walks on water

4. Boyhood home

5. Baptized by John

6. Transfiguration

7. Lazarus raised from the dead

8. Arrest and trials of Jesus

9. Crucifixion at at Golgotha

10. Empty tomb: "He is risen" Jesus ascends into heaven

A Mother Asks a Favor of Jesus

²⁰The mother of Zebedee's sons came to Jesus. Her sons came with her. Getting on her knees, she asked a favor of him.

²¹"What do you want?" Jesus asked.

She said, "Promise me that one of my two sons may sit at your right hand in your kingdom. Promise that the other one may sit at your left hand."

²²"You don't know what you're asking for," Jesus said to them. "Can you drink the cup of suffering I am going to drink?"

"We can," they answered.

²³Jesus said to them, "You will certainly drink from my cup. But it is not for me to say who will sit at my right or left hand. These places belong to those my Father has prepared them for."

²⁴The other ten disciples heard about this. They became angry at the two brothers.

²⁵Jesus called them together. He said, "You know about the rulers of the nations. They hold power over their people. Their high officials order them around. ²⁶Don't be like that. Instead, anyone who wants to be important among you must be your servant. ²⁷And anyone who wants to be first must be your slave.

²⁸"Be like the Son of Man. He did not come to be served. Instead, he came to serve others. He came to give his life as the price for setting many people free."

Two Blind Men Receive Their Sight

²⁹Jesus and his disciples were leaving Jericho. A large crowd followed him. ³⁰Two blind men were sitting by the side of the road. They heard that Jesus was going by. So they shouted, "Lord! Son of David! Have mercy on us!"

³¹The crowd commanded them to stop. They told them to be quiet. But the two men shouted even louder, "Lord! Son of David! Have mercy on us!"

³²Jesus stopped and called out to them. "What do you want me to do for you?" he asked.

³³"Lord," they answered, "we want to be able to see."

³⁴Jesus felt deep concern for them. He touched their eyes. Right away they could see. And they followed him.

Jesus Enters Jerusalem

21 As they all approached Jerusalem, they came to Bethphage. It was on the Mount of Olives. Jesus sent out two disciples. ²He said to them, "Go to the village ahead of you. As soon as you get there, you will find a donkey tied up. Her colt will be with her. Untie them and bring them to me. ³If anyone says anything to you, say that the Lord needs them. The owner will send them right away."

⁴This took place so that what was spoken through the prophet would come true. It says,

⁵"Say to the city of Zion,
'See, your king comes to you.
He is gentle and riding on a donkey.
He is riding on a donkey's colt.' "
(Zechariah 9:9)

⁶The disciples went and did what Jesus told them to do. ⁷They brought the donkey and the colt. They placed their coats on them. Then Jesus sat on the coats. ⁸A very large crowd spread their coats on the road. Others cut branches from the trees and spread them on the road. ⁹Some of the people went ahead of him, and some followed. They all shouted,

"Hosanna to the Son of David!"

"Blessed is the one who comes in the name of the Lord!" *(Psalm 118:26)*

"Hosanna in the highest heaven!"

¹⁰When Jesus entered Jerusalem, the whole city was stirred up. The people asked, "Who is this?"

¹¹The crowds answered, "This is Jesus. He is the prophet from Nazareth in Galilee."

Jesus Clears Out the Temple

¹²Jesus entered the temple area. He began chasing out all those who were buying and selling there. He turned over the tables of the people who were exchanging money. He also turned over the benches of those who were selling doves. ¹³He said to them, "It is written that the Lord said, 'My house will be called a house where people can pray.' *(Isaiah 56:7)* But you are making it a 'den for robbers.' " *(Jeremiah 7:11)*

¹⁴Blind people and those who were disabled came to Jesus at the temple. There he healed them. ¹⁵The chief priests and the teachers of the law saw the wonderful things he did. They also saw the children in the temple area shouting, "Hosanna to the Son of David!" But when they saw all of this, they became angry.

¹⁶"Do you hear what these children are saying?" they asked him.

"Yes," replied Jesus. "Haven't you ever read about it in Scripture? It says,

" 'You have made sure that children and infants
praise you.' " *(Psalm 8:2)*

¹⁷Then Jesus left the people and went out of the city to Bethany. He spent the night there.

The Fig Tree Dries Up

¹⁸Early in the morning, Jesus was on his way back to Jerusalem. He was hungry. ¹⁹He saw a fig tree by the road. He went up to it but found nothing on it except leaves. Then he said to it, "May you never bear fruit again!" Right away the tree dried up.

²⁰When the disciples saw this, they were amazed. "How did the fig tree dry up so quickly?" they asked.

²¹Jesus replied, "What I'm about to tell you is true. You must have faith and not doubt. Then you can do what was done to the fig tree. And you can say to this mountain, 'Go and throw yourself into the sea.' It will be done. ²²If you believe, you will receive what you ask for when you pray."

The Authority of Jesus Is Questioned

²³Jesus entered the temple courtyard. While he was teaching there, the chief priests and the elders of the people came to him. "By what authority are you doing these things?" they asked. "Who gave you this authority?"

²⁴Jesus replied, "I will also ask you one question. If you answer me, I will tell you by what authority I am doing these things. ²⁵Where did John's baptism come from? Was it from heaven? Or did it come from men?"

They talked to each other about it. They said, "If we say, 'From heaven,' he will ask, 'Then why didn't you believe him?' ²⁶But what if we say, 'From men'? We are afraid of the people. Everyone believes that John was a prophet."

²⁷So they answered Jesus, "We don't know."

Jesus said, "Then I won't tell you by what authority I am doing these things either.

The Story of the Two Sons

²⁸"What do you think about this? A man had two sons. He went to the first and said, 'Son, go and work today in the vineyard.'

²⁹" 'I will not,' the son answered. But later he changed his mind and went.

³⁰"Then the father went to the other son. He said the same thing. The son answered, 'I will, sir.' But he did not go.

³¹"Which of the two sons did what his father wanted?"

"The first," they answered.

Jesus said to them, "What I'm about to tell you is true. Tax collectors and prostitutes will enter the kingdom of God ahead of you. ³²John came to show you the right way to live. And you did not believe him. But the tax collectors and the prostitutes

Which One Are YOU?

The thermometer indicates the temperature and is controlled by its surroundings. It is **passive.**

The **thermostat** sets, controls and maintains the desired temperature. It is **purpose driven.**

The thermometer **Christian** ... looks and follows **the crowd.**

The **thermostat Christian** ... looks and follows **the cross.**

did. You saw this. But even then you did not turn away from your sins and believe him.

The Story of the Renters

³³"Listen to another story. A man who owned some land planted a vineyard. He put a wall around it. He dug a pit for a winepress in it. He also built a lookout tower. He rented the vineyard out to some farmers. Then he went away on a journey. ³⁴When harvest time approached, he sent

his servants to the renters. He told the servants to collect his share of the fruit.

³⁵"But the renters grabbed his servants. They beat one of them. They killed another. They threw stones at the third to kill him. ³⁶Then the man sent other servants to the renters. He sent more than he did the first time. The renters treated them the same way.

³⁷"Last of all, he sent his son to them. 'They will respect my son,' he said.

³⁸"But the renters saw the son coming. They said to each other, 'This is the one who will receive all the owner's property someday. Come, let's kill him. Then everything will be ours.' ³⁹So they took him and threw him out of the vineyard. Then they killed him.

⁴⁰"When the owner of the vineyard comes back, what will he do to those renters?"

⁴¹"He will destroy those evil people," they replied. "Then he will rent the vineyard out to other renters. They will give him his share of the crop at harvest time."

⁴²Jesus said to them, "Haven't you ever read what the Scriptures say,

" 'The stone the builders didn't accept
  has become the most important stone
  of all.
The Lord has done it.
It is wonderful in our eyes'?

(Psalm 118:22,23)

⁴³"So here is what I tell you. The kingdom of God will be taken away from you. It will be given to people who will produce its fruit. ⁴⁴Everyone who falls on that stone will be broken to pieces. But the stone will crush anyone it falls on."

⁴⁵The chief priests and the Pharisees heard Jesus' stories. They knew he was talking about them. ⁴⁶So they looked for a way to arrest him. But they were afraid of the crowd. The people believed that Jesus was a prophet.

The Story of the Wedding Dinner

22 Jesus told them more stories. He said, ²"Here is what the kingdom of heaven is like. A king prepared a wedding dinner for his son. ³He sent his servants to those who had been invited to the dinner.

The servants told them to come. But they refused.

⁴"Then he sent some more servants. He said, 'Tell those who were invited that I have prepared my dinner. I have killed my oxen and my fattest cattle. Everything is ready. Come to the wedding dinner.'

⁵"But the people paid no attention. One went away to his field. Another went away to his business. ⁶The rest grabbed his servants. They treated them badly and then killed them.

⁷"The king became very angry. He sent his army to destroy them. They killed those murderers and burned their city.

⁸"Then the king said to his servants, 'The wedding dinner is ready. But those I invited were not fit to come. ⁹Go to the street corners. Invite to the dinner anyone you can find.' ¹⁰So the servants went out into the streets. They gathered all the people they could find, both good and bad. Soon the wedding hall was filled with guests.

¹¹"The king came in to see the guests. He noticed a man there who was not wearing wedding clothes. ¹²'Friend,' he asked, 'how did you get in here without wedding clothes?' The man couldn't think of anything to say.

¹³"Then the king told his servants, 'Tie up his hands and feet. Throw him outside into the darkness. Out there people will sob and grind their teeth.'

¹⁴"Many are invited, but few are chosen."

Is It Right to Pay Taxes to Caesar?

¹⁵The Pharisees went out. They made plans to trap Jesus with his own words. ¹⁶They sent their followers to him. They sent the Herodians with them.

"Teacher," they said, "we know you are a man of honor. You teach the way of God truthfully. You don't let others tell you what to do or say. You don't care how important they are. ¹⁷Tell us then, what do you think? Is it right to pay taxes to Caesar or not?"

¹⁸But Jesus knew their evil plans. He said, "You pretenders! Why are you trying to trap me? ¹⁹Show me the coin people use for paying the tax."

They brought him a silver coin.

²⁰He asked them, "Whose picture is this?

"I'm not a Christian because ..."

"I live by the 10 Commandments."

The most important commandment is:

"Love the Lord your God with all your heart and with all your soul. Love him with all your mind." Matthew 22:37

How is it going?

- Ever wanted what someone else had?
- Ever tell a lie?
- Ever take something that was not yours?

"Suppose you keep the whole law but trip over just one part of it. Then you are guilty of breaking all of it." James 2:10

The Bible says if you break one ...

You're guilty.

Only a perfect person can keep them all - His name is Jesus.

And whose words?"

²¹"Caesar's," they replied.

Then he said to them, "Give to Caesar what belongs to Caesar. And give to God what belongs to God."

²²When they heard this, they were amazed. So they left him and went away.

Marriage When the Dead Rise

²³That same day the Sadducees came to Jesus with a question. They do not believe that people rise from the dead.

²⁴"Teacher," they said, "here is what Moses told us. If a man dies without having children, his brother must get married to the widow. He must have children to carry on his brother's name. ²⁵There were seven brothers among us. The first one got married and died. Since he had no children, he left his wife to his brother. ²⁶The same thing happened to the second and third brothers. It happened right on down to the seventh brother. ²⁷Finally, the woman died. ²⁸Now then, when the dead rise, whose wife will she be? All seven of them were married to her."

²⁹Jesus replied, "You are mistaken, because you do not know the Scriptures. And you do not know the power of God. ³⁰When the dead rise, they won't get married. And their parents won't give them to be married. They will be like the angels in heaven.

³¹"What about the dead rising? Haven't you read what God said to you? ³²He said, 'I am the God of Abraham. I am the God of Isaac. And I am the God of Jacob.' *(Exodus 3:6)* He is not the God of the dead. He is the God of the living."

³³When the crowds heard this, they were amazed by what he taught.

The Most Important Commandment

³⁴The Pharisees heard that the Sadducees weren't able to answer Jesus. So the

Pharisees got together. ³⁵One of them was an authority on the law. So he tested Jesus with a question. ³⁶"Teacher," he asked, "which is the most important commandment in the Law?"

³⁷Jesus replied, " 'Love the Lord your God with all your heart and with all your soul. Love him with all your mind.' *(Deuteronomy 6:5)* ³⁸This is the first and most important commandment. ³⁹And the second is like it. 'Love your neighbor as you love yourself.' *(Leviticus 19:18)* ⁴⁰Everything that is written in the Law and the Prophets is based on these two commandments."

Whose Son Is the Christ?

⁴¹The Pharisees were gathered together. Jesus asked them, ⁴²"What do you think about the Christ? Whose son is he?"

"The son of David," they replied.

⁴³He said to them, "Then why does David call him 'Lord'? The Holy Spirit spoke through David himself. David said,

⁴⁴" 'The Lord said to my Lord,
  "Sit at my right hand
  until I put your enemies
    under your control." '   *(Psalm 110:1)*

⁴⁵So if David calls him 'Lord,' how can he be David's son?"

⁴⁶No one could answer him with a single word. From that day on, no one dared to ask him any more questions.

Jesus Judges the Pharisees and the Teachers of the Law

23 Jesus spoke to the crowds and to his disciples. ²"The teachers of the law and the Pharisees sit in Moses' seat," he said. ³"So you must obey them. Do everything they tell you. But don't do what they do. They don't practice what they preach. ⁴They tie up heavy loads and put them on other people's shoulders. But they themselves aren't willing to lift a finger to move them.

⁵"Everything they do is done for others to see. On their foreheads and arms they wear little boxes that hold Scripture verses. They make the boxes very wide. And they make the tassels on their coats very long.

⁶"They love to sit down in the place of honor at dinners. They also love to have the most important seats in the synagogues. ⁷They love to be greeted in the market places. They love it when people call them 'Rabbi.'

⁸"But you shouldn't be called 'Rabbi.' You have only one Master, and you are all brothers. ⁹Do not call anyone on earth 'father.' You have one Father, and he is in heaven. ¹⁰You shouldn't be called 'teacher.' You have one Teacher, and he is the Christ. ¹¹The most important person among you will be your servant. ¹²Anyone who lifts himself up will be brought down. And anyone who is brought down will be lifted up.

Pharisee's Pompous Parade

You can call me "Rabbi"!

Are the cameras running?

We know everything about God!

¹³/¹⁴"How terrible it will be for you, teachers of the law and Pharisees! You pretenders! You shut the kingdom of heaven in people's faces. You yourselves do not enter. And you will not let those enter who are trying to.

¹⁵"How terrible for you, teachers of the law and Pharisees! You pretenders! You travel everywhere to win one person to your faith. Then you make him twice as much a son of hell as you are.

¹⁶"How terrible for you, blind guides! You say, 'If anyone takes an oath in the name of the temple, it means nothing. But anyone who takes an oath in the name of the gold of the temple must keep the oath.' ¹⁷You are blind and foolish! Which is more important? Is it the gold? Or is it the temple that makes the gold holy?

¹⁸"You also say, 'If anyone takes an oath in the name of the altar, it means nothing. But anyone who takes an oath in the name of the gift on it must keep the oath.' ¹⁹You blind men! Which is more important? Is it the gift? Or is it the altar that makes the gift holy?

²⁰"So anyone who takes an oath in the name of the altar takes an oath in the name of it and of everything on it. ²¹And anyone who takes an oath in the name of the temple takes an oath in the name of it and of the One who lives in it. ²²And anyone who takes an oath in the name of heaven takes an oath in the name of God's throne and of the One who sits on it.

²³"How terrible for you, teachers of the law and Pharisees! You pretenders! You give God a tenth of your spices, like mint, dill and cummin. But you have not practiced the more important things of the law, like fairness, mercy and faithfulness. You should have practiced the last things without failing to do the first. ²⁴You blind guides! You remove the smallest insect from your food. But you swallow a whole camel!

²⁵"How terrible for you, teachers of the law and Pharisees! You pretenders! You clean the outside of the cup and dish. But on the inside you are full of greed. You only want to satisfy yourselves. ²⁶Blind Pharisee! First clean the inside of the cup and dish. Then the outside will also be clean.

²⁷"How terrible for you, teachers of the law and Pharisees! You pretenders! You are like tombs that are painted white. They look beautiful on the outside. But on the inside they are full of the bones of the dead. They are also full of other things that are not pure and clean. ²⁸It is the same with you. On the outside you seem to be doing what is right. But on the inside you are full of what is wrong. You pretend to be what you are not.

²⁹"How terrible for you, teachers of the law and Pharisees! You pretenders! You build tombs for the prophets. You decorate the graves of the godly. ³⁰And you say, 'If

we had lived in the days of those who lived before us, we wouldn't have done what they did. We wouldn't have helped to kill the prophets.' ³¹So you give witness against yourselves. You admit that you are the children of those who murdered the prophets. ³²So finish the sins that those who lived before you started!

³³"You nest of poisonous snakes! How will you escape from being sentenced to hell? ³⁴So I am sending you prophets, wise men, and teachers. You will kill some of them. You will nail some to a cross. Others you will whip in your synagogues. You will chase them from town to town.

³⁵"So you will pay for all the godly people's blood spilled on earth. I mean from the blood of godly Abel to the blood of Zechariah, the son of Berekiah. Zechariah was the one you murdered between the temple and the altar. ³⁶What I'm about to tell you is true. All this will happen to those who are now living.

³⁷"Jerusalem! Jerusalem! You kill the prophets and throw stones in order to kill those who are sent to you. Many times I have wanted to gather your people together. I have wanted to be like a hen who gathers her chicks under her wings. But you would not let me! ³⁸Look, your house is left empty. ³⁹I tell you, you will not see me again until you say, 'Blessed is the one who comes in the name of the Lord.' " *(Psalm 118:26)*

Signs of the End

24 Jesus left the temple. He was walking away when his disciples came up to him. They wanted to call his attention to the temple buildings.

²"Do you see all these things?" Jesus asked. "What I'm about to tell you is true. Not one stone here will be left on top of another. Every stone will be thrown down."

³Jesus was sitting on the Mount of Olives. There the disciples came to him in private. "Tell us," they said. "When will this happen? And what will be the sign of your coming? What will be the sign of the end?"

⁴Jesus answered, "Keep watch! Be careful that no one fools you. ⁵Many will come in my name. They will claim, 'I am the Christ!' They will fool many people.

⁶"You will hear about wars. You will also hear people talking about future wars. Don't be alarmed. Those things must happen. But the end still isn't here. ⁷Nation will fight against nation. Kingdom will fight against kingdom. People will go hungry. There will be earthquakes in many places. ⁸All these are the beginning of birth pains.

⁹"Then people will hand you over to be treated badly and killed. All nations will hate you because of me. ¹⁰At that time, many will turn away from their faith. They will hate each other. They will hand each other over to their enemies. ¹¹Many false prophets will appear. They will fool many people. ¹²Because evil will grow, most people's love will grow cold. ¹³But the one who stands firm to the end will be saved. ¹⁴This good news of the kingdom will be preached in the whole world. It will be a witness to all nations. Then the end will come.

¹⁵"The prophet Daniel spoke about 'the hated thing that destroys.' *(Daniel 9:27; 11:31; 12:11)* Someday you will see it standing in the holy place. The reader should understand this. ¹⁶Then those who are in Judea should escape to the mountains. ¹⁷No one on the roof should go down into his house to take anything out. ¹⁸No one in the field should go back to get his coat. ¹⁹How awful it will be in those days for pregnant women! How awful for nursing mothers! ²⁰Pray that you will not have to escape in winter or on the Sabbath day. ²¹There will be terrible suffering in those days. It will be worse than any other from the beginning of the world until now. And there will never be anything like it again. ²²If the time had not been cut short, no one would live. But because of God's chosen people, it will be shortened.

You're as close to God as you choose to be.

²³"At that time someone may say to you, 'Look! Here is the Christ!' Or, 'There he is!' Do not believe it. ²⁴False Christs and false prophets will appear. They will do great signs and miracles. They will try to fool God's chosen people if possible. ²⁵See, I have told you ahead of time.

²⁶"So if anyone tells you, 'He is far out in the desert,' do not go out there. Or if anyone says, 'He is deep inside the house,' do not believe it. ²⁷Lightning that comes from the east can be seen in the west. It will be the same when the Son of Man comes. ²⁸The vultures will gather wherever there is a dead body.

²⁹"Right after the terrible suffering of those days,

" 'The sun will be darkened.
The moon will not shine.
The stars will fall from the sky.
The heavenly bodies will be shaken.'
(Isaiah 13:10; 34:4)

³⁰"At that time the sign of the Son of Man will appear in the sky. All the nations on earth will be sad. They will see the Son of Man coming on the clouds of the sky. He will come with power and great glory. ³¹He will send his angels with a loud trumpet call. They will gather his chosen people from all four directions. They will bring them from one end of the heavens to the other.

³²"Learn a lesson from the fig tree. As soon as its twigs get tender and its leaves come out, you know that summer is near. ³³In the same way, when you see all those things happening, you know that the end is near. It is right at the door. ³⁴What I'm about to tell you is true. The people living at that time will certainly not pass away until all those things have happened. ³⁵Heaven and earth will pass away. But my words will never pass away.

The Day and Hour Are Not Known

³⁶"No one knows about that day or hour. Not even the angels in heaven know. The Son does not know. Only the Father knows.

³⁷"Remember how it was in the days of Noah. It will be the same when the Son of Man comes.

³⁸"In the days before the flood, people were eating and drinking. They were getting married. They were giving their daughters to be married. They did all those things right up to the day Noah entered the ark. ³⁹They knew nothing about what would happen until the flood came and took them all away. That is how it will be when the Son of Man comes.

⁴⁰"Two men will be in the field. One will be taken and the other left. ⁴¹Two women will be grinding with a hand mill. One will be taken and the other left.

⁴²"So keep watch. You do not know on what day your Lord will come. ⁴³You must understand something. Suppose the owner of the house knew what time of night the robber was coming. Then he would have kept watch. He would not have let his house be broken into. ⁴⁴So you also must be ready. The Son of Man will come at an hour when you don't expect him.

⁴⁵"Suppose a master puts one of his servants in charge of the other servants in his house. The servant's job is to give them their food at the right time. The master wants a faithful and wise servant for this. ⁴⁶It will be good for the servant if the master finds him doing his job when the master returns. ⁴⁷What I'm about to tell you is true. The master will put that servant in charge of everything he owns.

⁴⁸"But suppose that servant is evil. Suppose he says to himself, 'My master is staying away a long time.' ⁴⁹Suppose he begins to beat the other servants. And suppose he eats and drinks with those who drink too much. ⁵⁰The master of that servant will come back on a day the servant doesn't expect him. He will return at an hour the servant does not know. ⁵¹Then the master will cut him to pieces. He will send him to the place where pretenders go. There people will sob and grind their teeth.

The Story of Ten Bridesmaids

25 "Here is what the kingdom of heaven will be like at that time. Ten bridesmaids took their lamps and went out to meet the groom. ²Five of them were fool-

ish. Five were wise. [3]The foolish ones took their lamps but didn't take any olive oil with them. [4]The wise ones took oil in jars along with their lamps. [5]The groom did not come for a long time. So the bridesmaids all grew tired and fell asleep.

[6]"At midnight someone cried out, 'Here's the groom! Come out to meet him!'

[7]"Then all the bridesmaids woke up and got their lamps ready. [8]The foolish ones said to the wise ones, 'Give us some of your oil. Our lamps are going out.'

[9]" 'No,' they replied. 'There may not be enough for all of us. Instead, go to those who sell oil. Buy some for yourselves.'

[10]"So they went to buy the oil. But while they were on their way, the groom arrived. The bridesmaids who were ready went in with him to the wedding dinner. Then the door was shut.

[11]"Later, the other bridesmaids also came. 'Sir! Sir!' they said. 'Open the door for us!'

[12]"But he replied, 'What I'm about to tell you is true. I don't know you.'

[13]"So keep watch. You do not know the day or the hour that the groom will come.

The Story of Three Servants

[14]"Again, here is what the kingdom of heaven will be like. A man was going on a journey. He sent for his servants and put them in charge of his property. [15]He gave $10,000 to one. He gave $4,000 to another. And he gave $2,000 to the third. The man gave each servant the amount of money he knew the servant could take care of. Then he went on his journey.

[16]"The servant who had received the $10,000 went at once and put his money to work. He earned $10,000 more. [17]The one with the $4,000 earned $4,000 more. [18]But the man who had received $2,000 went and dug a hole in the ground. He hid his master's money in it.

[19]"After a long time the master of those servants returned. He wanted to collect all the money they had earned. [20]The man who had received $10,000 brought the other $10,000. 'Master,' he said, 'you trusted me with $10,000. See, I have earned $10,000 more.'

[21]"His master replied, 'You have done well, good and faithful servant! You have been faithful with a few things. I will put you in charge of many things. Come and share your master's happiness!'

[22]"The man with $4,000 also came. 'Master,' he said, 'you trusted me with $4,000. See, I have earned $4,000 more.'

[23]"His master replied, 'You have done well, good and faithful servant! You have been faithful with a few things. I will put you in charge of many things. Come and share your master's happiness!'

[24]"Then the man who had received $2,000 came. 'Master,' he said, 'I knew that you are a hard man. You harvest where you have not planted. You gather crops where you have not scattered seed. [25]So I was afraid. I went out and hid your $2,000 in the ground. See, here is what belongs to you.'

[26]"His master replied, 'You evil, lazy servant! So you knew that I harvest where I have not planted? You knew that I gather crops where I have not scattered seed? [27]Well then, you should have put my money in the bank. When I returned, I would have received it back with interest.'

[28]"Then his master commanded the other servants, 'Take the $2,000 from him. Give it to the one who has $20,000. [29]Everyone who has will be given more. He will have more than enough. And what about anyone who doesn't have? Even what he has will be taken away from him. [30]Throw that worthless servant outside. There in the darkness, people will sob and grind their teeth.'

The Sheep and the Goats

[31]"The Son of Man will come in all his glory. All the angels will come with him. Then he will sit on his throne in the glory of heaven. [32]All the nations will be gathered in front of him. He will separate the people into two groups. He will be like a shepherd who separates the sheep from the goats. [33]He will put the sheep to his right and the goats to his left.

[34]"Then the King will speak to those on his right. He will say, 'My Father has blessed you. Come and take what is yours. It is the kingdom prepared for you since the world was created. [35]I was hungry. And

you gave me something to eat. I was thirsty. And you gave me something to drink. I was a stranger. And you invited me in. [36]I needed clothes. And you gave them to me. I was sick. And you took care of me. I was in prison. And you came to visit me.'

[37]"Then the people who have done what is right will answer him. 'Lord,' they will ask, 'when did we see you hungry and feed you? When did we see you thirsty and give you something to drink? [38]When did we see you as a stranger and invite you in? When did we see you needing clothes and give them to you? [39]When did we see you sick or in prison and go to visit you?'

[40]"The King will reply, 'What I'm about to tell you is true. Anything you did for one of the least important of these brothers of mine, you did for me.'

[41]"Then he will say to those on his left, 'You are cursed! Go away from me into the fire that burns forever. It has been prepared for the devil and his angels. [42]I was hungry. But you gave me nothing to eat. I was thirsty. But you gave me nothing to drink. [43]I was a stranger. But you did not invite me in. I needed clothes. But you did not give me any. I was sick and in prison. But you did not take care of me.'

[44]"They also will answer, 'Lord, when did we see you hungry or thirsty and not help you? When did we see you as a stranger or needing clothes or sick or in prison and not help you?'

[45]"He will reply, 'What I'm about to tell you is true. Anything you didn't do for one of the least important of these, you didn't do for me.'

[46]"Then they will go away to be punished forever. But those who have done what is right will receive eternal life."

The Plan to Kill Jesus

26 Jesus finished saying all these things. Then he said to his disciples, [2]"As you know, the Passover Feast is two days away. The Son of Man will be handed over to be nailed to a cross."

[3]Then the chief priests met with the elders of the people. They met in the palace of Caiaphas, the high priest. [4]They made

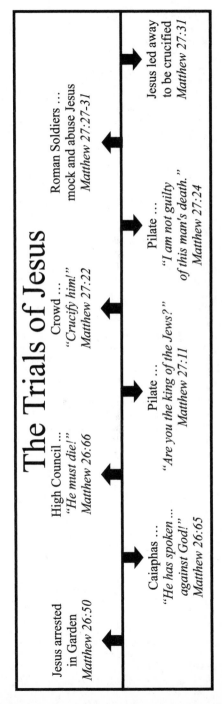

The Trials of Jesus

Jesus arrested in Garden
Matthew 26:50

Caiaphas ...
"He has spoken ... against God!"
Matthew 26:65

High Council ...
"He must die!"
Matthew 26:66

Pilate ...
"Are you the king of the Jews?"
Matthew 27:11

Crowd ...
"Crucify him!"
Matthew 27:22

Pilate ...
"I am not guilty of this man's death."
Matthew 27:24

Roman Soldiers ...
mock and abuse Jesus
Matthew 27:27-31

Jesus led away to be crucified
Matthew 27:31

plans to arrest Jesus in a clever way. They wanted to kill him. [5]"But not during the Feast," they said. "The people may stir up trouble."

A Woman Pours Perfume on Jesus

[6]Jesus was in Bethany. He was in the home of a man named Simon, who had a skin disease. [7]A woman came to Jesus with a special sealed jar of very expensive perfume. She poured the perfume on his head while he was at the table.

[8]When the disciples saw this, they became angry. "Why this waste?" they asked. [9]"The perfume could have been sold at a high price. The money could have been given to poor people."

[10]Jesus was aware of this. So he said to them, "Why are you bothering this woman? She has done a beautiful thing to me. [11]You will always have poor people with you. But you will not always have me. [12]She poured the perfume on my body to prepare me to be buried. [13]What I'm about to tell you is true. What she has done will be told anywhere this good news is preached all over the world. It will be told in memory of her."

Judas Agrees to Hand Jesus Over

[14]One of the Twelve went to the chief priests. His name was Judas Iscariot. [15]He asked, "What will you give me if I hand Jesus over to you?" So they counted out 30 silver coins for him. [16]From then on, Judas watched for the right time to hand Jesus over to them.

The Lord's Supper

[17]It was the first day of the Feast of Unleavened Bread. The disciples came to Jesus. They asked, "Where do you want us to prepare for you to eat the Passover meal?"

[18]He replied, "Go into the city to a certain man. Tell him, 'The Teacher says, "My time is near. I am going to celebrate the Passover at your house with my disciples."'"

[19]So the disciples did what Jesus had told them to do. They prepared the Passover meal.

[20]When evening came, Jesus was at the table with the Twelve. [21]While they were eating, he said, "What I'm about to tell you is true. One of you will hand me over to my enemies."

[22]The disciples became very sad. One after the other, they began to say to him, "It's not I, Lord, is it?"

[23]Jesus replied, "The one who has dipped his hand into the bowl with me will hand me over. [24]The Son of Man will go just as it is written about him. But how terrible it will be for the one who hands over the Son of Man! It would be better for him if he had not been born."

[25]Judas was the one who was going to hand him over. He said, "It's not I, Rabbi, is it?"

Jesus answered, "Yes. It is you."

[26]While they were eating, Jesus took bread. He gave thanks and broke it. He handed it to his disciples and said, "Take this and eat it. This is my body."

[27]Then he took the cup. He gave thanks and handed it to them. He said, "All of you drink from it. [28]This is my blood of the new covenant. It is poured out to forgive the sins of many. [29]Here is what I tell you. From now on, I won't drink wine with you again until the day I drink it with you in my Father's kingdom."

[30]Then they sang a hymn and went out to the Mount of Olives.

Jesus Says That Peter Will Fail

[31]Jesus told them, "This very night you will all turn away because of me. It is written that the Lord said,

" 'I will strike the shepherd down.
    Then the sheep of the flock will be
        scattered.'   *(Zechariah 13:7)*

[32]But after I rise from the dead, I will go ahead of you into Galilee."

[33]Peter replied, "All the others may turn away because of you. But I never will."

[34]"What I'm about to tell you is true," Jesus answered. "It will happen this very night. Before the rooster crows, you will say three times that you don't know me."

[35]But Peter said, "I may have to die with you. But I will never say I don't know you."

My Way or God's Way?

"If anyone wants to follow me, he must say no to himself. He must pick up his cross and follow me." Jesus (Matthew 16:24)

And all the other disciples said the same thing.

Jesus Prays in Gethsemane

[36]Then Jesus went with his disciples to a place called Gethsemane. He said to them, "Sit here while I go over there and pray."

[37]He took Peter and the two sons of Zebedee along with him. He began to be sad and troubled. [38]Then he said to them, "My soul is very sad. I feel close to death. Stay here. Keep watch with me."

[39]He went a little farther. Then he fell with his face to the ground. He prayed, "My Father, if it is possible, take this cup of suffering away from me. But let what you want be done, not what I want."

[40]Then he returned to his disciples and found them sleeping. "Couldn't you men keep watch with me for one hour?" he asked Peter. [41]"Watch and pray. Then you won't fall into sin when you are tempted. The spirit is willing. But the body is weak."

[42]Jesus went away a second time. He prayed, "My Father, is it possible for this cup to be taken away? But if I must drink it, may what you want be done."

[43]Then he came back. Again he found them sleeping. They couldn't keep their eyes open. [44]So he left them and went away once more.

For the third time he prayed the same thing.

[45]Then he returned to the disciples. He said to them, "Are you still sleeping and resting? Look! The hour is near. The Son of Man is about to be handed over to sinners. [46]Get up! Let us go! Here comes the one who is handing me over to them!"

Jesus Is Arrested

[47]While Jesus was still speaking, Judas arrived. He was one of the Twelve. A large crowd was with him. They were carrying swords and clubs. The chief priests and the elders of the people had sent them.

[48]Judas, who was going to hand Jesus over, had arranged a signal with them. "The one I kiss is the man," he said. "Arrest him."

[49]So Judas went to Jesus at once. He said, "Greetings, Rabbi!" And he kissed him.

[50]Jesus replied, "Friend, do what you came to do."

Then the men stepped forward. They grabbed Jesus and arrested him. [51]At that moment, one of Jesus' companions reached for his sword. He pulled it out and struck the servant of the high priest with it. He cut off the servant's ear.

[52]"Put your sword back in its place," Jesus said to him. "All who use the sword will die by the sword. [53]Do you think I can't ask my

Father for help? He would send an army of more than 70,000 angels right away. ⁵⁴But then how would the Scriptures come true? They say it must happen in this way."

⁵⁵At that time Jesus spoke to the crowd. "Am I leading a band of armed men against you?" he asked. "Do you have to come out with swords and clubs to capture me? Every day I sat in the temple courtyard teaching. And you didn't arrest me. ⁵⁶But all this has happened so that the words of the prophets would come true."

Then all the disciples left him and ran away.

Jesus Is Taken to the Sanhedrin

⁵⁷Those who had arrested Jesus took him to Caiaphas, the high priest. The teachers of the law and the elders had come together there. ⁵⁸Not too far away, Peter followed Jesus. He went right up to the courtyard of the high priest. He entered and sat down with the guards to see what would happen.

⁵⁹The chief priests and the whole Sanhedrin were looking for something to use against Jesus. They wanted to put him to death. ⁶⁰But they did not find any proof, even though many false witnesses came forward.

Finally, two other witnesses came forward. ⁶¹They said, "This fellow claimed, 'I am able to destroy the temple of God. I can build it again in three days.' "

⁶²Then the high priest stood up. He asked Jesus, "Aren't you going to answer? What are these charges that these men are bringing against you?"

⁶³But Jesus remained silent.

The high priest said to him, "I command you under oath by the living God. Tell us if you are the Christ, the Son of God."

⁶⁴"Yes. It is just as you say," Jesus replied. "But here is what I say to all of you. In days to come, you will see the Son of Man sitting at the right hand of the Mighty One. You will see the Son of Man coming on the clouds of heaven."

⁶⁵Then the high priest tore his clothes. He said, "He has spoken a very evil thing against God! Why do we need any more witnesses? You have heard him say this evil thing. ⁶⁶What do you think?"

"He must die!" they answered.

⁶⁷Then they spit in his face. They hit him with their fists. Others slapped him. ⁶⁸They said, "Prophesy to us, Christ! Who hit you?"

Peter Says He Does Not Know Jesus

⁶⁹Peter was sitting out in the courtyard. A female servant came to him. "You also were with Jesus of Galilee," she said.

⁷⁰But in front of all of them, Peter said he was not. "I don't know what you're talking about," he said.

⁷¹Then he went out to the gate leading into the courtyard. There another woman saw him. She said to the people, "This fellow was with Jesus of Nazareth."

⁷²Again he said he was not. With an oath he said, "I don't know the man!"

⁷³After a little while, those standing there went up to Peter. "You must be one of them," they said. "The way you talk gives you away."

⁷⁴Then Peter began to call down curses on himself. He took an oath and said to them, "I don't know the man!"

Right away a rooster crowed. ⁷⁵Then Peter remembered what Jesus had said. "The rooster will crow," Jesus had told him. "Before it does, you will say three times that you don't know me." Peter went outside. He broke down and sobbed.

Judas Hangs Himself

27 It was early in the morning. All the chief priests and the elders of the people decided to put Jesus to death. ²They tied him up and led him away. Then they handed him over to Pilate, who was the governor.

³Judas, who had handed him over, saw that Jesus had been sentenced to die. He felt deep shame and sadness for what he had done. So he returned the 30 silver coins to the chief priests and the elders. ⁴"I have sinned," he said. "I handed over a man who is not guilty."

"What do we care?" they replied. "That's your problem."

[5]So Judas threw the money into the temple and left. Then he went away and hanged himself.

[6]The chief priests picked up the coins. They said, "It's against the law to put this money into the temple fund. It is blood money. It has paid for a man's death." [7]So they decided to use the money to buy a potter's field. People from other countries would be buried there. [8]That is why it has been called The Field of Blood to this very day. [9]Then the words spoken by Jeremiah the prophet came true. He had said, "They took the 30 silver coins. That price was set for him by the people of Israel. [10]They used the coins to buy a potter's field, just as the Lord commanded me." (*Zechariah 11:12,13; Jeremiah 19:1–13; 32:6–9*)

Jesus Is Brought to Pilate

[11]Jesus was standing in front of the governor. The governor asked him, "Are you the king of the Jews?"

"Yes. It is just as you say," Jesus replied.

[12]But when the chief priests and the elders brought charges against him, he did not answer. [13]Then Pilate asked him, "Don't you hear the charges they are bringing against you?"

[14]But Jesus made no reply, not even to a single charge. The governor was really amazed.

[15]It was the governor's practice at the Passover Feast to let one prisoner go free. The people could choose the one they wanted. [16]At that time they had a well-known prisoner named Barabbas. [17]So when the crowd gathered, Pilate asked them, "Which one do you want me to set free? Barabbas? Or Jesus who is called Christ?" [18]Pilate knew that the leaders were jealous. He knew this was why they had handed Jesus over to him.

[19]While Pilate was sitting on the judge's seat, his wife sent him a message. It said, "Don't have anything to do with that man. He is not guilty. I have suffered a great deal in a dream today because of him."

[20]But the chief priests and the elders talked the crowd into asking for Barabbas and having Jesus put to death.

[21]"Which of the two do you want me to set free?" asked the governor.

"Barabbas," they answered.

[22]"Then what should I do with Jesus who is called Christ?" Pilate asked.

They all answered, "Crucify him!"

[23]"Why? What wrong has he done?" asked Pilate.

But they shouted even louder, "Crucify him!"

[24]Pilate saw that he wasn't getting anywhere. Instead, the crowd was starting to get angry. So he took water and washed his hands in front of them. "I am not guilty of this man's death," he said. "You are accountable for that!"

[25]All the people answered, "We and our children will accept the guilt for his death!"

[26]Pilate let Barabbas go free. But he had Jesus whipped. Then he handed him over to be nailed to a cross.

The Soldiers Make Fun of Jesus

[27]The governor's soldiers took Jesus into the palace, which was called the Praetorium. All the rest of the soldiers gathered around him. [28]They took off his clothes and put a purple robe on him. [29]Then they twisted thorns together to make a crown. They placed it on his head. They put a stick in his right hand. Then they fell on their knees in front of him and made fun of him. "We honor you, king of the Jews!" they said. [30]They spit on him. They hit him on the head with the stick again and again.

[31]After they had made fun of him, they took off the robe. They put his own clothes back on him. Then they led him away to nail him to a cross.

What have you done with what God has given you?

Jesus Is Nailed to a Cross

³²On their way out of the city, they met a man from Cyrene. His name was Simon. They forced him to carry the cross.

³³They came to a place called Golgotha. The word Golgotha means The Place of the Skull. ³⁴There they mixed wine with bitter spices and gave it to Jesus to drink. After tasting it, he refused to drink it.

³⁵When they had nailed him to the cross, they divided up his clothes by casting lots. ³⁶They sat down and kept watch over him there.

³⁷Above his head they placed the written charge against him. It read, THIS IS JESUS, THE KING OF THE JEWS.

³⁸Two robbers were crucified with him. One was on his right and one was on his left.

³⁹Those who passed by shouted at Jesus and made fun of him. They shook their heads ⁴⁰and said, "So you are going to destroy the temple and build it again in three days? Then save yourself! Come down from the cross, if you are the Son of God!"

⁴¹In the same way the chief priests, the teachers of the law and the elders made fun of him. ⁴²"He saved others," they said. "But he can't save himself! He's the King of Israel! Let him come down now from the cross! Then we will believe in him. ⁴³He trusts in God. Let God rescue him now if he wants him. He's the one who said, 'I am the Son of God.' "

⁴⁴In the same way the robbers who were being crucified with Jesus also made fun of him.

Jesus Dies

⁴⁵From noon until three o'clock, the whole land was covered with darkness. ⁴⁶About three o'clock, Jesus cried out in a loud voice. He said, *"Eloi, Eloi, lama sabachthani?"* This means "My God, my God, why have you deserted me?" *(Psalm 22:1)*

⁴⁷Some of those standing there heard Jesus cry out. They said, "He's calling for Elijah."

⁴⁸Right away one of them ran and got a sponge. He filled it with wine vinegar and put it on a stick. He offered it to Jesus to drink. ⁴⁹The rest said, "Leave him alone. Let's see if Elijah comes to save him."

⁵⁰After Jesus cried out again in a loud voice, he died.

⁵¹At that moment the temple curtain was torn in two from top to bottom. The earth shook. The rocks split. ⁵²Tombs broke open. The bodies of many holy people who had died were raised to life. ⁵³They came out of the tombs. After Jesus was raised to life, they went into the holy city. There they appeared to many people.

⁵⁴The Roman commander and those guarding Jesus saw the earthquake and all that had happened. They were terrified. They exclaimed, "He was surely the Son of God!"

⁵⁵Not very far away, many women were watching. They had followed Jesus from Galilee to take care of his needs. ⁵⁶Mary Magdalene was among them. Mary, the mother of James and Joses, was also there. So was the mother of Zebedee's sons.

Jesus Is Buried

⁵⁷As evening approached, a rich man came from the town of Arimathea. His name was Joseph. He had become a follower of Jesus. ⁵⁸He went to Pilate and asked for Jesus' body. Pilate ordered that it be given to him.

⁵⁹Joseph took the body and wrapped it in a clean linen cloth. ⁶⁰He placed it in his own new tomb that he had cut out of the rock. He rolled a big stone in front of the entrance to the tomb. Then he went away.

⁶¹Mary Magdalene and the other Mary were sitting there across from the tomb.

The Guards at the Tomb

⁶²The next day was the day after Preparation Day. The chief priests and the Pharisees went to Pilate. ⁶³"Sir," they said, "we remember something that liar said while he was still alive. He claimed, 'After three days I will rise again.' ⁶⁴So give the order to make the tomb secure until the third day. If you don't, his disciples might come and steal the body. Then they will tell the people that Jesus has been raised from the dead. This last lie will be worse than the first."

⁶⁵"Take some guards with you," Pilate answered. "Go. Make the tomb as secure as you can." ⁶⁶So they went and made the tomb secure. They put a seal on the stone and placed some guards on duty.

MATTHEW

Across

1. Washed his hands   ch. 27
5. Ask, seek, _____   ch. 7
8. First woman   ---
9. Rolled the stone away   ch. 28
10. Store treasures ____ heaven   ch. 6
11. Led the Wise Men   ch. 2
14. You are _____ of the world   ch. 5
16. Tempted Jesus   ch. 4
17. Street, avenue   ---
18. Satan crushed under a ___   ---
21. Rich man went away _____   ch. 19
23. Jesus, hope of the _____   ch. 12

Down

1. Enemies of Jesus   ch. 23
2. Need for walking   ch. 9
3. Abb. "avenue"   ---
4. Angel said "Go and ___"   ch. 28
6. Hometown of Jesus   ch. 2
7. Sign on the Cross   ch. 27
12. Jesus baptized in   ch. 3
13. One who obeys Jesus is   ch. 7
15. Jesus the Master   ch. 8
19. Lost in Gethsemane   ch. 26
20. Jesus ___ away to die   ch. 27
22. Left their nets __ once   ch. 4

Jesus Rises From the Dead

28 The Sabbath day was now over. It was dawn on the first day of the week. Mary Magdalene and the other Mary went to look at the tomb.

[2]There was a powerful earthquake. An angel of the Lord came down from heaven. The angel went to the tomb. He rolled back the stone and sat on it. [3]His body shone like lightning. His clothes were as white as snow. [4]The guards were so afraid of him that they shook and became like dead men.

[5]The angel said to the women, "Don't be afraid. I know that you are looking for Jesus, who was crucified. [6]He is not here! He has risen, just as he said he would! Come and see the place where he was lying. [7]Go quickly! Tell his disciples, 'He has risen from the dead. He is going ahead of you into Galilee. There you will see him.' Now I have told you."

[8]So the women hurried away from the tomb. They were afraid, but they were filled with joy. They ran to tell the disciples.

[9]Suddenly Jesus met them. "Greetings!" he said.

They came to him, took hold of his feet and worshiped him.

[10]Then Jesus said to them, "Don't be afraid. Go and tell my brothers to go to Galilee. There they will see me."

The Guards Report to the Chief Priests

[11]While the women were on their way, some of the guards went into the city. They reported to the chief priests all that had happened.

[12]When the chief priests met with the elders, they came up with a plan. They gave the soldiers a large amount of money. [13]They told the soldiers, "We want you to say, 'His disciples came during the night. They stole his body while we were sleeping.' [14]If the governor hears this report, we will pay him off. That will keep you out of trouble."

[15]So the soldiers took the money and did as they were told. This story has spread all around among the Jews to this very day.

Jesus' Final Orders to His Disciples

[16]Then the 11 disciples went to Galilee. They went to the mountain where Jesus had told them to go. [17]When they saw him, they worshiped him. But some still had their doubts.

[18]Then Jesus came to them. He said, "All authority in heaven and on earth has been given to me. [19]So you must go and make disciples of all nations. Baptize them in the name of the Father and of the Son and of the Holy Spirit. [20]Teach them to obey everything I have commanded you. And you can be sure that I am always with you, to the very end."

WORD Puzzle

EVERYTHING   COMMIT

PLANS   SUCCEED   DO   LORD   THE   YOUR

Place each word above in the proper space below to solve the message.

. _ _ _ _ _ _ _ . _ _ _ .   T _ O .

. _ _ _ _ .   . _ _ _ _ _ _ _ .

. _ _ _ _ _ _ _ _ _ _ .

. _ _ . O _ U _ . _ _ _ . • . T _ H _ E _ N .

. _ _ _ _ _ . _ _ _ _ _ _ _ .

. _ _ _ . I _ L _ L . _ _ _ _ _ _ _ _ _ _ • .

(Find answer on page 426 of The Illustrated New Testament)

THE GREAT COMMISSION

Matthew 28:18 • Acts 1:8

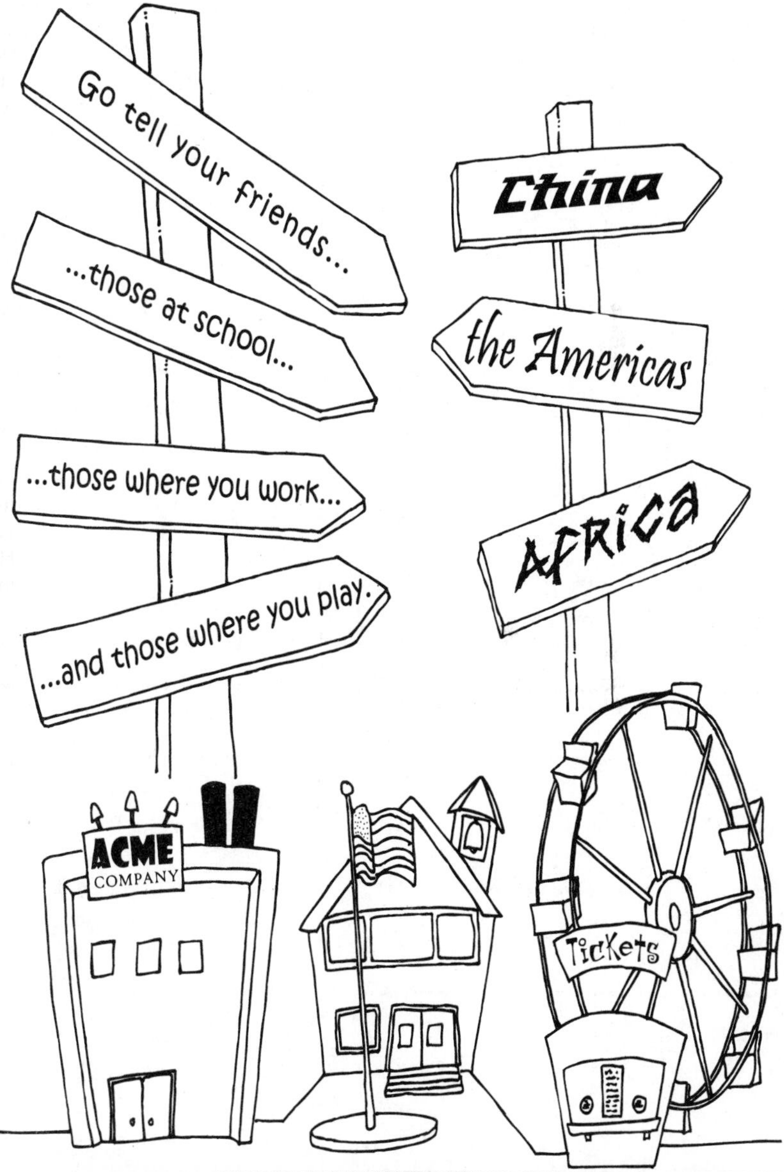

Open Book Quiz - The Book of Matthew

Read the letters from top to bottom and complete the answer below.

1 __K__ Throw yourself down   ch. 4

2 ____ Dogs eat the crumbs   ch. 15

3 ____ It is against the law   ch. 12

4 ____ 60 "quotes"   ch. 3

5 ____ Last commandment   ch. 28

6 ____ Even waves obey Him   ch. 8

7 ____ 5 + 2 =   ch. 14

8 ____ Never leave you   ch. 26

9 ____ Many invited but few ...   ch. 22

10 __H__ That's your problem   ch. 27

11 ____ Come down from cross   ch. 27

12 ____ Suffered in a dream   ch. 27

13 ____ Baptized Jesus   ch. 3

14 ____ We accept the guilt   ch. 27

15 ____ Last lie will be worst   ch. 27

Select the best answer from the right column which matches items 1-15 in the left column. Some letters are used more than once.

A - Pilate's wife
B - Adam and Eve
D - Go
E - People
F - ... are chosen
G - Isaiah
H - Chief priests
I - Canaan woman
K - Devil
L - Luke
M - 5000 fed
N - Pharisees
O - Disciples
P - Paul
V - John

Self-score

14 - 15	Great job!
12 - 13	"High-five" time
9 - 11	Turn off video games
5 - 8	Sell video games
1 - 4	Give the games away

Answer: __K__ __ __ __ __ __ __ • __ __

__H__ __ __ __ __

"The theme of the book of Matthew"

MARK

- *Written by John Mark - not an apostle*
- *Believed that Mark recorded Peter's account of the Gospel*
- *"Common man" Roman audience*
- *Style is brief, simple, fast-paced, and powerful*
- *Presents "Jesus as Servant" - Mark 10:45*

John the Baptist Prepares the Way

1 This is the beginning of the good news about Jesus Christ, the Son of God.

²Long ago Isaiah the prophet wrote,

"I will send my messenger ahead of you.
  He will prepare your way." *(Malachi 3:1)*
³"A messenger is calling out in the desert,
  'Prepare the way for the Lord.
  Make straight paths for him.'"

(Isaiah 40:3)

⁴And so John came. He baptized people in the desert. He also preached that people should be baptized and turn away from their sins. Then God would forgive them. ⁵All the people from the countryside of Judea went out to him. All the people from Jerusalem went too. When they admitted they had sinned, John baptized them in the Jordan River. ⁶John wore clothes made out of camel's hair. He had a leather belt around his waist. And he ate locusts and wild honey.

⁷Here is what John was preaching. "After me, one will come who is more powerful than I am. I'm not good enough to bend down and untie his sandals. ⁸I baptize you with water. But he will baptize you with the Holy Spirit."

Jesus Is Baptized and Tempted

⁹At that time Jesus came from Nazareth in Galilee. John baptized him in the Jordan River. ¹⁰Jesus was coming up out of the water. Just then he saw heaven being torn open. He saw the Holy Spirit coming down on him like a dove. ¹¹A voice spoke to him from heaven. It said, "You are my Son, and I love you. I am very pleased with you."

¹²At once the Holy Spirit sent Jesus out into the desert. ¹³He was in the desert 40 days. There Satan tempted him. The wild animals didn't harm Jesus. Angels took care of him.

Jesus Chooses the First Disciples

¹⁴After John was put in prison, Jesus went into Galilee. He preached God's good news. ¹⁵"The time has come," he said. "The kingdom of God is near. Turn away from your sins and believe the good news!"

¹⁶One day Jesus was walking beside the Sea of Galilee. There he saw Simon and his brother Andrew. They were throwing a net into the lake. They were fishermen. ¹⁷"Come. Follow me," Jesus said. "I will make you fishers of people."

¹⁸At once they left their nets and followed him.

¹⁹Then Jesus walked a little farther. As he did, he saw James, son of Zebedee, and his brother John. They were in a boat preparing their nets. ²⁰Right away he called out to them. They left their father Zebedee in the boat with the hired men. Then they followed Jesus.

Jesus Drives Out an Evil Spirit

²¹Jesus and those with him went to Capernaum. When the Sabbath day came, he went into the synagogue. There he began to teach. ²²The people were amazed at his teaching. He taught them like one who had authority. He did not talk like the teachers of the law.

²³Just then a man in their synagogue cried out. He was controlled by an evil spirit. He said, ²⁴"What do you want with us, Jesus of

Nazareth? Have you come to destroy us? I know who you are. You are the Holy One of God!"

²⁵"Be quiet!" said Jesus firmly. "Come out of him!"

²⁶The evil spirit shook the man wildly. Then it came out of him with a scream.

²⁷All the people were amazed. So they asked each other, "What is this? A new teaching! And with so much authority! He even gives orders to evil spirits, and they obey him." ²⁸News about Jesus spread quickly all over Galilee.

Jesus Heals Many People

²⁹Jesus and those with him left the synagogue. Right away they went with James and John to the home of Simon and Andrew. ³⁰Simon's mother-in-law was lying in bed. She had a fever. They told Jesus about her. ³¹So he went to her. He took her hand and helped her up. The fever left her. Then she began to serve them.

³²That evening after sunset, the people brought to Jesus all who were sick. They also brought all who were controlled by demons. ³³All the people in town gathered at the door. ³⁴Jesus healed many of them. They had all kinds of sicknesses. He also drove out many demons. But he would not let the demons speak, because they knew who he was.

Jesus Prays in a Quiet Place

³⁵It was very early in the morning and still dark. Jesus got up and left the house. He went to a place where he could be alone. There he prayed. ³⁶Simon and his friends went to look for Jesus. ³⁷When they found him, they called out, "Everyone is looking for you!"

³⁸Jesus replied, "Let's go somewhere else. I want to go to the nearby towns. I must preach there also. That is why I have come." ³⁹So he traveled all around Galilee. He preached in their synagogues. He also drove out demons.

Jesus Heals a Man Who Had a Skin Disease

⁴⁰A man who had a skin disease came to Jesus. On his knees he begged Jesus. He said, "If you are willing to make me 'clean,' you can do it."

⁴¹Jesus was filled with deep concern. He reached out his hand and touched the man. "I am willing to do it," he said. "Be 'clean'!"

You could be fishing for Men!

[42]Right away the disease left him. He was healed.

[43]Jesus sent him away at once. He gave the man a strong warning. [44]"Don't tell this to anyone," he said. "Go and show yourself to the priest. Offer the sacrifices that Moses commanded. It will be a witness to the priest and the people that you are 'clean.'"

[45]But the man went out and started talking right away. He spread the news to everyone. So Jesus could no longer enter a town openly. He stayed outside in lonely places. But people still came to him from everywhere.

Jesus Heals a Man Who Could Not Walk

2 A few days later, Jesus entered Capernaum again. The people heard that he had come home. [2]So many people gathered that there was no room left. There was not even room outside the door. And Jesus preached the word to them.

[3]Four of those who came were carrying a man who could not walk. [4]But they could not get him close to Jesus because of the crowd. So they made a hole in the roof above Jesus. Then they lowered the man through it on a mat.

[5]Jesus saw their faith. So he said to the man, "Son, your sins are forgiven."

[6]Some teachers of the law were sitting there. They were thinking, [7]"Why is this fellow talking like that? He's saying a very evil thing! Only God can forgive sins!"

[8]Right away Jesus knew what they were thinking. So he said to them, "Why are you thinking these things? [9]Is it easier to say to this man, 'Your sins are forgiven'? Or to say, 'Get up, take your mat and walk'? [10]I want you to know that the Son of Man has authority on earth to forgive sins."

Then Jesus spoke to the man who could not walk. [11]"I tell you," he said, "get up. Take your mat and go home."

[12]The man got up and took his mat. Then he walked away while everyone watched. All the people were amazed. They praised God and said, "We have never seen anything like this!"

Jesus Chooses Levi

[13]Once again Jesus went out beside the Sea of Galilee. A large crowd came to him. He began to teach them. [14]As he walked along he saw Levi, son of Alphaeus. Levi was sitting at the tax collector's booth. "Follow me," Jesus told him. Levi got up and followed him.

[15]Later Jesus was having dinner at Levi's house. Many tax collectors and "sinners" were eating with him and his disciples. They were part of the large crowd following Jesus.

[16]Some teachers of the law who were Pharisees were there. They saw Jesus eating with "sinners" and tax collectors. So they asked his disciples, "Why does he eat with tax collectors and 'sinners'?"

Jesus said, "Get up. Take your mat, and go home."

Sign him up for a 5K!

[17]Jesus heard that. So he said to them, "Those who are healthy don't need a doctor. Sick people do. I have not come to get those who think they are right with God to follow me. I have come to get sinners to follow me."

Jesus Is Asked About Fasting

[18]John's disciples and the Pharisees were going without eating. Some people came to Jesus. They said to him, "John's disciples are fasting. The disciples of the Pharisees are also fasting. But your disciples are not. Why aren't they?"

[19]Jesus answered, "How can the guests of the groom go without eating while he is with them? They will not fast as long as he is with them. [20]But the time will come when the groom will be taken away from them. On that day they will go without eating.

[21]"People don't sew a patch of new cloth on old clothes. If they do, the new piece will pull away from the old. That will make the tear worse. [22]People don't pour new wine into old wineskins. If they do, the wine will burst the skins. Then the wine and the wineskins will both be destroyed. No, everyone pours new wine into new wineskins."

Jesus Is Lord of the Sabbath Day

[23]One Sabbath day Jesus was walking with his disciples through the grainfields. The disciples began to break off some heads of grain. [24]The Pharisees said to Jesus, "Look! It is against the Law to do this on the Sabbath. Why are your disciples doing it?"

[25]He answered, "Haven't you ever read about what David did? He and his men were hungry. They needed food. [26]It was when Abiathar was high priest. David entered the house of God and ate the holy bread. Only priests were allowed to eat it. David also gave some to his men."

[27]Then Jesus said to them, "The Sabbath day was made for man. Man was not made for the Sabbath day. [28]So the Son of Man is Lord even of the Sabbath day."

3 Another time Jesus went into the synagogue. A man with a weak and twisted hand was there. [2]Some Pharisees were trying to find fault with Jesus. They watched him closely. They wanted to see if he would heal the man on the Sabbath day.

[3]Jesus spoke to the man with the weak and twisted hand. "Stand up in front of everyone," he said.

[4]Then Jesus asked them, "What does the Law say we should do on the Sabbath day? Should we do good? Or should we do evil? Should we save life? Or should we kill?" But no one answered.

[5]Jesus looked around at them in anger. He was very upset because their hearts were stubborn. Then he said to the man, "Stretch out your hand." He stretched it out, and his hand was as good as new.

[6]Then the Pharisees went out and began to make plans with the Herodians. They wanted to kill Jesus.

Crowds Follow Jesus

[7]Jesus went off to the Sea of Galilee with his disciples. A large crowd from Galilee followed. [8]People heard about all that Jesus was doing. And many came to him. They came from Judea, Jerusalem, and Idumea. They came from the lands east of the Jordan River. And they came from the area around Tyre and Sidon.

[9]Because of the crowd, Jesus told his disciples to get a small boat ready for him. This would keep the people from crowding him. [10]Jesus had healed many people. So those who were sick were pushing forward to touch him.

[11]When people with evil spirits saw him, they fell down in front of him. The spirits shouted, "You are the Son of God!" [12]But Jesus ordered them not to tell who he was.

Jesus Appoints the Twelve Apostles

[13]Jesus went up on a mountainside. He called for certain people to come to him, and they came. [14]He appointed 12 of them and called them apostles. From that time on they would be with him. He would also send them out to preach. [15]They would have authority to drive out demons.

[16]So Jesus appointed the Twelve. Simon was one of them. Jesus gave him the name Peter. [17]There were James, son of Zebedee,

"I'm not a Christian because ..."

"I don't believe that Jesus is God."

Of all the great persons who marched down the corridors of time, Jesus was unique!

Most people acknowledge Him as a great teacher, philosopher, example, and a man of honor. Yet of all the famous people of history, He alone claimed to be GOD! Jesus said:

"I have come [from heaven] to do what the One who sent me wants me to do." John 6:38

Even His enemies said, "He was even calling God his own Father. He was making himself equal with God." John 5:18

To be logical, one must reconcile these facts. Jesus was either INSANE, A LIAR, or who HE CLAIMED to BE.

How do you answer the question: "Who was Jesus?"

"Those who hear my word and believe him who sent me have eternal life." John 5:24

---

and his brother John. Jesus gave them the name Boanerges. Boanerges means Sons of Thunder. [18]There were also Andrew, Philip, Bartholomew, Matthew, Thomas, and James, son of Alphaeus. And there were Thaddaeus and Simon the Zealot. [19]Judas Iscariot was one of them too. He was the one who was later going to hand Jesus over to his enemies.

Jesus and Beelzebub

[20]Jesus entered a house. Again a crowd gathered. It was so large that Jesus and his disciples were not even able to eat. [21]His family heard about this. So they went to take charge of him. They said, "He is out of his mind."

[22]Some teachers of the law were there. They had come down from Jerusalem. They said, "He is controlled by Beelzebub! He is driving out demons by the power of the prince of demons."

[23]So Jesus called them over and spoke to them by using stories. He said, "How can Satan drive out Satan? [24]If a kingdom fights against itself, it can't stand. [25]If a family is divided, it can't stand. [26]And if Satan fights against himself, and his helpers are divided, he can't stand. That is the end of him. [27]In fact, none of you can enter a strong man's house and just take what the man owns. You must first tie him up. Then you can rob his house.

[28]"What I'm about to tell you is true. Everyone's sins and evil words against God will be forgiven. [29]But anyone who speaks evil things against the Holy Spirit will never be forgiven. His guilt will last forever."

[30]Jesus said this because the teachers of the law were saying, "He has an evil spirit."

Jesus' Mother and Brothers

[31]Jesus' mother and brothers came and stood outside. They sent someone in to get him. [32]A crowd was sitting around Jesus. They told him, "Your mother and your brothers are outside. They are looking for you."

[33]"Who is my mother? Who are my brothers?" he asked.

[34]Then Jesus looked at the people sitting in a circle around him. He said, "Here is my mother! Here are my brothers! [35]Anyone who does what God wants is my brother or sister or mother."

The Story of the Farmer

4 Again Jesus began to teach by the Sea of Galilee. The crowd that gathered around him was very large. So he got into a boat. He sat down in it out on the lake. All the people were along the shore at the water's edge. [2]He taught them many things by using stories.

In his teaching he said, [3]"Listen! A farmer went out to plant his seed. [4]He scattered the seed on the ground. Some fell on a path. Birds came and ate it up. [5]Some seed fell on rocky places, where there wasn't much soil. The plants came up quickly, because the soil wasn't deep. [6]When the sun came up, it burned the plants. They dried up because they had no roots. [7]Other seed fell among thorns. The thorns grew up and crowded out the plants. So the plants did not bear grain. [8]Still other seed fell on good soil. It grew up and produced a crop 30, 60, or even 100 times more than the farmer planted."

[9]Then Jesus said, "Those who have ears should listen."

[10]Later Jesus was alone. The Twelve asked him about the stories. So did the others around him. [11]He told them, "The secret of God's kingdom has been given to you. But to outsiders everything is told by using stories. [12]In that way,

" 'They will see but never know what
        they are seeing.
    They will hear but never understand.
    Otherwise they might turn and be
        forgiven!' "   *(Isaiah 6:9,10)*

[13]Then Jesus said to them, "Don't you understand this story? Then how will you understand any stories of this kind? [14]The seed the farmer plants is God's message. [15]What is seed scattered on a path like? The message is planted. The people hear the message. Then Satan comes. He takes away the message that was planted in them. [16]And what is seed scattered on rocky places like? The people hear the message. At once they receive it with joy. [17]But they have no roots. So they last only a short time. They quickly fall away from the faith when trouble or suffering comes because of the message. [18]And what is seed scattered among thorns like? The people hear the message. [19]But then the worries of this life come to them. Wealth comes with its false promises. The people also long for other things. All of those are the kinds of things that crowd out the message. They keep it from producing fruit. [20]And what is seed scattered on good soil like? The people hear the message. They accept it. They produce a good crop 30, 60, or even 100 times more than the farmer planted."

A Lamp on a Stand

[21]Jesus said to them, "Do you bring in a lamp to put it under a large bowl or a bed? Don't you put it on its stand? [22]What is hidden is meant to be seen. And what is put out of sight is meant to be brought out into the open. [23]Everyone who has ears should listen."

[24]"Think carefully about what you hear," he said. "As you give, so you will receive. In fact, you will receive even more. [25]If you have something, you will be given more. If you have nothing, even what you have will be taken away from you."

The Story of the Growing Seed

[26]Jesus also said, "Here is what God's kingdom is like. A farmer scatters seed on the ground. [27]Night and day the seed comes

up and grows. It happens whether the farmer sleeps or gets up. He doesn't know how it happens. ²⁸All by itself the soil produces grain. First the stalk comes up. Then the head appears. Finally, the full grain appears in the head. ²⁹Before long the grain ripens. So the farmer cuts it down, because the harvest is ready."

The Story of the Mustard Seed

³⁰Again Jesus said, "What can we say God's kingdom is like? What story can we use to explain it? ³¹It is like a mustard seed, which is the smallest seed planted in the ground. ³²But when you plant the seed, it grows. It becomes the largest of all garden plants. Its branches are so big that birds can rest in its shade."

³³Using many stories like those, Jesus spoke the word to them. He told them as much as they could understand. ³⁴He did not say anything to them without using a story. But when he was alone with his disciples, he explained everything.

Jesus Calms the Storm

³⁵When evening came, Jesus said to his disciples, "Let's go over to the other side of the lake." ³⁶They left the crowd behind. And they took him along in a boat, just as he was. There were also other boats with him.

³⁷A wild storm came up. Waves crashed over the boat. It was about to sink. ³⁸Jesus was in the back, sleeping on a cushion. The disciples woke him up. They said, "Teacher! Don't you care if we drown?"

³⁹He got up and ordered the wind to stop. He said to the waves, "Quiet! Be still!" Then the wind died down. And it was completely calm.

⁴⁰He said to his disciples, "Why are you so afraid? Don't you have any faith at all yet?"

⁴¹They were terrified. They asked each other, "Who is this? Even the wind and the waves obey him!"

Jesus Heals a Man Controlled by Demons

5 They went across the Sea of Galilee to the area of the Gerasenes. ²Jesus got out of the boat. A man with an evil spirit came from the tombs to meet him. ³The man lived in the tombs. No one could keep him tied up anymore. Not even a chain could hold him. ⁴His hands and feet had often been chained. But he tore the chains apart. And he broke the iron cuffs on his ankles. No one was strong enough to control him. ⁵Night and day he screamed among the tombs and in the hills. He cut himself with stones.

⁶When he saw Jesus a long way off, he ran to him. He fell on his knees in front of him. ⁷He shouted at the top of his voice, "Jesus, Son of the Most High God, what do you want with me? Promise before God that you won't hurt me!" ⁸This was because Jesus had said to him, "Come out of this man, you evil spirit!"

Famous Quotes

"I'm not good enough to ... untie his sandals."
John the Baptist - Mark 1:7

●

"Why does he eat with ... 'sinners'?"
Pharisees - Mark 2:16

●

"He is controlled by ... the power of the prince of demons."
Religious Leaders - Mark 3:22

●

"Everything is possible for the one who believes."
Jesus - Mark 9:23

●

"He has risen! He is not here!"
Angel - Mark 16:6

[9]Then Jesus asked the demon, "What is your name?"

"My name is Legion," he replied. "There are many of us." [10]And he begged Jesus again and again not to send them out of the area.

[11]A large herd of pigs was feeding on the nearby hillside. [12]The demons begged Jesus, "Send us among the pigs. Let us go into them." [13]Jesus allowed it. The evil spirits came out of the man and went into the pigs. There were about 2,000 pigs in the herd. The whole herd rushed down the steep bank. They ran into the lake and drowned.

[14]Those who were tending the pigs ran off. They told the people in the town and countryside what had happened. The people went out to see for themselves.

[15]Then they came to Jesus. They saw the man who had been controlled by many demons. He was sitting there. He was now dressed and thinking clearly. All this made the people afraid. [16]Those who had seen it told them what had happened to the man. They told about the pigs as well. [17]Then the people began to beg Jesus to leave their area.

[18]Jesus was getting into the boat. The man who had been controlled by demons begged to go with him. [19]Jesus did not let him. He said, "Go home to your family. Tell them how much the Lord has done for you. Tell them how kind he has been to you."

[20]So the man went away. In the area known as the Ten Cities, he began to tell how much Jesus had done for him. And all the people were amazed.

A Dying Girl and a Suffering Woman

[21]Jesus went across the Sea of Galilee in a boat. It landed at the other side. There a large crowd gathered around him. [22]Then a man named Jairus came. He was a synagogue ruler. Seeing Jesus, he fell at his feet. [23]He begged Jesus, "Please come. My little daughter is dying. Place your hands on her to heal her. Then she will live." [24]So Jesus went with him.

A large group of people followed. They crowded around him. [25]A woman was there who had a sickness that made her bleed. It had lasted for 12 years. [26]She had suffered a great deal, even though she had gone to many doctors. She had spent all the money she had. But she was getting worse, not better. [27]Then she heard about Jesus. She came up behind him in the crowd and touched his clothes. [28]She thought, "I just need to touch his clothes. Then I will be healed." [29]Right away her bleeding stopped. She felt in her body that her suffering was over.

[30]At once Jesus knew that power had gone out from him. He turned around in the crowd. He asked, "Who touched my clothes?"

[31]"You see the people," his disciples answered. "They are crowding against you. And you still ask, 'Who touched me?'"

[32]But Jesus kept looking around. He wanted to see who had touched him.

[33]Then the woman came and fell at his feet. She knew what had happened to her. She was shaking with fear. But she told him the whole truth.

[34]He said to her, "Dear woman, your faith has healed you. Go in peace. You are free from your suffering."

[35]While Jesus was still speaking, some people came from the house of Jairus. He was the synagogue ruler. "Your daughter is dead," they said. "Why bother the teacher anymore?"

[36]But Jesus didn't listen to them. He told the synagogue ruler, "Don't be afraid. Just believe."

[37]He let only Peter, James, and John, the brother of James, follow him. [38]They came to the home of the synagogue ruler. There Jesus saw a lot of confusion. People were crying and sobbing loudly. [39]He went inside. Then he said to them, "Why all this confusion and sobbing? The child is not dead. She is only sleeping." [40]But they laughed at him.

He made them all go outside. He took only the child's father and mother and the disciples who were with him. And he went in where the child was. [41]He took her by the hand. Then he said to her, *"Talitha koum!"* This means, "Little girl, I say to you, get up!" [42]The girl was 12 years old. Right away she stood up and walked around. They were totally amazed at this. ⁴³Jesus gave strict orders not to let anyone know what had happened. And he told them to give her something to eat.

A Prophet Without Honor

6 Jesus left there and went to his home-town of Nazareth. His disciples went with him. ²When the Sabbath day came, he began to teach in the synagogue. Many who heard him were amazed.

"Where did this man get these things?" they asked. "What's this wisdom that has been given to him? He even does miracles! ³Isn't this the carpenter? Isn't this Mary's son? Isn't this the brother of James, Joseph, Judas and Simon? Aren't his sisters here with us?" They were not pleased with him at all.

⁴Jesus said to them, "A prophet is not honored in his hometown. He doesn't receive any honor among his relatives. And he doesn't receive any in his own home."

⁵Jesus laid his hands on a few sick peo-ple and healed them. But he could not do any other miracles there. ⁶He was amazed because they had no faith.

Jesus Sends Out the Twelve Disciples

Jesus went around teaching from village to village. ⁷He called the Twelve to him. Then he sent them out two by two. He gave them authority to drive out evil spirits.

⁸Here were his orders. "Take only a walk-ing stick for your trip. Do not take bread or a bag. Take no money in your belts. ⁹Wear sandals. But do not take extra clothes. ¹⁰When you are invited into a house, stay there until you leave town. ¹¹Some places may not welcome you or listen to you. If they don't, shake the dust off your feet when you leave. That will be a witness against the people living there."

¹²They went out. And they preached that people should turn away from their sins. ¹³They drove out many demons. They poured olive oil on many sick people and healed them.

John the Baptist's Head Is Cut Off

¹⁴King Herod heard about this. Jesus' name had become well known. Some were saying, "John the Baptist has been raised from the dead! That is why he has the power to do miracles."

¹⁵Others said, "He is Elijah."

Still others claimed, "He is a prophet. He is like one of the prophets of long ago."

By The Numbers

4 men lowered their paralyzed friend through a hole in the roof - Mark 2:3

2000 pigs, possessed by evil spirits, ran off of a cliff and drowned - Mark 5:13

12 years of suffering by a woman in the crowd - Mark 5:25

2 pennies given - all a poor widow had to give - Mark 12:42

9 o'clock in the morning when the Crucifixion took place - Mark 15:25

[16]But when Herod heard this, he said, "I had John's head cut off. And now he has been raised from the dead!"

[17]In fact, it was Herod himself who had given orders to arrest John. He had him tied up and put in prison. He did this because of Herodias. She was the wife of Herod's brother Philip. But now Herod was married to her. [18]John had been saying to Herod, "It is against the Law for you to have your brother's wife." [19]Herodias held that against John. She wanted to kill him. But she could not, [20]because Herod was afraid of John. So he kept John safe. Herod knew John was a holy man who did what was right. When Herod heard him, he was very puzzled. But he liked to listen to him.

[21]Finally the right time came. Herod gave a big dinner on his birthday. He invited his high officials and military leaders. He also invited the most important men in Galilee. [22]Then the daughter of Herodias came in and danced. She pleased Herod and his dinner guests.

The king said to the girl, "Ask me for anything you want. I'll give it to you." [23]And he promised her with an oath, "Anything you ask for I will give you. I'll give you up to half of my kingdom."

[24]She went out and said to her mother, "What should I ask for?"

"The head of John the Baptist," she answered.

[25]At once the girl hurried to ask the king. She said, "I want you to give me the head of John the Baptist on a big plate right now."

[26]The king was very upset. But he thought of his promise and his dinner guests. So he did not want to say no to the girl. [27]He sent a man right away to bring John's head. The man went to the prison and cut off John's head. [28]He brought it back on a big plate. He gave it to the girl, and she gave it to her mother.

[29]John's disciples heard about this. So they came and took his body. Then they placed it in a tomb.

Jesus Feeds the Five Thousand

[30]The apostles gathered around Jesus. They told him all they had done and taught.

[31]But many people were coming and going. So they did not even have a chance to eat.

Then Jesus said to his apostles, "Come with me by yourselves to a quiet place. You need to get some rest." [32]So they went away by themselves in a boat to a quiet place.

[33]But many people who saw them leaving recognized them. They ran from all the towns and got there ahead of them. [34]When Jesus came ashore, he saw a large crowd. He felt deep concern for them. They were like sheep without a shepherd. So he began teaching them many things.

[35]By that time it was late in the day. His disciples came to him. "There is nothing here," they said. "It's already very late. [36]Send the people away. They can go and buy something to eat in the nearby countryside and villages."

[37]But Jesus answered, "You give them something to eat."

They said to him, "That would take eight months of a person's pay! Should we go and spend that much on bread? Are we supposed to feed them?"

[38]"How many loaves do you have?" Jesus asked. "Go and see."

When they found out, they said, "Five loaves and two fish."

[39]Then Jesus directed them to have all the people sit down in groups on the green grass. [40]So they sat down in groups of 100s and 50s.

[41]Jesus took the five loaves and the two fish. He looked up to heaven and gave thanks. He broke the loaves into pieces. Then he gave them to his disciples to set in front of the people. He also divided the two fish among them all.

[42]All of them ate and were satisfied. [43]The disciples picked up 12 baskets of broken pieces of bread and fish. [44]The number of men who had eaten was 5,000.

Jesus Walks on the Water

[45]Right away Jesus made his disciples get into the boat. He had them go on ahead of him to Bethsaida. Then he sent the crowd away. [46]After leaving them, he went up on a mountainside to pray.

[47]When evening came, the boat was in

the middle of the Sea of Galilee. Jesus was alone on land. [48]He saw the disciples pulling hard on the oars. The wind was blowing against them.

Early in the morning, he went out to them. He walked on the lake. When he was about to pass by them, [49]they saw him walking on the lake. They thought he was a ghost. They cried out. [50]They all saw him and were terrified.

Right away he said to them, "Be brave! It is I. Don't be afraid."

[51]Then he climbed into the boat with them. The wind died down. And they were completely amazed. [52]They had not understood about the loaves. They were stubborn.

[53]They crossed over the lake and landed at Gennesaret. There they tied up the boat. [54]As soon as Jesus and his disciples got out, people recognized him. [55]They ran through that whole area to bring to him those who were sick. They carried them on mats to where they heard he was.

[56]He went into the villages, the towns and the countryside. Everywhere he went, the people brought the sick to the market places. Those who were sick begged him to let them touch just the edge of his clothes. And all who touched him were healed.

What Makes People "Unclean"?

7 The Pharisees gathered around Jesus. So did some of the teachers of the law. All of them had come from Jerusalem. [2]They saw some of his disciples eating food with "unclean" hands. That means they were not washed.

[3]The Pharisees and all the Jews do not eat unless they wash their hands to make them pure. That's what the elders teach. [4]When they come from the market place, they do not eat unless they wash. And they follow many other teachings. For example, they wash cups, pitchers, and kettles in a special way.

[5]So the Pharisees and the teachers of the law questioned Jesus. "Why don't your disciples live by what the elders teach?" they asked. "Why do they eat their food with 'unclean' hands?"

[6]He replied, "Isaiah was right. He prophesied about you people who pretend to be good. He said,

" 'These people honor me by what they
say.
But their hearts are far away from me.
[7] Their worship doesn't mean anything
to me.
They teach nothing but human rules.'
(Isaiah 29:13)

[8]You have let go of God's commands. And you are holding on to the teachings that men have made up."

[9]Jesus then said to them, "You have a fine way of setting aside God's commands! You do this so you can follow your own teachings. [10]Moses said, 'Honor your father and mother.' *(Exodus 20:12; Deuteronomy 5:16)* He also said, 'If anyone calls down a curse on his father or mother, he will be put to death.' *(Exodus 21:17; Leviticus 20:9)* [11]But you allow people to say to their parents, 'Any help you might have received from us is Corban.' (Corban means 'a gift set apart for God.') [12]So you no longer let them do anything for their parents. [13]You make the word of God useless by putting your own teachings in its place. And you do many things like that."

[14]Again Jesus called the crowd to him. He said, "Listen to me, everyone. Understand this. [15/16]Nothing outside of you can make you 'unclean' by going into you. It is what comes out of you that makes you 'unclean.' "

[17]Then he left the crowd and entered the house. His disciples asked him about this teaching.

[18]"Don't you understand?" Jesus asked. "Don't you see? Nothing that enters people from the outside can make them

*Only one life will soon be past,
Only what you do for Christ will last.*

Created By God ...

... For A Purpose

"Love the Lord your God with all your heart and with all your soul. Love him with all your mind and all your strength." Mark 12:30

3 IN 1

PHYSICAL • MENTAL • SPIRITUAL

PHYSICAL — BODY

— This is the skin we live in. Bodies can be: tall, short, thin, chunky, strong, weak, hairy, scary, etc.

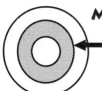

MENTAL — MIND

— This is the thinking machine. Minds can be: simple, complex, wise, foolish, serious, silly, etc. Some are naturally gifted in: music, math, arts, languages, while others are skilled in scientific, mechanical, interpersonal skills, and more.

SPIRITUAL — SOUL

— The soul is the driving force and CEO of the individual. It sets the core beliefs and directs the body and mind to pursue those convictions.

Our earthly bodies perish, our minds fail, and our spirits are in bondage to sin. Only in Christ is there hope for a freed spirit, a transformed mind, and a resurrected body. Jesus came to transform us from the "inside out".

FEED YOUR SOUL

"Nothing outside of you can make you 'unclean' ... Evil thoughts come from inside, from people's hearts."

"What good is it if someone gains the whole world but loses his soul?"

Mark 7:16, 21 and Mark 8:36

'unclean.' [19]It doesn't go into the heart. It goes into the stomach. Then it goes out of the body." In saying this, Jesus was calling all foods "clean."

[20]He went on to say, "What comes out of people makes them 'unclean.' [21]Evil thoughts come from the inside, from people's hearts. So do sexual sins, stealing and murder. Adultery, [22]greed, hate and cheating come from people's hearts too. So do desires that are not pure, and wanting what belongs to others. And so do telling lies about others and being proud and being foolish. [23]All those evil things come from inside a person. They make him 'unclean.' "

The Faith of a Greek Woman

[24]Jesus went from there to a place near Tyre. He entered a house. He did not want anyone to know where he was. But he could not keep it a secret.

[25]Soon a woman heard about him. An evil spirit controlled her little daughter. The woman came to Jesus and fell at his feet. [26]She was a Greek, born in Syrian Phoenicia. She begged Jesus to drive the demon out of her daughter.

[27]"First let the children eat all they want," he told her. "It is not right to take the children's bread and throw it to their dogs."

[28]"Yes, Lord," she replied. "But even the dogs under the table eat the children's crumbs."

[29]Then he told her, "That was a good reply. You may go. The demon has left your daughter."

[30]So she went home and found her child lying on the bed. And the demon was gone.

Jesus Heals a Man Who Could Not Hear or Speak

[31]Then Jesus left the area of Tyre and went through Sidon. He went down to the Sea of Galilee and into the area known as the Ten Cities.

[32]There some people brought a man to him. The man was deaf and could hardly speak. They begged Jesus to place his hand on him.

[33]Jesus took the man to one side, away from the crowd. He put his fingers into the man's ears. Then he spit and touched the man's tongue. [34]Jesus looked up to heaven. With a deep sigh, he said to the man, "*Ephphatha!*" That means "Be opened!" [35]The man's ears were opened. His tongue was freed up, and he began to speak clearly.

[36]Jesus ordered the people not to tell anyone. But the more he did so, the more they kept talking about it.

[37]People were really amazed. "He has done everything well," they said. "He even makes deaf people able to hear. And he makes those who can't speak able to talk."

Jesus Feeds the Four Thousand

8 During those days another large crowd gathered. They had nothing to eat. So Jesus called for his disciples to come to him. He said, [2]"I feel deep concern for these people. They have already been with me three days. They don't have anything to eat. [3]If I send them away hungry, they will become too weak on their way home. Some of them have come from far away."

[4]His disciples answered him. "There is nothing here," they said. "Where can anyone get enough bread to feed them?"

[5]"How many loaves do you have?" Jesus asked.

"Seven," they replied.

[6]He told the crowd to sit down on the ground. He took the seven loaves and gave thanks to God. Then he broke them and gave them to his disciples. They set the loaves down in front of the people. [7]The disciples also had a few small fish. Jesus gave thanks for them too. He told the disciples to pass them around. [8]The people ate and were satisfied.

After that, the disciples picked up seven baskets of leftover pieces. [9]About 4,000 men were there. Jesus sent them away. [10]Then he got into a boat with his disciples. He went to the area of Dalmanutha.

[11]The Pharisees came and began to ask Jesus questions. They wanted to put him to the test. So they asked him for a miraculous sign from heaven. [12]He sighed deeply. He said, "Why do you people ask for a sign? What I'm about to tell you is true. No sign

will be given to you."

¹³Then he left them. He got back into the boat and crossed to the other side of the lake.

The Yeast of the Pharisees and Herod

¹⁴The disciples had forgotten to bring bread. They had only one loaf with them in the boat.

¹⁵"Be careful," Jesus warned them. "Watch out for the yeast of the Pharisees. And watch out for the yeast of Herod."

¹⁶They talked about this with each other. They said, "He must be saying this because we don't have any bread."

¹⁷Jesus knew what they were saying. So he asked them, "Why are you talking about having no bread? Why can't you see or understand? Are you stubborn? ¹⁸Do you have eyes and still don't see? Do you have ears and still don't hear? And don't you remember? ¹⁹Earlier I broke five loaves for the 5,000. How many baskets of pieces did you pick up?"

"Twelve," they replied.

²⁰"Later I broke seven loaves for the 4,000. How many baskets of pieces did you pick up?"

"Seven," they answered.

²¹He said to them, "Can't you understand yet?"

Jesus Heals a Blind Man

²²Jesus and his disciples came to Bethsaida. Some people brought a blind man. They begged Jesus to touch him.

²³He took the blind man by the hand. Then he led him outside the village. He spit on the man's eyes and put his hands on him.

"Do you see anything?" Jesus asked.

²⁴The man looked up. He said, "I see people. They look like trees walking around."

²⁵Once more Jesus put his hands on the man's eyes. Then his eyes were opened so that he could see again. He saw everything clearly.

²⁶Jesus sent him home. He told him, "Don't go into the village."

Peter Says That Jesus Is the Christ

²⁷Jesus and his disciples went on to the villages around Caesarea Philippi. On the way he asked them, "Who do people say I am?"

²⁸They replied, "Some say John the Baptist. Others say Elijah. Still others say one of the prophets."

²⁹"But what about you?" he asked. "Who do you say I am?"

Peter answered, "You are the Christ."

³⁰Jesus warned them not to tell anyone about him.

"Rabbi, I want to be able to see."

Mark 10:51

It's not ...

W.W.J.D.

WHAT WOULD JESUS DO?

The real question is

W.W.Y.D.

WHAT WILL **YOU** DO?
THE CHOICE IS YOURS!

Jesus Tells About His Coming Death

31Jesus then began to teach his disciples. He taught them that the Son of Man must suffer many things. He taught them that the elders would not accept him. The chief priests and the teachers of the law would not accept him either. He must be killed and after three days rise again. 32He spoke clearly about this.

Peter took Jesus to one side and began to scold him.

33Jesus turned and looked at his disciples. He scolded Peter. "Get behind me, Satan!" he said. "You are not thinking about the things of God. Instead, you are thinking about human things."

34Jesus called the crowd to him along with his disciples. He said, "If anyone wants to come after me, he must say no to himself. He must pick up his cross and follow me. 35If he wants to save his life, he will lose it. But if he loses his life for me and for the good news, he will save it. 36What good is it if someone gains the whole world but loses his soul? 37Or what can anyone trade for his soul?

38"Suppose you are ashamed of me and my words among these adulterous and sinful people. Then the Son of Man will be ashamed of you when he comes in his Father's glory with the holy angels."

9 Jesus said to them, "What I'm about to tell you is true. Some who are standing here will not die before they see God's kingdom coming with power."

Jesus' Appearance Is Changed

2After six days Jesus took Peter, James and John with him. He led them up a high mountain. They were all alone. There in front of them his appearance was changed. 3His clothes became so white they shone. They were whiter than anyone in the world could bleach them. 4Elijah and Moses appeared in front of Jesus and his disciples. The two of them were talking with Jesus.

5Peter said to Jesus, "Rabbi, it is good for us to be here. Let us put up three shelters. One will be for you, one for Moses, and one for Elijah." 6Peter didn't really know what to say, because they were so afraid.

7Then a cloud appeared and surrounded them. A voice came from the cloud. It said, "This is my Son, and I love him. Listen to him!"

8They looked around. Suddenly they no longer saw anyone with them except Jesus.

9They came down the mountain. On the way down, Jesus ordered them not to tell anyone what they had seen. He told them to wait until the Son of Man had risen from the dead. 10So they kept the matter to themselves. But they asked each other what "rising from the dead" meant.

11Then they asked Jesus, "Why do the teachers of the law say that Elijah has to come first?"

12Jesus replied, "That's right. Elijah does come first. He makes all things new again. So why is it written that the Son of Man must suffer much and not be accepted? 13I tell you, Elijah has come. They have done to him everything they wanted to do. They did it just as it is written about him."

Jesus Heals a Boy Who Had an Evil Spirit

[14]When Jesus and those who were with him came to the other disciples, they saw a large crowd around them. The teachers of the law were arguing with them. [15]When all the people saw Jesus, they were filled with wonder. And they ran to greet him.

[16]"What are you arguing with them about?" Jesus asked.

[17]A man in the crowd answered. "Teacher," he said, "I brought you my son. He is controlled by a spirit. Because of this, my son can't speak anymore. [18]When the spirit takes hold of him, it throws him to the ground. He foams at the mouth. He grinds his teeth. And his body becomes stiff. I asked your disciples to drive out the spirit. But they couldn't do it."

[19]"You unbelieving people!" Jesus replied. "How long do I have to stay with you? How long do I have to put up with you? Bring the boy to me."

[20]So they brought him. As soon as the spirit saw Jesus, it threw the boy into a fit. He fell to the ground. He rolled around and foamed at the mouth.

[21]Jesus asked the boy's father, "How long has he been like this?"

"Since he was a child," he answered. [22]"The spirit has often thrown him into fire or water to kill him. But if you can do anything, take pity on us. Please help us."

[23]" 'If you can'?" said Jesus. "Everything is possible for the one who believes."

[24]Right away the boy's father cried out, "I do believe! Help me overcome my unbelief!"

[25]Jesus saw that a crowd was running over to see what was happening. Then he ordered the evil spirit to leave the boy. "You spirit that makes him unable to hear and speak!" he said. "I command you, come out of him. Never enter him again."

[26]The spirit screamed. It shook the boy wildly. Then it came out of him. The boy looked so lifeless that many people said,

"He's dead." [27]But Jesus took him by the hand. He lifted the boy to his feet, and the boy stood up.

[28]Jesus went indoors. Then his disciples asked him in private, "Why couldn't we drive out the evil spirit?"

[29]He replied, "This kind can come out only by prayer."

[30]They left that place and passed through Galilee. Jesus did not want anyone to know where they were. [31]That was because he was teaching his disciples.

He said to them, "The Son of Man is going to be handed over to men. They will kill him. After three days he will rise from the dead." [32]But they didn't understand what he meant. And they were afraid to ask him about it.

Who Is the Most Important Person?

[33]Jesus and his disciples came to a house in Capernaum. There he asked them, "What were you arguing about on the road?" [34]But they kept quiet. On the way, they had argued about which one of them was the most important person.

[35]Jesus sat down and called for the Twelve to come to him. Then he said, "If you want to be first, you must be the very last. You must be the servant of everyone."

[36]Jesus took a little child and had the child stand among them. Then he took the child in his arms. He said to them, [37]"Anyone who welcomes one of these little children in my name welcomes me. And anyone who welcomes me doesn't welcome only me but also the One who sent me."

Anyone Who Is Not Against Us Is for Us

[38]"Teacher," said John, "we saw a man driving out demons in your name. We told him to stop, because he was not one of us."

[39]"Do not stop him," Jesus said. "No one who does a miracle in my name can in the next moment say anything bad about me. [40]Anyone who is not against us is for us. [41]"What I'm about to tell you is true. Suppose someone gives you a cup of water in my name because you belong to me. That one will certainly not go without a reward.

Leading People to Sin

⁴²"What if someone leads one of these little ones who believe in me to sin? If he does, it would be better for him to be thrown into the sea with a large millstone tied around his neck.

⁴³/⁴⁴"If your hand causes you to sin, cut it off. It would be better for you to enter God's kingdom with only one hand than to go into hell with two hands. In hell the fire never goes out.

⁴⁵/⁴⁶"If your foot causes you to sin, cut it off. It would be better for you to enter God's kingdom with only one foot than to have two feet and be thrown into hell.

⁴⁷"If your eye causes you to sin, poke it out. It would be better for you to enter God's kingdom with only one eye than to have two eyes and be thrown into hell. ⁴⁸In hell,

" 'The worms do not die.
The fire is not put out.'   *(Isaiah 66:24)*

⁴⁹Everyone will be salted with fire.

⁵⁰"Salt is good. But suppose it loses its saltiness. How can you make it salty again? Have salt in yourselves. And be at peace with each other."

Jesus Teaches About Divorce

10 Jesus left that place and went into the area of Judea and across the Jordan River. Again crowds of people came to him. As usual, he taught them.

²Some Pharisees came to put him to the test. They asked, "Does the Law allow a man to divorce his wife?"

³"What did Moses command you?" he replied.

⁴They said, "Moses allowed a man to write a letter of divorce and send her away."

⁵"You were stubborn. That's why Moses wrote you this law," Jesus replied. ⁶"But at the beginning of creation, God 'made them male and female.' *(Genesis 1:27)* ⁷'That's why a man will leave his father and mother and be joined to his wife. ⁸The two of them will become one.' *(Genesis 2:24)* They are no longer two, but one. ⁹So a man must not separate what God has joined together."

¹⁰When they were in the house again, the disciples asked Jesus about this.

¹¹He answered, "What if a man divorces his wife and gets married to another woman? He commits adultery against her. ¹²And what if she divorces her husband and gets married to another man? She commits adultery."

Little Children Are Brought to Jesus

¹³People were bringing little children to Jesus. They wanted him to touch them. But the disciples told the people to stop.

¹⁴When Jesus saw this, he was angry. He said to his disciples, "Let the little children come to me. Don't keep them away. God's kingdom belongs to people like them. ¹⁵What I'm about to tell you is true. Anyone who will not receive God's kingdom like a little child will never enter it."

¹⁶Then he took the children in his arms. He put his hands on them and blessed them.

Jesus and the Rich Young Man

[17]As Jesus started on his way, a man ran up to him. He fell on his knees before Jesus. "Good teacher," he said, "what must I do to receive eternal life?"

[18]"Why do you call me good?" Jesus answered. "No one is good except God. [19]You know what the commandments say. 'Do not commit murder. Do not commit adultery. Do not steal. Do not give false witness. Do not cheat. Honor your father and mother.'" *(Exodus 20:12–16; Deuteronomy 5:16–20)*

[20]"Teacher," he said, "I have obeyed all those commandments since I was a boy."

[21]Jesus looked at him and loved him. "You are missing one thing," he said. "Go and sell everything you have. Give the money to those who are poor. You will have treasure in heaven. Then come and follow me."

[22]The man's face fell. He went away sad, because he was very rich.

[23]Jesus looked around. He said to his disciples, "How hard it is for rich people to enter God's kingdom!"

[24]The disciples were amazed at his words. But Jesus said again, "Children, how hard it is to enter God's kingdom! [25]Is it hard for a camel to go through the eye of a needle? It is even harder for the rich to enter God's kingdom!"

[26]The disciples were even more amazed. They said to each other, "Then who can be saved?"

[27]Jesus looked at them and said, "With man, that is impossible. But not with God. All things are possible with God."

[28]Peter said to him, "We have left everything to follow you!"

[29]"What I'm about to tell you is true," Jesus replied. "Has anyone left home or family or fields for me and the good news? [30]They will receive 100 times as much in this world. They will have homes and families and fields. But they will also be treated badly by others. In the world to come they will live forever. [31]But many who are first will be last. And the last will be first."

Jesus Again Tells About His Coming Death

[32]They were on their way up to Jerusalem. Jesus was leading the way. The disciples were amazed. Those who followed were afraid.

Again Jesus took the Twelve to one side. He told them what was going to happen to him. [33]"We are going up to Jerusalem," he said. "The Son of Man will be handed over to the chief priests and the teachers of the law. They will sentence him to death. Then they will hand him over to people who are not Jews. [34]The people will make fun of him and spit on him. They will whip him and kill him. Three days later he will rise from the dead!"

James and John Ask a Favor of Jesus

[35]James and John came to Jesus. They were the sons of Zebedee. "Teacher," they said, "we would like to ask a favor of you."

36"What do you want me to do for you?" he asked.

37They replied, "Let one of us sit at your right hand in your glorious kingdom. Let the other one sit at your left hand."

38"You don't know what you're asking for," Jesus said. "Can you drink the cup of suffering I drink? Or can you go through the baptism of suffering I must go through?"

39"We can," they answered.

Jesus said to them, "You will drink the cup I drink. And you will go through the baptism I go through. 40But it is not for me to say who will sit at my right or left hand. These places belong to those they are prepared for."

41The other ten disciples heard about it. They became angry at James and John.

42Jesus called them together. He said, "You know about those who are rulers of the nations. They hold power over their people. Their high officials order them around. 43Don't be like that. Instead, anyone who wants to be important among you must be your servant. 44And anyone who wants to be first must be the slave of everyone. 45Even the Son of Man did not come to be served. Instead, he came to serve others. He came to give his life as the price for setting many people free."

Blind Bartimaeus Receives His Sight

46Jesus and his disciples came to Jericho. They were leaving the city. A large crowd was with them.

A blind man was sitting by the side of the road begging. His name was Bartimaeus. Bartimaeus means Son of Timaeus. 47He heard that Jesus of Nazareth was passing by. So he began to shout, "Jesus! Son of David! Have mercy on me!"

48Many people commanded him to stop. They told him to be quiet. But he shouted even louder, "Son of David! Have mercy on me!"

49Jesus stopped and said, "Call for him." So they called out to the blind man, "Cheer up! Get up on your feet! Jesus is calling for you."

50He threw his coat to one side. Then he jumped to his feet and came to Jesus.

51"What do you want me to do for you?" Jesus asked him.

The blind man said, "Rabbi, I want to be able to see."

52"Go," said Jesus. "Your faith has healed you."

Right away he could see. And he followed Jesus along the road.

Jesus Enters Jerusalem

11 As they all approached Jerusalem, they came to Bethphage and Bethany at the Mount of Olives. Jesus sent out two of his disciples. 2He said to them, "Go to the village ahead of you. Just as you enter it, you will find a donkey's colt tied there. No one has ever ridden it. Untie it and bring it here. 3Someone may ask you, 'Why are you doing this?' If so, say, 'The Lord needs it. But he will send it back here soon.' "

4So they left. They found a colt out in the street. It was tied at a doorway. They untied it. 5Some people standing there asked, "What are you doing? Why are you untying that colt?" 6They answered as Jesus had told them to. So the people let them go.

7They brought the colt to Jesus. They threw their coats over it. Then he sat on it.

8Many people spread their coats on the road. Others spread branches they had cut in the fields. 9Those in front and those in back shouted,

"Hosanna!"

"Blessed is the one who comes in the
    name of the Lord!"

(Psalm 118:25,26)

10 "Blessed is the coming kingdom of
    our father David!"

"Hosanna in the highest heaven!"

11Jesus entered Jerusalem and went to the temple. He looked around at everything. But it was already late. So he went out to Bethany with the Twelve.

Jesus Clears the Temple

12The next day as Jesus and his disciples were leaving Bethany, they were hungry. 13Not too far away, he saw a fig tree. It was

	Gospel Highlights	Matt	Mark	Luke	John
1	John the Baptist	3:1	1:4	3:1	3:23
2	5,000 Fed	14:18	6:30	9:10	6:1
3	Triumphal Entry	21:8	11:1	19:28	12:12
4	Jesus Clears the Temple	21:12	11:15	19:45	2:13
5	Trial of Jesus	27:11	15:1	23:1	18:28
6	Crucifixion	27:35	15:25	23:33	19:16
7	Resurrection	28:1	16:1	24:1	20:1
8	The First Disciples	4:8	3:17	5:1	1:35
9	Paralyzed Man on Mat	9:1	2:3	5:17	-
10	Deformed Hand	12:10	3:1	6:6	-
11	Calms the Sea	8:23	4:39	8:22	-
12	Four Types of Soil	13:3	4:1	8:4	-
13	Walks on Water	14:25	6:45	-	6:16
14	Transfiguration	17:1	9:2	9:28	-
15	Demon-possessed Boy	17:15	9:17	9:37	-
16	Children Blessed	19:13	10:13	18:15	-
17	Last Supper	26:17	14:12	22:7	-
18	Baptism of Jesus	3:13	1:9	-	-
19	Man with leprosy	8:1	-	5:12	-
20	Officer's Son Healed	8:5	-	7:1	-
21	Blind are Healed	9:27	-	-	9:1
22	Demons sent from Man to Pigs	-	5:1	8:26	-
23	4,000 Fed	15:32	8:1	-	-
24	Narrow Gate vs. Wide Highway	7:13	-	-	-
25	Water to Wine	-	-	-	2:1
26	Woman Caught in Adultery	-	-	-	8:1
27	Lazarus	-	-	-	11:1
28	Good Samaritan	-	-	10:30	-
29	Prodigal Son	-	-	15:11	-
30	Pharisee vs. Tax Collector	-	-	18:10	-
31	Zacchaeus	-	-	19:1	-
32	The Great Commission	28:19	-	-	-

covered with leaves. He went to find out if it had any fruit. When he reached it, he found nothing but leaves. It was not the season for figs.

[14]Then Jesus said to the tree, "May no one ever eat fruit from you again!" And his disciples heard him say it.

[15]When Jesus reached Jerusalem, he entered the temple area. He began chasing out those who were buying and selling there. He turned over the tables of the people who were exchanging money. He also turned over the benches of those who were selling doves. [16]He would not allow anyone to carry items for sale through the temple courtyards.

[17]Then he taught them. He told them, "It is written that the Lord said,

" 'My house will be called
   a house where people from all nations
      can pray.'   (Isaiah 56:7)

But you have made it a 'den for robbers.' " (Jeremiah 7:11)

[18]The chief priests and the teachers of the law heard about this. They began looking for a way to kill Jesus. They were afraid of him, because the whole crowd was amazed at his teaching.

[19]When evening came, Jesus and his disciples left the city.

The Dried up Fig Tree

[20]In the morning as Jesus and his disciples walked along, they saw the fig tree. It was dried up all the way down to the roots.

[21]Peter remembered. He said to Jesus, "Rabbi, look! The fig tree you put a curse on has dried up!"

[22]"Have faith in God," Jesus said. [23]"What I'm about to tell you is true. Suppose one of you says to this mountain, 'Go and throw yourself into the sea.' You must not doubt in your heart. You must believe that what you say will happen. Then it will be done for you.

[24]"So I tell you, when you pray for something, believe that you have already received it. Then it will be yours. [25/26]And when you stand praying, forgive anyone you have anything against. Then your Father in heaven

will forgive your sins."

The Authority of Jesus Is Questioned

[27]Jesus and his disciples arrived again in Jerusalem. He was walking in the temple courtyards. Then the chief priests came to him. The teachers of the law and the elders came too.

[28]"By what authority are you doing these things?" they asked. "Who gave you authority to do this?"

[29]Jesus replied, "I will ask you one question. Answer me, and I will tell you by what authority I am doing these things. [30]Was John's baptism from heaven? Or did it come from men? Tell me!"

[31]They talked to each other about it. They said, "If we say, 'From heaven,' he will ask, 'Then why didn't you believe him?' [32]But what if we say, 'From men'?" They were afraid of the people. Everyone believed that John really was a prophet.

[33]So they answered Jesus, "We don't know."

Jesus said, "Then I won't tell you by what authority I am doing these things either."

The Story of the Renters

12 Jesus began to speak to the people by using stories. He said, "A man planted a vineyard. He put a wall around it. He dug a pit for a winepress. He also built a lookout tower. He rented the vineyard out to some farmers. Then he went away on a journey.

[2]"At harvest time he sent a servant to the renters. He told the servant to collect from them some of the fruit of the vineyard. [3]But they grabbed the servant and beat him up. Then they sent him away with nothing. [4]So the man sent another servant to the renters. They hit this one on the head and treated him badly. [5]The man sent still another servant. The renters killed him. The man sent many others. The renters beat up some of them. They killed the others.

[6]"The man had one person left to send. It was his son, and he loved him. He sent him last of all. He said, 'They will respect my son.'

[7]"But the renters said to each other, 'This is the one who will receive all the owner's property someday. Come, let's kill him. Then everything will be ours.' [8]So they took him and killed him. They threw him out of the vineyard.

[9]"What will the owner of the vineyard do then? He will come and kill those renters. He will give the vineyard to others.

[10]"Haven't you read what Scripture says,

" 'The stone the builders didn't accept
has become the most important stone
of all.
[11]The Lord has done it.
It is wonderful in our eyes'?"
(Psalm 118:22,23)

[12]Then the religious leaders looked for a way to arrest Jesus. They knew he had told the story against them. But they were afraid of the crowd. So they left him and went away.

Is It Right to Pay Taxes to Caesar?

[13]Later the religious leaders sent some of the Pharisees and Herodians to Jesus. They wanted to trap him with his own words.

[14]They came to him and said, "Teacher, we know you are a man of honor. You don't let others tell you what to do or say. You don't care how important they are. But you teach the way of God truthfully. Is it right to pay taxes to Caesar or not? [15]Should we pay or shouldn't we?"

But Jesus knew what they were trying to do. So he asked, "Why are you trying to trap me? Bring me a silver coin. Let me look at it."

[16]They brought the coin.

He asked them, "Whose picture is this? And whose words?"

"Caesar's," they replied.

[17]Then Jesus said to them, "Give to Caesar what belongs to Caesar. And give to God what belongs to God."

They were amazed at him.

Marriage When the Dead Rise

[18]The Sadducees came to Jesus with a question. They do not believe that people rise from the dead. [19]"Teacher," they said, "Moses wrote for us about a man who died and didn't have any children. But he did leave a wife behind. That man's brother must get married to the widow. He must have children to carry on his dead brother's name.

[20]"There were seven brothers. The first one got married. He died without leaving any children. [21]The second one got married to the widow. He also died and left no child. It was the same with the third one. [22]In fact, none of the seven left any children. Last of all, the woman died too. [23]When the dead rise, whose wife will she be? All seven of them were married to her."

[24]Jesus replied, "You are mistaken because you do not know the Scriptures. And you do not know the power of God. [25]When the dead rise, they won't get married. And their parents won't give them to be married. They will be like the angels in heaven.

[26]"What about the dead rising? Haven't you read in the scroll of Moses the story of the bush? God said to Moses, 'I am the God of Abraham. I am the God of Isaac. And I am the God of Jacob.' *(Exodus 3:6)* [27]He is not the God of the dead. He is the God of the living. You have made a big mistake!"

The Most Important Commandment

[28]One of the teachers of the law came and heard the Sadducees arguing. He noticed that Jesus had given the Sadducees a good answer. So he asked him, "Which is the most important of all the commandments?"

[29]Jesus answered, "Here is the most important one. Moses said, 'Israel, listen to me. The Lord is our God. The Lord is one. [30]Love the Lord your God with all your heart and with all your soul. Love him with all

God has loaned you a set of talents.
What you do with them is up to you.

your mind and with all your strength.' *(Deuteronomy 6:4,5)* ³¹And here is the second one. 'Love your neighbor as you love yourself.' *(Leviticus 19:18)* There is no commandment more important than these."

³²"You have spoken well, teacher," the man replied. "You are right in saying that God is one. There is no other God but him. ³³To love God with all your heart and mind and strength is very important. So is loving your neighbor as you love yourself. These things are more important than all burnt offerings and sacrifices."

³⁴Jesus saw that the man had answered wisely. He said to him, "You are not far from God's kingdom."

From then on, no one dared to ask Jesus any more questions.

Whose Son Is the Christ?

³⁵Jesus was teaching in the temple courtyard. He asked, "Why do the teachers of the law say that the Christ is the son of David? ³⁶The Holy Spirit spoke through David himself. David said,

" 'The Lord said to my Lord,
   "Sit at my right hand
until I put your enemies
   under your control." '   *(Psalm 110:1)*

³⁷David himself calls him 'Lord.' So how can he be David's son?"

The large crowd listened to Jesus with delight.

³⁸As he taught, he said, "Watch out for the teachers of the law. They like to walk around in long robes. They like to be greeted in the market places. ³⁹They love to have the most important seats in the synagogues. They also love to have the places of honor at dinners. ⁴⁰They take over the houses of widows. They say long prayers to show off. God will punish those men very much."

The Widow's Offering

⁴¹Jesus sat down across from the place where people put their temple offerings. He watched the crowd putting their money into the offering boxes. Many rich people threw large amounts into them.

⁴²But a poor widow came and put in two very small copper coins. They were worth much less than a penny.

⁴³Jesus asked his disciples to come to him. He said, "What I'm about to tell you is true. That poor widow has put more into the offering box than all the others. ⁴⁴They all gave a lot because they are rich. But she gave even though she is poor. She put in everything she had. She gave all she had to live on."

Signs of the End

13 Jesus was leaving the temple. One of his disciples said to him, "Look, Teacher! What huge stones! What wonderful buildings!"

²"Do you see these huge buildings?" Jesus asked. "Not one stone here will be left on top of another. Every stone will be thrown down."

³Jesus was sitting on the Mount of Olives, across from the temple. Peter, James, John and Andrew asked him a question in private. ⁴"Tell us," they said. "When will these things happen? And what will be the sign that they are all about to come true?"

⁵Jesus said to them, "Keep watch! Be careful that no one fools you. ⁶Many will come in my name. They will claim, 'I am he.' They will fool many people.

⁷"You will hear about wars. You will also hear people talking about future wars. Don't be alarmed. Those things must happen. But the end still isn't here. ⁸Nation will fight against nation. Kingdom will fight against kingdom. There will be earthquakes in many places. People will go hungry. All of those things are the beginning of birth pains.

⁹"Watch out! You will be handed over to the local courts. You will be whipped in the synagogues. You will stand in front of governors and kings because of me. In that way you will be witnesses to them. ¹⁰The good news has to be preached to all nations before the end comes. ¹¹You will be arrested and brought to trial. But don't worry ahead of time about what you will say. Just say what God brings to your mind at the time. It is not you speaking, but the Holy Spirit.

¹²"Brothers will hand over brothers to be

Who Were Those Guys?

"Apostles" (Emissaries)   AKA "Disciples" (Followers)

- Gathered by Jesus over a period of 1½ Years
- Traveled with Jesus for approximately 2 Years
- Most were martyred
- Most were from Galilee - an area considered to be the "wrong side of the tracks"

Peter AKA - Simon • Cephas
- Man of contrast and extremes
- Always heads the list of disciples
- Leader of the first church

James   First disciple to be martyred
- Along with his brother John called Sons of Thunder

John   "The disciple Jesus Loved"
- Bravest - only disciple at the cross
- Wrote 5 NT Books
- Youngest

Bartholomew AKA - Nathaniel
- "Here comes an honest man"
- "We have found the Messiah"

Matthew AKA - Levi
- Ex-tax collector
- Educated
- Wealthy

Judas Iscariot   The Betrayer
- Treasurer
- Committed Suicide
- Always listed last

Andrew   (Brother of Peter)
- Ex-disciple of John the Baptist
- "We have found the Messiah"

Philip
- Brought Nathaniel and some Greeks to Jesus
- "How to feed the 5,000"
- "Show us the way"

Thomas AKA - The Twin
- Doubting Thomas
- "I won't believe until I see"

James   Son of Alphaeus
- AKA "James the less"
(Because of his stature)

Judas AKA - Thaddaeus
- "Why are you going to reveal…?"
- (Not Judas Iscariot)

Simon AKA - The Zealot
- AKA - "The Cananaean"

Matthias   Judas Iscariots' replacement
- Chosen by lot

Matthew 10:3 • Mark 3:16 • Luke 6:14 • John 1:35 • Acts 1:26

killed. Fathers will hand over their children. Children will rise up against their parents and have them put to death. [13]Everyone will hate you because of me. But the one who stands firm to the end will be saved.

[14]"You will see 'the hated thing that destroys.' *(Daniel 9:27; 11:31; 12:11)* It will stand where it does not belong. The reader should understand this. Then those who are in Judea should escape to the mountains. [15]No one on the roof should go down into his house to take anything out. [16]No one in the field should go back to get his coat. [17]How awful it will be in those days for pregnant women! How awful for nursing mothers! [18]Pray that this will not happen in winter.

[19]"Those days will be worse than any others from the time God created the world until now. And there will never be any like them again. [20]If the Lord had not cut the time short, no one would live. But because of God's chosen people, he has shortened it.

[21]"At that time someone may say to you, 'Look! Here is the Christ!' Or, 'Look! There he is!' Do not believe it. [22]False Christs and false prophets will appear. They will do signs and miracles. They will try to fool God's chosen people if possible. [23]Keep watch! I have told you everything ahead of time.

[24]"So in those days there will be terrible suffering. After that, Scripture says,

" 'The sun will be darkened.
  The moon will not shine.
[25]The stars will fall from the sky.
  The heavenly bodies will be shaken.'
  (Isaiah 13:10; 34:4)

[26]"At that time people will see the Son of Man coming in clouds. He will come with great power and glory. [27]He will send his angels. He will gather his chosen people from all four directions. He will bring them from the ends of the earth to the ends of the heavens.

[28]"Learn a lesson from the fig tree. As soon as its twigs get tender and its leaves come out, you know that summer is near. [29]In the same way, when you see those things happening, you know that the end is near. It is right at the door. [30]What I'm about to tell you is true. The people living at that time will certainly not pass away until all those things have happened. [31]Heaven and earth will pass away. But my words will never pass away.

The Day and Hour Are Not Known

[32]"No one knows about that day or hour. Not even the angels in heaven know. The Son does not know. Only the Father knows.

[33]"Keep watch! Stay awake! You do not know when that time will come. [34]It's like a man going away. He leaves his house and puts his servants in charge. Each one is given a task to do. He tells the one at the door to keep watch.

[35]"So keep watch! You do not know when the owner of the house will come back. It may be in the evening or at midnight. It may be when the rooster crows or at dawn. [36]He may come suddenly. So do not let him find you sleeping.

[37]"What I say to you, I say to everyone. 'Watch!' "

A Woman Pours Perfume on Jesus

14 The Passover and the Feast of Unleavened Bread were only two days away. The chief priests and the teachers of the law were looking for a clever way to arrest Jesus. They wanted to kill him. [2]"But not during the Feast," they said. "The people may stir up trouble."

[3]Jesus was in Bethany. He was at the table in the home of a man named Simon, who had a skin disease. A woman came with a special sealed jar of very expensive perfume. It was made out of pure nard. She broke the jar open and poured the perfume on Jesus' head.

God would rather have you try and fail than to do nothing and succeed.

[4]Some of the people there became angry. They said to one another, "Why waste this perfume? [5]It could have been sold for more than a year's pay. The money could have been given to poor people." So they found fault with the woman.

[6]"Leave her alone," Jesus said. "Why are you bothering her? She has done a beautiful thing to me. [7]You will always have poor people with you. You can help them any time you want to. But you will not always have me. [8]She did what she could. She poured perfume on my body to prepare me to be buried. [9]What I'm about to tell you is true. What she has done will be told anywhere the good news is preached all over the world. It will be told in memory of her."

[10]Judas Iscariot was one of the Twelve. He went to the chief priests to hand Jesus over to them. [11]They were delighted to hear that he would do this. They promised to give Judas money. So he watched for the right time to hand Jesus over to them.

The Lord's Supper

[12]It was the first day of the Feast of Unleavened Bread. That was the time to sacrifice the Passover lamb.

Jesus' disciples asked him, "Where do you want us to go and prepare for you to eat the Passover meal?"

[13]So he sent out two of his disciples. He told them, "Go into the city. A man carrying a jar of water will meet you. Follow him. [14]He will enter a house. Say to its owner, 'The Teacher asks, "Where is my guest room? Where can I eat the Passover meal with my disciples?" ' [15]He will show you a large upstairs room. It will have furniture and will be ready. Prepare for us to eat there."

[16]The disciples left and went into the city. They found things just as Jesus had told them. So they prepared the Passover meal.

[17]When evening came, Jesus arrived with the Twelve. [18]While they were at the table eating, Jesus said, "What I'm about to tell you is true. One of you who is eating with me will hand me over to my enemies."

[19]The disciples became sad. One by one they said to him, "It's not I, is it?"

[20]"It is one of the Twelve," Jesus replied. "It is the one who dips bread into the bowl with me. [21]The Son of Man will go just as it is written about him. But how terrible it will be for the one who hands over the Son of Man! It would be better for him if he had not been born."

[22]While they were eating, Jesus took bread. He gave thanks and broke it. He handed it to his disciples and said, "Take it. This is my body."

[23]Then he took the cup. He gave thanks and handed it to them. All of them drank from it.

[24]"This is my blood of the new covenant," he said to them. "It is poured out for many. [25]What I'm about to tell you is true. I won't drink wine with you again until the day I drink it in God's kingdom."

[26]Then they sang a hymn and went out to the Mount of Olives.

Jesus Says That Peter Will Fail

[27]"You will all turn away," Jesus told the disciples. "It is written,

" 'I will strike the shepherd down.
    Then the sheep will be scattered.'
                              (*Zechariah 13:7*)

[28]But after I rise from the dead, I will go ahead of you into Galilee."

[29]Peter said, "All the others may turn away. But I will not."

[30]"What I'm about to tell you is true," Jesus answered. "It will happen today, this very night. Before the rooster crows twice, you yourself will say three times that you don't know me."

[31]But Peter would not give in. He said, "I may have to die with you. But I will never say I don't know you." And all the others said the same thing.

Jesus Prays in Gethsemane

[32]Jesus and his disciples went to a place called Gethsemane. Jesus said to them, "Sit here while I pray."

[33]He took Peter, James and John along with him. He began to be very upset and troubled. [34]"My soul is very sad. I feel close

to death," he said to them. "Stay here. Keep watch."

³⁵He went a little farther. Then he fell to the ground. He prayed that, if possible, the hour might pass by him. ³⁶"*Abba*," he said, "everything is possible for you. Take this cup of suffering away from me. But let what you want be done, not what I want." *Abba* means Father.

³⁷Then he returned to his disciples and found them sleeping. "Simon," he said to Peter, "are you asleep? Couldn't you keep watch for one hour? ³⁸Watch and pray. Then you won't fall into sin when you are tempted. The spirit is willing. But the body is weak."

³⁹Once more Jesus went away and prayed the same thing. ⁴⁰Then he came back. Again he found them sleeping. They couldn't keep their eyes open. They did not know what to say to him.

⁴¹Jesus returned the third time. He said to them, "Are you still sleeping and resting? Enough! The hour has come. Look! The Son of Man is about to be handed over to sinners. ⁴²Get up! Let us go! Here comes the one who is handing me over to them!"

Jesus Is Arrested

⁴³Just as Jesus was speaking, Judas appeared. He was one of the Twelve. A crowd was with him. They were carrying swords and clubs. The chief priests, the teachers of the law, and the elders had sent them.

⁴⁴Judas, who was going to hand Jesus over, had arranged a signal with them. "The one I kiss is the man," he said. "Arrest him and have the guards lead him away."

⁴⁵So Judas went to Jesus at once. He said, "Rabbi!" And he kissed him.

⁴⁶The men grabbed Jesus and arrested him.

⁴⁷Then one of those standing nearby pulled his sword out. He struck the servant of the high priest and cut off his ear.

⁴⁸"Am I leading a band of armed men against you?" asked Jesus. "Do you have to come out with swords and clubs to capture me? ⁴⁹Every day I was with you. I taught in the temple courtyard, and you didn't arrest me. But the Scriptures must come true."

⁵⁰Then everyone left him and ran away.

⁵¹A young man was following Jesus. The man was wearing nothing but a piece of linen cloth. When the crowd grabbed him, ⁵²he ran away naked. He left his clothing behind.

Jesus Is Taken to the Sanhedrin

⁵³The crowd took Jesus to the high priest. All of the chief priests, the elders, and the teachers of the law came together.

⁵⁴Not too far away, Peter followed Jesus. He went right into the courtyard of the high priest. There he sat with the guards. He warmed himself at the fire.

⁵⁵The chief priests and the whole Sanhedrin were looking for something to use against Jesus. They wanted to put him to death. But they did not find any proof. ⁵⁶Many witnesses lied about him. But their stories did not agree.

⁵⁷Then some stood up. They gave false witness about him. ⁵⁸"We heard him say, 'I will destroy this temple made by human hands. In three days I will build another temple, not made by human hands.' " ⁵⁹But what they said did not agree.

⁶⁰Then the high priest stood up in front of them. He asked Jesus, "Aren't you going to answer? What are these charges these men are bringing against you?"

⁶¹But Jesus remained silent. He gave no answer.

Again the high priest asked him, "Are you the Christ? Are you the Son of the Blessed One?"

⁶²"I am," said Jesus. "And you will see the Son of Man sitting at the right hand of the Mighty One. You will see the Son of Man coming on the clouds of heaven."

⁶³The high priest tore his clothes. "Why do we need any more witnesses?" he asked. ⁶⁴"You have heard him say a very evil thing against God. What do you think?"

They all found him guilty and said he must die.

⁶⁵Then some began to spit at him. They blindfolded him. They hit him with their fists. They said, "Prophesy!" And the guards took him and beat him.

"I'm not a Christian because ..."

"I'm sincere about my religion, so I'll get to heaven."

You may have genuine, earnest and fervent motivation and be ...

Sincerely RIGHT

Or

Sincerely WRONG

On September 11, 2001 a group of sincerely religious men crashed commercial jets into the Twin Towers in New York City. Over 3000 Americans died.

Those men were willing to sacrifice their lives in a dramatic demonstration of their sincerity.

Were they RIGHT or WRONG? Their actions were wicked and evil. Their "sincerity" caused destruction and DEATH.

**"There is a way that may seem right you.
But in the end it leads to death."** Proverbs 14:12

Peter Says He Does Not Know Jesus

66Peter was below in the courtyard. One of the high priest's female servants came by. 67When she saw Peter warming himself, she looked closely at him.

"You also were with Jesus, that Nazarene," she said.

68But Peter said he had not been with him. "I don't know or understand what you're talking about," he said. He went out to the entrance to the courtyard.

69The servant saw him there. She said again to those standing around, "This fellow is one of them."

70Again he said he was not.

After a little while, those standing nearby said to Peter, "You must be one of them. You are from Galilee."

71He began to call down curses on himself. He took an oath and said to them, "I don't know this man you're talking about!"

72Right away the rooster crowed the second time. Then Peter remembered what Jesus had spoken to him. "The rooster will crow twice," he had said. "Before it does, you will say three times that you don't know me." Peter broke down and sobbed.

Jesus Is Brought to Pilate

15 It was very early in the morning. The chief priests, with the elders, the teachers of the law, and the whole Sanhedrin, made a decision. They tied Jesus up and led him away. Then they handed him over to Pilate.

2"Are you the king of the Jews?" asked Pilate.

"Yes. It is just as you say," Jesus replied.

[3]The chief priests brought many charges against him. [4]So Pilate asked him again, "Aren't you going to answer? See how many things they charge you with."

[5]But Jesus still did not reply. Pilate was amazed.

[6]It was the usual practice at the Passover Feast to let one prisoner go free. The people could choose the one they wanted. [7]A man named Barabbas was in prison. He was there with some other people who had fought against the country's rulers. They had committed murder while they were fighting against the rulers. [8]The crowd came up and asked Pilate to do for them what he usually did.

[9]"Do you want me to let the king of the Jews go free?" asked Pilate. [10]He knew that the chief priests had handed Jesus over to him because they were jealous. [11]But the chief priests stirred up the crowd. So the crowd asked Pilate to let Barabbas go free instead.

[12]"Then what should I do with the one you call the king of the Jews?" Pilate asked them.

[13]"Crucify him!" the crowd shouted.

[14]"Why? What wrong has he done?" asked Pilate.

But they shouted even louder, "Crucify him!"

[15]Pilate wanted to satisfy the crowd. So he let Barabbas go free. He ordered that Jesus be whipped. Then he handed him over to be nailed to a cross.

The Soldiers Make Fun of Jesus

[16]The soldiers led Jesus away into the palace. It was called the Praetorium. They called together the whole company of soldiers. [17]The soldiers put a purple robe on Jesus. Then they twisted thorns together to make a crown. They placed it on his head. [18]They began to call out to him, "We honor you, king of the Jews!" [19]Again and again they hit him on the head with a stick. They spit on him. They fell on their knees and pretended to honor him.

[20]After they had made fun of him, they took off the purple robe. They put his own clothes back on him. Then they led him out to nail him to a cross.

Jesus Is Nailed to a Cross

[21]A man named Simon from Cyrene was passing by. He was the father of Alexander and Rufus. Simon was on his way in from the country. The soldiers forced him to carry the cross.

[22]They brought Jesus to the place called Golgotha. The word Golgotha means The Place of the Skull. [23]Then they gave him wine mixed with spices. But he did not take it.

[24]They nailed him to the cross. Then they divided up his clothes. They cast lots to see what each of them would get.

[25]It was nine o'clock in the morning when they crucified him. [26]They wrote out the charge against him. It read, THE KING OF THE JEWS.

[27/28]They crucified two robbers with him. One was on his right and one was on his left.

[29]Those who passed by shouted at Jesus and made fun of him. They shook their heads and said, "So you are going to destroy the temple and build it again in three days? [30]Then come down from the cross! Save yourself!"

[31]In the same way the chief priests and the teachers of the law made fun of him among themselves. "He saved others," they said. "But he can't save himself! [32]Let this Christ, this King of Israel, come down now from the cross! When we see that, we will believe."

Those who were being crucified with Jesus also made fun of him.

Jesus Dies

[33]At noon, darkness covered the whole land. It lasted three hours. [34]At three o'clock Jesus cried out in a loud voice, *"Eloi, Eloi, lama sabachthani?"* This means "My God, my God, why have you deserted me?" *(Psalm 22:1)*

[35]Some of those standing nearby heard Jesus cry out. They said, "Listen! He's calling for Elijah."

[36]One of them ran and filled a sponge with wine vinegar. He put it on a stick. He offered it to Jesus to drink. "Leave him alone," he said. "Let's see if Elijah comes to take him down."

[37]With a loud cry, Jesus took his last breath.

[38]The temple curtain was torn in two from top to bottom.

MARK

Grid:
- 1 J (Across 1, Down 1) ... 7 ... 12
- 2
- 3 F (Down 3) ... 8
- 4
- 5 ... 6 L ... 11
- 7
- 8 ... 13
- 9 ... 10
- 10
- 11

Across

1.	Sons of thunder	ch. 3
2.	Lost in the garden	ch. 14
3.	Going without food	ch. 2
4.	The unique you	---
5.	To point a weapon	---
6.	A large group of evil spirits	ch. 5
7.	a female deer	---
8.	Those who have ears should ...	ch. 4
9.	a male person	---
10.	Gain all but loses his ...	ch. 9
11.	The Holy Spirit is like a ...	ch. 1

Down

1.	John Baptized Jesus in	ch. 1
3.	He is out of his mind ...	ch. 3
6.	The first shall be ...	ch. 10
7.	To write down quickly	---
8.	Soil that produces	ch. 4
9.	All things are possible	ch. 10
10.	Repents blood of Jesus	ch. 14
11.	Levi didn't say __ to Jesus	ch. 2
12.	Represents body of Jesus	ch. 14
13.	Jesus betrayed by a ...	ch. 14

[39]A Roman commander was standing there in front of Jesus. He heard his cry and saw how Jesus died. Then he said, "This man was surely the Son of God!"

[40]Not very far away, some women were watching. Mary Magdalene was among them. Mary, the mother of the younger James and of Joses, was also there. So was Salome. [41]In Galilee those women had followed Jesus. They had taken care of his needs.

Many other women were also there. They had come up with him to Jerusalem.

Jesus Is Buried

[42]It was the day before the Sabbath. That day was called Preparation Day. As evening approached, [43]Joseph went boldly to Pilate and asked for Jesus' body. Joseph was from the town of Arimathea. He was a leading member of the Jewish Council. He was waiting for God's kingdom.

[44]Pilate was surprised to hear that Jesus was already dead. So he called for the Roman commander. He asked him if Jesus had already died. [45]The commander said it was true. So Pilate gave the body to Joseph.

[46]Then Joseph bought some linen cloth. He took the body down and wrapped it in the linen. He put it in a tomb cut out of rock. Then he rolled a stone against the entrance to the tomb.

[47]Mary Magdalene and Mary the mother of Joses saw where Jesus' body had been placed.

Jesus Rises From the Dead

16 The Sabbath day ended. Mary Magdalene, Mary the mother of James, and Salome bought spices. They were going to apply them to Jesus' body.

[2]Very early on the first day of the week, they were on their way to the tomb. It was just after sunrise. [3]They asked each other, "Who will roll the stone away from the entrance to the tomb?"

[4]Then they looked up and saw that the stone had been rolled away. The stone was very large.

[5]They entered the tomb. As they did, they saw a young man dressed in a white robe. He was sitting on the right side. They were alarmed.

[6]"Don't be alarmed," he said. "You are looking for Jesus the Nazarene, who was crucified. But he has risen! He is not here! See the place where they had put him. [7]Go! Tell his disciples and Peter, 'He is going ahead of you into Galilee. There you will see him. It will be just as he told you.'"

[8]The women were shaking and confused. They went out and ran away from the tomb. They said nothing to anyone, because they were afraid.

[9]Jesus rose from the dead early on the first day of the week. He appeared first to Mary Magdalene. He had driven seven demons out of her. [10]She went and told those who had been with him. She found them crying. They were very sad. [11]They heard that Jesus was alive and that she had seen him. But they did not believe it.

[12]After that, Jesus appeared in a different form to two of them. This happened while they were walking out in the country. [13]The two returned and told the others about it. But the others did not believe them either.

[14]Later Jesus appeared to the Eleven as they were eating. He spoke firmly to them because they had no faith. They would not believe those who had seen him after he rose from the dead.

[15]He said to them, "Go into all the world. Preach the good news to everyone. [16]Anyone who believes and is baptized will be saved. But anyone who does not believe will be punished. [17]Here are the miraculous signs that those who believe will do. In my name they will drive out demons. They will speak in languages they had not known before. [18]They will pick up snakes with their hands. And when they drink deadly poison, it will not hurt them at all. They will place their hands on sick people. And the people will get well."

[19]When the Lord Jesus finished speaking to them, he was taken up into heaven. He sat down at the right hand of God.

[20]Then the disciples went out and preached everywhere. The Lord worked with them. And he backed up his word by the signs that went with it.

LUKE

- *Written by Luke - not one of the original 12 apostles*
- *Luke was an educated Gentile physician and historian*
- *Written to the Gentile and intellectual community*
- *Traveled with Paul and wrote the book of Acts*
- *Theme: "Jesus as Perfect Man"*

Luke Writes an Orderly Report

1 Many people have attempted to write about the things that have taken place among us. ²Reports of these things were handed down to us. There were people who saw these things for themselves from the beginning and then passed the word on.

³I myself have carefully looked into everything from the beginning. So it seemed good also to me to write down an orderly report of exactly what happened. I am doing this for you, most excellent Theophilus. ⁴I want you to know that the things you have been taught are true.

The Coming Birth of John the Baptist

⁵Herod was king of Judea. During the time he was ruling, there was a priest named Zechariah. He belonged to a group of priests named after Abijah. His wife Elizabeth also came from the family line of Aaron. ⁶Both of them did what was right in God's eyes. They obeyed all the Lord's commandments and rules faithfully. ⁷But they had no children, because Elizabeth was not able to have any. And they were both very old.

⁸One day Zechariah's group was on duty. He was serving as a priest in God's temple. ⁹He happened to be chosen, in the usual way, to go into the temple of the Lord. There he was supposed to burn incense. ¹⁰The time came for this to be done. All who had gathered to worship were praying outside.

¹¹Then an angel of the Lord appeared to Zechariah. The angel was standing at the right side of the incense altar. ¹²When Zechariah saw him, he was amazed and terrified.

¹³But the angel said to him, "Do not be afraid, Zechariah. Your prayer has been heard. Your wife Elizabeth will have a child. It will be a boy, and you must name him John. ¹⁴He will be a joy and delight to you. His birth will make many people very glad. ¹⁵He will be important in the Lord's eyes.

"He must never use wine or other such drinks. He will be filled with the Holy Spirit from the time he is born. ¹⁶He will bring many of Israel's people back to the Lord their God. ¹⁷And he will prepare the way for the Lord. He will have the same spirit and power that Elijah had. He will teach parents how to love their children. He will also teach people who don't obey to be wise and do what is right. In this way, he will prepare a people who are ready for the Lord."

¹⁸Zechariah asked the angel, "How can I be sure of this? I am an old man, and my wife is old too."

¹⁹The angel answered, "I am Gabriel. I serve God. I have been sent to speak to you and to tell you this good news. ²⁰And now you will have to be silent. You will not be able to speak until after John is born. That's because you did not believe my words. They will come true when the time is right."

²¹During that time, the people were waiting for Zechariah to come out. They wondered why he stayed in the temple so long. ²²When he came out, he could not speak to them. They realized he had seen a vision in the temple. They knew this because he kept motioning to them. He still could not speak.

²³When his time of service was over, he

returned home. ²⁴After that, his wife Elizabeth became pregnant. She stayed at home for five months. ²⁵"The Lord has done this for me," she said. "In these days, he has been kind to me. He has taken away my shame among the people."

The Coming Birth of Jesus

²⁶In the sixth month after Elizabeth had become pregnant, God sent the angel Gabriel to Nazareth, a town in Galilee. ²⁷He was sent to a virgin. The girl was engaged to a man named Joseph. He came from the family line of David. The virgin's name was Mary. ²⁸The angel greeted her and said, "The Lord has given you special favor. He is with you."

²⁹Mary was very upset because of his words. She wondered what kind of greeting this could be. ³⁰But the angel said to her, "Do not be afraid, Mary. God is very pleased with you. ³¹You will become pregnant and give birth to a son. You must name him Jesus. ³²He will be great and will be called the Son of the Most High God. The Lord God will make him a king like his father David of long ago. ³³He will rule forever over his people, who came from Jacob's family. His kingdom will never end."

³⁴"How can this happen?" Mary asked the angel. "I am a virgin."

³⁵The angel answered, "The Holy Spirit will come to you. The power of the Most High God will cover you. So the holy one that is born will be called the Son of God. ³⁶Your relative Elizabeth is old. And even she is going to have a child. People thought she could not have children. But she has been pregnant for six months now. ³⁷Nothing is impossible with God."

³⁸"I serve the Lord," Mary answered. "May it happen to me just as you said it would." Then the angel left her.

Mary Visits Elizabeth

³⁹At that time Mary got ready and hurried to a town in Judea's hill country. ⁴⁰There she entered Zechariah's home and greeted Elizabeth. ⁴¹When Elizabeth heard Mary's greeting, the baby inside her jumped. And Elizabeth was filled with the Holy Spirit.

⁴²In a loud voice she called out, "God has blessed you more than other women. And blessed is the child you will have! ⁴³But why is God so kind to me? Why has the mother of my Lord come to me? ⁴⁴As soon as I heard the sound of your voice, the baby inside me jumped for joy. ⁴⁵You are a woman God has blessed. You have believed that what the Lord has said to you will be done!"

Mary's Song

⁴⁶Mary said,

"My soul gives glory to the Lord.
⁴⁷   My spirit delights in God my Savior.
⁴⁸He has taken note of me
      even though I am not important.
From now on all people will call me
      blessed.
⁴⁹   The Mighty One has done great things
      for me.
   His name is holy.
⁵⁰He shows his mercy to those who have
      respect for him,
      from parent to child down through the
      years.
⁵¹He has done mighty things with his arm.
   He has scattered those who are proud
      in their deepest thoughts.
⁵²He has brought down rulers from their
      thrones.
   But he has lifted up people who are
      not important.
⁵³He has filled those who are hungry with
      good things.
   But he has sent those who are rich
      away empty.
⁵⁴He has helped the people of Israel, who
      serve him.
   He has always remembered to be kind
⁵⁵to Abraham and his children down
      through the years.
   He has done it just as he said to our
      people of long ago."

⁵⁶Mary stayed with Elizabeth about three months. Then she returned home.

John the Baptist Is Born

⁵⁷The time came for Elizabeth to have her baby. She gave birth to a son. ⁵⁸Her neighbors and relatives heard that the Lord had

God wants to be the Center of your life...

hopes · school · family · prayers · relationships · tears · joys · Bible study · **LORD JESUS** · work · giving · thought life · struggles · serving · temptations · loneliness

... not at the top of a "to do list"!

"Trust in the LORD with all your heart ... In all your ways remember Him." Proverbs 3:5,6

been very kind to her. They shared her joy.

⁵⁹On the eighth day, they came to have the child circumcised. They were going to name him Zechariah, like his father. ⁶⁰But his mother spoke up. "No!" she said. "He must be called John."

⁶¹They said to her, "No one among your relatives has that name."

⁶²Then they motioned to his father. They wanted to find out what he would like to name the child. ⁶³He asked for something to write on. Then he wrote, "His name is John." Everyone was amazed.

⁶⁴Right away Zechariah could speak again. His first words gave praise to God. ⁶⁵The neighbors were all filled with fear and wonder. All through Judea's hill country, people were talking about all these things. ⁶⁶Everyone who heard this wondered about it. And because the Lord was with John, they asked, "What is this child going to be?"

Zechariah's Song

⁶⁷His father Zechariah was filled with the Holy Spirit. He prophesied,

⁶⁸"Give praise to the Lord, the God of Israel!

He has come and set his people free.

⁶⁹He has acted with great power and has saved us.

He did it for those who are from the family line of his servant David.

⁷⁰Long ago holy prophets said he would do it.

⁷¹He has saved us from our enemies.

We are rescued from all who hate us.

⁷²He has been kind to our people.

He has remembered his holy covenant.

⁷³He made an oath to our father Abraham.

⁷⁴He promised to save us from our enemies,

so that we could serve him without fear.

⁷⁵He wants us to be holy and godly as long as we live.

⁷⁶"And you, my child, will be called a prophet of the Most High God.

You will go ahead of the Lord to prepare the way for him.

⁷⁷You will tell his people how they can be saved.

You will tell them that their sins can be forgiven.

⁷⁸All of that will happen because our God

is tender and caring.
His kindness will bring the rising sun
    to us from heaven.
[79] It will shine on those living in darkness
    and in the shadow of death.
It will guide our feet on the path of
    peace."

[80]The child grew up, and his spirit became strong. He lived in the desert until he appeared openly to Israel.

Jesus Is Born

2 In those days, Caesar Augustus made a law. It required that a list be made of everyone in the whole Roman world. [2]It was the first time a list was made of the people while Quirinius was governor of Syria. [3]All went to their own towns to be listed.

[4]So Joseph went also. He went from the town of Nazareth in Galilee to Judea. That is where Bethlehem, the town of David, was. Joseph went there because he belonged to the family line of David. [5]He went there with Mary to be listed. Mary was engaged to him. She was expecting a baby.

[6]While Joseph and Mary were there, the time came for the child to be born. [7]She gave birth to her first baby. It was a boy. She wrapped him in large strips of cloth. Then she placed him in a manger. There was no room for them in the inn.

Angels Appear to the Shepherds

[8]There were shepherds living out in the fields nearby. It was night, and they were looking after their sheep. [9]An angel of the Lord appeared to them. And the glory of the Lord shone around them. They were terrified.

[10]But the angel said to them, "Do not be afraid. I bring you good news of great joy. It is for all the people. [11]Today in the town of David a Savior has been born to you. He is Christ the Lord. [12]Here is how you will know I am telling you the truth. You will find a baby wrapped in strips of cloth and lying in a manger."

[13]Suddenly a large group of angels from heaven also appeared. They were praising God. They said,

[14] "May glory be given to God in the
    highest heaven!
And may peace be given to those he is
    pleased with on earth!"

[15]The angels left and went into heaven. Then the shepherds said to one another, "Let's go to Bethlehem. Let's see this thing that has happened, which the Lord has told us about."

[16]So they hurried off and found Mary and Joseph and the baby. The baby was lying in the manger. [17]After the shepherds had seen him, they told everyone. They reported what the angel had said about this child. [18]All who heard it were amazed at what the shepherds said to them.

[19]But Mary kept all these things like a secret treasure in her heart. She thought about them over and over.

[20]The shepherds returned. They gave glory and praise to God. Everything they had seen and heard was just as they had been told.

Joseph and Mary Take Jesus to the Temple

[21]When the child was eight days old, he was circumcised. At the same time he was named Jesus. This was the name the angel had given him before his mother became pregnant.

[22]The time for making them pure came as it is written in the Law of Moses. So Joseph and Mary took Jesus to Jerusalem. There they presented him to the Lord. [23]In the Law of the Lord it says, "The first boy born in every family must be set apart for the Lord." *(Exodus 13:2,12)* [24]They also offered a sacrifice. They did it in keeping with the Law, which says, "a pair of doves or two young pigeons." *(Leviticus 12:8)*

[25]In Jerusalem there was a man named Simeon. He was a good and godly man. He was waiting for God's promise to Israel to happen. The Holy Spirit was with him. [26]The Spirit had told Simeon that he would not die before he had seen the Lord's Christ. [27]The Spirit led him into the temple courtyard.

Then Jesus' parents brought the child

in. They came to do for him what the Law required.

²⁸Simeon took Jesus in his arms and praised God. He said,

²⁹"Lord, you are the King over all.
  Now let me, your servant, go in peace.
  That is what you promised.
³⁰My eyes have seen your salvation.
³¹ You have prepared it in the sight of
    all people.
³²It is a light to be given to those who
    aren't Jews.
  It will bring glory to your people
    Israel."

³³The child's father and mother were amazed at what was said about him. ³⁴Then Simeon blessed them. He said to Mary, Jesus' mother, "This child is going to cause many people in Israel to fall and to rise. God has sent him. But many will speak against him. ³⁵The thoughts of many hearts will be known. A sword will wound your own soul too."

³⁶There was also a prophet named Anna. She was the daughter of Penuel from the tribe of Asher. Anna was very old. After getting married, she lived with her husband seven years. ³⁷Then she was a widow until she was 84. She never left the temple. She worshiped night and day, praying and going without eating.

³⁸Anna came up to Jesus' family at that very moment. She gave thanks to God. And she spoke about the child to all who were looking forward to the time when Jerusalem would be set free.

³⁹Joseph and Mary did everything the Law of the Lord required. Then they returned to Galilee. They went to their own town of Nazareth. ⁴⁰And the child grew and became strong. He was very wise. He was blessed by God's grace.

The Boy Jesus at the Temple

⁴¹Every year Jesus' parents went to Jerusalem for the Passover Feast. ⁴²When he was 12 years old, they went up to the Feast as usual.

⁴³After the Feast was over, his parents left to go back home. The boy Jesus stayed behind in Jerusalem. But they were not aware of it. ⁴⁴They thought he was somewhere in their group. So they traveled on for a day.

Then they began to look for him among their relatives and friends. ⁴⁵They did not find him. So they went back to Jerusalem to look for him. ⁴⁶After three days they found him in the temple courtyard. He was sitting with the teachers. He was listening to them and asking them questions. ⁴⁷Everyone who heard him was amazed at how much he understood. They also were amazed at his answers.

⁴⁸When his parents saw him, they were amazed. His mother said to him, "Son, why have you treated us like this? Your father and I have been worried about you. We have been looking for you everywhere."

⁴⁹"Why were you looking for me?" he asked. "Didn't you know I had to be in my Father's house?" ⁵⁰But they did not understand what he meant by that.

⁵¹Then he went back to Nazareth with them, and he obeyed them. But his mother kept all these things like a secret treasure in her heart. ⁵²Jesus became wiser and stronger. He also became more and more pleasing to God and to people.

John the Baptist Prepares the Way

3 Tiberius Caesar had been ruling for 15 years. Pontius Pilate was governor of Judea. Herod was the ruler of Galilee. His brother Philip was the ruler of Iturea and Traconitis. Lysanias was ruler of Abilene. ²Annas and Caiaphas were high priests. At that time God's word came to John, son of

You are a unique creation of God...
Don't compete • Don't compare

Zechariah, in the desert. [3]He went into all the countryside around the Jordan River. There he preached that people should be baptized and turn away from their sins. Then God would forgive them.

[4]Here is what is written in the scroll of the prophet Isaiah. It says,

"A messenger is calling out in the desert,
'Prepare the way for the Lord.
   Make straight paths for him.
[5]Every valley will be filled in.
      Every mountain and hill will be made level.
The crooked roads will become straight.
   The rough ways will become smooth.
[6]And everyone will see God's salvation.' "
(Isaiah 40:3–5)

[7]John spoke to the crowds coming to be baptized by him. He said, "You are like a nest of poisonous snakes! Who warned you to escape the coming of God's anger? [8]Produce fruit that shows you have turned away from your sins. And don't start saying to yourselves, 'Abraham is our father.' I tell you, God can raise up children for Abraham even from these stones. [9]The ax is already lying at the roots of the trees. All the trees that don't produce good fruit will be cut down. They will be thrown into the fire."

[10]"Then what should we do?" the crowd asked.

[11]John answered, "If you have extra clothes, you should share with those who have none. And if you have extra food, you should do the same."

[12]Tax collectors also came to be baptized. "Teacher," they asked, "what should we do?"

[13]"Don't collect any more than you are required to," John told them.

[14]Then some soldiers asked him, "And what should we do?"

John replied, "Don't force people to give you money. Don't bring false charges against people. Be happy with your pay."

[15]The people were waiting. They were expecting something. They were all wondering in their hearts if John might be the Christ.

[16]John answered them all, "I baptize you with water. But One who is more powerful than I am will come. I'm not good enough to untie the straps of his sandals. He will baptize you with the Holy Spirit and with fire. [17]His pitchfork is in his hand to toss the straw away from his threshing floor. He will gather the wheat into his storeroom. But he will burn up the husks with fire that can't be put out."

[18]John said many other things to warn the people. He also preached the good news to them.

[19]But John found fault with Herod, the ruler of Galilee, because of Herodias. She was the wife of Herod's brother. John also spoke strongly to Herod about all the other evil things he had done. [20]So Herod locked him up in prison. He added this sin to all his others.

The Baptism and Family Line of Jesus

[21]When all the people were being baptized, Jesus was baptized too. And as he was praying, heaven was opened. [22]The Holy Spirit came down on him in the form of a dove. A voice came from heaven. It said, "You are my Son, and I love you. I am very pleased with you."

[23]Jesus was about 30 years old when he began his special work for God and others. It was thought that he was the son of Joseph.

Joseph was the son of Heli.
[24]Heli was the son of Matthat.
Matthat was the son of Levi.
Levi was the son of Melki.
Melki was the son of Jannai.
Jannai was the son of Joseph.
[25]Joseph was the son of Mattathias.
Mattathias was the son of Amos.
Amos was the son of Nahum.
Nahum was the son of Esli.
Esli was the son of Naggai.
[26]Naggai was the son of Maath.
Maath was the son of Mattathias.
Mattathias was the son of Semein.
Semein was the son of Josech.
Josech was the son of Joda.
[27]Joda was the son of Joanan.
Joanan was the son of Rhesa.
Rhesa was the son of Zerubbabel.

Zerubbabel was the son of Shealtiel.
Shealtiel was the son of Neri.
²⁸ Neri was the son of Melki.
Melki was the son of Addi.
Addi was the son of Cosam.
Cosam was the son of Elmadam.
Elmadam was the son of Er.
²⁹ Er was the son of Joshua.
Joshua was the son of Eliezer.
Eliezer was the son of Jorim.
Jorim was the son of Matthat.
Matthat was the son of Levi.
³⁰ Levi was the son of Simeon.

Simeon was the son of Judah.
Judah was the son of Joseph.
Joseph was the son of Jonam.
Jonam was the son of Eliakim.
³¹ Eliakim was the son of Melea.
Melea was the son of Menna.
Menna was the son of Mattatha.
Mattatha was the son of Nathan.
Nathan was the son of David.
³² David was the son of Jesse.
Jesse was the son of Obed.
Obed was the son of Boaz.
Boaz was the son of Salmon.

Salmon was the son of Nahshon.
³³ Nahshon was the son of
Amminadab.
Amminadab was the son of Ram.
Ram was the son of Hezron.
Hezron was the son of Perez.
Perez was the son of Judah.
³⁴ Judah was the son of Jacob.
Jacob was the son of Isaac.
Isaac was the son of Abraham.
Abraham was the son of Terah.
Terah was the son of Nahor.
³⁵ Nahor was the son of Serug.
Serug was the son of Reu.
Reu was the son of Peleg.
Peleg was the son of Eber.
Eber was the son of Shelah.
³⁶ Shelah was the son of Cainan.
Cainan was the son of Arphaxad.
Arphaxad was the son of Shem.
Shem was the son of Noah.
Noah was the son of Lamech.
³⁷ Lamech was the son of Methuselah.
Methuselah was the son of Enoch.
Enoch was the son of Jared.
Jared was the son of Mahalalel.
Mahalalel was the son of Kenan.
³⁸ Kenan was the son of Enosh.
Enosh was the son of Seth.
Seth was the son of Adam.
Adam was the son of God.

Jesus Is Tempted

4 Jesus, full of the Holy Spirit, returned from the Jordan River. The Spirit led him into the desert. ²There the devil tempted him for 40 days.

Jesus ate nothing during that time. At the end of the 40 days, he was hungry.

³The devil said to him, "If you are the Son of God, tell this stone to become bread."

⁴Jesus answered, "It is written, 'Man doesn't live only on bread.' " *(Deuteronomy 8:3)*

⁵Then the devil led Jesus up to a high place. In an instant, he showed Jesus all the kingdoms of the world. ⁶He said to him, "I will give you all their authority and glory. It has been given to me, and I can give it to anyone I want to. ⁷So if you worship me, it will all be yours."

⁸Jesus answered, "It is written, 'Worship the Lord your God. He is the only one you should serve.' " *(Deuteronomy 6:13)*

⁹Then the devil led Jesus to Jerusalem. He had him stand on the highest point of the temple. "If you are the Son of God," he said, "throw yourself down from here. ¹⁰It is written,

" 'The Lord will command his angels to
take good care of you.
¹¹They will lift you up in their hands.
Then you won't trip over a stone.' "
(Psalm 91:11,12)

¹²Jesus answered, "Scripture says, 'Do not put the Lord your God to the test.' " *(Deuteronomy 6:16)*

¹³When the devil finished all this tempting, he left Jesus until a better time.

Jesus Is Not Accepted in Nazareth

¹⁴Jesus returned to Galilee in the power of the Holy Spirit. News about him spread through the whole countryside. ¹⁵He taught in their synagogues, and everyone praised him.

¹⁶Jesus went to Nazareth, where he had been brought up. On the Sabbath day he went into the synagogue as he usually did. And he stood up to read.

¹⁷The scroll of the prophet Isaiah was handed to him. He unrolled it and found the right place. There it is written,

¹⁸ "The Spirit of the Lord is on me.
He has anointed me
to tell the good news to poor people.
He has sent me to announce freedom for
prisoners.
He has sent me so that the blind will
see again.

Move ahead against your fears and God will honor you.

He wants me to free those who are
beaten down.

19   And he has sent me to announce the
year when he will set his people
free." *(Isaiah 61:1,2)*

²⁰Then Jesus rolled up the scroll. He gave
it back to the attendant and sat down. The
eyes of everyone in the synagogue were
staring at him.

²¹He began by saying to them, "Today this
passage of Scripture is coming true as you
listen."

²²Everyone said good things about him.
They were amazed at the gracious words
they heard from his lips. "Isn't this Joseph's
son?" they asked.

²³Jesus said, "Here is a saying you will
certainly apply to me. 'Doctor, heal yourself!
Do the things here in your hometown that
we heard you did in Capernaum.' "

²⁴"What I'm about to tell you is true," he
continued. "A prophet is not accepted in his
hometown. ²⁵I tell you for sure that there
were many widows in Israel in the days of
Elijah. And there had been no rain for three
and a half years. There wasn't enough food
to eat anywhere in the land. ²⁶But Elijah was
not sent to any of those widows. Instead,
he was sent to a widow in Zarephath near
Sidon. ²⁷And there were many in Israel who
had skin diseases in the days of Elisha the
prophet. But not one of them was healed
except Naaman the Syrian."

²⁸All the people in the synagogue were
very angry when they heard that. ²⁹They
got up and ran Jesus out of town. They
took him to the edge of the hill on which
the town was built. They planned to throw
him down the cliff. ³⁰But Jesus walked right
through the crowd and went on his way.

Jesus Drives Out an Evil Spirit

³¹Then Jesus went to Capernaum, a town
in Galilee. On the Sabbath day he began
to teach the people. ³²They were amazed
at his teaching, because his message had
authority.

³³In the synagogue there was a man
controlled by a demon, an evil spirit. He
cried out at the top of his voice. ³⁴"Ha!" he
said. "What do you want with us, Jesus of
Nazareth? Have you come to destroy us? I
know who you are. You are the Holy One
of God!"

³⁵"Be quiet!" Jesus said firmly. "Come out
of him!"

Then the demon threw the man down in
front of everybody. And it came out without hurting him.

³⁶All the people were amazed. They said
to each other, "What is this teaching? With
authority and power he gives orders to evil
spirits. And they come out!"

³⁷The news about Jesus spread throughout the whole area.

Jesus Heals Many People

³⁸Jesus left the synagogue and went to
the home of Simon. At that time, Simon's
mother-in-law was suffering from a high
fever. So they asked Jesus to help her. ³⁹He
bent over her and commanded the fever to
leave, and it left her. She got up at once and
began to serve them.

⁴⁰At sunset, people brought to Jesus all
who were sick. He placed his hands on each
one and healed them. ⁴¹Also, demons came
out of many people. The demons shouted,
"You are the Son of God!" But he commanded them to be quiet. He would not
allow them to speak, because they knew he
was the Christ.

⁴²At dawn, Jesus went out to a place
where he could be by himself. The people
went to look for him. When they found
him, they tried to keep him from leaving
them. ⁴³But he said, "I must announce the
good news of God's kingdom to the other
towns also. That is why I was sent." ⁴⁴And
he kept on preaching in the synagogues of
Judea.

Jesus Chooses the First Disciples

5 One day Jesus was standing by the Sea
of Galilee. The people crowded around
him and listened to the word of God. ²Jesus
saw two boats at the edge of the water.
They had been left there by the fishermen,
who were washing their nets. ³He got into
the boat that belonged to Simon. Jesus
asked him to go out a little way from shore.

Jesus said:
"Go out into deep water."
TRUST
and
OBEY

"You will catch people."
Luke 5:4-10

that their nets began to break. [7]So they motioned to their partners in the other boat to come and help them. They came and filled both boats so full that they began to sink.

[8]When Simon Peter saw this, he fell at Jesus' knees. "Go away from me, Lord!" he said. "I am a sinful man!"

[9]He and everyone with him were amazed at the number of fish they had caught. [10]So were James and John, the sons of Zebedee, who worked with Simon.

Then Jesus said to Simon, "Don't be afraid. From now on you will catch people."

[11]So they pulled their boats up on shore. Then they left everything and followed him.

Jesus Heals a Man With a Skin Disease

[12]While Jesus was in one of the towns, a man came along. He had a skin disease all over his body. When he saw Jesus, he fell with his face to the ground. He begged him, "Lord, if you are willing to make me 'clean,' you can do it."

[13]Jesus reached out his hand and touched the man. "I am willing to do it," he said. "Be 'clean'!" Right away the disease left him.

[14]Then Jesus ordered him, "Don't tell anyone. Go and show yourself to the priest. Offer the sacrifices that Moses commanded. It will be a witness to the priest and the people that you are 'clean.'"

[15]But the news about Jesus spread even more. So crowds of people came to hear him. They also came to be healed of their sicknesses. [16]But Jesus often went away to be by himself and pray.

Jesus Heals a Man Who Could Not Walk

[17]One day Jesus was teaching. Pharisees and teachers of the law were sitting there. They had come from every village of Galilee and from Judea and Jerusalem. They heard that the Lord had given Jesus the power to heal the sick.

[18]Some men came carrying a man who could not walk. He was lying on a mat. They tried to take him into the house to

Then he sat down in the boat and taught the people.

[4]When he finished speaking, he turned to Simon. He said, "Go out into deep water. Let the nets down so you can catch some fish."

[5]Simon answered, "Master, we've worked hard all night and haven't caught anything. But because you say so, I will let down the nets."

[6]When they had done so, they caught a large number of fish. There were so many

place him in front of Jesus. [19]They could not find a way to do this because of the crowd. So they went up on the roof. Then they lowered the man on his mat through the opening in the roof tiles. They lowered him into the middle of the crowd, right in front of Jesus.

[20]When Jesus saw that they had faith, he said, "Friend, your sins are forgiven."

[21]The Pharisees and the teachers of the law began to think, "Who is this fellow who says such an evil thing? Who can forgive sins but God alone?"

[22]Jesus knew what they were thinking. So he asked, "Why are you thinking these things in your hearts? [23]Is it easier to say, 'Your sins are forgiven'? Or to say, 'Get up and walk'? [24]I want you to know that the Son of Man has authority on earth to forgive sins." So he spoke to the man who could not walk. "I tell you," he said, "get up. Take your mat and go home."

[25]Right away, the man stood up in front of them. He took his mat and went home praising God. [26]Everyone was amazed and gave praise to God. They were filled with wonder. They said, "We have seen unusual things today."

Jesus Chooses Levi

[27]After this, Jesus left the house. He saw a tax collector sitting at the tax booth. The man's name was Levi.

"Follow me," Jesus said to him.

[28]Levi got up, left everything and followed him.

[29]Then Levi gave a huge dinner for Jesus at his house. A large crowd of tax collectors and others were eating with them. [30]But the Pharisees and their teachers of the law complained to Jesus' disciples. They said, "Why do you eat and drink with tax collectors and 'sinners'?"

[31]Jesus answered them, "Those who are healthy don't need a doctor. Sick people do. [32]I have not come to get those who think they are right with God to follow me. I have come to get sinners to turn away from their sins."

Jesus Is Asked About Fasting

[33]Some of the people who were there said to Jesus, "John's disciples often pray and go without eating. So do the disciples of the Pharisees. But yours go on eating and drinking."

[34]Jesus answered, "Can you make the guests of the groom go without eating while he is with them? [35]But the time will come when the groom will be taken away from them. In those days they will fast."

[36]Then Jesus gave them an example. He said, "People don't tear a patch from new clothes and sew it on old clothes. If they do, they will tear the new clothes. Also, the patch from the new clothes will not match the old clothes. [37]People don't pour new wine into old wineskins. If they do, the new wine will burst the skins. The wine will run out, and the wineskins will be destroyed. [38]No, new wine must be poured into new wineskins. [39]After people drink old wine, they don't want the new. They say, 'The old wine is better.'"

Jesus Is Lord of the Sabbath Day

6 One Sabbath day Jesus was walking through the grainfields. His disciples began to break off some heads of grain. They rubbed them in their hands and ate them.

[2]Some of the Pharisees said, "It is against the Law to do this on the Sabbath. Why are you doing it?"

[3]Jesus answered them, "Haven't you ever read about what David did? He and his men were hungry. [4]He entered the house of God and took the holy bread. He ate the bread that only priests were allowed to eat. David also gave some to his men."

[5]Then Jesus said to them, "The Son of Man is Lord of the Sabbath day."

[6]On another Sabbath day, Jesus went into the synagogue and was teaching. A man whose right hand was weak and twisted was there. [7]The Pharisees and the teachers of the law were trying to find fault with Jesus. So they watched him closely. They wanted to see if he would heal on the Sabbath.

[8]But Jesus knew what they were thinking. He spoke to the man who had the weak

and twisted hand. "Get up and stand in front of everyone," he said. So the man got up and stood there.

⁹Then Jesus said to them, "What does the Law say we should do on the Sabbath day? Should we do good? Or should we do evil? Should we save life? Or should we destroy it?"

¹⁰He looked around at all of them.

Then he said to the man, "Stretch out your hand."

He did, and his hand was as good as new.

¹¹But the Pharisees and the teachers of the law were very angry. They began to talk to each other about what they might do to Jesus.

Jesus Chooses the Twelve Apostles

¹²On one of those days, Jesus went out to a mountainside to pray. He spent the night praying to God. ¹³When morning came, he called for his disciples to come to him. He chose 12 of them and made them apostles.

¹⁴Simon was one of them. Jesus gave him the name Peter. There were also Simon's brother Andrew, James, John, Philip and Bartholomew. ¹⁵And there were Matthew, Thomas, and James, son of Alphaeus. There were also Simon who was called the Zealot ¹⁶and Judas, son of James. Judas Iscariot was one of them too. He was the one who would later hand Jesus over to his enemies.

Jesus Gives Blessings and Warnings

¹⁷Jesus went down the mountain with them and stood on a level place. A large crowd of his disciples was there. A large number of other people were there too. They came from all over Judea, including Jerusalem. They also came from the coast of Tyre and Sidon.

¹⁸They had all come to hear Jesus and to be healed of their sicknesses. People who were troubled by evil spirits were made well. ¹⁹Everyone tried to touch Jesus. Power was coming from him and healing them all.

²⁰Jesus looked at his disciples. He said to them,

"Blessed are you who are needy.
God's kingdom belongs to you.

²¹Blessed are you who are hungry now.
You will be satisfied.
Blessed are you who are sad now.
You will laugh.
²²Blessed are you when people hate you,
when they have nothing to do with you
and say bad things about you,
and when they treat your name as something evil.
They do all this because you are followers of the Son of Man.

²³"Their people treated the prophets the same way long ago. When these things happen to you, be glad and jump for joy. You will receive many blessings in heaven.

²⁴"But how terrible it will be for you who are rich!
You have already had your easy life.
²⁵How terrible for you who are well fed now!
You will go hungry.
How terrible for you who laugh now!
You will cry and be sad.
²⁶How terrible for you when everyone says good things about you!
Their people treated the false prophets the same way long ago.

Love Your Enemies

²⁷"But here is what I tell you who hear me. Love your enemies. Do good to those who hate you. ²⁸Bless those who call down curses on you. And pray for those who treat you badly.

²⁹"Suppose someone hits you on one cheek. Turn your other cheek to him also. Suppose someone takes your coat. Don't stop him from taking your shirt.

³⁰"Give to everyone who asks you. And if anyone takes what belongs to you, don't ask to get it back. ³¹Do to others as you want them to do to you.

³²"Suppose you love those who love you. Should anyone praise you for that? Even 'sinners' love those who love them. ³³And suppose you do good to those who are good to you. Should anyone praise you for that? Even 'sinners' do that. ³⁴And suppose you lend money to those who can pay you back. Should anyone praise you for that? Even a

'sinner' lends to 'sinners,' expecting them to pay everything back.

³⁵"But love your enemies. Do good to them. Lend to them without expecting to get anything back. Then you will receive a lot in return. And you will be sons of the Most High God. He is kind to people who are evil and are not thankful. ³⁶So have mercy, just as your Father has mercy.

Be Fair When You Judge Others

³⁷"If you do not judge others, then you will not be judged. If you do not find others guilty, then you will not be found guilty. Forgive, and you will be forgiven. ³⁸Give, and it will be given to you. A good amount will be poured into your lap. It will be pressed down, shaken together, and running over. The same amount you give will be measured out to you."

³⁹Jesus also gave them another example. He asked, "Can a blind person lead another blind person? Won't they both fall into a pit? ⁴⁰Students are not better than their teachers. But everyone who is completely trained will be like his teacher.

⁴¹"You look at the bit of sawdust in your friend's eye. But you pay no attention to the

First take the piece of wood out of your own eye...
Luke 6:42

piece of wood in your own eye. ⁴²How can you say to your friend, 'Let me take the bit of sawdust out of your eye'? How can you say this while there is a piece of wood in your own eye? You pretender! First take the piece of wood out of your own eye. Then you will be able to see clearly to take the bit of sawdust out of your friend's eye.

A Tree and Its Fruit

⁴³"A good tree doesn't bear bad fruit. And a bad tree doesn't bear good fruit. ⁴⁴You can tell each tree by the kind of fruit it bears. People do not pick figs from thorns. And they don't pick grapes from bushes.

⁴⁵"A good man says good things. These come from the good that is put away in his heart. An evil man says evil things. These come from the evil that is put away in his heart. Their mouths say everything that is in their hearts.

The Wise and Foolish Builders

⁴⁶"Why do you call me, 'Lord, Lord,' and still don't do what I say? ⁴⁷Some people come to me and listen to me and do what I say. I will show you what they are like. ⁴⁸They are like someone who builds a house. He digs down deep and sets it on solid rock. When a flood comes, the river rushes against the house. But the water can't shake it. The house is well built.

⁴⁹"But here is what happens when people listen to my words and do not obey them. They are like someone who builds a house on soft ground instead of solid rock. The moment the river rushes against that house, it falls down. It is completely destroyed."

A Roman Commander Has Faith

7 Jesus finished saying all those things to the people. Then he entered Capernaum.

²There the servant of a Roman commander was sick and about to die. His master thought highly of him. ³The commander heard about Jesus. So he sent some elders of the Jews to him. He told them to ask Jesus to come and heal his servant.

⁴They came to Jesus and begged him, "This man deserves to have you do this. ⁵He loves our nation and has built our synagogue." ⁶So Jesus went with them.

When Jesus came near the house, the Roman commander sent friends to him. He told them to say, "Lord, don't trouble yourself. I am not good enough to have you come into my house. ⁷That is why I did not even think I was fit to come to you. But just say the word, and my servant will be healed. ⁸I myself am a man who is under authority. And I have soldiers who obey my orders. I tell this one, 'Go,' and he goes. I tell that one, 'Come,' and he comes. I say to my servant, 'Do this,' and he does it."

⁹When Jesus heard this, he was amazed at him. He turned to the crowd that was following him. He said, "I tell you, even in Israel I have not found anyone whose faith is so strong."

¹⁰Then the men who had been sent to Jesus returned to the house. They found that the servant was healed.

Jesus Raises a Widow's Son From the Dead

¹¹Some time later, Jesus went to a town called Nain. His disciples and a large crowd went along with him. ¹²He approached the town gate. Just then, a dead person was being carried out. He was the only son of his mother. She was a widow. A large crowd from the town was with her.

¹³When the Lord saw her, he felt sorry for her. So he said, "Don't cry."

¹⁴Then he went up and touched the coffin. Those carrying it stood still.

Jesus said, "Young man, I say to you, get up!"

¹⁵The dead man sat up and began to talk. Then Jesus gave him back to his mother.

God's silence does not mean God's absence.

[16]The people were all filled with wonder and praised God. "A great prophet has appeared among us," they said. "God has come to help his people." [17]This news about Jesus spread all through Judea and the whole country.

Jesus and John the Baptist

[18]John's disciples told him about all these things. So he chose two of them. [19]He sent them to the Lord. They were to ask Jesus, "Are you the one who was supposed to come? Or should we look for someone else?"

[20]The men came to Jesus. They said, "John the Baptist sent us to ask you, 'Are you the one who was supposed to come? Or should we look for someone else?'"

[21]At that very time Jesus healed many people. They had illnesses, sicknesses and evil spirits. He also gave sight to many who were blind. [22]So Jesus replied to the messengers, "Go back to John. Tell him what you have seen and heard. Blind people receive sight. Disabled people walk. Those who have skin diseases are healed. Deaf people hear. Those who are dead are raised to life. And the good news is preached to those who are poor. [23]Blessed are those who do not give up their faith because of me."

[24]So John's messengers left. Then Jesus began to speak to the crowd about John. He said, "What did you go out into the desert to see? Tall grass waving in the wind? [25]If not, what did you go out to see? A man dressed in fine clothes? No. Those who wear fine clothes and have many expensive things are in palaces. [26]Then what did you go out to see? A prophet? Yes, I tell you, and more than a prophet.

[27]"He is the one written about in Scripture. It says,

" 'I will send my messenger ahead of you.
    He will prepare your way for you.'
                                    (Malachi 3:1)

[28]I tell you, no one more important than John has ever been born. But the least important person in God's kingdom is more important than he is."

[29]All the people who heard Jesus' words agreed that God's way was right. Even the tax collectors agreed. These people had all been baptized by John. [30]But the Pharisees and the authorities on the law did not accept God's purpose for themselves. They had not been baptized by John.

[31]"What can I compare today's people to?" Jesus asked. "What are they like? [32]They are like children sitting in the market place and calling out to each other. They say,

" 'We played a flute for you.
    But you didn't dance.
We sang a funeral song.
    But you didn't cry.'

[33]"That is how it has been with John the Baptist. When he came to you, he didn't eat bread or drink wine. And you say, 'He has a demon.' [34]But when the Son of Man came, he ate and drank as you do. And you say, 'This fellow is always eating and drinking far too much. He's a friend of tax collectors and "sinners." ' [35]All who follow wisdom prove that wisdom is right."

A Sinful Woman Pours Perfume on Jesus

[36]One of the Pharisees invited Jesus to have dinner with him. So he went to the Pharisee's house. He took his place at the table.

[37]There was a woman in that town who had lived a sinful life. She learned that Jesus was eating at the Pharisee's house. So she came with a special sealed jar of perfume. [38]She stood behind Jesus and cried at his feet. She began to wet his feet with her tears. Then she wiped them with her hair. She kissed them and poured perfume on them.

[39]The Pharisee who had invited Jesus saw this. He said to himself, "If this man were a prophet, he would know who is touching him. He would know what kind of woman she is. She is a sinner!"

[40]Jesus answered him, "Simon, I have something to tell you."

"Tell me, teacher," he said.

[41]"Two people owed money to a certain lender. One owed him 500 silver coins. The other owed him 50 silver coins. [42]Neither of

The Four Soils

Sower:	Jesus Christ
Seed:	The Word of God
Field:	The World
Soil:	Each Person

Matthew 13   Mark 4   Luke 8

Soil

The "spiritual soil" of each person is as unique as their fingerprints or DNA. This unseen mixture includes our personality, attitudes, and even our sin nature. These are "shaped" by our family, peer group, and life experiences of rejection, loneliness, trauma, etc. Into this "landscape of the heart" comes the Word of God . The soil can accept or reject God's Word.

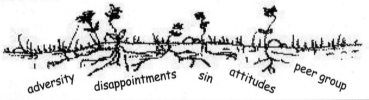

adversity   disappointments   sin   attitudes   peer group

Pathway Soil

The "pathway soil" has been pressed down by the steamroller of life's negative experiences. These hearts have been numbed by life's struggles. Because of the sinfulness of the heart, the soil becomes as hard as concrete pavement. The Word of God lands on the surface but goes no further.

They hear the message as it goes in one ear and out the other. The "birds come and quickly take the seed away."

Rocky Soil

The "rocky soil" hears and accepts the message with excitement. They rely on "feelings", "meetings", and "speakers". But the roots do not go deep.

They expect continual "blessings" and are unprepared for testing and hardship. They tasted a bite-size sample of the message, but are put off by the cost of following Christ. They have "talked the talk" but are not committed to "walk the walk." When the heat is turned up, they dry up and wither away.

Thorny Soil

The "thorny soil" goes further than the others, as it has some root system.

But the worries of the world, false promises of riches, and the pursuit of pleasure choke out the seed. The seed is neglected and crowded out.

Belief that is not deep causes the seed to be unfruitful.

Good Soil

The 'good soil" can be described by the words: commitment, action and sacrifice. They know following Christ is not a hobby or a leisure time activity. Rather, it is a matter of death and life.

And the harvest is plentiful!

them had the money to pay him back. So he let them go without paying. Which of them will love him more?"

⁴³Simon replied, "I suppose the one who owed the most money."

"You are right," Jesus said.

⁴⁴Then he turned toward the woman. He said to Simon, "Do you see this woman? I came into your house. You did not give me any water to wash my feet. But she wet my feet with her tears and wiped them with her hair. ⁴⁵You did not give me a kiss. But this woman has not stopped kissing my feet since I came in. ⁴⁶You did not put any olive oil on my head. But she has poured perfume on my feet. ⁴⁷So I tell you this. Her many sins have been forgiven. She has loved a lot. But the one who has been forgiven little loves only a little."

⁴⁸Then Jesus said to her, "Your sins are forgiven."

⁴⁹The other guests began to talk about this among themselves. They said, "Who is this who even forgives sins?"

⁵⁰Jesus said to the woman, "Your faith has saved you. Go in peace."

The Story of the Farmer

8 After this, Jesus traveled around from one town and village to another. He announced the good news of God's kingdom. The Twelve were with him. ²So were some women who had been healed of evil spirits and sicknesses. One was Mary Magdalene. Seven demons had come out of her. ³Another was Joanna, the wife of Cuza. He was the manager of Herod's household. Susanna and many others were there also. These women were helping to support Jesus and the Twelve with their own money.

⁴A large crowd gathered together. People came to Jesus from town after town. As they did, he told a story. He said, ⁵"A farmer went out to plant his seed. He scattered the seed on the ground. Some fell on a path. People walked on it, and the birds of the air ate it up. ⁶Some seed fell on rocky places. When it grew, the plants dried up because they had no water. ⁷Other seed fell among thorns. The thorns grew up with it and crowded out the plants. ⁸Still other seed fell on good soil. It grew up and produced a crop 100 times more than the farmer planted."

When Jesus said this, he called out, "Those who have ears should listen."

⁹His disciples asked him what the story meant.

¹⁰He said, "You have been given the chance to understand the secrets of God's kingdom. But to outsiders I speak by using stories. In that way,

" 'They see, but they will not know what they are seeing.
They hear, but they will not understand what they are hearing.'   *(Isaiah 6:9)*

¹¹"Here is what the story means. The seed is God's message. ¹²People on the path are those who hear. But then the devil comes. He takes away the message from their hearts. He does it so they won't believe. Then they can't be saved. ¹³Those on the rock are the ones who hear the message and receive it with joy. But they have no roots. They believe for a while. But when they are put to the test, they fall away from the faith. ¹⁴The seed that fell among thorns stands for those who hear the message. But as they go on their way, they are choked by life's worries, riches and pleasures. So they do not reach full growth.

¹⁵"But the seed on good soil stands for those with an honest and good heart. They hear the message. They keep it in their hearts. They remain faithful and produce a good crop.

A Lamp on a Stand

¹⁶"People do not light a lamp and then hide it in a jar or put it under a bed. Instead, they put it on a stand. Then those who come in can see its light. ¹⁷What is hidden will be seen. And what is out of sight will be brought into the open and made known.

¹⁸"So be careful how you listen. If you have something, you will be given more. If you have nothing, even what you think you have will be taken away from you."

Jesus' Mother and Brothers

¹⁹Jesus' mother and brothers came to see him. But they could not get near him because of the crowd. ²⁰Someone told him, "Your mother and brothers are standing outside. They want to see you."

²¹He replied, "My mother and brothers are those who hear God's word and do what it says."

Jesus Calms the Storm

²²One day Jesus said to his disciples, "Let's go over to the other side of the lake." So they got into a boat and left.

²³As they sailed, Jesus fell asleep. A storm came down on the lake. It was so bad that the boat was about to sink. They were in great danger.

²⁴The disciples went and woke Jesus up. They said, "Master! Master! We're going to drown!"

He got up and ordered the wind and the huge waves to stop. The storm quieted down. It was completely calm.

²⁵"Where is your faith?" he asked his disciples.

They were amazed and full of fear. They asked one another, "Who is this? He commands even the winds and the waves, and they obey him."

Jesus Heals a Man Controlled by Demons

²⁶Jesus and his disciples sailed to the area of the Gerasenes across the lake from Galilee. ²⁷When Jesus stepped on shore, he was met by a man from the town. The man was controlled by demons. For a long time he had not worn clothes or lived in a house. He lived in the tombs.

²⁸When he saw Jesus, he cried out and fell at his feet. He shouted at the top of his voice, "Jesus, Son of the Most High God, what do you want with me? I beg you, don't hurt me!"

²⁹This was because Jesus had commanded the evil spirit to come out of the man. Many times the spirit had taken hold of him. His hands and feet were chained, and he was kept under guard. But he had broken his chains. And then the demon had forced him to go out into lonely places in the countryside.

³⁰Jesus asked him, "What is your name?"

"Legion," he replied, because many demons had gone into him. ³¹And they begged Jesus again and again not to order them to go into the Abyss.

³²A large herd of pigs was feeding there on the hillside. The demons begged Jesus to let them go into the pigs. And he allowed it.

³³When the demons came out of the man, they went into the pigs. Then the herd rushed down the steep bank. They ran into the lake and drowned.

³⁴Those who were tending the pigs saw what had happened. They ran off and reported it in the town and countryside. ³⁵The people went out to see what had happened.

Then they came to Jesus. They found the man who was now free of the demons. He was sitting at Jesus' feet. He was dressed and thinking clearly. All this made the people afraid.

³⁶Those who had seen it told the others how the man who had been controlled by demons was now healed. ³⁷Then all the people who lived in the area of the Gerasenes asked Jesus to leave them. They were filled with fear. So he got into the boat and left.

³⁸The man who was now free of the demons begged to go with him. But Jesus sent him away. He said to him, ³⁹"Return home and tell how much God has done for you."

So the man went away. He told people all over town how much Jesus had done for him.

The best way to find the purpose of an invention... is to ask the creator to explain it.

A Dying Girl and a Suffering Woman

⁴⁰When Jesus returned, a crowd welcomed him. They were all expecting him.

⁴¹Then a man named Jairus came. He was a synagogue ruler. He fell at Jesus' feet. He begged Jesus to come to his house. ⁴²His only daughter was dying. She was about 12 years old.

As Jesus was on his way, the crowds almost crushed him.

⁴³A woman was there who had a sickness that made her bleed. Her sickness had lasted for 12 years. No one could heal her. ⁴⁴She came up behind Jesus and touched the edge of his clothes. Right away her bleeding stopped.

⁴⁵"Who touched me?" Jesus asked.

They all said they didn't do it. Then Peter said, "Master, the people are crowding and pushing against you."

⁴⁶But Jesus said, "Someone touched me. I know that power has gone out from me."

⁴⁷The woman realized that people would notice her. Shaking with fear, she came and fell at his feet. In front of everyone, she told why she had touched him. She also told how she had been healed in an instant.

⁴⁸Then he said to her, "Dear woman, your faith has healed you. Go in peace."

⁴⁹While Jesus was still speaking, someone came from the house of Jairus. Jairus was the synagogue ruler. "Your daughter is dead," the messenger said. "Don't bother the teacher anymore."

⁵⁰Hearing this, Jesus said to Jairus, "Don't be afraid. Just believe. She will be healed."

⁵¹When he arrived at the house of Jairus, he did not let everyone go in with him. He took only Peter, John and James, and the child's father and mother.

⁵²During this time, all the people were crying and sobbing loudly over the child. "Stop crying!" Jesus said. "She is not dead. She is sleeping."

⁵³They laughed at him. They knew she was dead.

⁵⁴But he took her by the hand and said, "My child, get up!"

⁵⁵Her spirit returned, and right away she stood up. Then Jesus told them to give her something to eat. ⁵⁶Her parents were amazed. But Jesus ordered them not to tell anyone what had happened.

Jesus Sends Out the Twelve Disciples

9 Jesus called the Twelve together. He gave them power and authority to drive out all demons and to heal sicknesses. ²Then he sent them out to preach about God's kingdom and to heal those who were sick.

³He told them, "Don't take anything for the journey. Do not take a walking stick or a bag. Do not take any bread, money or extra clothes. ⁴When you are invited into a house, stay there until you leave town. ⁵Some people may not welcome you. If they don't, shake the dust off your feet when you leave their town. This will be a witness against the people living there."

⁶So the Twelve left. They went from village to village. They preached the good news and healed people everywhere.

⁷Now Herod, the ruler of Galilee, heard about everything that was going on. He was bewildered, because some were saying that John the Baptist had been raised from the dead. ⁸Others were saying that Elijah had appeared. Still others were saying that a prophet of long ago had come back to life. ⁹But Herod said, "I had John's head cut off. So who is it that I hear such things about?" And he tried to see Jesus.

Jesus Feeds the Five Thousand

¹⁰The apostles returned. They told Jesus what they had done. Then he took them with him. They went off by themselves to a town called Bethsaida. ¹¹But the crowds learned about it and followed Jesus. He welcomed them and spoke to them about God's kingdom. He also healed those who needed to be healed.

¹²Late in the afternoon the Twelve came to him. They said, "Send the crowd away. They can go to the nearby villages and countryside. There they can find food and a place to stay. There is nothing here."

¹³Jesus replied, "You give them something to eat."

The disciples answered, "We have only five loaves of bread and two fish. We would have to go and buy food for all this crowd." [14]About 5,000 men were there.

But Jesus said to his disciples, "Have them sit down in groups of about 50 each." [15]The disciples did so, and everyone sat down.

[16]Jesus took the five loaves and the two fish. He looked up to heaven and gave thanks. He broke them into pieces. Then he gave them to the disciples to set in front of the people. [17]All of them ate and were satisfied. The disciples picked up 12 baskets of leftover pieces.

Peter Says That Jesus Is the Christ

[18]One day Jesus was praying alone. Only his disciples were with him. He asked them, "Who do the crowds say I am?"

[19]They replied, "Some say John the Baptist. Others say Elijah. Still others say that one of the prophets of long ago has come back to life."

[20]"But what about you?" he asked. "Who do you say I am?"

Peter answered, "The Christ of God."

[21]Jesus strongly warned them not to tell this to anyone. [22]He said, "The Son of Man must suffer many things. The elders will not accept him. The chief priests and teach-

Gospel Trivia

Who got "a head" by dancing?
Matthew 14:6

Do not feed the pigs ...
Matthew 7:6

Who got spit in their eye?
Mark 8:23

Who is more blessed than Mary?
Luke 11:28

Who ate honey covered insects?
Matthew 3:4

Do not swallow a camel.
Matthew 23:24

Why put a finger into an ear?
Mark 7:33

Who did not speak to his wife until she gave him a son?
Luke 1:21-22

ers of the law will not accept him either. He must be killed and on the third day rise from the dead."

²³Then he said to all of them, "If anyone wants to follow me, he must say no to himself. He must pick up his cross every day and follow me. ²⁴If he wants to save his life, he will lose it. But if he loses his life for me, he will save it. ²⁵What good is it if someone gains the whole world but loses or gives up his very self?

²⁶"Suppose you are ashamed of me and my words. The Son of Man will come in his glory and in the glory of the Father and the holy angels. Then he will be ashamed of you.

²⁷"What I'm about to tell you is true. Some who are standing here will not die before they see God's kingdom."

Jesus' Appearance Is Changed

²⁸About eight days after Jesus said this, he went up on a mountain to pray. He took Peter, John and James with him.

²⁹As he was praying, the appearance of his face changed. His clothes became as bright as a flash of lightning. ³⁰Two men, Moses and Elijah, ³¹appeared in shining glory. Jesus and the two of them talked together. They spoke about his coming death. He was going to die soon in Jerusalem.

³²Peter and his companions had been very sleepy. But then they became completely awake. They saw Jesus' glory and the two men standing with him.

³³As the men were leaving Jesus, Peter spoke up. "Master," he said to him, "it is good for us to be here. Let us put up three shelters. One will be for you, one for Moses, and one for Elijah." He didn't really know what he was saying.

³⁴While Jesus was speaking, a cloud appeared. It surrounded them. The disciples were afraid as they entered the cloud. ³⁵A voice came from the cloud. It said, "This is my Son, and I have chosen him. Listen to him." ³⁶When the voice had spoken, they found that Jesus was alone.

The disciples kept quiet about this. They didn't tell anyone at that time what they had seen.

Jesus Heals a Boy Who Had an Evil Spirit

³⁷The next day Jesus and those who were with him came down from the mountain. A large crowd met Jesus.

³⁸A man in the crowd called out. "Teacher," he said, "I beg you to look at my son. He is my only child. ³⁹A spirit takes hold of him, and he suddenly screams. It throws him into fits so that he foams at the mouth. It hardly ever leaves him. It is destroying him. ⁴⁰I begged your disciples to drive it out. But they couldn't do it."

⁴¹"You unbelieving and evil people!" Jesus replied. "How long do I have to stay with you? How long do I have to put up with you?"

Then he said to the man, "Bring your son here."

⁴²Even while the boy was coming, the demon threw him into a fit. The boy fell to the ground. But Jesus ordered the evil spirit to leave the boy. Then Jesus healed him and gave him back to his father. ⁴³They were all amazed at God's greatness.

Everyone was wondering about all that Jesus did. Then Jesus said to his disciples, ⁴⁴"Listen carefully to what I am about to tell you. The Son of Man is going to be handed over to men." ⁴⁵But they didn't understand what this meant. That was because it was hidden from them. And they were afraid to ask Jesus about it.

Who Is the Most Important Person?

⁴⁶The disciples began to argue about which one of them would be the most important person. ⁴⁷Jesus knew what they were thinking. So he took a little child and had the child stand beside him.

⁴⁸Then he spoke to them. "Anyone who welcomes this little child in my name welcomes me," he said. "And anyone who welcomes me welcomes the One who sent me. The least important person among all of you is the most important."

⁴⁹"Master," said John, "we saw a man driving out demons in your name. We tried to stop him, because he is not one of us."

⁵⁰"Do not stop him," Jesus said. "Anyone who is not against you is for you."

The Samaritans Do Not Welcome Jesus

⁵¹The time grew near for Jesus to be taken up to heaven. So he made up his mind to go to Jerusalem. ⁵²He sent messengers on ahead. They went into a Samaritan village to get things ready for him. ⁵³But the people there did not welcome Jesus. That was because he was heading for Jerusalem.

⁵⁴The disciples James and John saw this. They asked, "Lord, do you want us to call down fire from heaven to destroy them?"

⁵⁵But Jesus turned and commanded them not to do it. ⁵⁶They went on to another village.

It Costs to Follow Jesus

⁵⁷Once Jesus and those who were with him were walking along the road. A man said to Jesus, "I will follow you no matter where you go."

⁵⁸Jesus replied, "Foxes have holes. Birds of the air have nests. But the Son of Man has no place to lay his head."

⁵⁹He said to another man, "Follow me."

But the man replied, "Lord, first let me go and bury my father."

⁶⁰Jesus said to him, "Let dead people bury their own dead. You go and tell others about God's kingdom."

⁶¹Still another man said, "I will follow you, Lord. But first let me go back and say good-by to my family."

⁶²Jesus replied, "Suppose you start to plow and then look back. If you do, you are not fit for service in God's kingdom."

Jesus Sends Out the Seventy-two

10 After this the Lord appointed 72 others. He sent them out two by two ahead of him. They went to every town and place where he was about to go.

²He told them, "The harvest is huge, but the workers are few. So ask the Lord of the harvest to send out workers into his harvest field.

³"Go! I am sending you out like lambs among wolves. ⁴Do not take a purse or bag or sandals. And don't greet anyone on the road.

Famous Quotes

"I am a sinful man!"
Peter - Luke 5:8

"Inside you are full of greed."
Jesus - Luke 11:39

"How terrible for you!"
Jesus - Luke 11:47

"I have come to separate people."
Jesus - Luke 12:51

"She will wear me out."
Evil judge - Luke 18:5

"Jesus, remember me when you come into your kingdom."
Criminal on the cross - Luke 23:42

What? A criminal gets into the Kingdom of God?

⁵"When you enter a house, first say, 'May this house be blessed with peace.' ⁶If someone there loves peace, your blessing of peace will rest on him. If not, it will return to you. ⁷Stay in that house. Eat and drink anything they give you. Workers are worthy of their pay. Do not move around from house to house.

⁸"When you enter a town and are welcomed, eat what is set down in front of you. ⁹Heal the sick people who are there. Tell them, 'God's kingdom is near you.'

¹⁰"But what if you enter a town and are not welcomed? Then go into its streets and say, ¹¹'We wipe off even the dust of your town that sticks to our feet. We do it to show that God isn't pleased with you. But here is what you can be sure of. God's kingdom is near.'

¹²"I tell you this. On judgment day it will be easier for Sodom than for that town.

¹³"How terrible it will be for you, Korazin! How terrible for you, Bethsaida! Suppose the miracles done in you had been done in Tyre and Sidon. They would have turned away from their sins long ago. They would have put on black clothes. They would have sat down in ashes. ¹⁴On judgment day it will be easier for Tyre and Sidon than for you.

¹⁵"And what about you, Capernaum? Will you be lifted up to heaven? No! You will go down to the place of the dead.

¹⁶"Anyone who listens to you listens to me. Anyone who does not accept you does not accept me. And anyone who does not accept me does not accept the One who sent me."

¹⁷The 72 returned with joy. They said, "Lord, even the demons obey us when we speak in your name."

¹⁸Jesus replied, "I saw Satan fall like lightning from heaven. ¹⁹I have given you authority to walk all over snakes and scorpions. You will be able to destroy all the power of the enemy. Nothing will harm you. ²⁰But do not be glad when the evil spirits obey you. Instead, be glad that your names are written in heaven."

²¹At that time Jesus was full of joy through the Holy Spirit. He said, "I praise you, Father. You are Lord of heaven and earth. You have hidden these things from the wise and educated. But you have shown them to little children. Yes, Father. This is what you wanted.

²²"My Father has given all things to me. The Father is the only one who knows who the Son is. And the only ones who know the Father are the Son and those to whom the Son chooses to make the Father known."

²³Then Jesus turned to his disciples. He said to them in private, "Blessed are the eyes that see what you see. ²⁴I tell you, many prophets and kings wanted to see what you see. But they didn't see it. They wanted to hear what you hear. But they didn't hear it."

The Story of the Good Samaritan

²⁵One day an authority on the law stood up to put Jesus to the test. "Teacher," he asked, "what must I do to receive eternal life?"

²⁶"What is written in the Law?" Jesus replied. "How do you understand it?"

²⁷He answered, " 'Love the Lord your God with all your heart and with all your soul. Love him with all your strength and with all your mind.' *(Deuteronomy 6:5)* And, 'Love your neighbor as you love yourself.' " *(Leviticus 19:18)*

²⁸"You have answered correctly," Jesus replied. "Do that, and you will live."

²⁹But the man wanted to make himself look good. So he asked Jesus, "And who is my neighbor?"

³⁰Jesus replied, "A man was going down from Jerusalem to Jericho. Robbers attacked him. They stripped off his clothes and beat him. Then they went away, leaving him almost dead. ³¹A priest happened to be going down that same road. When he saw the man, he passed by on the other side. ³²A Levite also came by. When he saw the man, he passed by on the other side too.

³³But a Samaritan came to the place where the man was. When he saw the man, he felt sorry for him. ³⁴He went to him, poured olive oil and wine on his wounds and bandaged them. Then he put the man on his own donkey. He took him to an inn and took care of him. ³⁵The next day he took

Why Me?

As Christians, we are so blessed. God has provided so much to us. Sometimes we take it all for granted. We settle into our own comfort zone. We like our well-ordered world.

But when God changes things, we sometimes panic and cry out "Why me?" Maybe God is preparing us for the next step of His plan for our life.

Isn't it interesting that we rarely ask the question ...

Why Me?

... when blessings are pouring down on us from God? It is easy to panic when the "brook dries up." But hard to rejoice in all the "daily bread" and "living water" God has already given us.

We should begin each day with a thankful "Why me?" and count all our many blessings.

out two silver coins. He gave them to the owner of the inn. 'Take care of him,' he said. 'When I return, I will pay you back for any extra expense you may have.'

36"Which of the three do you think was a neighbor to the man who was attacked by robbers?"

37The authority on the law replied, "The one who felt sorry for him."

Jesus told him, "Go and do as he did."

Jesus at the Home of Martha and Mary

38Jesus and his disciples went on their way. Jesus came to a village where a woman named Martha lived. She welcomed him into her home. 39She had a sister named Mary.

Mary sat at the Lord's feet listening to what he said. 40But Martha was busy with all the things that had to be done. She came to Jesus and said, "Lord, my sister has left me to do the work by myself. Don't you care? Tell her to help me!"

41"Martha, Martha," the Lord answered. "You are worried and upset about many things. 42But only one thing is needed. Mary has chosen what is better. And it will not be taken away from her."

Jesus Teaches About Prayer

11 One day Jesus was praying in a certain place. When he finished, one of his disciples spoke to him. "Lord," he said, "teach us to pray, just as John taught his disciples."

2Jesus said to them, "When you pray, this is what you should say.

" 'Father,
may your name be honored.
May your kingdom come.
3 Give us each day our daily bread.
4 Forgive us our sins,
as we also forgive everyone who sins against us.
Keep us from falling into sin when we are tempted.' "

5Then Jesus said to them, "Suppose

someone has a friend. He goes to him at midnight. He says, 'Friend, lend me three loaves of bread. [6]A friend of mine on a journey has come to stay with me. I have nothing for him to eat.'

[7]"Then the one inside answers, 'Don't bother me. The door is already locked. My children are with me in bed. I can't get up and give you anything.'

[8]"I tell you, that person will not get up. And he won't give the man bread just because he is his friend. But because the man keeps on asking, he will get up. He will give him as much as he needs.

[9]"So here is what I say to you. Ask, and it will be given to you. Search, and you will find. Knock, and the door will be opened to you. [10]Everyone who asks will receive. He who searches will find. And the door will be opened to the one who knocks.

[11]"Fathers, suppose your son asks for a fish. Which of you will give him a snake instead? [12]Or suppose he asks for an egg. Which of you will give him a scorpion? [13]Even though you are evil, you know how to give good gifts to your children. How much more will your Father who is in heaven give the Holy Spirit to those who ask him!"

Jesus and Beelzebub

[14]Jesus was driving out a demon. The man who had the demon could not speak. When the demon left, the man began to speak. The crowd was amazed.

[15]But some of them said, "Jesus is driving out demons by the power of Beelzebub, the prince of demons." [16]Others put Jesus to the test by asking for a miraculous sign from heaven.

[17]Jesus knew what they were thinking. So he said to them, "Any kingdom that fights against itself will be destroyed. A family that is divided against itself will fall. [18]If Satan fights against himself, how can his kingdom stand?

"I say this because of what you claim. You say I drive out demons by the power of Beelzebub. [19]Suppose I do drive out demons with Beelzebub's help. With whose help do your followers drive them out? So then, they will be your judges. [20]But suppose I drive out demons with the help of God's powerful finger. Then God's kingdom has come to you.

[21]"When a strong man is completely armed and guards his house, what he owns is safe. [22]But when someone stronger attacks, he is overpowered. The attacker takes away the armor the man had trusted in. Then he divides up what he has stolen.

[23]"Anyone who is not with me is against me. Anyone who does not gather sheep with me scatters them.

[24]"What happens when an evil spirit comes out of a man? It goes through dry areas looking for a place to rest. But it doesn't find it. Then it says, 'I will return to the house I left.' [25]When it arrives there, it finds the house swept clean and put in order. [26]Then the evil spirit goes and takes seven other spirits more evil than itself. They go in and live there. That man is worse off than before."

[27]As Jesus was saying these things, a woman in the crowd called out. She shouted, "Blessed is the mother who gave you birth and nursed you."

[28]He replied, "Instead, blessed are those who hear God's word and obey it."

The Miraculous Sign of Jonah

[29]As the crowds grew larger, Jesus spoke to them. "The people of today are evil," he said. "They ask for a miraculous sign from God. But none will be given except the sign of Jonah. [30]He was a sign from God to the people of Nineveh. In the same way, the Son of Man will be a sign from God to the people of today.

[31]"The Queen of the South will stand up on judgment day with the men now living. And she will prove that they are guilty. She came from very far away to listen to Solomon's wisdom. And now one who is more important than Solomon is here.

[32]"The men of Nineveh will stand up on judgment day with the people now living. And the Ninevites will prove that those people are guilty. The men of Nineveh turned away from their sins when Jonah preached to them. And now one who is more important than Jonah is here.

The Eye Is the Lamp of the Body

[33]"No one lights a lamp and hides it. No one puts it under a bowl. Instead, people put a lamp on its stand. Then those who come in can see the light.

[34]"Your eye is like a lamp for your body. Suppose your eyes are good. Then your whole body also is full of light. But suppose your eyes are bad. Then your body also is full of darkness. [35]So make sure that the light inside you is not darkness.

[36]"Suppose your whole body is full of light. And suppose no part of it is dark. Then your body will be completely lit up. It will be as when the light of a lamp shines on you."

Six Warnings

[37]Jesus finished speaking. Then a Pharisee invited him to eat with him. So Jesus went in and took his place at the table. [38]But the Pharisee noticed that Jesus did not wash before the meal. He was surprised.

[39]Then the Lord spoke to him. "You Pharisees clean the outside of the cup and dish," he said. "But inside you are full of greed and evil. [40]You foolish people! Didn't the one who made the outside make the inside also? [41]Give to poor people what is inside the dish. Then everything will be clean for you.

[42]"How terrible it will be for you Pharisees! You give God a tenth of your garden plants, such as mint and rue. But you have forgotten to be fair and to love God. You should have practiced the last things without failing to do the first.

[43]"How terrible for you Pharisees! You love the most important seats in the synagogues. You love having people greet you in the market places.

[44]"How terrible for you! You are like graves that are not marked. People walk over them without knowing it."

[45]An authority on the law spoke to Jesus. He said, "Teacher, when you say things like that, you say bad things about us too."

[46]Jesus replied, "How terrible for you authorities on the law! You put such heavy loads on people that they can hardly carry them. But you yourselves will not lift one finger to help them.

[47]"How terrible for you! You build tombs for the prophets. It was your people of long ago who killed them. [48]So you give witness that you agree with what your people did long ago. They killed the prophets, and now you build the prophets' tombs.

[49]"So God in his wisdom said, 'I will send prophets and apostles to them. They will kill some. And they will try to hurt others.' [50]So the people of today will be punished. They will pay for all the prophets' blood

By the Numbers

7 demons cast out of Mary Magdalene
Luke 8:2

3 days later Jesus will be raised from the dead
Luke 9:22

72 other disciples sent out to spread the Gospel
Luke 10:1

18 years unable to stand straight
Luke 13:11

9 of **10** lepers failed to thank Jesus for healing them
Luke 17:17

spilled since the world began. [51]I mean from the blood of Abel to the blood of Zechariah, who was killed between the altar and the temple. Yes, I tell you, the people of today will be punished for all these things.

[52]"How terrible for you authorities on the law! You have taken away the key to the door of knowledge. You yourselves have not entered. And you have stood in the way of those who were entering."

[53]When Jesus left there, the Pharisees and the teachers of the law strongly opposed him. They threw a lot of questions at him. [54]They set traps for him. They wanted to catch him in something he might say.

Jesus Gives Words of Warning and Hope

12 During that time a crowd of many thousands had gathered. There were so many people that they were stepping on one another.

Jesus spoke first to his disciples. "Be on your guard against the yeast of the Pharisees," he said. "They just pretend to be godly. [2]Everything that is secret will be brought out into the open. Everything that is hidden will be uncovered. [3]What you have said in the dark will be heard in the daylight. What you have whispered to someone behind closed doors will be shouted from the rooftops.

[4]"My friends, listen to me. Don't be afraid of those who kill the body but can't do any more than that. [5]I will show you whom you should be afraid of. Be afraid of the One who can kill the body and also has the power to throw you into hell. Yes, I tell you, be afraid of him.

[6]"Aren't five sparrows sold for two pennies? But God does not forget even one of them. [7]In fact, he even counts every hair on your head! So don't be afraid. You are worth more than many sparrows.

[8]"What about someone who says in front of others that he knows me? I tell you, the Son of Man will say that he knows that person in front of God's angels. [9]But what about someone who says in front of others that he doesn't know me? I, the Son of Man, will say that I don't know him in front of God's angels.

[10]"Everyone who speaks a word against the Son of Man will be forgiven. But anyone who speaks evil things against the Holy Spirit will not be forgiven.

[11]"You will be brought before synagogues, rulers and authorities. But do not worry about how to stand up for yourselves or what to say. [12]The Holy Spirit will teach you at that time what you should say."

The Story of the Rich Man

[13]Someone in the crowd spoke to Jesus. "Teacher," he said, "tell my brother to divide the family property with me."

[14]Jesus replied, "Friend, who made me a judge or umpire between you?"

[15]Then he said to them, "Watch out! Be on your guard against wanting to have more and more things. Life is not made up of how much a person has."

[16]Then Jesus told them a story. He said, "A certain rich man's land produced a good crop. [17]He thought to himself, 'What should I do? I don't have any place to store my crops.'

[18]"Then he said, 'This is what I'll do. I will tear down my storerooms and build bigger ones. I will store all my grain and my other things in them. [19]I'll say to myself, "You have plenty of good things stored away for many years. Take life easy. Eat, drink and have a good time." '

[20]"But God said to him, 'You foolish man! This very night I will take your life away from you. Then who will get what you have prepared for yourself?'

[21]"That is how it will be for anyone who stores things away for himself but is not rich in God's eyes."

**Don't wait for the perfect time to act...
It will never come.**

Do Not Worry

²²Then Jesus spoke to his disciples. He said, "I tell you, do not worry. Don't worry about your life and what you will eat. And don't worry about your body and what you will wear. ²³There is more to life than eating. There are more important things for the body than clothes.

²⁴"Think about the ravens. They don't plant or gather crops. They don't have any storerooms at all. But God feeds them. You are worth much more than birds!

²⁵"Can you add even one hour to your life by worrying? ²⁶You can't do that very little thing. So why worry about the rest?

²⁷"Think about how the lilies grow. They don't work or make clothing. But here is what I tell you. Not even Solomon in all of his glory was dressed like one of those flowers. ²⁸If that is how God dresses the wild grass, how much better will he dress you! After all, the grass is here only today. Tomorrow it is thrown into the fire. Your faith is so small!

²⁹"Don't spend time thinking about what you will eat or drink. Don't worry about it. ³⁰People who are ungodly run after all of those things. Your Father knows that you need them.

³¹"But put God's kingdom first. Then those other things will also be given to you.

³²"Little flock, do not be afraid. Your Father has been pleased to give you the kingdom. ³³Sell what you own. Give to those who are poor. Provide purses for yourselves that will not wear out. Put away riches in heaven that will not be used up. There, no thief can come near it. There, no moth can destroy it. ³⁴Your heart will be where your riches are.

Be Ready

³⁵"Be dressed and ready to serve. Keep your lamps burning. ³⁶Be like servants waiting for their master to return from a wedding dinner. When he comes and knocks, they can open the door for him at once.

³⁷"It will be good for those servants whose master finds them ready when he comes. What I'm about to tell you is true. The master will then dress himself so he can serve them. He will have them take their places at the table. And he will come and wait on them. ³⁸It will be good for those servants whose master finds them ready. It will even be good if he comes very late at night.

³⁹"But here is what you must understand. Suppose the owner of the house knew at what hour the robber was coming. He would not have let his house be broken into. ⁴⁰You also must be ready. The Son of Man will come at an hour when you don't expect him."

⁴¹Peter asked, "Lord, are you telling this story to us, or to everyone?"

⁴²The Lord answered, "Suppose a master puts one of his servants in charge of his other servants. The servant's job is to give them the food they are to receive at the right time. The master wants a faithful and wise manager for this. ⁴³It will be good for the servant if the master finds him doing his job when the master returns. ⁴⁴What I'm about to tell you is true. The master will put that servant in charge of everything he owns.

⁴⁵"But suppose the servant says to himself, 'My master is taking a long time to come back.' Suppose he begins to beat the other servants. Suppose he feeds himself. And suppose he drinks until he gets drunk. ⁴⁶The master of that servant will come back on a day the servant doesn't expect him. He will return at an hour the servant doesn't know. Then the master will cut him to pieces. He will send him to the place where unbelievers go.

⁴⁷"Suppose a servant knows his master's wishes. But he doesn't get ready. And he doesn't do what his master wants. That servant will be beaten with many blows. ⁴⁸But suppose the servant does not know his master's wishes. And suppose he does things for which he should be punished. He will be beaten with only a few blows.

"Much will be required of everyone who has been given much. Even more will be asked of the person who is supposed to take care of much.

Jesus Will Separate People From One Another

[49]"I have come to bring fire on the earth. How I wish the fire had already started! [50]But I have a baptism of suffering to go through. And I will be very troubled until it is completed.

[51]"Do you think I came to bring peace on earth? No, I tell you. I have come to separate people. [52]From now on there will be five members in a family, each one against the other. There will be three against two and two against three. [53]They will be separated. Father will turn against son and son against father. Mother will turn against daughter and daughter against mother. Mother-in-law will turn against daughter-in-law and daughter-in-law against mother-in-law."

Understanding What Is Happening

[54]Jesus spoke to the crowd. He said, "You see a cloud rising in the west. Right away you say, 'It's going to rain.' And it does. [55]The south wind blows. So you say, 'It's going to be hot.' And it is. [56]You pretenders! You know how to understand the appearance of the earth and the sky. Why can't you understand the meaning of what is happening right now?

[57]"Why don't you judge for yourselves what is right? [58]Suppose someone has a claim against you, and you are on your way to court. Try hard to settle the matter on the way. If you don't, that person may drag you off to the judge. The judge may turn you over to the officer. And the officer may throw you into prison. [59]I tell you, you will not get out until you have paid the very last penny!"

Jesus Gives a Warning

13 Some people who were there at that time told Jesus about certain Galileans. Pilate had mixed their blood with their sacrifices.

[2]Jesus said, "These people from Galilee suffered greatly. Do you think they were worse sinners than all the other Galileans? [3]I tell you, no! But unless you turn away from your sins, you will all die too. [4]Or what about the 18 people in Siloam? They died when the tower fell on them. Do you think they were more guilty than all the others living in Jerusalem? [5]I tell you, no! But unless you turn away from your sins, you will all die too."

[6]Then Jesus told a story. "A man had a fig tree," he said. "It had been planted in his vineyard. When he went to look for fruit on it, he didn't find any. [7]So he went to the man who took care of the vineyard. He said, 'For three years now I've been coming to look for fruit on this fig tree. But I haven't found any. Cut it down! Why should it use up the soil?'

[8]"'Sir,' the man replied, 'leave it alone for one more year. I'll dig around it and feed it. [9]If it bears fruit next year, fine! If not, then cut it down.' "

Jesus Heals a Disabled Woman on the Sabbath Day

[10]Jesus was teaching in one of the synagogues on a Sabbath day. [11]A woman there had been disabled by an evil spirit for 18 years. She was bent over and could not stand up straight.

[12]Jesus saw her. He asked her to come to him. He said to her, "Woman, you will no longer be disabled. I am about to set you free." [13]Then he put his hands on her.

Right away she stood up straight and praised God.

[14]Jesus had healed the woman on the Sabbath day. This made the synagogue ruler angry. He told the people, "There are six days for work. So come and be healed on those days. But do not come on the Sabbath."

[15]The Lord answered him, "You pretenders! Doesn't each of you go to the barn and untie his ox or donkey on the Sabbath day? Then don't you lead it out to give it water? [16]This woman is a member of Abraham's family line. But Satan has kept her disabled for 18 long years. Shouldn't she be set free on the Sabbath day from what was keeping her disabled?"

[17]When Jesus said this, all those who opposed him were put to shame. But the people were delighted. They loved all the wonderful things he was doing.

The Stories of the Mustard Seed and the Yeast

[18]Then Jesus asked, "What is God's kingdom like? What can I compare it to? [19]It is like a mustard seed. Someone took the seed and planted it in a garden. It grew and became a tree. The birds sat in its branches."

[20]Again he asked, "What can I compare God's kingdom to? [21]It is like yeast that a woman used. She mixed it into a large amount of flour. The yeast worked its way all through the dough."

The Narrow Door

[22]Then Jesus went through the towns and villages, teaching the people. He was on his way to Jerusalem. [23]Someone asked him, "Lord, are only a few people going to be saved?"

He said to them, [24]"Try very hard to enter through the narrow door. I tell you, many will try to enter and will not be able to. [25]The owner of the house will get up and close the door. Then you will stand outside knocking and begging. You will say, 'Sir, open the door for us.'

"But he will answer, 'I don't know you. And I don't know where you come from.'

[26]"Then you will say, 'We ate and drank with you. You taught in our streets.'

[27]"But he will reply, 'I don't know you. And I don't know where you come from. Get away from me, all you who do evil!'

[28]"You will sob and grind your teeth when you see those who are in God's kingdom. You will see Abraham, Isaac and Jacob and all the prophets there. But you yourselves will be thrown out. [29]People will come from east and west and north and south. They will take their places at the feast in God's kingdom. [30]Then the last will be first. And the first will be last."

Jesus' Sadness Over Jerusalem

[31]At that time some Pharisees came to Jesus. They said to him, "Leave this place. Go somewhere else. Herod wants to kill you."

[32]He replied, "Go and tell that fox, 'I will drive out demons. I will heal people today and tomorrow. And on the third day I will reach my goal.' [33]In any case, I must keep going today and tomorrow and the next day. Certainly no prophet can die outside Jerusalem!

[34]"Jerusalem! Jerusalem! You kill the prophets and throw stones in order to kill those who are sent to you. Many times I have wanted to gather your people together. I have wanted to be like a hen who gathers her chicks under her wings. But you would not let me!

[35]"Look, your house is left empty. I tell you, you will not see me again until you say, 'Blessed is the one who comes in the name of the Lord.' " *(Psalm 118:26)*

Jesus Eats at a Pharisee's House

14 One Sabbath day, Jesus went to eat in the house of a well-known Pharisee. While he was there, he was being carefully watched. [2]In front of him was a man whose body was badly swollen.

[3]Jesus turned to the Pharisees and the authorities on the law. He asked them, "Is it breaking the Law to heal on the Sabbath?"

[4]But they remained silent.

So Jesus took hold of the man and healed him. Then he sent him away.

[5]He asked them another question. He said, "Suppose one of you has a son or an ox that falls into a well on the Sabbath day. Wouldn't you pull him out right away?" [6]And they had nothing to say.

[7]Jesus noticed how the guests picked the places of honor at the table. So he told them a story. [8]He said, "Suppose someone invites you to a wedding feast. Do not take

Read the Bible for *transformation,*
not just *information.*

the place of honor. A person more important than you may have been invited. [9]If so, the host who invited both of you will come to you. He will say, 'Give this person your seat.' Then you will be filled with shame. You will have to take the least important place.

[10]"But when you are invited, take the lowest place. Then your host will come over to you. He will say, 'Friend, move up to a better place.' Then you will be honored in front of all the other guests. [11]Anyone who lifts himself up will be brought down. And anyone who is brought down will be lifted up."

[12]Then Jesus spoke to his host. "Suppose you give a lunch or a dinner," he said. "Do not invite your friends, your brothers or sisters, or your relatives, or your rich neighbors. If you do, they may invite you to eat with them. So you will be paid back.

[13]"But when you give a big dinner, invite those who are poor. Also invite those who can't walk, the disabled and the blind. [14]Then you will be blessed. Your guests can't pay you back. But you will be paid back when those who are right with God rise from the dead."

The Story of the Big Dinner

[15]One of the people at the table with Jesus heard him say those things. So he said to Jesus, "Blessed is the one who will eat at the feast in God's kingdom."

[16]Jesus replied, "A certain man was preparing a big dinner. He invited many guests. [17]Then the day of the dinner arrived. He sent his servant to those who had been invited. The servant told them, 'Come. Everything is ready now.'

[18]"But they all had the same idea. They began to make excuses. The first one said, 'I have just bought a field. I have to go and see it. Please excuse me.'

[19]"Another said, 'I have just bought five pairs of oxen. I'm on my way to try them out. Please excuse me.'

[20]"Still another said, 'I just got married, so I can't come.'

[21]"The servant came back and reported this to his master.

"Then the owner of the house became angry. He ordered his servant, 'Go out quickly into the streets and lanes of the town. Bring in those who are poor. Also bring those who can't walk, the blind and the disabled.'

[22]" 'Sir,' the servant said, 'what you ordered has been done. But there is still room.'

[23]"Then the master told his servant, 'Go out to the roads. Go out to the country lanes. Make the people come in. I want my house to be full. [24]I tell you, not one of those men who were invited will get a taste of my dinner.' "

It Costs to Be a Disciple

[25]Large crowds were traveling with Jesus. He turned and spoke to them. He said, [26]"Anyone who comes to me must hate his father and mother. He must hate his wife and children. He must hate his brothers and sisters. And he must hate even his own life. Unless he does, he can't be my disciple. [27]Anyone who doesn't carry his cross and follow me can't be my disciple.

[28]"Suppose someone wants to build a tower. Won't he sit down first and figure out how much it will cost? Then he will see whether he has enough money to finish it. [29]Suppose he starts building and is not able to finish. Then everyone who sees what he has done will laugh at him. [30]They will say, 'This fellow started to build. But he wasn't able to finish.'

[31]"Or suppose a king is about to go to war against another king. And suppose he has 10,000 men, while the other has 20,000 coming against him. Won't he first sit down and think about whether he can win? [32]"And suppose he decides he can't win. Then he will send some men to ask how peace can be made. He will do this while the other king is still far away.

[33]"In the same way, you must give up everything you have. If you don't, you can't be my disciple.

[34]"Salt is good. But suppose it loses its saltiness. How can it be made salty again? [35]It is not good for the soil. And it is not good for the trash pile. It will be thrown out.

Luke 15:10

Angels
rejoice when one sinner
even repents.

"Those who have ears should listen."

The Story of the Lost Sheep

15 The tax collectors and "sinners" were all gathering around to hear Jesus. ²But the Pharisees and the teachers of the law were whispering among themselves. They said, "This man welcomes sinners and eats with them."

³Then Jesus told them a story. ⁴He said, "Suppose one of you has 100 sheep and loses one of them. Won't he leave the 99 in the open country? Won't he go and look for the one lost sheep until he finds it? ⁵When he finds it, he will joyfully put it on his shoulders ⁶and go home. Then he will call his friends and neighbors together. He will say, 'Be joyful with me. I have found my lost sheep.'

⁷"I tell you, it will be the same in heaven. There will be great joy when one sinner turns away from sin. Yes, there will be more joy than for 99 godly people who do not need to turn away from their sins.

The Story of the Lost Coin

⁸"Or suppose a woman has ten silver coins and loses one. She will light a lamp and sweep the house. She will search care- fully until she finds the coin. ⁹And when she finds it, she will call her friends and neigh- bors together. She will say, 'Be joyful with me. I have found my lost coin.'

¹⁰"I tell you, it is the same in heaven. There is joy in heaven over one sinner who turns away from sin."

The Story of the Lost Son

¹¹Jesus continued, "There was a man who had two sons. ¹²The younger son spoke to his father. He said, 'Father, give me my share of the family property.' So the father divided his property between his two sons.

¹³"Not long after that, the younger son packed up all he had. Then he left for a country far away. There he wasted his money on wild living. ¹⁴He spent everything he had.

"Then the whole country ran low on food. So the son didn't have what he needed. ¹⁵He went to work for someone who lived in that country, who sent him to the fields to feed the pigs. ¹⁶The son wanted to fill his stom- ach with the food the pigs were eating. But no one gave him anything.

¹⁷"Then he began to think clearly again. He said, 'How many of my father's hired work-

ers have more than enough food! But here I am dying from hunger! [18]I will get up and go back to my father. I will say to him, "Father, I have sinned against heaven. And I have sinned against you. [19]I am no longer fit to be called your son. Make me like one of your hired workers." ' [20]So he got up and went to his father.

"While the son was still a long way off, his father saw him. He was filled with tender love for his son. He ran to him. He threw his arms around him and kissed him.

[21]"The son said to him, 'Father, I have sinned against heaven and against you. I am no longer fit to be called your son.'

[22]"But the father said to his servants, 'Quick! Bring the best robe and put it on him. Put a ring on his finger and sandals on his feet. [23]Bring the fattest calf and kill it. Let's have a big dinner and celebrate. [24]This son of mine was dead. And now he is alive again. He was lost. And now he is found.'

"So they began to celebrate.

[25]"The older son was in the field. When he came near the house, he heard music and dancing. [26]So he called one of the servants. He asked him what was going on.

[27]" 'Your brother has come home,' the servant replied. 'Your father has killed the fattest calf. He has done this because your brother is back safe and sound.'

[28]"The older brother became angry. He refused to go in. So his father went out and begged him.

[29]"But he answered his father, 'Look! All these years I've worked like a slave for you. I have always obeyed your orders. You never gave me even a young goat so I could celebrate with my friends. [30]But this son of yours wasted your money with some prostitutes. Now he comes home. And for him you kill the fattest calf!'

[31]" 'My son,' the father said, 'you are always with me. Everything I have is yours. [32]But we had to celebrate and be glad. This brother of yours was dead. And now he is alive again. He was lost. And now he is found.' "

The Story of the Clever Manager

16 Jesus told his disciples another story. He said, "There was a rich man who had a manager. Some said that the manager was wasting what the rich man owned. [2]So the rich man told him to come in. He asked him, 'What is this I hear about you? Tell me exactly how you have handled what I own. You can't be my manager any longer.'

[3]"The manager said to himself, 'What will I do now? My master is taking away my job. I'm not strong enough to dig. And I'm too ashamed to beg. [4]I know what I'm going to do. I'll do something so that when I lose my job here, people will welcome me into their houses.'

[5]"So he called in each person who owed his master something. He asked the first one, 'How much do you owe my master?'

[6]" 'I owe 800 gallons of olive oil,' he replied.

"The manager told him, 'Take your bill. Sit down quickly and change it to 400 gallons.'

[7]"Then he asked the second one, 'And how much do you owe?'

" 'I owe 1,000 bushels of wheat,' he replied.

"The manager told him, 'Take your bill and change it to 800 bushels.'

[8]"The manager had not been honest. But the master praised him for being clever. The people of this world are clever in dealing with those who are like themselves. They are more clever than God's people.

[9]"I tell you, use the riches of this world to help others. In that way, you will make friends for yourselves. Then when your riches are gone, you will be welcomed into your eternal home in heaven.

[10]"Suppose you can be trusted with very little. Then you can be trusted with a lot. But suppose you are not honest with very little. Then you will not be honest with a lot.

[11]"Suppose you have not been worthy of trust in handling worldly wealth. Then who will trust you with true riches? [12]Suppose you have not been worthy of trust in handling someone else's property. Then who

will give you property of your own?

¹³"No servant can serve two masters at the same time. He will hate one of them and love the other. Or he will be faithful to one and dislike the other. You can't serve God and Money at the same time."

¹⁴The Pharisees loved money. They heard all that Jesus said and made fun of him. ¹⁵Jesus said to them, "You try to make yourselves look good in the eyes of other people. But God knows your hearts. What is worth a great deal among people is hated by God.

More Teachings

¹⁶"The teachings of the Law and the Prophets were preached until John came. Since then, the good news of God's kingdom is being preached. And everyone is trying very hard to enter it. ¹⁷It is easier for heaven and earth to disappear than for the smallest part of a letter to drop out of the Law.

¹⁸"Anyone who divorces his wife and gets married to another woman commits adultery. Also, the man who gets married to a divorced woman commits adultery.

The Rich Man and Lazarus

¹⁹"Once there was a rich man. He was dressed in purple cloth and fine linen. He lived an easy life every day. ²⁰A man named Lazarus was placed at his gate. Lazarus was a beggar. His body was covered with sores. ²¹Even dogs came and licked his sores. All he wanted was to eat what fell from the rich man's table.

²²"The time came when the beggar died. The angels carried him to Abraham's side. The rich man also died and was buried. ²³In hell, the rich man was suffering terribly. He looked up and saw Abraham far away. Lazarus was by his side. ²⁴So the rich man called out, 'Father Abraham! Have pity on me! Send Lazarus to dip the tip of his finger in water. Then he can cool my tongue with it. I am in terrible pain in this fire.'

²⁵"But Abraham replied, 'Son, remember what happened in your lifetime. You received your good things. Lazarus received bad things. Now he is comforted here, and you are in terrible pain. ²⁶Besides, a wide space has been placed between us and you.

Sooner or later...

...you'll have to decide which horse to ride.

"No one servant can serve two masters at the same time."

Luke 16:13

So those who want to go from here to you can't go. And no one can cross over from there to us.'

²⁷"The rich man answered, 'Then I beg you, father. Send Lazarus to my family. ²⁸I have five brothers. Let Lazarus warn them. Then they will not come to this place of terrible suffering.'

²⁹"Abraham replied, 'They have the teachings of Moses and the Prophets. Let your brothers listen to them.'

³⁰"'No, father Abraham,' he said. 'But if someone from the dead goes to them, they will turn away from their sins.'

[31]"Abraham said to him, 'They do not listen to Moses and the Prophets. So they will not be convinced even if someone rises from the dead.'"

Sin, Faith and Duty

17 Jesus spoke to his disciples. "Things that make people sin are sure to come," he said. "But how terrible it will be for the person who brings them! [2]Suppose people lead one of these little ones to sin. It would be better for those people to be thrown into the sea with a millstone tied around their neck. [3]So watch what you do.

"If your brother sins, tell him he is wrong. Then if he turns away from his sins, forgive him. [4]Suppose he sins against you seven times in one day. And suppose he comes back to you each time and says, 'I'm sorry.' Forgive him."

[5]The apostles said to the Lord, "Give us more faith!"

[6]He replied, "Suppose you have faith as small as a mustard seed. Then you can say to this mulberry tree, 'Be pulled up. Be planted in the sea.' And it will obey you.

[7]"Suppose one of you had a servant plowing or looking after the sheep. And suppose the servant came in from the field. Would you say to him, 'Come along now and sit down to eat'? [8]No. Instead, you would say, 'Prepare my supper. Get yourself ready. Wait on me while I eat and drink. Then after that you can eat and drink.' [9]Would you thank the servant because he did what he was told to do?

[10]"It's the same with you. Suppose you have done everything you were told to do. Then you should say, 'We are not worthy to serve you. We have only done our duty.'"

Jesus Heals Ten Men

[11]Jesus was on his way to Jerusalem. He traveled along the border between Samaria and Galilee. [12]As he was going into a village, ten men met him. They had a skin disease. They were standing close by. [13]And they called out in a loud voice, "Jesus! Master! Have pity on us!"

[14]Jesus saw them and said, "Go. Show yourselves to the priests." While they were on the way, they were healed.

[15]When one of them saw that he was healed, he came back. He praised God in a loud voice. [16]He threw himself at Jesus' feet and thanked him. The man was a Samaritan.

[17]Jesus asked, "Weren't all ten healed? Where are the other nine? [18]Didn't anyone else return and give praise to God except this outsider?"

[19]Then Jesus said to him, "Get up and go. Your faith has healed you."

The Coming of God's Kingdom

[20]Once the Pharisees asked Jesus when God's kingdom would come. He replied, "The coming of God's kingdom is not something you can see just by watching for it carefully. [21]People will not say, 'Here it is.' Or, 'There it is.' God's kingdom is among you."

[22]Then Jesus spoke to his disciples. "The time is coming," he said, "when you will long to see one of the days of the Son of Man. But you won't see it. [23]People will tell you, 'There he is!' Or, 'Here he is!' Don't go running off after them.

[24]"When the Son of Man comes, he will be like the lightning. It flashes and lights up the sky from one end to the other. [25]But first the Son of Man must suffer many things. He will not be accepted by the people of today.

[26]"Remember how it was in the days of Noah. It will be the same when the Son of Man comes. [27]People were eating and drinking. They were getting married. They were giving their daughters to be married. They did all those things right up to the day Noah entered the ark. Then the flood came and destroyed them all.

[28]"It was the same in the days of Lot. People were eating and drinking. They were buying and selling. They were planting and building. [29]But on the day Lot left Sodom, fire and sulfur rained down from heaven. And all the people were destroyed.

[30]"It will be just like that on the day the Son of Man is shown to the world. [31]Suppose someone is on the roof of his house on that day. And suppose his goods are inside

the house. He should not go down to get them. No one in the field should go back for anything either. ³²Remember Lot's wife! ³³Anyone who tries to keep his life will lose it. Anyone who loses his life will keep it.

³⁴"I tell you, on that night two people will be in one bed. One person will be taken and the other left. ³⁵/³⁶Two women will be grinding grain together. One will be taken and the other left."

³⁷"Where, Lord?" his disciples asked.

He replied, "The vultures will gather where there is a dead body."

The Story of the Widow Who Would Not Give Up

18 Jesus told his disciples a story. He wanted to show them that they should always pray and not give up. ²He said, "In a certain town there was a judge. He didn't have any respect for God or care about people. ³A widow lived in that town. She came to the judge again and again. She kept begging him, 'Make things right for me. Someone is doing me wrong.'

⁴"For some time the judge refused. But finally he said to himself, 'I don't have any respect for God. I don't care about people. ⁵But this widow keeps bothering me. So I will see that things are made right for her. If I don't, she will wear me out by coming again and again!' "

⁶The Lord said, "Listen to what the unfair judge says.

⁷"God's chosen people cry out to him day and night. Won't he make things right for

"Is it hard for a camel to go through the eye of a needle? It is even harder for the rich to enter God's kingdom!"
Luke 18:25

But with God ALL things are possible!

them? Will he keep putting them off? [8]I tell you, God will see that things are made right for them. He will make sure it happens quickly.

"But when the Son of Man comes, will he find people on earth who have faith?"

The Story of the Pharisee and the Tax Collector

[9]Jesus told a story to some people who were sure they were right with God. They looked down on everybody else. [10]He said to them, "Two men went up to the temple to pray. One was a Pharisee. The other was a tax collector.

[11]"The Pharisee stood up and prayed about himself. 'God, I thank you that I am not like other people,' he said. 'I am not like robbers or those who do other evil things. I am not like those who commit adultery. I am not even like this tax collector. [12]I fast twice a week. And I give a tenth of all I get.'

[13]"But the tax collector stood not very far away. He would not even look up to heaven. He beat his chest and said, 'God, have mercy on me. I am a sinner.'

[14]"I tell you, the tax collector went home accepted by God. But not the Pharisee. Everyone who lifts himself up will be brought down. And anyone who is brought down will be lifted up."

Little Children Are Brought to Jesus

[15]People were also bringing babies to Jesus. They wanted him to touch them. When the disciples saw this, they told the people to stop.

[16]But Jesus asked the children to come to him. "Let the little children come to me," he said. "Don't keep them away. God's kingdom belongs to people like them. [17]What I'm about to tell you is true. Anyone who will not receive God's kingdom like a little child will never enter it."

Jesus and the Rich Ruler

[18]A certain ruler asked Jesus a question. "Good teacher," he said, "what must I do to receive eternal life?"

[19]"Why do you call me good?" Jesus answered. "No one is good except God.

[20]You know what the commandments say. 'Do not commit adultery. Do not commit murder. Do not steal. Do not give false witness. Honor your father and mother.'" *(Exodus 20:12–16; Deuteronomy 5:16–20)*

[21]"I have obeyed all those commandments since I was a boy," the ruler said.

[22]When Jesus heard this, he said to him, "You are still missing one thing. Sell everything you have. Give the money to those who are poor. You will have treasure in heaven. Then come and follow me."

[23]When the ruler heard this, he became very sad. He was very rich.

[24]Jesus looked at him. Then he said, "How hard it is for rich people to enter God's kingdom! [25]Is it hard for a camel to go through the eye of a needle? It is even harder for the rich to enter God's kingdom!"

[26]Those who heard this asked, "Then who can be saved?"

[27]Jesus replied, "Things that are impossible with people are possible with God."

[28]Peter said to him, "We have left everything we had in order to follow you!"

[29]"What I'm about to tell you is true," Jesus said to them. "Has anyone left home or family for God's kingdom? [30]They will receive many times as much in this world. In the world to come they will live forever."

Jesus Again Tells About His Coming Death

[31]Jesus took the Twelve to one side. He told them, "We are going up to Jerusalem. Everything that the prophets wrote about the Son of Man will come true. [32]He will be handed over to people who are not Jews. They will make fun of him. They will laugh at him and spit on him. They will whip him and kill him. [33]On the third day, he will rise from the dead!"

[34]The disciples did not understand any of this. Its meaning was hidden from them. So they didn't know what Jesus was talking about.

A Blind Beggar Receives His Sight

[35]Jesus was approaching Jericho. A blind man was sitting by the side of the road

Some Highs and Lows of Peter in the Gospels

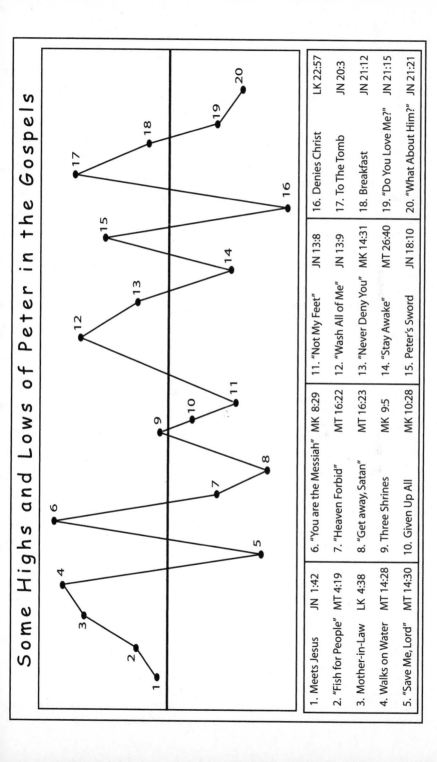

1. Meets Jesus	JN 1:42	6. "You are the Messiah"	MK 8:29	11. "Not My Feet"	JN 13:8	16. Denies Christ	LK 22:57
2. "Fish for People"	MT 4:19	7. "Heaven Forbid"	MT 16:22	12. "Wash All of Me"	JN 13:9	17. To The Tomb	JN 20:3
3. Mother-in-Law	LK 4:38	8. "Get away, Satan"	MT 16:23	13. "Never Deny You"	MK 14:31	18. Breakfast	JN 21:12
4. Walks on Water	MT 14:28	9. Three Shrines	MK 9:5	14. "Stay Awake"	MT 26:40	19. "Do You Love Me?"	JN 21:15
5. "Save Me, Lord"	MT 14:30	10. Given Up All	MK 10:28	15. Peter's Sword	JN 18:10	20. "What About Him?"	JN 21:21

begging. ³⁶The blind man heard the crowd going by. He asked what was happening. ³⁷They told him, "Jesus of Nazareth is passing by."

³⁸So the blind man called out, "Jesus! Son of David! Have mercy on me!"

³⁹Those who led the way commanded him to stop. They told him to be quiet. But he shouted even louder, "Son of David! Have mercy on me!"

⁴⁰Jesus stopped and ordered the man to be brought to him. When the man came near, Jesus spoke to him. ⁴¹"What do you want me to do for you?" Jesus asked.

"Lord, I want to be able to see," the blind man replied.

⁴²Jesus said to him, "Receive your sight. Your faith has healed you."

⁴³Right away he could see. He followed Jesus, praising God. When all the people saw it, they also praised God.

Zacchaeus the Tax Collector

19 Jesus entered Jericho and was passing through. ²A man named Zacchaeus lived there. He was a chief tax collector and was very rich.

³Zacchaeus wanted to see who Jesus was. But he was a short man. He could not see Jesus because of the crowd. ⁴So he ran ahead and climbed a sycamore-fig tree. He wanted to see Jesus, who was coming that way.

⁵Jesus reached the spot where Zacchaeus was. He looked up and said, "Zacchaeus, come down at once. I must stay at your house today." ⁶So Zacchaeus came down at once and welcomed him gladly.

⁷All the people saw this. They began to whisper among themselves. They said, "Jesus has gone to be the guest of a 'sinner.'"

⁸But Zacchaeus stood up. He said, "Look, Lord! Here and now I give half of what I own to those who are poor. And if I have cheated anybody out of anything, I will pay it back. I will pay back four times the amount I took."

⁹Jesus said to Zacchaeus, "Today salvation has come to your house. You are a member of Abraham's family line. ¹⁰The Son of Man came to look for the lost and save them."

The Story of Three Servants

¹¹While the people were listening to these things, Jesus told them a story. He was near Jerusalem. The people thought that God's kingdom was going to appear right away.

¹²Jesus said, "A man from an important family went to a country far away. He went there to be made king and then return home. ¹³So he sent for ten of his servants. He gave them each about three months' pay. 'Put this money to work until I come back,' he said.

¹⁴"But those he ruled over hated him. They sent some messengers after him. They were sent to say, 'We don't want this man to be our king.'

¹⁵"But he was made king and returned home. Then he sent for the servants he had given the money to. He wanted to find out what they had earned with it.

¹⁶"The first one came to him. He said, 'Sir, your money has earned ten times as much.'

¹⁷"'You have done well, my good servant!' his master replied. 'You have been faithful in a very small matter. So I will put you in charge of ten towns.'

¹⁸"The second servant came to his master. He said, 'Sir, your money has earned five times as much.'

¹⁹"His master answered, 'I will put you in charge of five towns.'

²⁰"Then another servant came. He said, 'Sir, here is your money. I have kept it hidden in a piece of cloth. ²¹I was afraid of you. You are a hard man. You take out what you did not put in. You harvest what you did not plant.'

²²"His master replied, 'I will judge you by your own words, you evil servant! So you knew that I am a hard man? You knew that I take out what I did not put in? You knew that I harvest what I did not plant? ²³Then why didn't you put my money in the bank? When I came back, I could have collected it with interest.'

²⁴"Then he said to those standing by, 'Take his money away from him. Give it to the one who has ten times as much.'

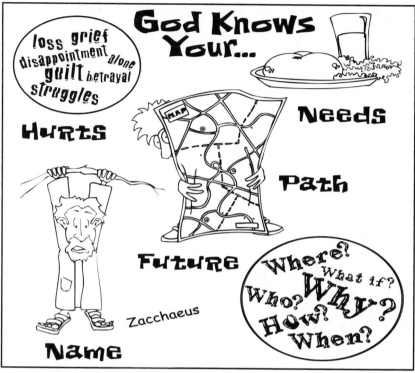

‘Sir,’ they said, ‘he already has ten times as much!’

26"He replied, ‘I tell you that everyone who has will be given more. But here is what will happen to anyone who has nothing. Even what he has will be taken away from him. 27And what about my enemies who did not want me to be king over them? Bring them here! Kill them in front of me!’ ”

Jesus Enters Jerusalem

28After Jesus had said this, he went on ahead. He was going up to Jerusalem.

29He approached Bethphage and Bethany. The hill there was called the Mount of Olives. Jesus sent out two of his disciples. He said to them, 30"Go to the village ahead of you. As soon as you get there, you will find a donkey's colt tied up. No one has ever ridden it. Untie it and bring it here. 31Someone may ask you, 'Why are you untying it?' If so, say, 'The Lord needs it.' ”

32Those who were sent ahead went and found the young donkey. It was there just as Jesus had told them. 33They were untying the colt when its owners came. The owners asked them, "Why are you untying the colt?"

34They replied, "The Lord needs it."

35Then the disciples brought the colt to Jesus. They threw their coats on the young donkey and put Jesus on it. 36As he went along, people spread their coats on the road.

37Jesus came near the place where the road goes down the Mount of Olives. There the whole crowd of disciples began to praise God with joy. In loud voices they praised him for all the miracles they had seen. They shouted,

38 "Blessed is the king who comes in the name of the Lord!" *(Psalm 118:26)*

"May there be peace and glory in the highest heaven!"

³⁹Some of the Pharisees in the crowd spoke to Jesus. "Teacher," they said, "tell your disciples to stop!"

⁴⁰"I tell you," he replied, "if they keep quiet, the stones will cry out."

⁴¹He approached Jerusalem. When he saw the city, he began to sob. ⁴²He said, "I wish you had known today what would bring you peace! But now it is hidden from your eyes.

⁴³"The days will come when your enemies will arrive. They will build a wall of dirt up against your city. They will surround you and close you in on every side. ⁴⁴You didn't recognize the time when God came to you. So your enemies will smash you to the ground. They will destroy you and all the people inside your walls. They will not leave one stone on top of another."

Jesus Clears Out the Temple

⁴⁵Then Jesus entered the temple area. He began chasing out those who were selling there. ⁴⁶He told them, "It is written that the Lord said, 'My house will be a house where people can pray.' *(Isaiah 56:7)* But you have made it a 'den for robbers.' " *(Jeremiah 7:11)*

⁴⁷Every day Jesus was teaching at the temple. But the chief priests and the teachers of the law were trying to kill him. So were the leaders among the people. ⁴⁸But they couldn't find any way to do it. All the people were paying close attention to his words.

The Authority of Jesus Is Questioned

20 One day Jesus was teaching the people in the temple courtyard. He was preaching the good news to them.

The chief priests and the teachers of the law came up to him. The elders came with them. ²"Tell us by what authority you are doing these things," they all said. "Who gave you this authority?"

³Jesus replied, "I will also ask you a question. Tell me, ⁴was John's baptism from heaven? Or did it come from men?"

⁵They talked to each other about it. They said, "If we say, 'From heaven,' he will ask, 'Why didn't you believe him?' ⁶But if we say, 'From men,' all the people will throw stones at us and kill us. They believe that John was a prophet."

⁷So they answered Jesus, "We don't know where John's baptism came from."

⁸Jesus said, "Then I won't tell you by what authority I am doing these things either."

The Story of the Renters

⁹Jesus went on to tell the people a story. "A man planted a vineyard," he said. "He rented it out to some farmers. Then he went away for a long time.

¹⁰"At harvest time he sent a servant to the renters. They were supposed to give him some of the fruit of the vineyard. But the renters beat the servant. Then they sent him away with nothing. ¹¹So the man sent another servant. They beat that one and treated him badly. They also sent him away with nothing. ¹²The man sent a third servant. The renters wounded him and threw him out.

¹³"Then the owner of the vineyard said, 'What should I do? I have a son, and I love him. I will send him. Maybe they will respect him.'

¹⁴"But when the renters saw the son, they talked the matter over. 'This is the one who will receive all the owner's property someday,' they said. 'Let's kill him. Then everything will be ours.' ¹⁵So they threw him out of the vineyard. And they killed him.

"What will the owner of the vineyard do to the renters? ¹⁶He will come and kill them. He will give the vineyard to others."

When the people heard this, they said, "We hope this never happens!"

¹⁷Jesus looked right at them and said, "Here is something I want you to explain the meaning of. It is written,

" 'The stone the builders didn't accept
    has become the most important stone
        of all.'   *(Psalm 118:22)*

¹⁸Everyone who falls on that stone will be broken to pieces. But the stone will crush anyone it falls on."

¹⁹The teachers of the law and the chief

priests looked for a way to arrest Jesus at once. They knew he had told that story against them. But they were afraid of the people.

Is It Right to Pay Taxes to Caesar?

²⁰The religious leaders sent spies to keep a close watch on Jesus. The spies pretended to be honest. They hoped they could trap Jesus with something he would say. Then they could hand him over to the power and authority of the governor.

²¹So the spies questioned Jesus. "Teacher," they said, "we know that you speak and teach what is right. We know you don't favor one person over another. You teach the way of God truthfully. ²²Is it right for us to pay taxes to Caesar or not?"

²³Jesus saw they were trying to trick him. So he said to them, ²⁴"Show me a silver coin. Whose picture and words are on it?"

²⁵"Caesar's," they replied.

He said to them, "Then give to Caesar what belongs to Caesar. And give to God what belongs to God."

²⁶They were not able to trap him with what he had said there in front of all the people. Amazed by his answer, they became silent.

Marriage When the Dead Rise

²⁷The Sadducees do not believe that people rise from the dead. Some of them came to Jesus with a question. ²⁸"Teacher," they said, "Moses wrote for us about a man's brother who dies. Suppose the brother leaves a wife but has no children. Then the man must get married to the widow. He must have children to carry on his dead brother's name.

²⁹"There were seven brothers. The first one got married to a woman. He died without leaving any children. ³⁰The second one got married to her. ³¹And then the third one got married to her. One after another, the seven brothers got married to her. They all died. None left any children. ³²Finally, the woman died too. ³³Now then, when the dead rise, whose wife will she be? All seven brothers were married to her."

³⁴Jesus replied, "People in this world get married. And their parents give them to get married. ³⁵But it will not be like that when the dead rise. Those who are considered worthy to take part in what happens at that time won't get married. And their parents won't give them to be married. ³⁶They can't die anymore. They are like the angels. They are God's children. They will be given a new form of life when the dead rise.

³⁷"Remember the story of Moses and the bush. Even Moses showed that the dead rise. The Lord said to him, 'I am the God of Abraham. I am the God of Isaac. And I am the God of Jacob.' *(Exodus 3:6)* ³⁸He is not the God of the dead. He is the God of the living. In his eyes, everyone is alive."

³⁹Some of the teachers of the law replied, "You have spoken well, teacher!" ⁴⁰And no one dared to ask him any more questions.

Whose Son Is the Christ?

⁴¹Jesus said to them, "Why do people say that the Christ is the Son of David? ⁴²David himself says in the Book of Psalms,

" 'The Lord said to my Lord,
  "Sit at my right hand
⁴³until I put your enemies
    under your control." '   *(Psalm 110:1)*

⁴⁴David calls him 'Lord.' So how can he be David's son?"

⁴⁵All the people were listening. Jesus said to his disciples, ⁴⁶"Watch out for the teachers of the law. They like to walk around in long robes. They love to be greeted in the market places. They love to have the most important seats in the synagogues. They also love to have the places of honor at dinners. ⁴⁷They take over the houses of widows. They say long prayers to show off. God will

God has a plan for your life...
Ask Him about it

punish those men very much."

The Widow's Offering

21 As Jesus looked up, he saw rich people putting their gifts into the temple offering boxes. [2]He also saw a poor widow put in two very small copper coins.

[3]"What I'm about to tell you is true," Jesus said. "That poor widow has put in more than all the others. [4]All of those other people gave a lot because they are rich. But even though she is poor, she put in everything. She had nothing left to live on."

Signs of the End

[5]Some of Jesus' disciples were talking about the temple. They spoke about how it was decorated with beautiful stones and with gifts that honored God. But Jesus asked, [6]"Do you see all this? The time will come when not one stone will be left on top of another. Every stone will be thrown down."

[7]"Teacher," they asked, "when will these things happen? And what will be the sign that they are about to take place?"

[8]Jesus replied, "Keep watch! Be careful that you are not fooled. Many will come in my name. They will claim, 'I am he!' And they will say, 'The time is near!' Do not follow them. [9]Do not be afraid when you hear about wars and about fighting against rulers. Those things must happen first. But the end will not come right away."

[10]Then Jesus said to them, "Nation will fight against nation. Kingdom will fight against kingdom. [11]In many places there will be powerful earthquakes. People will go hungry. There will be terrible sicknesses. Things will happen that will make people afraid. There will be great and miraculous signs from heaven.

[12]"But before all this, people will arrest you and treat you badly. They will hand you over to synagogues and prisons. You will be brought to kings and governors. All this will happen to you because of my name. [13]In that way you will be witnesses to them. [14]But make up your mind not to worry ahead of time about how to stand up for yourselves. [15]I will give you words of wisdom. None of your enemies will be able to withstand them or oppose them.

[16]"Even your parents, brothers, sisters, relatives and friends will hand you over to the authorities. They will put some of you to death. [17]Everyone will hate you because of me. [18]But not a hair on your head will be harmed. [19]If you stand firm, you will gain life.

[20]"A time is coming when you will see armies surround Jerusalem. Then you will know that it will soon be destroyed. [21]Those who are in Judea should then escape to the mountains. Those in the city should get out. Those in the country should not enter the city. [22]This is the time when God will punish Jerusalem. Everything will come true, just as it has been written.

[23]"How awful it will be in those days for pregnant women! How awful for nursing mothers! There will be terrible suffering in the land. There will be great anger against those people. [24]Some will be killed by the sword. Others will be taken as prisoners to all the nations. Jerusalem will be overrun by those who aren't Jews until the times of the non-Jews come to an end.

[25]"There will be miraculous signs in the sun, moon and stars. The nations of the earth will be in terrible pain. They will be puzzled by the roaring and tossing of the sea. [26]Terror will make people faint. They will be worried about what is happening in the world. The sun, moon and stars will be shaken from their places.

[27]"At that time people will see the Son of Man coming in a cloud. He will come with power and great glory. [28]When these things begin to take place, stand up. Hold your head up with joy and hope. The time when you will be set free will be very close."

[29]Jesus told them a story. "Look at the fig tree and all the trees," he said. [30]"When you see leaves appear on the branches, you know that summer is near. [31]In the same way, when you see these things happening, you will know that God's kingdom is near.

[32]"What I'm about to tell you is true. The people living at that time will certainly not pass away until all these things have happened. [33]Heaven and earth will pass away.

A Week in Jerusalem

About a third of each Gospel is given to the last eight days between Jesus' entering Jerusalem on Palm Sunday and rising from the grave on Easter Day

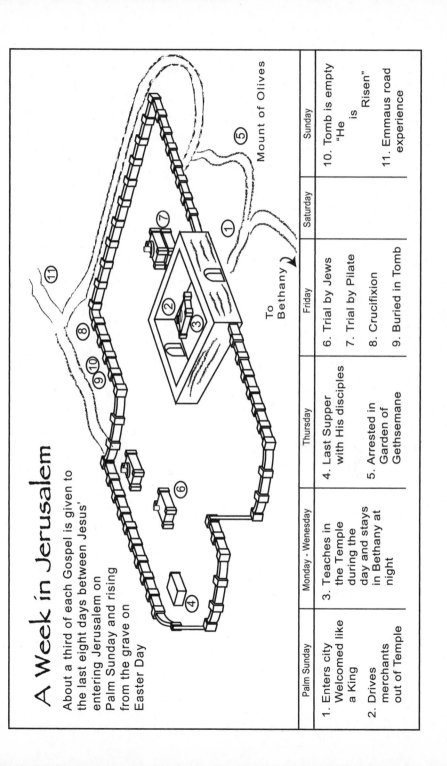

Mount of Olives

To Bethany

Palm Sunday	Monday - Wenesday	Thursday	Friday	Saturday	Sunday
1. Enters city Welcomed like a King 2. Drives merchants out of Temple	3. Teaches in the Temple during the day and stays in Bethany at night	4. Last Supper with His disciples 5. Arrested in Garden of Gethsemane	6. Trial by Jews 7. Trial by Pilate 8. Crucifixion 9. Buried in Tomb		10. Tomb is empty "He is Risen" 11. Emmaus road experience

But my words will never pass away.

³⁴"Be careful. If you aren't, your hearts will be loaded down with wasteful living, drunkenness and the worries of life. Then the day the Son of Man returns will close on you like a trap. You will not be expecting it. ³⁵That day will come upon every person who lives on the whole earth.

³⁶"Always keep watching. Pray that you will be able to escape all that is about to happen. Also, pray that you will not be judged guilty when the Son of Man comes."

³⁷Each day Jesus taught at the temple. And each evening he went to spend the night on the hill called the Mount of Olives. ³⁸All the people came to the temple early in the morning. They wanted to hear Jesus speak.

Judas Agrees to Hand Jesus Over

22 The Feast of Unleavened Bread, called the Passover, was near. ²The chief priests and the teachers of the law were looking for a way to get rid of Jesus. They were afraid of the people.

³Then Satan entered Judas, who was called Iscariot. Judas was one of the Twelve. ⁴He went to the chief priests and the officers of the temple guard. He talked with them about how he could hand Jesus over to them. ⁵They were delighted and agreed to give him money.

⁶Judas accepted their offer. He watched for the right time to hand Jesus over to them. He wanted to do it when no crowd was around.

The Last Supper

⁷Then the day of Unleavened Bread came. That was the time the Passover lamb had to be sacrificed. ⁸Jesus sent Peter and John on ahead. "Go," he told them. "Prepare for us to eat the Passover meal."

⁹"Where do you want us to prepare for it?" they asked.

¹⁰Jesus replied, "When you enter the city, a man carrying a jar of water will meet you. Follow him to the house he enters. ¹¹Then say to the owner of the house, 'The Teacher asks, "Where is the guest room? Where can I eat the Passover meal with my disciples?" ' ¹²He

will show you a large upstairs room with furniture in it. Prepare for us to eat there."

¹³Peter and John left. They found things just as Jesus had told them. So they prepared the Passover meal.

¹⁴When the hour came, Jesus and his apostles took their places at the table. ¹⁵He said to them, "I have really looked forward to eating this Passover meal with you. I wanted to do this before I suffer. ¹⁶I tell you, I will not eat the Passover meal again until it is celebrated in God's kingdom."

¹⁷After Jesus took the cup, he gave thanks. He said, "Take this cup and share it among yourselves. ¹⁸I tell you, I will not drink wine with you again until God's kingdom comes."

¹⁹Then Jesus took bread. He gave thanks and broke it. He handed it to them and said, "This is my body. It is given for you. Every time you eat it, do it in memory of me."

²⁰In the same way, after the supper he took the cup. He said, "This cup is the new covenant in my blood. It is poured out for you. ²¹But someone here is going to hand me over to my enemies. His hand is with mine on the table. ²²The Son of Man will go to his death, just as God has already decided. But how terrible it will be for the one who hands him over!"

²³The apostles began to ask each other about this. They wondered which one of them would do it.

²⁴They also started to argue. They disagreed about which of them was thought to be the most important person.

²⁵Jesus said to them, "The kings of the nations hold power over their people. And those who order them around call themselves Protectors. ²⁶But you must not be like that. Instead, the most important among you should be like the youngest. The one who rules should be like the one who serves.

²⁷"Who is more important? Is it the one at the table, or the one who serves? Isn't it the one who is at the table? But I am among you as one who serves. ²⁸You have stood by me during my troubles. ²⁹And I give you a kingdom, just as my Father gave me a kingdom. ³⁰Then you will eat and drink at my

LUKE

Across

1. Short and blessed — ch. 19
4. "___ you are the Son ..." — ch. 4
6. A promise at the Cross — ch. 23
7. A friend who betrayed — ch. 22
9. _____ your enemies — ch. 6
10. Too busy to listen — ch. 10
12. What you breathe — ---
13. First number — ---
14. Visited baby Jesus — ch. 2
18. Jesus healed a dead ___ — ch. 7
19. Resurrection day — ch. 24
20. "Lord, I want to ___" — ch. 18

Down

1. Father of John — ch. 1
2. A police officer — ---
3. Helped judge Jesus — ch. 23
5. First disciples were — ch. 5
7. His little girl died — ch. 8
8. Certain, no doubt — ---
10. Greater amount — ---
11. God counts every ____ — ch. 12
15. "Lord, teach us to ___" — ch. 11
16. Jesus rose after 3 ___ — ch. 24
17. Distress signal — ---

table in my kingdom. And you will sit on thrones, judging the 12 tribes of Israel.

³¹"Simon, Simon! Satan has asked to sift you disciples like wheat. ³²But I have prayed for you, Simon. I have prayed that your faith will not fail. When you have turned back, help your brothers to be strong."

³³But Simon replied, "Lord, I am ready to go with you to prison and to death."

³⁴Jesus answered, "I tell you, Peter, you will say three times that you don't know me. And you will do it before the rooster crows today."

³⁵Then Jesus asked the disciples, "Did you need anything when I sent you without a purse, bag or sandals?"

"Nothing," they answered.

³⁶He said to them, "But now if you have a purse, take it. And also take a bag. If you don't have a sword, sell your coat and buy one. ³⁷It is written, 'He was counted among those who had committed crimes.' *(Isaiah 53:12)* I tell you that what is written about me must come true. Yes, it is already coming true."

³⁸The disciples said, "See, Lord, here are two swords."

"That is enough," he replied.

Jesus Prays on the Mount of Olives

³⁹Jesus went out as usual to the Mount of Olives. His disciples followed him. ⁴⁰When they reached the place, Jesus spoke. "Pray that you won't fall into sin when you are tempted," he said to them.

⁴¹Then he went a short distance away from them. There he got down on his knees and prayed. ⁴²He said, "Father, if you are willing, take this cup of suffering away from me. But do what you want, not what I want."

⁴³An angel from heaven appeared to Jesus and gave him strength. ⁴⁴Because he was very sad and troubled, he prayed even harder. His sweat was like drops of blood falling to the ground.

⁴⁵After that, he got up from prayer and went back to the disciples. He found them sleeping. They were worn out because they were very sad.

⁴⁶"Why are you sleeping?" he asked them.

"Get up! Pray that you won't fall into sin when you are tempted."

Jesus Is Arrested

⁴⁷While Jesus was still speaking, a crowd came up. The man named Judas was leading them. He was one of the Twelve. Judas approached Jesus to kiss him.

⁴⁸But Jesus asked him, "Judas, are you handing over the Son of Man with a kiss?"

⁴⁹Jesus' followers saw what was going to happen. So they said, "Lord, should we use our swords against them?" ⁵⁰One of them struck the servant of the high priest and cut off his right ear.

⁵¹But Jesus answered, "Stop this!" And he touched the man's ear and healed him.

⁵²Then Jesus spoke to the chief priests, the officers of the temple guard, and the elders. They had all come for him. "Am I leading a band of armed men against you?" he asked. "Do you have to come with swords and clubs? ⁵³Every day I was with you in the temple courtyard. And you didn't lay a hand on me. But this is your hour. This is when darkness rules."

Peter Says He Does Not Know Jesus

⁵⁴Then the men arrested Jesus and led him away. They took him into the high priest's house. Peter followed from far away. ⁵⁵They started a fire in the middle of the courtyard. Then they sat down together. Peter sat down with them.

⁵⁶A female servant saw him sitting there in the firelight. She looked closely at him. Then she said, "This man was with Jesus."

⁵⁷But Peter said he had not been with him. "Woman, I don't know him," he said.

⁵⁸A little later someone else saw Peter. "You also are one of them," he said.

"No," Peter replied. "I'm not!"

⁵⁹About an hour later, another person spoke up. "This fellow must have been with Jesus," he said. "He is from Galilee."

⁶⁰Peter replied, "Man, I don't know what you're talking about!"

Just as he was speaking, the rooster crowed. ⁶¹The Lord turned and looked right at Peter. Then Peter remembered what the Lord had spoken to him. "The rooster will crow today," Jesus had said. "Before it does, you will say three times that you don't know me." [62]Peter went outside. He broke down and sobbed.

The Guards Make Fun of Jesus

[63]There were men guarding Jesus. They began laughing at him and beating him. [64]They blindfolded him. They said, "Prophesy! Who hit you?" [65]They also said many other things to make fun of him.

Jesus Is Brought to Pilate and Herod

[66]At dawn the elders of the people met together. These included the chief priests and the teachers of the law. Jesus was led to them. [67]"If you are the Christ," they said, "tell us."

Jesus answered, "If I tell you, you will not believe me. [68]And if I asked you, you would not answer. [69]But from now on, the Son of Man will be seated at the right hand of the mighty God."

[70]They all asked, "Are you the Son of God then?"

He replied, "You are right in saying that I am."

[71]Then they said, "Why do we need any more witnesses? We have heard it from his own lips."

23 Then the whole group got up and led Jesus off to Pilate. [2]They began to bring charges against Jesus. They said, "We have found this man misleading our people. He is against paying taxes to Caesar. And he claims to be Christ, a king."

[3]So Pilate asked Jesus, "Are you the king of the Jews?"

"Yes. It is just as you say," Jesus replied.

[4]Then Pilate spoke to the chief priests and the crowd. He announced, "I find no basis for a charge against this man."

[5]But they kept it up. They said, "His teaching stirs up the people all over Judea. He started in Galilee and has come all the way here."

[6]When Pilate heard this, he asked if the man was from Galilee. [7]He learned that Jesus was from Herod's area of authority. So Pilate sent Jesus to Herod. At that time Herod was also in Jerusalem.

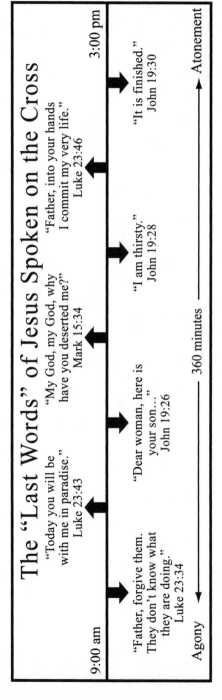

The "Last Words" of Jesus Spoken on the Cross

3:00 pm

"It is finished."
John 19:30

"Father, into your hands
I commit my very life."
Luke 23:46

"My God, my God, why
have you deserted me?"
Mark 15:34

"I am thirsty."
John 19:28

"Dear woman, here is
your son..."
John 19:26

"Today you will be
with me in paradise."
Luke 23:43

"Father, forgive them.
They don't know what
they are doing."
Luke 23:34

9:00 am

360 minutes

Agony ———————— Atonement

[8]When Herod saw Jesus, he was very pleased. He had been wanting to see Jesus for a long time. He had heard much about him. He hoped to see Jesus do a miracle.

[9]Herod asked him many questions, but Jesus gave him no answer. [10]The chief priests and the teachers of the law were standing there. With loud shouts they brought charges against him.

[11]Herod and his soldiers laughed at him and made fun of him. They dressed him in a beautiful robe. Then they sent him back to Pilate. [12]That day Herod and Pilate became friends. Before this time they had been enemies.

[13]Pilate called together the chief priests, the rulers and the people. [14]He said to them, "You brought me this man. You said he was turning the people against the authorities. I have questioned him in front of you. I have found no basis for your charges against him. [15]Herod hasn't either. So he sent Jesus back to us. As you can see, Jesus has done nothing that is worthy of death. [16/17]So I will just have him whipped and let him go."

[18]With one voice the crowd cried out, "Kill this man! Give Barabbas to us!" [19]Barabbas had been thrown into prison. He had taken part in a struggle in the city against the authorities. He had also committed murder.

[20]Pilate wanted to let Jesus go. So he made an appeal to the crowd again. [21]But they kept shouting, "Crucify him! Crucify him!"

[22]Pilate spoke to them for the third time. "Why?" he asked. "What wrong has this man done? I have found no reason to have him put to death. So I will just have him whipped and let him go."

[23]But with loud shouts they kept calling for Jesus to be crucified. The people's shouts won out.

[24]So Pilate decided to give them what they wanted. [25]He set free the man they asked for. The man had been thrown in prison for murder and for fighting against the authorities. Pilate gave Jesus over to them so they could carry out their plans.

Jesus Is Nailed to a Cross

[26]As they led Jesus away, they took hold of Simon. Simon was from Cyrene. He was on his way in from the country. They put a wooden cross on his shoulders. Then they made him carry it behind Jesus.

[27]A large number of people followed Jesus. Some were women whose hearts were filled with sorrow. They cried loudly because of him.

[28]Jesus turned and said to them, "Daughters of Jerusalem, do not cry for me. Cry for yourselves and for your children. [29]The time will come when you will say, 'Blessed are the women who can't have children! Blessed are those who never gave birth or nursed babies!' [30]It is written,

" 'The people will say to the mountains,
    "Fall on us!"
They'll say to the hills, "Cover us!" ' "
(Hosea 10:8)

[31]People do these things when trees are green. So what will happen when trees are dry?"

[32]Two other men were also led out with Jesus to be killed. Both of them had broken the law. [33]The soldiers brought them to the place called The Skull. There they nailed Jesus to the cross. He hung between the two criminals. One was on his right and one was on his left.

[34]Jesus said, "Father, forgive them. They don't know what they are doing." The soldiers divided up his clothes by casting lots.

[35]The people stood there watching. The rulers even made fun of Jesus. They said, "He saved others. Let him save himself if he is the Christ of God, the Chosen One."

[36]The soldiers also came up and poked fun at him. They offered him wine vinegar. [37]They said, "If you are the king of the Jews, save yourself."

[38]A written sign had been placed above him. It read, THIS IS THE KING OF THE JEWS.

[39]One of the criminals hanging there made fun of Jesus. He said, "Aren't you the Christ? Save yourself! Save us!"

[40]But the other criminal scolded him. "Don't you have any respect for God?" he said. "Remember, you are under the same

sentence of death. [41]We are being punished fairly. We are getting just what our actions call for. But this man hasn't done anything wrong."

[42]Then he said, "Jesus, remember me when you come into your kingdom."

[43]Jesus answered him, "What I'm about to tell you is true. Today you will be with me in paradise."

Jesus Dies

[44]It was now about noon. The whole land was covered with darkness until three o'clock. [45]The sun had stopped shining. The temple curtain was torn in two. [46]Jesus called out in a loud voice, "Father, into your hands I commit my very life." After he said this, he took his last breath.

[47]The Roman commander saw what had happened. He praised God and said, "Jesus was surely a man who did what was right."

[48]The people had gathered to watch that sight. When they saw what happened, they beat their chests and went away. [49]But all those who knew Jesus stood not very far away, watching those things. They included the women who had followed him from Galilee.

Jesus Is Buried

[50]A man named Joseph was a member of the Jewish Council. He was a good and honest man. [51]He had not agreed with what the leaders had decided and done. He was from Arimathea, a town in Judea. He was waiting for God's kingdom.

[52]Joseph went to Pilate and asked for Jesus' body. [53]He took it down and wrapped it in linen cloth. Then he put it in a tomb cut in the rock. No one had ever been buried there. [54]It was Preparation Day. The Sabbath was about to begin.

[55]The women who had come with Jesus from Galilee followed Joseph. They saw the tomb and how Jesus' body was placed in it. [56]Then they went home. There they prepared spices and perfumes. But they rested on the Sabbath day in order to obey the Law.

Jesus Rises From the Dead

24 It was very early in the morning on the first day of the week. The women took the spices they had prepared. Then they went to the tomb. [2]They found the stone rolled away from it. [3]When they entered the tomb, they did not find the body of the Lord Jesus. [4]They were wondering about this.

Suddenly two men in clothes as bright as lightning stood beside them. [5]The women were terrified. They bowed down with their faces to the ground.

Then the men said to them, "Why do you look for the living among the dead? [6]Jesus is not here! He has risen! Remember how he told you he would rise. It was while he was still with you in Galilee. [7]He said, 'The Son of Man must be handed over to sinful people. He must be nailed to a cross. On the third day he will rise from the dead.' "

[8]Then the women remembered Jesus' words.

[9]They came back from the tomb. They told all these things to the Eleven and to all the others. [10]Mary Magdalene, Joanna, Mary the mother of James, and the others with them were the ones who told the apostles. [11]But the apostles did not believe the women. Their words didn't make any sense to them.

[12]But Peter got up and ran to the tomb. He bent over and saw the strips of linen lying by themselves. Then he went away, wondering what had happened.

On the Road to Emmaus

[13]That same day two of Jesus' followers were going to a village called Emmaus. It was about seven miles from Jerusalem. [14]They were talking with each other about everything that had happened.

[15]As they talked about those things, Jesus himself came up and walked along with them. [16]But God kept them from recognizing him.

[17]Jesus asked them, "What are you talking about as you walk along?"

They stood still, and their faces were sad. [18]One of them was named Cleopas. He said to Jesus, "You must be a visitor to Jerusalem. If you lived there, you would know the things that have happened there in the last few days."

[19]"What things?" Jesus asked.

"About Jesus of Nazareth," they replied. "He was a prophet. He was powerful in what he said and did in the eyes of God and all of the people. [20]The chief priests and our rulers handed Jesus over to be sentenced to death. They nailed him to a cross. [21]But we had hoped that he was the one who was going to set Israel free. Also, it is the third day since all this happened.

[22]"Some of our women amazed us too. Early this morning they went to the tomb. [23]But they didn't find his body. So they came and told us what they had seen. They saw angels, who said Jesus was alive. [24]Then some of our friends went to the tomb. They saw it was empty, just as the women had said. They didn't see Jesus' body there."

[25]Jesus said to them, "How foolish you are! How long it takes you to believe all that the prophets said! [26]Didn't the Christ have to suffer these things and then receive his glory?"

[27]Jesus explained to them what was said about himself in all the Scriptures. He began with Moses and all the Prophets.

[28]The two men approached the village where they were going. Jesus acted as if he were going farther. [29]But they tried hard to keep him from leaving. They said, "Stay with us. It is nearly evening. The day is almost over." So he went in to stay with them.

[30]He joined them at the table. Then he took bread and gave thanks. He broke it and began to give it to them. [31]Their eyes were opened, and they recognized him. But then he disappeared from their sight.

[32]They said to each other, "He talked with us on the road. He opened the Scriptures to us. Weren't our hearts burning inside us during that time?"

[33]They got up and returned at once to Jerusalem. There they found the Eleven and those with them. They were all gathered together. [34]They were saying, "It's true! The Lord has risen! He has appeared to Simon!"

[35]Then the two of them told what had happened to them on the way. They told how they had recognized Jesus when he broke the bread.

Jesus Appears to the Disciples

[36]The disciples were still talking about this when Jesus himself suddenly stood among them. He said, "May peace be with you!"

[37]They were surprised and terrified. They thought they were seeing a ghost.

[38]Jesus said to them, "Why are you troubled? Why do you have doubts in your minds? [39]Look at my hands and my feet. It is really I! Touch me and see. A ghost does not have a body or bones. But you can see that I do."

[40]After he said that, he showed them his hands and feet. [41]But they still did not believe it. They were amazed and filled with joy.

So Jesus asked them, "Do you have anything here to eat?"

[42]They gave him a piece of cooked fish. [43]He took it and ate it in front of them.

[44]Jesus said to them, "This is what I told you while I was still with you. Everything written about me must happen. Everything written about me in the Law of Moses, the Prophets and the Psalms must come true."

[45]Then he opened their minds so they could understand the Scriptures. [46]He told them, "This is what is written. The Christ will suffer. He will rise from the dead on the third day. [47]His followers will preach in his name. They will tell others to turn away from their sins and be forgiven. People from every nation will hear it, beginning at Jerusalem. [48]You have seen these things with your own eyes.

[49]"I am going to send you what my Father has promised. But for now, stay in the city. Stay there until you have received power from heaven."

Jesus Is Taken Up Into Heaven

[50]Jesus led his disciples out to the area near Bethany. Then he lifted up his hands and blessed them. [51]While he was blessing them, he left them. He was taken up into heaven.

[52]Then they worshiped him. With great joy, they returned to Jerusalem. [53]Every day they went to the temple, praising God.

Open Book Quiz - The Book of Luke

Read the letters from top to bottom and complete the answer below.

1 __J__ Evil things come from ... ch. 6

2 ____ Waves obey Him   ch. 8

3 ____ Vultures will gather   ch. 17

4 ____ Prophet not accepted ... ch. 4

5 ____ You will catch people   ch. 5

6 ____ How can this happen?   ch. 1

7 ____ Follow Me   ch. 5

8 ____ You will be silent   ch. 1

9 ____ Send crowd away   ch. 9

10 ____ Now I can die happy   ch. 2

11 ____ Forgive & you will be ... ch. 6

12 ____ Teach us to pray   ch. 11

13 ____ Do to others as you ... ch. 6

14 __T__ Your heart is where ... ch. 12

15 ____ If they keep quite the ... ch. 19

16 ____ Why treat us like this? ch. 2

17 ____ Same named disciples ch. 6

Select the best answer from the right column which matches items 1-17 in the left column. Some letters are used more than once.

A - Mary

C - Want them to do to you

E - Disciples

F - Be forgiven

H - Zoo

J - Evil heart

M - Stones will cry out

N - James

P - Gabriel

R - Simeon

S - Jesus

T - Your riches are

U - In his hometown

W - Waldo

Self-score

16 - 17   "Swoosh"
13 - 15   Two pointer
10 - 12   Practice shooting
5 - 9   Work on dribbling
1 - 4   Pick-up the ball

Answer: __J__ __ __ __ __ • __ __

__ __ __ __ __ __ __T__ • __ __ __

"The theme of the book of Luke"

Who Wrote the New Testament?

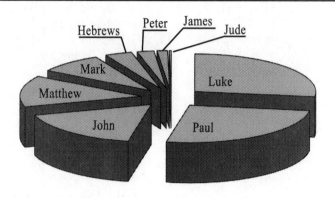

Author	Books	Verses	Percent **
Luke	2	2158	27.3
Paul	13	2033	25.9
John	5	1414	17.2
Matthew	1	1069	13.5
Mark	1	678	8.6
Hebrews*	1	302	3.7
Peter	2	166	2.1
James	1	108	1.4
Jude	1	25	.3
9	27	7953	100%

*Author unknown   ** Approximate

JOHN

- *Written by John, "the beloved disciple"*
- *Written to and for believers to enhance their spiritual growth*
- *Emphasizes the Resurrection of Jesus more than the other three Gospels combined*
- *Jesus' question to Peter (and us): "Do you love Me?"*
- *Theme: "Jesus as Son of God"*

The Word Became Human

1 In the beginning, the Word was already there. The Word was with God, and the Word was God. ²He was with God in the beginning.

³All things were made through him. Nothing that has been made was made without him. ⁴Life was in him, and that life was the light for all people. ⁵The light shines in the darkness. But the darkness has not understood it.

⁶A man came who was sent from God. His name was John. ⁷He came to give witness about that light. He gave witness so that all people could believe.

⁸John himself was not the light. He came only as a witness to the light. ⁹The true light that gives light to every man was coming into the world.

¹⁰The Word was in the world that was made through him. But the world did not recognize him. ¹¹He came to what was his own. But his own people did not accept him.

¹²Some people did accept him. They believed in his name. He gave them the right to become children of God. ¹³To be a child of God has nothing to do with human parents. Children of God are not born because of human choice or because a husband wants them to be born. They are born because of what God does.

¹⁴The Word became a human being. He made his home with us. We have seen his glory. It is the glory of the one and only Son.

He came from the Father. And he was full of grace and truth.

¹⁵John gives witness about him. He cries out and says, "This was the one I was talking about. I said, 'He who comes after me is more important than I am. He is more important because he existed before I was born.' "

¹⁶We have all received one blessing after another. God's grace is not limited. ¹⁷Moses gave us the law. Jesus Christ has given us grace and truth.

¹⁸No one has ever seen God. But God, the one and only Son, is at the Father's side. He has shown us what God is like.

John the Baptist Is Not the Christ

¹⁹The Jews of Jerusalem sent priests and Levites to ask John who he was. John gave witness to them. ²⁰He did not try to hide the truth. He spoke to them openly. He said, "I am not the Christ."

²¹They asked him, "Then who are you? Are you Elijah?"

He said, "I am not."

"Are you the Prophet we've been expecting?" they asked.

"No," he answered.

²²They asked one last time, "Who are you? Give us an answer to take back to those who sent us. What do you say about yourself?"

²³John replied, using the words of Isaiah the prophet. John said, "I'm the messenger who is calling out in the desert, 'Make the way for the Lord straight.' " *(Isaiah 40:3)*

²⁴Some Pharisees who had been sent ²⁵asked him, "If you are not the Christ, why are you baptizing people? Why are you doing that if you aren't Elijah or the Prophet we've been expecting?"

God Said ...

"Go tell them."

Repent
and Be Baptized

God is light
God is life
God is love
God is coming!

Jesus Is the Lamb of God

²⁹The next day John saw Jesus coming toward him. John said, "Look! The Lamb of God! He takes away the sin of the world! ³⁰This is the One I was talking about. I said, 'A man who comes after me is more important than I am. That's because he existed before I was born.' ³¹I did not know him. But God wants to make it clear to Israel who this person is. That's the reason I came baptizing with water."

³²Then John told them, "I saw the Holy Spirit come down from heaven like a dove. The Spirit remained on Jesus. ³³I would not have known him. But the One who sent me to baptize with water told me, 'You will see the Spirit come down and remain on someone. He is the One who will baptize with the Holy Spirit.' ³⁴I have seen it happen. I give witness that this is the Son of God."

Jesus Chooses the First Disciples

³⁵The next day John was again with two of his disciples. ³⁶He saw Jesus walking by. John said, "Look! The Lamb of God!"

³⁷The two disciples heard him say this. So they followed Jesus.

³⁸Then Jesus turned around and saw them following. He asked, "What do you want?"

They said, "Rabbi, where are you staying?" *Rabbi* means Teacher.

³⁹"Come," he replied. "You will see."

So they went and saw where he was staying. They spent the rest of the day with him. It was about four o'clock in the afternoon.

⁴⁰Andrew was Simon Peter's brother. Andrew was one of the two disciples who heard what John had said. He had also followed Jesus. ⁴¹The first thing Andrew did was to find his brother Simon. He told him, "We have found the Messiah." Messiah means Christ. ⁴²And he brought Simon to Jesus.

Jesus looked at him and said, "You are Simon, son of John. You will be called Cephas." Cephas means Peter (or rock).

²⁶"I baptize people with water," John replied. "But One is standing among you whom you do not know. ²⁷He is the One who comes after me. I am not good enough to untie his sandals."

²⁸This all happened at Bethany on the other side of the Jordan River. That was where John was baptizing.

Jesus Chooses Philip and Nathanael

⁴³The next day Jesus decided to leave for Galilee. He found Philip and said to him, "Follow me."

⁴⁴Philip was from the town of Bethsaida. So were Andrew and Peter. ⁴⁵Philip found Nathanael and told him, "We have found the One that Moses wrote about in the Law. The prophets also wrote about him. He is Jesus of Nazareth, the son of Joseph."

⁴⁶"Nazareth! Can anything good come from there?" Nathanael asked.

"Come and see," said Philip.

⁴⁷Jesus saw Nathanael approaching. Here is what Jesus said about him. "He is a true Israelite. There is nothing false in him."

⁴⁸"How do you know me?" Nathanael asked.

Jesus answered, "I saw you while you were still under the fig tree. I saw you there before Philip called you."

⁴⁹Nathanael replied, "Rabbi, you are the Son of God. You are the King of Israel."

⁵⁰Jesus said, "You believe because I told you I saw you under the fig tree. You will see greater things than that."

⁵¹Then he said to the disciples, "What I'm about to tell you is true. You will see heaven open. You will see the angels of God going up and coming down on the Son of Man."

Jesus Changes Water Into Wine

2 On the third day there was a wedding. It took place at Cana in Galilee. Jesus' mother was there. ²Jesus and his disciples had also been invited to the wedding. ³When the wine was gone, Jesus' mother said to him, "They have no more wine."

⁴"Dear woman, why do you bring me into this?" Jesus replied. "My time has not yet come."

⁵His mother said to the servants, "Do what he tells you."

⁶Six stone water jars stood nearby. The Jews used water from that kind of jar for special washings to make themselves pure. Each jar could hold 20 to 30 gallons.

⁷Jesus said to the servants, "Fill the jars with water." So they filled them to the top.

⁸Then he told them, "Now dip some out. Take it to the person in charge of the dinner."

They did what he said. ⁹The person in charge tasted the water that had been turned into wine. He didn't realize where it had come from. But the servants who had brought the water knew.

Then the person in charge called the groom to one side. ¹⁰He said to him, "Everyone brings out the best wine first. They

"Jesus changed the Water to Wine!"

Later He will serve fish sandwiches...

bring out the cheaper wine after the guests have had too much to drink. But you have saved the best until now."

¹¹That was the first of Jesus' miraculous signs. He did it at Cana in Galilee. Jesus showed his glory by doing it. And his disciples put their faith in him.

Jesus Clears Out the Temple

¹²After this, Jesus went down to Capernaum. His mother and brothers and disciples went with him. They all stayed there for a few days.

¹³It was almost time for the Jewish Passover Feast. So Jesus went up to Jerusalem. ¹⁴In the temple courtyard he found people who were selling cattle, sheep and doves. Others were sitting at tables exchanging money.

¹⁵So Jesus made a whip out of ropes. He chased all the sheep and cattle from the temple area. He scattered the coins of the people exchanging money. And he turned over their tables. ¹⁶He told those who were selling doves, "Get these out of here! How dare you turn my Father's house into a market!"

¹⁷His disciples remembered what had been written. It says, "My great love for your house will destroy me." *(Psalm 69:9)*

¹⁸Then the Jews asked him, "What miraculous sign can you show us? Can you prove your authority to do all of this?"

¹⁹Jesus answered them, "Destroy this temple. I will raise it up again in three days."

²⁰The Jews replied, "It has taken 46 years to build this temple. Are you going to raise it up in three days?"

²¹But the temple Jesus had spoken about was his body.

²²His disciples later remembered what he had said. That was after he had been raised from the dead. Then they believed the Scriptures. They also believed the words that Jesus had spoken.

²³Meanwhile, he was in Jerusalem at the Passover Feast. Many people saw the miraculous signs he was doing. And they believed in his name. ²⁴But Jesus did not fully trust them. He knew what people are like. ²⁵He

didn't need others to tell him what people are like. He already knew what was in the human heart.

Jesus Teaches Nicodemus

3 There was a Pharisee named Nicodemus. He was one of the Jewish rulers. ²He came to Jesus at night and said, "Rabbi, we know you are a teacher who has come from God. We know that God is with you. If he weren't, you couldn't do the miraculous signs you are doing."

³Jesus replied, "What I'm about to tell you is true. No one can see God's kingdom without being born again."

⁴"How can I be born when I am old?" Nicodemus asked. "I can't go back inside my mother! I can't be born a second time!"

⁵Jesus answered, "What I'm about to tell you is true. No one can enter God's kingdom without being born through water and the Holy Spirit. ⁶People give birth to people. But the Spirit gives birth to spirit. ⁷You should not be surprised when I say, 'You must all be born again.'

⁸"The wind blows where it wants to. You hear the sound it makes. But you can't tell where it comes from or where it is going. It is the same with everyone who is born through the Spirit."

⁹"How can this be?" Nicodemus asked.

¹⁰"You are Israel's teacher," said Jesus. "Don't you understand these things?

¹¹"What I'm about to tell you is true. We speak about what we know. We give witness to what we have seen. But still you people do not accept our witness. ¹²I have spoken to you about earthly things, and you do not believe. So how will you believe if I speak about heavenly things?

¹³"No one has ever gone into heaven except the One who came from heaven. He is the Son of Man. ¹⁴Moses lifted up the snake in the desert. The Son of Man must be lifted up also. ¹⁵Then everyone who believes in him can live with God forever.

¹⁶"God loved the world so much that he gave his one and only Son. Anyone who believes in him will not die but will have eternal life.

¹⁷"God did not send his Son into the

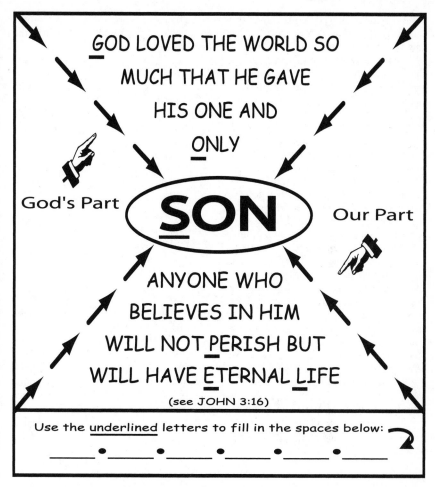

GOD LOVED THE WORLD SO MUCH THAT HE GAVE HIS ONE AND ONLY

God's Part

SON

Our Part

ANYONE WHO BELIEVES IN HIM WILL NOT PERISH BUT WILL HAVE ETERNAL LIFE

(see JOHN 3:16)

Use the <u>underlined</u> letters to fill in the spaces below:

_____ • _____ • _____ • _____ • _____

world to judge the world. He sent his Son to save the world through him. [18]Anyone who believes in him is not judged. But anyone who does not believe is judged already. He has not believed in the name of God's one and only Son.

[19]"Here is the judgment. Light has come into the world, but people loved darkness instead of light. They loved darkness because what they did was evil.

[20]"Everyone who does evil things hates the light. They will not come into the light. They are afraid that what they do will be seen. [21]But anyone who lives by the truth comes into the light. He does this so that it

will be easy to see that what he has done is with God's help."

John the Baptist Gives Witness About Jesus

[22]After this, Jesus and his disciples went out into the countryside of Judea. There he spent some time with them. And he baptized people there.

[23]John was also baptizing. He was at Aenon near Salim, where there was plenty of water. People were coming all the time to be baptized. [24]That was before John was put in prison.

[25]Some of John's disciples and a certain

Jew began to argue. They argued about special washings to make people "clean." [26]They came to John and said to him, "Rabbi, that man who was with you on the other side of the Jordan River is baptizing people. He is the one you gave witness about. Everyone is going to him."

[27]John replied, "A person can receive only what God gives him from heaven. [28]You yourselves are witnesses that I said, 'I am not the Christ. I was sent ahead of him.' [29]The bride belongs to the groom. The friend who helps the groom waits and listens for him. He is full of joy when he hears the groom's voice. That joy is mine, and it is now complete. [30]He must become more important. I must become less important.

[31]"The One who comes from above is above everything. The one who is from the earth belongs to the earth and speaks like someone from the earth. The One who comes from heaven is above everything. [32]He gives witness to what he has seen and heard. But no one accepts what he says. [33]Anyone who has accepted it has said, 'Yes. God is truthful.' [34]The One whom God has sent speaks God's words. God gives the Holy Spirit without limit.

[35]"The Father loves the Son and has put everything into his hands. [36]Anyone who believes in the Son has eternal life. Anyone who says no to the Son will not have life. God's anger remains on him."

Jesus Talks With a Woman From Samaria

4 The Pharisees heard that Jesus was winning and baptizing more disciples than John. [2]But in fact Jesus was not baptizing. His disciples were. [3]When the Lord found out about all this, he left Judea. He went back to Galilee again.

[4]Jesus had to go through Samaria. [5]He came to a town in Samaria called Sychar. It was near the piece of land Jacob had given his son Joseph. [6]Jacob's well was there. Jesus was tired from the journey. So he sat down by the well. It was about noon.

[7]A woman from Samaria came to get some water. Jesus said to her, "Will you give me a drink?" [8]His disciples had gone into the town to buy food.

[9]The Samaritan woman said to him, "You are a Jew. I am a Samaritan woman. How can you ask me for a drink?" She said this

---

"I'm not a Christian because ..."

"I'm good enough."

Once Jesus had a meeting with a man named Nicodemus, a ruler of the Jews. He was one of the most religious and honorable people in all of Jerusalem. Jesus, knowing all about him, said:

"No one can see God's kingdom without being born again."

Being good, trying hard, or being religious could not get Nicodemus into God's kingdom. The same is true for us today. Jesus says:

"You must all be born again."

The key to salvation is not my goodness, but God's ability to give us new life in Jesus.

See: John 3:1-21

because Jews don't have anything to do with Samaritans.

[10]Jesus answered her, "You do not know what God's gift is. And you do not know who is asking you for a drink. If you did, you would have asked him. He would have given you living water."

[11]"Sir," the woman said, "you don't have anything to get water with. The well is deep. Where can you get this living water? [12]Our father Jacob gave us the well. He drank from it himself. So did his sons and his flocks and herds. Are you more important than he is?"

[13]Jesus answered, "All who drink this water will be thirsty again. [14]But anyone who drinks the water I give him will never be thirsty. In fact, the water I give him will become a spring of water in him. It will flow up into eternal life."

[15]The woman said to him, "Sir, give me this water. Then I will never be thirsty. And I won't have to keep coming here to get water."

[16]He told her, "Go. Get your husband and come back."

[17]"I have no husband," she replied.

Jesus said to her, "You are right when you say you have no husband. [18]The fact is, you have had five husbands. And the man you have now is not your husband. What you have just said is very true."

[19]"Sir," the woman said, "I can see that you are a prophet. [20]Our people have worshiped on this mountain for a long time. But you Jews claim that the place where we must worship is in Jerusalem."

[21]Jesus said, "Believe me, woman. A time is coming when you will not worship the Father on this mountain or in Jerusalem. [22]You Samaritans worship what you do not know. We worship what we do know. Salvation comes from the Jews.

[23]But a new time is coming. In fact, it is already here. True worshipers will worship the Father in spirit and in truth. They are the kind of worshipers the Father is looking for.

[24]God is spirit. His worshipers must worship him in spirit and in truth."

[25]The woman said, "I know that Messiah is coming." (He is called Christ.) "When he comes, he will explain everything to us."

[26]Then Jesus said, "I, the one speaking to you, am he."

The Disciples Join Jesus Again

[27]Just then Jesus' disciples returned. They were surprised to find him talking with a woman. But no one asked, "What do you want from her?" No one asked, "Why are you talking with her?"

[28]The woman left her water jar and went back to the town. She said to the people, [29]"Come. See a man who told me everything I've ever done. Could this be the Christ?"

[30]The people came out of the town and made their way toward Jesus.

[31]His disciples were saying to him, "Rabbi, eat something!"

[32]But he said to them, "I have food to eat that you know nothing about."

[33]Then his disciples asked each other, "Did someone bring him food?"

[34]Jesus said, "My food is to do what my Father sent me to do. My food is to finish his work.

[35]You say, 'Four months more, and then it will be harvest time.' But I tell you, open your eyes! Look at the fields! They are ripe for harvest right now. [36]Those who gather the crop are already getting paid. They are already harvesting the crop for eternal life. So those who plant and those who gather can now be glad together.

[37]Here is a true saying. 'One plants and another gathers.' [38]I sent you to gather what you have not worked for. Others have done the hard work. You have gathered the benefits of their work."

Many Samaritans Believe in Jesus

[39]Many of the Samaritans from the town of Sychar believed in Jesus. They believed because of the woman's witness. She said, "He told me everything I've ever done."

[40]Then the Samaritans came to him and tried to get him to stay with them. So he stayed two days. [41]Because of his words, many more people became believers.

[42]They said to the woman, "We no longer believe just because of what you said. We

have now heard for ourselves. We know that this man really is the Savior of the world."

Jesus Heals the Official's Son

⁴³After the two days, Jesus left for Galilee. ⁴⁴He himself had pointed out that a prophet is not respected in his own country. ⁴⁵When he arrived in Galilee, the people living there welcomed him. They had seen everything he had done in Jerusalem at the Passover Feast. That was because they had also been there.

⁴⁶Once more, Jesus visited Cana in Galilee. Cana is where he had turned the water into wine. A royal official was there. His son was sick in bed at Capernaum. ⁴⁷The official heard that Jesus had arrived in Galilee from Judea. So he went to Jesus and begged him to come and heal his son. The boy was close to death.

⁴⁸Jesus told him, "You people will never believe unless you see miraculous signs and wonders."

⁴⁹The royal official said, "Sir, come down before my child dies."

⁵⁰Jesus replied, "You may go. Your son will live."

The man believed what Jesus said, and so he left. ⁵¹While he was still on his way home, his servants met him. They gave him the news that his boy was living. ⁵²He asked

what time his son got better. They said to him, "The fever left him yesterday afternoon at one o'clock."

[53]Then the father realized what had happened. That was the exact time Jesus had said to him, "Your son will live." So he and all his family became believers.

[54]This was the second miraculous sign that Jesus did after coming from Judea to Galilee.

Jesus Heals a Disabled Man

5 Some time later, Jesus went up to Jerusalem for a Jewish feast. [2]In Jerusalem near the Sheep Gate is a pool. In the Aramaic language it is called Bethesda. It is surrounded by five rows of columns with a roof over them. [3/4]Here a great number of disabled people used to lie down. Among them were those who were blind, those who could not walk, and those who could hardly move.

[5]One person who was there had been disabled for 38 years. [6]Jesus saw him lying there. He knew that the man had been in that condition for a long time. So he asked him, "Do you want to get well?"

[7]"Sir," the disabled man replied, "I have no one to help me into the pool when an angel stirs the water up. I try to get in, but someone else always goes down ahead of me."

[8]Then Jesus said to him, "Get up! Pick up your mat and walk."

[9]At once the man was healed. He picked up his mat and walked.

The day this happened was a Sabbath. [10]So the Jews said to the man who had been healed, "It is the Sabbath. The law does not allow you to carry your mat."

[11]But he replied, "The one who made me well said to me, 'Pick up your mat and walk.' "

[12]They asked him, "Who is this fellow? Who told you to pick it up and walk?"

[13]The one who was healed had no idea who it was. Jesus had slipped away into the crowd that was there.

[14]Later Jesus found him at the temple. Jesus said to him, "See, you are well again. Stop sinning, or something worse may happen to you." [15]The man went away. He told the Jews it was Jesus who had made him well.

Life Because of the Son

[16]Jesus was doing these things on the Sabbath day. So the Jews began to oppose him.

[17]Jesus said to them, "My Father is always doing his work. He is working right up to this very day. I am working too."

[18]For this reason the Jews tried even harder to kill him. Jesus was not only breaking the Sabbath. He was even calling God his own Father. He was making himself equal with God.

[19]Jesus answered, "What I'm about to tell you is true. The Son can do nothing by himself. He can do only what he sees his Father doing. What the Father does, the Son also does. [20]This is because the Father loves the Son. He shows him everything he does. Yes, you will be amazed! The Father will show him even greater things than these.

[21]"The Father raises the dead and gives them life. In the same way, the Son gives life to anyone he wants to.

[22]"Also, the Father does not judge anyone. He has given the Son the task of judging. [23]Then all people will honor the Son just as they honor the Father. Those who do not honor the Son do not honor the Father, who sent him.

[24]"What I'm about to tell you is true. Anyone who hears my word and believes him who sent me has eternal life. He will not be found guilty. He has crossed over from death to life.

[25]"What I'm about to tell you is true. A time is coming for me to give life. In fact, it has already begun. The dead will hear the voice of the Son of God. Those who hear it will live.

[26]"The Father has life in himself. He has also allowed the Son to have life in himself. [27]And the Father has given him the authority to judge. This is because he is the Son of Man.

[28]"Do not be amazed at this. A time is coming when all who are in the grave will hear his voice. [29]They will all come out of their graves. Those who have done good will

rise and live again. Those who have done evil will rise and be found guilty.

[30]"I can do nothing by myself. I judge only as I hear. And my judging is fair. I do not try to please myself. I try only to please the One who sent me.

Giving Witness About Jesus

[31]"If I give witness about myself, it doesn't count. [32]There is someone else who gives witness in my favor. And I know that his witness about me counts.

[33]"You have sent people to John. He has given witness to the truth. [34]I do not accept human witness. I only talk about it so you can be saved. [35]John was like a lamp that burned and gave light. For a while you chose to enjoy his light.

[36]"The witness I have is more important than John's. I am doing the very work the Father gave me to finish. It gives witness that the Father has sent me.

[37]"The Father who sent me has himself given witness about me. You have never heard his voice. You have never seen what he really looks like. [38]And his word does not live in you. This is because you do not believe the One he sent.

[39]"You study the Scriptures carefully. You study them because you think they will give you eternal life. The Scriptures you study give witness about me. [40]But you refuse to come to me and receive life.

[41]"I do not accept praise from people. [42]But I know you. I know that you do not have love for God in your hearts. [43]I have come in my Father's name, and you do not accept me. But if someone else comes in his own name, you will accept him.

[44]"You accept praise from one another. But you make no effort to receive the praise that comes from the only God. So how can you believe?

[45]"Do not think I will bring charges against you in front of the Father. Moses is the one who does that. And he is the one you build your hopes on.

[46]"Do you believe Moses? Then you should believe me. He wrote about me. [47]But you do not believe what he wrote. So how are you going to believe what I say?"

Jesus Feeds the Five Thousand

6 Some time after this, Jesus crossed over to the other side of the Sea of Galilee. It is also called the Sea of Tiberias. [2]A large crowd of people followed him. They had seen the miraculous signs he had done on those who were sick.

[3]Then Jesus went up on a mountainside. There he sat down with his disciples. [4]The Jewish Passover Feast was near.

[5]Jesus looked up and saw a large crowd coming toward him. So he said to Philip, "Where can we buy bread for these people to eat?" [6]He asked this only to put Philip to the test. He already knew what he was going to do.

[7]Philip answered him, "Eight months' pay would not buy enough bread for each one to have a bite!"

[8]Another of his disciples spoke up. It was Andrew, Simon Peter's brother. [9]He said, "Here is a boy with five small loaves of barley bread. He also has two small fish. But how far will that go in such a large crowd?"

[10]Jesus said, "Have the people sit down." There was plenty of grass in that place, and they sat down. The number of men among them was about 5,000.

[11]Then Jesus took the loaves and gave thanks. He handed out the bread to those who were seated. He gave them as much as they wanted. And he did the same with the fish.

[12]When all of them had enough to eat, Jesus spoke to his disciples. "Gather the leftover pieces," he said. "Don't waste anything."

[13]So they gathered what was left over from the five barley loaves. They filled 12 baskets with the pieces left by those who had eaten.

[14]The people saw the miraculous sign that Jesus did. Then they began to say, "This must be the Prophet who is supposed to come into the world." [15]But Jesus knew that they planned to come and force him to be their king. So he went away again to a mountain by himself.

Jesus Walks on the Water

[16]When evening came, Jesus' disciples went down to the Sea of Galilee. [17]There they got into a boat and headed across the lake toward Capernaum. By now it was dark. Jesus had not yet joined them.

[18]A strong wind was blowing, and the water became rough. [19]They rowed three or three and a half miles. Then they saw Jesus coming toward the boat. He was walking on the water. They were terrified.

[20]But he said to them, "It is I. Don't be afraid."

[21]Then they agreed to take him into the boat. Right away the boat reached the shore where they were heading.

[22]The next day the crowd that had stayed on the other side of the lake realized something. They saw that only one boat had been there. They knew that Jesus had not gotten into it with his disciples. And they knew that the disciples had gone away alone.

[23]Then some boats from Tiberias landed. It was near the place where the people had eaten the bread after the Lord gave thanks. [24]The crowd realized that Jesus and his disciples were not there. So they got into boats and went to Capernaum to look for Jesus.

Jesus Is the Bread of Life

[25]They found him on the other side of the lake. They asked him, "Rabbi, when did you get here?"

[26]Jesus answered, "What I'm about to tell you is true. You are not looking for me because you saw miraculous signs. You are looking for me because you ate the loaves until you were full. [27]Do not work for food that spoils. Work for food that lasts forever. That is the food the Son of Man will give you. God the Father has put his seal of approval on him."

[28]Then they asked him, "What does God want from us? What works does he want us to do?"

[29]Jesus answered, "God's work is to believe in the One he has sent."

[30]So they asked him, "What miraculous sign will you give us? What will you do so we can see it and believe you? [31]Long ago

WHEN DOES ...

5+2=5000?

WHEN Jesus says

GRACE

5 loaves and 2 fish feed 5000 people

our people ate the manna in the desert. It is written in Scripture, 'The Lord gave them bread from heaven to eat.'" *(Exodus 16:4; Nehemiah 9:15; Psalm 78:24,25)*

³²Jesus said to them, "What I'm about to tell you is true. It is not Moses who has given you the bread from heaven. It is my Father who gives you the true bread from heaven. ³³The bread of God is the One who comes down from heaven. He gives life to the world."

³⁴"Sir," they said, "give us this bread from now on."

³⁵Then Jesus said, "I am the bread of life. No one who comes to me will ever go hungry. And no one who believes in me will ever be thirsty.

³⁶"But it is just as I told you. You have seen me, and you still do not believe. ³⁷Everyone the Father gives me will come to me. I will never send away anyone who comes to me.

³⁸"I have not come down from heaven to do what I want to do. I have come to do what the One who sent me wants me to do. ³⁹The One who sent me doesn't want me to lose anyone he has given me. He wants me to raise them up on the last day. ⁴⁰My Father wants all who look to the Son and believe in him to have eternal life. I will raise them up on the last day."

⁴¹Then the Jews began to complain about Jesus. That was because he said, "I am the bread that came down from heaven." ⁴²They said, "Isn't this Jesus, the son of Joseph? Don't we know his father and mother? How can he now say, 'I came down from heaven'?"

⁴³"Stop complaining among yourselves," Jesus answered. ⁴⁴"No one can come to me unless the Father who sent me brings him. Then I will raise him up on the last day.

⁴⁵"It is written in the Prophets, 'God will teach all of them.' *(Isaiah 54:13)* Everyone who listens to the Father and learns from him comes to me.

⁴⁶"No one has seen the Father except the

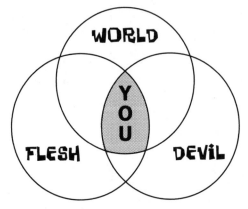

HOW CAN YOU SURVIVE AGAINST THE ENEMY?

WORLD

YOU

FLESH   DEVIL

"Our fight is not against human beings. It is against the rulers, the authorities and the powers of this dark world. It is against the spiritual forces of evil in the heavenly world." Ephesians 6:12

"In all these things we will do more than win! We owe it all to Christ, who has loved us." Romans 8:37

One who has come from God. Only he has seen the Father. [47]What I'm about to tell you is true. Everyone who believes has life forever.

[48]"I am the bread of life. [49]Long ago your people ate the manna in the desert, and they still died. [50]But here is the bread that comes down from heaven. A person can eat it and not die. [51]I am the living bread that came down from heaven. Everyone who eats some of this bread will live forever. The bread is my body. I will give it for the life of the world."

[52]Then the Jews began to argue sharply among themselves. They said, "How can this man give us his body to eat?"

[53]Jesus said to them, "What I'm about to tell you is true. You must eat the Son of Man's body and drink his blood. If you don't, you have no life in you. [54]Anyone who eats my body and drinks my blood has eternal life. I will raise him up on the last day.

[55]"My body is real food. My blood is real drink. [56]Anyone who eats my body and drinks my blood remains in me. And I remain in him.

[57]"The living Father sent me, and I live because of him. In the same way, those who feed on me will live because of me. [58]This is the bread that came down from heaven. Long ago your people ate manna and died. But those who feed on this bread will live forever."

[59]He said this while he was teaching in the synagogue in Capernaum.

Many Disciples Leave Jesus

[60]Jesus' disciples heard this. Many of them said, "This is a hard teaching. Who can accept it?"

[61]Jesus was aware that his disciples were complaining about his teaching. So he said to them, "Does this upset you? [62]What if you see the Son of Man go up to where he was before? [63]The Holy Spirit gives life. The body means nothing at all. The words I have spoken to you are from the Spirit. They give life. [64]But there are some of you who do not believe."

Jesus had known from the beginning which of them did not believe. And he had known who was going to hand him over to his enemies. [65]So he continued speaking. He said, "This is why I told you that no one can come to me unless the Father helps him."

[66]From this time on, many of his disciples turned back. They no longer followed him.

[67]"You don't want to leave also, do you?" Jesus asked the Twelve.

[68]Simon Peter answered him, "Lord, who can we go to? You have the words of eternal life. [69]We believe and know that you are the Holy One of God."

[70]Then Jesus replied, "Didn't I choose you, the 12 disciples? But one of you is a devil!" [71]He meant Judas, the son of Simon Iscariot. Judas was one of the Twelve. But later he was going to hand Jesus over to his enemies.

Jesus Goes to the Feast of Booths

7 After this, Jesus went around in Galilee. He stayed away from Judea on purpose. He knew that the Jews there were waiting to kill him.

[2]The Jewish Feast of Booths was near. [3]Jesus' brothers said to him, "You should leave here and go to Judea. Then your disciples will see the kinds of things you do. [4]No one who wants to be well known does things in secret. Since you are doing these things, show yourself to the world." [5]Even Jesus' own brothers did not believe in him.

[6]So Jesus told them, "The right time has not yet come for me. For you, any time is right. [7]The people of the world can't hate you. But they hate me. This is because I give witness that what they do is evil.

[8]"You go to the Feast. I am not yet going up to this Feast. For me, the right time has not yet come."

[9]After he said this, he stayed in Galilee. [10]When his brothers had left for the Feast, he went also. But he went secretly, not openly. [11]At the Feast the Jews were watching for him. They were asking, "Where is he?"

[12]Many people in the crowd were whispering about him. Some said, "He is a good man."

Others replied, "No. He fools the people."

[13]But no one would say anything about him openly. They were afraid of the Jews.

Jesus Teaches at the Feast

[14]Jesus did nothing until halfway through the Feast. Then he went up to the temple courtyard and began to teach. [15]The Jews were amazed. They asked, "How did this man learn so much without studying?"

[16]Jesus answered, "What I teach is not my own. It comes from the One who sent me. [17]Anyone who chooses to do what God wants him to do will find out whether my teaching comes from God or from me. [18]Someone who speaks on his own does it to get honor for himself. But someone who works for the honor of the One who sent him is truthful. There is nothing false about him.

[19]"Didn't Moses give you the law? But not one of you keeps the law. Why are you trying to kill me?"

[20]"You are controlled by demons," the crowd answered. "Who is trying to kill you?"

[21]Jesus said to them, "I did one miracle, and you are all amazed. [22]Moses gave you circumcision, and so you circumcise a child on the Sabbath day. But circumcision did not really come from Moses. It came from Abraham. [23]You circumcise a child on the Sabbath day. You think that if you do, you won't break the law of Moses. Then why are you angry with me? I healed a whole man on the Sabbath!

[24]"Stop judging only by what you see. Judge correctly."

Is Jesus the Christ?

[25]Then some of the people of Jerusalem began asking questions. They said, "Isn't this the man some people are trying to kill? [26]Here he is! He is speaking openly. They aren't saying a word to him. Have the authorities really decided that he is the Christ? [27]But we know where this man is from. When the Christ comes, no one will know where he is from."

[28]Jesus was still teaching in the temple courtyard. He cried out, "Yes, you know me. And you know where I am from. I am not here on my own. The One who sent me is true. You do not know him. [29]But I know him. I am from him, and he sent me."

[30]When he said this, they tried to arrest him. But no one laid a hand on him. His time had not yet come.

[31]Still, many people in the crowd put their faith in him. They said, "How will it be when the Christ comes? Will he do more miraculous signs than this man?"

[32]The Pharisees heard the crowd whispering things like this about him. Then the chief priests and the Pharisees sent temple guards to arrest him.

[33]Jesus said, "I am with you for only a short time. Then I will go to the One who sent me. [34]You will look for me, but you won't find me. You can't come where I am going."

[35]The Jews said to one another, "Where does this man plan to go? Does he think we can't find him? Will he go where our people live scattered among the Greeks? Will he go there to teach the Greeks? [36]What did he mean when he said, 'You will look for me, but you won't find me'? And, 'You can't come where I am going'?"

[37]It was the last and most important day of the Feast. Jesus stood up and spoke in a loud voice. He said, "Let anyone who is thirsty come to me and drink. [38]Does anyone believe in me? Then, just as Scripture says, streams of living water will flow from inside him."

[39]When he said this, he meant the Holy Spirit. Those who believed in Jesus would receive the Spirit later. Up to that time, the Spirit had not been given. This was because Jesus had not yet received glory.

[40]When some of the people heard his words, they said, "This man must be the Prophet we've been expecting."

[41]Others said, "He is the Christ."

Still others asked, "How can the Christ come from Galilee? [42]Doesn't Scripture say that the Christ will come from David's family? Doesn't it say that he will come from Bethlehem, the town where David lived?"

[43]So the people did not agree about who Jesus was. [44]Some wanted to arrest him. But no one laid a hand on him.

The Jewish Leaders Do Not Believe

⁴⁵Finally the temple guards went back to the chief priests and the Pharisees. They asked the guards, "Why didn't you bring him in?"

⁴⁶"No one ever spoke the way this man does," the guards replied.

⁴⁷"You mean he has fooled you also?" the Pharisees asked. ⁴⁸"Have any of the rulers or Pharisees believed in him? ⁴⁹No! But this mob knows nothing about the law. There is a curse on them."

You will know the TRUTH and the truth will set you FREE

John 8:32

⁵⁰Then Nicodemus, a Pharisee, spoke. He was the one who had gone to Jesus earlier. He asked, ⁵¹"Does our law find someone guilty without hearing him first? Doesn't it want to find out what he is doing?"

⁵²They replied, "Are you from Galilee too? Look into it. You will find that a prophet does not come out of Galilee."

---

⁵³Then each of them went home.

8 But Jesus went to the Mount of Olives. ²At sunrise he arrived in the temple courtyard again. All the people gathered around him there. He sat down to teach them.

³The teachers of the law and the Pharisees brought in a woman. She had been caught in adultery. They made her stand in front of the group. ⁴They said to Jesus, "Teacher, this woman was caught having sex with a man who was not her husband. ⁵In the Law, Moses commanded us to kill such women by throwing stones at them. Now what do you say?" ⁶They were trying to trap Jesus with that question. They wanted to have a reason to bring charges against him.

But Jesus bent down and started to write on the ground with his finger.

⁷They kept asking him questions. So he stood up and said to them, "Has any one of you not sinned? Then you be the first to throw a stone at her."

⁸He bent down again and wrote on the ground.

⁹Those who heard what he had said began to go away. They left one at a time, the older ones first. Soon only Jesus was left. The woman was still standing there.

¹⁰Jesus stood up and asked her, "Woman, where are they? Hasn't anyone found you guilty?"

¹¹"No one, sir," she said.

"Then I don't find you guilty either," Jesus said. "Go now and leave your life of sin."

Jesus' Witness Is True

¹²Jesus spoke to the people again. He said, "I am the light of the world. Those who follow me will never walk in darkness. They will have the light that leads to life."

¹³The Pharisees argued with him. "Here

you are," they said, "appearing as your own witness. But your witness does not count."

[14]Jesus answered, "Even if I give witness about myself, my witness does count. I know where I came from. And I know where I am going. But you have no idea where I come from or where I am going. [15]You judge by human standards. I don't judge anyone.

[16]"But if I do judge, what I decide is right. This is because I am not alone. I stand with the Father, who sent me. [17]Your own Law says that the witness of two is what counts. [18]I give witness about myself. My other witness is the Father, who sent me."

[19]Then they asked him, "Where is your father?"

"You do not know me or my Father," Jesus replied. "If you knew me, you would know my Father also."

[20]He spoke these words while he was teaching in the temple area. He was near the place where the offerings were put. But no one arrested him. His time had not yet come.

[21]Once more Jesus spoke to them. "I am going away," he said. "You will look for me, and you will die in your sin. You can't come where I am going."

[22]This made the Jews ask, "Will he kill himself? Is that why he says, 'You can't come where I am going'?"

[23]But Jesus said, "You are from below. I am from heaven. You are from this world. I am not from this world. [24]I told you that you would die in your sins. Do you believe that I am the one I claim to be? If you don't, you will certainly die in your sins."

[25]"Who are you?" they asked.

"Just what I have been claiming all along," Jesus replied. [26]"I have a lot to say that will judge you. But the One who sent me can be trusted. And I tell the world what I have heard from him."

[27]They did not understand that Jesus was telling them about his Father. [28]So Jesus said, "You will lift up the Son of Man. Then you will know that I am the one I claim to be. You will also know that I do nothing on my own. I speak just what the Father has taught me. [29]The One who sent me is

with me. He has not left me alone, because I always do what pleases him."

[30]Even while Jesus was speaking, many people put their faith in him.

The Children of Abraham

[31]Jesus spoke to the Jews who had believed him. "If you obey my teaching," he said, "you are really my disciples. [32]Then you will know the truth. And the truth will set you free."

[33]They answered him, "We are Abraham's children. We have never been slaves of anyone. So how can you say that we will be set free?"

[34]Jesus replied, "What I'm about to tell you is true. Everyone who sins is a slave of sin. [35]A slave has no lasting place in the family. But a son belongs to the family forever. [36]So if the Son of Man sets you free, you will really be free.

[37]"I know you are Abraham's children. But you are ready to kill me. You have no room for my word. [38]I am telling you what I saw when I was with my Father. You do what you have heard from your father."

[39]"Abraham is our father," they answered.

Jesus said, "Are you really Abraham's children? If you are, you will do the things Abraham did. [40]But you have decided to kill me. I am a man who has told you the truth I heard from God. Abraham didn't do the things you want to do. [41]You are doing the things your own father does."

"We are not children of people who weren't married to each other," they objected. "The only Father we have is God himself."

The Children of the Devil

[42]Jesus said to them, "If God were your Father, you would love me. I came from God, and now I am here. I have not come on my own. He sent me.

[43]"Why aren't my words clear to you? Because you can't really hear what I say. [44]You belong to your father, the devil. You want to obey your father's wishes.

"From the beginning, the devil was a murderer. He has never obeyed the truth.

There is no truth in him. When he lies, he speaks his natural language. He does this because he is a liar. He is the father of lies.

⁴⁵"But because I tell the truth, you don't believe me! ⁴⁶Can any of you prove I am guilty of sinning? Am I not telling the truth? Then why don't you believe me?

⁴⁷"Everyone who belongs to God hears what God says. The reason you don't hear is that you don't belong to God."

Jesus Makes Claims About Himself

⁴⁸The Jews answered Jesus, "Aren't we right when we say you are a Samaritan? Aren't you controlled by a demon?"

⁴⁹"I am not controlled by a demon," said Jesus. "I honor my Father. You do not honor me. ⁵⁰I am not seeking glory for myself. But there is One who brings glory to me. He is the judge. ⁵¹What I'm about to tell you is true. Anyone who obeys my word will never die."

⁵²Then the Jews cried out, "Now we know you are controlled by a demon! Abraham died. So did the prophets. But you say that anyone who obeys your word will never die. ⁵³Are you greater than our father Abraham? He died. So did the prophets. Who do you think you are?"

⁵⁴Jesus replied, "If I bring glory to myself, my glory means nothing. You claim that my Father is your God. He is the one who brings glory to me. ⁵⁵You do not know him. But I know him. If I said I did not, I would be a liar like you. But I do know him. And I obey his word.

⁵⁶"Your father Abraham was filled with joy at the thought of seeing my day. He saw it and was glad."

⁵⁷"You are not even 50 years old," the Jews said to Jesus. "And you have seen Abraham?"

⁵⁸"What I'm about to tell you is true," Jesus answered. "Before Abraham was born, I am!"

⁵⁹When he said this, they picked up stones to kill him. But Jesus hid himself. He slipped away from the temple area.

Jesus Heals a Man Born Blind

9 As Jesus went along, he saw a man who was blind. He had been blind since he was born. ²Jesus' disciples asked him, "Rabbi, who sinned? Was this man born blind because he sinned? Or did his parents sin?"

³"It isn't because this man sinned," said Jesus. "It isn't because his parents sinned. This happened so that God's work could be shown in his life. ⁴While it is still day, we must do the work of the One who sent me. Night is coming. Then no one can work. ⁵While I am in the world, I am the light of the world."

⁶After he said this, he spit on the ground. He made some mud with the spit. Then he put the mud on the man's eyes.

⁷"Go," he told him. "Wash in the Pool of Siloam." Siloam means Sent.

So the man went and washed. And he came home able to see.

⁸His neighbors and those who had earlier seen him begging asked questions. "Isn't this the same man who used to sit and beg?" they asked.

⁹Some claimed that he was.

Others said, "No. He only looks like him."

But the man who had been blind kept saying, "I am the man."

¹⁰"Then how were your eyes opened?" they asked.

¹¹He replied, "The man they call Jesus made some mud and put it on my eyes. He told me to go to Siloam and wash. So I went and washed. Then I could see."

¹²"Where is this man?" they asked him.

"I don't know," he said.

The Pharisees Want to Know What Happened

¹³They brought to the Pharisees the man who had been blind. ¹⁴The day Jesus made the mud and opened the man's eyes was a Sabbath. ¹⁵So the Pharisees also asked him

From God with love:
the peace of His presence

how he was able to see.

"He put mud on my eyes," the man replied. "Then I washed. And now I can see."

[16]Some of the Pharisees said, "Jesus has not come from God. He does not keep the Sabbath day."

But others asked, "How can a sinner do such miraculous signs?"

So the Pharisees did not agree with each other.

[17]Finally they turned again to the blind man. "What do you have to say about him?" they asked. "It was your eyes he opened."

The man replied, "He is a prophet."

[18]The Jews still did not believe that the man had been blind and now could see. So they sent for his parents. [19]"Is this your son?" they asked. "Is this the one you say was born blind? How is it that now he can see?"

[20]"We know he is our son," the parents answered. "And we know he was born blind. [21]But we don't know how he can now see. And we don't know who opened his eyes. Ask him. He is an adult. He can speak for himself."

[22]His parents said this because they were afraid of the Jews. The Jews had already decided that anyone who said Jesus was the Christ would be put out of the synagogue. [23]That was why the man's parents said, "He is an adult. Ask him."

[24]Again they called the man who had been blind to come to them. "Give glory to God by telling the truth!" they said. "We know that the man who healed you is a sinner."

[25]He replied, "I don't know if he is a sinner or not. I do know one thing. I was blind, but now I can see!"

[26]Then they asked him, "What did he do to you? How did he open your eyes?"

[27]He answered, "I have already told you. But you didn't listen. Why do you want to hear it again? Do you want to become his disciples too?"

[28]Then they began to attack him with their words. "You are this fellow's disciple!" they said. "We are disciples of Moses! [29]We know that God spoke to Moses. But we don't even know where this fellow comes from."

[30]The man answered, "That is really surprising! You don't know where he comes from, and yet he opened my eyes. [31]We know that God does not listen to sinners. He listens to godly people who do what he wants them to do. [32]Nobody has ever heard of anyone opening the eyes of a person born blind. [33]If this man had not come from God, he could do nothing."

[34]Then the Pharisees replied, "When you were born, you were already deep in sin. How dare you talk like that to us!" And they threw him out of the synagogue.

The Blind Will See

[35]Jesus heard that the Pharisees had thrown the man out. When he found him, he said, "Do you believe in the Son of Man?"

[36]"Who is he, sir?" the man asked. "Tell me, so I can believe in him."

[37]Jesus said, "You have now seen him. In fact, he is the one speaking with you."

[38]Then the man said, "Lord, I believe." And he worshiped him.

[39]Jesus said, "I have come into this world to judge it. I have come so that the blind will see and those who see will become blind."

[40]Some Pharisees who were with him heard him say this. They asked, "What? Are we blind too?"

[41]Jesus said, "If you were blind, you would not be guilty of sin. But since you claim you can see, you remain guilty.

The Shepherd and the Flock

10 "What I'm about to tell you is true. What if someone does not enter the sheep pen through the gate but climbs in another way? That person is a thief and a robber. [2]The one who enters through the gate is the shepherd of the sheep. [3]The gatekeeper opens the gate for him. The sheep listen to his voice. He calls his own sheep by name and leads them out. [4]When he has brought all of his own sheep out, he goes on ahead of them. His sheep follow him because they know his voice. [5]But they will never follow a stranger. In fact, they will

Open Book Quiz - The Book of John

Read the letters from top to bottom and complete the answer below.

1	____ Andrew	ch.	1
2	____ Assigns life & work	ch.	3
3	____ Their actions are evil	ch.	3
4	_S_ Jesus	ch.	1
5	____ Gave His only Son	ch.	3
6	____ Nathaniel	ch.	1
7	____ Obeys	ch.	8
8	____ Water-to-wine	ch.	2
9	____ Those who sin	ch.	8
10	____ I am not the Messiah	ch.	1
11	____ Wrath of God	ch.	3
12	____ Set you free	ch.	8
13	____ Voice in wilderness	ch.	1
14	____ Life	ch.	1
15	_L_ Salvation comes	ch.	5
16	____ Religious leaders	ch.	5
17	____ Holy Spirit	ch.	7
18	____ I must become less ...	ch.	3

Select the best answer from the right column which matches items 1-18 in the left column. Some letters are used more than once.

A - First miracle
D - Why men love darkness
E - He must become greater
F - Rivers of living water
G - First disciples mentioned
H - Light leads to ...
I - Wanted to kill Jesus
L - Moment one believes
N - An "honest man"
O - God
R - Rejecting the Son brings
S - The Messiah
T - John the Baptizer
U - The truth will ...
W - A genuine disciple
Y - Who is a slave?

Self-score
17 - 18 Great job!
15 - 16 "High-five" time
10 - 14 Turn off video games
5 - 9   Sell video games
1 - 4   Give the games away

Answer: __ __ __ • S __ __ • __ __ __

__ __ __ __ __ • L __ __ __

"Who Jesus Is"

run away from him. They don't recognize a stranger's voice."

⁶Jesus used this story. But the Jews who were there didn't understand what he was telling them.

⁷So Jesus said again, "What I'm about to tell you is true. I am like a gate for the sheep. ⁸All those who ever came before me were thieves and robbers. But the sheep did not listen to them. ⁹I'm like a gate. Anyone who enters through me will be saved. He will come in and go out. And he will find plenty of food. ¹⁰The thief comes only to steal and kill and destroy. I have come so they can have life. I want them to have it in the fullest possible way.

¹¹"I am the good shepherd. The good shepherd gives his life for the sheep. ¹²The hired man is not the shepherd who owns the sheep. So when the hired man sees the wolf coming, he leaves the sheep and runs away. Then the wolf attacks the flock and scatters it. ¹³The man runs away because he is a hired man. He does not care about the sheep.

¹⁴"I am the good shepherd. I know my sheep, and my sheep know me. ¹⁵They know me just as the Father knows me and I know the Father. And I give my life for the sheep. ¹⁶"I have other sheep that do not belong to this sheep pen. I must bring them in too. They also will listen to my voice. Then there will be one flock and one shepherd.

¹⁷"The reason my Father loves me is that I give up my life. But I will take it back again. ¹⁸No one takes it from me. I give it up myself. I have the authority to give it up. And I have the authority to take it back again. I received this command from my Father."

¹⁹After Jesus spoke these words, the Jews again could not agree with each other. ²⁰Many of them said, "He is controlled by a demon. He has gone crazy! Why should we listen to him?"

²¹But others said, "A person controlled by a demon does not say things like this. Can a demon open the eyes of someone who is blind?"

The Jews Do Not Believe

²²Then came the Feast of Hanukkah at Jerusalem. It was winter. ²³Jesus was in the temple area walking in Solomon's Porch. ²⁴The Jews gathered around him. They said, "How long will you keep us waiting? If you are the Christ, tell us plainly."

²⁵Jesus answered, "I did tell you. But you do not believe. The kinds of things I do in my Father's name speak for me. ²⁶But you do not believe, because you are not my sheep. ²⁷"My sheep listen to my voice. I know them, and they follow me. ²⁸I give them eternal life, and they will never die. No one can steal them out of my hand. ²⁹My Father, who has given them to me, is greater than anyone. No one can steal them out of my Father's hand. ³⁰I and the Father are one."

³¹Again the Jews picked up stones to kill him.

³²But Jesus said to them, "I have shown you many miracles from the Father. Which one of these are you throwing stones at me for?"

³³"We are not throwing stones at you for any of these," replied the Jews. "We are stoning you for saying a very evil thing. You are only a man. But you claim to be God."

³⁴Jesus answered them, "Didn't God say in your Law, 'I have said you are gods'? *(Psalm 82:6)* ³⁵We know that Scripture is always true. God spoke to some people and called them 'gods.' ³⁶If that is true, what about the One the Father set apart as his very own and sent into the world? Why do you charge me with saying a very evil thing? Is it because I said, 'I am God's Son'?

³⁷"Don't believe me unless I do what my Father does. ³⁸But what if I do it? Even if you don't believe me, believe the miracles. Then you will know and understand that the Father is in me and I am in the Father."

³⁹Again they tried to arrest him. But he escaped from them.

⁴⁰Then Jesus went back across the Jordan River. He went to the place where John had been baptizing in the early days. There he stayed. ⁴¹Many people came to him. They said, "John never did a miraculous sign. But everything he said about this man was true." ⁴²And in that place many believed in Jesus.

Lazarus Dies

11 A man named Lazarus was sick. He was from Bethany, the village where Mary and her sister Martha lived. ²Mary would later pour perfume on the Lord. She would also wipe his feet with her hair. Her brother Lazarus was sick in bed. ³So the sisters sent a message to Jesus. "Lord," they told him, "the one you love is sick."

⁴When Jesus heard this, he said, "This sickness will not end in death. No, it is for God's glory. God's Son will receive glory because of it."

⁵Jesus loved Martha and her sister and Lazarus. ⁶But after he heard Lazarus was sick, he stayed where he was for two more days.

⁷Then he said to his disciples, "Let us go back to Judea."

⁸"But Rabbi," they said, "a short time ago the Jews tried to kill you with stones. Are you still going back there?"

⁹Jesus answered, "Aren't there 12 hours of daylight? A person who walks during the day won't trip and fall. He can see because of this world's light. ¹⁰But when he walks at night, he'll trip and fall. He has no light."

¹¹After he said this, Jesus went on speaking to them. "Our friend Lazarus has fallen asleep," he said. "But I am going there to wake him up."

¹²His disciples replied, "Lord, if he's sleeping, he will get better."

¹³Jesus had been speaking about the death of Lazarus. But his disciples thought he meant natural sleep.

¹⁴So then he told them plainly, "Lazarus is dead. ¹⁵For your benefit, I am glad I was not there. Now you will believe. But let us go to him."

¹⁶Then Thomas, who was called Didymus, spoke to the rest of the disciples. "Let us go also," he said. "Then we can die with Jesus."

Jesus Comforts the Sisters

¹⁷When Jesus arrived, he found out that Lazarus had already been in the tomb for four days. ¹⁸Bethany was less than two miles from Jerusalem. ¹⁹Many Jews had come to

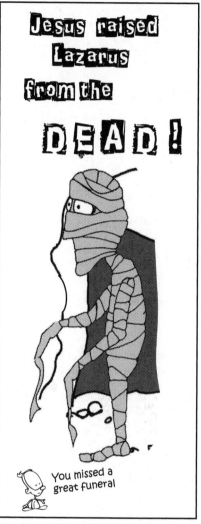

Jesus raised Lazarus from the DEAD!

You missed a great funeral

Martha and Mary. They had come to comfort them because their brother was dead.

²⁰When Martha heard that Jesus was coming, she went out to meet him. But Mary stayed at home.

²¹"Lord," Martha said to Jesus, "I wish you had been here! Then my brother would not have died. ²²But I know that even now God will give you anything you ask for."

²³Jesus said to her, "Your brother will rise again."

²⁴Martha answered, "I know he will rise

again. This will happen when people are raised from the dead on the last day."

²⁵Jesus said to her, "I am the resurrection and the life. Anyone who believes in me will live, even if he dies. ²⁶And those who live and believe in me will never die. Do you believe this?"

²⁷"Yes, Lord," she told him. "I believe that you are the Christ, the Son of God. I believe that you are the One who was supposed to come into the world."

²⁸After she said this, she went back home. She called her sister Mary to one side to talk to her. "The Teacher is here," Martha said. "He is asking for you."

²⁹When Mary heard this, she got up quickly and went to him. ³⁰Jesus had not yet entered the village. He was still at the place where Martha had met him. ³¹Some Jews had been comforting Mary in the house. They noticed how quickly she got up and went out. So they followed her. They thought she was going to the tomb to cry there.

³²Mary reached the place where Jesus was. When she saw him, she fell at his feet. She said, "Lord, I wish you had been here! Then my brother would not have died."

³³Jesus saw her crying. He saw that the Jews who had come along with her were crying also. His spirit became very sad, and he was troubled.

³⁴"Where have you put him?" he asked.

"Come and see, Lord," they replied.

³⁵Jesus sobbed.

³⁶Then the Jews said, "See how much he loved him!"

³⁷But some of them said, "He opened the eyes of the blind man. Couldn't he have kept this man from dying?"

Jesus Raises Lazarus From the Dead

³⁸Once more Jesus felt very sad. He came to the tomb. It was a cave with a stone in front of the entrance.

³⁹"Take away the stone," he said.

"But, Lord," said Martha, the sister of the dead man, "by this time there is a bad smell. Lazarus has been in the tomb for four days."

⁴⁰Then Jesus said, "Didn't I tell you that if you believed, you would see God's glory?"

⁴¹So they took away the stone.

Then Jesus looked up. He said, "Father, I thank you for hearing me. ⁴²I know that you always hear me. But I said this for the benefit of the people standing here. I said it so they will believe that you sent me."

⁴³Then Jesus called in a loud voice. He said, "Lazarus, come out!"

⁴⁴The dead man came out. His hands and feet were wrapped with strips of linen. A cloth was around his face.

Jesus said to them, "Take off the clothes he was buried in and let him go."

The Plan to Kill Jesus

⁴⁵Many of the Jews who had come to visit Mary saw what Jesus did. So they put their faith in him.

⁴⁶But some of them went to the Pharisees. They told the Pharisees what Jesus had done. ⁴⁷Then the chief priests and the Pharisees called a meeting of the Sanhedrin.

"What can we do?" they asked. "This man is doing many miraculous signs. ⁴⁸If we let him keep on doing this, everyone will believe in him. Then the Romans will come. They will take away our temple and our nation."

⁴⁹One of them spoke up. His name was Caiaphas. He was high priest at that time. He said, "You don't know anything at all! ⁵⁰You don't realize what is good for you. It is better if one man dies for the people than if the whole nation is destroyed."

⁵¹He did not say this on his own. But he was high priest at that time. So he told ahead of time that Jesus would die for the Jewish nation. ⁵²He also prophesied that Jesus would die for God's children scattered everywhere. He would die to bring them together and make them one.

⁵³So from that day on, the Jewish rulers planned to kill Jesus.

⁵⁴Jesus no longer moved around openly among the Jews. Instead, he went away to an area near the desert. He went to a village called Ephraim. There he stayed with his disciples.

⁵⁵It was almost time for the Jewish Passover Feast. Many people went up from the country to Jerusalem. They went there for

Match the Drawings
Which verse listed at the bottom fits the drawing?

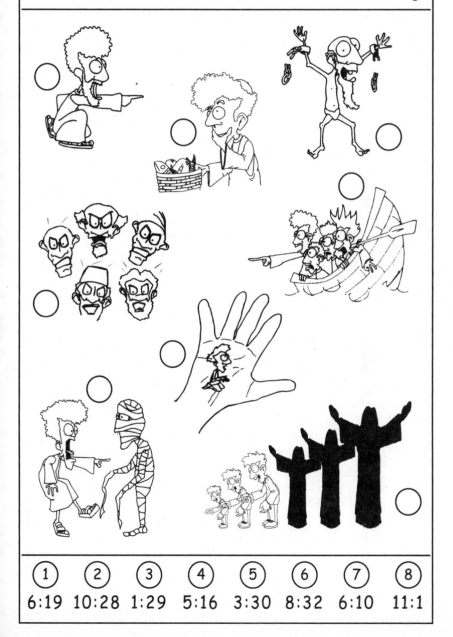

①	②	③	④	⑤	⑥	⑦	⑧
6:19	10:28	1:29	5:16	3:30	8:32	6:10	11:1

the special washing that would make them pure before the Passover Feast. [56]They kept looking for Jesus as they stood in the temple area. They asked one another, "What do you think? Isn't he coming to the Feast at all?"

[57]But the chief priests and the Pharisees had given orders. They had commanded anyone who found out where Jesus was staying to report it. Then they could arrest him.

Mary Pours Perfume on Jesus

12 It was six days before the Passover Feast. Jesus arrived at Bethany, where Lazarus lived. Lazarus was the one Jesus had raised from the dead. [2]A dinner was given at Bethany to honor Jesus. Martha served the food. Lazarus was among those at the table with Jesus.

[3]Then Mary took about a pint of pure nard. It was an expensive perfume. She poured it on Jesus' feet and wiped them with her hair. The house was filled with the sweet smell of the perfume.

[4]But Judas Iscariot didn't like what Mary did. He was one of Jesus' disciples. Later he was going to hand Jesus over to his enemies. Judas said, [5]"Why wasn't this perfume sold? Why wasn't the money given to poor people? It was worth a year's pay."

[6]He didn't say this because he cared about the poor. He said it because he was a thief. Judas was in charge of the money bag. He used to help himself to what was in it.

[7]"Leave her alone," Jesus replied. "The perfume was meant for the day I am buried. [8]You will always have the poor among you. But you won't always have me."

[9]Meanwhile a large crowd of Jews found out that Jesus was there, so they came. But they did not come only because of Jesus. They also came to see Lazarus. After all, Jesus had raised him from the dead.

[10]So the chief priests made plans to kill Lazarus too. [11]Because of Lazarus, many of the Jews were starting to follow Jesus. They were putting their faith in him.

Jesus Enters Jerusalem

[12]The next day the large crowd that had come for the Feast heard that Jesus was on his way to Jerusalem. [13]So they took branches from palm trees and went out to meet him. They shouted,

"Hosanna! "

"Blessed is the one who comes in the name of the Lord!"

(Psalm 118:25,26)

"Blessed is the King of Israel!"

[14]Jesus found a young donkey and sat on it. This is just as it is written in Scripture. It says,

[15]"City of Zion, do not be afraid.
See, your king is coming.
He is sitting on a donkey's colt."

(Zechariah 9:9)

[16]At first, Jesus' disciples did not understand all this. They realized it only after he had received glory. Then they realized that these things had been written about him. They realized that the people had done these things to him.

[17]A crowd had been with Jesus when he called Lazarus from the tomb and raised him from the dead. So they continued to tell everyone about what had happened. [18]Many people went out to meet him. They had heard that he had done this miraculous sign.

[19]So the Pharisees said to one another, "This isn't getting us anywhere. Look how the whole world is following him!"

Jesus Tells About His Coming Death

[20]There were some Greeks among the people who went up to worship during the Feast. [21]They came to ask Philip for a favor. Philip was from Bethsaida in Galilee.

"Sir," they said, "we would like to see Jesus."

[22]Philip went to tell Andrew. Then Andrew and Philip told Jesus.

[23]Jesus replied, "The hour has come for the Son of Man to receive glory. [24]What I'm about to tell you is true. Unless a grain of wheat falls to the ground and dies, it remains only one seed. But if it dies, it produces many seeds.

[25]"Anyone who loves his life will lose it. But anyone who hates his life in this world will keep it and have eternal life. [26]Anyone who serves me must follow me. And where

I am, my servant will also be. My Father will honor the one who serves me.

²⁷"My heart is troubled. What should I say? 'Father, save me from this hour'? No. This is the very reason I came to this hour. ²⁸Father, bring glory to your name!"

Then a voice came from heaven. It said, "I have brought glory to my name. I will bring glory to it again."

²⁹The crowd there heard the voice. Some said it was thunder. Others said an angel had spoken to Jesus.

³⁰Jesus said, "This voice was for your benefit, not mine. ³¹Now it is time for the world to be judged. Now the prince of this world will be thrown out. ³²But I am going to be lifted up from the earth. When I am, I will bring all people to myself." ³³He said this to show them how he was going to die.

³⁴The crowd spoke up. "The Law tells us that the Christ will remain forever," they said. "So how can you say, 'The Son of Man must be lifted up'? Who is this 'Son of Man'?"

³⁵Then Jesus told them, "You are going to have the light just a little while longer. Walk while you have the light. Do this before darkness catches up with you. Anyone who walks in the dark does not know where he is going. ³⁶While you have the light, put your trust in it. Then you can become sons of light."

When Jesus had finished speaking, he left and hid from them.

The Jews Still Do Not Believe

³⁷Jesus had done all these miraculous signs in front of them. But they still would not believe in him. ³⁸This happened as Isaiah the prophet had said it would. He had said,

> "Lord, who has believed what we've
> been saying?
> Who has seen the Lord's saving
> power?"   (Isaiah 53:1)

³⁹For this reason, they could not believe. As Isaiah says in another place,

⁴⁰"The Lord has blinded their eyes.
> He has closed their minds.
> So they can't see with their eyes.
> They can't understand with their minds.

Famous Quotes

"Do what he tells you."
Mary
John 2:5

●

"Then you will know the truth. And the truth will set you free."
Jesus
John 8:32

●

"Before Abraham was born, I am!"
Jesus
John 8:58

●

"You don't know anything at all!"
Caiaphas
John 11:49

●

"Feed my lambs."
Jesus
John 21:15

They can't turn to the Lord. If they could, he would heal them."

(Isaiah 6:10)

[41]Isaiah said this because he saw Jesus' glory and spoke about him.

[42]At the same time that Jesus did those miracles, many of the leaders believed in him. But because of the Pharisees, they would not admit they believed. They were afraid they would be thrown out of the synagogue. [43]They loved praise from people more than praise from God.

[44]Then Jesus cried out, "Anyone who believes in me does not believe in me only. He also believes in the One who sent me. [45]When he looks at me, he sees the One who sent me.

[46]"I have come into the world to be a light. No one who believes in me will stay in darkness.

[47]"I don't judge a person who hears my words but does not obey them. I didn't come to judge the world. I came to save it. [48]But there is a judge for anyone who does not accept me and my words. The very words I have spoken will judge him on the last day.

[49]"I did not speak on my own. The Father who sent me commanded me what to say. He also told me how to say it. [50]I know that his command leads to eternal life. So everything I say is just what the Father has told me to say."

Jesus Washes His Disciples' Feet

13 It was just before the Passover Feast. Jesus knew that the time had come for him to leave this world. It was time for him to go to the Father. Jesus loved his disciples who were in the world. So he now showed them how much he really loved them.

[2]The evening meal was being served. The devil had already tempted Judas Iscariot, son of Simon. He had told Judas to hand Jesus over to his enemies. [3]Jesus knew that the Father had put everything under his power. He also knew he had come from God and was returning to God.

[4]So he got up from the meal and took off his outer clothes. He wrapped a towel around his waist. [5]After that, he poured water into a large bowl. Then he began to wash his disciples' feet. He dried them with the towel that was wrapped around him.

[6]He came to Simon Peter.

"Lord," Peter said to him, "are you going to wash my feet?"

[7]Jesus replied, "You don't realize now what I am doing. But later you will understand."

[8]"No," said Peter. "You will never wash my feet."

By the Numbers

150 gallons of water turned into wine
John 2:6

1:00 pm exact time official's son was healed
John 4:52

4 days after his death, Lazarus brought back to life
John 11:39

12 ounces of perfume used to anoint Jesus
John 12:3

153 large fish caught when Jesus said "Fish"
John 21:11

Jesus answered, "Unless I wash you, you can't share life with me."

⁹"Lord," Simon Peter replied, "not just my feet! Wash my hands and my head too!"

¹⁰Jesus answered, "A person who has had a bath needs to wash only his feet. The rest of his body is clean. And you are clean. But not all of you are."

¹¹Jesus knew who was going to hand him over to his enemies. That was why he said not every one was clean.

¹²When Jesus finished washing their feet, he put on his clothes. Then he returned to his place.

"Do you understand what I have done for you?" he asked them. ¹³"You call me 'Teacher' and 'Lord.' You are right. That is what I am. ¹⁴I, your Lord and Teacher, have washed your feet. So you also should wash one another's feet. ¹⁵I have given you an example. You should do as I have done for you.

¹⁶"What I'm about to tell you is true. A servant is not more important than his master. And a messenger is not more important than the one who sends him. ¹⁷Now you know these things. So you will be blessed if you do them.

Jesus Tells What Judas Will Do

¹⁸"I am not talking about all of you. I know those I have chosen. But this will happen so that Scripture will come true. It says, 'The one who shares my bread has deserted me.' *(Psalm 41:9)*

¹⁹"I am telling you now, before it happens. When it does happen, you will believe that I am he. ²⁰What I'm about to tell you is true. Anyone who accepts someone I send accepts me. And anyone who accepts me accepts the One who sent me."

²¹After he had said this, Jesus' spirit was troubled. Here is the witness he gave. "What I'm about to tell you is true," he said. "One of you is going to hand me over to my enemies."

²²His disciples stared at one another. They had no idea which one of them he meant. ²³The disciple Jesus loved was next to him at the table. ²⁴Simon Peter motioned to that disciple. He said, "Ask Jesus which one he means."

²⁵The disciple was leaning back against Jesus. He asked him, "Lord, who is it?"

²⁶Jesus answered, "It is the one I will give this piece of bread to. I will give it to him after I have dipped it in the dish."

He dipped the piece of bread. Then he gave it to Judas Iscariot, son of Simon. ²⁷As soon as Judas took the bread, Satan entered into him.

"Do quickly what you are going to do," Jesus told him.

²⁸But no one at the meal understood why Jesus said this to him. ²⁹Judas was in charge of the money. So some of the disciples thought Jesus was telling him to buy what was needed for the Feast. Others thought Jesus was talking about giving something to poor people.

³⁰As soon as Judas had taken the bread, he went out. And it was night.

Jesus Says That Peter Will Fail

³¹After Judas was gone, Jesus spoke. He said, "Now the Son of Man receives glory. And he brings glory to God. ³²If the Son brings glory to God, God himself will bring glory to the Son. God will do it at once.

³³"My children, I will be with you only a little longer. You will look for me. Just as I told the Jews, so I am telling you now. You can't come where I am going.

³⁴"I give you a new command. Love one another. You must love one another, just as I have loved you. ³⁵If you love one another, everyone will know you are my disciples."

³⁶Simon Peter asked him, "Lord, where are you going?"

Jesus replied, "Where I am going you can't follow now. But you will follow me later."

³⁷"Lord," Peter asked, "why can't I follow you now? I will give my life for you."

³⁸Then Jesus answered, "Will you really give your life for me? What I'm about to tell you is true. Before the rooster crows, you will say three times that you don't know me!

Jesus Comforts His Disciples

14 "Do not let your hearts be troubled. Trust in God. Trust in me also.

²"There are many rooms in my Father's house. If this were not true, I would have told you. I am going there to prepare a place

for you. [3]If I go and do that, I will come back. And I will take you to be with me. Then you will also be where I am.

[4]"You know the way to the place where I am going."

Jesus Is the Way to the Father

[5]Thomas said to him, "Lord, we don't know where you are going. So how can we know the way?"

[6]Jesus answered, "I am the way and the truth and the life. No one comes to the Father except through me. [7]If you really knew me, you would know my Father also. From now on, you do know him. And you have seen him."

[8]Philip said, "Lord, show us the Father. That will be enough for us."

[9]Jesus answered, "Don't you know me, Philip? I have been among you such a long time! Anyone who has seen me has seen the Father. So how can you say, 'Show us the Father'?

[10]"Don't you believe that I am in the Father? Don't you believe that the Father is in me? The words I say to you are not just my own. The Father lives in me. He is the One who is doing his work. [11]Believe me when I say I am in the Father. Also believe that the Father is in me. Or at least believe what the miracles show about me.

[12]"What I'm about to tell you is true. Anyone who has faith in me will do what I have been doing. In fact, he will do even greater things. That is because I am going to the Father.

[13]"And I will do anything you ask in my name. Then the Son will bring glory to the Father. [14]You may ask me for anything in my name. I will do it.

The Father Will Send the Holy Spirit

[15]"If you love me, you will obey what I command. [16]I will ask the Father. And he will give you another Friend to help you and to be with you forever. [17]The Friend is the Spirit of truth. The world can't accept him. That is because the world does not see him or know him. But you know him. He lives with you, and he will be in you.

[18]"I will not leave you like children who don't have parents. I will come to you.

[19]"Before long, the world will not see me anymore. But you will see me. Because I live, you will live also. [20]On that day you will realize that I am in my Father. You will know that you are in me, and I am in you.

[21]"Anyone who has my commands and obeys them loves me. My Father will love the one who loves me. I too will love him. And I will show myself to him."

[22]Then Judas spoke. "Lord," he said, "why do you plan to show yourself only to us? Why not also to the world?" The Judas who spoke those words was not Judas Iscariot.

[23]Jesus replied, "Anyone who loves me will obey my teaching. My Father will love him. We will come to him and make our home with him. [24]Anyone who does not love me will not obey my teaching. The words you hear me say are not my own. They belong to the Father who sent me.

[25]"I have spoken all these things while I am still with you. [26]But the Father will send the Friend in my name to help you. The Friend is the Holy Spirit. He will teach you all things. He will remind you of everything I have said to you.

[27]"I leave my peace with you. I give my peace to you. I do not give it to you as the world does. Do not let your hearts be troubled. And do not be afraid.

[28]"You heard me say, 'I am going away. And I am coming back to you.' If you loved me, you would be glad I am going to the Father. The Father is greater than I am. [29]I have told you now before it happens. Then when it does happen, you will believe.

[30]"I will not speak with you much longer. The prince of this world is coming. He has no power over me. [31]But the world must learn that I love the Father. They must also learn that I do exactly what my Father has commanded me to do.

"Come now. Let us leave.

The Vine and the Branches

15 "I am the true vine. My Father is the gardener. [2]He cuts off every branch joined to me that does not bear fruit. He trims every branch that does bear fruit. Then it will bear even more fruit.

[3]"You are already clean because of the word I have spoken to you. [4]Remain

joined to me, and I will remain joined to you. No branch can bear fruit by itself. It must remain joined to the vine. In the same way, you can't bear fruit unless you remain joined to me.

⁵"I am the vine. You are the branches. If anyone remains joined to me, and I to him, he will bear a lot of fruit. You can't do anything without me. ⁶If anyone does not remain joined to me, he is like a branch that is thrown away and dries up. Branches like those are picked up. They are thrown into the fire and burned.

⁷"If you remain joined to me and my words remain in you, ask for anything you wish. And it will be given to you. ⁸When you bear a lot of fruit, it brings glory to my Father. It shows that you are my disciples.

⁹"Just as the Father has loved me, I have loved you. Now remain in my love. ¹⁰If you obey my commands, you will remain in my love. In the same way, I have obeyed my Father's commands and remain in his love. ¹¹I have told you this so that my joy will be in you. I also want your joy to be complete.

¹²"Here is my command. Love each other, just as I have loved you. ¹³No one has greater love than the one who gives his life for his

friends. [14]You are my friends if you do what I command.

[15]"I do not call you servants anymore. Servants do not know their master's business. Instead, I have called you friends. I have told you everything I learned from my Father.

[16]"You did not choose me. Instead, I chose you. I appointed you to go and bear fruit. It is fruit that will last. Then the Father will give you anything you ask for in my name.

[17]"Here is my command. Love each other.

The World Hates the Disciples

[18]"Does the world hate you? Remember that it hated me first. [19]If you belonged to the world, it would love you like one of its own. But you do not belong to the world. I have chosen you out of the world. That is why the world hates you.

[20]"Remember the words I spoke to you. I said, 'A servant is not more important than his master.' *(John 13:16)* If people hated me and tried to hurt me, they will do the same to you. If they obeyed my teaching, they will obey yours also. [21]They will treat you like that because of my name. They do not know the One who sent me.

[22]"If I had not come and spoken to them, they would not be guilty of sin. But now they have no excuse for their sin. [23]Those who hate me hate my Father also.

[24]"I did miracles among them that no one else did. If I hadn't, they would not be guilty of sin. But now they have seen those miracles. And still they have hated both me and my Father. [25]This has happened so that what is written in their Law would come true. It says, 'They hated me without any reason.' *(Psalms 35:19; 69:4)*

[26]"I will send the Friend to you from the Father. He is the Spirit of truth, who comes out from the Father. When the Friend comes to help you, he will give witness about me.

[27]"You also must give witness. This is because you have been with me from the beginning.

16 "I have told you all of this so that you will not go down the wrong path. [2]You will be thrown out of the synagogue. In fact, a time is coming when those who kill you will think they are doing God a favor. [3]They will do things like that because they do not know the Father or me.

[4]"Why have I told you this? So that when the time comes, you will remember that I warned you. I didn't tell you this at first because I was with you.

What the Holy Spirit Will Do

[5]"Now I am going to the One who sent me. But none of you asks me, 'Where are you going?' [6]Because I have said these things, you are filled with sadness.

[7]"But what I'm about to tell you is true. It is for your good that I am going away. Unless I go away, the Friend will not come to help you. But if I go, I will send him to you. [8]When he comes, he will prove that the world's people are guilty. He will prove their guilt concerning sin and godliness and judgment.

[9]"The world is guilty as far as sin is concerned. That is because people do not believe in me. [10]The world is guilty as far as godliness is concerned. That is because I am going to the Father, where you can't see me anymore. [11]The world is guilty as far as judgment is concerned. That is because the devil, the prince of this world, has already been judged.

[12]"I have much more to say to you. It is more than you can handle right now. [13]But when the Spirit of truth comes, he will guide you into all truth. He will not speak on his own. He will speak only what he hears. And he will tell you what is still going to happen.

[14]"He will bring me glory by receiving something from me and showing it to you. [15]Everything that belongs to the Father is mine. That is why I said the Holy Spirit will receive something from me and show it to you.

[16]"In a little while, you will no longer see me. Then after a little while, you will see me."

The Disciples' Sadness Will Turn Into Joy

[17]Some of his disciples spoke to one another. They said, "What does he mean by saying, 'In a little while, you will no longer

see me. Then after a little while, you will see me'? And what does he mean by saying, 'I am going to the Father'?" [18]They kept asking, "What does he mean by 'a little while'? We don't understand what he is saying."

[19]Jesus saw that they wanted to ask him about those things. So he said to them, "Are you asking one another what I meant? Didn't you understand when I said, 'In a little while, you will no longer see me. Then after a little while, you will see me'? [20]What I'm about to tell you is true. You will cry and be full of sorrow while the world is full of joy. You will be sad, but your sadness will turn into joy.

[21]"A woman giving birth to a baby has pain. This is because her time to give birth has come. But when her baby is born, she forgets the pain. She forgets because she is so happy that a baby has been born into the world.

[22]"That's the way it is with you. Now it's your time to be sad. But I will see you again. Then you will be full of joy. And no one will take your joy away.

[23]"When that day comes, you will no longer ask me for anything. What I'm about to tell you is true. My Father will give you anything you ask for in my name. [24]Until now you have not asked for anything in my name. Ask, and you will receive what you ask for. Then your joy will be complete.

[25]"I have not been speaking to you plainly. But a time is coming when I will speak clearly. Then I will tell you plainly about my Father. [26]When that day comes, you will ask for things in my name. I am not saying I will ask the Father instead of you asking him. [27]No, the Father himself loves you because you have loved me. He also loves you because you have believed that I came from God.

[28]"I came from the Father and entered the world. Now I am leaving the world and going back to the Father."

[29]Then Jesus' disciples said, "Now you are speaking plainly. You are using examples that are clear. [30]Now we can see that you know everything. You don't even need anyone to ask you questions. This makes us believe that you came from God."

[31]"At last you believe!" Jesus said. [32]"But a

The Work of the HOLY SPIRIT

Convict the World of Its Sin

Warn of Coming Judgment

Reveal God's Godliness

Godliness

Sin

Judgment

The World's Sin is Unbelief
John 16:8

time is coming when you will be scattered and go to your own homes. In fact, that time is already here. You will leave me all alone. But I am not really alone. My Father is with me.

[33]"I have told you these things, so that you can have peace because of me. In this world you will have trouble. But cheer up! I have won the battle over the world."

Open Book Quiz - The Land of Jesus

Read the letters from top to bottom and complete the answer below.

1	___	Jesus Begins to Preach	Mt	4
2	___	Women at the Well	Jn.	4
3	___	Zacchaeus Converted	Lk.	19
4	___	Lazarus Raised	Jn.	11
5	_L_	Evil Spirit Cast Out	Mk.	1
6	___	Water to Wine	Jn.	2
7	___	Jesus is Tempted	Lk.	4
8	___	Walks on Water	Mt.	14
9	___	Nicodemus at Night	Jn.	3
10	___	Safety for Jesus	Mt.	2
11	___	Bartimaeus Healed	Mk.	10
12	___	Judas Betrays Jesus	Lk.	22
13	___	Mary Anoints Jesus	Jn.	12
14	_S_	Jesus Clears Temple	Lk.	19
15	___	"A Prophet w/o Honor"	Mk.	6
16	___	Resurrection	Mt.	28

Select the best answer from the right column which matches items 1-16 in the left column. Some letters are used more than once.

A - Cana
D - Sea of Galilee
E - Bethany
F - Jericho
I - Sychar
J - Mt. of Olives
L - Capernaum
M - Bethlehem
N - Desert
O - Egypt
P - Jordan River
S - Jerusalem
U - Nazareth

Self-score
15 - 16	Ace Geographer
13 - 14	Be our Guide
10 - 12	Follow the Guide
5 - 9	Get a Compass
1 - 4	Take a Map Class

Answer: ___ ___ ___ ___ • L ___ ___ ___ ___

___ ___ • ___ ___ S ___ ___

"Come and Walk With Jesus"

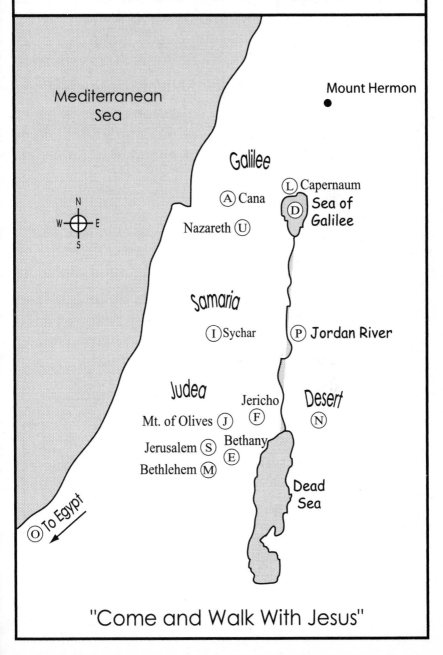

Try Prayer

When you need help
John 5:7, 8

When Others Oppose You
John 9:24-34

When Troubled
John 14:1

To Be Fruitful
John 15:4

When You Fail God
John 21:15-17

Need Security
John 10:28

For Peace of Mind
John 14:27

For Assurance
John 5:24

When the World Hates You
John 17:15

Jesus Prays for Himself

17 After Jesus said this, he looked toward heaven and prayed. He said,

"Father, the time has come. Bring glory to your Son. Then your Son will bring glory to you. ²You gave him authority over all people. He gives eternal life to all those you have given him.

³"And what is eternal life? It is knowing you, the only true God, and Jesus Christ, whom you have sent. ⁴I have brought you glory on earth. I have finished the work you gave me to do. ⁵So now, Father, give glory to me in heaven where your throne is. Give me the glory I had with you before the world began.

Jesus Prays for His Disciples

⁶"I have shown you to the disciples you gave me out of the world. They were yours. You gave them to me. And they have obeyed your word. ⁷Now they know that everything you have given me comes from you. ⁸I gave them the words you gave me. And they accepted them. They knew for certain that I came from you. They believed that you sent me.

⁹"I pray for them. I am not praying for the world. I am praying for those you have given me, because they are yours. ¹⁰All I have is yours, and all you have is mine. Glory has come to me because of my disciples.

¹¹"I will not remain in the world any longer. But they are still in the world, and I am coming to you. Holy Father, keep them safe by the power of your name. It is the name you gave me. Keep them safe so they can be one, just as you and I are one.

¹²"While I was with them, I guarded them. I kept them safe through the name you gave me. None of them has been lost, except the one who was sentenced to be destroyed. It happened so that Scripture would come true.

¹³"I am coming to you now. But I say these things while I am still in the

world. I say them so that those you gave me can have all my joy inside them. ¹⁴I have given them your word. The world has hated them. This is because they are not part of the world any more than I am. ¹⁵I do not pray that you will take them out of the world. I pray that you will keep them safe from the evil one. ¹⁶"They do not belong to the world, just as I do not belong to it. ¹⁷Use the truth to make them holy. Your word is truth. ¹⁸You sent me into the world. In the same way, I have sent them into the world. ¹⁹I make myself holy for them so that they too can be made holy in a true sense.

Jesus Prays for All Believers

²⁰"I do not pray only for them. I pray also for those who will believe in me because of their message. ²¹Father, I pray that all of them will be one, just as you are in me and I am in you. I want them also to be in us. Then the world will believe that you have sent me. ²²"I have given them the glory you gave me. I did this so they would be one, just as we are one. ²³I will be in them, just as you are in me. I want them to be brought together perfectly as one. This will let the world know that you sent me. It will also show the world that you have loved those you gave me, just as you have loved me. ²⁴"Father, I want those you have given me to be with me where I am. I want them to see my glory, the glory you have given me. You gave it to me because you loved me before the world was created.

²⁵"Father, you are holy. The world does not know you, but I know you. Those you have given me know you have sent me. ²⁶I have shown you to them. And I will continue to show you to them. Then the love you have for me will be in them. I myself will be in them."

Jesus Is Arrested

18 When Jesus had finished praying, he left with his disciples. They crossed the Kidron Valley. On the other side there was a grove of olive trees. Jesus and his disciples went into it.

²Judas knew the place. He was going to hand Jesus over to his enemies. Jesus had often met in that place with his disciples. ³So Judas came to the grove. He was guiding a group of soldiers and some officials. The chief priests and the Pharisees had sent them. They were carrying torches, lanterns and weapons.

⁴Jesus knew everything that was going to happen to him. So he went out and asked them, "Who is it that you want?"

⁵"Jesus of Nazareth," they replied.

"I am he," Jesus said.

Judas, who was going to hand Jesus over, was standing there with them. ⁶When Jesus said, "I am he," they moved back. Then they fell to the ground.

⁷He asked them again, "Who is it that you want?"

They said, "Jesus of Nazareth."

⁸"I told you I am he," Jesus answered. "If you are looking for me, then let these men go." ⁹This happened so that the words Jesus had spoken would come true. He had said, "I have not lost anyone God has given me." *(John 6:39)*

¹⁰Simon Peter had a sword and pulled it out. He struck the high priest's servant and cut off his right ear. The servant's name was Malchus.

¹¹Jesus commanded Peter, "Put your sword away! Shouldn't I drink the cup of suffering the Father has given me?"

Jesus Is Taken to Annas

¹²Then the group of soldiers, their leader and the Jewish officials arrested Jesus. They tied him up ¹³and brought him first to Annas. He was the father-in-law of Caiaphas, the high priest at that time. ¹⁴Caiaphas had advised the Jews that it would be good if one man died for the people.

Peter Says He Is Not Jesus' Disciple

¹⁵Simon Peter and another disciple were following Jesus. The high priest knew the other disciple. So that disciple went with Jesus into the high priest's courtyard. ¹⁶But Peter had to wait outside by the door.

The other disciple came back. He was the one the high priest knew. He spoke to the woman who was on duty there. Then he brought Peter in.

[17] The woman at the door spoke to Peter. "You are not one of Jesus' disciples, are you?" she asked him.

"I am not," he replied.

[18] It was cold. The servants and officials stood around a fire. They had made it to keep warm. Peter was also standing with them. He was warming himself.

The High Priest Questions Jesus

[19] Meanwhile, the high priest questioned Jesus. He asked him about his disciples and his teaching.

[20] "I have spoken openly to the world," Jesus replied. "I always taught in synagogues or at the temple, where all the Jews come together. I didn't say anything in secret. [21] Why question me? Ask the people who heard me. They certainly know what I said."

[22] When Jesus said that, one of the officials nearby hit him in the face. "Is this any way to answer the high priest?" he asked.

[23] "Have I said something wrong?" Jesus replied. "If I have, give witness to it. But if I spoke the truth, why did you hit me?"

[24] While Jesus was still tied up, Annas sent him to Caiaphas, the high priest.

Peter Again Says He Is Not Jesus' Disciple

[25] Simon Peter stood there. He was warming himself. Then someone asked him, "You aren't one of Jesus' disciples, are you?"

He said, "I am not."

[26] One of the high priest's servants was a relative of the man whose ear Peter had cut off. He said to Peter, "Didn't I see you with Jesus in the olive grove?"

[27] Again Peter said no.

At that very moment a rooster began to crow.

Jesus Is Brought to Pilate

[28] Then the Jews led Jesus from Caiaphas to the palace of the Roman governor. By now it was early morning. The Jews did not want to be made "unclean." They wanted to be able to eat the Passover meal. So they did not enter the palace.

[29] Pilate came out to them. He asked, "What charges are you bringing against this man?"

[30] "He has committed crimes," they replied. "If he hadn't, we would not have handed him over to you."

[31] Pilate said, "Take him yourselves. Judge him by your own law."

"But we don't have the right to put anyone to death," the Jews complained. [32] This happened so that the words Jesus had spoken about how he was going to die would come true.

[33] Then Pilate went back inside the palace. He ordered Jesus to be brought to him. Pilate asked him, "Are you the king of the Jews?"

[34] "Is that your own idea?" Jesus asked. "Or did others talk to you about me?"

[35] "Am I a Jew?" Pilate replied. "It was your people and your chief priests who handed you over to me. What have you done?"

[36] Jesus said, "My kingdom is not part of this world. If it were, those who serve me would fight. They would try to keep the Jews from arresting me. My kingdom is from another place."

[37] "So you are a king, then!" said Pilate.

Jesus answered, "You are right to say I am a king. In fact, that's the reason I was born. I came into the world to give witness to the truth. Everyone who is on the side of truth listens to me."

[38] "What is truth?" Pilate asked.

Then Pilate went out again to the Jews. He said, "I find no basis for any charge against him. [39] But it is your practice for me to set one prisoner free for you at Passover time. Do you want me to set 'the king of the Jews' free?"

[40] They shouted back, "No! Not him! Give us Barabbas!" Barabbas had taken part in an armed struggle against the country's rulers.

Jesus Is Sentenced to Be Crucified

19 Then Pilate took Jesus and had him whipped. [2] The soldiers twisted thorns together to make a crown. They put it on Jesus' head. Then they put a purple robe on him. [3] They went up to him again and again. They kept saying, "We honor you, king of the Jews!" And they hit him in the face.

"... Told You So ..."

The Old Testament was written hundreds of years before the New Testament. There are over 250 predictions and prophecies written by different men who wrote of the things to come. Most of these future events centered on the coming Messiah - Jesus Christ - and the End Times. Here in John chapter 19 are examples of events that occurred just as they had been foretold.

New Testament	Old Testament
23When the soldiers had <u>crucified</u> Jesus, They <u>divided his clothes</u> among the four of them. They also took his robe, but it was seamless, woven in one piece from the top. 24So they said, "Let's not tear it but throw dice to see who gets it." This fulfilled the Scripture that says, "They <u>divided my clothes</u> among themselves and <u>threw dice</u> for my robe." 25So that is what they did. 31The Jewish leaders didn't want the victims hanging there the next day, which was the Sabbath (and a very special Sabbath at that, because it was Passover), so they asked Pilate to hasten their deaths by ordering that their legs be broken. Then their bodies could be taken down. 32So soldiers came and broke the legs of the two men crucified with Jesus. 33But when they came to Jesus, they saw that he was dead already, so <u>they didn't break his legs</u>. 34One of the soldiers, however, <u>pierced his side</u> with a spear, and blood and water flowed out. 35This report is from an eyewitness giving an accurate account; it is presented so that you also can believe. 36These things happened in fulfillment of the Scriptures that say, "Not one of his bones will be broken," 37and "They will <u>look on him who they pierced</u>." <div align="right">John 19:23-25, 31-37 (NLT)</div>	*"They have pierced my hands and feet." (crucifixion)* *-- Psalm 22:16 (NLT)* *"They divide my clothes among themselves and throw dice for my garments." -- Psalm 22:18 (NLT)* *"Not one of his bones will be broken!" -- Psalm 34:20 (NLT) (These Psalms were written 600 years before the coming of Jesus)* *"They will look upon me whom they have pierced." -- Zechariah 12:10 (NLT) (Written 500 years before the coming of Jesus)*

[4]Once more Pilate came out. He said to the Jews, "Look, I am bringing Jesus out to you. I want to let you know that I find no basis for a charge against him."

[5]Jesus came out wearing the crown of thorns and the purple robe. Then Pilate said to them, "Here is the man!"

[6]As soon as the chief priests and their officials saw him, they shouted, "Crucify him! Crucify him!"

But Pilate answered, "You take him and crucify him. I myself find no basis for a charge against him."

[7]The Jews replied, "We have a law. That law says he must die. He claimed to be the Son of God."

[8]When Pilate heard that, he was even more afraid. [9]He went back inside the palace. "Where do you come from?" he asked Jesus.

But Jesus did not answer him.

[10]"Do you refuse to speak to me?" Pilate said. "Don't you understand? I have the power to set you free or to nail you to a cross."

[11]Jesus answered, "You were given power from heaven. If you weren't, you would have no power over me. So the one who handed me over to you is guilty of a greater sin."

[12]From then on, Pilate tried to set Jesus free. But the Jews kept shouting, "If you let this man go, you are not Caesar's friend! Anyone who claims to be a king is against Caesar!"

[13]When Pilate heard that, he brought Jesus out. Pilate sat down on the judge's seat. It was at a place called The Stone Walkway. In the Aramaic language it was called Gabbatha. [14]It was about noon on Preparation Day in Passover Week.

"Here is your king," Pilate said to the Jews.

[15]But they shouted, "Kill him! Kill him! Crucify him!"

"Should I crucify your king?" Pilate asked.

"We have no king but Caesar," the chief priests answered.

[16]Finally, Pilate handed Jesus over to them to be nailed to a cross.

Jesus Is Nailed to a Cross

So the soldiers took charge of Jesus. [17]He had to carry his own cross. He went out to a place called The Skull. In the Aramaic language it was called Golgotha. [18]There they nailed Jesus to the cross. Two other men were crucified with him. One was on each side of him. Jesus was in the middle.

[19]Pilate had a notice prepared. It was fastened to the cross. It read, JESUS OF NAZARETH, THE KING OF THE JEWS. [20]Many of the Jews read the sign. The place where Jesus was crucified was near the city. The sign was written in the Aramaic, Latin and Greek languages.

[21]The chief priests of the Jews argued with Pilate. They said, "Do not write 'The King of the Jews.' Write that this man claimed to be king of the Jews."

[22]Pilate answered, "I have written what I have written."

[23]When the soldiers crucified Jesus, they took his clothes. They divided them into four parts. Each soldier got one part. Jesus' long, inner robe was left. It did not have any seams. It was made out of one piece of cloth from top to bottom.

[24]"Let's not tear it," they said to one another. "Let's cast lots to see who will get it."

This happened so that Scripture would come true. It says,

"They divided up my clothes among them.
They cast lots for what I was wearing."   *(Psalm 22:18)*

So that is what the soldiers did.

[25]Jesus' mother stood near his cross. So did his mother's sister, Mary the wife of Clopas, and Mary Magdalene. [26]Jesus saw his mother there. He also saw the disciple he loved standing nearby. Jesus said to his mother, "Dear woman, here is your son." [27]He said to the disciple, "Here is your mother." From that time on, the disciple took her into his home.

Jesus Dies

[28]Later Jesus said, "I am thirsty." He knew that everything was now finished. He knew that what Scripture said must come true. [29]A jar of wine vinegar was there. So they soaked a sponge in it. They put the sponge on a stem of the hyssop plant. Then they

lifted it up to Jesus' lips.

[30]After Jesus drank he said, "It is finished." Then he bowed his head and died.

[31]It was Preparation Day. The next day would be a special Sabbath. The Jews did not want the bodies left on the crosses during the Sabbath. So they asked Pilate to have the legs broken and the bodies taken down. [32]The soldiers came and broke the legs of the first man who had been crucified with Jesus. Then they broke the legs of the other man.

[33]But when they came to Jesus, they saw that he was already dead. So they did not break his legs. [34]Instead, one of the soldiers stuck his spear into Jesus' side. Right away, blood and water flowed out. [35]The man who saw it has given witness. And his witness is true. He knows that he tells the truth. He gives witness so that you also can believe.

[36]These things happened in order that Scripture would come true. It says, "Not one of his bones will be broken." *(Exodus 12:46; Numbers 9:12; Psalm 34:20)* [37]Scripture also says, "They will look to the one they have pierced." *(Zechariah 12:10)*

Jesus Is Buried

[38]Later Joseph asked Pilate for Jesus' body. Joseph was from the town of Arimathea. He was a follower of Jesus. But he followed Jesus secretly because he was afraid of the Jews. After Pilate gave him permission, Joseph came and took the body away.

[39]Nicodemus went with Joseph. He was the man who had earlier visited Jesus at night. Nicodemus brought some mixed spices, about 75 pounds. [40]The two men took Jesus' body. They wrapped it in strips of linen cloth, along with the spices. That was the way the Jews buried people's bodies.

[41]At the place where Jesus was crucified, there was a garden. A new tomb was there. No one had ever been put in it before. [42]That day was the Jewish Preparation Day, and the tomb was nearby. So they placed Jesus there.

The Tomb Is Empty

20 Early on the first day of the week, Mary Magdalene went to the tomb. It was still dark. She saw that the stone had

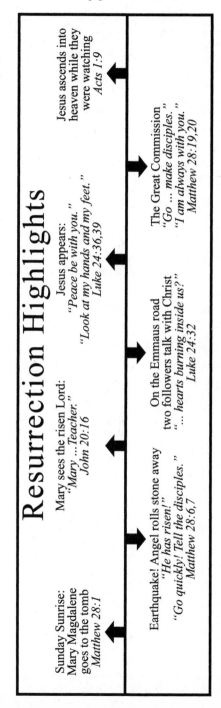

Resurrection Highlights

Jesus ascends into heaven while they were watching
Acts 1:9

The Great Commission
"Go ... make disciples."
"I am always with you."
Matthew 28:19,20

Jesus appears:
"Peace be with you."
"Look at my hands and my feet."
Luke 24:36,39

On the Emmaus road two followers talk with Christ
"... hearts burning inside us?"
Luke 24:32

Mary sees the risen Lord:
"Mary ...Teacher."
John 20:16

Earthquake! Angel rolls stone away
"He has risen!"
"Go quickly! Tell the disciples."
Matthew 28:6,7

Sunday Sunrise:
Mary Magdalene goes to the tomb
Matthew 28:1

been moved away from the entrance. [2]So she ran to Simon Peter and another disciple, the one Jesus loved. She said, "They have taken the Lord out of the tomb! We don't know where they have put him!"

[3]So Peter and the other disciple started out for the tomb. [4]Both of them were running. The other disciple ran faster than Peter. He reached the tomb first. [5]He bent over and looked in at the strips of linen lying there. But he did not go in.

[6]Then Simon Peter, who was behind him, arrived. He went into the tomb. He saw the strips of linen lying there. [7]He also saw the burial cloth that had been around Jesus' head. The cloth was folded up by itself. It was separate from the linen.

[8]The disciple who had reached the tomb first also went inside. He saw and believed. [9]They still did not understand from Scripture that Jesus had to rise from the dead.

Jesus Appears to Mary Magdalene

[10]Then the disciples went back to their homes. [11]But Mary stood outside the tomb crying. As she cried, she bent over to look into the tomb. [12]She saw two angels dressed in white. They were seated where Jesus' body had been. One of them was where Jesus' head had been laid. The other sat where his feet had been placed.

[13]They asked her, "Woman, why are you crying?"

"They have taken my Lord away," she said. "I don't know where they have put him."

[14]Then she turned around and saw Jesus standing there. But she didn't realize that it was Jesus.

[15]"Woman," he said, "why are you crying? Who are you looking for?"

She thought he was the gardener. So she said, "Sir, did you carry him away? Tell me where you put him. Then I will go and get him."

[16]Jesus said to her, "Mary."

She turned toward him. Then she cried out in the Aramaic language, "Rabboni!" Rabboni means Teacher.

[17]Jesus said, "Do not hold on to me. I have not yet returned to the Father. Instead, go to those who believe in me. Tell them, 'I am returning to my Father and your Father, to my God and your God.' "

[18]Mary Magdalene went to the disciples with the news. She said, "I have seen the Lord!" And she told them that he had said these things to her.

Jesus Appears to His Disciples

[19]On the evening of that first day of the week, the disciples were together. They had locked the doors because they were afraid of the Jews.

Jesus came in and stood among them. He said, "May peace be with you!" [20]Then he showed them his hands and his side. The disciples were very happy when they saw the Lord.

[21]Again Jesus said, "May peace be with you! The Father has sent me. So now I am sending you." [22]He then breathed on them. He said, "Receive the Holy Spirit. [23]If you forgive anyone's sins, they are forgiven. If you do not forgive them, they are not forgiven."

Jesus Appears to Thomas

[24]Thomas was one of the Twelve. He was called Didymus. He was not with the other disciples when Jesus came. [25]So they told him, "We have seen the Lord!"

But he said to them, "First I must see the nail marks in his hands. I must put my finger where the nails were. I must put my hand into his side. Only then will I believe what you say."

[26]A week later, Jesus' disciples were in the house again. Thomas was with them. Even though the doors were locked, Jesus came in and stood among them.

He said, "May peace be with you!" [27]Then he said to Thomas, "Put your finger here. See my hands. Reach out your hand and put it into my side. Stop doubting and believe."

[28]Thomas said to him, "My Lord and my God!"

[29]Then Jesus told him, "Because you have seen me, you have believed. Blessed are those who have not seen me but still have believed."

[30]Jesus did many other miraculous signs in front of his disciples. They are not written down in this book. [31]But these are written down so that you may believe that Jesus is the Christ, the Son of God. If you believe this, you will have life because you belong to him.

Gospel of John
Who said ...

Across

1. "What will happen to Him?"   ch. 21
2. "I'm not good enough"   ch. 1
3. "No one ever spoke ... "   ch. 8
4. To sight a weapon   ---
5. An English drink   ---
6. Head to lean forward   ---
7. "Come and _____"   ch. 1
8. Next to, near   ---
9. Tall shade tree   ---
10. "He has gone crazy"   ch. 10
11. A choice of two   ---
12. "There is a bad smell"   ch. 11
13. "No more wine"   ch. 2

Down

1. "What is truth?"   ch. 18
2. Round candies   ---
3. "we would see Jesus"   ch. 12
4. "I must see the nail marks"   ch. 20
5. What Peter cut off   ch. 18
6. "He fooled you too"   ch. 7
7. Woman caught in adultery   ch. 8
8. "Back inside my mother?"   ch. 3

Jesus Does a Miracle at the Sea

21 After this, Jesus appeared to his disciples again. It was by the Sea of Galilee. Here is what happened.

²Simon Peter and Thomas, who was called Didymus, were there together. Nathanael from Cana in Galilee and the sons of Zebedee were with them. So were two other disciples.

³"I'm going out to fish," Simon Peter told them. They said, "We'll go with you." So they went out and got into the boat. That night they didn't catch anything.

⁴Early in the morning, Jesus stood on the shore. But the disciples did not realize that it was Jesus.

⁵He called out to them, "Friends, don't you have any fish?"

"No," they answered.

⁶He said, "Throw your net on the right side of the boat. There you will find some fish."

When they did, they could not pull the net into the boat. There were too many fish in it.

⁷Then the disciple Jesus loved said to Simon Peter, "It is the Lord!"

As soon as Peter heard that, he put his coat on. He had taken it off earlier. Then he jumped into the water.

⁸The other disciples followed in the boat. They were towing the net full of fish. The shore was only about 100 yards away. ⁹When they landed, they saw a fire of burning coals. There were fish on it. There was also some bread.

¹⁰Jesus said to them, "Bring some of the fish you have just caught."

¹¹Simon Peter climbed into the boat. He dragged the net to shore. It was full of large fish. There were 153 of them. But even with that many fish the net was not torn.

¹²Jesus said to them, "Come and have breakfast."

None of the disciples dared to ask him, "Who are you?" They knew it was the Lord.

¹³Jesus came, took the bread and gave it to them. He did the same thing with the fish.

¹⁴This was the third time Jesus appeared to his disciples after he was raised from the dead.

Jesus Takes Peter Back

¹⁵When Jesus and the disciples had finished eating, Jesus spoke to Simon Peter. He asked, "Simon, son of John, do you really love me more than these others do?"

"Yes, Lord," he answered. "You know that I love you."

Jesus said, "Feed my lambs."

¹⁶Again Jesus asked, "Simon, son of John, do you really love me?"

He answered, "Yes, Lord. You know that I love you."

Jesus said, "Take care of my sheep."

¹⁷Jesus spoke to him a third time. He asked, "Simon, son of John, do you love me?"

Peter felt bad because Jesus asked him the third time, "Do you love me?" He answered, "Lord, you know all things. You know that I love you."

Jesus said, "Feed my sheep. ¹⁸What I'm about to tell you is true. When you were younger, you dressed yourself. You went wherever you wanted to go. But when you are old, you will stretch out your hands. Someone else will dress you. Someone else will lead you where you do not want to go."

¹⁹Jesus said this to point out how Peter would die. His death would bring glory to God.

Then Jesus said to him, "Follow me!"

²⁰Peter turned around. He saw that the disciple Jesus loved was following them. He was the one who had leaned back against Jesus at the supper. He had said, "Lord, who is going to hand you over to your enemies?" ²¹When Peter saw that disciple, he asked, "Lord, what will happen to him?"

²²Jesus answered, "Suppose I want him to remain alive until I return. What does that matter to you? You must follow me."

²³Because of what Jesus said, a false report spread among the believers. The story was told that the disciple Jesus loved wouldn't die. But Jesus did not say he would not die. He only said, "Suppose I want him to remain alive until I return. What does that matter to you?"

²⁴This is the disciple who gives witness to these things. He also wrote them down. We know that his witness is true.

²⁵Jesus also did many other things. What if every one of them were written down? I suppose that even the whole world would not have room for the books that would be written.

ACTS

- *Written by Dr. Luke, who also wrote the Gospel of Luke*
- *Acts records the beginning and growth of the early church*
- *Peter is the central person in the first part of the book*
- *Paul's travels are central in the second part of the book*
- *Begins in Jerusalem, ends in Rome*
- *Theme: "The work of the Holy Spirit"*

Jesus Is Taken Up Into Heaven

1 Theophilus, I wrote about Jesus in my earlier book. I wrote about all he did and taught ²until the day he was taken up to heaven. Before Jesus left, he gave orders to the apostles he had chosen. He did this through the Holy Spirit. ³After his suffering and death, he appeared to them. In many ways he proved that he was alive. He appeared to them over a period of 40 days. During that time he spoke about God's kingdom.

⁴One day Jesus was eating with them. He gave them a command. "Do not leave Jerusalem," he said. "Wait for the gift my Father promised. You have heard me talk about it. ⁵John baptized with water. But in a few days you will be baptized with the Holy Spirit."

⁶When the apostles met together, they asked Jesus a question. "Lord," they said, "are you going to give the kingdom back to Israel now?"

⁷He said to them, "You should not be concerned about times or dates. The Father has set them by his own authority. ⁸But you will receive power when the Holy Spirit comes on you. Then you will be my witnesses in Jerusalem. You will be my witnesses in all Judea and Samaria. And you will be my witnesses from one end of the earth to the other."

⁹After Jesus said this, he was taken up to heaven. They watched until a cloud hid him from their sight.

¹⁰While he was going up, they kept on looking at the sky. Suddenly two men dressed in white clothing stood beside them. ¹¹"Men of Galilee," they said, "why do you stand here looking at the sky? Jesus has been taken away from you into heaven. But he will come back in the same way you saw him go."

Matthias Is Chosen to Take the Place of Judas

¹²The apostles returned to Jerusalem from the Mount of Olives. It is almost a mile from the city. ¹³When they arrived, they went upstairs to the room where they were staying. Peter, John, James and Andrew were there. Philip, Thomas, Bartholomew and Matthew were there too. So were James, son of Alphaeus, Simon the Zealot, and Judas, son of James. ¹⁴They all came together regularly to pray. The women joined them too. So did Jesus' mother Mary and his brothers.

¹⁵In those days Peter stood up among the believers. About 120 of them were there. ¹⁶Peter said, "Brothers, a long time ago the Holy Spirit spoke through David's mouth about Judas. What he said in Scripture had to come true. Judas was the guide for the men who arrested Jesus. ¹⁷But Judas was one of us. He shared with us in our work for God."

¹⁸Judas bought a field with the reward he got for the evil thing he had done. He fell down headfirst in the field. His body burst open. All his insides spilled out. ¹⁹Everyone in Jerusalem heard about this. So they called that field Akeldama. In their language, Akeldama means The Field of Blood.

²⁰Peter said, "Here is what is written in the book of Psalms. It says,

" 'May his home be deserted.
May no one live in it.' *(Psalm 69:25)*

The Psalms also say,

" 'Let someone else take his place as
leader.' *(Psalm 109:8)*

²¹So we need to choose someone to take his place. It will have to be a man who was with us the whole time the Lord Jesus lived among us. ²²That time began when John was baptizing. It ended when Jesus was taken up from us. The one we choose must join us in giving witness that Jesus rose from the dead."

²³So they suggested two men. One was Joseph, who was called Barsabbas. He was also called Justus. The other man was Matthias. ²⁴Then they prayed. "Lord," they said, "you know everyone's heart. Show us which of these two you have chosen. ²⁵Show us who should take the place of Judas as an apostle. He gave up being an apostle to go where he belongs." ²⁶Then they cast lots. Matthias was chosen. So he was added to the 11 apostles.

The Holy Spirit Comes at Pentecost

2 The day of Pentecost came. The believers all gathered in one place. ²Suddenly a sound came from heaven. It was like a strong wind blowing. It filled the whole house where they were sitting. ³They saw something that looked like tongues of fire. The flames separated and settled on each of them. ⁴All of them were filled with the Holy Spirit. They began to speak in languages they had not known before. The Spirit gave them the ability to do this.

⁵Godly Jews from every country in the world were staying in Jerusalem. ⁶A crowd came together when they heard the sound. They were bewildered because they each heard the believers speaking in their own language. ⁷The crowd was really amazed. They asked, "Aren't all these people from Galilee? ⁸Why, then, do we each hear them speaking in our own native language? ⁹We are Parthians, Medes and Elamites. We live in Mesopotamia, Judea and Cappadocia. We are from Pontus, Asia, ¹⁰Phrygia and Pamphylia. Others of us are from Egypt and the parts of Libya near Cyrene. Still others are visitors from Rome. ¹¹Some of the visitors are Jews. Others have accepted the Jewish faith. Also, Cretans and Arabs are here. We hear all these people speaking about God's wonders in our own languages!" ¹²They were amazed and bewildered. They asked one another, "What does this mean?"

¹³But some people in the crowd made fun of the believers. "They've had too much wine!" they said.

Peter Speaks to the Crowd

¹⁴Then Peter stood up with the Eleven. In a loud voice he spoke to the crowd. "My Jewish friends," he said, "let me explain this to you. All of you who live in Jerusalem, listen carefully to what I say. ¹⁵You think these people are drunk. But they aren't. It's only nine o'clock in the morning! ¹⁶No, here is what the prophet Joel meant. ¹⁷He said,

the **Holy Spirit**
gives power to believers

Power Up!

Acts 1:8

" 'In the last days, God says,
   I will pour out my Holy Spirit on all
      people.
Your sons and daughters will prophesy.
   Your young men will see visions.
   Your old men will have dreams.
¹⁸ In those days I will pour out my Spirit
      even on those who serve me, both men
      and women.
   When I do, they will prophesy.
¹⁹ I will show wonders in the heavens
      above.
   I will show miraculous signs on the
      earth below.
   There will be blood and fire and
      clouds of smoke.
²⁰ The sun will become dark.
   The moon will turn red like blood.
   This will happen before the coming of
      the great and glorious day of the
      Lord.
²¹ Everyone who calls
   on the name of the Lord will be saved.'
                              (Joel 2:28–32)

²²"Men of Israel, listen to this! Jesus of Nazareth was a man who had God's approval. God did miracles, wonders and signs among you through Jesus. You yourselves know this. ²³Long ago God planned that Jesus would be handed over to you. With the help of evil people, you put Jesus to death. You nailed him to the cross. ²⁴But God raised him from the dead. He set him free from the suffering of death. It wasn't possible for death to keep its hold on Jesus. ²⁵David spoke about him. He said,

" 'I know that the Lord is always with
      me.
   He is at my right hand.
   I will always be secure.
²⁶ So my heart is glad. Joy is on my tongue.
   My body also will be full of hope.
²⁷ You will not leave me in the grave.
   You will not let your Holy One rot
      away.
²⁸ You always show me the path that leads
      to life.
   You will fill me with joy when I am
      with you.'   *(Psalm 16:8–11)*

²⁹"Brothers, you can be sure that King David died. He was buried. His tomb is still here today. ³⁰But David was a prophet. He knew that God had made a promise to him. He had taken an oath that someone in David's family line would be king after him. ³¹David saw what was ahead. So he spoke about the Christ rising from the dead. He said that the Christ would not be left in the grave. His body wouldn't rot in the ground. ³²God has raised this same Jesus back to life. We are all witnesses of this. ³³Jesus has been given a place of honor at the right hand of God. He has received the Holy Spirit from the Father. This is what God had promised. It is Jesus who has poured out what you now see and hear. ³⁴David did not go up to heaven. But he said,

" 'The Lord said to my Lord,
   "Sit at my right hand.
³⁵ I will put your enemies
      under your control." '   *(Psalm 110:1)*

³⁶"So be sure of this, all you people of Israel. You nailed Jesus to the cross. But God has made him both Lord and Christ."

³⁷When the people heard this, their hearts were filled with shame. They said to Peter and the other apostles, "Brothers, what should we do?"

³⁸Peter replied, "All of you must turn away from your sins and be baptized in the name of Jesus Christ. Then your sins will be forgiven. You will receive the gift of the Holy Spirit. ³⁹The promise is for you and your children. It is also for all who are far away. It is for all whom the Lord our God will choose."

⁴⁰Peter said many other things to warn them. He begged them, "Save yourselves from these evil people." ⁴¹Those who accepted his message were baptized. About 3,000 people joined the believers that day.

The Believers Share Life Together

⁴²The believers studied what the apostles taught. They shared life together. They broke bread and ate together. And they prayed. ⁴³Everyone felt that God was near. The apostles did many wonders and miraculous signs. ⁴⁴All the believers were together. They shared everything they had.

[45]They sold what they owned. They gave each other everything they needed. [46]Every day they met together in the temple courtyard. In their homes they broke bread and ate together. Their hearts were glad and honest and true. [47]They praised God. They were respected by all the people. Every day the Lord added to their group those who were being saved.

Peter Heals the Disabled Beggar

3 One day Peter and John were going up to the temple. It was three o'clock in the afternoon. It was the time for prayer. [2]A man unable to walk was being carried to the temple gate called Beautiful. He had been that way since he was born. Every day someone put him near the gate. There he would beg from people going into the temple courtyards.

[3]He saw that Peter and John were about to enter. So he asked them for money. [4]Peter looked straight at him, and so did John. Then Peter said, "Look at us!" [5]So the man watched them closely. He expected to get something from them.

[6]Peter said, "I don't have any silver or gold. But I'll give you what I have. In the name of Jesus Christ of Nazareth, get up and walk." [7]Then Peter took him by the right hand and helped him up. At once the man's feet and ankles became strong. [8]He jumped to his feet and began to walk. He went with Peter and John into the temple courtyards. He walked and jumped and praised God. [9]All the people saw him walking and praising God. [10]They recognized him as the same man who used to sit and beg at the temple gate called Beautiful. They were filled with wonder. They were amazed at what had happened to him.

GOD CALLS US TO FOLLOW AND HE GUIDES OUR STEPS

Peter Speaks to the Jews

[11]The beggar was holding on to Peter and John. All the people were amazed. They came running to them at Solomon's Porch. [12]When Peter saw this, he said, "Men of Israel, why does this surprise you? Why do you stare at us? We haven't made this man walk by our own power or godliness. [13]The God of our fathers, Abraham, Isaac and Jacob, has done this. He has brought glory to Jesus, who serves him. But you handed Jesus over to be killed. Pilate had decided to let him go. But you spoke against Jesus when he was in Pilate's court. [14]You spoke against the Holy and Blameless One. You asked for a murderer to be set free instead. [15]You killed the one who gives life. But God raised him from the dead. We are witnesses of this. [16]This man whom you see and know was made strong because of faith in Jesus' name. Faith in Jesus has healed him completely. You can see it with your own eyes.

[17]"My friends, I know you didn't realize what you were doing. Neither did your leaders. [18]But God had given a promise through all the prophets. And this is how he has made his promise come true. He said that his Christ would suffer. [19]So turn away from your sins. Turn to God. Then your sins will be wiped away. The time will come when the Lord will make everything new. [20]He will send the Christ. Jesus has been appointed as the Christ for you. [21]He must remain in heaven until the time when God makes everything new. He promised this long ago through his holy prophets. [22]Moses said, 'The Lord your God will raise up for you a prophet like me. He will be one of your own people. You must listen to everything he tells you. [23]Those who do not listen to him will be completely cut off from their people.' *(Deuteronomy 18:15,18,19)*

[24]"Samuel and all the prophets after him spoke about this. They said these days would come. [25]What the prophets said was meant for you. The covenant God made with your people long ago is yours also. He said to Abraham, 'All nations on earth will be blessed through your children.' *(Genesis 22:18; 26:4)* [26]God raised up Jesus, who serves him. God sent him first to you. He did it to bless you. He wanted to turn each of you from your evil ways."

Peter and John Are Taken to the Sanhedrin

4 Peter and John were speaking to the people. The priests, the captain of the temple guard, and the Sadducees came up to the apostles. [2]They were very upset by what the apostles were teaching the people. The apostles were saying that because Jesus rose from the dead, people can be raised from the dead. [3]So the temple authorities arrested Peter and John. It was already evening, so they put them in prison until the next day. [4]But many who heard the message believed. The number of men who believed grew to about 5,000.

[5]The next day the rulers, the elders and the teachers of the law met in Jerusalem. [6]Annas, the high priest, was there. So were Caiaphas, John, Alexander and others in the high priest's family. [7]They had Peter and John brought to them. They wanted to question them. "By what power did you do this?" they asked. "And through whose name?"

[8]Peter was filled with the Holy Spirit. He said to them, "Rulers and elders of the people! [9]Are you asking us to explain our actions today? Do you want to know why we were kind to a disabled man? Are you asking how he was healed? [10]Then listen to this, you and all the people of Israel! You nailed Jesus Christ of Nazareth to the cross. But God raised him from the dead. It is through Jesus' name that this man stands healed in front of you. [11]Scripture says that Jesus is

" 'the stone you builders did not accept.
But it has become the most important
stone of all.' *(Psalm 118:22)*

[12]You can't be saved by believing in anyone else. God has given us no other name under heaven that will save us."

[13]The leaders saw how bold Peter and John were. They also realized that Peter and John were ordinary men with no training. This surprised the leaders. They real-

ized that these men had been with Jesus. [14]The leaders could see the man who had been healed standing there with them. So there was nothing they could say. [15]They ordered Peter and John to leave the Sanhedrin. Then they talked things over. [16]"What can we do with these men?" they asked. "Everybody in Jerusalem knows they have done an outstanding miracle. We can't say it didn't happen. [17]We have to stop this thing. It must not spread any further among the people. We have to warn these men. They must never speak to anyone in Jesus' name again."

[18]Once again the leaders called in Peter and John. They commanded them not to speak or teach at all in Jesus' name. [19]But Peter and John replied, "Judge for yourselves. Which is right from God's point of view? Should we obey you? Or God? [20]There's nothing else we can do. We have to speak about the things we've seen and heard."

[21]The leaders warned them again. Then they let them go. They couldn't decide how to punish Peter and John. They knew that all the people were praising God for what had happened. [22]The man who had been healed by the miracle was over 40 years old.

The Believers Pray

[23]Peter and John were allowed to leave. They went back to their own people. They reported everything the chief priests and the elders had said to them. [24]When the believers heard this, they raised their voices together in prayer to God. "Lord and King," they said, "you made the heavens, the earth and the sea. You made everything in them. [25]Long ago you spoke by the Holy Spirit through the mouth of our father David, who served you. You said,

" 'Why are the nations angry?
  Why do the people make useless
    plans?
[26]The kings of the earth take their stand
    against the Lord.
  The rulers of the earth gather together
    against his Anointed King.' *(Psalm 2:1,2)*

In the time it takes to count these numbers ...

10 precious souls have passed either into a blissful heaven or a horrible hell.

What are you doing to win souls to Christ?

- Yesterday is gone
- Tomorrow is God's
- Today is mine ...

To live and labor for the Savior and souls

[27]"In fact, Herod and Pontius Pilate met together in this city with those who weren't Jews. They also met with the people of Israel. All of them made plans against your holy servant Jesus. He is the one you anointed. [28]They did what your power and purpose had already decided should happen. [29]Now, Lord, consider the bad things

they say they are going to do. Help us to be very bold when we speak your word. [30]Stretch out your hand to heal. Do miraculous signs and wonders through the name of your holy servant Jesus."

[31]After they prayed, the place where they were meeting was shaken. They were all filled with the Holy Spirit. They were bold when they spoke God's word.

The Believers Share What They Own

[32]All the believers were agreed in heart and mind. They didn't claim that anything they had was their own. They shared everything they owned. [33]With great power the apostles continued their teaching. They gave witness that the Lord Jesus had risen from the dead. And they were greatly blessed by God.

[34]There were no needy persons among them. From time to time, those who owned land or houses sold them. They brought the money from the sales. [35]They put it down at the apostles' feet. It was then given out to anyone who needed it.

[36]Joseph was a Levite from Cyprus. The apostles called him Barnabas. The name Barnabas means Son of Help. [37]Barnabas sold a field he owned. He brought the money from the sale. He put it down at the apostles' feet.

Ananias and Sapphira

5 A man named Ananias and his wife, Sapphira, also sold some land. [2]He kept part of the money for himself. Sapphira knew he had kept it. He brought the rest of it and put it down at the apostles' feet.

[3]Then Peter said, "Ananias, why did you let Satan fill your heart? He made you lie to the Holy Spirit. You have kept some of the money you received for the land. [4]Didn't the land belong to you before it was sold? After it was sold, you could have used the money as you wished. What made you think of doing such a thing? You haven't lied to just anyone. You've lied to God."

[5]When Ananias heard this, he fell down and died. All who heard what had happened were filled with fear. [6]Some young

men came and wrapped up his body. They carried him out and buried him.

[7]About three hours later, the wife of Ananias came in. She didn't know what had happened. [8]Peter asked her, "Tell me. Is this the price you and Ananias sold the land for?"

"Yes," she said. "That's the price."

[9]Peter asked her, "How could you agree to test the Spirit of the Lord? Listen! You can hear the steps of the men who buried your husband. They are at the door. They will carry you out also."

[10]At that very moment she fell down at his feet and died. Then the young men came in. They saw that Sapphira was dead. So they carried her out and buried her beside her husband. [11]The whole church and all who heard about these things were filled with fear.

The Apostles Heal Many People

[12]The apostles did many miraculous signs and wonders among the people. All the believers used to meet together at Solomon's Porch. [13]No outsider dared to join them. But the people thought highly of them. [14]More and more men and women believed in the Lord. They joined the other believers. [15]So people brought those who were sick into the streets. They placed them on beds and mats. They hoped that at least Peter's shadow might fall on some of them as he walked by. [16]Crowds even gathered from the towns around Jerusalem. They brought their sick. They also brought those who were suffering because of evil spirits. All of them were healed.

An Angel Opens the Prison Doors

[17]The high priest and all his companions were Sadducees. They were very jealous of the apostles. [18]So they arrested them and put them in the public prison. [19]But during the night an angel of the Lord came. He opened the prison doors and brought the apostles out. [20]"Go! Stand in the temple courtyard," the angel said. "Tell the people all about this new life."

[21]Early the next day they did as they had been told. They entered the temple court-

WHO ARE YOU GOING TO OBEY?

The WORLD?

Don't preach Jesus!

OR the LORD?

"We must obey God instead of people!"

Peter
(Acts 5:29)

Jesus is my Savior!

yard. There they began to teach the people.

The high priest and his companions arrived. They called the Sanhedrin together. The Sanhedrin was a gathering of all the elders of Israel. They sent for the apostles who were in prison. [22]The officers arrived at the prison. But they didn't find the apostles there. So they went back and reported it. [23]"We found the prison locked up tight," they said. "The guards were standing at the doors. But when we opened the doors, we didn't find anyone inside." [24]When the captain of the temple guard and the chief priests heard this report, they were bewildered. They wondered what would happen next.

[25]Then someone came and said, "Look! The men you put in prison are standing in the temple courtyard. They are teaching the people." [26]So the captain went with his officers and brought the apostles back. But they didn't use force. They were afraid the people would kill them by throwing stones at them.

[27]They brought the apostles to be judged by the Sanhedrin. The high priest questioned them. [28]"We gave you clear orders not to teach in Jesus' name," he said. "But you have filled Jerusalem with your teaching. You want to make us guilty of this man's death."

[29]Peter and the other apostles replied, "We must obey God instead of people! [30]You had Jesus killed by nailing him to a cross. But the God of our people raised Jesus from the dead. [31]Now Jesus is Prince and Savior. God has proved this by giving him a place of honor at his own right hand. He did it so that he could turn Israel away from their sins and forgive them. [32]We are witnesses of these things. And so is the Holy Spirit. God has given the Spirit to those who obey him."

[33]When the leaders heard this, they became very angry. They wanted to put the apostles to death. [34]But a Pharisee named Gamaliel stood up in the Sanhedrin. He was a teacher of the law. He was honored by all the people. He ordered the men to be taken outside for a little while. [35]Then he spoke to the Sanhedrin. "Men of Israel," he said, "think

carefully about what you plan to do to these men. [36]Some time ago Theudas appeared. He claimed he was really somebody. About 400 people followed him. But he was killed. All his followers were scattered. So they accomplished nothing. [37]After this, Judas from Galilee came along. This was in the days when the Romans made a list of all the people. Judas led a gang of men against the Romans. He too was killed. All his followers were scattered. [38]So let me give you some advice. Leave these men alone! Let them go! If their plans and actions are only human, they will fail. [39]But if their plans come from God, you won't be able to stop these men. You will only find yourselves fighting against God."

[40]His speech won the leaders over. They called the apostles in and had them whipped. The leaders ordered them not to speak in Jesus' name. Then they let the apostles go.

[41]The apostles were full of joy as they left the Sanhedrin. They considered it an honor to suffer shame for the name of Jesus. [42]Day after day, they kept teaching in the temple courtyards and from house to house. They never stopped telling the good news that Jesus is the Christ.

Seven Leaders Are Chosen

6 In those days the number of believers was growing. The Jews who followed Greek practices complained against the Jews who followed only Jewish practices. They said that the widows of men who followed Greek practices were not being taken care of. They weren't getting their fair share of food each day. [2]So the Twelve gathered all the believers together. They said, "It wouldn't be right for us to give up teaching God's word in order to wait on tables. [3]Brothers, choose seven of your men. They must be known as men who are wise and full of the Holy Spirit. We will turn this important work over to them. [4]Then we can give our attention to prayer and to teaching the word."

[5]This plan pleased the whole group. They chose Stephen. He was full of faith and of the Holy Spirit. Philip, Procorus, Nicanor, Timon and Parmenas were chosen too. The group also chose Nicolas from Antioch. He had accepted the Jewish faith. [6]The group brought them to the apostles. Then the apostles prayed and placed their hands on them.

[7]So God's word spread. The number of believers in Jerusalem grew quickly. Also, a large number of priests began to obey Jesus' teachings.

Stephen Is Arrested

[8]Stephen was full of God's grace and power. He did great wonders and miraculous signs among the people. [9]But members of the group called the Synagogue of the Freedmen began to oppose him. Some of them were Jews from Cyrene and Alexandria. Others were Jews from Cilicia and Asia Minor. They all began to argue with Stephen. [10]But he was too wise for them. They couldn't stand up against the Holy Spirit who spoke through him.

[11]Then in secret they talked some men into lying about Stephen. They said, "We heard Stephen speak evil things against Moses. He also spoke evil things against God."

[12]So the people were stirred up. The elders and the teachers of the law were stirred up too. They arrested Stephen and brought him to the Sanhedrin. [13]They found people who were willing to tell lies. The false witnesses said, "This fellow never stops speaking against this holy place. He also speaks against the law. [14]We have heard him say that this Jesus of Nazareth will destroy this place. He says Jesus will change the practices that Moses handed down to us."

[15]All who were sitting in the Sanhedrin looked right at Stephen. They saw that his face was like the face of an angel.

Stephen Speaks to the Sanhedrin

7 Then the high priest questioned Stephen. "Is what these people are saying true?" he asked.

[2]"Brothers and fathers, listen to me!" Stephen replied. "The God of glory appeared to our father Abraham. At that time Abraham was still in Mesopotamia. He had not yet begun living in Haran. [3]'Leave your country and your people,' God said. 'Go to the land

I will show you.' *(Genesis 12:1)*

⁴"So Abraham left the land of Babylonia. He settled in Haran. After his father died, God sent Abraham to this land where you are now living. ⁵God didn't give him any property here. He didn't give him even a foot of land. But God made a promise to him and to all his family after him. He said they would possess the land. The promise was made even though at that time Abraham had no child.

⁶"Here is what God said to him. 'Your family after you will be strangers in a country that is not their own. They will be slaves and will be treated badly for 400 years. ⁷But I will punish the nation that makes them slaves,' God said. 'After that, they will leave that country and worship me here.' *(Genesis 15:13,14)*

⁸"Then God made a covenant with Abraham. God told him that circumcision would show who the members of the covenant were. Abraham became Isaac's father. He circumcised Isaac eight days after he was born. Later, Isaac became Jacob's father. Jacob had 12 sons. They became the founders of the 12 tribes of Israel.

⁹"Jacob's sons were jealous of their brother Joseph. So they sold him as a slave. He was taken to Egypt. But God was with him. ¹⁰He saved Joseph from all his troubles. God made Joseph wise. He helped him to become the friend of Pharaoh, the king of Egypt. So Pharaoh made Joseph ruler over Egypt and his whole palace.

¹¹"There was not enough food for all Egypt and Canaan. This brought great suffering. Jacob and his sons couldn't find food. ¹²But Jacob heard that there was grain in Egypt. So he sent his sons on their first visit. ¹³On their second visit, Joseph told his brothers who he was. Pharaoh learned about Joseph's family.

¹⁴"After this, Joseph sent for his father Jacob and his whole family. The total number of people was 75. ¹⁵Then Jacob went down to Egypt. There he and his family died. ¹⁶Some of their bodies were brought back to Shechem. They were placed in a tomb Abraham had bought. He had purchased it from Hamor's sons at Shechem

for a certain amount of money.

¹⁷"In Egypt the number of our people grew and grew. It was nearly time for God to make his promise to Abraham come true. ¹⁸Another king became ruler of Egypt. He knew nothing about Joseph. ¹⁹He was very evil and dishonest with our people. He beat them down. He forced them to throw out their newborn babies to die.

²⁰"At that time Moses was born. He was not an ordinary child. For three months he was taken care of by his family. ²¹Then he was placed outside. But Pharaoh's daughter took him home. She brought him up as her own son. ²²Moses was taught all the knowledge of the people of Egypt. He became a powerful speaker and a man of action.

²³"When Moses was 40 years old, he decided to visit the people of Israel. They were his own people. ²⁴He saw one of them being treated badly by a man of Egypt. So he went to help him. He got even by killing the man. ²⁵Moses thought his own people would realize that God was using him to save them. But they didn't.

²⁶"The next day Moses saw two men of Israel fighting. He tried to make peace between them. 'Men, you are both of Israel,' he said. 'Why do you want to hurt each other?'

²⁷"But the man who was treating the other one badly pushed Moses to one side. He said, 'Who made you ruler and judge over us? ²⁸Do you want to kill me as you killed the Egyptian yesterday?' *(Exodus 2:14)* ²⁹When Moses heard this, he escaped to Midian. He lived there as a stranger. He became the father of two sons there.

³⁰"Forty years passed. Then an angel appeared to Moses in the flames of a burning bush. This happened in the desert near Mount Sinai. ³¹When Moses saw the bush, he was amazed. He went over for a closer look. There he heard the Lord's voice. ³²'I am the God of your fathers,' the Lord said. 'I am the God of Abraham, Isaac and Jacob.' *(Exodus 3:6)* Moses shook with fear. He didn't dare to look.

³³"Then the Lord said to him, 'Take off your sandals. The place you are standing on is holy ground. ³⁴I have seen my people

beaten down in Egypt. I have heard their groans. I have come down to set them free. Now come. I will send you back to Egypt.' *(Exodus 3:5,7,8,10)*

35"This is the same Moses the two men of Israel would not accept. They had said, 'Who made you ruler and judge?' But God himself sent Moses to rule the people of Israel and set them free. He spoke to Moses through the angel who had appeared to him in the bush. 36So Moses led them out of Egypt. He did wonders and miraculous signs in Egypt, at the Red Sea, and for 40 years in the desert.

37"This is the same Moses who spoke to the people of Israel. 'God will send you a prophet,' he said. 'He will be like me. He will come from your own people.' *(Deuteronomy 18:15)* 38Moses was with the Israelites in the desert. He was with the angel who spoke to him on Mount Sinai. Moses was with our people of long ago. He received living words to pass on to us.

39"But our people refused to obey Moses. They would not accept him. In their hearts, they wished they were back in Egypt. 40They told Aaron, 'Make us a god who will lead us. This fellow Moses led us out of Egypt. But we don't know what has happened to him!' *(Exodus 32:1)* 41That was the time they made a statue to be their god. It looked like a calf. They brought sacrifices to it. They were glad because of what they had made with their own hands. 42But God turned away from them. He left them to worship the sun, moon and stars. This agrees with what is written in the book of the prophets. There it says,

" 'People of Israel, did you bring me
      sacrifices and offerings
   for 40 years in the desert?
43You lifted up the place where Molech
      was worshiped.
   You lifted up the star of your god
      Rephan.
   You made statues of them to worship.
So I will send you away from your
      country.' *(Amos 5:25–27)*
   God sent them to Babylon and even
      farther.

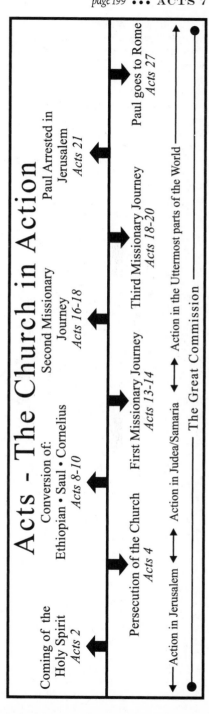

Acts - The Church in Action

Coming of the Holy Spirit — *Acts 2*

Conversion of: Ethiopian • Saul • Cornelius — *Acts 8-10*

Paul Arrested in Jerusalem — *Acts 21*

Paul goes to Rome — *Acts 27*

Persecution of the Church — *Acts 4*

First Missionary Journey — *Acts 13-14*

Second Missionary Journey — *Acts 16-18*

Third Missionary Journey — *Acts 18-20*

Action in Jerusalem

Action in Judea/Samaria

Action in the Uttermost parts of the World

The Great Commission

44"Long ago our people had with them in the desert the holy tent where the tablets of the covenant were kept. Moses had made the holy tent as God had commanded him. It was made like the pattern he had seen. 45Our people received the tent from God. They brought it with them when they took the land of Canaan. God drove out the nations that were in their way. At that time Joshua was Israel's leader.

"The tent remained in the land until David's time. 46David was blessed by God. So David asked if he could build a house for the God of Jacob. 47Instead, it was Solomon who built it for him.

48"But the Most High God does not live in houses made by human hands. As God says through the prophet,

49" 'Heaven is my throne.
The earth is under my control.
What kind of house will you build for
    me?
                        says the Lord.
Where will my resting place be?
50Didn't my hand make all these things?'
                        (Isaiah 66:1,2)

51"You people! You won't obey! You are stubborn! You won't listen! You are just like your people of long ago! You always oppose the Holy Spirit! 52Was there ever a prophet your people didn't try to hurt? They even killed those who told about the coming of the Blameless One. And now you have handed him over to his enemies. You have murdered him. 53The law you received was brought by angels. But you haven't obeyed it."

Stephen Is Killed

54When the Sanhedrin heard this, they became very angry. They ground their teeth at Stephen. 55But he was full of the Holy Spirit. He looked up to heaven and saw God's glory. He saw Jesus standing at God's right hand. 56"Look!" he said. "I see heaven open. The Son of Man is standing at God's right hand."

57When the Sanhedrin heard this, they covered their ears. They yelled at the top of their voices. They all rushed at him. 58They dragged him out of the city. They began to throw stones at him to kill him. The witnesses took off their coats. They placed them at the feet of a young man named Saul.

59While the members of the Sanhedrin were throwing stones at Stephen, he prayed. "Lord Jesus, receive my spirit," he said. 60Then he fell on his knees. He cried out, "Lord! Don't hold this sin against them!" When he had said this, he died.

8 Saul was there. He had agreed that Stephen should die.

The Church Is Scattered

On that day the church in Jerusalem began to be attacked and treated badly. All except the apostles were scattered throughout Judea and Samaria.

2Godly Jews buried Stephen. They sobbed and sobbed over him.

3But Saul began to destroy the church. He went from house to house. He dragged men and women away and put them in prison.

Philip Goes to Samaria

4The believers who had been scattered preached the word everywhere they went. 5Philip went down to a city in Samaria. There he preached about the Christ. 6The crowds listened to Philip. They saw the miraculous signs he did. They all paid close attention to what he said. 7Evil spirits screamed and came out of many people. Many who were disabled or who couldn't walk were healed. 8So there was great joy in that city.

Simon the Evil Magician

9A man named Simon lived in the city. For quite a while he had practiced evil magic there. He amazed all the people of Samaria. He claimed to be someone great. 10All of the people listened to him, from the least important of them to the most important. They exclaimed, "This man is known as the Great Power of God!" 11He had amazed them for a long time with his magic. So they followed him.

12But Philip preached the good news of God's kingdom. He preached the name of

Jesus Christ. So men and women believed and were baptized. [13]Simon himself believed and was baptized. He followed Philip everywhere. He was amazed by the great signs and miracles he saw.

[14]The apostles in Jerusalem heard that people in Samaria had accepted God's word. So they sent Peter and John to them. [15]When they arrived there, they prayed that the believers would receive the Holy Spirit. [16]The Holy Spirit had not yet come on any of them. They had only been baptized in the name of the Lord Jesus. [17]Then Peter and John placed their hands on them. And they received the Holy Spirit.

[18]Simon watched as the apostles placed their hands on them. He saw that the Spirit was given to them. So he offered money to Peter and John. [19]He said, "Give me this power too. Then everyone I place my hands on will receive the Holy Spirit."

[20]Peter answered, "May your money be destroyed with you! Do you think you can buy God's gift with money? [21]You have no part or share in this holy work. Your heart is not right with God. [22]Turn away from this evil sin of yours. Pray to the Lord. Perhaps he will forgive you for having such a thought in your heart. [23]I see that you are very bitter. You are a prisoner of sin."

[24]Then Simon answered, "Pray to the Lord for me. Pray that nothing you have said will happen to me."

[25]Peter and John gave witness and preached the Lord's word. Then they returned to Jerusalem. On the way they preached the good news in many villages in Samaria.

Philip and the Man From Ethiopia

[26]An angel of the Lord spoke to Philip. "Go south to the desert road," he said. "It's the road that goes down from Jerusalem to Gaza." [27]So Philip started out. On his way he met an Ethiopian official. The man had an important position. He was in charge of all the wealth of Candace. She was the queen of Ethiopia. He had gone to Jerusalem to worship. [28]On his way home he was sitting in his chariot. He was reading the book of Isaiah the prophet. [29]The Holy Spirit told Philip, "Go to that chariot. Stay near it."

[30]So Philip ran up to the chariot. He heard the man reading Isaiah the prophet. "Do you understand what you're reading?" Philip asked.

[31]"How can I?" he said. "I need someone to explain it to me." So he invited Philip to come up and sit with him.

[32]Here is the part of Scripture the official was reading. It says,

"He was led like a sheep to be killed.
    Just as lambs are silent while their
        wool is being cut off,

Famous Quotes

"They've had too much wine!"
Unbelievers - Acts 2:13

●

"Should we obey you? Or God?"
Peter - Acts 4:19

●

"Do you want to kill me...?"
Man of Israel - Acts 7:28

●

"I know Jesus. And I know about Paul. But who are you?"
Evil Spirit - Acts 19:15

●

"God will hit you!"
Paul - Acts 23:3

he did not open his mouth.
33 When he was treated badly, he was
    refused a fair trial.
Who can say anything about his
    children?
His life was cut off from the earth."
                                (Isaiah 53:7,8)

34 The official said to Philip, "Tell me, please. Who is the prophet talking about? Himself, or someone else?" 35 Then Philip began with that same part of Scripture. He told him the good news about Jesus.

36/37 As they traveled along the road, they came to some water. The official said, "Look! Here is water! Why shouldn't I be baptized?" 38 He gave orders to stop the chariot. Then both Philip and the official went down into the water. Philip baptized him. 39 When they came up out of the water, the Spirit of the Lord suddenly took Philip away. The official did not see him again. He went on his way full of joy. 40 Philip was seen next at Azotus. From there he traveled all around. He preached the good news in all the towns. Finally he arrived in Caesarea.

Saul Becomes a Believer

9 Meanwhile, Saul continued to oppose the Lord's followers. He said they would be put to death. He went to the high priest. 2 He asked the priest for letters to the synagogues in Damascus. He wanted to find men and women who belonged to the Way of Jesus. The letters would allow him to take them as prisoners to Jerusalem.

3 On his journey, Saul approached Damascus. Suddenly a light from heaven flashed around him. 4 He fell to the ground. He heard a voice speak to him. "Saul! Saul!" the voice said. "Why are you opposing me?"

5 "Who are you, Lord?" Saul asked.

"I am Jesus," he replied. "I am the one you are opposing. 6 Now get up and go into the city. There you will be told what you must do."

7 The men traveling with Saul stood there. They weren't able to speak. They had heard the sound. But they didn't see anyone. 8 Saul got up from the ground. He opened his eyes, but he couldn't see. So they led him by the hand into Damascus. 9 For three days he was blind. He didn't eat or drink anything.

10 In Damascus there was a believer named Ananias. The Lord called out to him in a vision. "Ananias!" he said.

"Yes, Lord," he answered.

11 The Lord told him, "Go to the house of Judas on Straight Street. Ask for a man from Tarsus named Saul. He is praying. 12 In a vision he has seen a man named Ananias. The man has come and placed his hands on him. Now he will be able to see again."

13 "Lord," Ananias answered, "I've heard many reports about this man. They say he has done great harm to God's people in Jerusalem. 14 Now he has come here to arrest all those who worship you. The chief priests have given him authority to do this."

15 But the Lord said to Ananias, "Go! I have chosen this man to work for me. He will carry my name to those who aren't Jews and to their kings. He will bring my name to the people of Israel. 16 I will show him how much he must suffer for me."

17 Then Ananias went to the house and entered it. He placed his hands on Saul. "Brother Saul," he said, "you saw the Lord Jesus. He appeared to you on the road as you were coming here. He has sent me so that you will be able to see again. You will be filled with the Holy Spirit."

18 Right away something like scales fell from Saul's eyes. And he could see again. He got up and was baptized. 19 After eating some food, he got his strength back.

Saul in Damascus and Jerusalem

Saul spent several days with the believers in Damascus. 20 At once he began to preach in the synagogues. He taught that Jesus is the Son of God. 21 All who heard him were

Christianity is a movement, not a condition;
    a voyage, not a harbor.

amazed. They asked, "Isn't he the man who caused great trouble in Jerusalem for those who worship Jesus? Hasn't he come here to take them as prisoners to the chief priests?" [22]But Saul grew more and more powerful. The Jews living in Damascus couldn't believe what was happening. Saul proved to them that Jesus is the Christ.

[23]After many days, the Jews had a meeting. They planned to kill Saul. [24]But he learned about their plan. Day and night they watched the city gates closely in order to kill him. [25]But his followers helped him escape by night. They lowered him in a basket through an opening in the wall.

[26]When Saul came to Jerusalem, he tried to join the believers. But they were all afraid of him. They didn't believe he was really one of Jesus' followers. [27]But Barnabas took him to the apostles. He told them about Saul's journey. He said that Saul had seen the Lord. He told how the Lord had spoken to Saul. Barnabas also said that Saul had preached without fear in Jesus' name in Damascus.

[28]So Saul stayed with the believers. He moved about freely in Jerusalem. He spoke boldly in the Lord's name. [29]He talked and argued with Jews who followed Greek practices. But they tried to kill him. [30]The other believers heard about this. They took Saul down to Caesarea. From there they sent him off to Tarsus.

[31]Then the church throughout Judea, Galilee and Samaria enjoyed a time of peace. The Holy Spirit gave the church strength and boldness. So they grew in numbers. And they worshiped the Lord.

Peter Goes to Lydda and Joppa

[32]As Peter traveled around the country, he went to visit God's people in Lydda. [33]There he found a disabled man named Aeneas. For eight years the man had spent most of his time in bed. [34]"Aeneas," Peter said to him, "Jesus Christ heals you. Get up! Take care of your mat!" So Aeneas got up right away. [35]Everyone who lived in Lydda and Sharon saw him. They turned to the Lord.

[36]In Joppa there was a believer named Tabitha. Her name in the Greek language was Dorcas. She was always doing good and helping poor people.

[37]About that time she became sick and died. Her body was washed and placed in a room upstairs. [38]Lydda was near Joppa. The believers heard that Peter was in Lydda. So they sent two men to him. They begged him, "Please come at once!"

[39]Peter went with them. When he arrived, he was taken upstairs to the room. All the widows stood around him crying. They showed him the robes and other clothes Dorcas had made while she was still alive. [40]Peter sent them all out of the room. Then he got down on his knees and prayed. He turned toward the dead woman. He said, "Tabitha, get up." She opened her eyes. When she saw Peter, she sat up. [41]He took her by the hand and helped her to her feet. Then he called the believers and the widows. He brought her to them. They saw that she was alive. [42]This became known all over Joppa. Many people believed in the Lord. [43]Peter stayed in Joppa for some time. He stayed with Simon, a man who worked with leather.

Cornelius Calls for Peter

10 A man named Cornelius lived in Caesarea. He was a Roman commander in the Italian Regiment. [2]Cornelius and all his family were faithful and worshiped God. He gave freely to people who were in need. He prayed to God regularly. [3]One day about three o'clock in the afternoon he had a vision. He saw an angel of God clearly. The angel came to him and said, "Cornelius!"

[4]Cornelius was afraid. He stared at the angel. "What is it, Lord?" he asked.

The angel answered, "Your prayers and gifts to poor people have come up like an offering to God. So he has remembered you. [5]Now send men to Joppa. Have them bring back a man named Simon. He is also called Peter. [6]He is staying with another Simon, a man who works with leather. His house is by the sea."

[7]The angel who spoke to him left. Then Cornelius called two of his servants. He also called a godly soldier who was one of his attendants. [8]He told them everything that had happened. Then he sent them to Joppa.

Peter Has a Vision

[9]It was about noon the next day. The men were on their journey and were approaching the city. Peter went up on the roof to pray. [10]He became hungry. He wanted something to eat. While the meal was being prepared, Peter had a vision. [11]He saw heaven open up. There he saw something that looked like a large sheet. It was being let down to earth by its four corners. [12]It had all kinds of four-footed animals in it. It also had reptiles of the earth and birds of the air. [13]Then a voice told him, "Get up, Peter. Kill and eat."

[14]"No, Lord! I will not!" Peter replied. "I have never eaten anything that is not pure and 'clean.' "

[15]The voice spoke to him a second time. "Do not say anything is not pure that God has made 'clean,' " it said.

[16]This happened three times. Right away the sheet was taken back up to heaven.

[17]Peter was wondering what the vision meant. At that very moment the men sent by Cornelius found Simon's house. They stopped at the gate [18]and called out. They asked if Simon Peter was staying there.

[19]Peter was still thinking about the vision. The Holy Spirit spoke to him. "Simon," he said, "three men are looking for you. [20]Get up and go downstairs. Don't let anything keep you from going with them. I have sent them."

[21]Peter went down and spoke to the men. "I'm the one you're looking for," he said. "Why have you come?"

[22]The men replied, "We have come from Cornelius, the Roman commander. He is a good man who worships God. All the Jewish people respect him. A holy angel told him to invite you to his house. Cornelius wants to hear what you have to say." [23]Then Peter invited the men into the house to be his guests.

Peter Goes to the House of Cornelius

The next day Peter went with the three men. Some of the believers from Joppa went along. [24]The following day he arrived in Caesarea. Cornelius was expecting them. He had called together his relatives and close friends.

[25]When Peter entered the house, Cornelius met him. As a sign of respect, he fell at Peter's feet. [26]But Peter made him get up. "Stand up," he said. "I am only a man myself."

[27]Talking with Cornelius, Peter went inside. There he found a large group of people. [28]He said to them, "You know that it is against our law for a Jew to have anything to do with those who aren't Jews. But God has shown me that I should not say anyone is not pure and 'clean.' [29]So when you sent for me, I came without asking any questions. May I ask why you sent for me?"

[30]Cornelius answered, "Four days ago at this very hour I was in my house praying. It was three o'clock in the afternoon. Suddenly a man in shining clothes stood in front

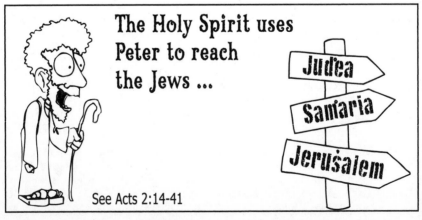

The Holy Spirit uses Peter to reach the Jews ...

Judea
Samaria
Jerusalem

See Acts 2:14-41

of me. [31]He said, 'Cornelius, God has heard your prayer. He has remembered your gifts to poor people. [32]Send someone to Joppa to get Simon Peter. He is a guest in the home of another Simon, who works with leather. He lives by the sea.' [33]So I sent for you right away. It was good of you to come. Now we are all here. And God is here with us. We are ready to listen to everything the Lord has commanded you to tell us."

[34]Then Peter began to speak. "I now realize how true it is that God treats everyone the same," he said. [35]"He accepts people from every nation. He accepts all who have respect for him and do what is right.

[36]"You know the message God sent to the people of Israel. It is the good news of peace through Jesus Christ. He is Lord of all. [37]You know what has happened all through Judea. It started in Galilee after John preached about baptism. [38]You know how God anointed Jesus of Nazareth with the Holy Spirit and with power. Jesus went around doing good. He healed all who were under the devil's power. God was with him.

[39]"We are witnesses of everything he did in the land of the Jews and in Jerusalem. They killed him by nailing him to a cross. [40]But on the third day God raised him from the dead. God allowed Jesus to be seen. [41]But he wasn't seen by all the people. He was seen only by us. We are witnesses whom God had already chosen. We ate and drank with him after he rose from the dead.

[42]"He commanded us to preach to the people. He told us to give witness that he is the one appointed by God to judge the living and the dead. [43]All the prophets give witness about him. They say that all who believe in him have their sins forgiven through his name."

[44]While Peter was still saying these things, the Holy Spirit came on all who heard the message. [45]Some Jewish believers had come with Peter. They were amazed because the gift of the Holy Spirit had been poured out even on those who weren't Jews. [46]They heard them speaking in languages they had not known before. They also heard them praising God.

Then Peter said, [47]"Can anyone keep these people from being baptized with water? They have received the Holy Spirit just as we have." [48]So he ordered that they be baptized in the name of Jesus Christ. Then they asked Peter to stay with them for a few days.

Peter Explains His Actions

11 The apostles and the believers all through Judea heard that people who were not Jews had also received God's word. [2]Peter went up to Jerusalem. There the Jewish believers found fault with him. [3]They said, "You went into the house of those who aren't Jews. You ate with them."

[4]Peter explained everything to them. He told them exactly what had happened. [5]"I was in the city of Joppa praying," he said. "There I had a vision. I saw something that looked like a large sheet. It was being let

... and Paul to reach the Gentiles.

Athens

Corinth

Rome

Antioch

See Acts 17:16-34

down from heaven by its four corners. It came down to where I was. [6]I looked into it and saw four-footed animals of the earth. There were also wild animals, reptiles and birds. [7]Then I heard a voice speaking to me. 'Get up, Peter,' the voice said. 'Kill and eat.'

[8]"I replied, 'No, Lord! I will not! Nothing that is not pure and "clean" has ever entered my mouth.'

[9]"A second time the voice spoke from heaven. 'Do not say anything is not pure that God has made "clean," ' the voice said. [10]This happened three times. Then the sheet was pulled up into heaven.

[11]"Just then three men stopped at the house where I was staying. They had been sent to me from Caesarea. [12]The Holy Spirit told me not to let anything keep me from going with them. These six brothers here went with me. We entered the man's house. [13]He told us how he had seen an angel appear in his house. The angel said, 'Send to Joppa for Simon Peter. [14]He has a message to bring to you. You and your whole family will be saved through it.'

[15]"As I began to speak, the Holy Spirit came on them. He came just as he had come on us at the beginning. [16]Then I remembered the Lord's words. 'John baptized with water,' he had said. 'But you will be baptized with the Holy Spirit.' [17]God gave them the same gift he gave those of us who believed in the Lord Jesus Christ. So who was I to think that I could oppose God?"

[18]When they heard this, they didn't object anymore. They praised God. They said, "So then, God has allowed even those who aren't Jews to turn away from their sins and live."

Believers Are Called Christians for the First Time

[19]Some believers had been scattered by the suffering that came to them after Stephen's death. They traveled as far as Phoenicia, Cyprus and Antioch. But they told the message only to Jews. [20]Some believers from Cyprus and Cyrene went to Antioch. There they began to speak to Greeks also. They told them the good news about the Lord Jesus. [21]The Lord's power was with them. Large numbers of people believed and turned to the Lord.

[22]The church in Jerusalem heard about this. So they sent Barnabas to Antioch. [23]When he arrived and saw what the grace of God had done, he was glad. He told them all to remain true to the Lord with all their hearts. [24]Barnabas was a good man. He was full of the Holy Spirit and of faith. Large numbers of people came to know the Lord.

[25]Then Barnabas went to Tarsus to look for Saul. [26]He found him there. Then he brought him to Antioch. For a whole year Barnabas and Saul met with the church. They taught large numbers of people. At Antioch the believers were called Christians for the first time.

[27]In those days some prophets came down from Jerusalem to Antioch. [28]One of them was named Agabus. He stood up and spoke through the Spirit. He said there would not be nearly enough food anywhere in the Roman world. This happened while Claudius was the emperor. [29]The believers decided to provide help for the brothers and sisters living in Judea. All of them helped as much as they could. [30]They sent their gift to the elders through Barnabas and Saul.

An Angel Helps Peter Escape From Prison

12 About this time, King Herod arrested some people who belonged to the church. He planned to make them suffer greatly. [2]He had James killed with a sword. James was John's brother. [3]Herod saw that the death of James pleased the Jews. So he arrested Peter also. This happened during the Feast of Unleavened Bread. [4]After Herod arrested Peter, he put him in prison. Peter was placed under guard. He was watched by four groups of four soldiers each. Herod planned to put Peter on public trial. It would take place after the Passover Feast.

[5]So Peter was kept in prison. But the church prayed hard to God for him.

[6]It was the night before Herod was going to bring him to trial. Peter was sleeping

between two soldiers. Two chains held him there. Lookouts stood guard at the entrance. [7]Suddenly an angel of the Lord appeared. A light shone in the prison cell. The angel struck Peter on his side. Peter woke up. "Quick!" the angel said. "Get up!" The chains fell off Peter's wrists.

[8]Then the angel said to him, "Put on your clothes and sandals." Peter did so. "Put on your coat," the angel told him. "Follow me." [9]Peter followed him out of the prison. But he had no idea that what the angel was doing was really happening. He thought he was seeing a vision. [10]They passed the first and second guards. Then they came to the iron gate leading to the city. It opened for them by itself. They went through it. They walked the length of one street. Suddenly the angel left Peter.

[11]Then Peter realized what had happened. He said, "Now I know for sure that the Lord sent his angel. He set me free from Herod's power. He saved me from everything the Jewish people were hoping for."

[12]When Peter understood what had happened, he went to Mary's house. Mary was the mother of John Mark. Many people had gathered in her home. They were praying there. [13]Peter knocked at the outer entrance. A servant named Rhoda came to answer the door. [14]She recognized Peter's voice. She was so excited that she ran back without opening the door. "Peter is at the door!" she exclaimed.

[15]"You're out of your mind," they said to her. But she kept telling them it was true. So they said, "It must be his angel."

[16]Peter kept on knocking. When they opened the door and saw him, they were amazed. [17]Peter motioned with his hand for them to be quiet. He explained how the Lord had brought him out of prison. "Tell James and the others about this," he said. Then he went to another place.

[18]In the morning the soldiers were bewildered. They couldn't figure out what had happened to Peter. [19]So Herod had them look everywhere for Peter. But they didn't find him. Then Herod questioned the guards closely. He ordered that they be put to death.

Herod Dies

Herod went from Judea to Caesarea. He stayed there awhile. [20]He had been quarreling with the people of Tyre and Sidon. So they got together and asked for a meeting with him. This was because they depended on the king's country to supply them with food. They gained the support of Blastus and asked for peace. Blastus was a trusted personal servant of the king.

[21]The appointed day came. Herod was seated on his throne. He was wearing his royal robes. He made a speech to the people. [22]Then they shouted, "This is the voice of a god. It's not the voice of a man." [23]Right away an angel of the Lord struck Herod down. Herod had not given praise to God. So he was eaten by worms and died.

[24]But God's word continued to increase and spread.

[25]Barnabas and Saul finished their task. Then they returned from Jerusalem. They took John Mark with them.

Barnabas and Saul Are Sent Off

13 In the church at Antioch there were prophets and teachers. Among them were Barnabas, Simeon, and Lucius from Cyrene. Simeon was also called Niger. Another was Manaen. He had been brought up with Herod, the ruler of Galilee. Saul was among them too. [2]While they were worshiping the Lord and fasting, the Holy Spirit spoke. "Set apart Barnabas and Saul for me," he said. "I have appointed them to do special work." [3]The prophets and teachers fasted and prayed. They placed their

Just think how happy you'd be if you lost everything you now have, and then suddenly got it back

hands on Barnabas and Saul. Then they sent them off.

Events on Cyprus

[4]Barnabas and Saul were sent on their way by the Holy Spirit. They went down to Seleucia. From there they sailed to Cyprus. [5]They arrived at Salamis. There they preached God's word in the Jewish synagogues. John was with them as their helper.

[6]They traveled all across the island until they came to Paphos. There they met a Jew named Bar-Jesus. He was an evil magician and a false prophet. [7]He was an attendant of Sergius Paulus, the governor. Paulus was a man of understanding. He sent for Barnabas and Saul. He wanted to hear God's word.

[8]But Elymas, the evil magician, opposed them. The name Elymas means "magician." He tried to keep the governor from becoming a believer. [9]Saul was also known as Paul. He was filled with the Holy Spirit. He looked straight at Elymas. He said to him, [10]"You are a child of the devil! You are an enemy of everything that is right! You cheat people. You use all kinds of tricks. Won't you ever stop twisting the right ways of the Lord? [11]Now the Lord's hand is against you. You are going to go blind. You won't be able to see the light of the sun for a while."

Right away mist and darkness came over him. He tried to feel his way around. He wanted to find someone to lead him by the hand. [12]When the governor saw what had happened, he believed. He was amazed at what Paul was teaching about the Lord.

Paul Preaches in Pisidian Antioch

[13]From Paphos, Paul and his companions sailed to Perga in Pamphylia. There John left them and returned to Jerusalem. [14]From Perga they went on to Pisidian Antioch. On the Sabbath day they entered the synagogue and sat down. [15]The Law and the Prophets were read aloud. Then the synagogue rulers sent word to Paul and his companions. They said, "Brothers, do you have a message of hope for the people? If you do, please speak."

[16]Paul stood up and motioned with his hand. Then he said, "Men of Israel, and you non-Jews who worship God, listen to me! [17]The God of Israel chose our people who lived long ago. He blessed them greatly while they were in Egypt. With his mighty power he led them out of that country. [18]He put up with them for about 40 years in the desert. [19]He destroyed seven nations in Canaan. Then he gave the land to his people as their rightful share. [20]All of this took about 450 years.

"After this, God gave them judges until the time of Samuel the prophet. [21]Then the people asked for a king. He gave them Saul, son of Kish. Saul was from the tribe of Benjamin. He ruled for 40 years. [22]God removed him and made David their king. Here is God's witness about him. 'David, son of Jesse, is a man dear to my heart,' he said. 'He will do everything I want him to do.'

[23]"From this man's family line God has brought to Israel the Savior Jesus. This is what he had promised. [24]Before Jesus came, John preached that we should turn away from our sins and be baptized. He preached this to all Israel. [25]John was coming to the end of his work. 'Who do you think I am?' he said. 'I am not the one you are looking for. No, he is coming after me. I am not good enough to untie his sandals.'

[26]"Listen, brothers, you children of Abraham! Listen, you non-Jews who worship God! This message of salvation has been sent to us. [27]The people of Jerusalem and their rulers did not recognize Jesus. By finding him guilty, they made the prophets' words come true. These are read every Sabbath day. [28]The people and their rulers had no reason at all for sentencing Jesus to death. But they asked Pilate to have him killed. [29]They did everything that had been written about Jesus. Then they took him down from the cross. They laid him in a tomb. [30]But God raised him from the dead. [31]For many days he was seen by those who had traveled with him from Galilee to Jerusalem. Now they are his witnesses to our people.

[32]"We are telling you the good news. What God promised our people long ago [33]he has done for us, their children. He has raised up Jesus. This is what is written in

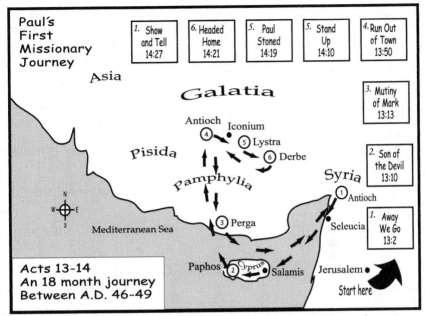

Paul's First Missionary Journey

Asia
Galatia
Pisida
Antioch Iconium
Lystra
Derbe
Pamphylia
Syria
Antioch
Perga
Seleucia
Mediterranean Sea
Paphos Cyprus Salamis
Jerusalem
Start here

1. Show and Tell 14:27
6. Headed Home 14:21
5. Paul Stoned 14:19
5. Stand Up 14:10
4. Run Out of Town 13:50
3. Mutiny of Mark 13:13
2. Son of the Devil 13:10
1. Away We Go 13:2

Acts 13-14
An 18 month journey
Between A.D. 46-49

the second Psalm. It says,

" 'You are my Son.
Today I have become your Father.'
(Psalm 2:7)

³⁴God raised Jesus from the dead. He will never rot in the grave. This is what is written in Scripture. It says,

" 'Holy and sure blessings were promised to David.
I will give them to you.' (Isaiah 55:3)

³⁵In another place it says,

" 'You will not let your Holy One rot away.' (Psalm 16:10)

³⁶"David carried out God's purpose while he lived. Then he died. He was buried with his people. His body rotted away. ³⁷But the One whom God raised from the dead did not rot away.

³⁸"My brothers, here is what I want you to know. I announce to you that your sins can be forgiven because of what Jesus has done. ³⁹Through him everyone who believes is made right with God. Moses' law could not make you right in God's eyes. ⁴⁰Be careful! Don't let what the prophets spoke

about happen to you. They said,

⁴¹" 'Look, you who make fun of the truth! Wonder and die!
I am going to do something in your days that you would never believe.
You wouldn't believe it even if someone told you.' "
(Habakkuk 1:5)

⁴²Paul and Barnabas started to leave the synagogue. The people invited them to say more about these things on the next Sabbath day. ⁴³The people were told they could leave the service. Many Jews followed Paul and Barnabas. Many non-Jews who faithfully worshiped the God of the Jews did the same. Paul and Barnabas talked with them. They tried to get them to keep living in God's grace.

⁴⁴On the next Sabbath day, almost the whole city gathered to hear the word of the Lord. ⁴⁵When the Jews saw the crowds, they became very jealous. They said evil things against what Paul was saying.

⁴⁶Then Paul and Barnabas answered them boldly. "We had to speak God's word to you first," they said. "But you don't accept it. You don't think you are good enough for

eternal life. So now we are turning to those who aren't Jews. ⁴⁷This is what the Lord has commanded us to do. He said,

" 'I have made you a light for those who
aren't Jews.
You will bring salvation to the
whole earth.' "   *(Isaiah 49:6)*

⁴⁸When the non-Jews heard this, they were glad. They honored the word of the Lord. All who were appointed for eternal life believed.

⁴⁹The word of the Lord spread through the whole area. ⁵⁰But the Jews stirred up the important women who worshiped God. They also stirred up the men who were leaders in the city. They tried to get them to attack Paul and Barnabas. They threw them out of that area. ⁵¹Paul and Barnabas didn't like this. So they shook the dust from their feet. They went on to Iconium. ⁵²The believers were filled with joy and with the Holy Spirit.

Paul and Barnabas Preach in Iconium

14 At Iconium, Paul and Barnabas went into the Jewish synagogue as usual. They spoke there with great power. Large numbers of Jews and non-Jews became believers. ²But the Jews who refused to believe stirred up those who weren't Jews. They poisoned their minds against the two men and the new believers. ³So Paul and Barnabas spent a lot of time there. They spoke boldly for the Lord. He gave them the ability to do miraculous signs and wonders. In this way the Lord showed that they were telling the truth about his grace.

⁴The people of the city did not agree with each other. Some were on the side of the Jews. Others were on the side of the apostles. ⁵Jews and non-Jews alike planned to treat Paul and Barnabas badly. Their leaders agreed. They planned to kill them by throwing stones at them. ⁶But Paul and

Barnabas found out about the plan. They escaped to the Lycaonian cities of Lystra and Derbe and to the surrounding area. ⁷There they continued to preach the good news.

Paul Preaches in Lystra

⁸In Lystra there sat a man who couldn't walk. He hadn't been able to use his feet since the day he was born. ⁹He listened as Paul spoke. Paul looked right at him. He saw that the man had faith to be healed. ¹⁰So he called out, "Stand up on your feet!" Then the man jumped up and began to walk.

¹¹The crowd saw what Paul had done. They shouted in the Lycaonian language. "The gods have come down to us in human form!" they exclaimed. ¹²They called Barnabas Zeus. Paul was the main speaker. So they called him Hermes. ¹³Just outside the city was the temple of the god Zeus. The priest of Zeus brought bulls and wreaths to the city gates. He and the crowd wanted to offer sacrifices to Paul and Barnabas.

¹⁴But the apostles Barnabas and Paul heard about this. So they tore their clothes. They rushed out into the crowd. They shouted, ¹⁵"Why are you men doing this? We are only human, just like you. We are bringing you good news. Turn away from these worthless things. Turn to the living God. He is the one who made the heavens and the earth and the sea. He made everything in them. ¹⁶In the past, he let all nations go their own way. ¹⁷But he has given proof of what he is like. He has shown kindness by giving you rain from heaven. He gives you crops in their seasons. He provides you with plenty of food. He fills your hearts with joy." ¹⁸Paul and Barnabas told them all these things. But they had trouble keeping the crowd from offering sacrifices to them.

¹⁹Then some Jews came from Antioch and Iconium. They won the crowd over to their side. They threw stones at Paul. They

It is not a question as to who is right,
but, rather, what is right

thought he was dead, so they dragged him out of the city. [20]The believers gathered around Paul. Then he got up and went back into the city. The next day he and Barnabas left for Derbe.

Paul and Barnabas Return to Antioch

[21]Paul and Barnabas preached the good news in the city of Derbe. They won large numbers of followers. Then they returned to Lystra, Iconium and Antioch. [22]There they helped the believers gain strength. They told them to remain true to what they had been taught. "We must go through many hard times to enter God's kingdom," they said. [23]Paul and Barnabas appointed elders for them in each church. The elders had trusted in the Lord. Paul and Barnabas prayed and fasted. They placed the elders in the Lord's care.

[24]After going through Pisidia, Paul and Barnabas came into Pamphylia. [25]They preached the word in Perga. Then they went down to Attalia.

[26]From Attalia they sailed back to Antioch. That was where they had been committed to God's grace. They had now completed the work God had given them to do. [27]When they arrived at Antioch, they gathered the church together. They reported all that God had done through them. They told how he had opened the way for non-Jews to believe. [28]And they stayed there a long time with the believers.

Church Leaders Meet in Jerusalem

15 Certain people came down from Judea to Antioch. Here is what they were teaching the believers. "Moses commanded you to be circumcised," they said. "If you aren't, you can't be saved." [2]But Paul and Barnabas didn't agree with this. They argued strongly with them. So Paul and Barnabas were appointed to go up to Jerusalem. Some other believers were chosen to go with them. They were supposed to see the apostles and elders about this question.

[3]The church sent them on their way. As they traveled through Phoenicia and Samaria, they told how those who weren't Jews had turned to God. This news made all the believers very glad.

[4]When they arrived in Jerusalem, the church welcomed them. The apostles and elders welcomed them too. Then Paul and Barnabas reported everything God had done through them.

[5]Some of the believers were Pharisees. They stood up and said, "Those who aren't Jews must be circumcised. They must obey the law of Moses."

[6]The apostles and elders met to consider this question. [7]After they had talked it over, Peter got up and spoke to them.

"Brothers," he said, "you know that some time ago God chose me to take the good news to those who aren't Jews. He wanted them to hear the good news and believe. [8]God knows the human heart. By giving the Holy Spirit to non-Jews, he showed that he accepted them. He did the same for them as he had done for us. [9]He showed that there is no difference between us and them. He made their hearts pure because of their faith.

[10]"Now then, why are you trying to test God? You test him when you put a heavy load on the believers' shoulders. Our people of long ago couldn't carry that load. We can't either. [11]No! We believe we are saved through the grace of our Lord Jesus. Those who aren't Jews are saved in the same way."

[12]Everyone became quiet as they listened to Barnabas and Paul. They were telling about the miraculous signs and wonders God had done through them among non-Jews.

[13]When they finished, James spoke up. "Brothers," he said, "listen to me. [14]Simon Peter has explained to us how God first showed his concern for those who aren't Jews. He chose some of them to be his very own people.

[15]"The prophets' words agree with that. They say,

[16] " 'After this I will return
        and rebuild David's fallen tent.
    I will rebuild what was destroyed.
        I will make it what it used to be.
[17] Then the rest of the people can look
        to the Lord.

This means all the non-Jews who belong to me.

The Lord says this. He is the one who does these things.' *(Amos 9:11,12)*

[18] The Lord does things that have been known for a long time.

[19]"Now here is my opinion. We should not make it hard for the non-Jews who are turning to God. [20]Here is what we should write to them. They must not eat food polluted by being offered to statues of gods. They must not commit sexual sins. They must not eat the meat of animals that have been choked to death. And they must not drink blood. [21]These laws of Moses have been preached in every city from the earliest times. They are read out loud in the synagogues every Sabbath day."

A Letter Is Written to Non-Jewish Believers

[22]Then the apostles, the elders and the whole church decided what to do. They would choose some of their own men. They would send them to Antioch with Paul and Barnabas. So they chose two leaders among the believers. Their names were Judas Barsabbas and Silas. [23]Here is the letter they sent with them.

The apostles and elders, your brothers, are writing this letter.

We are sending it to the non-Jewish believers in Antioch, Syria and Cilicia.

Greetings.

[24]We have heard that some of our people came to you and caused trouble. You were upset by what they said. But we had given them no authority to go. [25]So we all agreed to send our dear friends Barnabas and Paul to you. We chose some others to go with them. [26]Barnabas and Paul have put their lives in danger for the name of our Lord Jesus Christ. [27]So we are sending Judas and Silas with them. What they say will agree with this letter.

[28]It seemed good to the Holy Spirit and to us not to give you a load that is too heavy. So here are a few basic rules. [29]Don't eat food that has been offered to statues of gods. Don't drink blood. Don't eat the meat of animals that have been choked to death. And don't commit sexual sins. You will do well to keep away from these things.

Farewell.

[30]The men were sent down to Antioch. There they gathered the church together. They gave the letter to them. [31]The people read it. They were glad for its message of hope. [32]Judas and Silas were prophets. They said many things to give strength and hope to the believers. [33/34]Judas and Silas stayed there for some time. Then the believers sent them away with the blessing of peace. They sent them back to those who had sent them out.

[35]Paul and Barnabas remained in Antioch. There they and many others taught and preached the word of the Lord.

Paul and Barnabas Do Not Agree

[36]Some time later Paul spoke to Barnabas. "Let's go back to all the towns where we preached the word of the Lord," he said. "Let's visit the believers and see how they are doing." [37]Barnabas wanted to take John Mark with them. [38]But Paul didn't think it was wise to take him. Mark had deserted them in Pamphylia. He hadn't continued with them in their work. [39]Barnabas and Paul strongly disagreed with each other. So they went their separate ways. Barnabas took Mark and sailed for Cyprus. [40]But Paul chose Silas. The believers asked the Lord to give his grace to Paul and Silas as they went. [41]Paul traveled through Syria and Cilicia. He gave strength to the churches there.

Timothy Joins Paul and Silas

16 Paul came to Derbe. Then he went on to Lystra. A believer named Timothy lived there. His mother was Jewish and a believer. His father was a Greek. [2]The believers at Lystra and Iconium said good things about Timothy. [3]Paul wanted to take him along on the journey. So he circumcised Timothy because of the Jews who lived in that area. They all knew that Timothy's father was a Greek. [4]Paul and his companions traveled from town to town.

They reported what the apostles and elders in Jerusalem had decided. The people were supposed to obey what was in the report. [5]So the churches were made strong in the faith. The number of believers grew every day.

Paul's Vision of the Man From Macedonia

[6]Paul and his companions traveled all through the area of Phrygia and Galatia. The Holy Spirit had kept them from preaching the word in Asia Minor. [7]They came to the border of Mysia. From there they tried to enter Bithynia. But the Spirit of Jesus would not let them. [8]So they passed by Mysia. Then they went down to Troas.

[9]During the night Paul had a vision. He saw a man from Macedonia standing and begging him. "Come over to Macedonia!" the man said. "Help us!" [10]After Paul had seen the vision, we got ready at once to leave for Macedonia. We decided that God had called us to preach the good news there.

Lydia Becomes a Believer

[11]At Troas we got into a boat. We sailed straight for Samothrace. The next day we went on to Neapolis. [12]From there we traveled to Philippi, a Roman colony. It is an important city in that part of Macedonia. We stayed there several days.

[13]On the Sabbath day we went outside the city gate. We walked down to the river. There we expected to find a place of prayer. We sat down and began to speak to the women who had gathered together. [14]One of those listening was a woman named Lydia. She was from the city of Thyatira. Her business was selling purple cloth. She was a worshiper of God. The Lord opened her heart to accept Paul's message. [15]She and her family were baptized. Then she invited us to her home. "Do you consider me a believer in the Lord?" she asked. "If you do, come and stay at my house." She succeeded in getting us to go home with her.

Paul and Silas Are Thrown Into Prison

[16]One day we were going to the place of prayer. On the way we were met by a female

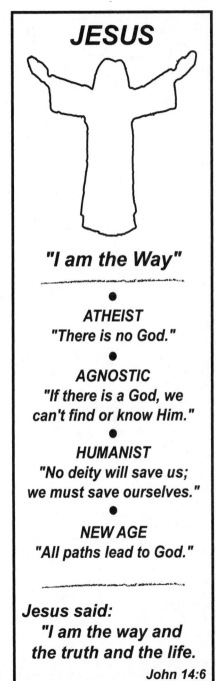

JESUS

"I am the Way"

●

ATHEIST
"There is no God."

●

AGNOSTIC
"If there is a God, we can't find or know Him."

●

HUMANIST
"No deity will save us; we must save ourselves."

●

NEW AGE
"All paths lead to God."

Jesus said:
"I am the way and the truth and the life.
John 14:6

slave. She had a spirit that helped her to tell ahead of time what was going to happen. She earned a lot of money for her owners by telling fortunes. [17]The woman followed Paul and the rest of us around. She shouted, "These men serve the Most High God. They are telling you how to be saved." [18]She kept this up for many days. Finally Paul became upset. Turning around, he spoke to the spirit. "In the name of Jesus Christ," he said, "I command you to come out of her!" At that very moment the spirit left her.

[19]The female slave's owners realized that their hope of making money was gone. So they grabbed Paul and Silas. They dragged them into the market place to face the authorities. [20]They brought them to the judges. "These men are Jews," her owners said. "They are making trouble in our city. [21]They are suggesting practices that are against Roman law. These are practices we can't accept or take part in."

[22]The crowd joined the attack against Paul and Silas. The judges ordered that Paul and Silas be stripped and beaten. [23]They were whipped without mercy. Then they were thrown into prison. The jailer was commanded to guard them carefully. [24]When he received his orders, he put Paul and Silas deep inside the prison. He fastened their feet so they couldn't get away.

[25]About midnight Paul and Silas were praying. They were also singing hymns to God. The other prisoners were listening to them. [26]Suddenly there was a powerful earthquake. It shook the prison from top to bottom. All at once the prison doors flew open. Everybody's chains came loose.

[27]The jailer woke up. He saw that the prison doors were open. He pulled out his sword and was going to kill himself. He thought the prisoners had escaped. [28]"Don't harm yourself!" Paul shouted. "We are all here!"

[29]The jailer called out for some lights. He rushed in, shaking with fear. He fell down in front of Paul and Silas. [30]Then he brought them out. He asked, "Sirs, what must I do to be saved?"

[31]They replied, "Believe in the Lord Jesus. Then you and your family will be saved."

[32]They spoke the word of the Lord to him. They also spoke to all the others in his house.

[33]At that hour of the night, the jailer took Paul and Silas and washed their wounds. Right away he and his whole family were baptized. [34]The jailer brought them into his house. He set a meal in front of them. He and his whole family were filled with joy. They had become believers in God.

[35]Early in the morning the judges sent their officers to the jailer. They ordered him, "Let those men go." [36]The jailer told Paul, "The judges have ordered me to set you and Silas free. You can leave now. Go in peace."

[37]But Paul replied to the officers. "They beat us in public," he said. "We weren't given a trial. And we are Roman citizens! They threw us into prison. And now do they want to get rid of us quietly? No! Let them come themselves and personally lead us out."

[38]The officers reported this to the judges. When the judges heard that Paul and Silas were Roman citizens, they became afraid. [39]So they came and said they were sorry. They led them out of the prison. Then they asked them to leave the city. [40]After Paul and Silas came out of the prison, they went to Lydia's house. There they met with the believers. They told them to be brave. Then they left.

Paul and Silas Arrive in Thessalonica

17 Paul and Silas passed through Amphipolis and Apollonia. They came to Thessalonica. A Jewish synagogue was there. [2]Paul went into the synagogue as he usually did. For three Sabbath days in a row he talked about the Scriptures with the Jews. [3]He explained and proved that the Christ had to suffer and rise from the dead. "This Jesus I am telling you about is the Christ!" he said. [4]His words won some of the Jews over. They joined Paul and Silas. A large number of Greeks who worshiped God joined them too. So did quite a few important women.

[5]But the Jews were jealous. So they rounded up some evil fellows from the mar-

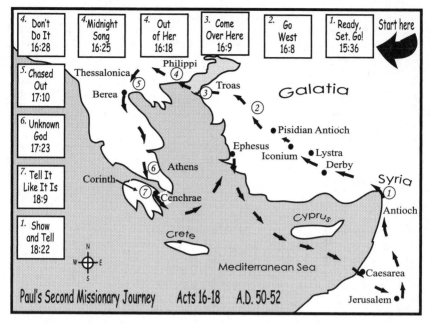

| 4. Don't Do It 16:28 | 4. Midnight Song 16:25 | 4. Out of Her 16:18 | 3. Come Over Here 16:9 | 2. Go West 16:8 | 1. Ready, Set, Go! 15:36 | Start here |

Paul's Second Missionary Journey   Acts 16-18   A.D. 50-52

ket place. Forming a crowd, they started all kinds of trouble in the city. The Jews rushed to Jason's house. They were looking for Paul and Silas. They wanted to bring them out to the crowd. [6]But they couldn't find them. So they dragged Jason and some other believers to the city officials. "These men have caused trouble all over the world," they shouted. "Now they have come here. [7]Jason has welcomed them into his house. They are all disobeying Caesar's commands. They say there is another king. He is called Jesus."

[8]When the crowd and the city officials heard this, they became very upset. [9]They made Jason and the others give them money. They wanted to make sure they would return to the court. Then they let them go.

Paul and Silas Are Sent to Berea

[10]As soon as it was night, the believers sent Paul and Silas away to Berea. When they arrived, they went to the Jewish synagogue.

[11]The Bereans were very glad to receive Paul's message. They studied the Scriptures carefully every day. They wanted to see if what Paul said was true. So they were more noble than the Thessalonians. [12]Many of the Jews believed. A number of important Greek women also became believers. And so did many Greek men.

[13]The Jews in Thessalonica found out that Paul was preaching God's word in Berea. So they went there too. They stirred up the crowds and got them all worked up.

[14]Right away the believers sent Paul to the coast. But Silas and Timothy stayed in Berea. [15]The men who went with Paul took him to Athens. Then they returned with orders that Silas and Timothy were supposed to join him as soon as they could.

Paul Preaches in Athens

[16]Paul was waiting for Silas and Timothy in Athens. He was very upset to see that the city was full of statues of gods. [17]So he went to the synagogue. There he talked with Jews and with Greeks who worshiped God. Each day he spoke with anyone who happened to be in the market place.

[18]A group of Epicurean and Stoic thinkers began to argue with him. Some of them asked, "What is this fellow chattering

about?" Others said, "He seems to be telling us about gods we've never heard of." They said this because Paul was preaching the good news about Jesus. He was telling them that Jesus had risen from the dead.

[19]They took him to a meeting of the Areopagus. There they said to him, "What is this new teaching you're giving us? [20]You have some strange ideas. We've never heard them before. We want to know what they mean."

[21]All the people of Athens spent their time talking about and listening to the latest ideas. People from other lands who lived there did the same.

[22]Then Paul stood up in the meeting of the Areopagus. He said, "Men of Athens! I see that you are very religious in every way. [23]As I walked around, I looked carefully at the things you worship. I even found an altar with TO AN UNKNOWN GOD written on it. Now I am going to tell you about this 'unknown god' that you worship.

[24]"He is the God who made the world. He also made everything in it. He is the Lord of heaven and earth. He doesn't live in temples built by hands. [25]He is not served by human hands. He doesn't need anything. He himself gives life and breath to all people. He also gives them everything else they have. [26]From one man he made all the people of the world. Now they live all over the earth. He decided exactly when they should live. And he decided exactly where they should live. [27]God did this so that people would seek him. Then perhaps they would reach out for him and find him. They would find him even though he is not far from any of us. [28]'In him we live and move and exist.' As some of your own poets have also said, 'We are his children.'

[29]"Yes, we are God's children. So we shouldn't think that God is made out of gold or silver or stone. He isn't a statue planned and made by clever people. [30]In the past, God didn't judge people for what they didn't know. But now he commands all people everywhere to turn away from their sins. [31]He has set a day when he will judge the world fairly. He has appointed a man to be its judge. God has proved this to all people by raising that man from the dead."

[32]When they heard Paul talk about the dead rising, some of them made fun of it. But others said, "We want to hear you speak about this again." [33]So Paul left the meeting of the Areopagus. [34]A few men became followers of Paul and believed in Jesus. Dionysius was one of them. He was a member of the Areopagus. A woman named Damaris also became a believer. And so did some others.

Paul Goes to Corinth

18 After this, Paul left Athens and went to Corinth. [2]There he met a Jew named Aquila, who was a native of Pontus. Aquila had recently come from Italy with his wife Priscilla. The emperor Claudius had ordered all the Jews to leave Rome. Paul went to see Aquila and Priscilla. [3]They were tentmakers, just as he was. So he stayed and worked with them. [4]Every Sabbath day he went to the synagogue. He was trying to get both Jews and Greeks to believe in the Lord.

[5]Silas and Timothy came from Macedonia. Then Paul spent all his time preaching. He gave witness to the Jews that Jesus was the Christ. [6]But the Jews opposed Paul. They treated him badly. He didn't like this. So he shook out his clothes. Then he said to them, "Anything that happens to you will be your own fault! Don't blame me for it! From now on I will go to people who are not Jews."

[7]Then Paul left the synagogue. He went next door to the house of Titius Justus, a man who worshiped God. [8]Crispus was the synagogue ruler. He and his whole family came to believe in the Lord. Many others who lived in Corinth heard Paul. They too believed and were baptized.

[9]One night the Lord spoke to Paul in a vision. "Don't be afraid," he said. "Keep on speaking. Don't be silent. [10]I am with you. No one will attack you and harm you. I have many people in this city." [11]So Paul stayed there for a year and a half. He taught them God's word.

[12]At that time Gallio was governor of Achaia. The Jews got together and attacked Paul. They brought him into court. [13]"This

man," they charged, "is trying to talk people into worshiping God in ways that are against the law."

[14]Paul was about to speak up for himself. But just then Gallio spoke to the Jews. "You Jews are not claiming that Paul has committed a crime, whether large or small," he said. "If you were, it would make sense for me to listen to you. [15]But this is about your own law. It is a question of words and names. Settle the matter yourselves. I will not be a judge of such things." [16]So he had them thrown out of the court. [17]Then all the Jews turned against Sosthenes. He was the synagogue ruler. They beat him up in front of the court. But Gallio didn't care at all.

Priscilla and Aquila Teach Apollos

[18]Paul stayed in Corinth for some time.

Then he left the believers and sailed for Syria. Priscilla and Aquila went with him. Before he sailed, he had his hair cut off at Cenchrea. He did this because he had made a promise to God. [19]They arrived at Ephesus. There Paul said good-by to Priscilla and Aquila. He himself went into the synagogue and talked with the Jews. [20]The Jews asked him to spend more time with them. But he said no. [21]As he left, he made them a promise. "If God wants me to," he said, "I will come back." Then he sailed from Ephesus. [22]When he landed at Caesarea, he went up to Jerusalem. There he greeted the church. He then went down to Antioch.

[23]Paul spent some time in Antioch. Then he left and traveled all over Galatia and Phrygia. He gave strength to all the believers there.

[24]At that time a Jew named Apollos came to Ephesus. He was an educated man from

---

"I'm not a Christian because ..."

"I can make my own way to God."

"If you want to get a job done right - do it yourself!" This may work in day-to-day living, but it doesn't work in spiritual matters.

Why is a sailor on a naval ship told when to get up, when to sleep, when to eat, what to wear, what job to do? Because the ship belongs to the navy and they make the rules.

The same is true for sports teams, jobs, schools and families ... the one who establishes the system, makes the rules.

Now God, the One who created the world, said that the only way to Him was through Jesus.

"Do you believe that I am the one I claim to be? If you don't, you will certainly die in your sins." Jesus - John 8:24

Alexandria. He knew the Scriptures very well. [25]Apollos had been taught the way of the Lord. He spoke with great power. He taught the truth about Jesus. But he only knew about John's baptism. [26]He began to speak boldly in the synagogue. Priscilla and Aquila heard him. So they invited him to their home. There they gave him a better understanding of the way of God.

[27]Apollos wanted to go to Achaia. The brothers agreed with him. They wrote to the believers there. They asked them to welcome him. When he arrived, he was a great help to those who had become believers by God's grace. [28]He argued strongly against the Jews in public meetings. He proved from the Scriptures that Jesus was the Christ.

Paul Goes to Ephesus

19 While Apollos was at Corinth, Paul took the road to Ephesus. When he arrived, he found some believers there. [2]He asked them, "Did you receive the Holy Spirit when you became believers?"

"No," they answered. "We haven't even heard that there is a Holy Spirit."

[3]So Paul asked, "Then what baptism did you receive?"

"John's baptism," they replied.

[4]Paul said, "John baptized people, calling them to turn away from their sins. He told them to believe in the one who was coming after him. Jesus is that one." [5]After hearing this, they were baptized in the name of the Lord Jesus. [6]Paul placed his hands on them. Then the Holy Spirit came on them. They spoke in languages they had not known before. They also prophesied. [7]There were about 12 of them in all.

[8]Paul entered the synagogue. There he spoke boldly for three months. He tried to talk the people into accepting his teaching about God's kingdom. [9]But some of them wouldn't listen. They refused to believe. In public they said evil things about the Way of Jesus. So Paul left them. He took the believers with him. Each day he talked with people in the lecture hall of Tyrannus. [10]This went on for two years. So all the Jews and Greeks who lived in Asia Minor heard the word of the Lord.

[11]God did amazing miracles through Paul. [12]Even handkerchiefs and aprons that had touched him were taken to those who were sick. When this happened, their sicknesses were healed and evil spirits left them.

[13]Some Jews went around driving out evil spirits. They tried to use the name of the Lord Jesus to set free those who were controlled by demons. They said, "In Jesus' name I command you to come out. He is the Jesus that Paul is preaching about." [14]Seven sons of Sceva were doing this. Sceva was a Jewish chief priest. [15]One day the evil spirit answered them, "I know Jesus. And I know about Paul. But who are you?" [16]Then the man who had the evil spirit jumped on Sceva's sons. He overpowered them all. He gave them a terrible beating. They ran out of the house naked and bleeding.

[17]The Jews and Greeks living in Ephesus heard about this. They were all overcome with fear. They held the name of the Lord Jesus in high honor. [18]Many who believed now came and openly admitted the evil they had done. [19]A number of those who had practiced evil magic brought their scrolls together. They set them on fire out in the open. They added up the value of the scrolls. They found that it would take more than two lifetimes to earn what the scrolls were worth.

[20]The word of the Lord spread everywhere. It became more and more powerful.

[21]After all this had happened, Paul decided to go to Jerusalem. He went through Macedonia and Achaia. "After I have been to Jerusalem," he said, "I must visit Rome also." [22]He sent Timothy and Erastus, two of his helpers, to Macedonia. But he stayed a little longer in Asia Minor.

Trouble in Ephesus

[23]At that time many people became very upset about the Way of Jesus. [24]There was a man named Demetrius who made things out of silver. He made silver models of the temple of the goddess Artemis. He brought in a lot of business for the other skilled workers. [25]One day he called them together. He also called others who were in the same kind of business. "Men," he said, "you know that

we make good money from our work. [26]You have seen and heard what this fellow Paul is doing. He has talked to large numbers of people here in Ephesus. Almost everywhere in Asia Minor he has led people away from our gods. He says that the gods we make are not gods at all. [27]Our work is in danger of losing its good name. People's faith in the temple of the great goddess Artemis will be weakened. Now she is worshiped through all of Asia Minor and the whole world. But soon she will be robbed of her greatness."

[28]When they heard this, they became very angry. They began shouting, "Great is Artemis of the Ephesians!" [29]Soon people were making trouble in the whole city. They all rushed into the theater. They dragged Gaius and Aristarchus along with them. These two men had come with Paul from Macedonia. [30]Paul wanted to appear in front of the crowd. But the believers wouldn't let him. [31]Some of the officials in Asia Minor were friends of Paul. They sent him a message, begging him not to go into the theater.

[32]The crowd didn't know what was going on. Some were shouting one thing and some another. Most of the people didn't even know why they were there. [33]The Jews pushed Alexander to the front. Some of the crowd tried to tell him what to say. But he motioned for them to be quiet. He wanted to speak up for himself in front of the people. [34]But then they realized that he was a Jew. So they all shouted the same thing for about two hours. "Great is Artemis of the Ephesians!" they yelled.

[35]The city clerk quieted the crowd down. "Men of Ephesus!" he said. "The whole world knows that the city of Ephesus guards the temple of the great Artemis. They know that Ephesus guards her statue, which fell from heaven. [36]These facts can't be questioned. So calm down. Don't do anything foolish.

[37]"These men haven't robbed any temples. They haven't said evil things against our goddess. But you have brought them here anyhow. [38]Demetrius and the other skilled workers may feel they have been wronged by someone. Let them bring charges. The courts are open. We have our governors. [39]Is there anything else you want to bring up? Settle it in a court of law. [40]As it is, today we are in danger of being charged with causing all this trouble. But there is no reason for it. We wouldn't be able to explain what has happened." [41]After he said this, he sent the people away.

Paul Travels Through Macedonia and Greece

20 All the trouble came to an end. Then Paul sent for the believers. After cheering them up, he said good-by. He then left for Macedonia. [2]He traveled through that area, speaking many words of hope to the people. Finally he arrived in Greece.

By the Numbers

3000 become believers
when Peter preached
Acts 2:41

3 days of blindness
for Saul
Acts 9:9

$1,000,000
of magic books burned
Acts 19:19

40 men take an oath
to kill Paul
Acts 23:13

³There he stayed for three months. He was just about to sail for Syria. But the Jews were making plans against him. So he decided to go back through Macedonia. ⁴Sopater, son of Pyrrhus, from Berea went with him. Aristarchus and Secundus from Thessalonica, Gaius from Derbe, and Timothy went too. Tychicus and Trophimus from Asia Minor also went with him. ⁵These men went on ahead. They waited for us at Troas. ⁶But we sailed from Philippi after the Feast of Unleavened Bread. Five days later we joined the others at Troas. We stayed there for seven days.

Eutychus Is Raised From the Dead

⁷On the first day of the week we met to break bread and eat together. Paul spoke to the people. He kept on talking until midnight because he planned to leave the next day. ⁸There were many lamps in the room upstairs where we were meeting. ⁹A young man named Eutychus was sitting in a window. He sank into a deep sleep as Paul talked on and on. Sound asleep, Eutychus fell from the third floor. When they picked him up from the ground, he was dead.

¹⁰Paul went down and threw himself on the young man. He put his arms around him. "Don't be alarmed," he told them. "He's alive!" ¹¹Then Paul went upstairs again. He broke bread and ate with them. He kept on talking until daylight. Then he left. ¹²The people took the young man home. They were greatly comforted because he was alive.

Paul Says Good-by to the Ephesian Elders

¹³We went on ahead to the ship. We sailed for Assos. There we were going to take Paul on board. He had planned it this way because he wanted to go there by land. ¹⁴So he met us at Assos. We took him on board and went on to Mitylene. ¹⁵The next day we sailed from there. We arrived near Kios. The day after that we crossed over to Samos. We arrived at Miletus the next day. ¹⁶Paul had decided to sail past Ephesus. He didn't want to spend time in Asia Minor. He was in a hurry to get to Jerusalem. If he could, he wanted to be there by the day of Pentecost.

¹⁷From Miletus, Paul sent for the elders of the church at Ephesus. ¹⁸When they arrived, he spoke to them. "You know how I lived the whole time I was with you," he said. "From the first day I came into Asia Minor, ¹⁹I was free of pride. I served the Lord with tears. I served him even though I was greatly tested by the evil plans of the Jews. ²⁰You know I haven't let anyone keep me from preaching anything that would be helpful to you. I have taught you in public and from house to house. ²¹I have told both Jews and Greeks that they must turn away from their sins to God. They must have faith in our Lord Jesus.

²²"Now I am going to Jerusalem. The Holy Spirit compels me. I don't know what will happen to me there. ²³I only know that in every city the Spirit warns me. He tells me that I will face prison and suffering. ²⁴But my life means nothing to me. I only want to finish the race. I want to complete the work the Lord Jesus has given me. He wants me to give witness to others about the good news of God's grace.

²⁵"I have spent time with you preaching about the kingdom. I know that none of you will ever see me again. ²⁶So I tell you today that I am not guilty if anyone has not believed. ²⁷I haven't let anyone keep me from telling you everything God wants you to do.

²⁸"Keep watch over yourselves. Keep watch over all the believers. The Holy Spirit has made you leaders over them. Be shepherds of God's church. He bought it with his own blood.

²⁹"I know that after I leave, wild wolves will come in among you. They won't spare any of the sheep. ³⁰Even men from your own people will rise up and twist the truth. They want to get the believers to follow them. ³¹So be on your guard! Remember that for three years I never stopped warning you. Night and day I warned each of you with tears.

³²"Now I commit you to God's care. I commit you to the word of his grace. It can build you up. Then you will share in what God plans to give all his people. ³³I haven't longed for anyone's silver or gold or clothing. ³⁴You yourselves know that I have used

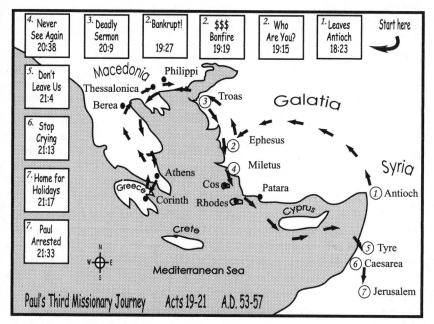

Paul's Third Missionary Journey   Acts 19-21   A.D. 53-57

Map labels:
4. Never See Again 20:38
3. Deadly Sermon 20:9
2. Bankrupt! 19:27
2. $$$ Bonfire 19:19
2. Who Are You? 19:15
1. Leaves Antioch 18:23
Start here

5. Don't Leave Us 21:4
6. Stop Crying 21:13
7. Home for Holidays 21:17
7. Paul Arrested 21:33

Macedonia
Philippi
Thessalonica
Berea
Troas
Galatia
Ephesus
Miletus
Syria
Athens
Cos
Greece
Corinth
Rhodes
Patara
Cyprus
Antioch
Crete
Mediterranean Sea
Tyre
Caesarea
Jerusalem

my own hands to meet my needs. I have also met the needs of my companions. ³⁵In everything I did, I showed you that we must work hard and help the weak. We must remember the words of the Lord Jesus. He said, 'It is more blessed to give than to receive.' "

³⁶When Paul had said this, he got down on his knees with all of them and prayed. ³⁷They all cried as they hugged and kissed him. ³⁸What hurt them the most was that he had said they would never see his face again. Then they went with him to the ship.

Paul Continues His Journey

21 After we had torn ourselves away from the Ephesian elders, we headed out to sea. We sailed straight to Cos. The next day we went to Rhodes. From there we continued on to Patara. ²We found a ship crossing over to Phoenicia. So we went on board and headed out to sea. ³We came near Cyprus and passed to the south of it. Then we sailed on to Syria. We landed at Tyre. There our ship was supposed to unload. ⁴We found the believers there and stayed with them for seven days. Led by the Holy Spirit, they tried to get Paul not to

go on to Jerusalem. ⁵But when it was time to leave, we continued on our way. All the believers and their families went with us out of the city. There on the beach we got down on our knees to pray. ⁶We said goodby to each other. Then we went on board the ship. And they returned home.

⁷Continuing on from Tyre, we landed at Ptolemais. There we greeted the brothers and sisters. We stayed with them for a day. ⁸The next day we left and arrived at Caesarea. We stayed at the house of Philip the evangelist. He was one of the seven deacons. ⁹He had four unmarried daughters who prophesied.

¹⁰We stayed there several days. Then a prophet named Agabus came down from Judea. ¹¹He came over to us. Then he took Paul's belt and tied his own hands and feet with it. He said, "The Holy Spirit says, 'This is how the Jews of Jerusalem will tie up the owner of this belt. They will hand him over to people who are not Jews.' "

¹²When we heard this, we all begged Paul not to go up to Jerusalem. ¹³He asked, "Why are you crying? Why are you breaking my heart? I'm ready to be put in prison. In fact,

I'm ready to die in Jerusalem for the Lord Jesus." [14]We couldn't change his mind. So we gave up. We said, "May what the Lord wants to happen be done."

[15]After this, we got ready and went up to Jerusalem. [16]Some of the believers from Caesarea went with us. They brought us to Mnason's home. We were supposed to stay there. Mnason was from Cyprus. He was one of the first believers.

Paul Arrives in Jerusalem

[17]When we arrived in Jerusalem, the brothers and sisters gave us a warm welcome. [18]The next day Paul and the rest of us went to see James. All the elders were there. [19]Paul greeted them. Then he reported everything God had done among the non-Jews through his work.

[20]When they heard this, they praised God. Then they spoke to Paul. "Brother," they said, "you see that thousands of Jews have become believers. All of them try very hard to obey the law. [21]They have been told that you teach all the Jews who live among the non-Jews to turn away from Moses. They think that you teach them not to circumcise their children. They think that you teach them to give up our Jewish ways.

[22]"What should we do? They will certainly hear that you have come. [23]So do what we tell you. There are four men with us who have made a promise to God. [24]Take them with you. Join them in the Jewish practice that makes people pure and clean. Pay their expenses so they can have their heads shaved. Then everybody will know that these reports about you are not true in any way. They will know that you yourself obey the law.

[25]"We have already given written directions to the believers who are not Jews. They must not eat food that has been offered to statues of gods. They must not drink blood. They must not eat the meat of animals that have been choked to death. And they must not commit sexual sins."

[26]The next day Paul took the men with him. They all made themselves pure and clean in the usual way. Then Paul went to the temple. There he reported the date when the days of cleansing would end. At that time the proper offering would be made for each of them.

Paul Is Arrested

[27]The seven days of cleansing were almost over. Some Jews from Asia Minor saw Paul at the temple. They stirred up the whole crowd. They arrested Paul. [28]"Men of Israel, help us!" they shouted. "This is the man who teaches everyone in all places against our people. He speaks against our law and against this holy place. Besides, he has brought Greeks into the temple area. He has made this holy place unclean." [29]They said this because they had seen Trophimus the Ephesian in the city with Paul. They thought Paul had brought him into the temple area.

[30]The whole city was stirred up. People came running from all directions. They grabbed Paul and dragged him out of the temple. Right away the temple gates were shut. [31]The people were trying to kill Paul. But news reached the commander of the Roman troops. He heard that people were making trouble in the whole city of Jerusalem. [32]At once he took some officers and soldiers with him. They ran down to the crowd. The people causing the trouble saw the commander and his soldiers. So they stopped beating Paul.

[33]The commander came up and arrested Paul. He ordered him to be held with two chains. Then he asked who Paul was and what he had done. [34]Some in the crowd shouted one thing, some another. But the commander couldn't get the facts because of all the noise. So he ordered that Paul be taken into the fort. [35]Paul reached the steps. But then the mob became so wild that he had to be carried by the soldiers. [36]The crowd that followed kept shouting, "Kill him!"

Paul Speaks to the Crowd

[37]The soldiers were about to take Paul into the fort. Then he asked the commander, "May I say something to you?"

"Do you speak Greek?" he replied. [38]"Aren't you the Egyptian who turned some of our people against their leaders? Didn't

ACTS

The crossword grid with starting letters: 1 across begins with **J**, 12 down begins with **F**.

Across

#	Clue	Reference
1.	Central city	ch. 1
5.	Sound of doves	---
6.	Wrote second Gospel book	---
7.	Preached to Gentiles	ch. 15
8.	First to die for Christ	ch. 7
13.	Enemy of the Church	ch. 9
14.	Tentmaker, preacher	ch. 18
15.	"Jesus _____"	ch. 4
17.	Holy _____ gives power	ch. 2
18.	City of "unknown god" altar	ch. 17

Down

#	Clue	Reference
1.	Killed by a sword	ch. 12
2.	Abb. "south"	---
3.	Opposite of truth	---
4.	Called for Peter	ch. 10
5.	Shed tears, weep	---
9.	Helped an Ethiopian	ch. 8
10.	Scales fell from Saul's ____	ch. 9
11.	"I _____ to Caesar!"	ch. 25
12.	"You are out of your mind"	ch. 26
16.	_____ that cannot hear	ch. 28

you lead 4,000 terrorists out into the desert some time ago?"

³⁹Paul answered, "I am a Jew from Tarsus in Cilicia. I am a citizen of an important city. Please let me speak to the people."

⁴⁰The commander told him he could. So Paul stood on the steps and motioned to the crowd. When all of them were quiet, he spoke to them in the Aramaic language. 22 ¹"Brothers and fathers," Paul began, "listen to me now. I want to speak up for myself."

²When they heard that he was speaking to them in Aramaic, they became very quiet.

Then Paul said, ³"I am a Jew. I was born in Tarsus in Cilicia. But I grew up here in Jerusalem. I was well trained by Gamaliel in the law of our people. I wanted to serve God as much as any of you do today. ⁴I hurt the followers of the Way of Jesus. I sent many of them to their death. I arrested men and women. I threw them into prison. ⁵The high priest and the whole Council can give witness to this. I even had some official letters they had written to their friends in Damascus. So I went there to bring these people as prisoners to Jerusalem to be punished.

⁶"I had almost reached Damascus. About noon a bright light from heaven suddenly flashed around me. ⁷I fell to the ground and heard a voice speak to me. 'Saul! Saul!' it said. 'Why are you opposing me?'

⁸" 'Who are you, Lord?' I asked.

" 'I am Jesus of Nazareth,' he replied. 'I am the one you are opposing.'

⁹"The light was seen by my companions. But they didn't understand the voice of the one speaking to me.

¹⁰" 'What should I do, Lord?' I asked.

" 'Get up,' the Lord said. 'Go into Damascus. There you will be told everything you have been given to do.' ¹¹The brightness of the light had blinded me. So my companions led me by the hand into Damascus.

¹²"A man named Ananias came to see me. He was a godly Jew who obeyed the law. All the Jews living there respected him very much. ¹³He stood beside me and said, 'Brother Saul, receive your sight!' At that very moment I was able to see him.

¹⁴"Then he said, 'The God of our people has chosen you. He wanted to tell you his plans for you. You have seen the Blameless One. You have heard words from his mouth. ¹⁵Now you will give witness to all people about what you have seen and heard. ¹⁶So what are you waiting for? Get up and call on his name. Be baptized. Have your sins washed away.'

¹⁷"I returned to Jerusalem and was praying at the temple. Then it seemed to me that I was dreaming. ¹⁸I saw the Lord speaking to me. 'Quick!' he said. 'Leave Jerusalem at once. These people will not accept your witness about me.'

¹⁹" 'Lord,' I replied, 'these people know what I used to do. I went from one synagogue to another and put believers in prison. I also beat them. ²⁰Stephen was a man who gave witness to others about you. I stood there when he was killed. I had agreed that he should die. I even guarded the coats of those who were killing him.'

²¹"Then the Lord said to me, 'Go. I will send you far away to people who are not Jews.' "

Paul the Roman Citizen

²²The crowd listened to Paul until he said this. Then they shouted, "Kill him! He isn't fit to live!"

²³They shouted and threw off their coats. They threw dust into the air. ²⁴So the commanding officer ordered Paul to be taken into the fort. He gave orders for Paul to be whipped and questioned. He wanted to find out why the people were shouting at him like this.

²⁵A commander was standing there as they stretched Paul out to be whipped. Paul said to him, "Does the law allow you to whip a Roman citizen who hasn't even been found guilty?"

²⁶When the commander heard this, he went to the commanding officer and reported it. "What are you going to do?" the commander asked. "This man is a Roman citizen."

²⁷So the commanding officer went to Paul. "Tell me," he asked. "Are you a Roman citizen?"

"Yes, I am," Paul answered.

[28]Then the officer said, "I had to pay a lot of money to become a citizen."

"But I was born a citizen," Paul replied.

[29]Right away those who were about to question him left. Even the officer was alarmed. He realized that he had put Paul, a Roman citizen, in chains.

Paul Is Taken to the Sanhedrin

[30]The commanding officer wanted to find out exactly what the Jews had against Paul. So the next day he let Paul out of prison. He ordered a meeting of the chief priests and all the Sanhedrin. Then he brought Paul and had him stand in front of them.

23 Paul looked straight at the Sanhedrin. "My brothers," he said, "I have always done my duty to God. To this very day I feel that I have done nothing wrong."

[2]Ananias the high priest heard this. So he ordered the men standing near Paul to hit him on the mouth.

[3]Then Paul said to him, "You pretender! God will hit you! You sit there and judge me by the law. But you yourself broke the law when you commanded them to hit me!"

[4]Those who were standing near Paul said, "How dare you talk like that to God's high priest!"

[5]Paul replied, "Brothers, I didn't realize he was the high priest. It is written, 'Do not speak evil about the ruler of your people.'" (Exodus 22:28)

[6]Paul knew that some of them were Sadducees and the others Pharisees. So he called out in the Sanhedrin. "My brothers," he said, "I am a Pharisee. I am the son of a Pharisee. I believe that people will rise from the dead. That's why I am on trial."

[7]When he said this, the Pharisees and the Sadducees started to argue. They began to take sides. [8]The Sadducees say that people will not rise from the dead. They don't believe there are angels or spirits either. But the Pharisees believe all these things.

[9]People were causing trouble and making a lot of noise. Some of the teachers of the law who were Pharisees stood up. They argued strongly. "We find nothing wrong with this man," they said. "What if a spirit or an angel has spoken to him?" [10]The arguing got out of hand. The commanding officer was afraid that Paul would be torn to pieces by those who were arguing. So he ordered the soldiers to go down and take him away from them by force. They were supposed to bring him into the fort.

[11]The next night the Lord stood near Paul. He said, "Be brave! You have given witness about me in Jerusalem. You must do the same in Rome."

The Plan to Kill Paul

[12]The next morning the Jews gathered secretly to make plans against Paul. They took an oath that they would not eat or drink anything until they had killed him. [13]More than 40 men took part in this plan. [14]They went to the chief priests and the elders. They said, "We have taken a strong oath. We have made a special promise to God. We will not eat anything until we have killed Paul. [15]Now then, you and the Sanhedrin must make an appeal to the commanding officer. Ask him to bring Paul to you. Pretend you want more facts about his case. We are ready to kill him before he gets here."

[16]But Paul's nephew heard about this plan. So he went into the fort and told Paul.

[17]Then Paul called one of the commanders. He said to him, "Take this young man to the commanding officer. He has something to tell him." [18]So the commander took Paul's nephew to the officer.

The commander said, "Paul, the prisoner, sent for me. He asked me to bring this young man to you. The young man has something

God gives his best to those who leave the choice with Him.

to tell you."

[19]The commanding officer took the young man by the hand. He spoke to him in private. "What do you want to tell me?" the officer asked.

[20]He said, "The Jews have agreed to ask you to bring Paul to the Sanhedrin tomorrow. They will pretend they want more facts about him. [21]Don't give in to them. More than 40 of them are waiting in hiding to attack him. They have taken an oath that they will not eat or drink anything until they have killed him. They are ready now. All they need is for you to bring Paul to the Sanhedrin."

[22]The commanding officer let the young man go. But he gave him a warning. "Don't tell anyone you have reported this to me," he said.

Paul Is Taken to Caesarea

[23]Then the commanding officer called for two of his commanders. He ordered them, "Gather a company of 200 soldiers, 70 horsemen and 200 men armed with spears. Get them ready to go to Caesarea at nine o'clock tonight. [24]Provide horses for Paul so that he may be taken safely to Governor Felix."

[25]Here is the letter the officer wrote.

[26]I, Claudius Lysias, am writing this letter.

I am sending it to His Excellency, Governor Felix.

Greetings.

[27]The Jews grabbed Paul. They were about to kill him. But I came with my soldiers and saved him. I had learned that he is a Roman citizen. [28]I wanted to know why they were bringing charges against him. So I brought him to their Sanhedrin. [29]I found out that the charge against him was based on questions about their law. But there was no charge against him worthy of death or prison. [30]Then I was told about a plan against the man. So I sent him to you at once. I also ordered those bringing charges against him to tell you their case.

[31]The soldiers followed their orders. During the night they took Paul with them. They brought him as far as Antipatris. [32]The next day they let the horsemen go on with him. The soldiers returned to the fort. [33]The horsemen arrived in Caesarea. They gave the letter to the governor. Then they handed Paul over to him. [34]The governor read the letter. He asked Paul where he was from. He learned that Paul was from Cilicia. [35]So he said, "I will hear your case when those bringing charges against you get here." Then he ordered that Paul be kept under guard in Herod's palace.

Paul's Trial in Front of Felix

24 Five days later Ananias the high priest went down to Caesarea. Some elders and a lawyer named Tertullus went with him. They brought their charges against Paul to the governor. [2]So Paul was

called in. Tertullus began to bring the charges against Paul. He said to Felix, "We have enjoyed a long time of peace while you have been ruling. You are a wise leader. You have made this a better nation. ³Most excellent Felix, we gladly admit this everywhere and in every way. And we are very thankful. ⁴I don't want to bother you. But would you be kind enough to listen to us for a short time?

⁵"We have found that Paul is a trouble-maker. He stirs up trouble among Jews all over the world. He is a leader of those who follow Jesus of Nazareth. ⁶/⁷He even tried to pollute our temple. So we arrested him. ⁸Question him yourself. Then you will learn the truth about all these charges we are bringing against him."

⁹The Jews said the same thing. They agreed that the charges were true.

¹⁰The governor motioned for Paul to speak. Paul said, "I know that you have been a judge over this nation for quite a few years. So I am glad to stand up for myself. ¹¹About 12 days ago I went up to Jerusalem to worship. You can easily check on this. ¹²Those bringing charges against me did not find me arguing with anyone at the temple. I wasn't stirring up a crowd in the synagogues or anywhere else in the city. ¹³They can't prove to you any of the charges they are making against me.

¹⁴"It is true that I worship the God of our people. I am a follower of the Way of Jesus. Those bringing charges against me call it a cult. I believe everything that agrees with the Law. I believe everything written in the Prophets. ¹⁵I have the same hope in God that these men have. I believe that both the godly and the ungodly will rise from the dead. ¹⁶So I always try not to do anything wrong in the eyes of God and man.

¹⁷"I was away for several years. Then I came to Jerusalem to bring my people gifts for those who were poor. I also came to offer sacrifices. ¹⁸They found me doing this in the temple courtyard. I had already been made pure and clean in the usual way. There was no crowd with me. I didn't stir up any trouble.

¹⁹"But there are some other Jews who should be here in front of you. They are from Asia Minor. They should bring charges if they have anything against me. ²⁰Let the Jews who are here tell you what crime I am guilty of. After all, I was put on trial by the Sanhedrin. ²¹Perhaps they blame me for what I said when I was on trial. I shouted, 'I believe that people will rise from the dead. That is why I am on trial here today.'"

²²Felix knew all about the Way of Jesus. So he put off the trial for the time being. "Lysias the commanding officer will come," he said. "Then I will decide your case." ²³He ordered the commander to keep Paul under guard. He told him to give Paul some freedom. He also told him to allow Paul's friends to take care of his needs.

²⁴Several days later Felix came with his wife Drusilla. She was a Jew. Felix sent for Paul and listened to him speak about faith in Christ Jesus. ²⁵Paul talked about how to live right. He talked about how people should control themselves. He also talked

... 4 REACTIONS TO THE GOSPEL

about the time when God will judge everyone. Then Felix became afraid. "That's enough for now!" he said. "You may leave. When I find the time, I will send for you." 26He was hoping that Paul would offer him some money to let him go. So he often sent for Paul and talked with him.

27Two years passed. Porcius Festus took the place of Felix. But Felix wanted to do the Jews a favor. So he left Paul in prison.

Paul's Trial in Front of Festus

25 Three days after Festus arrived, he went up from Caesarea to Jerusalem. 2There the chief priests and Jewish leaders came to him and brought their charges against Paul. 3They tried to get Festus to have Paul taken to Jerusalem. They asked for this as a favor. They were planning to hide and attack Paul along the way. They wanted to kill him. 4Festus answered, "Paul is being held at Caesarea. Soon I'll be going there myself. 5Let some of your leaders come with me. If the man has done anything wrong, they can bring charges against him there."

6Festus spent eight or ten days in Jerusalem with them. Then he went down to Caesarea. The next day he called the court together. He ordered Paul to be brought to him. 7When Paul arrived, the Jews who had come down from Jerusalem stood around him. They brought many strong charges against him. But they couldn't prove them.

8Then Paul spoke up for himself. He said, "I've done nothing wrong against the law of the Jews or against the temple. I've done nothing wrong against Caesar."

9But Festus wanted to do the Jews a favor. So he said to Paul, "Are you willing to go up to Jerusalem? Are you willing to go on trial there? Are you willing to face these charges in my court?"

10Paul answered, "I'm already standing in Caesar's court. This is where I should go on trial. I haven't done anything wrong to the Jews. You yourself know that very well. 11If I am guilty of anything worthy of death, I'm willing to die. But the charges brought against me by these Jews are not true. No one has the right to hand me over to them. I make my appeal to Caesar!"

12Festus talked it over with the members of his court. Then he said, "You have made an appeal to Caesar. To Caesar you will go!"

Festus Talks With King Agrippa

13A few days later King Agrippa and Bernice arrived in Caesarea. They came to pay a visit to Festus. 14They were spending many days there. So Festus talked with the king about Paul's case. He said, "There's a man here that Felix left as a prisoner. 15When I went to Jerusalem, the Jewish chief priests and the elders brought charges against the man. They wanted him to be found guilty.

16"I told them that this is not the way Romans do things. We don't judge people before they have faced those bringing charges against them. They must have a chance to speak up for themselves. 17When the Jews came back with me, I didn't waste any time. I called the court together the next day. I ordered the man to be brought in. 18Those bringing charges against him got up to speak. But they didn't charge him with any of the crimes I had expected. 19Instead, they argued with him about their own beliefs. They didn't agree about a dead man named Jesus. Paul claimed Jesus was alive.

20"I had no idea how to look into such matters. So I asked Paul if he would be willing to go to Jerusalem. There he could be tried on these charges. 21But Paul made an appeal to have the Emperor decide his case. So I ordered him to be held until I could send him to Caesar."

22Then Agrippa said to Festus, "I would like to hear this man myself."

Festus replied, "Tomorrow you will hear him."

Paul Speaks to Agrippa

23The next day Agrippa and Bernice arrived. They acted like very important people. They entered the courtroom. The most important officers and the leading men of the city came with them. When Festus gave the command, Paul was brought in. 24Festus said, "King Agrippa, and all who are here with us, take a good look at this man! Both in Jerusalem and here in Caes-

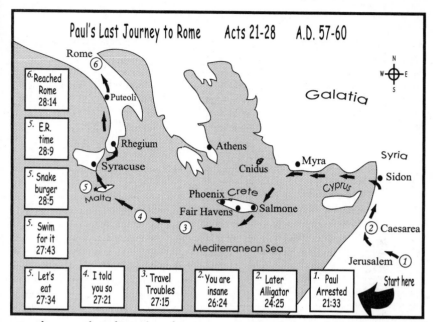

Paul's Last Journey to Rome   Acts 21-28   A.D. 57-60

Rome
6
Galatia
6. Reached Rome 28:14
Puteoli
5. E.R. time 28:9
Rhegium
Athens
Myra
Syria
5. Snake burger 28:5
Syracuse
Cnidus
Sidon
5
Cyprus
Malta
Phoenix Crete
Caesarea
4
Fair Havens
Salmone
2
3
5. Swim for it 27:43
Mediterranean Sea
Jerusalem 1
5. Let's eat 27:34
4. I told you so 27:21
3. Travel Troubles 27:15
2. You are insane 26:24
2. Later Alligator 24:25
1. Paul Arrested 21:33
Start here

area a large number of Jews have come to me about him. They keep shouting that he shouldn't live any longer. [25]I have found that he hasn't done anything worthy of death. But he made his appeal to the Emperor. So I decided to send him to Rome.

[26]"I don't have anything certain to write about him to His Majesty. So I have brought him here today. Now all of you will be able to hear him. King Agrippa, it will also be very good for you to hear him. As a result of this hearing, I will have something to write. [27]It doesn't make sense to send a prisoner to Rome without listing the charges against him."

26 Agrippa said to Paul, "You may now speak for yourself."

So Paul motioned with his hand. Then he began to stand up for himself. [2]"King Agrippa," he said, "I am happy to be able to stand here today. I will speak up for myself against all the charges brought by the Jews. [3]I am very pleased that you are familiar with Jewish ways. You know the kinds of things they argue about. So I beg you to be patient as you listen to me.

[4]"The Jews all know how I have lived

ever since I was a child. They know all about me from the beginning of my life. They know how I lived in my own country and in Jerusalem. [5]They have known me for a long time. So if they wanted to, they could give witness that I lived by the rules of the Pharisees. Those rules are harder to obey than the rules of any other group in the Jewish faith.

[6]"Today I am on trial because of the hope I have. I believe in what God promised our people long ago. [7]It is the promise that our 12 tribes are hoping to see come true. Because of this hope they serve God with a true and honest heart day and night. King Agrippa, it is also because of this hope that the Jews are bringing charges against me. [8]Why should any of you think it is impossible for God to raise the dead?

[9]"I myself believed that I should do everything I could to oppose the name of Jesus of Nazareth. [10]That's just what I was doing in Jerusalem. On the authority of the chief priests, I put many of God's people in prison. I agreed that they should die. [11]I often went from one synagogue to another to have them punished. I tried to force them

to speak evil things against Jesus. I hated them so much that I even went to cities in other lands to hurt them.

[12]"On one of these journeys I was on my way to Damascus. I had the authority and commission of the chief priests. [13]About noon, King Agrippa, I was on the road. I saw a light coming from heaven. It was brighter than the sun. It was shining around me and my companions. [14]We all fell to the ground. I heard a voice speak to me in the Aramaic language. 'Saul! Saul!' it said. 'Why are you opposing me? It is hard for you to go against what you know is right.'

[15]"Then I asked, 'Who are you, Lord?'

" 'I am Jesus,' the Lord replied. 'I am the one you are opposing. [16]Now get up. Stand on your feet. I have appeared to you to appoint you to serve me and be my witness. You will tell others that you have seen me today. You will also tell them that I will show myself to you again.

[17]" 'I will save you from your own people and from those who aren't Jews. I am sending you to them [18]to open their eyes. I want you to turn them from darkness to light. I want you to turn them from Satan's power to God. I want their sins to be forgiven. They will be forgiven when they believe in me. They will have their place among God's people.'

[19]"So then, King Agrippa, I obeyed the vision that appeared from heaven. [20]First I preached to people in Damascus. Then I preached in Jerusalem and in all Judea. I preached also to people who are not Jews. I told them to turn away from their sins to God. The way they live must prove that they have turned away from their sins. [21]That's why the Jews grabbed me in the temple courtyard and tried to kill me.

[22]"But God has helped me to this very day. So I stand here and give witness to both small and great. I have been saying nothing different from what the prophets and Moses said would happen. [23]They said the Christ would suffer. He would be the first to rise from the dead. He would announce the light of life to his own people and to those who aren't Jews."

[24]While Paul was still speaking up for himself, Festus interrupted. "You are out of your mind, Paul!" he shouted. "Your great learning is driving you crazy!"

[25]"I am not crazy, most excellent Festus," Paul replied. "What I am saying is true and reasonable. [26]The king is familiar with these things. So I can speak openly to him. I am certain he knows everything that has been going on. After all, it was not done in secret. [27]King Agrippa, do you believe the prophets? I know you do."

[28]Then Agrippa spoke to Paul. "Are you trying to talk me into becoming a Christian?" he said. "Do you think you can do that in such a short time?"

[29]Paul replied, "I don't care if it takes a short time or a long time. I pray to God for you and all who are listening to me today. I pray that you may become like me, except for these chains."

[30]The king stood up. The governor and Bernice and those sitting with them stood up too. [31]They left the room and began to talk with one another. "Why should this man die or be put in prison?" they said. "He has done nothing worthy of that!"

[32]Agrippa said to Festus, "This man could have been set free. But he has made an appeal to Caesar."

Paul Sails for Rome

27 It was decided that we would sail for Italy. Paul and some other prisoners were handed over to a Roman commander named Julius. He belonged to the Imperial Guard. [2]We boarded a ship from Adramyttium. It was about to sail for ports along the coast of Asia Minor. We headed out to sea. Aristarchus was with us. He was a Macedonian from Thessalonica.

[3]The next day we landed at Sidon. There Julius was kind to Paul. He let Paul visit his friends so they could give him what he needed. [4]From there we headed out to sea again. We passed the calmer side of Cyprus because the winds were against us.

[5]We sailed across the open sea off the coast of Cilicia and Pamphylia. Then we landed at Myra in Lycia. [6]There the commander found a ship from Alexandria sailing for Italy. He put us on board. [7]We moved along slowly for many days. We had trouble getting to Cnidus. The wind did

not let us stay on course. So we passed the calmer side of Crete, opposite Salmone. [8]It was not easy to sail along the coast. Then we came to a place called Fair Havens. It was near the town of Lasea.

[9]A lot of time had passed. Sailing had already become dangerous. By now it was after the Day of Atonement, a day of fasting. So Paul gave them a warning. [10]"Men," he said, "I can see that our trip is going to be dangerous. The ship and everything in it will be lost. Our own lives will be in danger also."

[11]But the commander didn't listen to what Paul said. Instead, he followed the advice of the pilot and the ship's owner. [12]The harbor wasn't a good place for ships to stay during winter. So most of the people decided we should sail on. They hoped we would reach Phoenix. They wanted to spend the winter there. Phoenix was a harbor in Crete. It faced both southwest and northwest.

The Storm

[13]A gentle south wind began to blow. They thought that this was what they had been waiting for. So they pulled up the anchor and sailed along the shore of Crete. [14]Before very long, a wind blew down from the island. It had the force of a hurricane. It was called a "northeaster."

[15]The ship was caught by the storm. We could not keep it sailing into the wind. So we gave up and were driven along. [16]We passed the calmer side of a small island called Cauda. We almost lost the lifeboat. [17]So the men lifted it on board. Then they tied ropes under the ship itself to hold it together. They were afraid it would get stuck on the sandbars of Syrtis. They lowered the sea anchor and let the ship be driven along.

[18]We took a very bad beating from the storm. The next day the crew began to throw the ship's contents overboard. [19]On the third day, they even threw the ship's gear overboard with their own hands. [20]The sun and stars didn't appear for many days. The storm was terrible. So we gave up all hope of being saved.

[21]The men had not eaten for a long time. Paul stood up in front of them. "Men," he said, "you should have taken my advice not to sail from Crete. Then you would have avoided this harm and loss.

[22]"Now I beg you to be brave. Not one of you will die. Only the ship will be destroyed. [23]I belong to God and serve him. Last night his angel stood beside me. [24]The angel said, 'Do not be afraid, Paul. You must go on trial in front of Caesar. God has shown his grace by sparing the lives of all those sailing with you.' [25]"Men, continue to be brave. I have faith in God. It will happen just as he told me. [26]But we must run the ship onto the beach of some island."

The Ship Is Destroyed

[27]On the 14th night we were still being driven across the Sea of Adria. About midnight the sailors had a feeling that they were approaching land. [28]They measured how deep the water was. They found that it was 120 feet deep. A short time later they measured the water again. This time it was 90 feet deep. [29]They were afraid we would crash against the rocks. So they dropped four anchors from the back of the ship. They prayed that daylight would come.

[30]The sailors wanted to escape from the ship. So they let the lifeboat down into the sea. They pretended they were going to lower some anchors from the front of the ship. [31]But Paul spoke to the commander and the soldiers. "These men must stay with the ship," he said. "If they don't, you can't be saved." [32]So the soldiers cut the ropes that held the lifeboat. They let it drift away.

[33]Just before dawn Paul tried to get them all to eat. "For the last 14 days," he said, "you have wondered what would happen. You have gone without food. You haven't eaten anything. [34]Now I am asking you to eat

In going the second mile, we find no traffic jams.

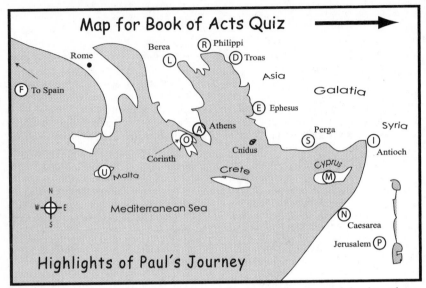

Map for Book of Acts Quiz

Berea
(R) Philippi
Rome
(L)
(D) Troas
(F) To Spain
Asia
Galatia
(E) Ephesus
(A) Athens
Perga
Syria
(O)
(S)
(I)
Corinth
Cnidus
Antioch
(U) Malta
Crete
Cyprus
(M)
N
W—E
S
Mediterranean Sea
(N)
Caesarea
Jerusalem (P)

Highlights of Paul's Journey

some food. You need it to live. Not one of you will lose a single hair from your head."

³⁵After Paul said this, he took some bread and gave thanks to God. He did this where they all could see him. Then he broke it and began to eat. ³⁶All of them were filled with hope. So they ate some food. ³⁷There were 276 of us on board. ³⁸They ate as much as they wanted. They needed to make the ship lighter. So they threw the rest of the grain into the sea.

³⁹When daylight came, they saw a bay with a sandy beach. They didn't recognize the place. But they decided to run the ship onto the beach if they could. ⁴⁰So they cut the anchors loose and left them in the sea. At the same time, they untied the ropes that held the rudders. They lifted the sail at the front of the ship to the wind. Then they headed for the beach. ⁴¹But the ship hit a sandbar. So the front of it got stuck and wouldn't move. The back of the ship was broken to pieces by the pounding of the waves.

⁴²The soldiers planned to kill the prisoners. They wanted to keep them from swimming away and escaping. ⁴³But the commander wanted to save Paul's life. So he kept the soldiers from carrying out their plan. He ordered those who could swim to jump overboard first and swim to land. ⁴⁴The rest were supposed to get there on

boards or other pieces of the ship. That is how everyone reached land safely.

On Shore at Malta

28 When we were safe on shore, we found out that the island was called Malta. ²The people of the island were unusually kind. It was raining and cold. So they built a fire and welcomed all of us.

³Paul gathered some sticks and put them on the fire. A poisonous snake was driven out by the heat. It fastened itself on Paul's hand. ⁴The people of the island saw the snake hanging from his hand. They said to each other, "This man must be a murderer. He escaped from the sea. But Justice won't let him live." Justice was the name of a goddess.

⁵Paul shook the snake off into the fire. He was not harmed. ⁶The people expected him to swell up. They thought he would suddenly fall dead. They waited for a long time. But they didn't see anything unusual happen to him. So they changed their minds. They said he was a god.

⁷Publius owned property nearby. He was the chief official on the island. He welcomed us to his home. For three days he took care of us. He treated us with kindness. ⁸His father was sick in bed. The man suffered from fever and dysentery. So Paul

Open Book Quiz - The Book of Acts

Use Map on Previous Page

Read the letters from top to bottom and complete the answer below.

1 _____ Oath to Kill Paul   ch. 23

2 _____ Altar to Unknown God   ch. 17

3 _____ Shipwrecked But Safe   ch. 28

4 _____ Daily Bible Study   ch. 17

5 _____ Million Dollar Fire   ch. 19

6 _____ I Appeal to Caesar   ch. 25

7 _____ Deadly Sermon   ch. 20

8 _____ Mutiny of John Mark   ch. 13

9 _____ Snake Holding On   ch. 28

10 _____ Paul Arrested   ch. 21

11 _____ Paul & Barnabas Split ch. 15

12 _____ You're Out of Your Mind ch. 26

13 _____ Earthquake = Freedom   ch. 16

14 _____ Keep Preaching   ch. 18

15 _____ Son of the Devil   ch. 13

16 _____ Naked and Bleeding   ch. 19

Select the best answer from the right column which matches items 1-16 in the left column. Some letters are used more than once

A - Athens

D - Troas

E - Ephesus

F - Spain

I - Antioch

L - Berea

M - Cyprus

N - Caesarea

O - Corinth

P - Jerusalem

R - Philippi

S - Perga

U - Malta

Self-score

15 - 16 Great Job, Captain!

13 - 14 Nice Job, Mate

10 - 12 Set the Sails!

5 - 9   Prepare a Life Boat

1 - 4   Swab the deck

Answer:

__ __ __ __ • __ __ __ __ __ • __ __ __

__ __ __ • __ __ __ __

"An Adventurous Journey"

went in to see him. Paul prayed for him. He placed his hands on him and healed him.

⁹Then the rest of the sick people on the island came. They too were healed. ¹⁰The people of the island honored us in many ways. When we were ready to sail, they gave us the supplies we needed.

Paul Arrives in Rome

¹¹After three months we headed out to sea. We sailed in a ship that had stayed at the island during the winter. It was a ship from Alexandria. On the front of it the figures of twin gods were carved. Their names were Castor and Pollux. ¹²We landed at Syracuse and stayed there for three days.

¹³From there we sailed to Rhegium. The next day the south wind came up. The day after that, we reached Puteoli. ¹⁴There we found some believers. They invited us to spend a week with them.

At last we came to Rome. ¹⁵The brothers and sisters there had heard we were coming. They traveled as far as the Forum of Appius and the Three Taverns to meet us. When Paul saw these people, he thanked God and was cheered up. ¹⁶When we got to Rome, Paul was allowed to live by himself. But a soldier guarded him.

Paul Preaches in Rome

¹⁷Three days later Paul called a meeting of the Jewish leaders. So they came. Paul said to them, "My brothers, I have done nothing against our people. I have also done nothing against what our people of long ago practiced. But I was arrested in Jerusalem. I was handed over to the Romans.

¹⁸"They questioned me. And they wanted to let me go. They saw I wasn't guilty of any crime worthy of death. ¹⁹But the Jews objected. So I had to make an appeal to Caesar.

"It wasn't that I had anything against my own people. ²⁰I share Israel's hope. That is why I am held with this chain. So I have asked to see you and talk with you."

²¹They replied, "We have not received any letters from Judea about you. None of our companions who came from there has reported or said anything bad about you. ²²But we want to hear what your ideas are. We know that people everywhere are talking against those who believe as you do."

²³They decided to meet Paul on a certain day. At that time even more people came to the place where he was staying. From morning until evening, he told them about God's kingdom and explained it to them. Using the Law of Moses and the Prophets, he tried to get them to believe in Jesus.

²⁴Some believed what he said. Others did not. ²⁵They didn't agree with each other. They began to leave after Paul had made a final statement. He said, "The Holy Spirit was right when he spoke to your people long ago. Through Isaiah the prophet the Spirit said,

²⁶" 'Go to your people. Say to them,
"You will hear but never understand.
You will see but never know what you are seeing."
²⁷These people's hearts have become stubborn.
They can barely hear with their ears.
They have closed their eyes.
Otherwise they might see with their eyes.
They might hear with their ears.
They might understand with their hearts.
They might turn, and then I would heal them.'
(Isaiah 6:9,10)

²⁸/²⁹"Here is what I want you to know. God has sent his salvation to people who are not Jews. And they will listen!"

³⁰For two whole years Paul stayed there in a house he rented. He welcomed all who came to see him. ³¹He preached boldly about God's kingdom. No one could keep him from teaching people about the Lord Jesus Christ.

If you seek first the Lord...
You won't have time to seek anything else.

ROMANS

- *Written by Paul to both Gentile and Jewish audiences*
- *Paul wrote 12 other New Testament books*
- *Considered to be the "masterpiece of the New Testament," the most profound writing that exists*
- *Reveals the way to a right relationship with God*
- *Theme: "Justification by Faith"*

1 I, Paul, am writing this letter. I serve Christ Jesus. I have been appointed to be an apostle. God set me apart to tell others his good news. ²He promised the good news long ago. He announced it through his prophets in the Holy Scriptures.

³The good news is about God's Son. As a human being, the Son of God belonged to King David's family line. ⁴By the power of the Holy Spirit, he was appointed to be the mighty Son of God because he rose from the dead. He is Jesus Christ our Lord.

⁵I received God's grace because of what Jesus did so that I could bring glory to him. He made me an apostle to all those who aren't Jews. I must invite them to have faith in God and obey him. ⁶You also are among those who are appointed to belong to Jesus Christ.

⁷I am sending this letter to all of you in Rome who are loved by God and appointed to be his people.

May God our Father and the Lord Jesus Christ give you grace and peace.

Paul Longs to Visit Rome

⁸First, I thank my God through Jesus Christ for all of you. People all over the world are talking about your faith. ⁹I serve God with my whole heart. I preach the good news about his Son. God knows that I always remember you ¹⁰in my prayers. I pray that now at last it may be God's plan to open the way for me to visit you.

¹¹I long to see you. I want to make you strong by giving you a gift from the Holy Spirit. ¹²I want us to cheer each other up by sharing our faith.

¹³Brothers and sisters, I want you to know that I planned many times to visit you. But until now I have been kept from coming. My work has produced results among others who are not Jews. In the same way, I want to see results among you.

¹⁴I have a duty both to Greeks and to non-Greeks. I have a duty both to wise people and to foolish people. ¹⁵So I really want to preach the good news also to you who live in Rome.

¹⁶I am not ashamed of the good news. It is God's power. And it will save everyone who believes. It is meant first for the Jews. It is meant also for those who aren't Jews.

¹⁷The good news shows how God makes people right with himself. From beginning to end, becoming right with God depends on a person's faith. It is written, "Those who are right with God will live by faith." *(Habakkuk 2:4)*

God's Anger Against Sinners

¹⁸God shows his anger from heaven. It is against all the godless and evil things people do. They are so evil that they say no to the truth. ¹⁹The truth about God is plain to them. God has made it plain.

²⁰Ever since the world was created it has been possible to see the qualities of God that are not seen. I'm talking about his eternal power and about the fact that he is God. Those things can be seen in what he has made. So people have no excuse for what they do.

²¹They knew God. But they didn't honor him as God. They didn't thank him. Their thinking became worthless. Their foolish

The Fall of Man
Romans, Chapter 1

SPIRITUAL
- Creation seen
- Evidence given
- Truth is clear
- Heart is touched

Decision

ABANDONMENT
- Reject God
- Turn away
- Choose own way
- Say "NO" to God

MORAL
- A decline of a basic code of ethics and conduct

Inner Decay

CORRUPTION
- Lie
- Cheat
- Hate
- Pride

POLITICAL
- A complete breakdown of any system or behavioral guidelines

Outward Action

ANARCHY
- Anything goes
- Lawlessness
- Anti-authority
- Sexual perversion

The fall of man begins with his personal decision to reject God. God allows him to go his own way. Man's mind and heart become dark as inner decay and corruption begin. The inner collapse of guidelines results in outward action of violence, drugs, abuse, crime and acts of disorder and personal destruction.

hearts became dark. [22]They claimed to be wise. But they made fools of themselves. [23]They would rather have statues of gods than the glorious God who lives forever. Their statues of gods are made to look like people, birds, animals and reptiles.

[24]So God let them go. He allowed them to do what their sinful hearts wanted to. He let them commit sexual sins. They polluted one another's bodies by what they did.

[25]They chose a lie instead of God's truth. They worshiped and served created things. They didn't worship the Creator. But he must be praised forever. Amen.

[26]So God let them go. They were filled with shameful longings. Their women committed sexual acts that were not natural. [27]In the same way, the men turned away from their natural love for women. They burned with sexual longing for each other. Men did shameful things with other men. They suffered in their bodies for all the twisted things they did.

[28]They didn't think it was important to know God. So God let them go. He allowed them to have dirty minds. They did things they shouldn't do.

[29]They are full of every kind of sin, evil and ungodliness. They want more than they need. They commit murder. They want what belongs to other people. They fight and cheat. They hate others. They say mean things about other people. [30]They tell lies about them. They hate God. They are rude and proud. They brag. They think of new ways to do evil. They don't obey their parents. [31]They are foolish. They can't be trusted. They are not loving and kind.

[32]They know that God's commands are right. They know that those who do evil things should die. But they continue to do those very things. They also approve of others who do them.

God Judges Fairly

2 If you judge someone else, you have no excuse for it. When you judge another person, you are judging yourself. You do the same things you blame others for doing.

[2]We know that when God judges those who do evil things, he judges fairly. [3]Though you are only a human being, you judge others. But you yourself do the same things. So how do you think you will escape when God judges you?

[4]Do you make fun of God's great kindness and favor? Do you make fun of God when he is patient with you? Don't you realize that God's kindness is meant to turn you away from your sins?

[5]But you are stubborn. In your heart you are not sorry for your sins. You are storing up anger against yourself. The day of God's anger is coming. Then his way of judging fairly will be shown. [6]God "will give to each person in keeping with what he has done." *(Psalm 62:12; Proverbs 24:12)*

[7]God will give eternal life to those who keep on doing good. They want glory, honor, and life that never ends. [8]But there are others who only look out for themselves. They don't accept the truth. They go down an evil path. God will pour out his burning anger on them. [9]There will be trouble and suffering for everyone who does evil. That is meant first for the Jews. It is also meant for the non-Jews. [10]But there will be glory, honor and peace for everyone who does good. That is meant first for the Jews. It is also meant for the non-Jews. [11]God treats everyone the same.

[12]Some people do not know God's law when they sin. They will not be judged by the law when they die. Others do know God's law when they sin. They will be judged by the law. [13]Hearing the law does not make a person right with God. People are considered to be right with God only when they obey the law.

[14]Those who aren't Jews do not have the law. Sometimes they just naturally do what the law requires. They are a law for themselves. This is true even though they don't have the law. [15]They show that what the law requires is written on their hearts. The way their minds judge them gives witness to that fact. Sometimes their thoughts find them guilty. At other times their thoughts find them not guilty.

[16]People will be judged on the day God appoints Jesus Christ to judge their secret thoughts. That's part of my good news.

The Jews and the Law

[17]Suppose you call yourself a Jew. You trust in the law. You brag that you are close to God. [18]You know what God wants. You agree with what is best because the law teaches you. [19]You are sure you can lead people who are blind. You are sure you are a light for those who are in the dark. [20]You claim to be able to teach foolish people. You can even teach babies. You think that in the law you have all knowledge and truth.

[21]You teach others. But you don't teach yourself! You preach against stealing. But you steal! [22]You say that people should not commit adultery. But you commit adultery! You hate statues of gods. But you rob temples! [23]You brag about the law. But when you break it, you rob God of his honor! [24]It is written, "Those who aren't Jews say evil things against God's name because of you." *(Isaiah 52:5; Ezekiel 36:22)*

[25]Circumcision has value if you obey the law. But if you break the law, it is just as if you hadn't been circumcised.

[26]Sometimes those who aren't circumcised do what the law requires. Won't God accept them as if they had been circumcised? [27]Many are not circumcised physically, but they obey the law. They will prove that you are guilty. You are breaking the law, even though you have the written law and are circumcised.

[28]A man is not a Jew if he is a Jew only on the outside. And circumcision is more than just something done to the outside of a man's body.

[29]No, a man is a Jew only if he is a Jew on the inside. And true circumcision means that the heart has been circumcised. It is done by the Holy Spirit. It is more than just obeying the written Law. Then a man's praise will not come from others. It will come from God.

God Is Faithful

3 Is there any advantage in being a Jew? Is there any value in being circumcised?

[2]There is great value in every way! First of all, the Jews have been given the very words of God.

[3]What if some Jews did not believe? Will the fact that they don't have faith keep God from being faithful? [4]Not at all! God is true, even though every human being is a liar. It is written,

"You are right when you sentence me.
    You are fair when you judge me."

(Psalm 51:4)

WORD Puzzle

LORD   DO   TRUST

HEART   THE   ALL   UNDERSTANDING   DEPEND   YOUR

Place each word above in the proper space below to solve the message.

_ _ _ _ . I N . _ _ _ _ _

_ _ _ . W I T H . _ _ _ _

Y O U R . _ _ _ _ _ _ _ . _ _

N O T _ _ _ _ _ O N

_ _ _ O W N .

_ _ _ _ _ . _ _ _ _ _ _ _ _ _

(Find answer on page 425 of The Illustrated New Testament)

⁵Doesn't the fact that we are wrong prove more clearly that God is right? Then what can we say? Can we say that God is not fair when he brings his anger down on us? As you can tell, I am just using human ways of thinking. ⁶God is certainly fair! If he weren't, how could he judge the world?

⁷Someone might argue, "When I lie, it becomes clearer that God is truthful. It makes his glory shine more brightly. Why then does he find me guilty of sin?"

⁸Why not say, "Let's do evil things so that good things will happen"? Some people actually lie by reporting that this is what we say. They are the ones who should be found guilty.

No One Is Right With God

⁹What should we say then? Are we Jews any better? Not at all! We have already claimed that Jews are sinners. The same is true of those who aren't Jews.

¹⁰It is written,

"No one is right with God, no one at all.
¹¹ No one understands.
  No one trusts in God.
¹² All of them have turned away.
  They have all become worthless.
  No one does anything good,
    no one at all."

(Psalms 14:1–3; 53:1–3;
Ecclesiastes 7:20)

¹³ "Their throats are like open graves.
  With their tongues they tell lies."
(Psalm 5:9)
"The words from their lips are like the
    poison of a snake."   *(Psalm 140:3)*
¹⁴ "Their mouths are full of curses and
    bitterness."   *(Psalm 10:7)*
¹⁵ "They run quickly to commit murder.
¹⁶ They leave a trail of failure and pain.
¹⁷ They do not know the way of peace."
(Isaiah 59:7,8)
¹⁸ "They don't have any respect for God."
(Psalm 36:1)

¹⁹What the law says, it says to those who are ruled by the law. Its purpose is to shut every mouth and make the whole world accountable to God. ²⁰So it can't be said that anyone will be made right with God by obeying the law. Not at all! The law makes us more aware of our sin.

Becoming Right With God

²¹But now God has shown us how to become right with him. The Law and the Prophets give witness to this. It has nothing to do with obeying the law. ²²We are made right with God by putting our faith in Jesus Christ. That happens to all who believe.

It is no different for the Jews than for anyone else. ²³Everyone has sinned. No one measures up to God's glory. ²⁴The free gift of God's grace makes all of us right with him. Christ Jesus paid the price to set us free. ²⁵God gave him as a sacrifice to pay for sins. So he forgives the sins of those who have faith in his blood.

God did all of that to prove that he is fair. Because of his mercy he did not punish people for the sins they had committed before Jesus died for them. ²⁶God did that to prove in our own time that he is fair. He proved that he is right. He also made right with himself those who believe in Jesus.

²⁷So who can brag? No one! Are people saved by obeying the law? Not at all! They are saved because of their faith. ²⁸We firmly believe that people are made right with God because of their faith. They are not saved by obeying the law.

²⁹Is God the God of Jews only? Isn't he also the God of those who aren't Jews? Yes, he is their God too. ³⁰There is only one God. When those who are circumcised believe in him, he makes them right with himself. When those who are not circumcised believe in him, he also makes them right with himself. ³¹Does faith make the law useless? Not at all! We agree with the law.

Abraham's Faith Made Him Right With God

4 What should we say about those things? What did our father Abraham discover about being right with God? ²Did he become right with God because of something he did? If so, he could brag about it. But he couldn't brag to God. ³What do we

find in Scripture? It says, "Abraham believed God. God accepted Abraham's faith, and so his faith made him right with God." (*Genesis 15:6*)

⁴When a man works, his pay is not considered a gift. It is owed to him. ⁵But things are different with God. He makes evil people right with himself. If people trust in him, their faith is accepted even though they do not work. Their faith makes them right with God.

⁶King David says the same thing. He tells us how blessed some people are. God makes those people right with himself. But they don't have to do anything in return. David says,

⁷"Blessed are those
    whose lawless acts are forgiven.
Blessed are those
    whose sins are taken away.
⁸Blessed is the man
    whose sin the Lord never counts
        against him." (*Psalm 32:1,2*)

⁹Is that blessing only for those who are circumcised? Or is it also for those who are not circumcised? We have been saying that God accepted Abraham's faith, and so his faith made him right with God. ¹⁰When did it happen? Was it after Abraham was circumcised, or before? It was before he was circumcised, not after! ¹¹He was circumcised as a sign of the covenant God had made with him. It showed that his faith had made him right with God before he was circumcised.

So Abraham is the father of all believers who have not been circumcised. God accepts their faith. So their faith makes them right with him. ¹²Abraham is also the father of the circumcised who believe. So just being circumcised is not enough. Those who are circumcised must also follow the steps of our father Abraham. He had faith before he was circumcised.

¹³Abraham and his family received a promise. God promised that Abraham would receive the world. It would not come to him because he obeyed the law. It would come because of his faith, which made him right with God.

¹⁴Do those who obey the law receive the promise? If they do, faith would have no value. God's promise would be worthless. ¹⁵The law brings God's anger. Where there is no law, the law can't be broken.

¹⁶The promise is based on God's grace. The promise comes by faith. All of Abraham's children will certainly receive the promise. And it is not only for those who are ruled by the law. Those who have the same faith that Abraham had are also included. He is the father of us all.

¹⁷It is written, "I have made you a father of many nations." (*Genesis 17:5*) God considers Abraham to be our father. The God that Abraham believed in gives life to the dead. Abraham's God also speaks of things that do not exist as if they do exist.

¹⁸When there was no reason for hope, Abraham believed because he had hope. He became the father of many nations, exactly as God had promised. God said, "That is how many children you will have." (*Genesis 15:5*)

¹⁹Without becoming weak in his faith, Abraham accepted the fact that he was past the time when he could have children. At that time he was about 100 years old. He also realized that Sarah was too old to have children.

²⁰But he kept believing in God's promise. He became strong in his faith. He gave glory to God. ²¹He was absolutely sure that God had the power to do what he had promised. ²²That's why "God accepted Abraham because he believed. So his faith made him right with God."

²³The words "God accepted Abraham's faith" were written not only for Abraham. ²⁴They were written also for us. We believe in the God who raised Jesus our Lord from the dead. So God will accept our faith and make us right with himself.

²⁵Jesus was handed over to die for our sins. He was raised to life in order to make us right with God.

Peace and Joy

5 We have been made right with God because of our faith. Now we have

peace with him because of our Lord Jesus Christ. [2]Through faith in Jesus we have received God's grace. In that grace we stand. We are full of joy because we expect to share in God's glory.

[3]And that's not all. We are full of joy even when we suffer. We know that our suffering gives us the strength to go on. [4]The strength to go on produces character. Character produces hope. [5]And hope will never let us down. God has poured his love into our hearts. He did it through the Holy Spirit, whom he has given to us.

[6]At just the right time Christ died for ungodly people. He died for us when we had no power of our own. [7]It is unusual for anyone to die for a godly person. Maybe someone would be willing to die for a good person. [8]But here is how God has shown his love for us. While we were still sinners, Christ died for us.

[9]The blood of Christ has made us right with God. So we are even more sure that Jesus will save us from God's anger. [10]Once we were God's enemies. But we have been brought back to him because his Son has died for us. Now that God has brought us back, we are even more secure. We know that we will be saved because Christ lives.

[11]And that is not all. We are full of joy in God because of our Lord Jesus Christ. Because of him, God has brought us back to himself.

Death Through Adam, Life Through Christ

[12]Sin entered the world because one man sinned. And death came because of sin. Everyone sinned, so death came to all people.

[13]Before the law was given, sin was in the world. But sin is not judged when there is no law. [14]Death ruled from the time of Adam to the time of Moses. Death ruled even over those who did not sin as Adam did. He broke God's command. But he also became a pattern of the One who was going to come.

[15]God's gift is different from Adam's sin. Many people died because of the sin of that one man. But it was even more sure that

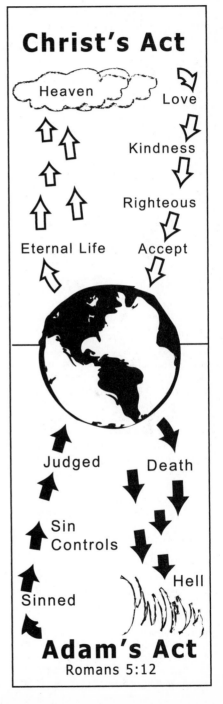

God's grace would also come through one man. That man is Jesus Christ. God's gift of grace was more than enough for the whole world.

[16]The result of God's gift is different from the result of Adam's sin. God judged one sin. That brought guilt. But after many sins, God's gift made people right with him.

[17]One man sinned, and death ruled because of his sin. But we are even more sure of what will happen because of what the one man, Jesus Christ, has done. Those who receive the rich supply of God's grace will rule with Christ in his kingdom. They have received God's gift and have been made right with him.

[18]One man's sin brought guilt to all people. So also one right act made all people right with God. And all who are right with God will live. [19]Many people were made sinners because one man did not obey. But one man did obey. That is why many people will be made right with God.

[20]The law was given so that sin would increase. But where sin increased, God's grace increased even more. [21]Sin ruled because of death. So also grace rules in the lives of those who are right with God. The grace of God brings eternal life because of what Jesus Christ our Lord has done.

Living a New Life

6 What should we say then? Should we keep on sinning so that God's grace can increase? [2]Not at all! As far as sin is concerned, we are dead. So how can we keep on sinning? [3]All of us were baptized into Christ Jesus. Don't you know that we were baptized into his death? [4]By being baptized, we were buried with Christ into his death. Christ has been raised from the dead by the Father's glory. And like Christ we also can live a new life.

[5]By being baptized, we have been joined with him in his death. We will certainly also be joined with him in his resurrection. [6]We know that what we used to be was nailed to the cross with him. That happened so our sinful bodies would lose their power. We are no longer slaves of sin. [7]Those who have died have been set free from sin.

[8]We died with Christ. So we believe

Wages of sin ... eternal death

eternal Life

Gift of God

that we will also live with him. [9]We know that Christ was raised from the dead and will never die again. Death doesn't control him anymore. [10]When he died, he died once and for all time as far as sin is concerned. Now that he lives, he lives as far as God is concerned.

[11]In the same way, consider yourselves to be dead as far as sin is concerned. Now that you believe in Christ Jesus, consider yourselves to be alive as far as God is concerned.

[12]So don't let sin rule your body, which is going to die. Don't obey its evil longings. [13]Don't give the parts of your body to serve sin. Don't let them be used to do

evil. Instead, give yourselves to God. You have been brought from death to life. Give the parts of your body to him to do what is right. [14]Sin will not be your master. Law does not rule you. God's grace has set you free.

Slaves to Right Living

[15]What should we say then? Should we sin because we are not ruled by law but by God's grace? Not at all! [16]Don't you know that when you give yourselves to obey someone you become that person's slave? You can be slaves of sin. Then you will die. Or you can be slaves who obey God. Then you will live a godly life. [17]You used to be slaves of sin. But thank God that with your whole heart you obeyed the teachings you were given! [18]You have been set free from sin. You have become slaves to right living.

[19]Because you are human, you find this hard to understand. So I have said it in a way that will help you understand it. You used to give the parts of your body to be slaves to unclean living. You were becoming more and more evil. Now give your bodies to be slaves to right living. Then you will become holy. [20]Once you were slaves of sin. At that time right living did not control you. [21]What benefit did you gain from doing the things you are now ashamed of? Those things lead to death! [22]You have been set free from sin. God has made you his slaves. The benefit you gain leads to holy living. And the end result is eternal life. [23]When you sin, the pay you get is death. But God gives you the gift of eternal life because of what Christ Jesus our Lord has done.

An Example From Marriage

7 Brothers and sisters, I am speaking to you who know the law. Don't you know that the law has authority over us only as long as we are alive? [2]For example, by law a married woman is joined to her husband as long as he is living. But suppose her husband dies. Then the marriage law no longer applies to her. [3]But suppose that married woman gets married again while her husband is still alive. Then she is called a woman who commits adultery. But suppose her husband dies. Then she is free from that law. She is not guilty of adultery even if she marries another man.

[4]My brothers and sisters, when Christ died you also died as far as the law is concerned. Then it became possible for you to belong to him. He was raised from the dead. Now our lives can be useful to God. [5]Our sinful nature used to control us. The law stirred up sinful longings in our bodies. So the things we did resulted in death.

[6]But now we have died to what used to control us. We have been set free from the law. Now we serve in the new way of the Holy Spirit. We no longer serve in the old way of the written law.

Struggling With Sin

[7]What should we say then? That the law is sin? Not at all! I wouldn't have known what sin was unless the law had told me. The law said, "Do not want what belongs to other people." *(Exodus 20:17; Deuteronomy 5:21)* If the law hadn't said that, I would not have known what it was like to want what belonged to others. [8]But the commandment gave sin an opportunity. Sin caused me to want all kinds of things that belonged to others. No one can break a law that doesn't exist.

[9]Before I knew about the law, I was alive. But then the commandment came. Sin came to life, and I died. [10]I found that the commandment that was supposed to bring life actually brought death. [11]When the commandment gave sin the opportunity, sin tricked me. It used the commandment to put me to death. [12]So the law is holy. The commandment also is holy and right and good.

[13]Did what is good cause me to die? Not at all! Sin had to be recognized for what it really is. So it produced death in me through what was good. Because of the commandment, sin became totally sinful.

[14]We know that the law is holy. But I am not. I have been sold to be a slave of sin. [15]I don't understand what I do. I don't do what I want to do. Instead, I do what I hate to do. [16]I do what I don't want to do. So I agree

that the law is good. [17]As it is, I am no longer the one who does these things. It is sin living in me that does them.

[18]I know there is nothing good in my sinful nature. I want to do what is good, but I can't. [19]I don't do the good things I want to do. I keep on doing the evil things I don't want to do. [20]I do what I don't want to do. But I am not really the one who is doing it. It is sin living in me.

[21]Here is the law I find working in me. When I want to do good, evil is right there with me. [22]Deep inside me I find joy in God's law. [23]But I see another law working in the parts of my body. It fights against the law of my mind. It makes me a prisoner of the law of sin. That law controls the parts of my body.

[24]What a terrible failure I am! Who will save me from this sin that brings death to my body? [25]I give thanks to God. He will do it through Jesus Christ our Lord.

So in my mind I am a slave to God's law. But in my sinful nature I am a slave to the law of sin.

The Holy Spirit Gives Life

8 Those who belong to Christ Jesus are no longer under God's sentence. [2]I am now controlled by the law of the Holy Spirit. That law gives me life because of what Christ Jesus has done. It has set me free from the law of sin that brings death.

[3]The written law was made weak by our sinful nature. But God did what the written law could not do. He made his Son to be like those who have a sinful nature. He sent him to be an offering for sin. In that way, he judged sin in his Son's human body. [4]Now we can do everything the law requires. Our sinful nature no longer controls the way we live. The Holy Spirit now controls the way we live.

[5]Don't live under the control of your sinful nature. If you do, you will think about what your sinful nature wants. Live under the control of the Holy Spirit. If you do, you will think about what the Spirit wants.

[6]The way a sinful person thinks leads to death. But the mind controlled by the Spirit brings life and peace. [7]The sinful mind is at war with God. It does not obey God's law. It can't. [8]Those who are controlled by their sinful nature can't please God.

[9]But your sinful nature does not control you. The Holy Spirit controls you. The Spirit of God lives in you. Anyone who does not have the Spirit of Christ does not belong to Christ.

[10]Christ lives in you. So your body is dead because of sin. But your spirit is alive because you have been made right with God. [11]The Spirit of the One who raised Jesus from the dead is living in you. So the God who raised Christ from the dead will also give life to your bodies, which are going to die. He will do this by the power of his Spirit, who lives in you.

[12]Brothers and sisters, we have a duty. Our duty is not to live under the control of our sinful nature. [13]If you live under the control of your sinful nature, you will die. But by the power of the Holy Spirit you can put to death the sins your body commits. Then you will live.

[14]Those who are led by the Spirit of God are children of God. [15]You didn't receive a spirit that makes you a slave to fear once again. Instead you received the Holy Spirit, who makes you God's child. By the Spirit's power we call God "*Abba*." *Abba* means Father. [16]The Spirit himself joins with our spirits. Together they give witness that we are God's children.

[17]As his children, we will receive all that he has for us. We will share what Christ receives. But we must share in his sufferings if we want to share in his glory.

The Hope of Future Glory

[18]What we are suffering now is nothing compared with the glory that will be shown in us. [19]Everything God created looks forward to the time when his children will appear in their full and final glory. [20]The created world was bound to fail. But that was not the result of its own choice. It was planned that way by the One who made it. God planned [21]to set the created world free. He didn't want it to rot away completely. Instead, he wanted it to have the same glo-

rious freedom that his children have.

²²We know that all that God created has been groaning. It is in pain as if it were giving birth to a child. The created world continues to groan even now. ²³And that's not all. We have the Holy Spirit as the promise of future blessing. But we also groan inside ourselves as we look forward to the time when God will adopt us as full members of his family. Then he will give us everything he has for us. He will raise our bodies and give glory to them.

²⁴That's the hope we had when we were saved. But hope that can be seen is no hope at all. Who hopes for what he already has? ²⁵We hope for what we don't have yet. So we are patient as we wait for it.

²⁶In the same way, the Holy Spirit helps us when we are weak. We don't know what we should pray for. But the Spirit himself prays for us. He prays with groans too deep for words. ²⁷God, who looks into our hearts, knows the mind of the Spirit. And the Spirit prays for God's people just as God wants him to pray.

We Will Win

²⁸We know that in all things God works for the good of those who love him. He appointed them to be saved in keeping with his purpose.

²⁹God planned that those he had chosen would become like his Son. In that way, Christ will be the first and most honored among many brothers. ³⁰And those God has planned for, he has also appointed to be saved. Those he has appointed, he has made right with himself. To those he has made right with himself, he has given his glory.

³¹What should we say then? Since God is on our side, who can be against us? ³²God did not spare his own Son. He gave him up for us all. Then won't he also freely give us everything else?

³³Who can bring any charge against God's chosen ones? God makes us right with himself. ³⁴Who can sentence us to death? Christ Jesus is at the right hand of God and is also praying for us. He died. More than that, he was raised to life.

³⁵Who can separate us from Christ's love? Can trouble or hard times or harm or hunger? Can nakedness or danger or war? ³⁶It is written,

> "Because of you, we face death all day
>   long.
> We are considered as sheep to be
>   killed."   *(Psalm 44:22)*

³⁷No! In all these things we will do even more than win! We owe it all to Christ, who has loved us.

³⁸I am absolutely sure that not even death or life can separate us from God's love. Not even angels or demons, the present or the future, or any powers can do that. ³⁹Not even the highest places or the lowest, or anything else in all creation can do that. Nothing at all can ever separate us from God's love because of what Christ Jesus our Lord has done.

God's Free Choice

9 I speak the truth in Christ. I am not lying. My mind tells me that what I say is true. It is guided by the Holy Spirit. ²My heart is full of sorrow. My sadness never ends. ³I am so concerned about my people, who are members of my own race. I am ready to be cursed, if that would help them. I am even willing to be separated from Christ.

⁴They are the people of Israel. They have been adopted as God's children. God's glory belongs to them. So do the covenants. They received the law. They were taught to worship in the temple. They were given the promises. ⁵The founders of our nation belong to them. Christ comes from their family line. He is God over all. May he always be praised! Amen.

⁶Their condition does not mean that

Lincoln was not great because he lived in a log cabin, but because he was able to get out of the cabin.

God's word has failed. Not everyone in the family line of Israel really belongs to Israel. [7]Not everyone in Abraham's family line is really his child. Not at all! Scripture says, "Your family line will continue through Isaac." *(Genesis 21:12)*

[8]In other words, God's children are not just Abraham's natural children. Instead, they are the children God promised to him. They are the ones considered to be Abraham's children. [9]God promised, "I will return at the appointed time. Sarah will have a son." *(Genesis 18:10,14)*

[10]And that's not all. Rebekah's children had the same father. He was our father Isaac.

[11]Here is what happened. Rebekah's twins had not even been born. They hadn't done anything good or bad yet. So they show that God's purpose is based firmly on his free choice. [12]It was not because of anything they did but because of God's choice. So Rebekah was told, "The older son will serve the younger one." *(Genesis 25:23)* [13]It is written, "I chose Jacob instead of Esau." *(Malachi 1:2,3)*

[14]What should we say then? Is God unfair? Not at all! [15]He said to Moses,

> "I will have mercy on whom I have mercy.
> I will show love to those I love."
> *(Exodus 33:19)*

[16]So it doesn't depend on what we want or do. It depends on God's mercy.

[17]In Scripture, God says to Pharaoh, "I had a special reason for making you king. I decided to use you to show my power. I wanted my name to become known everywhere on earth." *(Exodus 9:16)* [18]So God does what he wants to do. He shows mercy to one person and makes another stubborn.

[19]One of you will say to me, "Then why does God still blame us? Who can oppose what he wants to do?" [20]But you are a mere man. So who are you to talk back to God? Scripture says, "Can what is made say to the one who made it, 'Why did you make me like this?'" *(Isaiah 29:16; 45:9)* [21]Isn't the potter free to make different kinds of pots out of the same lump of clay? Some are for special purposes. Others are for ordinary use.

[22]What if God chose to show his great anger? What if he chose to make his power known? That is why he put up with people he was angry with. They had been made to be destroyed. [23]What if he did that to show the riches of his glory to others? Those are the people he shows his mercy to. He had prepared them to receive his glory. [24]We are those people. He has chosen us. We do not come only from the Jewish race. Many of us are not Jews. [25]God says in Hosea,

> "I will call those who are not my people
> 'my people.'
> I will call the one who is not my loved
> one 'my loved one.'" *(Hosea 2:23)*

[26]He also says,

> "Once it was said to them,
> 'You are not my people.'
> In that very place they will be called
> 'children of the living God.'" *(Hosea 1:10)*

[27]Isaiah cries out concerning Israel. He says,

Nothing can separate us from God's love

"The number of people from Israel may
be like the sand by the sea.
But only a few of them will be saved.
²⁸The Lord will carry out his sentence.
He will be quick to carry it out on
earth, once and for all."

(Isaiah 10:22,23)

²⁹Earlier Isaiah had said,

"The Lord who rules over all
left us children and grandchildren.
If he hadn't, we would have become
like Sodom.
We would have been like Gomorrah."

(Isaiah 1:9)

Israel Does Not Believe

³⁰What should we say then? Those who
aren't Jews did not look for a way to be
right with God. But they found it by having
faith. ³¹Israel did look for a law that could
make them right with God. But they didn't
find it.

³²Why not? Because they didn't look for it
by faith. They tried to get it by working for
it. They tripped over the stone that causes
people to trip and fall. ³³It is written,

"Look! In Zion I am laying a stone that
causes people to trip.
It is a rock that makes them fall.
The one who trusts in him will never be
put to shame." *(Isaiah 8:14; 28:16)*

10 Brothers and sisters, with all my
heart I long for the people of Israel to
be saved. I pray to God for them. ²I can give
witness about them that they really want to
serve God. But how they are trying to do it
is not based on what they know.

³They didn't know how God makes people right with himself. They tried to get
right with God in their own way. They
didn't do it in God's way.

⁴Christ has completed the law. So now
everyone who believes can be right with
God.

⁵Moses explained how the law could
help a person do what God requires. He
said, "The one who does those things will
live by them." *(Leviticus 18:5)*

⁶But the way to do what God requires
must begin by having faith in him. Scripture
says, "Do not say in your heart, 'Who will
go up into heaven?'" *(Deuteronomy 30:12)* That
means to go up into heaven and bring Christ
down. ⁷"And do not say, 'Who will go down
into the grave?'" *(Deuteronomy 30:13)* That
means to bring Christ up from the dead.

⁸But what does it say? "The word is near
you. It's in your mouth and in your heart."
(Deuteronomy 30:14) That means the word
we are preaching. You must put your faith
in it.

⁹Say with your mouth, "Jesus is Lord."
Believe in your heart that God raised him
from the dead. Then you will be saved.
¹⁰With your heart you believe and are made
right with God. With your mouth you say
that Jesus is Lord. And so you are saved.
¹¹Scripture says, "The one who trusts in him
will never be put to shame." *(Isaiah 28:16)*

¹²There is no difference between those
who are Jews and those who are not. The
same Lord is Lord of all. He richly blesses
everyone who calls on him. ¹³Scripture says,
"Everyone who calls on the name of the
Lord will be saved." *(Joel 2:32)*

[14]How can they call on him unless they believe in him? How can they believe in him unless they hear about him? How can they hear about him unless someone preaches to them? [15]And how can anyone preach without being sent? It is written, "How beautiful are the feet of those who bring good news!" *(Isaiah 52:7)*

[16]But not all the people of Israel accepted the good news. Isaiah says, "Lord, who has believed our message?" *(Isaiah 53:1)* [17]So faith comes from hearing the message. And the message that is heard is the word of Christ.

[18]But I ask, "Didn't the people of Israel hear?" Of course they did. It is written,

"Their voice has gone out into the whole
     earth.
     Their words have gone out from one
          end of the world to the other."
                    (Psalm 19:4)

[19]Again I ask, "Didn't Israel understand?" First, Moses says,

"I will use people who are not a nation to
     make you jealous.
     I will use a nation that has no
          understanding to make you
          angry."   *(Deuteronomy 32:21)*

[20]Then Isaiah boldly speaks about what God says. God said,

"I was found by those who were not
     trying to find me.
     I made myself known to those who
          were not asking for me."
                    (Isaiah 65:1)

[21]But Isaiah also speaks about what God says concerning Israel. God said,

"All day long I have held out my hands.
     I have held them out to a stubborn
          people who do not obey me."
                    (Isaiah 65:2)

God's Faithful People in Israel

11 So here is what I ask. Did God turn his back on his people? Not at all! I myself belong to Israel. I am one of Abraham's children. I am from the tribe of Benjamin. [2]God didn't turn his back on his people. After all,

he chose them.

Don't you know what Scripture says about Elijah? He complained to God about Israel. [3]He said, "Lord, they have killed your prophets. They have torn down your altars. I'm the only one left. And they are trying to kill me." *(1 Kings 19:10,14)*

[4]How did God answer him? God said, "I have kept 7,000 people for myself. They have not bowed down to Baal." *(1 Kings 19:18)*

[5]Some are also faithful today. They have been chosen by God's grace. [6]And if they are chosen by grace, it is no longer a matter of working for it. If it were, grace wouldn't be grace anymore.

[7]What should we say then? Israel did not receive what they wanted so badly. But those who were chosen did. God made the rest of them stubborn.

[8]It is written,

"God made it hard for them to
     understand.
     He gave them eyes that could not see.
     He gave them ears that could not hear.
     And they are still like that today."
                    (Deuteronomy 29:4; Isaiah 29:10)

[9]David says,

"Let their feast be a trap and a snare.
     Let it make Israel trip and fall. Let
          Israel get what's coming to them.
[10] Let their eyes grow dark so they can't
          see.
     Let their backs be bent forever."
                    (Psalm 69:22,23)

Two Kinds of Olive Branches

[11]Again, here is what I ask. They didn't trip and fall once and for all time, did they? Not at all! Because Israel sinned, those who aren't Jews can be saved. That will make Israel jealous of them. [12]Israel's sin brought riches to the world. Their loss brought riches to the non-Jews. What greater riches will come when all Israel turns to God!

[13]I am talking to you who are not Jews. I am the apostle to the non-Jews. So I think the work I do for God and others is very important.

[14]I hope somehow to stir up my own peo-

The Transformation Process

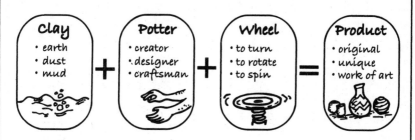

Clay		Potter		Wheel		Product
• earth		• creator		• to turn		• original
• dust	**+**	• designer	**+**	• to rotate	**=**	• unique
• mud		• craftsman		• to spin		• work of art

Clay is ordinary, ugly, messy, formless, lifeless, with no real value, ability or purpose.

Potter is the master designer with absolute control of the clay and the wheel.

Wheel is the turning platform controlled by the potter who turns it on, sets the speed and determines how long it spins.

Process The potter places the clay on the turning wheel to bring into reality what he desires to accomplish.

SPIRITUAL TRUTH: Each of us is worthless clay!

Unlike actual clay that is lifeless, we have free will to either:

- <u>resist</u> the process and say, "No" to God, **or**
- <u>yield</u> to his divine plan for our lives.

The turning wheel represents your life's journey with the everchanging circumstances, events, issues, challenges, relationships, etc.

The potter has a purpose unknown to the clay and so it is with us.

The process of shaping and forming sometimes includes pain, loss, disappointment, insecurity, silence, etc. At every turn and change, God is challenging us to yield to him.

Within each heart lurks some dark and hard areas of ownership. What is God asking you to yield to him today?

ple to want what you have. Perhaps I can save some of them. [15]When they were not accepted, it became possible for the whole world to be brought back to God. So what will happen when they are accepted? It will be like life from the dead.

[16]The first handful of dough that is offered is holy. This makes all of the dough holy.

If the root is holy, so are the branches.

[17]Some of the natural branches have been broken off. You are a wild olive branch. But you have been joined to the tree with the other branches. Now you enjoy the life-giving sap of the olive tree root. [18]So don't think you are better than the other branches. Remember, you don't give life to the root. The root gives life to you.

[19]You will say, "Some branches were broken off so that I could be joined to the tree." [20]That's true. But they were broken off because they didn't believe. You stand only because you do believe. So don't be proud. Be afraid. [21]God didn't spare the natural branches. He won't spare you either.

[22]Think about how kind God is! Also think about how firm he is! He was hard on those who stopped following him. But he is kind to you. So you must continue to live in his kindness. If you don't, you also will be cut off.

[23]If the people of Israel do not continue in their unbelief, they will again be joined to the tree. God is able to join them to the tree again.

[24]After all, weren't you cut from a wild olive tree? Weren't you joined to an olive tree that was taken care of? And wasn't that the opposite of how things should be done? How much more easily will the natural branches be joined to their own olive tree!

All Israel Will Be Saved

[25]Brothers and sisters, here is a mystery I want you to understand. It will keep you from being proud. Part of Israel has refused to obey God. That will continue until the full number of non-Jews has entered God's kingdom. [26]And so all Israel will be saved. It is written,

"The One who saves will come from
    Mount Zion.
He will remove sin from Jacob.
[27]Here is my covenant with them.
    I will take away their sins."
        (Isaiah 59:20,21; 27:9;
        Jeremiah 31:33,34)

[28]As far as the good news is concerned, the people of Israel are enemies. That is for your good. But as far as God's choice is concerned, the people of Israel are loved. That is because of God's promises to the founders of our nation. [29]God does not take back his gifts. He does not change his mind about those he has chosen.

[30]At one time you did not obey God. But now you have received mercy because Israel did not obey. [31]In the same way, Israel has not been obeying God. But now they receive mercy because of God's mercy to you. [32]God has found everyone guilty of not obeying him. So now he can have mercy on everyone.

Praise to God

[33] How very rich are God's wisdom and
    knowledge!
    How he judges is more than we
        can understand!
    The way he deals with people is more
        than we can know!
[34] "Who can ever know what is in the
    Lord's mind?
    Or who can ever give him advice?"
        (Isaiah 40:13)
[35] "Has anyone ever given anything to God,
    so that God has to pay him back?"
        (Job 41:11)
[36] All things come from him.
    All things are directed by him.
    All things are for his good.
    May God be given the glory forever!
    Amen.

Living for God

12 Brothers and sisters, God has shown you his mercy. So I am asking you to offer up your bodies to him while you are still alive. Your bodies are a holy sacrifice that is pleasing to God. When you offer

GOD IS ONE GOD IN THREE PERSONS

The 3-in-1 God (the Trinity) means there is One God in three distinct Persons: Father - Son - Holy Spirit

The Father plans all things
Ephesians 3:11

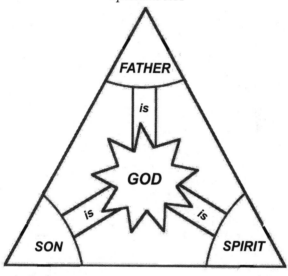

The Son is God
in human form
John 1:14

The Holy Spirit
works in and
through people
Romans 8:14, 15

Distinct ● Equal Value ● Different Work

"As soon as Jesus was baptized, he came up out of the water. At that moment heaven was opened. Jesus saw the Spirit of God coming down on him like a dove. A voice from heaven said, 'This is my Son, and I love him. I am very pleased with him.'"   Matthew 3:16,17

The **Father** spoke from heaven
       The **Son** was baptized in water
              The **Holy Spirit** came down like a dove

your bodies to God, you are worshiping him. ²Don't live any longer the way this world lives. Let your way of thinking be completely changed. Then you will be able to test what God wants for you. And you will agree that what he wants is right. His plan is good and pleasing and perfect.

³God's grace has been given to me. So here is what I say to every one of you. Don't think of yourself more highly than you should. Be reasonable when you think about yourself. Keep in mind the amount of faith God has given you.

⁴Each of us has one body with many parts. And the parts do not all have the same purpose. ⁵So also we are many persons. But in Christ we are one body. And each part of the body belongs to all the other parts.

⁶We all have gifts. They differ in keeping with the grace that God has given each of us. Do you have the gift of prophecy? Then use it in keeping with the faith you have. ⁷Is it your gift to serve? Then serve. Is it teaching? Then teach. ⁸Is it telling others how they should live? Then tell them. Is it giving to those who are in need? Then give freely. Is it being a leader? Then work hard at it. Is it showing mercy? Then do it cheerfully.

Love

⁹Love must be honest and true. Hate what is evil. Hold on to what is good. ¹⁰Love each other deeply. Honor others more than yourselves. ¹¹Never let the fire in your heart go out. Keep it alive. Serve the Lord. ¹²When you hope, be joyful. When you suffer, be patient. When you pray, be faithful. ¹³Share with God's people who are in need. Welcome others into your homes.

¹⁴Bless those who hurt you. Bless them, and do not call down curses on them. ¹⁵Be joyful with those who are joyful. Be sad with those who are sad. ¹⁶Agree with each other. Don't be proud. Be willing to be a friend of people who aren't considered important. Don't think that you are better than others.

¹⁷Don't pay back evil with evil. Be careful to do what everyone thinks is right. ¹⁸If possible, live in peace with everyone. Do that as much as you can.

¹⁹My friends, don't try to get even. Leave room for God to show his anger. It is written, "I am the One who judges people. I will pay them back," *(Deuteronomy 32:35)* says the Lord. ²⁰Do just the opposite. Scripture says,

"If your enemies are hungry, give them
  food to eat.
If they are thirsty, give them
  something to drink.
By doing those things, you will pile up
  burning coals on their heads."
(Proverbs 25:21,22)

²¹Don't let evil overcome you. Overcome evil by doing good.

Do not **conform**, but be **transformed!**
Romans 12:1,2 (NIV)

Obey Those in Authority

13 All of you must be willing to obey completely those who rule over you. There are no authorities except the ones God has chosen. Those who now rule have been chosen by God. ²So when you oppose the authorities, you are opposing those whom God has appointed. Those who do that will be judged.

³If you do what is right, you won't need to be afraid of your rulers. But watch out if you do what is wrong! You don't want to be afraid of those in authority, do you? Then do what is right. The one in authority will praise you. ⁴He serves God and will do you good. But if you do wrong, watch out! The ruler doesn't carry a sword for no reason at all. He serves God. And God is carrying out his anger through him. The ruler punishes anyone who does wrong.

⁵You must obey the authorities. Then you will not be punished. You must also obey them because you know it is right.

⁶That's also why you pay taxes. The authorities serve God. Ruling takes up all their time. ⁷Give to everyone what you owe. Do you owe taxes? Then pay them. Do you owe anything else to the government? Then pay it. Do you owe respect? Then give it. Do you owe honor? Then show it.

Love, Because the Day Is Near

⁸Pay everything you owe. But you can never pay back all the love you owe each other. Those who love others have done everything the law requires. ⁹Here are some commandments to think about. "Do not commit adultery." "Do not commit murder." "Do not steal." "Do not want what belongs to others." *(Exodus 20:13–15,17; Deuteronomy 5:17–19,21)* These and other commandments are all included in one rule. Here's what it is. "Love your neighbor as you love yourself." *(Leviticus 19:18)* ¹⁰Love does not harm its neighbor. So love does everything the law requires.

¹¹When you do those things, keep in mind the times we are living in. The hour has come for you to wake up from your sleep. Our full salvation is closer now than it was when we first believed in Christ.

¹²The dark night of evil is nearly over. The day of Christ's return is almost here. So let us get rid of the works of darkness. Let us put on the armor of light.

¹³Let us act as we should, like people living in the daytime. Have nothing to do with wild parties. Don't get drunk. Don't take part in sexual sins or evil conduct. Don't fight with each other. Don't be jealous of anyone.

¹⁴Instead, put on the Lord Jesus Christ as your clothing. Don't think about how to satisfy what your sinful nature wants.

The Weak and the Strong

14 Accept those whose faith is weak. Don't judge them where you have differences of opinion.

²The faith of some people allows them to eat anything. But others eat only vegetables because their faith is weak. ³People who eat everything must not look down on those who do not. And people who don't eat everything must not judge those who do. God has accepted them.

⁴Who are you to judge someone else's servants? Whether they are faithful or not is their own master's concern. They will be faithful, because the Lord has the power to make them faithful.

⁵Some people consider one day to be more holy than another. Others think all days are the same. Each person should be absolutely sure in his own mind. ⁶Those who think one day is special do it to honor the Lord. Those who eat meat do it to honor the Lord. They give thanks to God. Those who don't eat meat do it to honor the Lord. They also give thanks to God.

⁷We don't live for ourselves alone. And we don't die all by ourselves. ⁸If we live, we live to honor the Lord. If we die, we die to honor the Lord. So whether we live or die, we belong to the Lord.

⁹Christ died and came back to life. He did this to become the Lord of both the dead and the living.

¹⁰Now then, who are you to judge your brother or sister? Why do you look down on them? We will all stand in God's courtroom to be judged. ¹¹It is written,

" 'You can be sure that I live,' says the Lord.

'And you can be just as sure that every knee will bow down in front of me. Every tongue will tell the truth to God.'"

(*Isaiah 45:23*)

¹²So we will all have to explain to God the things we have done.

¹³Let us stop judging one another. Instead, make up your mind not to put anything in your brother's way that would make him trip and fall.

¹⁴I am absolutely sure that no food is "unclean" in itself. I say this as one who belongs to the Lord Jesus. But some people may consider a thing to be "unclean." If they do, it is "unclean" for them. ¹⁵Your brothers and sisters may be upset by what you eat. If they are, you are no longer acting as though you love them. So don't destroy them by what you eat. Christ died for them. ¹⁶Don't let something you consider good be spoken of as if it were evil.

¹⁷God's kingdom has nothing to do with eating or drinking. It is a matter of being right with God. It brings the peace and joy the Holy Spirit gives.

¹⁸Those who serve Christ in this way are pleasing to God. They are pleasing to people too.

¹⁹So let us do all we can to live in peace. And let us work hard to build each other up.

²⁰Don't destroy the work of God because of food. All food is "clean." But it is wrong for you to eat anything that causes someone else to trip and fall. ²¹Don't eat meat if it will cause your brothers and sisters to fall. Don't drink wine or do anything else that will make them fall.

²²No matter what you think about those things, keep it between yourself and God. Blessed are those who do not have to feel guilty for what they allow.

²³But those who have doubts are guilty if they eat. Their eating is not based on faith. Everything that is not based on faith is sin.

15 We who have strong faith should help the weak with their problems. We should not please only ourselves. ²We should all please our neighbors. Let us do what is good for them. Let us build them up.

³Even Christ did not please himself. It is written, "Those who make fun of you have made fun of me also." (*Psalm 69:9*) ⁴Everything that was written in the past was written to teach us. The Scriptures give us strength to go on. They cheer us up and give us hope.

⁵Our God is a God who strengthens you and cheers you up. May he help you agree with each other as you follow Christ Jesus. ⁶Then you can give glory to God with one heart and voice. He is the God and Father of our Lord Jesus Christ.

⁷Christ has accepted you. So accept one another in order to bring praise to God.

⁸I tell you that Christ has become a servant of the Jews. He teaches us that God is true. He shows us that God will keep the promises he made to the founders of our nation. ⁹Jesus became a servant of the Jews so that people who are not Jews could give glory to God for his mercy. It is written,

"I will praise you among those who aren't Jews.
I will sing praises to you."

(*2 Samuel 22:50; Psalm 18:49*)

¹⁰Again it says,

"You non-Jews, be full of joy.
Be joyful together with God's people."

(*Deuteronomy 32:43*)

¹¹And again it says,

"All you non-Jews, praise the Lord.
All you nations, sing praises to him."

(*Psalm 117:1*)

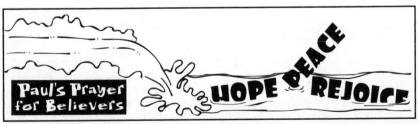

Paul's Prayer for Believers — HOPE PEACE REJOICE

[12]And Isaiah says,

"The Root of Jesse will grow up quickly.
    He will rule over the nations.
Those who aren't Jews will put their
        hope in him."   *(Isaiah 11:10)*

[13]May the God who gives hope fill you with great joy. May you have perfect peace as you trust in him. May the power of the Holy Spirit fill you with hope.

Paul Serves the Non-Jews

[14]My brothers and sisters, I am sure that you are full of goodness. What you know is complete. You are able to teach one another.

[15]I have written to you very boldly about some things. I wanted you to think about them again. The grace of God has allowed me [16]to serve Christ Jesus among those who aren't Jews. My duty as a priest is to preach God's good news. Then the non-Jews will become an offering that pleases God. The Holy Spirit will make the offering holy.

[17]Because I belong to Christ Jesus, I can take pride in my work for God. [18]I will not try to speak of anything except what Christ has done through me. He has been leading those who aren't Jews to obey God. He has been doing this by what I have said and done.

[19]He has given me power to do signs and miracles. He has given me the power of the Holy Spirit.

From Jerusalem all the way around to Illyricum I have finished preaching the good news about Christ. [20]I have always wanted to preach the good news where Christ was not known. I don't want to build on what someone else has started. [21]It is written,

    "Those who were not told about
him will understand.
Those who have not heard will know
    what it all means."   *(Isaiah 52:15)*

[22]That's why I have often been kept from coming to you.

Paul Plans to Visit Rome

[23]Now there is no more place for me to work in those areas. For many years I have been longing to see you. [24]So I plan to see you when I go to Spain. I hope to visit you while I am passing through. And I hope you will help me on my journey there. But first I want to enjoy being with you for a while.

[25]Now I am on my way to Jerusalem to serve God's people there. [26]The believers in Macedonia and Achaia were pleased to take an offering for those who were poor among God's people in Jerusalem. [27]They were happy to do it. And of course they owe it to them. Those who aren't Jews have shared from the Jews' spiritual blessings. So the non-Jews should share their earthly blessings with the Jews.

[28]I want to finish my task. I want to make sure that the poor in Jerusalem have received the offering. Then I will go to Spain. On my way I will visit you. [29]I know that when I come to you, I will come with the full blessing of Christ.

[30]Brothers and sisters, I am asking you through the authority of our Lord Jesus Christ to join me in my struggle by praying to God for me. Pray for me with the love the Holy Spirit provides. [31]Pray that I will be saved from those in Judea who do not believe. Pray that my work in Jerusalem will be accepted by God's people there. [32]Then, as God has planned, I will come to you with joy. Together we will be renewed.

[33]May the God who gives peace be with you all. Amen.

Personal Greetings

16 I would like you to welcome our sister Phoebe. She serves the church in

ROMANS

Across

1. Preached the Good News — ch. 1
2. A messenger sent by God — ch. 1
3. Given by God to be used — ch. 12
4. We are saved by ____ — ch. 3
5. "Abba" means ... — ch. 8
6. Automobile — ---
7. First woman — ---
8. ____ of sin is death — ch. 6
9. The Gospel is the ____ News — ch. 1
10. Abraham & Sarah's problem — ch. 4
11. Put on the armor of ____ — ch. 13

Down

1. When you suffer be ____ — ch. 12
2. Christ's ____ brought life — ch. 5
3. God's ____ set us free — ch. 6
4. "May ____ our Father ..." — ch. 1
5. Christ has set me ____ — ch. 8
6. No excuse for what we __ — ch. 1
7. Unbelieving branches cut _ — ch. 11
8. Sinful mind is at ____ — ch. 8
9. They __ down an evil path — ch. 2
10. Higher than a "king" — ---
11. Don't ____ sin rule — ch. 6
12. Sound of grief or sadness — ---
13. Not heaven, but ____ — ---

Cenchrea. [2]I ask you to receive her as one who belongs to the Lord. Receive her in the way God's people should. Give her any help she may need from you. She has been a great help to many people, including me.

[3]Greet Priscilla and Aquila. They work together with me in serving Christ Jesus. [4]They have put their lives in danger for me. I am thankful for them. So are all the non-Jewish churches.

[5]Greet also the church that meets in the house of Priscilla and Aquila.

Greet my dear friend Epenetus. He was the first person in Asia Minor to become a believer in Christ.

[6]Greet Mary. She worked very hard for you.

[7]Greet Andronicus and Junias, my relatives. They have been in prison with me. They are leaders among the apostles. They became believers in Christ before I did.

[8]Greet Ampliatus. I love him as a brother in the Lord.

[9]Greet Urbanus. He works together with me in serving Christ. And greet my dear friend Stachys.

[10]Greet Apelles. Even though he was put to the test, he remained faithful as one who belonged to Christ.

Greet those who live in the house of Aristobulus.

[11]Greet Herodion, my relative.

Greet the believers who live in the house of Narcissus.

[12]Greet Tryphena and Tryphosa. Those women work hard for the Lord.

Greet my dear friend Persis. She is another woman who has worked very hard for the Lord.

[13]Greet Rufus. He is a choice believer in the Lord. And greet his mother. She has been like a mother to me too.

[14]Greet Asyncritus, Phlegon and Hermes. Greet Patrobas, Hermas and the believers with them.

[15]Greet Philologus, Julia, Nereus and his sister. Greet Olympas and all of God's people with them.

[16]Greet one another with a holy kiss.

All the churches of Christ send their greetings.

[17]I am warning you, brothers and sisters, to watch out for those who try to keep you from staying together. They want to trip you up. They teach you things opposite to what you have learned. Stay away from them. [18]People like that are not serving Christ our Lord. They are serving only themselves. With smooth talk and with words they don't mean they fool people who don't know any better.

[19]Everyone has heard that you obey God. So you have filled me with joy. I want you to be wise about what is good. And I want you to have nothing to do with what is evil.

[20]The God who gives peace will soon crush Satan under your feet.

May the grace of our Lord Jesus be with you.

[21]Timothy works together with me. He sends his greetings to you. So do Lucius, Jason and Sosipater, my relatives.

[22]I, Tertius, wrote down this letter. I greet you as a believer in the Lord.

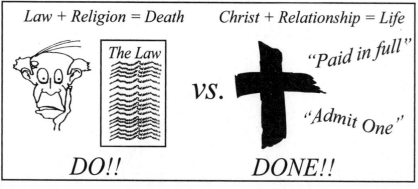

Law + Religion = Death   *Christ + Relationship = Life*

The Law   VS.   *"Paid in full"*

"Admit One"

DO!!   *DONE!!*

And He shall be called

Mighty God • King • Everlasting Father
Wonderful Counselor • Good Shepherd
Lion of Judah • Savior • Lamb of God
Son of God • Rock • Alpha and Omega
Son of Man • Word • Living Water
Creator • Chief Cornerstone • Lord
Branch of David • Servant • Teacher
Friend • Light of the World • Rabbi
The Door • Holy One • Bread of Life
Carpenter • Great Physician • Jesus
High Priest • Vine • Everlasting God
Righteous Judge • Bright Morning Star
Bridegroom • The Amen • Faithful
Emmanuel • Messiah • Prince of Peace
Anointed One • I Am • Resurrection

Jesus Christ
The Way, the Truth, and the Life

[23/24]Gaius sends you his greetings. He has welcomed me and the whole church here into his house.

Erastus is the director of public works here in the city. He sends you his greetings. Our brother Quartus also greets you.

[25]May God receive glory. He is able to strengthen your faith because of the good news I preach. It is the message about Jesus Christ. It is in keeping with the mystery that was hidden for a very long time. [26]The mystery has now been made known through the writings of the prophets. The eternal God commanded that it be made known. He wanted all nations to believe and obey him. [27]May the only wise God receive glory forever through Jesus Christ. Amen.

1 CORINTHIANS

- *Written by Paul to the church in Corinth*
- *Corinth was a major center of culture and trade*
- *The city was filled with temples, idolatry and immorality*
- *The church was established during his second missionary trip*
- *He wrote to encourage and correct these "baby" Christians*
- *Theme: "The Lordship of Christ"*

1 I, Paul, am writing this letter. I have been chosen to be an apostle of Christ Jesus just as God planned. Our brother Sosthenes joins me in writing.

²We are sending this letter to you, the members of God's church in Corinth. You have been made holy because you belong to Christ Jesus. God has chosen you to be his holy people. He has done the same for all those everywhere who pray to our Lord Jesus Christ. Jesus is their Lord and ours.

³May God our Father and the Lord Jesus Christ give you grace and peace.

Paul Gives Thanks

⁴I always thank God for you. I thank him because of the grace he has given to you who belong to Christ Jesus. ⁵You have been blessed in every way because of him. All your teaching of the truth is better. Your understanding of it is more complete. ⁶Our witness about Christ has been proved to be true in you.

⁷There is no gift of the Holy Spirit that you don't have. You are full of hope as you wait for our Lord Jesus Christ to come again. ⁸God will keep you strong to the very end. Then you will be without blame on the day our Lord Jesus Christ returns.

⁹God is faithful. He has chosen you to share life with his Son, Jesus Christ our Lord.

Taking Sides in the Church

¹⁰Brothers and sisters, I ask all of you to agree with one another. I make my appeal in the name of our Lord Jesus Christ. Then you won't take sides. You will be in complete agreement in all that you think.

¹¹My brothers and sisters, some people who live in Chloe's house have told me you are arguing with each other. ¹²Here is what I mean. One of you says, "I follow Paul." Another says, "I follow Apollos." Another says, "I follow Peter." And still another says, "I follow Christ."

¹³Does Christ take sides? Did Paul die on the cross for you? Were you baptized in the name of Paul? ¹⁴I'm thankful that I didn't baptize any of you except Crispus and Gaius. ¹⁵No one can say that you were baptized in my name.

¹⁶It's true that I also baptized those who live in the house of Stephanas. Besides that, I don't remember if I baptized anyone else.

¹⁷Christ did not send me to baptize. He sent me to preach the good news. He commanded me not to use the kind of wisdom that people commonly use. That would take all the power away from the cross of Christ.

Christ Is God's Power and Wisdom

¹⁸The message of the cross seems foolish to those who are lost and dying. But it is God's power to us who are being saved. ¹⁹It is written,

"I will destroy the wisdom of those who
    are wise.
I will do away with the cleverness
    of those who think they are so
    smart." *(Isaiah 29:14)*

²⁰Where is the wise person? Where is the educated person? Where are the great thinkers of this world? Hasn't God made the wisdom of the world foolish? ²¹God wisely planned that the world would not know him through its own wisdom. It

pleased God to use the foolish things we preach to save those who believe.

²²Jews require miraculous signs. Greeks look for wisdom. ²³But we preach about Christ and his death on the cross. That is very hard for Jews to accept. And everyone else thinks it's foolish.

²⁴But there are those God has chosen, both Jews and others. To them Christ is God's power and God's wisdom. ²⁵The foolish things of God are wiser than human wisdom. The weakness of God is stronger than human strength.

²⁶Brothers and sisters, think of what you were when God chose you. Not many of you were considered wise by human standards. Not many of you were powerful. Not many of you belonged to important families.

²⁷But God chose the foolish things of the world to shame the wise. He chose the weak things of the world to shame the strong. ²⁸God chose the things of this world that are common and looked down on. He chose what is not considered to be important to do away with what is considered to be important. ²⁹So no one can brag to God.

³⁰Because of what God has done, you belong to Christ Jesus. He has become God's wisdom for us. He makes us right with God. He makes us holy and sets us free. ³¹It is written, "The one who brags should brag about what the Lord has done." (*Jeremiah 9:24*)

2 Brothers and sisters, when I came to you I didn't come with fancy words or great wisdom. I preached to you the truth about God's love. ²I made up my mind to pay attention to only one thing while I was with you. That one thing was Jesus Christ and his death on the cross.

³When I came to you, I was weak and afraid and trembling all over. ⁴I didn't preach my message with clever and compelling words. As I preached, the Holy Spirit showed his power. ⁵That was so you would believe not because of human wisdom but because of God's power.

Wisdom From the Holy Spirit

⁶The words we speak to those who have grown in the faith are wise. Our words are different from the words of the wise people or rulers of this world. People like that aren't going anywhere. ⁷No, we speak about God's secret wisdom. His wisdom has been hidden. But before time began, God planned that his wisdom would bring us heavenly glory.

⁸None of the rulers of this world understood God's wisdom. If they had, they would not have nailed the Lord of glory to the cross. ⁹It is written,

"No eye has seen,
    no ear has heard,
no mind has known
    what God has prepared for those who
        love him."   (*Isaiah 64:4*)

¹⁰But God has shown it to us through his Spirit.

On judgment day your work will be shown for what it is...

Smoldering ashes?

1 Corinthians 3:12-15

Or priceless treasure?

The Spirit understands all things. He understands even the deep things of God. [11]Who can know the thoughts of another person? Only a person's own spirit can know them. In the same way, only the Spirit of God knows God's thoughts.

[12]We have not received the spirit of the world. We have received the Spirit who is from God. The Spirit helps us understand what God has freely given us.

[13]That is what we speak about. We don't use words taught to us by people. We use words taught to us by the Holy Spirit. We use the words of the Spirit to teach the truths of the Spirit.

[14]Some people don't have the Holy Spirit. They don't accept the things that come from the Spirit of God. Things like that are foolish to them. They can't understand them. In fact, such things can't be understood without the Spirit's help.

[15]Everyone who has the Spirit can judge all things. But no one can judge those who have the Spirit. It is written,

[16]"Who can ever know what is in the
Lord's mind?
Can anyone ever teach him?"
(Isaiah 40:13)

But we have the mind of Christ.

Taking Sides in the Church

3 Brothers and sisters, I couldn't speak to you as if you were guided by the Holy Spirit. I had to speak to you as if you were following the ways of the world. You aren't growing as Christ wants you to. You are still like babies. [2]The words I spoke to you were like milk, not like solid food. You weren't ready for solid food yet. And you still aren't ready for it.

[3]You are still following the ways of the world. Some of you are jealous. Some of you argue. So aren't you following the ways of the world? Aren't you acting like ordinary human beings? [4]One of you says, "I follow Paul." Another says, "I follow Apollos." Aren't you acting like ordinary human beings?

[5]After all, what is Apollos? And what is Paul? We are only people who serve. We helped you to believe. The Lord has given

each of us our own work to do. ⁶I planted the seed. Apollos watered it. But God made it grow.

⁷So the one who plants is not important. The one who waters is not important. It is God who makes things grow. He is the One who is important. ⁸The one who plants and the one who waters have the same purpose. The Lord will give each of us a reward for our work. ⁹We work together with God. You are like God's field. You are like his building.

¹⁰God has given me the grace to lay a foundation as a master builder. Now someone else is building on it. But each one should build carefully. ¹¹No one can lay any other foundation than the one that has already been laid. That foundation is Jesus Christ.

¹²A person may build on it using gold, silver, jewels, wood, hay or straw. ¹³But each person's work will be shown for what it is. On judgment day it will be brought to light. It will be put through fire. The fire will test how good everyone's work is. ¹⁴If the building doesn't burn up, God will give the builder a reward for his work. ¹⁵If the building burns up, the builder will lose everything. The builder will be saved, but only like one escaping through the flames.

¹⁶Don't you know that you yourselves are God's temple? God's Spirit lives in you. ¹⁷If anyone destroys God's temple, God will destroy him. God's temple is holy. And you are that temple.

¹⁸Don't fool yourselves. Suppose some of you think you are wise by the standards of the world. Then you should become a "fool" so that you can become wise.

¹⁹The wisdom of this world is foolish in God's eyes. It is written, "God catches wise people in their own tricks." *(Job 5:13)* ²⁰It is also written, "The Lord knows that the thoughts of the wise don't amount to anything." *(Psalm 94:11)*

²¹So no more bragging about human beings! All things are yours. ²²That means Paul or Apollos or Peter or the world or life or death or the present or the future. All are yours. ²³You are joined to Christ and belong to him. And Christ is joined to God.

Apostles of Christ

4 Here is how you should think of us. We serve Christ. We are trusted with God's secret truth. ²Those who have been given a trust must prove that they are faithful.

³I care very little if I am judged by you or by any human court. I don't even judge myself. ⁴I don't feel I have done anything wrong. But that doesn't mean I'm not guilty. The Lord judges me.

⁵So don't judge anything before the appointed time. Wait until the Lord returns. He will bring to light what is hidden in the dark. He will show the real reasons why people do what they do. At that time each person will receive praise from God.

⁶Brothers and sisters, I have used myself and Apollos as examples to help you. You can learn from us the meaning of the saying, "Don't go beyond what is written." Then you won't be proud that you follow one person instead of another.

⁷Who makes you different from anyone else? What do you have that you did not receive? And if you did receive it, why do you brag as though you did not?

⁸You already have everything you want, don't you? Have you already become rich? Have you begun to rule as kings? And did you do that without us? I wish that you really had begun to rule. Then we could rule with you!

⁹It seems to me that God has put us apostles on display at the end of a parade. We are like men sentenced to die in front of a crowd. We have been made a show for the whole creation to see. Angels and people are staring at us.

¹⁰We are fools for Christ. But you are so wise in Christ! We are weak. But you are so strong! You are honored. But we are looked down on! ¹¹Up to this very hour we are hungry and thirsty. We are dressed in rags. We are being treated badly. We have no homes. ¹²We work hard with our own hands. When others call down a curse on us, we bless them. When we are attacked, we put up with it. ¹³When others say bad things about us, we answer kindly. Up to

this moment we have become the world's garbage. We are everybody's trash.

[14] I am not writing this to shame you. You are my dear children, and I want to warn you. [15] You may have 10,000 believers in Christ watching over you. But you don't have many fathers. I became your father by serving Christ Jesus and telling you the good news. [16] So I'm asking you to follow my example.

[17] That's the reason I'm sending Timothy to you. He is like a son to me, and I love him. He is faithful in serving the Lord. He will remind you of my way of life in serving Christ Jesus. And that agrees with what I teach everywhere in every church.

[18] Some of you have become proud. You act as if I weren't coming to you. [19] But I will come very soon, if that's what the Lord wants. Then I will find out how those proud people are talking. I will also find out what power they have. [20] The kingdom of God is not a matter of talk. It is a matter of power.

[21] Which do you want? Should I come to you with a whip? Or should I come in love and with a gentle spirit?

Throw the Evil Person Out!

5 It is actually reported that there is sexual sin among you. I'm told that a man is living with his father's wife and is having sex with her. Even people who do not know God don't commit that sin. [2] And you are proud! Shouldn't you be filled with sadness instead? Shouldn't you have put the man who did that out of your church?

[3] Even though I am not right there with you, I am with you in spirit. And I have already judged the one who did that, just as if I were there.

[4] When you come together in the name of our Lord Jesus, I will be with you in spirit. The power of our Lord Jesus will also be with you. [5] When you come together like that, hand that man over to Satan. Then his sinful nature will be destroyed. His spirit will be saved on the day the Lord returns.

[6] Your bragging is not good. It is like yeast. Don't you know that just a little yeast works its way through the whole batch of dough? [7] Get rid of the old yeast. Be like a

Jesus Christ is our Foundation

Be careful how you build on it!

"Bummer"

1 Corinthians 3:11

new batch of dough without yeast. That is what you really are, because Christ has been offered up for us. He is our Passover lamb.

[8] So let us keep the Feast, but not with the old yeast. I'm talking about yeast that is full of hatred and evil. Let us keep the Feast with bread made without yeast. Let us do it with bread that is honest and true.

[9] I wrote a letter to you to tell you to stay away from people who commit sexual sins. [10] I didn't mean the people of this world who sin that way or who always want more and more. I didn't mean those who cheat or who worship statues of gods. In that case you would have to leave this world!

[11]But here is what I am writing to you. You must stay away from anyone who claims to be a believer but who does those things. Stay away from anyone who commits sexual sins or who always wants more and more things. Stay away from a person who worships statues of gods or who tells lies about others. Stay away from anyone who gets drunk or who cheats. Don't even eat with a person like that.

[12]Is it my business to judge those outside the church? Aren't you supposed to judge those inside the church? [13]God will judge those outside. Scripture says, "Get rid of that evil person!" *(Deuteronomy 17:7; 19:19; 21:21; 22:21,24; 24:7)*

Do Not Take Believers to Court

6 Suppose one of you wants to bring a charge against another believer. Should you take it to the ungodly to be judged? Why not take it to God's people?

[2]Don't you know that God's people will judge the world? And if you are going to judge the world, aren't you able to judge small cases? [3]Don't you know that we will judge angels? Then we should be able to judge the things of this life even more!

[4]So if you want to press charges in matters like that, appoint as judges members of the church who aren't very important! [5]I say this to shame you. Is it possible that no one among you is wise enough to judge matters between believers? [6]Instead, one believer goes to court against another. And this happens in front of unbelievers!

[7]The very fact that you take another believer to court means you have lost the battle already. Why not be treated wrongly? Why not be cheated? [8]Instead, you yourselves cheat and do wrong. And you do it to your brothers and sisters.

[9]Don't you know that evil people will not receive God's kingdom? Don't be fooled. Those who commit sexual sins will not receive the kingdom. Neither will those who worship statues of gods or commit adultery. Neither will men who are prostitutes or who commit homosexual acts. [10]Neither will thieves or those who always want more and more. Neither will those who are often drunk or tell lies or cheat. People who live like that will not receive God's kingdom.

[11]Some of you used to do those things. But your sins were washed away. You were made holy. You were made right with God. All of that was done in the name of the Lord Jesus Christ and by the Spirit of our God.

Sexual Sins

[12]Some of you say, "Everything is permitted for me." But not everything is good for me. Again some of you say, "Everything is permitted for me." But I will not be controlled by anything. [13]Some of you say, "Food

God's Wonderful Plan for Sex

MARRIAGE   PURITY   COMMITMENT
FAMILY   FUTURE OF HUMANKIND   CHILDREN

is for the stomach. And the stomach is for food." But God will destroy both of them.

The body is not meant for sexual sins. The body is meant for the Lord. And the Lord is meant for the body. [14]By his power God raised the Lord from the dead. He will also raise us up.

[15]Don't you know that your bodies belong to the body of Christ? Should I take what belongs to Christ and join it to a prostitute? Never! [16]Don't you know that when you join yourself to a prostitute, you become one with her in body? Scripture says, "The two will become one." *(Genesis 2:24)* [17]But anyone who is joined to the Lord becomes one with him in spirit.

[18]Keep far away from sexual sins. All the other sins a person commits are outside his body. But sexual sins are sins against one's own body.

[19]Don't you know that your bodies are temples of the Holy Spirit? The Spirit is in you. You have received him from God. You do not belong to yourselves. [20]Christ has paid the price for you. So use your bodies in a way that honors God.

Marriage

7 Now I want to deal with the things you wrote me about.

Some of you say, "It is good for a man not to have sex with a woman." [2]But since there is so much sexual sin, each man should have his own wife. And each woman should have her own husband. [3]A husband should satisfy his wife's sexual needs. And a wife should satisfy her husband's sexual needs.

[4]The wife's body does not belong only to her. It also belongs to her husband. In the same way, the husband's body does not belong only to him. It also belongs to his wife. [5]You shouldn't stop giving yourselves to each other except when you both agree to do so. And that should be only to give yourselves time to pray for a while. Then you should come together again. In that way, Satan will not tempt you when you can't control yourselves.

[6]I say those things to you as my advice, not as a command. [7]I wish all of you were like me. But you each have your own gift from God. One has this gift. Another has that.

[8]I speak to those who are not married. I also speak to widows. It is good for you to stay single like me. [9]But if you can't control yourselves, you should get married. It is better to get married than to burn with sexual longing.

[10]I give a command to those who are married. It is a direct command from the Lord, not from me. A wife must not leave her husband. [11]But if she does, she must not get married again. Or she can go back to her husband. And a husband must not divorce his wife.

Satan's Destructive Plan for Sex

¹²I also have something to say to everyone else. It is from me, not a direct command from the Lord. Suppose a brother has a wife who is not a believer. If she is willing to live with him, he must not divorce her. ¹³And suppose a woman has a husband who is not a believer. If he is willing to live with her, she must not divorce him. ¹⁴The unbelieving husband has been made holy through his wife. The unbelieving wife has been made holy through her believing husband. If that were not the case, your children would not be pure and clean. But as it is, they are holy.

¹⁵If the unbeliever leaves, let that person go. In that case, a believing man or woman does not have to stay married. God wants us to live in peace. ¹⁶Wife, how do you know if you can save your husband? Husband, how do you know if you can save your wife?

¹⁷But each of you should remain in the place in life that the Lord has given you. Stay as you were when God chose you. That's the rule all the churches must follow.

¹⁸Was a man already circumcised when God chose him? Then he should not become uncircumcised. Was he uncircumcised when God chose him? Then he should not be circumcised. ¹⁹Being circumcised means nothing. Being uncircumcised means nothing. Doing what God commands is what counts.

²⁰Each of you should stay as you were when God chose you.

²¹Were you a slave when God chose you? Don't let it trouble you. But if you can get your master to set you free, do it. ²²Those who were slaves when the Lord chose them are now the Lord's free people. Those who were free when God chose them are now slaves of Christ. ²³Christ has paid the price for you. Don't become slaves of human beings.

²⁴Brothers and sisters, you are accountable to God. So all of you should stay as you were when God chose you.

²⁵Now I want to say something about virgins. I have no direct command from the Lord. But I give my opinion. Because of the Lord's mercy, I give it as one who can be trusted.

²⁶Times are hard for you right now. So I think it's good for you to stay as you are. ²⁷Are you married? Then don't get a divorce. Are you single? Then don't look for a wife. ²⁸But if you get married, you have not sinned. And if a virgin gets married, she has not sinned. But those who get married will have many troubles in this life. I want to save you from that.

²⁹Brothers and sisters, what I mean is that the time is short. From now on, those who have a husband or wife should live as if they did not. ³⁰Those who are sad should live as if they were not. Those who are happy should live as if they were not. Those who buy something should live as if it were not theirs to keep. ³¹Those who use the things of the world should not become all wrapped up in them. The world as it now exists is passing away.

³²I don't want you to have anything to worry about. A single man is concerned about the Lord's matters. He wants to know how he can please the Lord. ³³But a married man is concerned about the matters of this world. He wants to know how he can please his wife. ³⁴His concerns pull him in two directions.

A single woman or a virgin is concerned

about the Lord's matters. She wants to serve the Lord with both body and spirit. But a married woman is concerned about the matters of this world. She wants to know how she can please her husband.

³⁵I'm saying those things for your own good. I'm not trying to hold you back. I want you to be free to live in a way that is right. I want you to give yourselves completely to the Lord.

³⁶Suppose a man thinks he is not acting properly toward the virgin he has promised to marry. Suppose she is getting old, and he feels that he should marry her. He should do as he wants. He is not sinning. They should get married.

³⁷But suppose the man has decided not to marry the virgin. And suppose he has no compelling need to get married and can control himself. If he has made up his mind not to get married, he also does the right thing.

³⁸So then, the man who marries the virgin does the right thing. But the man who doesn't marry her does an even better thing.

³⁹A woman has to stay married to her husband as long as he lives. If he dies, she is free to marry anyone she wants to. But the one she marries must belong to the Lord. ⁴⁰In my opinion, she is happier if she stays single. And I also think that I am led by the Spirit of God in saying that.

Food Offered to Statues of Gods

8 Now I want to deal with food offered to statues of gods.

We know that we all have knowledge. Knowledge makes people proud. But love builds them up. ²Those who think they know something still don't know as they should. ³But those who love God are known by God.

⁴So then, here is what I say about eating food that is offered to statues of gods. We know that a god made by human hands is really nothing at all in the world. We know there is only one God. ⁵There may be so-called gods either in heaven or on earth. In fact, there are many "gods" and many "lords." ⁶But for us there is only one God. He is the Father. All things came from him, and we live for him. And there is only one Lord. He is Jesus Christ. All things came because of him, and we live because of him.

⁷But not everyone knows that. Some people still think that statues of gods are real gods. When they eat food that was offered to statues of gods, they think of it as food that was offered to real gods. And because they have a weak sense of what is right and wrong, they feel guilty. ⁸But food doesn't bring us close to God. We are no worse if we don't eat. We are no better if we do eat.

⁹But be careful how you use your freedom. Be sure it doesn't trip up someone who is weaker than you.

¹⁰Suppose you who have that knowledge are eating in a temple of one of those gods. And suppose someone who has a weak sense of what is right and wrong sees you. Won't that person become bold and eat what has been offered to statues of gods? ¹¹If so, then your knowledge destroys that weak brother or sister for whom Christ died.

¹²When you sin against other believers in that way, you harm their weak sense of what is right and wrong. By doing that you sin against Christ.

¹³So what should I do if what I eat causes my brother or sister to fall into sin? I will

Stop competing! Be ONE in... Christ

never eat meat again. In that way, I will not cause them to fall.

The Rights of an Apostle

9 Am I not free? Am I not an apostle? Haven't I seen Jesus our Lord? Aren't you the result of my work for the Lord? ²Even though others may not think of me as an apostle, I am certainly one to you! You are the proof that I am the Lord's apostle. ³That is what I say to stand up for myself when people judge me.

⁴Don't we have the right to eat and drink? ⁵Don't we have the right to take a believing wife with us when we travel? The other apostles do. The Lord's brothers do. Peter does. ⁶Or are Barnabas and I the only ones who have to work for a living?

⁷Who serves as a soldier but doesn't get paid? Who plants a vineyard but doesn't eat any of its grapes? Who takes care of a flock but doesn't drink any of the milk? ⁸Do I say that from only a human point of view? The Law says the same thing.

⁹Here is what is written in the Law of Moses. "Do not stop an ox from eating while it helps separate the grain from the straw." *(Deuteronomy 25:4)* Is it oxen that God is concerned about? ¹⁰Doesn't he say that for us? Yes, it was written for us. When a farmer plows and separates the grain, he does it because he hopes to share in the crop.

¹¹We have planted spiritual seed among you. Is it too much to ask that we receive from you some of the things we need? ¹²Others have the right to receive help from you. Don't we have even more right to do so?

But we didn't use that right. No, we have put up with everything. We didn't want to keep the good news of Christ from spreading.

¹³Don't you know that those who work in the temple get their food from the temple? Don't you know that those who serve at the altar eat from what is offered on the altar? ¹⁴In the same way, those who preach the good news should receive their living from their work. That is what the Lord has commanded.

¹⁵But I haven't used any of those rights. And I'm not writing because I hope you will do things like that for me. I would rather die than have anyone take away my pride in my work. ¹⁶But when I preach the good news, I can't brag. I have to preach it. How terrible it will be for me if I do not preach the good news!

¹⁷If I preach because I want to, I get a reward. If I preach because I have to, I'm only doing my duty. ¹⁸Then what reward do I get? Here is what it is. I am able to preach the good news free of charge. And I can do it without making use of my rights when I preach it.

¹⁹I am free. I don't belong to anyone. But I make myself a slave to everyone. I do it to win as many as I can to Christ.

²⁰To the Jews I became like a Jew. That was to win the Jews. To those under the law I became like one who was under the law, even though I myself am not under the law. That was to win those under the law. ²¹To those who don't have the law I became like one who doesn't have the law. I am not free from God's law. I am under Christ's law. Now I can win those who

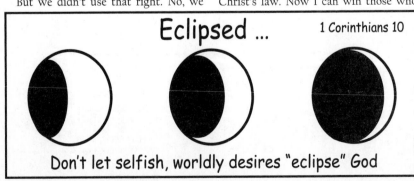

Eclipsed ... 1 Corinthians 10

Don't let selfish, worldly desires "eclipse" God

don't have the law. [22]To those who are weak I became weak. That was to win the weak.

I have become all things to all people so that in all possible ways I might save some. [23]I do all of that because of the good news. And I want to share in its blessings.

[24]In a race all the runners run. But only one gets the prize. You know that, don't you? So run in a way that will get you the prize. [25]All who take part in the games train hard. They do it to get a crown that will not last. But we do it to get a crown that will last forever.

[26]So I do not run like someone who doesn't run toward the finish line. I do not fight like a boxer who hits nothing but air. [27]No, I train my body and bring it under control. Then after I have preached to others, I myself will not break the rules and fail to win the prize.

Warnings From Israel's History

10 Brothers and sisters, here is what I want you to know about our people who lived long ago. They were all led by the cloud. They all walked through the Red Sea. [2]They were all baptized into Moses in the cloud and in the sea. [3]They all ate the same supernatural food. [4]They all drank the same supernatural water. They drank from the supernatural rock that went with them. That rock was Christ.

[5]But God was not pleased with most of them. Their bodies were scattered all over the desert.

[6]Now those things happened as examples for us. They are supposed to keep us from longing for evil things, as the people of Israel did.

[7]So don't worship statues of gods, as some of them did. It is written, "The people sat down to eat and drink. Then they got up to dance wildly in front of their god." *(Exodus 32:6)* [8]We should not commit sexual sins, as some of them did. In one day 23,000 of them died. [9]We should not put the Lord to the test, as some of them did. They were killed by snakes. [10]Don't tell your leaders how unhappy you are with them. That's what some of the people of Israel did. And they were killed by the destroying angel.

[11]Those things happened to them as examples for us. They were written down to warn us who are living at the time when God's work is being completed. [12]So be careful. When you think you are standing firm, you might fall.

[13]You are tempted in the same way all other human beings are. God is faithful. He will not let you be tempted any more than you can take. But when you are tempted, God will give you a way out so that you can stand up under it.

Sharing in the Body and Blood of Christ

[14]My dear friends, run away from statues of gods. Don't worship them. [15]I'm talking to people who are reasonable. Judge for yourselves what I say.

[16]When we give thanks for the cup at the Lord's Supper, aren't we sharing in the blood of Christ? When we break the bread, aren't we sharing in the body of Christ? [17]Just as there is one loaf, so we who are many are one body. We all eat from the one loaf.

... By The World

False religions   Fame   Money   Career   Sex   Possessions   Addictions

Eclipse brings darkness to the soul

Choose to "Lift off" with the Lord

Throw off the baggage of this world

Let it go and lighten the load

Loaded down or Lifted Up?

[18]Think about the people of Israel. Don't those who eat the offerings share in the altar? [19]Do I mean that what is offered to a statue of a god is anything? Do I mean that a statue of a god is anything? [20]No! But what is offered by those who worship statues of gods is really offered to demons. It is not offered to God. I don't want you to be sharing with demons.

[21]You can't drink the cup of the Lord and the cup of demons too. You can't have a part in both the Lord's table and the table of demons. [22]Are we trying to make the Lord jealous? Are we stronger than he is?

The Believer's Freedom

[23]You say, "Everything is permitted." But not everything is good for us. Again you say, "Everything is permitted." But not everything builds us up. [24]We should not look out for our own interests. Instead, we should look out for the interests of others.

[25]Eat anything that is sold in the meat market. Don't ask if it's right or wrong. [26]Scripture says, "The earth belongs to the Lord. And so does everything in it." *(Psalm 24:1)*

[27]Suppose an unbeliever invites you to a meal and you want to go. Then eat anything that is put in front of you. Don't ask if it's right or wrong.

[28]But suppose someone says to you, "This food has been offered to a statue of a god." Then don't eat it. Keep in mind the good of the one who told you. And don't eat because of a sense of what is right and wrong. [29]I'm talking about the other person's sense of what is right and wrong, not yours.

Why should my freedom be judged by what someone else thinks? [30]Suppose I give thanks when I eat. Then why should I be blamed for eating food I thank God for?

[31]So eat and drink and do everything else for the glory of God. [32]Don't do anything that causes another person to trip and fall. It doesn't matter if that person is a Jew or a Greek or a member of God's church. [33]Follow my example. I try to please everyone in every way. I'm not looking out for what is good for me. I'm looking out for the interests of others. I do it so that they might be saved.

11 Follow my example, just as I follow the example of Christ.

Proper Worship

[2]I praise you for being faithful in remembering me. I also praise you for staying true to all my teachings, just as I gave them to you.

[3]Now I want you to know that the head of every man is Christ. The head of the woman is the man. And the head of Christ is God. [4]Every man who prays or prophesies with his head covered brings shame on his head. [5]And every woman who prays or

prophesies with her head uncovered brings shame on her head. It is just as if her head were shaved.

⁶What if a woman does not cover her head? She should have her hair cut off. But it is shameful for her to cut her hair or shave it off. So she should cover her head.

⁷A man should not cover his head. He is the likeness and glory of God. But the woman is the glory of the man. ⁸The man did not come from the woman. The woman came from the man.

⁹Also, the man was not created for the woman. The woman was created for the man. ¹⁰That's why a woman should have her head covered. It shows that she is under authority. She should also cover her head because of the angels.

¹¹But here is how things are for those who belong to the Lord. The woman is not independent of the man. And the man is not independent of the woman. ¹²The woman came from the man, and the man is born from the woman. But everything comes from God.

¹³You be the judge. Is it proper for a woman to pray to God without covering her head? ¹⁴Suppose a man has long hair. Doesn't the very nature of things teach you that it is shameful? ¹⁵And suppose a woman has long hair. Doesn't the very nature of things teach you that it is her glory? Long hair is given to her as a covering.

¹⁶If anyone wants to argue about that, we don't have any other practice. And God's churches don't either.

The Lord's Supper

¹⁷In the following matters, I don't praise you. Your meetings do more harm than good.

¹⁸First, here is what people are telling me. When you come together as a church, you take sides. And in some ways I believe it. ¹⁹No doubt you need to take sides in order to show which of you God agrees with!

²⁰When you come together, it is not the Lord's Supper you eat. ²¹As you eat, each of you goes ahead without waiting for anyone else. One remains hungry and another gets drunk. ²²Don't you have homes to eat and drink in? Or do you think so little of God's church that you shame those in it who have nothing? What should I say to you? Should I praise you for that? Certainly not!

²³I passed on to you what I received from the Lord. On the night the Lord Jesus was handed over to his enemies, he took bread. ²⁴When he had given thanks, he broke it. He said, "This is my body. It is given for you. Every time you eat it, do it in memory of me." ²⁵In the same way, after supper he took the cup. He said, "This cup is the new covenant in my blood. Every time you drink it, do it in memory of me."

²⁶When you eat the bread and drink the cup, you are announcing the Lord's death until he comes again.

²⁷So do not eat the bread or drink the cup of the Lord in a way that isn't worthy of him. If you do, you will be guilty of sinning against the body and blood of the Lord. ²⁸A person should take a careful look at himself before he eats the bread and drinks from the cup. ²⁹Anyone who eats and drinks must recognize the body of the Lord. If he doesn't, God will judge him for it. ³⁰That is why many of you are weak and sick. That is why a number of you have died.

³¹We should judge ourselves. Then we would not be found guilty. ³²When the Lord judges us, he corrects us. Then we will not be judged along with the rest of the world.

³³My brothers and sisters, when you come together to eat, wait for each other. ³⁴Those who are hungry should eat at home. Then when you come together, you will not be judged.

When I come, I will give you more directions.

What you are is God's gift to you.
What you make of yourself is your gift to God.

Gifts of the Holy Spirit

12 Brothers and sisters, I want you to know about the gifts of the Holy Spirit.

²You know that at one time you were unbelievers. You were somehow drawn away to worship statues of gods that couldn't even speak. ³So I tell you that no one who is speaking with the help of God's Spirit says, "May Jesus be cursed." And without the help of the Holy Spirit no one can say, "Jesus is Lord."

⁴There are different kinds of gifts. But they are all given by the same Spirit. ⁵There are different ways to serve. But they all come from the same Lord. ⁶There are different ways to work. But the same God makes it possible for all of us to have all those different things.

⁷The Holy Spirit is given to each of us in a special way. That is for the good of all. ⁸To some people the Spirit gives the message of wisdom. To others the same Spirit gives the message of knowledge. ⁹To others the same Spirit gives faith. To others that one Spirit gives gifts of healing. ¹⁰To others he gives the power to do miracles. To others he gives the ability to prophesy. To others he gives the ability to tell the spirits apart. To others he gives the ability to speak in different kinds of languages they had not known before. And to still others he gives the ability to explain what was said in those languages.

¹¹All of the gifts are produced by one and the same Spirit. He gives them to each person, just as he decides.

One Body but Many Parts

¹²There is one body. But it has many parts. Even though it has many parts, they make up one body. It is the same with Christ. ¹³We were all baptized by one Holy Spirit into one body. It didn't matter whether we were Jews or Greeks, slaves or free people. We were all given the same Spirit to drink.

¹⁴The body is not made up of just one part. It has many parts. ¹⁵Suppose the foot says, "I am not a hand. So I don't belong to the body." It is still part of the body. ¹⁶And suppose the ear says, "I am not an eye. So I don't belong to the body." It is still part of the body.

¹⁷If the whole body were an eye, how could it hear? If the whole body were an ear, how could it smell? ¹⁸God has placed each part in the body just as he wanted it to be. ¹⁹If all the parts were the same, how could there be a body? ²⁰As it is, there are many parts. But there is only one body.

²¹The eye can't say to the hand, "I don't need you!" The head can't say to the feet, "I don't need you!" ²²In fact, it is just the opposite. The parts of the body that seem to be weaker are the ones we can't do without. ²³The parts that we think are less important we treat with special honor. The private parts aren't shown. But they are treated with special care. ²⁴The parts that can be shown don't need special care.

But God has joined together all the parts of the body. And he has given more honor to the parts that didn't have any. ²⁵In that way, the parts of the body will not take sides. All of them will take care of each other. ²⁶If one part suffers, every part suffers with it. If one part is honored, every part shares in its joy.

²⁷You are the body of Christ. Each one of you is a part of it. ²⁸First, God has appointed apostles in the church. Second, he has appointed prophets. Third, he has appointed teachers. Then he has appointed people who do miracles and those who have gifts of healing. He also appointed those able to help others, those able to direct things, and those who can speak in different kinds of languages they had not known before.

²⁹Is everyone an apostle? Is everyone a prophet? Is everyone a teacher? Do all work miracles? ³⁰Do all have gifts of healing? Do all speak in languages they had not known before? Do all explain what is said in those languages? ³¹But above all, you should want the more important gifts.

Love

And now I will show you the best way of all.

13 Suppose I speak in the languages of human beings and of angels. If I don't have love, I am only a loud gong or a noisy cymbal. ²Suppose I have the gift of prophecy. Suppose I can understand all the secret things of God and know everything about him. And suppose I have enough faith to move mountains. If I don't have love, I am nothing at all. ³Suppose I give everything I have to poor people. And suppose I give my body to be burned. If I don't have love, I get nothing at all.

⁴Love is patient. Love is kind. It does not want what belongs to others. It does not brag. It is not proud. ⁵It is not rude. It does not look out for its own interests. It does not easily become angry. It does not keep track of other people's wrongs.

⁶Love is not happy with evil. But it is full of joy when the truth is spoken. ⁷It always protects. It always trusts. It always hopes. It never gives up.

⁸Love never fails. But prophecy will pass away. Speaking in languages that had not been known before will end. And knowledge will pass away.

⁹What we know now is not complete. What we prophesy now is not perfect. ¹⁰But when what is perfect comes, the things that are not perfect will pass away.

¹¹When I was a child, I talked like a child. I thought like a child. I had the understanding of a child. When I became a man, I put childish ways behind me.

¹²Now we see only a dim likeness of things. It is as if we were seeing them in a mirror. But someday we will see clearly. We will see face to face. What I know now is not complete. But someday I will know completely, just as God knows me completely.

¹³The three most important things to have are faith, hope and love. But the greatest of them is love.

The Gifts the Holy Spirit Gives

14 Follow the way of love. You should also want the gifts the Holy Spirit gives. Most of all, you should want the gift of prophecy.

²Anyone who speaks in a language he had not known before doesn't speak to people. He speaks only to God. In fact, no

Spiritual Gifts are to be used to build up the Church.

prophecy wisdom serving faith knowledge miracles

The Church was designed to be a smooth running "revival machine" with all believers functioning with the power of the Holy Spirit.

1 Corinthians 12

one understands that person. What he says with his spirit remains a mystery. ³But anyone who prophesies speaks to people. He says things to make them stronger, to give them hope and to comfort them. ⁴Those who speak in other languages build themselves up. But those who prophesy build up the church.

⁵I would like all of you to speak in other languages. But I would rather have you prophesy. Those who prophesy are more helpful than those who speak in other languages. But that is not the case if those who speak in other languages explain what they have said. Then the whole church can be built up.

⁶Brothers and sisters, suppose I were to come to you and speak in other languages. What good would I be to you? None! I would need to come with new truth or knowledge, or a prophecy or a teaching.

⁷Here are some examples. Certain objects make sounds. Take a flute or a harp. No one will know what the tune is unless different notes are played. ⁸Also, if the trumpet call isn't clear, who will get ready for battle?

⁹It's the same with you. You must speak words that people understand. If you don't, no one will know what you are saying. You will just be speaking into the air.

¹⁰It is true that there are all kinds of languages in the world. And they all have meaning. ¹¹But if I don't understand what someone is saying, I am a stranger to that person. And that person is a stranger to me.

¹²It's the same with you. You want to have gifts of the Spirit. So try to do your best in using gifts that build up the church.

¹³For that reason, those who speak in languages they had not known before should pray that they can explain what they say. ¹⁴If I pray in another language, my spirit prays. But my mind does not pray. ¹⁵So what should I do? I will pray with my spirit. But I will also pray with my mind. I will sing with my spirit. But I will also sing with my mind.

¹⁶Suppose you are praising God with your spirit. And suppose there are visitors among you who don't understand what's going on. How can they say "Amen" when you give thanks? They don't know what you are saying. ¹⁷You might be giving thanks well enough. But the others are not being built up.

¹⁸I thank God that I speak in other languages more than all of you do. ¹⁹But in the church I would rather speak five words that people can understand than 10,000 words in another language. Then I would be teaching others.

²⁰Brothers and sisters, stop thinking like children. Be like babies as far as evil is concerned. But be grown up in your thinking. ²¹In the Law it is written,

"Through people who speak unfamiliar
        languages
    and through the lips of strangers
I will speak to these people.
    But even then they will not listen
        to me."   *(Isaiah 28:11,12)*

That is what the Lord says.

²²So speaking in other languages is a sign for those who don't believe. It is not a sign for those who do believe. But prophecy is for believers. It is not for those who don't believe.

²³Suppose the whole church comes together and everyone speaks in other languages. And suppose visitors or unbelievers come in. Won't they say you are out of your minds? ²⁴But suppose unbelievers or visitors come in while everyone is prophesying. Then they will be shown by all who speak that they are sinners. They will be judged by all. ²⁵The secrets of their hearts will be brought out into the open. They will fall down and worship God. They will exclaim, "God is really here among you!"

Proper Worship

²⁶Brothers and sisters, what should we say then? When you come together, every one of you brings something. You bring a hymn or a teaching or a word from God. You bring a message in another language or explain what was said. All of those things must be done to make the church strong.

²⁷No more than two or three people should speak in another language. And they

Match the Drawings
Which verse listed at the bottom fits the drawing?

Extra verses were added to challenge the experts.

① John 3:30

② James 1:23

③ Acts 2:10

④ John 10:28

⑤ Luke 3:30

⑥ Matthew 26:62

⑦ James 2:19

⑧ Ephesians 6:11

⑨ Jude 25

⑩ Luke 5:12

⑪ 2 Timothy 2:22

should speak one at a time. Then someone must explain what was said. 28If there is no one to explain, the speakers should keep quiet in the church. They can speak to themselves and to God.

29Only two or three prophets are supposed to speak. Others should decide if what is being said is true. 30What if a message from God comes to someone else who is sitting there? Then the one who is speaking should stop.

31Those who prophesy can all take turns. In that way, everyone can be taught and be given hope. 32Those who prophesy should control their speaking. 33God is not a God of disorder. He is a God of peace.

As in all the churches of God's people, 34women should remain silent in the meetings. They are not allowed to speak. They must follow the lead of those who are in authority, as the Law says. 35If they have a question about something, they should ask their own husbands at home. It is shameful for women to speak in church meetings.

36Did the word of God begin with you? Or are you the only people it has reached? 37Suppose some think they are prophets or have gifts of the Holy Spirit. They should agree that what I am writing to you is the Lord's command. 38Anyone who does not recognize that will not be recognized.

39Brothers and sisters, you should want to prophesy. And don't stop people from speaking in languages they had not known before. 40But everything should be done in a proper and orderly way.

Paul Explains the Good News

15 Brothers and sisters, I want to remind you of the good news I preached to you. You received it and have put your faith in it. 2Because you believed the good news, you are saved. But you must hold firmly to the message I preached to you. If you don't, you have believed it for nothing.

3What I received I passed on to you. And it is the most important of all. Here is what it is. Christ died for our sins, just as Scripture said he would. 4He was buried. He was raised from the dead on the third day, just as Scripture said he would be. 5He appeared to Peter.

Then he appeared to the Twelve. 6After that, he appeared to more than 500 believers at the same time. Most of them are still living. But some have died. 7He appeared to James. Then he appeared to all the apostles. 8Last of all, he also appeared to me. I was like someone who wasn't born at the right time or in a normal way.

9I am the least important of the apostles. I'm not even fit to be called an apostle. I tried to destroy God's church. 10But because of God's grace I am what I am. And his grace was not wasted on me. No, I have worked harder than all the other apostles. But I didn't do the work. God's grace was with me.

11So whether it was I or the other apostles who preached to you, that is what we preach. And that is what you believed.

Believers Will Rise From the Dead

12We have preached that Christ has been raised from the dead. So how can some of you say that no one rises from the dead? 13If no one rises from the dead, then not even Christ has been raised. 14And if Christ has not been raised, what we preach doesn't mean anything. Your faith doesn't mean anything either. 15More than that, we would be lying about God. We have given witness that God raised Christ from the dead. But he did not raise him if the dead are not raised.

16If the dead are not raised, then Christ has not been raised either. 17And if Christ has not been raised, your faith doesn't mean anything. Your sins have not been forgiven. 18Those who have died believing in Christ are also lost.

19Do we have hope in Christ only for this life? Then people should pity us more than anyone else.

20But Christ really has been raised from the dead. He is the first of all those who will rise.

21Death came because of what a man did. Rising from the dead also comes because of what a man did. 22Because of Adam, all people die. So because of Christ, all will be made alive.

23But here is the order of events. Christ

is the first of those who rise from the dead. When he comes back, those who belong to him will be raised. ²⁴Then the end will come. Christ will destroy all rule, authority and power. He will hand over the kingdom to God the Father.

²⁵Christ must rule until he has put all his enemies under his control. ²⁶The last enemy that will be destroyed is death. ²⁷Scripture says that God "has put everything under his control." *(Psalm 8:6)* It says that "everything" has been put under him. But it is clear that this does not include God himself, who puts everything under Christ. ²⁸When he has done that, the Son also will be under God's rule. God puts everything under the Son. In that way, God will be all in all.

²⁹Suppose no one rises from the dead. Then what will people do who are baptized for the dead? Suppose the dead are not raised at all. Then why are people baptized for them? ³⁰And why would we put ourselves in danger every hour?

³¹I die every day. I really mean that, brothers and sisters. Here is something you can be sure of. I take pride in what Christ Jesus our Lord has done for you through my work. ³²Did I fight wild animals in Ephesus for only human reasons? Then what have I gotten for it? If the dead are not raised,

"Let us eat and drink,
   because tomorrow we will die."
                          (Isaiah 22:13)

³³Don't let anyone fool you. "Bad companions make a good person bad." ³⁴You should come back to your senses and stop sinning. Some of you don't know anything about God. I say this to make you ashamed.

The Body That Rises From the Dead

³⁵But someone might ask, "How are the dead raised? What kind of body will they have?" ³⁶How foolish! What you plant doesn't come to life unless it dies. ³⁷When

you plant something, it isn't a completely grown plant that you put in the ground. You only plant a seed. Maybe it's wheat or something else. ³⁸But God gives the seed a body just as he has planned. And to each kind of seed he gives its own body.

³⁹All earthly creatures are not the same. People have one kind of body. Animals have another. Birds have another kind. Fish have still another.

⁴⁰There are also heavenly bodies as well as earthly bodies. Heavenly bodies have one kind of glory. Earthly bodies have another. ⁴¹The sun has one kind of glory. The moon has another kind. The stars have still another. And one star's glory is different from that of another star.

⁴²It will be like that with bodies that are raised from the dead. The body that is planted does not last forever. The body that is raised from the dead lasts forever. ⁴³It is planted without honor. But it is raised in glory. It is planted in weakness. But it is raised in power. ⁴⁴It is planted as an earthly body. But it is raised as a spiritual body.

Just as there is an earthly body, there is also a spiritual body. ⁴⁵It is written, "The first man Adam became a living person." *(Genesis 2:7)* The last Adam became a spirit that gives life. ⁴⁶What is spiritual did not come first. What is earthly came first. What is spiritual came after that. ⁴⁷The first man came from the dust of the earth. The second man came from heaven.

⁴⁸Those who belong to the earth are like the one who came from the earth. And those who are spiritual are like the one who came from heaven. ⁴⁹We are like the earthly man. And we will be like the man from heaven.

⁵⁰Brothers and sisters, here is what I'm telling you. Bodies made of flesh and blood can't share in the kingdom of God. And what dies can't share in what never dies.

⁵¹Listen! I am telling you a mystery. We will not all die. But we will all be changed. ⁵²That will happen in a flash, as quickly as

To have the Lord's smile
will mean the frown of man.

you can wink an eye. It will happen when the last trumpet sounds. The trumpet will sound, and the dead will be raised to live forever. And we will be changed.

[53]Our natural bodies don't last forever. They must be dressed with what does last forever. What dies must be dressed with what does not die. [54]In fact, that is going to happen. What does not last will be dressed with what lasts forever. What dies will be dressed with what does not die. Then what is written will come true. It says, "Death has been swallowed up. It has lost the battle." *(Isaiah 25:8)*

[55]"Death, where is the battle you thought
     you were winning?
   Death, where is your sting?"

                                    (Hosea 13:14)

[56]The sting of death is sin. And the power of sin is the law. [57]But let us give thanks to God! He wins the battle for us because of what our Lord Jesus Christ has done.

[58]My dear brothers and sisters, stand firm. Don't let anything move you. Always give yourselves completely to the work of the Lord. Because you belong to the Lord, you know that your work is not worthless.

The Offering for God's People

16 Now I want to deal with the offering of money for God's people.

Do what I told the churches in Galatia to do. [2]On the first day of every week, each of you should put some money away. The amount should be in keeping with how much money you make. Save the money so that you won't have to take up an offering when I come. [3]When I arrive, I will send some people with your gift to Jerusalem. They will be people you consider to be good. And I will give them letters that explain who they are. [4]If it seems good for me to go also, they will go with me.

What Paul Asks for Himself

[5]After I go through Macedonia, I will come to you. I will only be passing through Macedonia. [6]But I might stay with you for a while. I might even spend the winter. Then you can help me on my journey everywhere

I go.

[7]I don't want to see you now while I am just passing through. I hope to spend some time with you, if the Lord allows it. [8]But I will stay at Ephesus until the day of Pentecost. [9]A door has opened wide for me to do some good work here. There are many people who oppose me.

[10]Timothy might come to you. Make sure he has nothing to worry about while he is with you. He is doing the work of the Lord, just as I am. [11]No one should refuse to accept him. Send him safely on his way so he can return to me. I'm expecting him to come back along with the others.

[12]I want to say something about our brother Apollos. I tried my best to get him to go to you with the others. But he didn't want to go right now. He will go when he can.

[13]Be on your guard. Stand firm in the faith. Be brave. Be strong. [14]Be loving in everything you do.

[15]You know that the first believers in Achaia were from the family of Stephanas. They have spent all their time serving God's people. Brothers and sisters, I am asking you [16]to follow the lead of people like them. Follow everyone who joins in the task and works hard at it.

[17]I was glad when Stephanas, Fortunatus and Achaicus arrived. They have supplied me with what you couldn't give me. [18]They renewed my spirit, and yours also. People like that are worthy of honor.

Final Greetings

[19]The churches in Asia Minor send you greetings. Aquila and Priscilla greet you warmly because of the Lord's love. So does the church that meets in their house. [20]All the brothers and sisters here send you greetings. Greet one another with a holy kiss.

[21]I, Paul, am writing this greeting with my own hand.

[22]If anyone does not love the Lord, let a curse be on that person! Come, Lord!

[23]May the grace of the Lord Jesus be with you.

[24]I give my love to all of you who belong to Christ Jesus. Amen.

2 CORINTHIANS

- *Written by Paul to the church in Corinth*
- *Paul defends his motives and authority as an apostle*
- *This letter reveals much about Paul's suffering*
- *Some in the church were being led astray by false teachers and discouraged by Paul's delay in visiting them*
- *Theme: "Being Ambassadors for God"*

1 I, Paul, am writing this letter. I am an apostle of Christ Jesus just as God planned. Timothy our brother joins me in writing.

We are sending this letter to you, the members of God's church in Corinth. It is also for all of God's people everywhere in Achaia.

²May God our Father and the Lord Jesus Christ give you grace and peace.

God Gives Comfort

³Give praise to the God and Father of our Lord Jesus Christ! He is the Father who gives tender love. All comfort comes from him. ⁴He comforts us in all our troubles. Now we can comfort others when they are in trouble. We ourselves have received comfort from God. ⁵We share the sufferings of Christ. We also share his comfort.

⁶If we are having trouble, it is so that you will be comforted and renewed. If we are comforted, it is so that you will be comforted. Then you will be able to put up with the same suffering we have gone through. ⁷Our hope for you remains firm. We know that you suffer just as we do. In the same way, God comforts you just as he comforts us.

⁸Brothers and sisters, we want you to know about the hard times we suffered in Asia Minor. We were having a lot of trouble. It was far more than we could stand. We even thought we were going to die. ⁹In fact, in our hearts we felt as if we were under the sentence of death.

But that happened so that we would not depend on ourselves but on God. He raises the dead to life. ¹⁰God has saved us from deadly dangers. And he will continue to do it. We have put our hope in him. He will continue to save us.

¹¹You must help us by praying for us. Then many people will give thanks because of what will happen to us. They will thank God for his kindness to us in answer to the prayers of many.

Paul Changes His Plans

¹²Here is what we take pride in. Our sense of what is right and wrong gives witness that we have acted in God's holy and honest ways. That is how we live in the world. We live that way most of all when we are dealing with you. Our way of living is not wise in the eyes of the world. But it is in keeping with God's grace.

¹³We are writing only what you can read and understand. And here is what I hope. ¹⁴Up to this point you have understood some of the things we have said. But now I hope that someday you will be able to take pride in us, just as we will take pride in you on the day the Lord Jesus returns. When you are able to do that, you will understand us completely.

¹⁵I was sure of those things. So I planned to visit you first. Here is how I thought you would be helped twice. ¹⁶I planned to visit you on my way to Macedonia. I would have come back to you from there. Then you would have sent me on my way to Judea.

¹⁷When I planned all of that, did I do it without much thought? No. I don't make my plans the way the world makes theirs. In the same breath the world says, "Yes! Yes!" and "No! No!"

[18]But just as sure as God is faithful, our message to you is not "Yes" and "No." [19]Silas, Timothy and I preached to you about the Son of God, Jesus Christ. Our message did not say "Yes" and "No" at the same time. The message of Christ has always been "Yes."

[20]God has made a great many promises. They are all "Yes" because of what Christ has done. So through Christ we say "Amen." We want God to receive glory.

[21]He makes both us and you stand firm because we belong to Christ. He anointed us. [22]He put his Spirit in our hearts and marked us as his own. We can now be sure that he will give us everything he promised us.

[23]I call God as my witness. I wanted to spare you. So I didn't return to Corinth. [24]Your faith is not under our control. You stand firm in your own faith. But we work together with you for your joy.

2 So I made up my mind that I would not make another painful visit to you. [2]If I make you sad, who is going to make me glad? Only you, the one I made sad.

[3]I wrote what I did for a special reason. When I came, I didn't want to be troubled by those who should make me glad. I was sure that all of you would share my joy. [4]I was very troubled when I wrote to you. My heart was sad. My eyes were full of tears. I didn't want to make you sad. I wanted to let you know that I love you very deeply.

Forgive Those Who Make You Sad

[5]Suppose someone has made us sad. In some ways, he hasn't made me sad so much as he has made all of you sad. But I don't want to put this too strongly. [6]He has been punished because most of you decided he should be. That is enough for him.

[7]Now you should forgive him and comfort him. Then he won't be sad more than he can stand. [8]So I'm asking you to tell him again that you still love him.

[9]I wrote to you for a special reason. I wanted to see if you could stand the test. I wanted to see if you could obey everything that was asked of you.

[10]Anyone you forgive I also forgive. Was there anything to forgive? If so, I have forgiven it for your benefit, knowing that Christ is watching. [11]We don't want Satan to outsmart us. We know how he does his evil work.

Serving Under the New Covenant

[12]I went to Troas to preach the good news about Christ. There I found that the Lord had opened a door of opportunity for me. [13]But I still had no peace of mind. I couldn't find my brother Titus there. So I said goodby to the believers at Troas and went on to Macedonia.

[14]Give thanks to God! He always leads us in the winners' parade because we belong to Christ. Through us, God spreads the knowledge of Christ everywhere like perfume. [15]God considers us to be the sweet smell that Christ is spreading among people who are being saved and people who are dying. [16]To the one, we are the smell of death. To the other, we are the perfume of life. Who is able to do that work?

[17]Unlike many people, we aren't selling God's word to make money. In fact, it is just the opposite. Because of Christ we speak honestly before God. We speak like people God has sent.

3 Are we beginning to praise ourselves again? Some people need letters that speak well of them. Do we need those kinds of letters, either to you or from you?

[2]You yourselves are our letter. You are written on our hearts. Everyone knows you and reads you. [3]You make it clear that you are a letter from Christ. You are the result of our work for God. You are a letter written not with ink but with the Spirit of the living God. You are a letter written not on tablets made out of stone but on human hearts.

[4]Through Christ, we can be sure of this because of our faith in God's power. [5]In ourselves we are not able to claim anything for ourselves. The power to do what we do comes from God. [6]He has given us the power to serve under a new covenant. The covenant is not based on the written Law of Moses. It comes from the Holy Spirit. The written Law kills, but the Spirit gives life.

The Glory of the New Covenant

[7]The Law was written in letters on stone. Even though it was a way of serving God, it led to death. But even that way of serving God came with glory. And even though the glory was fading, the people of Israel couldn't look at Moses' face very long.

[8]Since all of that is true, won't the work of the Holy Spirit be even more glorious? [9]The Law that sentences people to death is glorious. How much more glorious is the work of the Spirit! His work makes people right with God.

[10]The glory of the old covenant is nothing compared with the far greater glory of the new. [11]The glory of the old is fading away. How much greater is the glory of the new! It will last forever.

[12]Since we have that kind of hope, we are very bold. [13]We are not like Moses. He used to cover his face with a veil. That was to keep the people of Israel from looking at his face while the brightness was fading away.

[14]But their minds were made stubborn. To this very day, the same veil remains when the old covenant is read. The veil has not been removed. Only faith in Christ can take it away. [15]To this very day, when the Law of Moses is read, a veil covers the minds of those who hear it.

[16]But when anyone turns to the Lord, the veil is taken away. [17]Now the Lord is the Holy Spirit. And where the Spirit of the Lord is, freedom is also there. [18]Our faces are not covered with a veil. We all display the Lord's glory. We are being changed to become more like him so that we have more and more glory. And the glory comes from the Lord, who is the Holy Spirit.

A Treasure in Clay Jars

4 So because of God's mercy, we have work to do. He has given it to us. And we don't give up. [2]Instead, we have given up doing secret and shameful things. We don't twist God's word. In fact, we do just the opposite. We present the truth plainly. In the sight of God, we make our appeal to everyone's sense of what is right and wrong.

[3]Suppose our good news is covered with a veil. Then it is veiled to those who are dying. [4]The god of this world has blinded the minds of those who don't believe. They can't see the light of the good news of Christ's glory. He is the likeness of God.

[5]We do not preach about ourselves. We preach about Jesus Christ. We say that he is Lord. And we serve you because of him.

[6]God said, "Let light shine out of darkness." (*Genesis 1:3*) He made his light shine in our hearts. It shows us the light of God's glory in the face of Christ.

[7]Treasure is kept in clay jars. In the same way, we have the treasure of the good news in these earthly bodies of ours. That shows that the mighty power of the good news comes from God. It doesn't come from us.

[8]We are pushed hard from all sides. But we are not beaten down. We are bewildered. But that doesn't make us lose hope. [9]Others make us suffer. But God does not desert us. We are knocked down. But we

Satan blinds the minds of those who **reject Jesus.**

are not knocked out. [10]We always carry around the death of Jesus in our bodies. In that way, the life of Jesus can be shown in our bodies.

[11]We who are alive are always in danger of death because we are serving Jesus. So his life can be shown in our earthly bodies. [12]Death is at work in us. But life is at work in you.

[13]It is written, "I believed, and so I have spoken." *(Psalm 116:10)* With that same spirit of faith we also believe. And we also speak.

[14]We know that God raised the Lord Jesus from the dead. And he will also raise us up with Jesus. He will bring us with you to God in heaven. [15]All of that is for your benefit. God's grace is reaching more and more people. So they will become more and more thankful. They will give glory to God.

[16]We don't give up. Our bodies are becoming weaker and weaker. But our spirits are being renewed day by day. [17]Our troubles are small. They last only for a short time. But they are earning for us a glory that will last forever. It is greater than all our troubles.

[18]So we don't spend all our time looking at what we can see. Instead, we look at what we can't see. What can be seen lasts only a short time. But what can't be seen will last forever.

Our Home in Heaven

5 We know that the earthly tent we live in will be destroyed. But we have a building made by God. It is a house in heaven that lasts forever. Human hands did not build it.

[2]During our time on earth we groan. We long to put on our house in heaven as if it were clothing. [3]Then we will not be naked. [4]While we live in this tent of ours, we groan under our heavy load. We don't want to be naked. We want to be dressed with our house in heaven. What must die will be swallowed up by life.

[5]God has made us for that very purpose. He has given us the Holy Spirit as a down payment. The Spirit makes us sure of what is still to come.

[6]So here is what we can always be certain about. As long as we are at home in our bodies, we are away from the Lord. [7]We live by believing, not by seeing. [8]We are certain about that. We would rather be away from our bodies and at home with the Lord. [9]So we try our best to please him. We want to please him whether we are at home in our bodies or away from them.

[10]We must all stand in front of Christ to be judged. Each one of us will be judged for the good things and the bad things we do while we are in our bodies. Then each of us will receive what we are supposed to get.

Christ Brings Us Back to God

[11]We know what it means to have respect for the Lord. So we try to help other people to understand it.

What we are is plain to God. I hope it is also plain to your way of thinking. [12]We are not trying to make an appeal to you again. But we are giving you a chance to take pride in us. Then you can answer those who take pride in how people look rather than in what is really in their hearts.

[13]Are we out of our minds? That is because we want to serve God. Does what we say make sense? That is because we want to serve you.

[14]Christ's love controls us. We are sure that one person died for everyone. And so everyone died.

[15]Christ died for everyone. He died so that those who live should not live for themselves anymore. They should live for Christ. He died for them and was raised again.

[16]So from now on we don't look at anyone the way the world does. At one time we looked at Christ in that way. But we don't anymore.

[17]Anyone who believes in Christ is a new creation. The old is gone! The new has come! [18]It is all from God. He brought us back to himself through Christ's death on the cross. And he has given us the task of bringing others back to him through Christ.

[19]God was bringing the world back to himself through Christ. He did not hold people's sins against them. God has trusted us with the message that people may be

---

"I'm not a Christian because ..."

"I don't care... I'm just not interested."

In the great scheme of life, there are factors and laws that function whether or not you care, are interested in, or are even aware of them.

For example, you didn't get to vote on gravity, seasons, tides, the weather, etc. But you are subject to their influence and power.

If you try to defy the law of gravity by jumping off a tall building, you suffer the consequences - whether you believe in gravity or not!

God made this world...

...and He makes the rules!

Jesus said: "I am the way and the truth and the life. No one comes to the Father except through me." John 14:6

Don't ignore God ... there are consequences.

---

brought back to him. [20]So we are Christ's official messengers. It is as if God were making his appeal through us. Here is what Christ wants us to beg you to do. Come back to God!

[21]Christ didn't have any sin. But God made him become sin for us. So we can be made right with God because of what Christ has done for us.

6 We work together with God. So we are asking you not to receive God's grace and then do nothing with it. [2]He says,

"When I showed you my favor, I heard you.
On the day I saved you, I helped you."
(Isaiah 49:8)

I tell you, now is the time God shows his favor. Now is the day he saves.

Paul's Sufferings

[3]We don't put anything in anyone's way. So no one can find fault with our work for God. [4]Instead, we make it clear that we serve God in every way. We serve him by holding steady. We stand firm in all kinds of trouble, hard times and suffering.

[5]We don't give up when we are beaten or put in prison. When people stir up trouble in the streets, we continue to serve God. We work hard for him. We go without sleep and food. [6]We remain pure. We understand completely what it means to serve God. We are patient and kind. We serve him in the power of the Holy Spirit. We serve him with true love. [7]We speak the truth. We serve in the power of God. We hold the weapons of godliness in the right hand and in the left. [8]We serve God in times of glory and shame. We serve him whether the news about us is bad or good. We are true to our calling.

But people treat us as if we were pretenders. [9]We are known, but people treat us as if we were unknown. We are dying, but we continue to live. We are beaten, but we are not killed. [10]We are sad, but we are always full of joy. We are poor, but we make many people rich. We have nothing, but we own everything.

[11]Believers at Corinth, we have spoken freely to you. We have opened our hearts wide to you. [12]We are not holding back our love from you. But you are holding back your love from us. [13]I speak to you as if you were my children. It is only fair that you open your hearts wide to us also.

Do Not Be Joined to Unbelievers

[14]Do not be joined to unbelievers. What do right and wrong have in common? Can light and darkness be friends? [15]How can Christ and Satan agree? What does a believer have in common with an unbeliever? [16]How can the temple of the true God and the statues of other gods agree?

We are the temple of the living God. God has said, "I will live with them. I will walk among them. I will be their God. And they will be my people." *(Leviticus 26:12; Jeremiah 32:38; Ezekiel 37:27)*

[17]"So come out from among them
  and be separate,
                        says the Lord.
Do not touch anything that is not pure
  and clean.
  Then I will receive you."
                        (Isaiah 52:11; Ezekiel 20:34,41)
[18]"I will be your Father.
You will be my sons and daughters,
                        says the Lord
                        who rules over all."
                        (2 Samuel 7:14; 7:8)

7 Dear friends, we have these promises from God. So let us make ourselves pure from everything that pollutes our bodies and spirits. Let us be completely holy. We want to honor God.

Paul's Joy

[2]Make room for us in your hearts. We haven't done anything wrong to anyone. We haven't caused anyone to sin. We haven't taken advantage of anyone.

[3]I don't say this to judge you. I have told you before that you have an important place

in our hearts. We would live or die with you. [4]I have great faith in you. I am very proud of you. I am very happy. Even with all our troubles, my joy has no limit.

[5]When I came to Macedonia, my body wasn't able to rest. I was attacked no matter where I went. I had battles on the outside and fears on the inside.

[6]But God comforts those who are sad. He comforted me when Titus came. [7]I was comforted not only when he came but also by the comfort you had given him. He told me how much you longed for me. He told me about your deep sadness and concern for me. That made my joy greater than ever.

[8]Even if my letter made you sad, I'm not sorry I sent it. At first I was sorry. I see that my letter hurt you, but only for a little while. [9]Now I am happy. I'm not happy because you were made sad. I'm happy because your sadness led you to turn away from your sins. You became sad just as God wanted you to. So you were not hurt in any way by us.

[10]Godly sadness causes us to turn away from our sins and be saved. And we are certainly not sorry about that! But worldly sadness brings death.

[11]Look at what that godly sadness has produced in you. You are working hard to clear yourselves. You are angry and alarmed. You are longing to see me. You are concerned. You are ready to make sure that the right thing is done. In every way you have proved that you are not guilty in that matter.

[12]So even though I wrote to you, it wasn't because of the one who did the wrong. It wasn't because of the one who was hurt. Instead, I wrote you so that in the sight of God you could see for yourselves how faithful you are to us. [13]All of that cheers us up.

We were also very glad to see how happy Titus was. You have all renewed his spirit. [14]I had bragged about you to him. And you have not let us down. Everything we said to you was true. In the same way, our bragging about you to Titus has also turned out to be true. [15]His love for you is even greater when he remembers that you all obeyed his teaching. You received him with fear and trembling. [16]I am glad I can have complete faith in you.

Giving Freely to Others

8 Brothers and sisters, we want you to know about the grace that God has given to the churches in Macedonia. ²They have suffered a great deal. But their joy was more than full. Even though they were very poor, they gave very freely.

³I give witness that they gave as much as they could. In fact, they gave even more than they could. Completely on their own, ⁴they begged us for the chance to share in serving God's people in that way. ⁵They did more than we expected. First they gave themselves to the Lord. Then they gave themselves to us in keeping with what God wanted.

⁶Titus had already started collecting money from you. So we asked him to get you to finish making your kind gift.

⁷You do well in everything else. You do well in faith and in speaking. You do well in knowledge and in complete commitment. And you do well in your love for us. So make sure that you also do well in the grace of giving to others.

⁸I am not commanding you to do it. But I want to put you to the test. I want to find out if you really love God. I want to compare your love with that of others.

⁹You know the grace shown by our Lord Jesus Christ. Even though he was rich, he became poor to help you. Because he became poor, you can become rich.

¹⁰Here is my advice about what is best for you in that matter. Last year you were the first to give. You were also the first to want to give. ¹¹So finish the work. Then your longing to do it will be matched by your finishing it. Give on the basis of what you have.

¹²Do you really want to give? Then the gift is received in keeping with what you have, not with what you don't have.

¹³We don't want others to have it easy at your expense. We want things to be equal. ¹⁴Right now you have plenty in order to take care of what they need. Then they will have plenty to take care of what you need. That will make things equal. ¹⁵It is written, "Those who gathered a lot didn't have too much. And those who gathered a little had enough." (Exodus 16:18)

By the Numbers

783,137 words

1600 years to be written

40 different authors many different lands

66 books: letters, prophecies & history

39 in the Hebrew Old Testament

27 in the Greek New Testament

1 Way to God Jesus Christ

0 contradictions

Fits together like a Divine jigsaw puzzle

Paul Sends Titus to Corinth

¹⁶God put into the heart of Titus the same concern I have for you. I am thankful to God for this. ¹⁷Titus welcomed our appeal. He is also excited about coming to you. It was his own idea.

¹⁸Along with Titus, we are sending another brother. All the churches praise him for his service in telling the good news. ¹⁹He was also chosen by the churches to go with us as we bring the offering. We are in charge of it. We want to honor the Lord himself. We want to show how ready we are to help.

²⁰We want to keep anyone from blaming us for how we take care of that large gift. ²¹We are trying hard to do what is right in the Lord's eyes and in the eyes of people.

²²We are also sending another one of our brothers with them. He has often proved to us in many ways that he is very committed. He is now even more committed because he has great faith in you.

²³Titus is my helper. He and I work together among you. Our brothers are messengers from the churches. They honor Christ. ²⁴So show them that you really love them. Show them why we are proud of you. Then the churches can see it.

9 I don't need to write to you about giving to God's people. ²I know how much you want to help. I have been bragging about it to the people in Macedonia. I have been telling them that since last year you who live in Achaia were ready to give. You are so excited that it has stirred up most of them to take action.

³But I am sending the brothers. Then our bragging about you in this matter will have a good reason. You will be ready, just as I said you would be.

⁴Suppose people from Macedonia come with me and find out that you are not prepared. Then we, as well as you, would be ashamed of being so certain.

⁵So I thought I should try to get the brothers to visit you ahead of time. They

will finish the plans for the large gift you had promised. Then it will be ready as a gift that is freely given. It will not be given by force.

Planting Many Seeds

[6]Here is something to remember. The one who plants only a little will gather only a little. And the one who plants a lot will gather a lot. [7]You should each give what you have decided in your heart to give. You shouldn't give if you don't want to. You shouldn't give because you are forced to. God loves a cheerful giver.

[8]And God is able to shower all kinds of blessings on you. In all things and at all times you will have everything you need. You will do more and more good works. [9]It is written,

"They have spread their gifts around to
     poor people.
Their good works continue forever."
                                   (Psalm 112:9)

[10]God supplies seed to the planter. He supplies bread for food. God will also supply and increase the amount of your seed. He will increase the results of your good works. [11]You will be made rich in every way. Then you can always give freely. We will take your many gifts to the people who need them. And they will give thanks to God.

[12]Your gifts meet the needs of God's people. And that's not all. Your gifts also cause many people to thank God.

[13]You have shown yourselves to be worthy by what you have given. So people will praise God because you obey him. That proves that you really believe the good news about Christ. They will also praise God because you share freely with them and with everyone else. [14]Their hearts will be filled with longing for you when they pray for you. God has given you grace that is better than anything.

[15]Let us give thanks to God for his gift. It is so great that no one can tell how wonderful it really is!

Don't let anything stand in your way!

God is ...

Bigger than your problems!

Paul Speaks Up for Himself

10 Christ is gentle and free of pride. So I make my appeal to you. I, Paul, am the one you call shy when I am face to face with you. But when I am away from you, you call me bold. [2]I beg you that when I come I won't have to be as bold as I expect

to be toward some people. They think that I live the way the people of this world live.

[3]I do live in the world. But I don't fight my battles the way the people of the world do. [4]The weapons I fight with are not the weapons the world uses. In fact, it is just the opposite. My weapons have the power of God to destroy the camps of the enemy.

[5]I destroy every claim and every reason that keeps people from knowing God. I keep every thought under control in order to make it obey Christ. [6]Until you have obeyed completely, I will be ready to punish you every time you don't obey.

[7]You are looking only at what appears on the surface of things. Suppose you are sure you belong to Christ. Then you should consider again that I belong to Christ just as much as you do.

[8]Do I brag too much about the authority the Lord gave me? If I do, it's because I want to build you up, not pull you down. And I'm not ashamed of that kind of bragging.

[9]Don't think that I'm trying to scare you with my letters. [10]Some say, "His letters sound important. They are powerful. But in person he doesn't seem like much. And what he says doesn't amount to anything." [11]People like that have a lot to learn. What I say in my letters when I'm away from you, I will do in my actions when I'm with you.

[12]I don't dare to compare myself with those who praise themselves. I'm not that kind of person. They measure themselves by themselves. They compare themselves with themselves. When they do that, they are not wise.

[13]But I won't brag more than I should. Instead, I will brag only about what I have done in the area God has given me. It is an area that reaches all the way to you. [14]I am not going too far in my bragging. I would be going too far if I hadn't come to where you live. But I did get there with the good news about Christ.

[15]And I won't brag about work done by others. If I did, I would be bragging more than I should. As your faith continues to grow, I hope that my work among you will greatly increase. [16]Then I will be able to preach the good news in the areas beyond

Paul's Hardships...

jailed
whipped
faced death
39 lashes
robbed
beaten with a rod
thirsty
hungry
shipwrecked
stoned
stranded at sea
faced angry mobs
exhausted
called an impostor
heart-aches
suffered in the cold
despised
sleepless nights
in pain

Resulted in
JOY
in the Lord

you. I don't want to brag about work already done in someone else's territory.

[17]But, "The one who brags should brag about what the Lord has done." *(Jeremiah 9:24)* [18]Those who praise themselves are not accepted. Those the Lord praises are accepted.

Paul and Those Who Pretend to Be Apostles

11 I hope you will put up with a little of my foolish bragging. But you are already doing that.

[2]My jealousy for you comes from God himself. I promised to give you to only one husband. That husband is Christ. I wanted to be able to give you to him as if you were a pure virgin. [3]But Eve was tricked by the snake's clever lies. And I'm afraid that in the same way your minds will somehow be led down the wrong path. They will be led away from your true and pure love for Christ.

[4]Suppose someone comes to you and preaches about a Jesus different from the Jesus we preached about. Or suppose you receive a spirit different from the one you received before. Or suppose you receive a message of good news different from the one you accepted earlier. You put up with those kinds of things easily enough.

[5]But I don't think I'm in any way less important than those "super-apostles." [6]I may not be a trained speaker. But I do have knowledge. I've made that very clear to you in every way.

[7]When I preached God's good news to you free of charge, I put myself down in order to lift you up. Was that a sin? [8]Did I rob other churches when I received help from them so that I could serve you? [9]When I was with you and needed something, I didn't cause you any expense. The believers who came from Macedonia gave me what I needed. I haven't caused you any expense at all. And I won't ever do it.

[10]I'm sure that the truth of Christ is in me. And I'm just as sure that nobody in Achaia will keep me from bragging. [11]Why? Because I don't love you? No! God knows I do! [12]And I will keep on doing what I'm doing. That

will stop those who claim they have things to brag about. They think they have a chance to be considered equal with us.

[13]People like that are false apostles. They work hard to trick others. They only pretend to be apostles of Christ.

[14]That comes as no surprise. Even Satan himself pretends to be an angel of light. [15]So it doesn't surprise us that those who serve Satan pretend to be serving God. They will finally get exactly what they should.

Paul Brags About His Sufferings

[16]I will say it again. Don't let anyone think I'm a fool. But if you do, receive me just as you would receive a fool. Then I can do a little bragging.

[17]When I brag about myself like this, I'm not talking the way the Lord would. I'm talking like a fool. [18]Many are bragging the way the people of the world do. So I will brag like that too.

[19]You are so wise! You gladly put up with fools! [20]In fact, you even put up with anyone who makes you a slave or uses you. You put up with those who take advantage of you. You put up with those who claim to be better than you. You put up with those who slap you in the face.

[21]I'm ashamed to have to say that I was too weak for that!

What anyone else dares to brag about, I also dare to brag about. I'm speaking like a fool! [22]Are they Hebrews? So am I. Do they belong to the people of Israel? So do I. Are they Abraham's children? So am I. [23]Are they serving Christ? I am serving him even more. I'm out of my mind to talk like this! I have worked much harder. I have been in prison more often. I have suffered terrible beatings. Again and again I almost died. [24]Five times the Jews gave me 39 strokes with a whip. [25]Three times I was beaten with sticks. Once they tried to kill me by throwing stones at me. Three times I was shipwrecked. I spent a night and a day in the open sea.

[26]I have had to keep on the move. I have been in danger from rivers. I have been in danger from robbers. I have been in danger from people from my own country. I

have been in danger from those who aren't Jews. I have been in danger in the city, in the country, and at sea. I have been in danger from people who pretended they were believers.

²⁷I have worked very hard. Often I have gone without sleep. I have been hungry and thirsty. Often I have gone without food. I have been cold and naked.

²⁸Besides everything else, every day I am concerned about all the churches. It is a very heavy load. ²⁹If anyone is weak, I feel weak. If anyone is led into sin, I burn on the inside.

³⁰If I have to brag, I will brag about the things that show how weak I am. ³¹I am not lying. The God and Father of the Lord Jesus knows this. May God be praised forever. ³²In Damascus the governor who served under King Aretas had their city guarded. He wanted to arrest me. ³³But I was lowered in a basket from a window in the wall. So I slipped through the governor's hands.

Paul's Vision and His Painful Problem

12 We can't gain anything by bragging. But I have to do it anyway. I am going to tell you what I've seen. I want to talk about what the Lord has shown me.

²I know a believer in Christ who was taken up to the third heaven 14 years ago. I don't know if his body was taken up or not. Only God knows. ³I don't know if that man was in his body or out of it. Only God knows. But I do know that ⁴he was taken up to paradise. He heard things that couldn't be put into words. They were things that people aren't allowed to talk about.

⁵I will brag about a man like that. But I won't brag about myself. I will brag only about how weak I am.

⁶Suppose I decide to brag. That would not make me a fool, because I would be telling the truth. But I don't do it. Then no one will think more of me than he should because of what I do or say.

⁷I could have become proud of myself because of the amazing and wonderful things God has shown me. So I was given a problem that caused pain in my body. It is a messenger from Satan to make me suffer. ⁸Three times I begged the Lord to take it away from me. ⁹But he said to me, "My grace is all you need. My power is strongest when you are weak."

So I am very happy to brag about how weak I am. Then Christ's power can rest on me. ¹⁰Because of how I suffered for Christ, I'm glad that I am weak. I am glad in hard times. I am glad when people say mean things about me. I am glad when things are difficult. And I am glad when people make me suffer. When I am weak, I am strong.

Paul's Concern for the People of Corinth

¹¹I have made a fool of myself. But you made me do it. You should have praised me. Even though I am nothing, I am in no way less important than the "super-apostles." ¹²You can recognize apostles by the signs, wonders and miracles they do. Those things were faithfully done among you no matter what happened.

¹³How were you less important than the other churches? The only difference was that I didn't cause you any expense. Forgive me for that wrong!

¹⁴Now I am ready to visit you for the third time. I won't cause you any expense. I don't want what you have. What I really want is you. After all, children shouldn't have to save up for their parents. Parents should save up for their children. ¹⁵So I will be very happy to spend everything I have for you. I will even spend myself. If I love you more, will you love me less?

¹⁶In any case, I haven't caused you any expense. But I'm such a tricky fellow! I have caught you by tricking you!

¹⁷Did I take advantage of you through any of the men I sent to you? ¹⁸I asked Titus to go to you. And I sent our brother with him. Titus didn't take advantage of you, did he? Didn't I act in the same spirit? Didn't I follow the same path?

¹⁹All this time, have you been thinking that I've been speaking up for myself? No, I've been speaking with God as my witness. I've been speaking like a believer in Christ. Dear friends, everything I do is to help you

become stronger.

[20]I'm afraid that when I come I won't find you as I want you to be. I'm afraid that you won't find me as you want me to be. I'm afraid there will be arguing, jealousy and fits of anger. I'm afraid you will separate into your own little groups. Then you will tell lies about each other. You will talk about each other. I'm afraid you will be proud and cause trouble.

[21]I'm afraid that when I come again my God will put me to shame in front of you. Then I will be sad about many who sinned earlier and have not turned away from it. They have not turned away from uncleanness, sexual sins and wild living. They have done all those things.

Final Warnings

13 This will be my third visit to you. Scripture says, "Every matter must be proved by the words of two or three witnesses." *(Deuteronomy 19:15)* [2]I already warned you during my second visit. I now say it again while I'm away. When I return, I won't spare those who sinned earlier. I won't spare any of the others either.

[3]You are asking me to prove that Christ is speaking through me. He is not weak in dealing with you. He is powerful among you. [4]It is true that Christ was nailed to the cross because he was weak. But he lives by God's power. In the same way, I share his weakness. But by God's power I will live with him to serve you.

[5]Take a good look at yourselves to see if you are really believers. Test yourselves. Don't you realize that Christ Jesus is in you? Unless, of course, you fail the test! [6]I hope you will discover that I haven't failed the test.

[7]I pray to God that you won't do anything wrong. I don't pray so that people will see that I have passed the test. Instead, I pray so that you will do what is right, even if it seems I have failed. [8]I can't do anything to stop the truth. I can only work for the truth.

[9]I'm glad when I am weak but you are strong. I pray that you will become perfect. [10]That's why I write these things before I come to you. Then when I do come, I won't have to be hard on you when I use my authority.

The Lord gave me the authority to build you up. He didn't give it to me to tear you down.

Final Greetings

[11]Finally, brothers and sisters, good-by. Try to be perfect. Pay attention to what I'm saying. Agree with one another. Live in peace. And the God who gives love and peace will be with you.

[12]Greet one another with a holy kiss. [13]All of God's people send their greetings.

[14]May the grace shown by the Lord Jesus Christ, and the love that God has given us, and the sharing of life brought about by the Holy Spirit be with you all.

Possible Corinthian "Report Card"

Quarreling	- A	Faith	- F	What does
Jealousy	- A	Humility	- D-	YOUR
Gossip	- A	Witnessing	- F	report card
Strife	- A	Giving	- D-	look like?
Anger	- A+	Love	- F	

Hidden Message Puzzle

Find the hidden words on the tape below that make up the complete message

SECRET, KEEP OUT!

WLTGODBRNRHASR

JHLOANEDBHWCBYOUJFLPMSKTKMDARST

GHWJKMSPBSETWSOFQZLGFHPJTALENTS

BKLWMWHATLMKGWPYOUSGDFGHRJKNDO

MGZWITHSRVWXBZRTHEMGXOWNKLISQZ

PDMGHUPRXDSTOHCDTSPLMSRMYOUST

Circle each hidden word on the tape and place in the space below. Check your decoding skills with the answer at the bottom of page 83 in the Illustrated New Testament.

1._ _ _ _   2._ _ _ _   3._ _ _ _ _ _ _

4._ _ _   5._   6._ _ _   7._ _

8._ _ _ _ _ _ _ .   9._ _ _ _

10._ _ _   11._ _ _   12._ _ _ _

13._ _ _ _ _   14._ _   15._ _   16._ _

17._ _ _ .

GALATIANS

- Written by Paul to the various churches in Galatia
- Concerned that "Judaizers" preaching legalism had made inroads into the churches
- Present the true Gospel vs. a false gospel of works
- Paul established these churches on his first missionary trip
- Theme: "Saved by Grace - Live by Grace"

I, Paul, am writing this letter. I am an apostle. People have not sent me. No human authority has sent me. I have been sent by Jesus Christ and by God the Father. God raised Jesus from the dead. ²All the brothers who are with me join me in writing.

We are sending this letter to you, the members of the churches in Galatia.

³May God our Father and the Lord Jesus Christ give you grace and peace. ⁴Jesus gave his life for our sins. He set us free from this evil world. That was what our God and Father wanted. ⁵Give glory to God for ever and ever. Amen.

There Is No Other Good News

⁶I am amazed. You are so quickly deserting the One who chose you because of the grace that Christ has provided. You are turning to a different "good news." ⁷What you are accepting is really not the good news at all.

It seems that some people have gotten you all mixed up. They are trying to twist the good news about Christ.

⁸But suppose even we should preach a different "good news." Suppose even an angel from heaven should preach it. I'm talking about a different one than the good news we gave you. Let anyone who does that be judged by God forever. ⁹I have already said it. Now I will say it again. Anyone who preaches a "good news" that is different from the one you accepted should be judged by God forever.

¹⁰Am I now trying to get people to think well of me? Or do I want God to think well of me? Am I trying to please people? If I were, I would not be serving Christ.

Paul Was Appointed by God

¹¹Brothers and sisters, here is what I want you to know. The good news I preached is not something a human being made up. ¹²No one gave it to me. No one taught it to me. Instead, I received it from Jesus Christ. He showed it to me.

¹³You have heard of my earlier way of life as a Jew. With all my strength I attacked the church of God. I tried to destroy it. ¹⁴I was moving ahead in my Jewish way of life. I went beyond many Jews who were my own age. I held firmly to the teachings passed down by my people.

¹⁵But God set me apart from the time I was born. He showed me his grace by appointing me. He was pleased ¹⁶to show his Son in my life. He wanted me to preach about Jesus among those who aren't Jews.

When God appointed me, I didn't talk to anyone. ¹⁷I didn't go up to Jerusalem to see those who were apostles before I was. Instead, I went at once into Arabia. Later I returned to Damascus.

¹⁸Then after three years I went up to Jerusalem. I went there to get to know Peter. I stayed with him for 15 days. ¹⁹I didn't see any of the other apostles. I only saw James, the Lord's brother. ²⁰Here is what you can be sure of. And God gives witness to it. What I am writing you is not a lie.

²¹Later I went to Syria and Cilicia. ²²The members of Christ's churches in Judea did not know me in a personal way. ²³They only heard others say, "The man who used to attack us has changed. He is now preaching the faith he once tried to destroy." ²⁴And they praised God because of me.

Paul Is Accepted by the Apostles

2 Fourteen years later I went up again to Jerusalem. This time I went with Barnabas. I took Titus along also. [2]I went because God showed me what he wanted me to do. I told the people there the good news that I preach among those who aren't Jews. But I spoke in private to those who seemed to be leaders. I was afraid that I was running or had run my race for nothing.

[3]Titus was with me. He was a Greek. But even he was not forced to be circumcised.

[4]That matter came up because some who pretended to be believers had slipped in among us. They wanted to find out about the freedom we have because we belong to Christ Jesus. They wanted to make us slaves again.

[5]We didn't give in to them for a moment. We wanted the truth of the good news to remain with you.

[6]Some people in Jerusalem seemed to be important. It makes no difference to me what they were. God does not judge by what he sees on the outside. Those people added nothing to my message.

[7]In fact, it was just the opposite. They saw that I had been trusted with the task of preaching the good news just as Peter had been. My task was to preach to the non-Jews. Peter's task was to preach to the Jews. [8]God was working through Peter as an apostle to the Jews. He was also working through me as an apostle to the non-Jews.

[9]James, Peter and John are considered to be pillars in the church. They recognized the special grace that was given to me. So they shook my hand and the hand of Barnabas. They wanted to show they accepted us. They agreed that we should go to the non-Jews. They would go to the Jews. [10]They asked only one thing. They wanted us to continue to remember poor people. That was what I really wanted to do anyway.

Paul Opposes Peter

[11]When Peter came to Antioch, I told him to his face that I was against what he was doing. He was clearly wrong. [12]He used to eat with those who weren't Jews. But certain men came from the group that was led by James. When they arrived, Peter began to draw back. He separated himself from the non-Jews. He was afraid of the circumcision group.

[13]Peter's actions were not honest. The other Jews joined him. Even Barnabas was led down the wrong path.

[14]I saw what they were doing. It was not

Garbage in... Rebellion Me! My Way Selfishness Grinder 2010 anger envy Lust gluttony Coveting pride sloth garbage OUT!

in line with the truth of the good news. So I spoke to Peter in front of them all. "You are a Jew," I said. "But you live like one who is not. So why do you force non-Jews to follow Jewish ways?"

God's Grace and Our Faith

¹⁵We are Jews by birth. We are not "non-Jewish sinners." ¹⁶We know that no one is made right with God by obeying the law. It is by believing in Jesus Christ. So we too have put our faith in Christ Jesus. That is so we can be made right with God by believing in Christ, not by obeying the law. No one can be made right with God by obeying the law.

¹⁷We are trying to be made right with God through Christ. But it is clear that we are sinners. So does that mean that Christ causes us to sin? Certainly not! ¹⁸Suppose I build again what I had destroyed. Then I prove that I break the Law.

¹⁹Because of the law, I died as far as the law is concerned. I died so that I might live for God. ²⁰I have been crucified with Christ. I don't live any longer. Christ lives in me. My faith in the Son of God helps me to live my life in my body. He loved me. He gave himself for me.

²¹I do not get rid of the grace of God. What if a person could become right with God by obeying the law? Then Christ died for nothing!

Faith or Obeying the Law

3 You foolish people of Galatia! Who has put you under an evil spell? When I preached, I clearly showed you that Jesus Christ had been nailed to the cross.

²I would like to learn just one thing from you. Did you receive the Holy Spirit by obeying the law? Or did you receive the Spirit by believing what you heard? ³Are you so foolish? You began with the Holy Spirit. Are you now trying to complete God's work in you by your own strength?

⁴Have you suffered so much for nothing? And was it really for nothing? ⁵Why does God give you his Spirit? Why does he work miracles among you? Is it because you do what the law says? Or is it because you believe what you have heard?

⁶Think about Abraham. Scripture says, "Abraham believed God. God accepted Abraham because he believed. So his faith made him right with God." *(Genesis 15:6)* ⁷So you see, those who have faith are children of Abraham.

⁸Long ago, Scripture knew that God would make non-Jews right with himself by believing in him. He announced the good news ahead of time to Abraham. He said, "All nations will be blessed because of you." *(Genesis 12:3; 18:18; 22:18)* ⁹So those who have faith are blessed along with Abraham. He was the man of faith.

¹⁰All who depend on obeying the law are under a curse. It is written, "May everyone who doesn't continue to do everything that is written in the Book of the Law be under God's curse." *(Deuteronomy 27:26)* ¹¹We know that no one is made right with God by keeping the law. Scripture says, "Those who are right with God will live by faith." *(Habakkuk 2:4)*

¹²The law is not based on faith. In fact, it is just the opposite. It teaches that "the one who does those things will live by them." *(Leviticus 18:5)*

¹³Christ set us free from the curse of the law. He did it by becoming a curse for us. It is written, "Everyone who is hung on a pole is under God's curse." *(Deuteronomy 21:23)* ¹⁴Christ Jesus set us free so that the blessing given to Abraham would come to non-Jews through Christ. He did it so that we might receive the promise of the Holy Spirit by believing in Christ.

What ever you put first in your life...
that is your god.

The Law and the Promise

[15]Brothers and sisters, let me give you an example from everyday life. No one can get rid of an official agreement between people. No one can add to it. It can't be changed after it has been made. It is the same with God's covenant. [16]The promises were given to Abraham. They were also given to his seed. Scripture does not say, "and to seeds." That means many people. It says, "and to your seed." *(Genesis 12:7; 13:15; 24:7)* That means one person. And that one person is Christ.

[17]Here is what I mean. The law came 430 years after the promise. But the law does not get rid of God's covenant and promise. The covenant had already been made by God. So the law does not do away with the promise.

[18]The great gift that God has for us does not depend on the law. If it did, it would no longer depend on a promise. But God gave it to Abraham as a free gift through a promise.

[19]Then what was the purpose of the law? It was added because of human sin. And it was supposed to control us until the promised Seed had come. The law was put into effect through angels by a go-between. [20]A go-between does not take sides. God didn't use a go-between when he made his promise to Abraham. But the same God was at work in both the law and the promise.

[21]So is the law opposed to God's promises? Certainly not! What if a law had been given that could give life? Then people could become right with God by obeying the law. [22]But Scripture announces that the whole world is a prisoner because of sin. It does so in order that what was promised might be given to those who believe. The promise comes through faith in Jesus Christ.

[23]Before faith in Christ came, we were held prisoners by the law. We were locked up until faith was made known. [24]So the law was put in charge until Christ came. He came so that we might be made right with God by believing in Christ.

[25]But now faith in Christ has come. So we are no longer under the control of the law.

Children of God

[26]You are all children of God by believing in Christ Jesus. [27]All of you who were baptized into Christ have put on Christ as if he were your clothes. [28]There is no Jew or Greek. There is no slave or free person. There is no male or female. Because you belong to Christ Jesus, you are all one.

[29]You who belong to Christ are Abraham's seed. You will receive what God has promised.

4 Here is what I have been saying. As long as your own children are young, they are no different from slaves in your house. They are no different, even though they own all of the property. [2]They are under the care of guardians and those who manage the property. They are under their care until the time when their fathers give them the property. [3]It is the same with us.

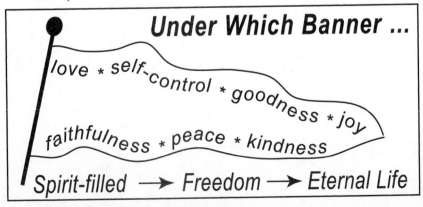

When we were children, we were slaves to the basic things the people of the world believe.

4But then the right time came. God sent his Son. A woman gave birth to him. He was born under the authority of the law. 5He came to set free those who were under the law. He wanted us to be adopted as children with all the rights children have.

6Because you are his children, God sent the Spirit of his Son into our hearts. He is the Holy Spirit. By his power we call God "Abba." Abba means Father.

7So you aren't slaves any longer. You are God's children. Because you are his children, he gives you what he promised to give his people.

Paul's Concern for the Believers in Galatia

8At one time you didn't know God. You were slaves to gods that are really not gods at all. 9But now you know God. Even better, God knows you. So why are you turning back to those weak and worthless beliefs? Do you want to be slaves to them all over again?

10You are observing special days and months and seasons and years! 11I am afraid for you. I am afraid that somehow I have wasted my efforts on you.

Paul's Appeal to the Believers

12I make my appeal to you, brothers and sisters. I'm asking you to become like me. After all, I became like you. You didn't do anything wrong to me.

13As you know, it was because I was sick that I first preached the good news to you. 14My sickness was hard on you. But you didn't put me off. You didn't make fun of me. Instead, you welcomed me as if I were an angel of God. You welcomed me as if I were Christ Jesus himself.

15What has happened to all of your joy? If you could have torn out your own eyes and given them to me, you would have. I can give witness to that. 16Have I become your enemy now by telling you the truth?

17Those people are trying hard to win you over. But it is not for your good. They want to take you away from us. They want you to commit yourselves to them. 18It is fine to be committed to something, if the purpose is good. And you shouldn't be committed only when I am with you. You should always be committed.

19My dear children, I am in pain for you. Once again I have pain like a woman giving birth. And my pain will continue until Christ makes you like himself.

20I wish I could be with you now. I wish I could change my tone of voice. As it is, you bewilder me.

Hagar and Sarah

21You who want to be under the authority of the law, tell me something. Don't you know what the law says? 22It is written that Abraham had two sons. The slave woman gave birth to one of them. The free woman gave birth to the other one. 23Abraham's son

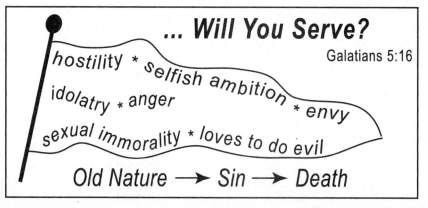

by the slave woman was born in the usual way. But his son by the free woman was born because of God's promise.

²⁴Those things can be taken as examples. The two women stand for two covenants. One covenant comes from Mount Sinai. It gives birth to children who are going to be slaves. It is Hagar. ²⁵Hagar stands for Mount Sinai in Arabia. She stands for the present city of Jerusalem. That's because she and her children are slaves.

²⁶But the Jerusalem that is above is free. She is our mother. ²⁷It is written,

> "Be glad, woman,
> you who have no children.
> Start shouting,
> you who have no labor pains.
> The woman who is all alone has more children
> than the woman who has a husband."
> *(Isaiah 54:1)*

²⁸Brothers and sisters, you are children because of God's promise just as Isaac was. ²⁹At that time, the son born in the usual way tried to hurt the son born by the power of the Holy Spirit. It is the same now.

³⁰But what does Scripture say? "Get rid of the slave woman. Get rid of her son. The slave woman's son will never have a share of the family's property with the free woman's son." *(Genesis 21:10)*

³¹Brothers and sisters, we are not the slave woman's children. We are the free woman's children.

Christ Sets Us Free

5 Christ has set us free. He wants us to enjoy freedom. So stand firm. Don't let the chains of slavery hold you again.

²Here is what I, Paul, say to you. Don't let yourselves be circumcised. If you do, Christ won't be of any value to you. ³I say it again. Every man who lets himself be circumcised must obey the whole law.

⁴Some of you are trying to be made right with God by obeying the law. You have been separated from Christ. You have fallen away from God's grace.

⁵But we expect to be made completely holy because of our faith in Christ. Through the Holy Spirit we wait in hope. ⁶Circumcision and uncircumcision aren't worth anything to those who believe in Christ Jesus. The only thing that really counts is faith that shows itself through love.

⁷You were running a good race. Who cut in on you and kept you from obeying the truth? ⁸The One who chooses you does not keep you from obeying the truth. ⁹You should know that "just a little yeast works its way through the whole batch of dough."

¹⁰The Lord makes me certain that you will not think in any other way. The one who has gotten you all mixed up will pay the price. It doesn't matter who that may be.

¹¹Brothers and sisters, I am not still preaching that people must be circumcised. If I were, why am I still being opposed? If that were what I preach, then the cross wouldn't upset anyone.

¹²So then, what about troublemakers who try to get others to be circumcised? I wish they would go the whole way! I wish they would cut off everything that marks them as men!

Chosen to Be Free

¹³My brothers and sisters, you were chosen to be free. But don't use your freedom as an excuse to live in sin. Instead, serve one another in love. ¹⁴The whole law can be found in a single command. "Love your neighbor as you love yourself." *(Leviticus 19:18)*

¹⁵You must not keep on biting each other. You must not keep eating each other up. Watch out! You might destroy each other.

Living by the Holy Spirit's Power

¹⁶So I say, live by the Holy Spirit's power. Then you will not do what your sinful nature wants you to do.

The fire of God in your heart
will melt the lead in your feet.

¹⁷The sinful nature does not want what the Spirit delights in. And the Spirit does not want what the sinful nature delights in. The two are at war with each other. That's what makes you do what you don't want to do. ¹⁸But if you are led by the Spirit, you are not under the authority of the law.

¹⁹What the sinful nature does is clear. It enjoys sexual sins, impure acts and wild living. ²⁰It worships statues of gods. It also worships evil powers. It is full of hatred and fighting. It is full of jealousy and fits of anger. It is interested only in getting ahead. It stirs up trouble. It separates people into their own little groups. ²¹It wants what others have. It gets drunk and takes part in wild parties. It does many things of that kind. I warn you now as I did before. People who live like that will not receive God's kingdom.

²²But the fruit the Holy Spirit produces is love, joy and peace. It is being patient, kind and good. It is being faithful ²³and gentle and having control of oneself. There is no law against things of that kind.

²⁴Those who belong to Christ Jesus have nailed their sinful nature to his cross. They don't want what their sinful nature loves and longs for.

²⁵Since we live by the Spirit, let us march in step with the Spirit. ²⁶Let us not become proud. Let us not make each other angry. Let us not want what belongs to others.

Do Good to Everyone

6 Brothers and sisters, what if someone is caught in a sin? Then you who are guided by the Spirit should correct that person. Do it in a gentle way. But be careful. You could be tempted too. ²Carry each other's heavy loads. If you do, you will give the law of Christ its full meaning.

³If you think you are somebody when you are nobody, you are fooling yourselves. ⁴Each of you should put your own actions to the test. Then you can take pride in yourself. You won't be comparing yourself to somebody else. ⁵Each of you should carry your own load.

⁶Those who are taught the word must share all good things with their teacher.

⁷Don't be fooled. You can't outsmart

God. A man gathers a crop from what he plants. ⁸Some people plant to please their sinful nature. From that nature they will harvest death. Others plant to please the Holy Spirit. From the Spirit they will harvest eternal life.

⁹Let us not become tired of doing good. At the right time we will gather a crop if we don't give up. ¹⁰So when we can do good to everyone, let us do it. Let us make a special point of doing good to those who belong to the family of believers.

The Creation of a New Nature

¹¹Look at the big letters I'm using as I write to you with my own hand!

¹²Some people want others to think well of them. They are trying to force you to be circumcised. They do it for only one reason. They don't want to suffer by being connected with the cross of Christ. ¹³Even those who are circumcised don't obey the law. But they want you to be circumcised. Then they can brag about what has been done to your body.

¹⁴I never want to brag about anything except the cross of our Lord Jesus Christ. Through that cross the ways of the world have been crucified as far as I am concerned. And I have been crucified as far as the ways of the world are concerned.

¹⁵Circumcision and uncircumcision don't mean anything. What really counts is the creation of a new nature.

¹⁶May peace and mercy be given to all who follow this rule. May peace and mercy be given to the Israel that belongs to God.

¹⁷Finally, let no one cause trouble for me. My body has marks that show I belong to Jesus.

¹⁸Brothers and sisters, may the grace of our Lord Jesus Christ be with your spirit. Amen.

EPHESIANS

- *Written by Paul while a prisoner in Rome*
- *Paul spent three years in Ephesus due to their openness*
- *Paul portrays the Church as the "bride of Christ"*
- *Written to encourage and build up the believers*
- *Takes the reader from spiritual blessings to spiritual battle*
- *Theme: "The Church as the Body of Christ"*

1 I, Paul, am writing this letter. I am an apostle of Christ Jesus just as God planned.

I am sending this letter to you, God's people in Ephesus. Because you belong to Christ Jesus, you are faithful.

²May God our Father and the Lord Jesus Christ give you grace and peace.

God Gives Spiritual Blessings

³Give praise to the God and Father of our Lord Jesus Christ. He has blessed us with every spiritual blessing. Those blessings come from the heavenly world. They belong to us because we belong to Christ.

⁴God chose us to belong to Christ before the world was created. He chose us to be holy and without blame in his eyes. He loved us. ⁵So he decided long ago to adopt us as his children. He did it because of what Jesus Christ has done. It pleased God to do it. ⁶All those things bring praise to his glorious grace. God freely gave us his grace because of the One he loves.

⁷We have been set free because of what Christ has done. Through his blood our sins have been forgiven. We have been set free because God's grace is so rich. ⁸He poured his grace on us by giving us great wisdom and understanding.

⁹He showed us the mystery of his plan. It was in keeping with what he wanted to do. It was what he had planned through Christ. ¹⁰It will all come about when history has been completed. God will then bring together all things in heaven and on earth under one ruler. The ruler is Christ.

¹¹We were also chosen to belong to him.

God decided to choose us long ago in keeping with his plan. He works out everything to fit his plan and purpose. ¹²We were the first to put our hope in Christ. We were chosen to bring praise to his glory.

¹³You also became believers in Christ. That happened when you heard the message of truth. It was the good news about how you could be saved. When you believed, he marked you with a seal. The seal is the Holy Spirit that he promised.

¹⁴The Spirit marks us as God's own. We can now be sure that someday we will receive all that God has promised. That will happen after God sets all of his people completely free. All of those things will bring praise to his glory.

Paul Prays and Gives Thanks

¹⁵I have heard about your faith in the Lord Jesus. I have also heard about your love for all of God's people. That is why ¹⁶I have not stopped thanking God for you. I always remember you in my prayers.

¹⁷I pray to the God of our Lord Jesus Christ. God is the glorious Father. I keep asking him to give you the wisdom and understanding that come from the Holy Spirit. I want you to know God better.

¹⁸I also pray that your mind might see more clearly. Then you will know the hope God has chosen you to receive. You will know that the things God's people will receive are rich and glorious. ¹⁹And you will know his great power. It can't be compared with anything else. It is at work for us who believe. It is like the mighty strength ²⁰God showed when he raised Christ from the dead.

He seated him at his right hand in his heavenly kingdom. [21]There Christ sits far above all who rule and have authority. He also sits far above all powers and kings. He is above every title that can be given in this world and in the world to come.

[22]God placed all things under Christ's rule. He appointed him to be ruler over everything for the church. [23]The church is Christ's body. It is filled by Christ. He fills everything in every way.

God Has Given Us New Life Through Christ

2 You were living in your sins and lawless ways. But in fact you were dead. [2]You used to live as sinners when you followed the ways of this world. You served the one who rules over the spiritual forces of evil. He is the spirit who is now at work in those who don't obey God.

[3]At one time we all lived among them. We tried to satisfy what our sinful nature wanted to do. We followed its longings and thoughts. God was angry with us and everyone else because of the kind of people we were.

[4]But God loves us deeply. He is full of mercy. [5]So he gave us new life because of what Christ has done. He gave us life even when we were dead in sin. God's grace has saved you.

[6]God raised us up with Christ. He has seated us with him in his heavenly kingdom because we belong to Christ Jesus. [7]He has done it to show the riches of his grace for all time to come. His grace can't be compared with anything else. He has shown it by being kind to us because of what Christ Jesus has done.

[8]God's grace has saved you because of your faith in Christ. Your salvation doesn't come from anything you do. It is God's gift. [9]It is not based on anything you have done. No one can brag about earning it. [10]God made us. He created us to belong to Christ Jesus. Now we can do good things. Long ago God prepared them for us to do.

God's New Family

[11]You who are not Jews by birth, here is what I want you to remember. You are called "uncircumcised" by those who call themselves "circumcised." But they have only been circumcised in their bodies by human hands.

[12]Before you believed in Christ, you were separated from him. You were not considered to be citizens of Israel. You were not included in what the covenants promised. You were without hope and without God in the world. [13]At one time you were far

away from God. But now you belong to Christ Jesus. He spilled his blood for you. That has brought you near to God.

¹⁴Christ himself is our peace. He has made Jews and non-Jews into one group of people. He has destroyed the hatred that was like a wall between us. ¹⁵Through his body on the cross, Christ put an end to the law with all its commands and rules. He wanted to create one new group of people out of the two. He wanted to make peace between them.

¹⁶He planned to bring both of them as one body back to God because of the cross. Christ put their hatred to death on that cross.

¹⁷He came and preached peace to you who were far away. He also preached peace to those who were near. ¹⁸Through Christ we both come to the Father by the power of one Holy Spirit.

¹⁹So you are no longer strangers and outsiders. You are citizens together with God's people. You are members of God's family.

²⁰You are a building that is built on the apostles and prophets. They are the foundation. Christ Jesus himself is the most important stone in the building. ²¹The whole building is held together by him. It rises to become a holy temple because it belongs to the Lord.

²²And because you belong to him, you too are being built together. You are being made into a house where God lives through his Spirit.

Paul Is the Messenger to Non-Jews

3 I, Paul, am a prisoner because of Christ Jesus. I am in prison because of my work among you who are not Jews.

²I am sure you have heard that God appointed me to share his grace with you. ³I'm talking about the mystery God showed me. I have already written a little about it. ⁴By reading it you will be able to understand what I know about the mystery of Christ.

⁵The mystery was not made known to people of other times. But now the Holy Spirit has made it known to God's holy apostles and prophets.

⁶Here is the mystery. Because of the good news, God's promises are for non-Jews as well as for Jews. Both groups are parts of one body. They share in the promise. It belongs to them because they belong to Christ Jesus.

⁷I now serve the good news because God gave me his grace. His power is at work in me. ⁸I am by far the least important of all of God's people. But he gave me the grace to preach to the non-Jews about the wonderful riches that Christ gives.

⁹God told me to make clear to everyone how the mystery came about. In times past it was kept hidden in the mind of God, who created all things. ¹⁰He wanted the rulers and authorities in the heavenly world to come to know his great wisdom. The church would make it known to them.

¹¹That was God's plan from the beginning. He has worked it out through Christ Jesus our Lord. ¹²Through him and through faith in him we can approach God. We can come to him freely. We can come without fear.

¹³So here is what I'm asking you to do. Don't lose hope because I am suffering for you. It will lead to the time when God will give you his glory.

Paul Prays for God's People

¹⁴I bow in prayer to the Father because of my work among you. ¹⁵From the Father his whole family in heaven and on earth gets its name.

¹⁶I pray that he will use his glorious riches to make you strong. May his Holy Spirit give you his power deep down inside you. ¹⁷Then Christ will live in your hearts because you believe in him.

Don't be a carbon copy of someone else... make your own impression.

And I pray that your love will have deep roots. I pray that it will have a strong foundation. [18]May you have power with all God's people to understand Christ's love. May you know how wide and long and high and deep it is. [19]And may you know his love, even though it can't be known completely. Then you will be filled with everything God has for you.

[20]God is able to do far more than we could ever ask for or imagine. He does everything by his power that is working in us. [21]Give him glory in the church and in Christ Jesus. Give him glory through all time and for ever and ever. Amen.

The Body of Christ Is One

4 I am a prisoner because of the Lord. So I am asking you to live a life worthy of what God chose you for.

[2]Don't be proud at all. Be completely gentle. Be patient. Put up with one another in love. [3]The Holy Spirit makes you one in every way. So try your best to remain as one. Let peace keep you together.

[4]There is one body. There is one Spirit. You were appointed to one hope when you were chosen. [5]There is one Lord. There is one faith and one baptism. [6]There is one God and Father of all. He is over everything. He is through everything. He is in everything.

[7]But each one of us has received a gift of grace, just as Christ wanted us to have it. [8]That is why Scripture says,

"When he went up to his place on high,
he led a line of prisoners.
He gave gifts to people."   *(Psalm 68:18)*

[9]What does "he went up" mean? It can

Paul's Prayer for Believers

Deep Roots in God's love

Filled with life and power

Strength through the Holy Spirit

Ephesians 1:18

only mean that he also came down to the lower, earthly places. [10]The One who came down is the same as the One who went up higher than all the heavens. He did it in order to fill all of creation. [11]He is the One who gave some the gift to be apostles. He gave some the gift to be prophets. He gave some the gift of preaching the good news. And he gave some the gift to be pastors and teachers. [12]He did it so that they might prepare God's people to serve. If they do, the body of Christ will be built up.

[13]That will continue until we all become one in the faith and in the knowledge of God's Son. Then we will be grown up in the faith. We will receive everything that Christ has for us.

[14]We will no longer be babies in the faith. We won't be like ships tossed around by the waves. We won't be blown here and there by every new teaching. We won't be blown around by the cleverness and tricks of people who try to hide their evil plans. [15]Instead, we will speak the truth in love. We will grow up into Christ in every way.

He is the Head. [16]He makes the whole body grow and build itself up in love. Under the control of Christ, each part of the body does its work. It supports the other parts. In that way, the body is joined and held together.

Living as Children of Light

[17]Here is what I'm telling you. I am speaking for the Lord as I warn you. You must no longer live like those who aren't Jews. Their thoughts don't have any purpose. [18]They can't understand the truth. They are separated from the life of God. That is because they don't know him. And they don't know him because their hearts are stubborn.

[19]They have lost all feeling for what is right. They have given themselves over to the evil pleasures of their bodies. They take part in every kind of unclean act. And they always long for more.

[20]But that is not what you have learned about Christ. [21]I'm sure you heard of him. I'm sure you were taught by him. What you learned was the truth about Jesus.

[22]You were taught not to live the way you used to. You must get rid of your old way of life. That's because it is polluted by longing for things that lead you down the wrong path.

[23]You were taught to be made new in your thinking. [24]You were taught to start living a new life. It is created to be truly good and holy, just as God is.

[25]So each of you must get rid of your lying. Speak the truth to your neighbor. We are all parts of one body.

[26]Scripture says, "When you are angry, do not sin." *(Psalm 4:4)* Do not let the sun go down while you are still angry. [27]Don't give the devil a chance.

[28]Those who have been stealing must never steal again. Instead, they must work. They must do something useful with their own hands. Then they will have something to give to people in need.

[29]Don't let any evil talk come out of your mouths. Say only what will help to build others up and meet their needs. Then what you say will help those who listen.

[30]Do not make God's Holy Spirit sad. He marked you with a seal for the day when God will set you completely free.

[31]Get rid of all hard feelings, anger and rage. Stop all fighting and lying. Put away every form of hatred. [32]Be kind and tender to one another. Forgive each other, just as God forgave you because of what Christ has done.

5 You are the children that God dearly loves. So be just like him. [2]Lead a life of love, just as Christ did. He loved us. He gave himself up for us. He was a sweet-smelling offering and sacrifice to God.

[3]There should not be even a hint of sexual

Giving is a thermometer of our love.

sin among you. Don't do anything unclean. And do not always want more and more. Things like that are not what God's holy people should do.

⁴There must not be any unclean speech or foolish talk or dirty jokes. All of them are out of place. Instead, you should give thanks.

⁵Here is what you can be sure of. Those who give themselves over to sexual sins are lost. So are people whose lives are not pure. The same is true of those who always want more and more. People who do those things might as well worship statues of gods. No one who does them will receive a share in the kingdom of Christ and of God.

⁶Don't let anyone fool you with words that don't mean anything. Because of things like that, God is angry with those who don't obey. ⁷So don't go along with people like that.

⁸At one time you were in the dark. But now you are in the light because of what the Lord has done. Live like children of the light. ⁹The light produces what is completely good, right and true. ¹⁰Find out what pleases the Lord.

¹¹Have nothing to do with the acts of darkness. They don't produce anything good. Show what they are really like. ¹²It is shameful even to talk about what people who don't obey do in secret.

¹³But everything the light shines on can

be seen. [14]Light makes everything clear. That is why it is said,

"Wake up, sleeper.
　Rise from the dead.
Then Christ will shine on you."

[15]So be very careful how you live. Do not live like people who aren't wise. Live like people who are wise. [16]Make the most of every opportunity. The days are evil. [17]So don't be foolish. Instead, understand what the Lord wants.

[18]Don't fill yourself up with wine. Getting drunk will lead to wild living. Instead, be filled with the Holy Spirit.

[19]Speak to each other with psalms, hymns and spiritual songs. Sing and make music in your heart to the Lord. [20]Always give thanks to God the Father for everything. Give thanks to him in the name of our Lord Jesus Christ.

[21]Follow the lead of one another because of your respect for Christ.

Wives and Husbands

[22]Wives, follow the lead of your husbands as you follow the Lord. [23]The husband is the head of the wife, just as Christ is the head of the church. The church is Christ's body. He is its Savior. [24]The church follows the lead of Christ. In the same way, wives should follow the lead of their husbands in everything.

[25]Husbands, love your wives. Love them just as Christ loved the church. He gave himself up for her. [26]He did it to make her holy. He made her clean by washing her with water and the word. [27]He did it to bring her to himself as a brightly shining church. He wants a church that has no stain or wrinkle or any other flaw. He wants a church that is holy and without blame.

[28]In the same way, husbands should love their wives. They should love them as they love their own bodies. Any man who loves his wife loves himself. [29]After all, people have never hated their own bodies. Instead, they feed and care for their bodies. And that is what Christ does for the church. [30]We are parts of his body.

[31]Scripture says, "That's why a man will leave his father and mother and be joined to his wife. The two will become one." *(Genesis 2:24)* [32]That is a deep mystery. But I'm talking about Christ and the church.

[33]A husband also must love his wife. He must love her just as he loves himself. And a wife must respect her husband.

Children and Parents

6 Children, obey your parents as believers in the Lord. Obey them because it's the right thing to do. [2]Scripture says, "Honor your father and mother." That is the first commandment that has a promise. [3]"Then things will go well with you. You will live a long time on the earth." *(Deuteronomy 5:16)*

[4]Fathers, don't make your children angry. Instead, train them and teach them the ways of the Lord as you raise them.

Slaves and Masters

[5]Slaves, obey your masters here on earth. Respect them and honor them with a heart that is true. Obey them just as you would obey Christ. [6]Don't obey them only to please them when they are watching. Do it because you are slaves of Christ. Be sure your heart does what God wants.

[7]Serve your masters with all your heart. Work as if you were not serving people but the Lord. [8]You know that the Lord will give you a reward. He will give to each of you in keeping with the good you do. It doesn't matter whether you are slaves or free.

[9]Masters, treat your slaves in the same way. When you warn them, don't be too hard on them. You know that the One who is their Master and yours is in heaven. And he treats everyone the same.

God's Armor

[10]Finally, let the Lord make you strong. Depend on his mighty power. [11]Put on all of God's armor. Then you can stand firm against the devil's evil plans. [12]Our fight is not against human beings. It is against the rulers, the authorities and the powers of this dark world. It is against the spiritual forces of evil in the heavenly world.

Put on the Full Armor of God

Ephesians 6:10-18

Sword of the Holy Spirit

Helmet of salvation

Body armor of godliness

Shield of faith

Belt of truth

"Where do we enlist?"

Shoes of peace

"We already know who wins the war!"

Pray at all times

[13]So put on all of God's armor. Evil days will come. But you will be able to stand up to anything. And after you have done everything you can, you will still be standing.

[14]So stand firm. Put the belt of truth around your waist. Put the armor of godliness on your chest. [15]Wear on your feet what will prepare you to tell the good news of peace. [16]Also, pick up the shield of faith. With it you can put out all of the flaming arrows of the evil one. [17]Put on the helmet of salvation. And take the sword of the Holy Spirit. The sword is God's word.

[18]At all times, pray by the power of the Spirit. Pray all kinds of prayers. Be watchful, so that you can pray. Always keep on praying for all of God's people.

[19]Pray also for me. Pray that when I open my mouth, the right words will be given to me. Then I can be bold as I tell the mystery of the good news. [20]Because of the good news, I am being held by chains as the Lord's messenger. So pray that I will be bold as I preach the good news. That's what I should do.

Final Greetings

[21]Tychicus is a dear brother. He is faithful in serving the Lord. He will tell you everything about me. Then you will know how I am and what I am doing. [22]That's why I am sending him to you. I want you to know how we are. And I want him to cheer you up.

[23]May God the Father and the Lord Jesus Christ give peace to the brothers and sisters. May they also give them love and faith.

[24]May grace be given to everyone who loves our Lord Jesus Christ with a love that will never die.

PHILIPPIANS

- Links Old Testament prophecies with Jesus as the Messiah
- Written by Paul while a prisoner in Rome
- Paul came from Asia Minor to found the first church in Europe
- This church was closer to Paul than any other
- Established on his second missionary trip
- Theme: "Living a joyful life as a Christian"

1 We, Paul and Timothy, are writing this letter. We serve Christ Jesus.

We are sending this letter to you, all of God's people in Philippi. You belong to Christ Jesus. We are also sending this letter to your leaders and deacons.

[2]May God our Father and the Lord Jesus Christ give you grace and peace.

Paul Prays and Gives Thanks

[3]I thank my God every time I remember you. [4]In all my prayers for all of you, I always pray with joy. [5]I am happy because you have joined me in spreading the good news. You have done so from the first day until now.

[6]I am sure that the One who began a good work in you will carry it on until it is completed. That will be on the day Christ Jesus returns.

[7]It is right for me to feel this way about all of you. I love you with all my heart. I may be held by chains, or I may be standing up for the truth of the good news. Either way, all of you share in God's grace together with me. [8]God can give witness that I long for all of you. I love you with the love that Christ Jesus gives.

[9]I pray that your love will grow more and more. And let it be based on knowledge and understanding. [10]Then you will be able to know what is best. You will be pure and without blame until the day Christ returns. [11]You will be filled with the fruit of right living produced by Jesus Christ. All of those things bring glory and praise to God.

Paul Honors Christ in Prison

[12]Brothers and sisters, here is what I want you to know. What has happened to me has really helped to spread the good news. [13]One thing has become clear. I am being held by chains because of my stand for Christ. All of the palace guards and everyone else know it.

[14]Because I am being held by chains, most of the believers in the Lord have become bolder. They now speak God's word more boldly and without fear.

[15]It's true that some preach about Christ because they are jealous. But others preach about Christ to help me in my work. [16]The last group acts out of love. They know I have been put here to stand up for the good news. [17]But the others preach about Christ only to get ahead. They are not honest and true. They think they can stir up trouble for me while I am being held by chains.

[18]But what does it matter? Here is the important thing. Whether for reasons that are right or wrong, Christ is being preached about. That makes me very glad.

And I will continue to be glad. [19]I know that you are praying for me. I also know that the Spirit of Jesus Christ will help me. So no matter what happens, I'm sure I will still be saved.

[20]I completely expect and hope that I won't be ashamed in any way. I'm sure I will be brave enough. Now as always Christ will be lifted high through my body. He will be lifted up whether I live or die.

[21]For me, life finds all of its meaning in Christ. Death also has its benefits.

[22]Suppose I go on living in my body. Then I will be able to carry on my work. It will

bear a lot of fruit. But what should I choose? I don't know. ²³I can't decide between the two. I long to leave this world and be with Christ. That is better by far.

²⁴But it is more important for you that I stay alive. ²⁵I'm sure of that. So I know I will remain with you. And I will continue with all of you to help you grow and be joyful in what you have been taught. ²⁶I'm sure I will be with you again. Then your joy in Christ Jesus will be greater than ever because of me.

²⁷No matter what happens, live in a way that brings honor to the good news about Christ. Then I will know that you stand firm with one purpose. I may come and see you or only hear about you. But I will know that you work together as one person. And I will know that you work to spread the teachings of the good news.

²⁸So don't be afraid in any way of those who oppose you. That will show them that they will be destroyed and that you will be saved. That's what God will do.

²⁹Here is what he has given you to do for Christ. You must not only believe in him. You must also suffer for him.

³⁰You are going through the same struggle you saw me go through. As you have heard, I am still struggling.

Thinking Like Christ

2 Are you cheerful because you belong to Christ? Does his love comfort you? Is the Holy Spirit your companion? Has Christ been gentle and loving toward you? ²Then make my joy complete by agreeing with each other. Have the same love. Be one in spirit and purpose.

³Don't do anything only to get ahead. Don't do it because you are proud. Instead, be free of pride. Think of others as better than yourselves.

⁴None of you should look out just for your own good. You should also look out for the good of others.

⁵You should think in the same way Christ Jesus does.

⁶In his very nature he was God.
But he did not think that being equal
with God was something he
should hold on to.
⁷Instead, he made himself nothing.
He took on the very nature of a
servant.
He was made in human form.
⁸He appeared as a man.
He came down to the lowest level.
He obeyed God completely, even
though it led to his death.
In fact, he died on a cross.
⁹So God lifted him up to the highest
place.
He gave him the name that is above
every name.
¹⁰When the name of Jesus is spoken,
everyone's knee will bow to
worship him.
Every knee in heaven and on earth
and under the earth will bow to
worship him.
¹¹Everyone's mouth will say that Jesus
Christ is Lord.
And God the Father will receive the
glory.

Living Like Christ

¹²My dear friends, you have always obeyed God. You obeyed while I was with you. And you have obeyed even more while I am not with you. So continue to work out your own salvation. Do it with fear and trembling. ¹³God is working in you. He wants your plans and your acts to be in keeping with his good purpose.

¹⁴Do everything without finding fault or arguing. ¹⁵Then you will be pure and without blame. You will be children of God without fault in a sinful and evil world. Among the people of the world you shine like stars in the heavens. ¹⁶You shine as you hold out to them the word of life. So I can brag about you on the day Christ returns. I can be happy that I didn't run or work for nothing.

¹⁷But my life might even be poured out like a drink offering on your sacrifices. I'm talking about the way you serve because you believe. Even so, I am glad. I am joyful

Leave it all behind to know Christ!

with all of you. ¹⁸So you too should be glad and joyful with me.

Timothy and Epaphroditus

¹⁹I hope to send Timothy to you soon if the Lord Jesus allows it. Then I will be cheered up when I receive news about you. ²⁰I have no one else like Timothy. He truly cares about how you are doing.

²¹All the others are looking out for their own interests. They are not looking out for the interests of Jesus Christ. ²²But you know that Timothy has proved himself. He has served with me like a son with his father in spreading the good news.

²³So I hope to send him as soon as I see how things go with me. ²⁴And I'm sure I myself will come soon if the Lord allows it.

²⁵But I think it's necessary to send Epaphroditus back to you. He is my brother in the Lord. He is a worker and a soldier of Christ together with me. He is also your messen-

ger. You sent him to take care of my needs. ²⁶He longs for all of you. He is troubled because you heard he was sick.

²⁷He was very sick. In fact, he almost died. But God had mercy on him. He also had mercy on me. God spared me sadness after sadness. ²⁸So I want even more to send him to you. Then when you see him again, you will be glad. And I won't worry so much.

²⁹Welcome him as a brother in the Lord with great joy. Honor people like him. ³⁰He almost died for the work of Christ. He put his life in danger to make up for the help you couldn't give me.

Do Not Trust Human Nature

3 Finally, my brothers and sisters, be joyful because you belong to the Lord. It is no trouble for me to write about some important matters to you again. If you know about them, you will have a safe path to follow.

[2]Watch out for those dogs. They do evil things. When they circumcise, it is nothing more than a useless cutting of the body.

[3]But we have been truly circumcised. We worship God by the power of his Spirit. We brag about what Christ Jesus has done.

Drop the Dead Weight!

Focus on the Goal!

We don't put our trust in our weak human nature.

[4]I have many reasons to trust in my human nature. Others may think they have reasons to trust in theirs. But I have even more. [5]I was circumcised on the eighth day. I am part of the people of Israel. I am from the tribe of Benjamin. I am a pure Hebrew. As far as the law is concerned, I am a Pharisee. [6]As far as being committed is concerned, I opposed and attacked the church. As far as keeping the Law is concerned, I kept it perfectly.

[7]I thought things like that were for my benefit. But now I consider them to be nothing because of Christ. [8]Even more, I consider everything to be nothing compared to knowing Christ Jesus my Lord. To know him is the best thing of all. Because of him I have lost everything. But I consider all of it to be garbage so I can get to know Christ. [9]I want to be joined to him.

For me, being right with God does not come from the law. It comes because I believe in Christ. It comes from God. It is received by faith.

[10]I want to know Christ better. I want to know the power that raised him from the dead. I want to share in his sufferings. I want to become like him by sharing in his death. [11]Then by God's grace I will rise from the dead.

Moving on Toward the Goal

[12]I have not yet received all of those things. I have not yet been made perfect. But I move on to take hold of what Christ Jesus took hold of me for.

[13]Brothers and sisters, I don't consider that I have taken hold of it yet. But here is the one thing I do. I forget what is behind me. I push hard toward what is ahead of me. [14]I move on toward the goal to win the prize. God has appointed me to win it. The heavenly prize is Christ Jesus himself.

[15]All of us who are grown up in the faith should see things that way. Maybe you think differently about something. But God will make it clear to you. [16]Only let us live up to what we have already reached.

[17]Brothers and sisters, join with others in following my example. Pay close attention

to those who live in keeping with the pattern we gave you.

[18]I have told you those things many times before. Now I say it again with tears in my eyes. Many people live like enemies of the cross of Christ. [19]The only thing they have coming to them is death. Their stomach is their god. They brag about what they should be ashamed of. They think only about earthly things.

[20]But we are citizens of heaven. And we can hardly wait for a Savior from there. He is the Lord Jesus Christ. [21]He has the power to bring everything under his control. By his power he will change our earthly bodies. They will become like his glorious body.

4 My brothers and sisters, that is how you should stand firm in the Lord's strength. I love you and long for you. Dear friends, you are my joy and my crown.

Do What Is Best

[2]Here is what I'm asking Euodia and Syntyche to do. I want them to agree with each other because they belong to the Lord.

[3]My true companion, here is what I ask you to do. Help those women. They have served at my side. They have helped me spread the good news. So have Clement and the rest of those who have worked together with me. Their names are all written in the Book of Life.

[4]Always be joyful because you belong to the Lord. I will say it again. Be joyful. [5]Let everyone know how gentle you are. The Lord is coming soon.

[6]Don't worry about anything. Instead, tell God about everything. Ask and pray. Give thanks to him. [7]Then God's peace will watch over your hearts and your minds because you belong to Christ Jesus. God's peace can never be completely understood.

[8]Finally, my brothers and sisters, always think about what is true. Think about what is noble, right and pure. Think about what is lovely and worthy of respect. If anything is excellent or worthy of praise, think about those kinds of things. [9]Do what you have learned or received or heard from me. Follow my example.

The God who gives peace will be with you.

Prayer conquers WORLD

weakness money job guilt habits relationships past future

Get your head out of the clouds and focus!

love joy God truth excellence goodness patience purity

His peace will surround you!

Paul Gives Thanks for Help Received

[10]At last you are concerned about me again. That makes me very happy. We belong to the Lord. I know that you have been concerned. But you had no chance to show it.

[11]I'm not saying that because I need anything. I have learned to be content no matter what happens to me. [12]I know what it's like not to have what I need. I also know what it's like to have more than I need. I have learned the secret of being content no matter what happens. I am content whether I am well fed or hungry. I am content whether I have more than enough or not enough. [13]I can do everything by the power of Christ. He gives me strength.

[14]But it was good of you to share in my troubles. [15]And you believers at Philippi know what happened when I left Macedonia. Not one church helped me in the matter of giving and receiving. You were the only one that did. That was in the early days when you first heard the good news. [16]Even when I was in Thessalonica, you sent me help when I needed it. You did it again and again.

[17]I'm not looking for a gift. I'm looking for what is best for you. [18]I have received my full pay, and even more than that. I have everything I need. That's because Epaphroditus brought me the gifts you sent. They are a sweet-smelling offering. They are a gift that God accepts. He is pleased with it.

[19]My God will meet all your needs. He will meet them in keeping with his wonderful riches that come to you because you belong to Christ Jesus.

[20]Give glory to our God and Father for ever and ever. Amen.

Final Greetings

[21]Greet all of God's people. They belong to Christ Jesus. The brothers who are with me send greetings. [22]All of God's people here send you greetings. Most of all, those who live in the palace of Caesar send you greetings.

[23]May the grace of the Lord Jesus Christ be with your spirit. Amen.

"I'm not a Christian because ..."
"I can't make up my mind."

Life is a series of choices. Each decision molds you and makes you the person you are.

Some choices are trivial: coffee or soda - hot dogs or tacos.

Some choices are important: college - career - marriage.

However, the most significant decision is:

"What will YOU do with Jesus?"

You can live for self or live for Jesus. Jesus said:

"Those who love their life will lose it. But those who hate their life in this world will keep it and have eternal life."

John 12:25

The choice and the consequences are yours.

Open Book Quiz - The Book of Philippians

Read the letters from top to bottom and complete the answer below.

1 ____ Attacked the church   ch. 3

2 ____ Heavenly prize   ch. 3

3 ____ Forget the past and ...   ch. 3

4 ____ Life's full meaning is in   ch. 1

5 ____ Soldier of Christ   ch. 2

6 ____ Every knee will ...   ch. 2

7 ____ Without Christ all is ...   ch. 3

8 ____ Don't worry about ...   ch. 4

9 ____ Helped Paul write   ch. 1

10 ____ Your love based on   ch. 1

11 ____ God's riches will meet   ch. 4

12 ____ Founded the church   Intro.

13 ____ Held in chains   ch. 1

14 ____ Like a son   ch. 2

Select the best answer from the right column which matches items 1-14 in the left column. Some letters are used more than once

A - Athens
B - Bethlehem
F - Knowledge
G - Bow
I - Christ Jesus
J - Garbage
L - Paul
N - Epaphoditus
O - Anything
Q - Rome
U - Your needs
V - Move on!
W - Waldo
Y -- Timothy

Self-score
13 - 14	Shinning Star
10 - 12	Bright Star
7 - 9	Star
4 - 6	Falling Star
1 - 3	Black Hole

Answer:

__ __ __ __ __ __

__ __ __ __ __ __ __ __

"The theme of the book of Philippians"

PHILIPPIANS

Across

1. Heavenly ___ is Christ Jesus   ch. 3
2. First Church in ___   Intro.
3. Faithful will ___ for Christ   ch. 1
4. Not ___ made perfect   ch. 3
5. God's wonderful ___   ch. 4
6. Neither one   ---
7. Confess "Jesus is Lord"   ch. 2
8. I owe you   ---
9. Timothy, like a ___   ch. 2
10. Christ is being ___   ch. 1

Down

1. Don't worry. Ask and ___   ch. 4
2. First woman   ---
3. God's children shine like   ch. 2
4. Move ___ towards the goal   ch. 3
5. Written from ___   Intro.
6. God will meet all your ___   ch. 4
7. Tiny fairy   ---
8. Personal pronoun   ---
9. Impact, strike   ---
10. Greeting   ---
11. Be ___ in spirit & purpose   ch. 2
12. Follow my ___   ch. 4

COLOSSIANS

- *Written by Paul while a prisoner in Rome*
- *Paul had never visited the church in Colosse*
- *Written to counter false teachings that infiltrated the church*
- *Presents Christ as the fullness of God and Head of the Church*
- *Theme: "Christ is All"*

1 I, Paul, am writing this letter. I am an apostle of Christ Jesus just as God planned. Our brother Timothy joins me in writing.

²We are sending this letter to you, our brothers and sisters in Colosse. You belong to Christ. You are holy and faithful.

May God our Father give you grace and peace.

Paul Prays and Gives Thanks

³We always thank God, the Father of our Lord Jesus Christ, when we pray for you. ⁴We thank him because we have heard about your faith in Christ Jesus. We have also heard that you love all of God's people.

⁵Your faith and love are based on the hope you have. What you hope for is stored up for you in heaven. You have already heard about it. You were told about it when the message of truth was given to you. I'm talking about the good news ⁶that has come to you.

All over the world the good news is bearing fruit and growing. It has been doing that among you since the day you heard it. That is when you understood God's grace in all its truth.

⁷You learned the good news from Epaphras. He is dear to us. He serves Christ together with us. He faithfully works for Christ and for us among you. ⁸He also told us about your love that comes from the Holy Spirit.

⁹That's why we have not stopped praying for you. We have been praying for you since the day we heard about you. We have been asking God to fill you with the knowledge of what he wants. We pray that he will give you spiritual wisdom and understanding.

¹⁰We pray that you will lead a life that is worthy of the Lord. We pray that you will please him in every way. So we want you to bear fruit in every good thing you do. We want you to grow to know God better. ¹¹We want you to be very strong, in keeping with his glorious power. We want you to be patient. Never give up. Be joyful ¹²as you give thanks to the Father.

He has made you fit to share with all his people. You will all receive a share in the kingdom of light.

¹³He has saved us from the kingdom of darkness. He has brought us into the kingdom of the Son he loves. ¹⁴Because of what the Son has done, we have been set free. Because of him, all of our sins have been forgiven.

Christ Is Far Above Everything

¹⁵Christ is the exact likeness of God, who can't be seen. He is first, and he is over all of creation. ¹⁶All things were created by him. He created everything in heaven and on earth. He created everything that can be seen and everything that can't be seen. He created kings, powers, rulers and authorities. Everything was created by him and for him. ¹⁷Before anything was created, he was already there. He holds everything together.

¹⁸And he is the head of the body, which is the church. He is the beginning. He is the first to be raised from the dead. That happened so that he would be far above everything. ¹⁹God was pleased to have his whole

nature living in Christ. [20]God was pleased to bring all things back to himself because of what Christ has done. That includes all things on earth and in heaven. God made peace through Christ's blood, through his death on the cross.

[21]At one time you were separated from God. You were enemies in your minds because of your evil ways. [22]But because Christ died, God has brought you back to himself. Christ's death has made you holy in God's sight. So now you don't have any flaw. You are free from blame.

[23]But you must keep your faith steady and firm. Don't move away from the hope that the good news holds out to you. It is the good news that you heard. It has been preached to every creature under heaven. I, Paul, now serve the good news.

Paul's Work for the Church

[24]I am happy because of what was suffered for you. And in my body I fill up my share in Christ's sufferings. I do it for his body, which is the church. [25]I serve the church. God appointed me to bring all of his word to you.

[26]That word contains the mystery that has been hidden for many ages. But now it has been made known to God's people. [27]God has chosen to make known to them the glorious riches of that mystery. He has made it known among those who aren't Jews. And here is what it is. Christ is in you. He is your hope of glory.

[28]We preach about him. With all the wisdom we have, we warn and teach everyone. When we bring them to God, we want them to be perfect as people who belong to Christ.

[29]That's what I'm working for. I work hard with all of Christ's strength. His strength works powerfully in me.

2 I want you to know how hard I am working for you. I'm concerned for those who are in Laodicea. I'm also concerned for everyone who has not met me in person. [2]I want their hearts to be made cheerful and strong. I want them to be joined together in love. Then their understanding will be rich and complete. They will know the mystery of God. That mystery is Christ.

[3]All the treasures of wisdom and knowledge are hidden in him.

[4]But I don't want anyone to fool you with fast talk that only sounds good. [5]So even though I am away from you in body, I am with you in spirit. I am glad to see that you are doing everything in good order. And

Freedom at the Cross

REGULATIONS * MAN MADE LAW
LAW 10 COMMANDMENTS * FOLL
LEGALISM ... ES * EARN YOUR
REGULATI... MAN MADE RUL
EARN YOU... VATION * OBEY
LISM RUL... RN YOUR SALV
LA... WS * D
C... ADE
LI... ALV
MA... ION * OBEY TH
DO THE 10... ANDMENTS * S
FOLLOW A... ES * EARN YOU
REGULATI... AN MADE LAW
LAW *10 C... DMENTS * DO
FOLLOW L... TIC RULES * M
SALVATION... OD WORKS A
10 COMMA... TS * DO GOOD
LISM RUL... ARN YOUR SALV
LATIONS * MAN MADE LAWS * O
OBEY THE 10 COMMANDMENTS *
FOLLOW RELIGIOUS RULES * EA

I am happy that your faith in Christ is so strong.

Freedom From Human Rules

[6]You received Christ Jesus as Lord. So keep on living in him. [7]Have your roots in him. Build yourselves up in him. Grow strong in what you believe, just as you were taught. Be more thankful than ever before.

[8]Make sure no one captures you. They will try to capture you by using false reasoning that has no meaning. Their ideas depend on human teachings. They also depend on the basic things the people of this world believe. They don't depend on Christ.

[9]God's whole nature is living in Christ in human form. [10]Because you belong to Christ, you have everything you need. He is the ruler over every power and authority.

[11]When you received Christ, you were also circumcised by putting away your sinful nature. Human hands didn't circumcise you. Christ did.

[12]When you were baptized, you were buried together with him. You were raised to life together with him by believing in God's power. God raised Jesus from the dead.

[13]At one time you were dead in your sins. Your sinful nature was not circumcised. But God gave you new life together with Christ. He forgave us all of our sins.

[14]He wiped out the written Law with its rules. The Law was against us. It opposed us. He took it away and nailed it to the cross. [15]He took away the weapons of the powers and authorities. He made a public show of them. He won the battle over them by dying on the cross.

[16]So don't let anyone judge you because of what you eat or drink. Don't let anyone judge you about holy days. I'm talking about special feasts and New Moons and Sabbath days. [17]They are only a shadow of the things that were going to come. But what is real is found in Christ.

[18]Some people enjoy pretending they aren't proud. They worship angels. But don't let people like that hold you back from winning the prize. They tell you every little thing about what they have seen. Their minds are not guided by the Holy Spirit. So they are proud of their useless ideas.

[19]They aren't connected to the Head. But the whole body grows from the Head. The muscles and tendons hold the body together. And God causes it to grow.

[20]The people of the world believe certain basic things. You died with Christ as far as things like that are concerned. So why do you act as if you still belong to the world? Here are the rules you follow. [21]"Do not handle! Do not taste! Do not touch!" [22]Rules like that are all going to die out as time goes by. They are only based on human rules and teachings.

[23]It is true that those rules seem wise. Because of them, people give themselves over to their own kind of worship. They pretend they aren't proud. They treat their bodies very badly. But rules like that don't help. They don't stop people from chasing after sinful pleasures.

Rules for Holy Living

3 You have been raised up with Christ. So think about things that are in heaven. That is where Christ is. He is sitting at God's right hand. [2]Think about things that are in heaven. Don't think about things that are on earth.

[3]You died. Now your life is hidden with Christ in God. [4]Christ is your life. When he appears again, you also will appear with him in heaven's glory.

[5]So put to death anything that belongs to your earthly nature. Get rid of your sexual sins and unclean acts. Don't let your feelings get out of control. Remove from your life all evil longings. Stop always wanting more and more. You might as well be worshiping statues of gods. [6]God's anger is going to come because of these things. [7]That's the way you lived at one time in your life.

[8]But now here are the kinds of things you must get rid of. You must put away anger, rage, hate and lies. Let no dirty words come out of your mouths. [9]Don't lie to each other.

You have gotten rid of your old way of life and its habits. [10]You have started living a new life. It is being made new so that what you know has the Creator's likeness.

[11]Here there is no Greek or Jew. There is no difference between those who are circumcised and those who are not. There is no rude outsider, or even a Scythian. There is no slave or free person. But Christ is everything. And he is in everything.

[12]You are God's chosen people. You are holy and dearly loved. So put on tender mercy and kindness as if they were your clothes. Don't be proud. Be gentle and patient. [13]Put up with each other. Forgive the things you are holding against one another. Forgive, just as the Lord forgave you.

[14]And over all of those good things put on love. Love holds them all together perfectly as if they were one.

[15]Let the peace that Christ gives rule in your hearts. As parts of one body, you were appointed to live in peace. And be thankful.

[16]Let Christ's word live in you like a rich treasure. Teach and correct each other wisely. Sing psalms, hymns and spiritual songs. Sing with thanks in your hearts to God. [17]Do everything you say or do in the name of the Lord Jesus. Always give thanks to God the Father through Christ.

Rules for Christian Families

[18]Wives, follow the lead of your husbands. That's what the Lord wants you to do.

[19]Husbands, love your wives. Don't be mean to them.

[20]Children, obey your parents in everything. That pleases the Lord.

[21]Fathers, don't make your children bitter. If you do, they will lose hope.

[22]Slaves, obey your earthly masters in everything. Don't do it just to please them when they are watching you. Obey them with an honest heart. Do it out of respect for the Lord.

[23]Work at everything you do with all your heart. Work as if you were working for the Lord, not for human masters. [24]Work because you know that you will finally receive as a reward what the Lord wants you to have. You are serving the Lord Christ.

[25]Anyone who does wrong will be paid back for what he does. God treats everyone the same.

4 Masters, give your slaves what is right and fair. Do it because you know that you also have a Master in heaven.

More Directions

[2]Spend a lot of time in prayer. Always be watchful and thankful.

[3]Pray for us too. Pray that God will open a door for our message. Then we can preach the mystery of Christ. Because I preached it, I am being held by chains. [4]Pray that I will preach it clearly, as I should.

[5]Be wise in the way you act toward out-

Work or play ... do all to please God.
Colossians 3:17

Thank you, Lord!

Amen!

God is GREAT!

Work hard and cheerfully at whatever you do.

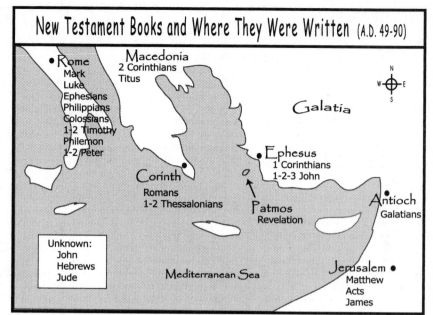

New Testament Books and Where They Were Written (A.D. 49-90)

siders. Make the most of every opportunity. [6]Let the words you speak always be full of grace. Season them with salt. Then you will know how to answer everyone.

Final Greetings

[7]Tychicus will tell you all the news about me. He is a dear brother. He is a faithful worker. He serves the Lord together with us. [8]I am sending him to you for one reason. I want you to know what is happening here. I want him to cheer you up and make your hearts strong.

[9]He is coming with Onesimus, our faithful and dear brother. He is one of you. They will tell you everything that is happening here.

[10]Aristarchus is in prison with me. He sends you his greetings. So does Mark, the cousin of Barnabas. You have been given directions about him. If he comes to you, welcome him. [11]Jesus, who is called Justus, also sends greetings. They are the only Jews who work together with me for God's kingdom. They have been a comfort to me.

[12]Epaphras sends greetings. He is one of you. He serves Christ Jesus. He is always praying hard for you. He prays that you will stand firm in holding to all that God has in mind for us. He prays that you will continue to grow in your knowledge of what God wants you to do. He also prays that you will be completely sure about it. [13]I am happy to tell you that he is working very hard for you. He is also working hard for everyone in Laodicea and Hierapolis.

[14]Our dear friend Luke, the doctor, sends greetings. So does Demas.

[15]Give my greetings to the brothers and sisters in Laodicea. Also give my greetings to Nympha and the church that meets in her house.

[16]After this letter has been read to you, send it on. Be sure that it is also read to the church in Laodicea. And be sure that you read the letter from Laodicea.

[17]Tell Archippus, "Be sure that you complete the work the Lord gave you to do."

[18]I, Paul, am writing this greeting with my own hand. Remember that I am being held by chains. May grace be with you.

THE THREE ENEMIES
OF THE BELIEVER

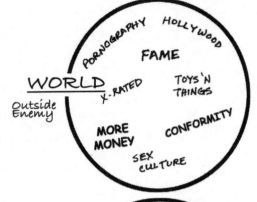

WORLD

Outside
Enemy

PORNOGRAPHY HOLLYWOOD
FAME
X-RATED TOYS 'N THINGS
MORE MONEY CONFORMITY
SEX CULTURE

Strategy
for Victory

"Who is it that has
won the battle over
the world? Only the
persdon who believes
that Jesus is the Son
of God."

1 John 5:5

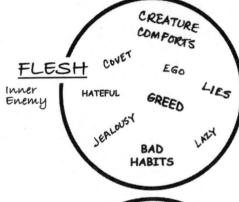

FLESH

Inner
Enemy

CREATURE COMFORTS
COVET EGO
HATEFUL GREED LIES
JEALOUSY
BAD HABITS LAZY

"Our sinful nature
no longer controls
the way we live.
The Holy Spirit now
controls the way we
live."

Romans 8:4

DEVIL

Spiritual
Enemy

COUNTERFEITER
TEMPTOR
RULER OF THIS WORLD
LIAR SATAN
SERPENT
MURDERER
PRINCE OF DARKNESS

"Put on all of God's
armor. Then you
can stand firm
against the devil's
evil plans."

Ephesians 6:11

1 THESSALONIANS

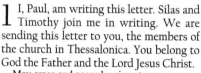

- *First letter written by Paul*
- *Paul's stay in Thessalonica was less than a month due to the great opposition, yet the church was strong and grew*
- *The church was established during his second missionary trip*
- *Theme: "The Second Coming of Christ"*

1 I, Paul, am writing this letter. Silas and Timothy join me in writing. We are sending this letter to you, the members of the church in Thessalonica. You belong to God the Father and the Lord Jesus Christ.

May grace and peace be given to you.

Paul Gives Thanks

²We always thank God for all of you. We pray for you. ³We never forget you when we pray to our God and Father. Your work is produced by your faith. Your service is the result of your love. Your strength to continue comes from your hope in our Lord Jesus Christ.

⁴Brothers and sisters, you are loved by God. We know that he has chosen you. ⁵Our good news didn't come to you only in words. It came with power. It came with the Holy Spirit's help. He gave us complete faith in what we were preaching. You know how we lived among you for your good.

⁶We and the Lord were your examples. You followed us. You suffered terribly. Even so, you welcomed our message with the joy the Holy Spirit gives. ⁷So you became a model to all the believers in the lands of Macedonia and Achaia.

⁸The Lord's message rang out from you. That was true not only in Macedonia and Achaia. Your faith in God has also become known everywhere. So we don't have to say anything about it. ⁹The believers themselves report the kind of welcome you gave us. They tell about how you turned away from statues of gods to serve the living and true God. ¹⁰They tell about how you are waiting for his Son to come from heaven.

God raised him from the dead. He is Jesus. He saves us from God's anger, and his anger is sure to come.

Paul's Work for God in Thessalonica

2 Brothers and sisters, you know that our visit to you was not a failure. ²You know what happened earlier in the city of Philippi. We suffered, and people treated us badly there. But God gave us the boldness to tell you his good news. We preached to you even though people opposed us strongly.

³The appeal we make is based on truth. It comes from a pure heart. We are not trying to trick you. ⁴In fact, it is just the opposite. God has accepted us to preach. He has trusted us with the good news. We aren't trying to please people. We want to please God. He puts our hearts to the test.

⁵As you know, we never praised you if we didn't mean it. We didn't put on a mask to cover up any sinful longing. God is our witness that this is true. ⁶We were not expecting people to praise us. We were not looking for praise from you or anyone else.

As Christ's apostles, we could have caused you some expense. ⁷But we were gentle among you. We were like a mother caring for her little children. ⁸We loved you so much that we were happy to share with you God's good news. We were also happy to share our lives with you. You had become very special to us.

⁹Brothers and sisters, I am sure you remember how hard we worked. We labored night and day while we preached to you God's good news. We didn't want to cause you any expense.

¹⁰You are witnesses of how we lived among you believers. God is also a witness

that we were holy and godly and without blame. [11]You know that we treated each of you as a father treats his own children.

[12]We gave you hope and strength. We comforted you. We really wanted you to live in a way that is worthy of God. He chooses you to enter his glorious kingdom.

[13]We never stop thanking God for the way you received his word. You heard it from us. But you didn't accept it as a human word. You accepted it for what it really is. It is God's word. It is at work in you who believe.

[14]Brothers and sisters, you became like the members of God's churches in Judea. They are believers in Christ Jesus, just as you are. People in your own country made you suffer. You went through the same things the church members in Judea suffered from the Jews.

[15]The Jews who killed the Lord Jesus and the prophets also forced us to leave. They do not please God. They are enemies of everyone. [16]They try to keep us from speaking to those who aren't Jews. The Jews don't want them to be saved. In that way, the Jews always increase their sins to the limit. God's anger has come on them at last.

Paul Longs to See the Believers in Thessalonica

[17]Brothers and sisters, we were torn away from you for a short time. We were no longer with you in person, but we kept you in our thoughts. We really longed to see you. So we tried very hard to do so. [18]We wanted to come to you. Again and again I, Paul, wanted to come. But Satan stopped us.

[19]What is our hope? What is our joy? When our Lord Jesus returns, what is the crown we will delight in? Isn't it you? [20]Yes, you are our glory and our joy.

3 We couldn't wait any longer. So we thought it was best to be left by ourselves in Athens. [2]We sent our brother Timothy to give you strength and hope in your faith. He works together with God in spreading the good news about Christ. [3]We sent him so that no one would be upset by times of testing.

You know very well that we have to go through them. [4]In fact, when we were with you, we kept telling you that our enemies would make us suffer. As you know very well, it has turned out that way.

[5]That's the reason I sent someone to find out about your faith. I couldn't wait any longer. I was afraid that Satan might have tempted you in some way. Then our efforts would have been useless.

Timothy Brings a Good Report

[6]But Timothy has come to us from you just now. He has brought good news about your faith and love. He has told us that you always have happy memories of us. He has also said that you long to see us, just as we long to see you.

[7]Brothers and sisters, in all our trouble and suffering your faith cheered us up. [8]Now we really live, because you are standing firm in the Lord.

[9]How can we thank God enough for you because of all the joy that comes only from our God? [10]Night and day we pray very hard that we will see you again. We want to give you what is missing in your faith.

[11]Now may our God and Father himself and our Lord Jesus open up a way for us to come to you. [12]May the Lord make your love grow. May it be like a rising flood. May your love for one another increase. May it

Stay "On Track" For Jesus...

Faithful   Honest   Pure

also increase for everyone else. May it be just like our love for you. ¹³May the Lord give you strength in your hearts. Then you will be holy and without blame in the sight of our God and Father. May that be true when our Lord Jesus comes with all his holy ones.

Living in a Way That Pleases God

4 Finally, brothers and sisters, we taught you how to live in a way that pleases God. In fact, that is how you are living. In the name of the Lord Jesus we ask and beg you to do it more and more.

²You know the directions we gave you. They were given by the authority of the Lord Jesus.

³God wants you to be made holy. He wants you to stay away from sexual sins. ⁴He wants all of you to learn to control your own bodies. You must live in a way that is holy. You must live with honor. ⁵Don't long to commit sexual sins like those who don't know God. ⁶None of you should sin against your brother by doing that. You should not take advantage of him. The Lord will punish everyone who commits those kinds of sins. We have already told you and warned you about that. ⁷God chose us to live pure lives. He wants us to be holy.

⁸So if you refuse to accept my teaching, you turn your back on God, not on people. God gives you his Holy Spirit.

⁹We don't need to write to you about love among believers. God himself has taught you to love each other. ¹⁰In fact, you do love all the brothers and sisters all around Macedonia. But we are asking you to love each other more and more.

¹¹Do everything you can to live a quiet life. Mind your own business. Work with your hands, just as we told you to. ¹²Then unbelievers will have respect for your everyday life. And you won't have to depend on anyone.

The Lord Is Coming

¹³Brothers and sisters, we want you to know what happens to those who die. We don't want you to be sad, as other people are. They don't have any hope.

¹⁴We believe that Jesus died and rose again. When he returns, many who believe in him will have died already. We believe that God will bring them back with Jesus.

¹⁵That agrees with what the Lord has said. When the Lord comes, many of us will still be alive. We tell you that we will certainly not go up before those who have died.

¹⁶The Lord himself will come down from heaven. We will hear a loud command. We will hear the voice of the leader of the angels. We will hear a blast from God's trumpet. Many who believe in Christ will have died already. They will rise first. ¹⁷After that, we who are still alive and are left will be caught up together with them. We will be taken up in the clouds. We will meet the Lord in the air. And we will be with him forever.

¹⁸So cheer each other up with these words of comfort.

5 Brothers and sisters, we don't have to write to you about times and dates. ²You know very well that the day of the Lord will come like a thief in the night. ³People will be saying that everything is peaceful and safe. Then suddenly they will be destroyed. It will happen like birth pains coming on a pregnant woman. None of the people will escape.

⁴Brothers and sisters, you are not in darkness. So that day should not surprise you as

a thief would. [5]All of you are children of the light. You are children of the day. We don't belong to the night. We don't belong to the darkness.

[6]So let us not be like the others. They are asleep. Instead, let us be wide awake and in full control of ourselves.

[7]Those who sleep, sleep at night. Those who get drunk, get drunk at night. [8]But we belong to the day. So let us control ourselves. Let us put the armor of faith and love on our chest. Let us put on the hope of salvation like a helmet.

[9]God didn't choose us to receive his anger. He chose us to receive salvation because of what our Lord Jesus Christ has done.

[10]Jesus died for us. Some will be alive when he comes. Others will be dead. Either way, we will live together with him. [11]So cheer each other up with the hope you have. Build each other up. In fact, that's what you are doing.

Final Directions

[12]Brothers and sisters, we ask you to have respect for the godly leaders who work hard among you. They have authority over you. They correct you. [13]Have a lot of respect for them. Love them because of what they do. Live in peace with each other.

[14]Brothers and sisters, we are asking you to warn those who don't want to work. Cheer up those who are shy. Help those who are weak. Put up with everyone. [15]Make sure that nobody pays back one wrong act with another. Always try to be kind to each other and to everyone else.

[16]Always be joyful. [17]Never stop praying. [18]Give thanks no matter what happens. God wants you to thank him because you believe in Christ Jesus.

[19]Don't put out the Holy Spirit's fire. [20]Don't treat prophecies as if they amount to nothing. [21]Put everything to the test. Hold on to what is good. [22]Stay away from every kind of evil.

[23]God is the God who gives peace. May he make you holy through and through. May your whole spirit, soul and body be kept free from blame. May you be without blame from now until our Lord Jesus Christ comes. [24]The One who has chosen you is faithful. He will do all these things.

[25]Brothers and sisters, pray for us. [26]Greet all the believers with a holy kiss. [27]While the Lord is watching, here is what I command you. Have this letter read to all the believers.

[28]May the grace of our Lord Jesus Christ be with you.

the **Second Coming** of **Christ**

step **1**

step **3**

step **2**

If He came today, would you be ready?

2 THESSALONIANS

- *Written by Paul shortly after he wrote 1 Thessalonians*
- *Speaks of their perseverance in the midst of persecution*
- *Paul counters false reports that claimed the second coming of Jesus had already transpired and they had missed the "rapture"*
- *Theme: "Christ's Return in Judgment"*

1 I, Paul, am writing this letter. Silas and Timothy join me in writing.

We are sending this letter to you, the members of the church in Thessalonica. You belong to God our Father and the Lord Jesus Christ.

²May God the Father and the Lord Jesus Christ give you grace and peace.

Paul Prays and Gives Thanks

³Brothers and sisters, we should always thank God for you. That is only right, because your faith is growing more and more. The love you all have for each other is increasing. ⁴So among God's churches we brag about the fact that you don't give up easily. We brag about your faith in all the suffering and testing you are going through.

⁵All of this proves that when God judges, he is fair. So you will be considered worthy to enter God's kingdom. You are suffering for his kingdom.

⁶God is fair. He will pay back trouble to those who give you trouble. ⁷He will help you who are troubled. And he will also help us.

All of those things will happen when the Lord Jesus appears from heaven. He will come in blazing fire. He will come with the angels who are given the power to do what God wants. ⁸He will punish those who don't know God. He will punish those who don't obey the good news about our Lord Jesus. ⁹They will be destroyed forever. They will be shut out of heaven. They will never see the glory of the Lord's power.

¹⁰All of those things will happen when he comes. On that day his glory will be seen in his holy people. Everyone who has believed will be amazed when they see him. That includes you, because you believed the witness we gave you.

¹¹Keeping this in mind, we never stop praying for you. Our God has chosen us. We pray that he will consider you worthy of his choice. We pray that by his power he will make every good thing you have planned come true. We pray that he will make perfect all that you have done by faith. ¹²We pray this so that the name of our Lord Jesus will receive glory through what you have done. We also pray that you will receive glory through what he has done. We pray all these things in keeping with the grace of our God and the Lord Jesus Christ.

The Man of Sin

2 Brothers and sisters, we want to ask you something. It has to do with the coming of our Lord Jesus Christ. It concerns the time when we will go to be with him.

²What if you receive a prophecy, report or letter that is supposed to have come from us? What if it says that the day of the Lord has already come? If it does, we ask you not to become easily upset or alarmed.

³Don't let anyone trick you in any way. That day will not come until people rise up against God. It will not come until the man of sin appears. He is a marked man. He is sentenced to be destroyed. ⁴He will oppose everything that is called God. He will oppose everything that is worshiped. He will give himself power over everything. He will set himself up in God's temple. He will announce that he himself is God.

⁵Don't you remember? When I was with you, I used to tell you those things.

⁶Now you know what is holding the man of sin back. He is held back so that he can make his appearance at the right time. ⁷The secret power of sin is already at work. But the one who now holds that power back will keep doing it until he is taken out of the way.

⁸Then the man of sin will appear. The Lord Jesus will overthrow him with the breath of his mouth. The glorious brightness of Jesus' coming will destroy the man of sin.

⁹The coming of the man of sin will be Satan's work. His work will be seen in all kinds of fake miracles, signs and wonders. ¹⁰It will be seen in every kind of evil that fools people who are dying. They are dying because they refuse to love the truth. The truth would save them.

¹¹So God will fool them completely. Then they will believe the lie. ¹²Many will not believe the truth. They will take pleasure in evil. They will be judged.

Stand Firm

¹³Brothers and sisters, we should always thank God for you. The Lord loves you. God chose you from the beginning. He wanted you to be saved. Salvation comes through the Holy Spirit's work. He makes people holy. It also comes through believing the truth. ¹⁴He chose you to be saved by accepting the good news that we preach. And you will share in the glory of our Lord Jesus Christ.

¹⁵Brothers and sisters, stand firm. Hold on to what we taught you. We passed our teachings on to you by what we preached and wrote.

¹⁶Our Lord Jesus Christ and God our Father loved us. By his grace God gave us comfort that will last forever. The hope he gave us is good.

May our Lord Jesus Christ and God our Father ¹⁷comfort your hearts. May they make you strong in every good thing you do and say.

Paul Asks for Prayer

3 Finally, brothers and sisters, pray for us. Pray that the Lord's message will spread quickly. Pray that others will honor it just as you did. ²And pray that we will be saved from sinful and evil people. Not everyone is a believer.

³But the Lord is faithful. He will strengthen you. He will guard you from the evil one.

⁴We trust in the Lord. So we are sure that you are doing the things we tell you to do. And we are sure that you will keep on doing them.

⁵May the Lord fill your hearts with God's love. May Christ give you the strength to go on.

Paul Warns Those Who Do Not Want to Work

[6]Brothers and sisters, here is a command we give you in the name of the Lord Jesus Christ. Keep away from every believer who doesn't want to work. Keep away from anyone who doesn't live up to the teaching you received from us.

[7]You know how you should follow our example. We worked when we were with you. [8]We didn't eat anyone's food without paying for it. In fact, it was just the opposite. We worked night and day. We worked very hard so that we wouldn't cause any expense to any of you.

[9]We worked, even though we have the right to receive help from you. We did it in order to be a model for you to follow. [10]Even when we were with you, we gave you a rule. We said, "Anyone who will not work will not eat."

[11]We hear that some people among you don't want to work. They aren't really busy. Instead, they are bothering others. [12]We belong to the Lord Jesus Christ. So we strongly command people like that to settle down. They have to earn the food they eat.

[13]Brothers and sisters, don't ever get tired of doing the right thing.

[14]Keep an eye on anyone who doesn't obey the directions in our letter. Watch that person closely. Have nothing to do with him. Then he will feel ashamed. [15]But don't think of him as an enemy. Instead, warn him as a brother or sister.

Final Greetings

[16]May the Lord who gives peace give you peace at all times and in every way. May the Lord be with all of you.

[17]I, Paul, write this greeting in my own handwriting. That's how I prove that I am the author of all my letters. I always do it that way.

[18]May the grace of our Lord Jesus Christ be with you all.

1 & 2 THESSALONIANS

| | | | | | 6 | | 2 | | | |
|C| | | | | | | | | | |

(Crossword grid with starting letters: 1-C, 8-R, 7-H)

Across

#	Clue	Ref
1.	Believers are Paul's ...	1 Th. 2
2.	Will rise first	1 Th. 4
3.	May your love be like a ...	1 Th. 3
4.	To hear the Good News	---
5.	Who stopped Paul	1 Th. 2
6.	Keep an ___ on disobedient	2 Th. 3
7.	Hope of salvation	1 Th. 5
8.	Believers become a ___	1 Th. 1
9.	abb. for a "knock out"	---

Down

#	Clue	Ref
1.	God's action towards us	1 Th. 5
2.	The ___ of the Lord	1 Th. 5
3.	Jesus returns in blazing ...	2 Th. 1
4.	Produced by faith	1 Th. 1
5.	___ from evil people	2 Th. 3
6.	Sorrow for the hopeless	1 Th. 4
7.	Chosen to be ...	1 Th. 4
8.	Jews showed ___	1 Th. 2
9.	Put on armor of faith & ...	1 Th. 5
10.	Many take pleasure in ...	2 Th. 2
11.	We are children of ...	1 Th. 5

1 TIMOTHY

- *First of three pastoral epistles written by Paul to two young pastors (Timothy and Titus)*
- *Provides instructions for the functioning of the local church*
- *Theme: "Creed and Conduct"*
  Creed (doctrine) - Worship in the Church
  Conduct (good works) - Living in the World

1 I, Paul, am writing this letter. I am an apostle of Christ Jesus, just as God our Savior commanded. Christ Jesus also commanded it. We have put our hope in him.

²Timothy, I am sending you this letter. You are my true son in the faith.

May God the Father and Christ Jesus our Lord give you grace, mercy and peace.

Paul Warns Against Certain Teachers of the Law

³Stay there in Ephesus. That is what I told you to do when I went into Macedonia. I want you to command certain people not to teach things that aren't true. ⁴Command them not to spend their time on stories that aren't completely true. They must not waste time on family histories that never end. Things like that cause people to argue instead of doing God's work. His work is done by faith.

⁵Love is the purpose of my command. Love comes from a pure heart. It comes from a good sense of what is right and wrong. It comes from faith that is honest and true.

⁶Some have wandered away from those teachings. They would rather talk about things that have no meaning. ⁷They want to be teachers of the law. And they are very sure about that law. But they don't know what they are talking about.

⁸We know that the law is good if it is used properly. ⁹We also know that the law isn't made for godly people. It is made for those who break the law. It is for those who refuse to obey. It is for ungodly and sinful people. It is for those who aren't holy and who don't believe. It is for those who kill their fathers or mothers. It is for murderers.

¹⁰It is for those who commit adultery. It is for those who have a twisted view of sex. It is for people who buy and sell slaves. It is for liars. It is for those who give witness to things that aren't true. And it is for anything else that is the opposite of true teaching.

¹¹True teaching agrees with the glorious good news of the blessed God. He trusted me with that good news.

The Lord Pours Out His Grace on Paul

¹²I am thankful to Christ Jesus our Lord. He has given me strength. I thank him that he considered me faithful. And I thank him for appointing me to serve him.

¹³I used to speak evil things against Jesus. I tried to hurt his followers. I really pushed them around. But God showed me mercy anyway. I did those things without knowing any better. I wasn't a believer.

¹⁴Our Lord poured out more and more of his grace on me. Along with it came faith and love from Christ Jesus.

¹⁵Here is a saying that you can trust. It should be accepted completely. Christ Jesus came into the world to save sinners.

And I am the worst sinner of all. ¹⁶But for that very reason, God showed me mercy. And I am the worst of sinners. He showed me mercy so that Christ Jesus could show that he is very patient. I was an example for those who would come to believe in him. Then they would receive eternal life.

¹⁷The eternal King will never die. He can't be seen. He is the only God. Give him honor and glory for ever and ever. Amen.

¹⁸My son Timothy, I give you these teachings. They are in keeping with the prophecies that were once made about you. By

following them, you can fight the good fight. [19]Then you will hold on to faith. You will hold on to a good sense of what is right and wrong.

Some have not accepted these teachings. By doing that, they have destroyed their faith. They are like a ship that has sunk. [20]Hymenaeus and Alexander are among them. I have handed them over to Satan. That will teach them not to speak evil things against God.

Directions for Worship

2 First, I want all of you to pray for everyone. Ask God to bless them. Give thanks for them.

[2]Pray for kings. Pray for all who are in authority. Pray that we will live peaceful and quiet lives. And pray that we will be godly and holy.

[3]That is good. It pleases God our Savior. [4]He wants everyone to be saved. He wants them to come to know the truth.

[5]There is only one God. And there is only one go-between for God and human beings. He is the man Christ Jesus. [6]He gave himself to pay for the sins of everyone. That was a witness given by God at just the right time.

[7]I was appointed to be a messenger and an apostle to preach the good news. I am telling the truth. I'm not lying. God appointed me to be a teacher of the true faith to those who aren't Jews.

[8]I want men everywhere to pray. I want them to lift up holy hands. I don't want them to be angry when they pray. I don't want them to argue.

[9]I also want women to dress simply. They should wear clothes that are right and proper. They shouldn't braid their hair. They shouldn't wear gold or pearls. They shouldn't spend too much on clothes. [10]Instead, they should put on good works as if they were their clothes. That is proper for women who claim to worship God.

[11]When a woman is learning, she should be quiet. She should follow the leaders in every way. [12]I do not let women teach. I do not let them have authority over men. They must be quiet.

[13]Adam was made first. Then Eve was made. [14]Adam was not the one who was tricked. The woman was tricked and became a sinner. [15]Will women be saved by having children? Only if they keep on believing, loving, and leading a holy life in a proper way.

Leaders and Deacons

3 Here is a saying you can trust. If anyone wants to be a leader in the church, he wants to do a good work for God and people.

[2]A leader must be free from blame. He must be faithful to his wife. In anything he does, he must not go too far. He must control himself. He must be worthy of respect. He must welcome people into his home. He must be able to teach. [3]He must not get drunk. He must not push people around. He must be gentle. He must not be a person who likes to argue. He must not love money.

[4]He must manage his own family well. He must make sure that his children obey him and show him proper respect. [5]Suppose someone doesn't know how to manage his own family. Then how can he take care of God's church?

[6]The leader must not be a new believer. If he is, he might become proud. Then he would be judged just like the devil.

[7]The leader must also be respected by those who are outside the church. Then he will not be put to shame. He will not fall into the devil's trap.

[8]Deacons also must be worthy of respect. They must be honest and true. They must not drink too much wine. They must not try to get money by cheating people. [9]They must hold on to the deep truths of the faith. Even their own minds tell them to do that. [10]First they must be tested. Then let them serve as deacons if there is nothing against them.

[11]In the same way, their wives must be worthy of respect. They must not say things that harm others. In anything they do, they must not go too far. They must be worthy of trust in everything.

[12] A deacon must be faithful to his wife. He must manage his children and family well. [13] Those who have served well earn the full respect of others. They also become more sure of their faith in Christ Jesus.

[14] I hope I can come to you soon. But now I am writing these directions to you. [15] Then if I have to put off my visit, you will know how you should act in God's family. The family of God is the church of the living God. It is the pillar and foundation of the truth.

[16] There is no doubt that godliness is a great mystery.

> Jesus appeared in a body.
> The Holy Spirit proved that he was
> the Son of God.
> He was seen by angels.

"I'm not a Christian because ..."

"Of the evil in the world."

Some people ask: "Where did all the evil in our world come from? If God created everything, does that mean He created evil?"

God created both the seen and unseen things - the cosmos and the spiritual heavenly sphere. God could have created preprogrammed "robots" with no ability to choose to love and serve Him. Instead, God created us with the "computer chip" of "free will".

Free will leads to choices and choices lead to negative consequences or positive rewards.

Because we have chosen to reject God and to do evil, we are responsible for the evil in our world.

Only through accepting the Lord Jesus Christ as our Savior and God's spiritual healing can we be set free from the evil we bring on each other.

> God created a perfect cosmos
>
> God allowed "free will"
>
> What is your choice for eternity?

Jesus "gave himself for us. By doing that, he set us free from all evil." Titus 2:14

He was preached among the nations.
People in the world believed in him.
He was taken up to heaven in glory.

Directions for Timothy

4 The Holy Spirit clearly says that in the last days some people will leave the faith. They will follow spirits that will fool them. They will believe things that demons will teach them.

²Teachings like those come from liars who pretend to be what they are not. Their sense of what is right and wrong has been burned as if with a hot iron. ³They do not allow people to get married. They order them not to eat certain foods. But God created those foods. So people who believe and know the truth should receive them and give thanks for them.

⁴Everything God created is good. You shouldn't turn anything down. Instead, you should thank God for it. ⁵The word of God and prayer make it holy.

⁶Point these things out to the brothers and sisters. Then you will serve Christ Jesus well. You were brought up in the truths of the faith. You received good teaching. You followed it.

⁷Don't have anything to do with godless stories and silly tales. Instead, train yourself to be godly. ⁸Training the body has some value. But being godly has value in every way. It promises help for the life you are now living and the life to come.

⁹Here is a saying you can trust. You can accept it completely. ¹⁰We work hard for it. Here is the saying. We have put our hope in the living God. He is the Savior of all people. Most of all he is the Savior of those who believe.

¹¹Command those things. Teach them. ¹²Don't let anyone look down on you because you are young. Set an example for the believers in what you say and in how you live. Also set an example in how you love and in what you believe. Show the believers how to be pure.

¹³Until I come, spend your time reading Scripture out loud to one another. Spend your time preaching and teaching. ¹⁴Don't fail to use the gift the Holy Spirit gave you.

He gave it to you through a message from God. It was given when the elders placed their hands on you.

[15]Keep on doing those things. Give them your complete attention. Then everyone will see how you are coming along. [16]Be careful of how you live and what you believe. Never give up. Then you will save yourself and those who hear you.

Advice About Widows, Elders and Slaves

5 Don't tell an older man off. Make an appeal to him as if he were your father. Treat younger men as if they were your brothers. [2]Treat older women as if they were your mothers. Treat younger women as if they were your sisters. Be completely pure in the way you treat them.

[3]Take care of the widows who really need help. [4]But suppose a widow has children or grandchildren. They should first learn to put their faith into practice. They should care for their own family. In that way they will pay back their parents and grandparents. That pleases God.

[5]The widow who really needs help and is left all alone puts her hope in God. Night and day she keeps on praying. Night and day she asks God for help. [6]But the widow who lives for pleasure is dead even while she is still living.

[7]Give those directions to the people also. Then no one can be blamed. [8]Everyone should provide for his own relatives. Most of all, everyone should take care of his own family. If he doesn't, he has left the faith. He is worse than someone who doesn't believe.

[9]No widow should be put on the list of widows unless she is more than 60 years old. She must also have been faithful to her husband. [10]She must be well known for the good things she does. That includes bringing up children. It includes inviting guests into her home. It includes washing the feet of God's people. It includes helping those who are in trouble. A widow should spend her time doing all kinds of good things.

[11]Don't put younger widows on that kind of list. They might want pleasure more than they want Christ. Then they would want to get married again. [12]If they do that, they will be judged. They have broken their first promise.

[13]Besides, they get into the habit of having nothing to do. They go around from house to house. They waste time. They talk about others. They bother people. They say things they shouldn't say.

[14]So here is the advice I give to younger widows. Get married. Have children. Take care of your own homes. Don't give the enemy the chance to tell lies about you. [15]In fact, some have already turned away to follow Satan.

[16]Suppose a woman is a believer and has widows in her family. She should help them. She shouldn't let the church pay the expenses. Then the church can help the widows who really need it.

[17]The elders who do the church's work well are worth twice as much honor. That is true in a special way of elders who preach and teach. [18]Scripture says, "Do not stop the ox from eating while it helps separate the grain from the straw." (Deuteronomy 25:4) Scripture also says, "Workers are worthy of their pay." (Luke 10:7)

[19]Don't believe a charge against an elder unless two or three witnesses bring it. [20]Elders who sin should be corrected in front of the other believers. That will be a warning to the others.

[21]I command you to follow those directions. I command you in the sight of God and Christ Jesus and the chosen angels. Treat everyone the same. Don't favor one person over another.

[22]Don't be too quick to place your hands on others to set them apart to serve God. Don't take part in the sins of others. Keep yourself pure.

[23]Stop drinking only water. If your stomach is upset, drink a little wine. It can also help the other sicknesses you often have.

[24]The sins of some people are easy to see. They are already being judged. Others will be judged later. [25]In the same way, good works are easy to see. But even good works that are hard to see can't stay hidden.

6 All who are forced to serve as slaves should consider their masters worthy of full respect. Then people will not speak

evil things against God's name and against what we teach.

²Some slaves have masters who are believers. They shouldn't show less respect for their masters just because they are believers. Instead, they should serve them even better. That's because those who benefit from their service are believers. They are loved by them.

Teach the slaves those things. Try hard to get them to do them.

Love for Money

³Suppose someone teaches ideas that are false. He doesn't agree with the true teaching of our Lord Jesus Christ. He doesn't agree with godly teaching. ⁴People like that are proud. They don't understand anything. They like to argue more than they should. They can't agree about what words mean.

All of that results in wanting what others have. It causes fighting, harmful talk, and evil distrust. ⁵It stirs up trouble all the time among people whose minds are twisted by sin. The truth they once had has been taken away from them. They think they can get rich by being godly.

⁶You gain a lot when you live a godly life. But you must be happy with what you have. ⁷We didn't bring anything into the world. We can't take anything out of it. ⁸If we have food and clothing, we will be happy with that.

⁹People who want to get rich are tempted. They fall into a trap. They are tripped up by wanting many foolish and harmful things. Those who live like that are dragged down by what they do. They are destroyed and die.

¹⁰Love for money causes all kinds of evil. Some people want to get rich. They have wandered away from the faith. They have wounded themselves with many sorrows.

Paul Gives a Command to Timothy

¹¹But you are a man of God. Run away from all of those things. Try hard to do what is right and godly. Have faith, love and gentleness. Hold on to what you believe. ¹²Fight the good fight along with all other believers. Take hold of eternal life. You were chosen for it when you openly told others what you believe. Many witnesses heard you.

¹³God gives life to everything. Christ Jesus told the truth when he gave witness to Pontius Pilate. In the sight of God and Christ, I give you a command. ¹⁴Obey it until our Lord Jesus Christ appears. Obey it completely. Then no one can find fault with it or you.

¹⁵God will bring Jesus back at a time that pleases him. God is the blessed and only Ruler. He is the greatest King of all. He is the most powerful Lord of all. ¹⁶God is the only one who can't die. He lives in light that no one can get close to. No one has seen him. No one can see him.

Give honor and power to him forever. Amen.

¹⁷Command people who are rich in this world not to be proud. Tell them not to put their hope in riches. Wealth is so uncertain. Command those who are rich to put their hope in God. He richly provides us with everything to enjoy.

¹⁸Command the rich to do what is good. Tell them to be rich in doing good things. They must give freely. They must be willing to share. ¹⁹In that way they will put riches away for themselves. It will provide a firm basis for the next life. Then they will take hold of the life that really is life.

²⁰Timothy, guard what God has trusted you with. Turn away from godless chatter. Stay away from opposing ideas that are falsely called knowledge. ²¹Some people believe them. By doing that they have wandered away from the faith.

May God's grace be with you.

We cannot all be apostles...
but we *can* be living epistles!

2 TIMOTHY

- *Written by Paul just prior to his execution in Rome*
- *Timothy was a pastor in the church in Ephesus*
- *Paul's final words and personal farewell*
- *Theme: "Preach the Word"*
  "Work hard so that God can approve you ..."

1 I, Paul, am writing this letter. I am an apostle of Christ Jesus just as God planned. He sent me to tell about the promise of life that is found in Christ Jesus.

²Timothy, I am sending you this letter. You are my dear son.

May God the Father and Christ Jesus our Lord give you grace, mercy and peace.

Paul Tells Timothy to Be Faithful

³I serve God, knowing that what I have done is right. That is how our people served him long ago. Night and day I thank God for you. Night and day I always remember you in my prayers.

⁴I remember your tears. I long to see you so that I can be filled with joy. ⁵I remember your honest and true faith. It was alive first in your grandmother Lois and in your mother Eunice. And I am certain that it is now alive in you also.

⁶That is why I remind you to help God's gift grow, just as a small spark grows into a fire. God put his gift in you when I placed my hands on you.

⁷God didn't give us a spirit that makes us weak and fearful. He gave us a spirit that gives us power and love. It helps us control ourselves.

⁸So don't be ashamed to give witness about our Lord. And don't be ashamed of me, his prisoner. Instead, join with me as I suffer for the good news. God's power will help us do that.

⁹God has saved us. He has chosen us to live a holy life. It wasn't because of anything we have done. It was because of his own purpose and grace. Through Christ Jesus, God gave us that grace even before

time began. ¹⁰It has now been made known through the coming of our Savior, Christ Jesus. He has destroyed death. Because of the good news, he has brought life out into the light. That life never dies.

¹¹I was appointed to announce the good news. I was appointed to be an apostle and a teacher. ¹²That's why I'm suffering the way I am. But I'm not ashamed. I know the One I have believed in. I am sure he is able to take care of what I have given him. I can trust him with it until the day he returns as judge.

¹³Follow what you heard from me as the pattern of true teaching. Follow it with faith and love because you belong to Christ Jesus. ¹⁴Guard the truth of the good news that you were trusted with. Guard it with the help of the Holy Spirit who lives in us.

¹⁵You know that all the believers in Asia Minor have deserted me. They include Phygelus and Hermogenes.

¹⁶May the Lord show mercy to all who live in the house of Onesiphorus. He often cheered me up. He was not ashamed that I was being held by chains. ¹⁷In fact, it was just the opposite. When he was in Rome, he looked everywhere for me. At last he found me.

¹⁸May Onesiphorus find mercy from the Lord on the day Jesus returns as judge. You know very well how many ways Onesiphorus helped me in Ephesus.

2 My son, be strong in the grace that is found in Christ Jesus. ²You have heard me teach in front of many witnesses. Pass on to men you can trust the things you've heard me say. Then they will be able to teach others also. ³Like a good soldier of Christ Jesus, share in the hard times with us.

[4]A soldier does not take part in things that don't have anything to do with the army. He wants to please his commanding officer. [5]In the same way, anyone who takes part in a sport doesn't receive the winner's crown unless he plays by the rules. [6]The farmer who works hard should be the first to receive a share of the crops.

[7]Think about what I'm saying. The Lord will help you understand what all of it means.

[8]Remember Jesus Christ. He came from David's family line. He was raised from the dead. That is my good news. [9]I am suffering for it. I have even been put in chains like someone who has committed a crime. But God's word is not held back by chains.

[10]So I put up with everything for the good of God's chosen people. Then they also can be saved. Christ Jesus saves them. He gives them glory that will last forever.

[11]Here is a saying you can trust.

If we died with him,
    we will also live with him.
[12]If we don't give up,
    we will also rule with him.
If we say we don't know him,
    he will also say he doesn't know us.
[13]Even if we are not faithful,
    he will remain faithful.
    He must be true to himself.

A Worker Who Pleases God

[14]Keep reminding the believers of those things. While God is watching, warn them not to argue about words. That doesn't have any value. It only destroys those who listen.

[15]Do your best to please God. Be a worker who doesn't need to be ashamed. Teach the message of truth correctly.

[16]Stay away from godless chatter. Those who take part in it will become more and more ungodly. [17]Their teaching will spread like a deadly sickness.

Hymenaeus and Philetus are two of those teachers. [18]They have wandered away from the truth. They say that the time when people will rise from the dead has already come. They destroy the faith of some people.

[19]But God's solid foundation stands firm. Here is the message written on it. "The Lord knows who his own people are." *(Numbers 16:5)* Also, "All who say they believe in the Lord must turn away from evil."

[20]In a large house there are things made out of gold and silver. But there are also things made out of wood and clay. Some have honorable purposes. Others do not. [21]Suppose someone stays away from what is not honorable. Then the Master will be able to use him for honorable purposes. He

"Pass on to men you can trust the things you've heard me say. Then they will be able to teach others also."

Pass the baton!

2 Timothy 2:2

will be made holy. He will be ready to do any good work.

²²Run away from the evil things that young people long for. Try hard to do what is right. Have faith, love and peace. Do these things together with those who call on the Lord from a pure heart. ²³Don't have anything to do with arguing. It is dumb and foolish. You know it only leads to fights.

²⁴Anyone who serves the Lord must not fight. Instead, he must be kind to everyone. He must be able to teach. He must not hold anything against anyone. ²⁵He must gently teach those who oppose him.

Maybe God will give a change of heart to those who are against you. That will lead them to know the truth. ²⁶Maybe they will come to their senses. Maybe they will escape the devil's trap. He has taken them prisoner to do what he wanted.

Terrible Times in the Last Days

3 Here is what I want you to know. There will be terrible times in the last days. ²People will love themselves. They will love money. They will brag and be proud. They will tear others down. They will not obey their parents. They won't be thankful or holy. ³They won't love others. They won't forgive others. They will tell lies about people. They will be out of control. They will be wild. They will hate what is good.

⁴They will turn against their friends. They will act without thinking. They will think they are better than others. They will love what pleases them instead of loving God. ⁵They will act as if they were serving God. But what they do will show that they have turned their backs on God's power. Have nothing to do with those people.

⁶They are the kind who worm their way into the homes of silly women. They get control over them. Women like that are loaded down with sins. They give in to all kinds of evil longings. ⁷They are always learning. But they never come to know the truth.

⁸Jannes and Jambres opposed Moses. In the same way, the teachers I'm talking about oppose the truth. Their minds are twisted. As far as the faith is concerned, God doesn't accept them. ⁹They won't get

very far. Just like Jannes and Jambres, their foolish ways will be clear to everyone.

Paul Gives a Command to Timothy

¹⁰But you know all about my teaching. You know how I live and what I live for. You know about my faith and love. You know how patient I am. You know I haven't given up. ¹¹You know that I was treated badly. You know that I suffered greatly. You know what kinds of things happened to me in Antioch, Iconium and Lystra. You know how badly I have been treated. But the Lord saved me from all of my troubles.

¹²In fact, everyone who wants to live a godly life in Christ Jesus will be treated

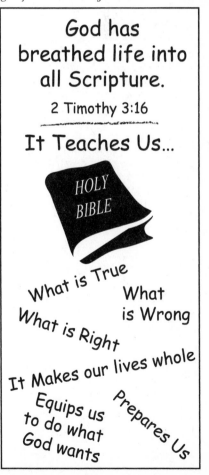

God has breathed life into all Scripture.

2 Timothy 3:16

It Teaches Us...

HOLY BIBLE

What is True
What is Wrong
What is Right
It Makes our lives whole
Equips us to do what God wants
Prepares Us

badly. [13]Evil people and pretenders will go from bad to worse. They will fool others, and others will fool them.

[14]But I want you to continue to follow what you have learned. Don't give up what you are sure of. You know the people you learned it from. [15]You have known the Holy Scriptures ever since you were a little child. They are able to teach you how to be saved by believing in Christ Jesus.

[16]God has breathed life into all of Scripture. It is useful for teaching us what is true. It is useful for correcting our mistakes. It is useful for making our lives whole again. It is useful for training us to do what is right. [17]By using Scripture, a man of God can be completely prepared to do every good thing.

4 I give you a command in the sight of God and Christ Jesus. Christ will judge the living and the dead. Because he and his kingdom are coming, here is the command I give you. [2]Preach the word. Be ready to serve God in good times and bad. Correct people's mistakes. Warn them. Cheer them up with words of hope. Be very patient as you do these things. Teach them carefully.

[3]The time will come when people won't put up with true teaching. Instead, they will try to satisfy their own longings. They will gather a large number of teachers around them. The teachers will say what the people want to hear. [4]The people will turn their ears away from the truth. They will turn to stories that aren't completely true.

[5]But I want you to keep your head no matter what happens. Don't give up when times are hard. Work to spread the good news. Do everything God has given you to do.

[6]I am already being poured out like a drink offering. The time has come for me to leave.

[7]I have fought the good fight. I have finished the race. I have kept the faith. [8]Now there is a crown waiting for me. It is given to those who are right with God. The Lord, who judges fairly, will give it to me on the day he returns. He will not give it only to me. He will also give it to all those who are longing for him to return.

Personal Words

[9]Do your best to come to me quickly.

[10]Demas has deserted me. He has gone to Thessalonica. He left me because he loved this world. Crescens has gone to Galatia. Titus has gone to Dalmatia. [11]Only Luke is with me. Get Mark and bring him with you. He helps me in my work for the Lord. [12]I sent Tychicus to Ephesus.

[13]When you come, bring my coat. I left it with Carpus at Troas. Also bring my scrolls. Most of all, bring the ones made out of animal skins.

[14]Remember Alexander, the one who works with metal? He did me a great deal of harm. The Lord will pay him back for what he has done. [15]You too should watch out for him. He strongly opposed our message.

[16]The first time I was put on trial, no one came to help me. Everyone deserted me. I hope they will be forgiven for it.

[17]The Lord stood at my side. He gave me the strength to preach the whole message. Then all those who weren't Jews heard it. I was saved from the lion's mouth. [18]The Lord will save me from every evil attack. He will bring me safely to his heavenly kingdom.

Give him glory for ever and ever. Amen.

Final Greetings

[19]Greet Priscilla and Aquila. Greet those who live in the house of Onesiphorus.

[20]Erastus stayed in Corinth. I left Trophimus sick in Miletus.

[21]Do your best to get here before winter.

Eubulus greets you. So do Pudens, Linus, Claudia and all the brothers.

[22]May the Lord be with your spirit. May God's grace be with you.

Have you felt the Holy Spirit nudging you lately?

TITUS

- *Written by Paul, probably from Macedonia*
- *Paul advises Titus of his responsibilities in overseeing the churches on the island of Crete*
- *The healthy church is properly organized, teaches and preaches the Word of God and performs good works*
- *Theme: "Godly Leadership Produces Healthy Churches"*

1 I, Paul, am writing this letter. I serve God. I am an apostle of Jesus Christ. God sent me to help his chosen people believe in Christ. I have been sent to help them understand the truth that leads to godly living. ²Faith and understanding rest on the hope of eternal life. Before time began, God promised to give that life. And he does not lie. ³At just the right time he made his word plain. He did it through the preaching that he trusted me with. God our Savior has commanded all those things.

⁴Titus, I am sending you this letter. You are my true son in the faith we share.

May God the Father and Christ Jesus our Savior give you grace and peace.

The Work of Titus on Crete

⁵I left you on the island of Crete. There were some things that hadn't been finished. You needed to sort them out. You also had to appoint elders in every town. I told you how to do it.

⁶An elder must be without blame. He must be faithful to his wife. His children must be believers. They must not give anyone a reason to say that they are wild and don't obey.

⁷A church leader is trusted with God's work. That's why he must be without blame. He must not look after only his own interests. He must not get angry easily. He must not get drunk. He must not push peo-

ple around. He must not try to get money by cheating people.

⁸Instead, he must welcome people into his home. He must love what is good. He must control his mind and feelings. He must do what is right. He must be holy. He must control what his body longs for. ⁹The message as it has been taught can be trusted. He must hold firmly to it. Then he will be able to use true teaching to comfort others and build them up. He will be able to prove that people who oppose it are wrong.

¹⁰Many people refuse to obey God. All they do is talk a lot. They try to fool others. No one does these things more than the circumcision group. ¹¹They must be stopped. They are destroying entire families. They are teaching things they shouldn't. They do it to get money by cheating people.

¹²Even one of their own prophets has said, "People from Crete are always liars. They are evil beasts. They don't want to work. They live only to eat." ¹³What I have just said is true. So give them a strong warning. Then they will understand the faith correctly. ¹⁴They will pay no attention to Jewish stories that aren't completely true. They won't listen to the commands of those who turn away from the truth.

¹⁵To people who are pure, all things are pure. But to those who have twisted minds and don't believe, nothing is pure. In fact, their minds and their sense of what is right

Being faithful means taking risks

and wrong are twisted. [16]They claim to know God. But their actions show they don't know him. They are hated by God. They refuse to obey him. They aren't fit to do anything good.

Teaching God's People

2 What you teach must agree with true teaching.

[2]Tell the older men that in anything they do, they must not go too far. They must be worthy of respect. They must control themselves. They must have true faith. They must love others. They must not give up.

[3]In the same way, teach the older women to lead a holy life. They must not tell lies about others. They must not let wine control them. Instead, they must teach what is good. [4]Then they can train the younger women to love their husbands and children.

[5]The younger women must control themselves. They must be pure. They must take good care of their homes. They must be kind. They must follow the lead of their husbands. Then no one will be able to speak evil things against God's word.

[6]In the same way, help the young men to control themselves. [7]Do what is good. Set an example for them in everything. When you teach, be honest and serious. [8]No one can question the truth. So teach what is true. Then those who oppose you will be ashamed. That's because they will have nothing bad to say about us.

[9]Teach slaves to obey their masters in everything they do. Tell them to try to please their masters. They must not talk back to them. [10]They must not steal from them. Instead, they must show that they can be trusted completely. Then they will make the teaching about God our Savior appealing in every way.

[11]God's saving grace has appeared to all people. [12]It teaches us to say no to godless ways and sinful longings. We must control ourselves. We must do what is right. We must lead godly lives in today's world. [13]That's how we should live as we wait for the blessed hope God has given us.

We are waiting for Jesus Christ to appear in all his glory. He is our great God and Savior. [14]He gave himself for us. By doing that, he set us free from all evil. He wanted to make us pure. He wanted us to be his very own people. He wanted us to long to do what is good.

[15]Those are the things you should teach. Cheer people up and give them hope. Correct them with full authority. Don't let anyone look down on you.

Do What Is Good

3 Remind God's people to obey rulers and authorities. Remind them to be ready to do what is good. [2]Tell them not to speak evil things against

WHAT GOES AROUND ... COMES AROUND

LOVE SELF AND DIE

walk in darkness * reject Jesus Christ as Lord * evil deeds * hatred * lie * deceitfulness * please self * quarrel * love of money * envy * pride * love the world * cruel * serve self * prideful

ETERNAL DEATH

anyone. Remind them to live in peace. They must consider the needs of others. They must be kind and gentle toward all people.

[3]At one time we too acted like fools. We didn't obey God. We were tricked. We were controlled by all kinds of longings and pleasures. We were full of evil. We wanted what belongs to others. People hated us, and we hated one another.

[4]But the kindness and love of God our Savior appeared. [5]He saved us. It wasn't because of the good things we had done. It was because of his mercy. He saved us by washing away our sins. We were born again. The Holy Spirit gave us new life.

[6]God poured out the Spirit on us freely because of what Jesus Christ our Savior has done. [7]His grace made us right with God. So now we have received the hope of eternal life as God's children.

[8]You can trust that saying. Those things are important. Treat them that way. Then those who have trusted in God will be careful to commit themselves to doing what is good. Those things are excellent. They are for the good of everyone.

[9]But keep away from foolish disagree-ments. Don't argue about family histories. Don't make trouble. Don't fight about what the law teaches. Don't argue about things like that. It doesn't do any good. It doesn't help anyone.

[10]Warn anyone who tries to get believers to take sides and separate into their own lit-tle groups. Warn him more than once. After that, have nothing to do with him. [11]You can be sure that someone like that is twisted and sinful. His own actions judge him.

Final Words

[12]I will send Artemas or Tychicus to you. Then do your best to come to me at Nicop-olis. I've decided to spend the winter there.

[13]Do everything you can to help Zenas the lawyer and Apollos. Send them on their way. See that they have everything they need.

[14]Our people must learn to commit them-selves to doing what is good. Then they will be able to provide for the daily needs of oth-ers. If they do that, their lives won't turn out to be useless.

[15]Everyone who is with me sends you greetings. Greet those who love us in the faith.

May God's grace be with you all.

"Jesus Christ ... is our great God and Savior. He gave himself for us ... he set us free from all evil. He wanted to make us pure [and] to be his very own people." Titus 2:13,14

THE CHOICES YOU MAKE ... DECIDE YOUR FATE

LOVE GOD AND LIVE

compassion * accept Jesus Christ as Savior * wisdom * please God * peace * walking in the truth * kindness * humility * serve others * self-control * faithfulness * love * pure * patience * ETERNAL LIFE

PHILEMON

- *Written by Paul from Rome to a friend in Colosse*
- *While imprisoned, Paul leads a runaway slave to Christ*
- *The slave's name, Onesimus, means "useful"*
- *Paul sends Onesimus back to Philemon as a beloved brother in the Lord*
- *Theme: "No Barriers in Christ"*

[1]I, Paul, am writing this letter. I am a prisoner because of Christ Jesus. Our brother Timothy joins me in writing.

Philemon, we are sending you this letter. You are our dear friend. You work together with us. [2]We are also sending it to our sister Apphia and to Archippus. He is a soldier of Christ together with us. And we are sending it to the church that meets in your home.

[3]May God our Father and the Lord Jesus Christ give you grace and peace.

Paul Prays and Gives Thanks

[4]I always thank my God when I remember you in my prayers. [5]That's because I hear about your faith in the Lord Jesus. I hear about your love for all of God's people. [6]I pray that you will be active in sharing what you believe. Then you will completely understand every good thing we have in Christ.

[7]Your love has given me great joy. It has cheered me up. My brother, you have renewed the hearts of God's people.

Paul Makes an Appeal for Onesimus

[8]Because of the authority Christ has given me, I could be bold. I could order you to do what you should do anyway. [9]But I make my appeal to you on the basis of our love for each other.

I, Paul, am an old man. I am now also a prisoner because of Christ Jesus. [10]I make an appeal to you for my son Onesimus. He became a son to me while I was being held by chains. [11]Before that, he was useless to you. But now he has become useful to you and to me.

[12]I'm sending Onesimus back to you. My very heart goes with him. [13]I would have liked to keep him with me. Then he could have taken your place in helping me while I'm being held by chains because of the good news. [14]But I didn't want to do anything unless you agreed. Any favor you do must be done because you want to do it, not because you have to.

[15]Onesimus was separated from you for a little while. Maybe that was so you could have him back for good. [16]You could have him back not as a slave. Instead, he would be better than a slave. He would be a dear brother. He is very dear to me. But he is even more dear to you, both as a man and as a brother in the Lord.

[17]Do you think of me as a believer who works together with you? Then welcome Onesimus as you would welcome me. [18]Has he done anything wrong to you? Does he owe you anything? Then charge it to me. [19]I'll pay it back. I, Paul, am writing this with my own hand. I won't even mention that you owe me your very life.

[20]My brother, I wish I could receive some benefit from you because we both belong to the Lord. Renew my heart. We know that Christ is the one who really renews it. [21]I'm sure you will obey. So I'm writing to you. I know you will do even more than I ask.

[22]There is one more thing. Have a guest room ready for me. I hope I can return to all of you in answer to your prayers.

[23]Epaphras sends you greetings. Together with me, he is a prisoner because of Christ Jesus. [24]Mark, Aristarchus, Demas and Luke work together with me. They also send you greetings.

[25]May the grace of the Lord Jesus Christ be with your spirit.

HEBREWS

- *Author unknown*
- *Written to immature believers to exhort them to grow from spiritual "babies" to mature followers of Christ*
- *Presented as a sermon, rather than a letter*
- *Theme: "Jesus Christ is Superior to the Law, Religion, Prophets, Priests, and Angels"*

The Son Is Greater Than the Angels

1 In the past, God spoke to our people through the prophets. He spoke at many times. He spoke in different ways. ²But in these last days, he has spoken to us through his Son. He is the one whom God appointed to receive all things. God made everything through him. ³The Son is the gleaming brightness of God's glory. He is the exact likeness of God's being. He uses his powerful word to hold all things together. He provided the way for people to be made pure from sin. Then he sat down at the right hand of the King, the Majesty in heaven. ⁴So he became higher than the angels. The name he received is more excellent than theirs.

⁵God never said to any of the angels,

"You are my Son.
Today I have become your Father."
(Psalm 2:7)

Or,

"I will be his Father.
And he will be my Son."
(2 Samuel 7:14; 1 Chronicles 17:13)

⁶God's first and only Son is over all things. When God brings him into the world, he says,

"Let all of God's angels worship him."
(Deuteronomy 32:43)

⁷Here is something else God says about the angels.

"God makes his angels to be like winds.
He makes those who serve him to be like flashes of lightning."
(Psalm 104:4)

⁸But here is what he says about the Son.

"You are God. Your throne will last for ever and ever.
Your kingdom will be ruled by what is right.
⁹You have loved what is right and hated what is evil.
So your God has placed you above your companions.
He has filled you with joy by pouring the sacred oil on your head."
(Psalm 45:6,7)

¹⁰He also says,

"Lord, in the beginning you made the earth secure. You placed it on its foundations.
The heavens are the work of your hands.
¹¹They will pass away. But you remain.
They will all wear out like a piece of clothing.
¹²You will roll them up like a robe.
They will be changed as a person changes clothes.
But you remain the same.
Your years will never end."
(Psalm 102:25–27)

¹³God never said to an angel,

"Sit at my right hand
until I put your enemies
under your control."
(Psalm 110:1)

¹⁴All angels are spirits who serve. God sends them to serve those who will receive salvation.

A Warning to Pay Attention

2 So we must pay more careful attention to what we have heard. Then we will not drift away from it. [2]Even the message God spoke through angels had to be obeyed. Every time people broke the Law, they were punished. Every time they didn't obey, they were punished. [3]Then how will we escape if we don't pay attention to God's great salvation?

The Lord first announced that salvation. Those who heard him gave us the message about it. [4]God gave witness to it through signs and wonders. He gave witness through different kinds of miracles. He also gave witness through the gifts of the Holy Spirit. He gave them out as it pleased him.

Jesus Was Made Like His Brothers

[5]God has not put angels in charge of the world that is going to come. We are talking about that world. [6]There is a place where someone has given witness to it. He said,

"What is a human being that you think
    about him?
What is the son of man that you take
    care of him?
[7]You made him a little lower than the
    angels.
You placed on him a crown of glory
    and honor.
[8]   You have put everything under his
    control."   (Psalm 8:4–6)

So God has put everything under him. Everything is under his control.

We do not now see everything under his control. [9]But we do see Jesus already given a crown of glory and honor. He was made a little lower than the angels. He suffered death. By the grace of God, he tasted death for everyone. That is why he was given his crown.

[10]God has made everything. He has acted in exactly the right way. He is bringing his many sons and daughters to share in his glory. To do so, he has made the One who saved them perfect because of his sufferings.

[11]The One who makes people holy and the people he makes holy belong to the same family. So Jesus is not ashamed to call them his brothers and sisters. [12]He says,

"I will announce your name to my
    brothers and sisters.
I will sing your praises among those
    who worship you."   (Psalm 22:22)

[13]Again he says,

"I will put my trust in him."   (Isaiah 8:17)

And again he says,

"Here I am. Here are the children God
    has given me."   (Isaiah 8:18)

[14]Those children have bodies made out of flesh and blood. So Jesus became human like them in order to die for them. By doing that, he could destroy the one who rules over the kingdom of death. I'm talking about the devil. [15]Jesus could set people free who were afraid of death. All their lives they were held as slaves by that fear.

[16]It is certainly Abraham's children that he helps. He doesn't help angels. [17]So he had to be made like his brothers in every way. Then he could serve God as a kind and faithful high priest. And then he could pay for the sins of the people by dying for them.

[18]He himself suffered when he was tempted. Now he is able to help others who are being tempted.

Jesus Is Greater Than Moses

3 Holy brothers and sisters, God chose you to be his people. So keep thinking about Jesus. He is our apostle. He is our high priest. We believe in him.

[2]Moses was faithful in everything he did in the house of God. In the same way, Jesus was faithful to the One who appointed him.

[3]The person who builds a house has greater honor than the house itself. In the same way, Jesus has been found worthy of greater honor than Moses. [4]Every house is built by someone. But God is the builder of everything.

[5]Moses was faithful as one who serves in the house of God. He gave witness to what God would say in days to come. [6]But Christ

is faithful as a son over God's house. We are his house if we continue to come boldly to God. We must also hold on to the hope we take pride in.

A Warning Against Unbelief

⁷The Holy Spirit says,

"Listen to his voice today.
⁸   If you hear it, don't be stubborn.
You were stubborn when you opposed me.
   You did that when you were put to the test in the desert.
⁹There your people of long ago put me to the test.
   For 40 years they saw what I did.
¹⁰That is why I was angry with them.
   I said, 'Their hearts are always going down the wrong path.
   They have not known my ways.'
¹¹So in my anger I took an oath.
   I said, 'They will never enjoy the rest I planned for them.' "
(Psalm 95:7–11)

¹²Brothers and sisters, make sure that none of you has a sinful heart. Do not let an unbelieving heart turn you away from the living God. ¹³But build one another up every day. Do it as long as there is still time. Then none of you will become stubborn. You won't be fooled by sin's tricks. ¹⁴We belong to Christ if we hold firmly to the faith we had at first. But we must hold to it until the end. ¹⁵It has just been said,

"Listen to his voice today.
   If you hear it, don't be stubborn.
You were stubborn when you opposed me."
(Psalm 95:7,8)

¹⁶Who were those who heard and refused to obey? Weren't they all the people Moses led out of Egypt? ¹⁷Who was God angry with for 40 years? Wasn't it with those who sinned? They died in the desert. ¹⁸What people did God promise with an oath that they would never enjoy the rest he planned for them? Wasn't it those who didn't obey? ¹⁹So we see that they weren't able to enter. That's because they didn't believe.

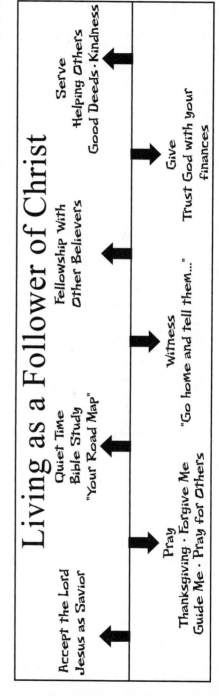

Living as a Follower of Christ

Serve
Helping Others
Good Deeds · Kindness

Give
Trust God with your finances

Fellowship With Other Believers

Witness
"Go home and tell them..."

Quiet Time
Bible Study
"Your Road Map"

Pray
Thanksgiving · Forgive Me
Guide Me · Pray for Others

Accept the Lord
Jesus as Savior

Sometimes Unseen things can bring you Down!

fear

worries

the past

sin

Jesus can help you.

Hebrews 4:16

God's People Enter His Sabbath Rest

4 God's promise of enjoying his rest still stands. So be careful that none of you fails to receive it.

²The good news was preached to our people long ago. It has also been preached to us. The message they heard didn't have any value for them. They didn't combine it with faith. ³Now we who have believed enjoy that rest. God said,

"When I was angry I took an oath.
　I said, 'They will never enjoy the rest I
　　planned for them.' "　　*(Psalm 95:11)*

Ever since God created the world, his work has been finished.

⁴Somewhere he spoke about the seventh day. He said, "On the seventh day God rested from all his work." *(Genesis 2:2)* ⁵In the part of Scripture I talked about earlier God said, "They will never enjoy the rest I planned for them." *(Psalm 95:11)*

⁶It is still true that some will enjoy that rest. But those who had the good news preached to them earlier didn't go in. That was because they didn't obey.

⁷So God again chose a certain day. He named it Today. He did that when he spoke through David a long time later. As it was said earlier,

"Listen to his voice today.
　If you hear it, don't be stubborn."
　　　　　　　　　　(Psalm 95:7,8)

⁸Suppose Joshua had given them rest. If he had, God would not have spoken later about another day. ⁹So there is still a Sabbath rest for God's people.

¹⁰God rested from his work. Those who enjoy God's rest also rest from their work. ¹¹So let us make every effort to enjoy that rest. Then no one will fall into sin by following the example of those who didn't obey God.

¹²The word of God is living and active. It is sharper than any sword that has two edges. It cuts deep enough to separate soul from spirit. It can separate joints from bones. It judges the thoughts and purposes of the heart. ¹³Nothing God created is hidden from him. His eyes see everything. He will hold us accountable for everything we do.

Jesus Is the Great High Priest

¹⁴We have a great high priest. He has gone up into the heavens. He is Jesus the Son of God. So let us hold firmly to what we say we believe.

¹⁵We have a high priest who can feel it when we are weak and hurting. We have a high priest who has been tempted in every way, just as we are. But he did not sin. ¹⁶So let us boldly approach the throne of grace. Then we will receive mercy. We will find grace to help us when we need it.

5 Every high priest is chosen from among men. He is appointed to act for them in everything that has to do with God. He offers gifts and sacrifices for their sins. ²He is able to deal gently with those who have gone down the wrong path without knowing it. He can do that because he himself is weak. ³That's why he has to offer sacrifices for his own sins. He must also do it for the sins of the people.

⁴No one can take that honor for himself. He must be appointed by God, just as Aaron was.

⁵Even Christ did not take the glory of becoming a high priest for himself. God said to him,

"You are my Son.
Today I have become your Father." *(Psalm 2:7)*

⁶In another place he said,

"You are a priest forever,
just like Melchizedek." *(Psalm 110:4)*

⁷Jesus prayed while he lived on earth. He made his appeal with loud cries and tears. He prayed to the One who could save him from death. God heard him because he truly honored God.

⁸Jesus was God's Son. But by suffering he learned what it means to obey. ⁹In that way he was made perfect. Eternal salvation comes from him. He saves all those who obey him.

¹⁰God appointed him to be the high priest, just like Melchizedek.

A Warning Against Falling Away

¹¹We have a lot to say about that. But it is hard to explain it to you. You learn too slowly. ¹²By this time you should be teachers. But in fact, you need someone to teach you all over again. You need even the simple truths of God's word. You need milk, not solid food.

¹³Anyone who lives on milk is still a baby. That person does not want to learn about living a godly life. ¹⁴Solid food is for those who are grown up. They have trained themselves with a lot of practice. They can tell the difference between good and evil.

6 So let us leave the simple teachings about Christ. Let us grow up as believers. Let us not start all over again with the basic teachings. They taught us that we need to turn away from doing things that lead to death. They taught us that we must have faith in God. ²They taught us about different kinds of baptism. They taught us about placing hands on people. They taught

*Knowing your purpose
gives meaning to your life.*

us that people will rise from the dead. They taught us that God will judge everyone. And they taught us that what he decides will last forever.

³If God permits, we will go beyond those teachings and grow up.

⁴What if some people fall away from the faith? It won't be possible to bring them back. It is true that they have seen the light. They have tasted the heavenly gift. They have shared in the Holy Spirit. ⁵They have tasted the good things of God's word. They have tasted the powers of the age to come. ⁶But they have fallen away from the faith. So it won't be possible to bring them back. They won't be able to turn away from their sins. They are losing everything. That's because they are nailing the Son of God to the cross all over again. They are bringing shame on him in front of everyone.

⁷Some land drinks the rain that falls on it. It produces a crop that is useful to those who farm the land. That land receives God's blessing. ⁸But other land produces only thorns and weeds. That land isn't worth anything. It is in danger of coming under God's curse. In the end, it will be burned.

⁹Dear friends, we have to say these things. But we are sure of better things in your case. We are talking about the things that go along with being saved.

¹⁰God is fair. He will not forget what you have done. He will remember the love you have shown him. You showed it when you helped his people. And you show it when you keep on helping them.

¹¹We want each of you to be faithful to the very end. We want you to be sure of what you hope for. ¹²We don't want you to slow down. Instead, be like those who have faith and are patient. They will receive what God promised.

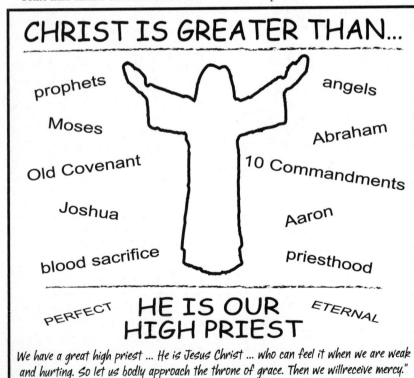

CHRIST IS GREATER THAN...

prophets

angels

Moses

Abraham

Old Covenant

10 Commandments

Joshua

Aaron

blood sacrifice

priesthood

PERFECT   **HE IS OUR**   ETERNAL
           HIGH PRIEST

We have a great high priest ... He is Jesus Christ ... who can feel it when we are weak and hurting. So let us boldly approach the throne of grace. Then we will receive mercy."

Hebrews 4:14-16

God Keeps His Promise

[13]When God made his promise to Abraham, he took an oath to keep it. But there was no one greater than himself to take an oath by. So he took his oath by making an appeal to himself.

[14]He said, "I will certainly bless you. I will give you many children." *(Genesis 22:17)* [15]Abraham was patient while he waited. Then he received what God promised him.

[16]People take oaths by someone greater than themselves. An oath makes a promise certain. It puts an end to all arguing. [17]So God took an oath when he made his promise. He wanted to make it very clear that his purpose does not change. He wanted those who would receive what was promised to know that.

[18]God took an oath so we would have good reason not to give up. We have run away from everything else to take hold of the hope offered to us in God's promise. So God gave his promise and his oath. Those two things can't change. He couldn't lie about them.

[19]Our hope is certain. It is something for the soul to hold on to. It is strong and secure. It goes all the way into the Most Holy Room behind the curtain. [20]That is where Jesus has gone. He went there to open the way ahead of us. He has become a high priest forever, just like Melchizedek.

Melchizedek the Priest

7 Melchizedek was the king of Salem. He was the priest of God Most High. He met Abraham, who was returning from winning a battle over some kings. Melchizedek blessed him. [2]Abraham gave him a tenth of everything.

First, the name Melchizedek means "king of what is right." Also, "king of Salem" means "king of peace." [3]Melchizedek has no father or mother. He has no family line. His days have no beginning. His life has no end. He remains a priest forever, just like the Son of God.

[4]Think how great Melchizedek was. Even our father Abraham gave him a tenth of what he had captured. [5]Now the law lays down a rule for the sons of Levi who become priests.

They must collect a tenth from the people. They must collect it even from those who belong to the family line of Abraham.

[6]Melchizedek did not trace his family line from Levi. But he collected a tenth from Abraham. Melchizedek blessed the one who had received the promises. [7]Without a doubt, the more important person blesses the less important one. [8]In the one case, the tenth is collected by men who die. But in the other case, it is collected by the one who is said to be living.

[9]Levi collects the tenth. But we might say that Levi paid the tenth through Abraham. [10]That's because when Melchizedek met Abraham, Levi was still in Abraham's body.

Jesus Is Like Melchizedek

[11]Suppose the Levites who were priests could have made people perfect. The law was given to the people so they could become perfect through the priests. Then why was there still a need for another priest to come? And why did he need to be like Melchizedek? Why wasn't he from Aaron's family line?

[12]A change of priests requires a change of law. [13]Those things are said about one who is from a different tribe. No one from that tribe has ever served at the altar. [14]It is clear that our Lord came from the family line of Judah. Moses said nothing about priests who were from that tribe.

[15]But suppose another priest like Melchizedek appears. Then what we have said is even more clear. [16]He has not become a priest because of a rule about his family line. He has become a priest because of his powerful life. His life can never be destroyed. [17]Scripture says,

"You are a priest forever,
    just like Melchizedek." *(Psalm 110:4)*

[18]The old rule is done away with. It was weak and useless. [19]The law didn't make anything perfect. Now a better hope has been given to us. That hope brings us near to God.

[20]The change of priests was made with an oath. Others became priests without any oath. [21]But Jesus became a priest with an

oath. God said to him,

> "The Lord has taken an oath and made
> a promise.
> He will not change his mind. He has
> said,
> 'You are a priest forever.'"   (*Psalm 110:4*)

²²Because of that oath, Jesus makes the promise of a better covenant certain.

²³There were many priests in Levi's family line. Death kept them from continuing in office. ²⁴But Jesus lives forever. So he always holds the office of priest. ²⁵People now come to God through him. And he is able to save them completely and for all time. Jesus lives forever. He prays for them.

²⁶A high priest like that meets our need. He is holy, pure and without blame. He isn't like other people. He does not sin. He is lifted high above the heavens.

²⁷He isn't like the other high priests. They need to offer sacrifices day after day. First they bring offerings for their own sins. Then they do it for the sins of the people. But Jesus gave one sacrifice for the sins of the people. He gave it once and for all time. He did it by offering himself.

²⁸The law appoints men who are weak to be high priests. But God's oath came after the law. The oath appointed the Son. He has been made perfect forever.

The High Priest of a New Covenant

8 Here is the point of what we are saying. We have a high priest like that. He sat down at the right hand of the throne of the King, the Majesty in heaven. ²He serves in the sacred tent. The Lord set up the true holy tent. A mere man did not set it up.

³Every high priest is appointed to offer gifts and sacrifices. So that priest also had to have something to offer.

⁴What if he were on earth? Then he would not be a priest. There are already priests who offer the gifts required by the law. ⁵They serve at a sacred tent. But it is only a copy and shadow of what is in heaven. That's why God warned Moses when he was about to build the holy tent. God said, "Be sure to make everything just like the pattern I showed you on the mountain." (*Exodus 25:40*)

⁶Jesus has been given a greater work to do for God. He is the go-between for the new covenant. That covenant is better than the old one. It is based on better promises.

⁷Suppose nothing had been wrong with that first covenant. Then no one would have looked for another covenant. ⁸But God found fault with the people. He said,

> "A new day is coming, says the Lord.
> I will make a new covenant
> with the people of Israel.
> I will also make it with the people of
> Judah.
> ⁹It will not be like the covenant
> I made with their people of long ago.
> That was when I took them by the hand.
> I led them out of Egypt.
> My new covenant will be different
> because they didn't remain
> faithful to my old covenant.
> So I turned away from them,
> says the Lord.
> ¹⁰This is the covenant I will make with
> Israel
> after that time, says the Lord.
> I will put my laws in their minds.
> I will write them on their hearts.
> I will be their God.
> And they will be my people.
> ¹¹A man will not teach his neighbor
> anymore.
> And he will not teach his friend
> anymore.
> He will not say, 'Know the Lord.'
> Everyone will know me.
> From the least important of them to
> the most important,
> all of them will know me.

*Don't doubt in the dark...
what the Lord has shown you in the light.*

[12] I will forgive their evil ways.
I will not remember their sins
anymore." *(Jeremiah 31:31–34)*

[13] God called that covenant "new." So he has made the first one out of date. And what is out of date and getting older will soon disappear.

Worship in the Holy Tent on Earth

9 The first covenant had rules for worship. It also had a sacred tent on earth. [2] A holy tent was set up. The lampstand was in the first room. So were the table and the holy bread. That was called the Holy Room. [3] Behind the second curtain was a room called the Most Holy Room. [4] It had the golden altar for incense. It also had the wooden chest called the ark of the covenant. The ark was covered with gold. It held the gold jar of manna. It held Aaron's wooden staff that had budded. It also held the stone tablets. The words of the covenant were written on them.

[5] The cherubim were above the ark. God showed his glory there. The cherubim spread their wings over the place where sin was paid for. But we can't deal with those things more completely now.

[6] That's how everything was arranged in the holy tent. The priests entered it at regular times. They went into the outer room to do their work for God and others. [7] But only the high priest went into the inner room. He went in only once a year. He never entered without taking blood with him. He offered the blood for himself. He also offered it for the sins the people had committed because they didn't know any better.

[8] Here is what the Holy Spirit was showing us. He was telling us that God had not yet clearly shown the way into the Most Holy Room. It would not be clearly shown as long as the first holy tent was still standing.

The cemetery is your last stop!

too busy to believe

?

I'm good enough

I must decrease so He can increase

I was ashamed of Christ

Saved by Grace!

What will be written on your tombstone?

[9]That's an example for the present time. It shows us that the gifts and sacrifices they offered were not enough. They were not able to remove the worshiper's feelings of guilt. [10]They deal only with food and drink and different kinds of special washings. They are rules that deal with things outside our bodies. People had to obey them only until the new covenant came.

The Blood of Christ

[11]Christ came to be the high priest of the good things that are already here. When he came, he went through the greater and more perfect holy tent. The tent was not made by people. In other words, it is not a part of this creation. [12]He did not enter by spilling the blood of goats and calves. He entered the Most Holy Room by spilling his own blood. He did it once and for all time. He paid the price to set us free from sin forever.

[13]The blood of goats and bulls is sprinkled on people. So are the ashes of a young cow. They are sprinkled on people the Law called unclean. The people are sprinkled to make them holy. That makes them clean on the outside. [14]But Christ offered himself to God without any flaw. He did this through the power of the eternal Holy Spirit. So how much more will his blood wash from our minds our feelings of guilt for committing sin! Sin always leads to death. But now we can serve the living God.

[15]That's why Christ is the go-between of a new covenant. Now those God calls to himself will receive the eternal gift he promised. They will receive it now that Christ has died to save them. He died to set them free from the sins they committed under the first covenant.

[16]What happens in the case of a will? It is necessary to prove that the person who made the will has died. [17]A will is in effect only when somebody has died. It never takes effect while the one who made it is still living. [18]That's why even the first covenant was not put into effect without the spilling of blood.

[19]Moses first announced every commandment of the law to all the people. Then he took the blood of calves. He also took water, bright red wool and branches of a hyssop plant. He sprinkled the scroll. He also sprinkled all of the people. [20]He said, "This is the blood of the covenant God has commanded you to keep." *(Exodus 24:8)* [21]In the same way, he sprinkled the holy tent with blood. He also sprinkled everything that was used in worship there.

[22]In fact, the law requires that nearly everything be made clean with blood. Without the spilling of blood, no one can be forgiven.

[23]So the copies of the heavenly things had to be made pure with those sacrifices. But the heavenly things themselves had to be made pure with better sacrifices.

[24]Christ did not enter a sacred tent made by people. That tent was only a copy of the true one. He entered heaven itself. He did it to stand in front of God for us. He is there right now.

[25]The high priest enters the Most Holy Room every year. He enters with blood that is not his own. But Christ did not enter heaven to offer himself again and again. [26]If he had, he would have had to suffer many times since the world was created. But now he has appeared once and for all time. He has come at the end of the ages to do away with sin. He has done that by offering himself.

[27]People have to die once. After that, God will judge them. [28]In the same way, Christ was offered up once. He took away the sins of many people.

He will also come a second time. At that time he will not suffer for sin. Instead, he will come to bring salvation to those who are waiting for him.

In making decisions...
The good is always the enemy of the best.

Christ's Sacrifice Is Once and for All Time

10 The law is only a shadow of the good things that are coming. It is not the real things themselves. The same sacrifices have to be offered over and over again. They must be offered year after year. That's why the law can never make perfect those who come near to worship. [2]If it could, wouldn't the sacrifices have stopped being offered? The worshipers would have been made clean once and for all time. They would not have felt guilty for their sins anymore.

[3]But those offerings remind people of their sins every year. [4]It isn't possible for the blood of bulls and goats to take away sins.

[5]So when Christ came into the world, he said,

"You didn't want sacrifices and offerings.
    Instead, you prepared a body for me.
[6]You weren't pleased
    with burnt offerings and sin offerings.
[7]Then I said, 'Here I am. It is written
        about me in the scroll.
    God, I have come to do what you
        want.'"   (Psalm 40:6–8)

[8]First Christ said, "You didn't want sacrifices and offerings. You didn't want burnt offerings and sin offerings. You weren't pleased with them." He said that even though the law required people to bring them. [9]Then he said, "Here I am. I have come to do what you want." He did away with the first. He did it to put the second in place.

[10]We have been made holy by what God wanted. We have been made holy because Jesus Christ offered his body once and for all time.

[11]Day after day every priest stands and does his special duties. He offers the same sacrifices again and again. But they can never take away sins.

[12]Jesus our priest offered one sacrifice for sins for all time. Then he sat down at the right hand of God. [13]Since that time, he waits for his enemies to be put under his control. [14]By that one sacrifice he has made perfect forever those who are being made holy.

[15]The Holy Spirit also gives witness to us about this. First he says,

[16]"This is the covenant I will make with
        them
    after that time, says the Lord.
I will put my laws in their hearts.
    I will write my laws on their minds."
                        (Jeremiah 31:33)

[17]Then he adds,

"I will not remember their sins anymore.
    I will not remember the evil things
        they have done."   (Jeremiah 31:34)

[18]Where those have been forgiven, there is no longer any offering for sin.

A Warning to Remain Faithful

[19]Brothers and sisters, we are not afraid to enter the Most Holy Room. We enter boldly because of the blood of Jesus. [20]His way is new because he lives. It has been opened for us through the curtain. I'm talking about his body.

[21]We also have a great priest over the house of God. [22]So let us come near to God with an honest and true heart. Let us come near with a faith that is sure and strong. Our hearts have been sprinkled. Our minds have been cleansed from a sense of guilt. Our bodies have been washed with pure water.

[23]Let us hold firmly to the hope we claim to have. The One who promised is faithful.

[24]Let us consider how we can stir up one another to love. Let us help one another to do good works. [25]Let us not give up meeting together. Some are in the habit of doing this. Instead, let us cheer each other up with words of hope. Let us do it all the more as you see the day coming when Christ will return.

[26]What if we keep sinning on purpose? What if we do it even after we know the truth? Then there is no offering for our sins. [27]All we can do is to wait in fear for God to judge. His blazing fire will burn up his enemies.

[28]Anyone who did not obey the law of Moses died without mercy if there were two or three witnesses. [29]What should be done to anyone who has hated the Son of God or has said no to him? What should be done to a person who treated as an unholy

thing the blood of the covenant that makes him holy? What should be done to someone who has made fun of the Holy Spirit who brings God's grace? Don't you think people like that should be punished more than anyone else?

³⁰We know the One who said, "I am the One who judges people. I will pay them back." *(Deuteronomy 32:35)* Scripture also says, "The Lord will judge his people." *(Deuteronomy 32:36; Psalm 135:14)*

³¹It is a terrible thing to fall into the hands of the living God.

³²Remember those earlier days after you received the light. At that time you stood firm in a great struggle. You did it even in the face of suffering.

³³Sometimes you were made fun of in front of others. You were treated badly. At other times you stood side by side with people who were being treated like that. ³⁴You suffered together with people in prison. When your property was taken from you, you accepted it with joy. You knew that God had given you better and more lasting things.

³⁵So don't throw away your bold faith. It will bring you rich rewards. ³⁶You need to be faithful. Then you will do what God wants. You will receive what he has promised. ³⁷In just a very little while,

"The one who is coming will come. He
 will not wait.
³⁸   The one who is in the right will live
      by faith.
  If he pulls back,
    I will not be pleased with him."
                                    (Habakkuk 2:3,4)

³⁹But we aren't people who pull back and are destroyed. We are people who believe and are saved.

Living by Faith

11 Faith is being sure of what we hope for. It is being certain of what we do not see. ²That is what the people of long ago were praised for.

³We have faith. So we understand that everything was made when God commanded it. That's why we believe that what we see was not made out of what could be seen.

⁴Abel had faith. So he offered to God a better sacrifice than Cain did. Because of his faith Abel was praised as a godly man. God said good things about his offerings. Because of his faith Abel still speaks. He speaks even though he is dead.

⁵Enoch had faith. So he was taken from this life. He didn't die. He just couldn't be found. God had taken him away. Before God took him, Enoch was praised as one who pleased God.

⁶Without faith it isn't possible to please God. Those who come to God must believe that he exists. And they must believe that he rewards those who look to him.

⁷Noah had faith. So he built an ark to save his family. He built it because of his great respect for God. God had warned him about things that could not yet be seen. Because of his faith he showed the world that it was guilty. Because of his faith he was considered right with God.

⁸Abraham had faith. So he obeyed God. God called him to go to a place he would later receive as his own. So he went. He did it even though he didn't know where he was going. ⁹Because of his faith he made his home in the land God had promised him. He was like an outsider in a strange country. He lived there in tents. So did Isaac and Jacob. They received the same promise he did. ¹⁰Abraham was looking forward to the city that has foundations. He was waiting for the city that God planned and built.

¹¹Abraham had faith. So God made it possible for him to become a father. He became a father even though he was too old. Sarah also was too old to have children. But Abra-

God was thinking about you...
even before He made the world.

ham believed that the One who made the promise was faithful. ¹²Abraham was past the time when he could have children. But many children came from that one man. They were as many as the stars in the sky. They were as many as the sand on the seashore. No one could count them.

¹³All those people were still living by faith when they died. They didn't receive the things God had promised. They only saw them and welcomed them from a long way off. They openly said that they were outsiders and strangers on earth.

¹⁴People who say things like that show that they are looking for a country of their own. ¹⁵What if they had been thinking of the country they had left? Then they could have returned to it. ¹⁶Instead, they longed for a better country. They wanted one in heaven.

So God is pleased when they call him their God. In fact, he has prepared a city for them.

¹⁷Abraham had faith. So he offered Isaac as a sacrifice. That happened when God put him to the test. Abraham had received the promises. But he was about to offer his one and only son. ¹⁸God had said to him, "Your family line will continue through Isaac." *(Genesis 21:12)* Even so, Abraham was going to offer him up. ¹⁹Abraham believed that God could raise the dead. In a way, he did receive Isaac back from death.

²⁰Isaac had faith. So he blessed Jacob and Esau. He told them what was ahead for them.

²¹Jacob had faith. So he blessed each of Joseph's sons. He blessed them when he was dying. Because of his faith he worshiped God as he leaned on the top of his wooden staff.

²²Joseph had faith. So he spoke to the people of Israel about their leaving Egypt. He gave directions about his bones. He did that toward the end of his life.

²³Moses' parents had faith. So they hid him for three months after he was born. They saw he was a special child. They were not afraid of the king's command.

²⁴Moses had faith. So he refused to be called the son of Pharaoh's daughter. That happened after he had grown up. ²⁵He chose to be treated badly together with the people of God. He chose that instead of enjoying sin's pleasures for a short time. ²⁶He suffered shame because of Christ. He thought it had great value. He considered it better than the riches of Egypt. He was looking ahead to God's reward.

²⁷Because of his faith he left Egypt. It wasn't because he was afraid of the king's anger. He didn't let anything stop him. He saw the One who can't be seen.

²⁸Because of his faith he was the first to keep the Passover Feast. He commanded the people of Israel to sprinkle blood on their doorways. He did it so that the destroying angel would not touch their oldest sons.

²⁹The people had faith. So they passed through the Red Sea. They went through it as if it were dry land. The Egyptians tried to do it also. But they drowned.

³⁰The people had faith. So the walls of Jericho fell down. It happened after they had marched around the city for seven days.

³¹Rahab, the prostitute, had faith. So she welcomed the spies. That's why she wasn't killed with those who didn't obey God.

³²What more can I say? I don't have time to tell about all the others. I don't have time to talk about Gideon, Barak, Samson and Jephthah. I don't have time to tell about David, Samuel and the prophets. ³³Because of their faith they took over kingdoms. They ruled fairly. They received the blessings God had promised. They shut the mouths of lions. ³⁴They put out great fires. They escaped being killed by the sword. Their weakness was turned to strength. They became powerful in battle. They beat back armies from other countries.

³⁵Women received their dead back. The dead were raised to life again. Others were made to suffer greatly. But they refused to be set free. They did that so that after death they would be raised to a better life.

³⁶Some were laughed at. Some were whipped. Still others were held by chains. They were put in prison. ³⁷Some were killed with stones. They were sawed in two. They were put to death by the sword. They went around wearing the skins of sheep and

goats. They were poor. They were attacked. They were treated badly. ³⁸The world was not worthy of them. They wandered in deserts and mountains. They lived in caves. They lived in holes in the ground.

³⁹All of those people were praised because they had faith. But none of them received what God had promised. ⁴⁰God had planned something better for us. So they would only be made perfect together with us.

12 A huge cloud of witnesses is all around us. So let us throw off everything that stands in our way. Let us throw off any sin that holds on to us so tightly. Let us keep on running the race marked out for us.

²Let us keep looking to Jesus. He is the author of faith. He also makes it perfect. He paid no attention to the shame of the cross. He suffered there because of the joy he was looking forward to. Then he sat down at the right hand of the throne of God.

³He put up with attacks from sinners. So think about him. Then you won't get tired. You won't lose hope.

God Trains His Children

⁴You struggle against sin. But you have not yet fought to the point of spilling your blood. ⁵You have forgotten that word of hope. It speaks to you as children. It says,

"My son, think of the Lord's training as
    important.
  Do not lose hope when he corrects
      you.
⁶ The Lord trains those he loves.
  He punishes everyone he accepts as a
    son."   *(Proverbs 3:11,12)*

⁷Put up with hard times. God uses them to train you. He is treating you as children. What children are not trained by their parents? ⁸God trains all of his children. But what if he doesn't train you? Then you are like children of people who weren't married to each other. You are not truly God's children.

⁹Besides, we have all had human parents who trained us. We respected them for it. How much more should we be trained by the Father of our spirits and live!

¹⁰Our parents trained us for a little while. They did what they thought was best. But God trains us for our good. He wants us to share in his holiness.

¹¹No training seems pleasant at the time. In fact, it seems painful. But later on it produces a harvest of godliness and peace. It does that for those who have been trained by it.

¹²So lift your sagging arms. Strengthen your weak knees. ¹³"Make level paths for your feet to walk on." *(Proverbs 4:26)* Then those who have trouble walking won't be disabled. Instead, they will be healed.

A Warning Against Saying No to God

¹⁴Try your best to live in peace with everyone. Try to be holy. Without holiness no one will see the Lord.

¹⁵Be sure that no one misses God's grace. See to it that a bitter plant doesn't grow up. If it does, it will cause trouble. And it will pollute many people. ¹⁶See to it that no one commits sexual sins.

See to it that no one is godless like Esau. He sold the rights to what he would receive as the oldest son. He sold them for a single meal. ¹⁷As you know, after that he wanted to receive his father's blessing. But he was turned away. With tears he tried to get the blessing. But he couldn't get his father to change his mind.

¹⁸You haven't come to a mountain that can be touched. You haven't come to a mountain that is burning with fire. You haven't come to darkness, gloom and storm. ¹⁹You haven't come to a blast from God's trumpet. You haven't come to a voice speaking to you. When people heard that voice long ago, they begged it not to say anything more to them. ²⁰What God commanded was too much for them. He said, "If even an animal touches the mountain, it must be killed with stones." *(Exodus 19:12,13)* ²¹The sight was terrifying. Moses said, "I am trembling with fear." *(Deuteronomy 9:19)*

²²But you have come to Mount Zion. You have come to the Jerusalem in heaven. It is the city of the living God. You have come to a joyful gathering of angels. There are

thousands and thousands of them. ²³You have come to the church of God's people. God's first and only Son is over all things. God's people share in what belongs to his Son. Their names are written in heaven. You have come to God. He is the judge of all people.

You have come to the spirits of godly people who have been made perfect. ²⁴You have come to Jesus. He is the go-between of a new covenant. You have come to the sprinkled blood. It promises better things than the blood of Abel.

²⁵Be sure that you don't say no to the One who speaks. People did not escape when they said no to the One who warned them on earth. And what if we turn away from the One who warns us from heaven? How much less will we escape!

²⁶At that time his voice shook the earth. But now he has promised, "Once more I will shake the earth. I will also shake the heavens." *(Haggai 2:6)* ²⁷The words "once more" point out that what can be shaken can be taken away. I'm talking about created things. Then what can't be shaken will remain.

²⁸We are receiving a kingdom that can't be shaken. So let us be thankful. Then we can worship God in a way that pleases him. We will worship him with deep respect and wonder. ²⁹Our "God is like a fire that burns everything up." *(Deuteronomy 4:24)*

Final Words

13 Keep on loving each other as brothers and sisters. ²Don't forget to welcome strangers. By doing that, some people have welcomed angels without knowing it.

³Remember those in prison as if you were in prison with them. And remember those who are treated badly as if you yourselves were suffering.

⁴All of you should honor marriage. You should keep the marriage bed pure. God will judge the person who commits adultery. He will judge everyone who commits sexual sins.

⁵Don't be controlled by love for money. Be happy with what you have. God has said,

"I will never leave you.
    I will never desert you."
(Deuteronomy 31:6)

There's a huge cloud of **Witnesses**...

Go!

Yes!

You can do it!

...so Run the Race that's set before You! Hebrews 12:1

[6]So we can say boldly,

"The Lord helps me. I will not be afraid.
What can a mere man do to me?"

(Psalm 118:6,7)

[7]Remember your leaders. They spoke God's word to you. Think about the results of their way of life. Copy their faith.

[8]Jesus Christ is the same yesterday and today and forever.

[9]Don't be carried away by all kinds of strange teachings. It is good that God's grace makes our hearts strong. Don't depend on foods the Law requires. They have no value for the people who eat them. [10]Some worship at the holy tent. But we have an altar that they have no right to eat from.

[11]The high priest carries the blood of animals into the Most Holy Room. He brings their blood as a sin offering. But the bodies are burned outside the camp. [12]Jesus also suffered outside the city gate. He suffered to make the people holy by spilling his own blood.

[13]So let us go to him outside the camp. Let us be willing to suffer the shame he suffered. [14]Here we do not have a city that lasts. But we are looking for the city that is going to come.

[15]So let us never stop offering to God our praise through Jesus. Let us offer it as the fruit of lips that say they believe in him.

[16]Don't forget to do good. Don't forget to share with others. God is pleased with those kinds of offerings.

[17]Obey your leaders. Put yourselves under their authority. They keep watch over you. They know they are accountable to God for everything they do. Obey them so that their work will be a joy. If you make their work a heavy load, it won't do you any good.

[18]Pray for us. We feel sure we have done what is right. We long to live as we should in every way.

[19]I beg you to pray that I may return to you soon.

[20]Our Lord Jesus is the great Shepherd of the sheep. The God who gives peace brought him back from the dead. He did it because of the blood of the eternal covenant. May God [21]supply you with everything good. Then you can do what he wants. May he do in us what is pleasing to him. We can do it only with the help of Jesus Christ. Give him glory for ever and ever. Amen.

[22]Brothers and sisters, I beg you to accept my word. It tells you to be faithful. I have written you only a short letter.

[23]I want you to know that our brother Timothy has been set free. If he arrives soon, I will come with him to see you.

[24]Greet all of your leaders. Greet all of God's people. The believers from Italy send you their greetings.

[25]May grace be with you all.

As a believer, you can bring your OWN sacrifices to God!

Altar of Sacrifice

Romans 12:1
Hebrews 13:16

HEBREWS LINE-UP PUZZLE

1 Statement (from Intro., boxes & headlines)	2 Clue Page	3 Clue Letters	4 Draw lines Column 3 & 5	5 Answers	6 Clue Letters
1 reaction to unbelief	349	A		● Old Covenant	___
2 falling away response	351	A		● New Covenant	___
3 Christ sacrifice for	357	B		● unknown	___
4 What you can't do	346	C		● witnesses	___
5 Don't say ___ to God	360	E		● faithful	___
6 What Christ has done	346	H		● promises	___
7 Huge crowd of	361	I		● warning	**B**
8 Great High priest	351	L		● all time	___
9 superior to all	Intro.	L		● cemetery	___
10 your last stop	355	O		● children	___
11 author of Hebrews	Intro.	R		● No	___
12 remain ...	357	S		● warning	___
13 God keeps His	353	T		● Jesus	___
14 God trains His	360	V		● Jesus	___

CHRIST ABOVE ALL

Directions:

Column   1   -   Read incomplete statement
Column   2   -   Look up clue page
Columns 3-5 -   Draw line from clue Letters to list of answers
Column   6   -   Place letters in space for solution

HEBREWS

Across

1. Same - Past, Present, Future — ch. 13
2. Remember those in _____ — ch. 13
3. Disaster signal — ---
4. Jesus is higher than _____ — ch. 1
5. Consume food — ---
6. In Ark of Covenant — ch. 9
7. Short for "Alfred" — ---
8. Selection of meals — ---
9. Listen __ His voice — ch. 3
10. Either, __ — ---
11. Contract with God — ch. 8

Down

1. The Hebrew people — ---
2. Most quoted OT book — ch. 1
3. Can't please God without — ch. 11
4. Here today, ____ tomorrow — ---
5. Godless like _____ — ch. 12
6. Unholy will not ____ Jesus — ch. 12
7. At end of prayer — ch. 13
8. As in our race — ch. 12
9. Abb. "south" — ---
10. Greater than angel — ch. 1
11. Peace, trust, salvation — ch. 4
12. Burn up His enemies — ch. 10

JAMES

- *Written by James - the Lord's brother*
- *He was a leader in the church of Jerusalem*
- *Considered the first New Testament book written*
- *Calls true Christians to be doers of the Word*
- *Theme: "Faith is the root of Salvation"*
  "Works are the fruit of Salvation"

1 I, James, am writing this letter. I serve God and the Lord Jesus Christ.

I am sending this letter to you, the 12 tribes that are scattered among the nations.

Greetings.

Facing All Kinds of Trouble

²My brothers and sisters, you will face all kinds of trouble. When you do, think of it as pure joy. ³Your faith will be put to the test. You know that when that happens it will produce in you the strength to continue. ⁴The strength to keep going must be allowed to finish its work. Then you will be all you should be. You will have everything you need.

⁵If any of you need wisdom, ask God for it. He will give it to you. God gives freely to everyone. He doesn't find fault.

⁶But when you ask, you must believe. You must not doubt. People who doubt are like waves of the sea. The wind blows and tosses them around. ⁷A man like that shouldn't expect to receive anything from the Lord. ⁸He can't make up his mind. He can never decide what to do.

⁹A believer who finds himself in a low position in life should be proud that God has given him a high position. ¹⁰But someone who is rich should take pride in his low position. That's because he will fade away like a wild flower.

¹¹The sun rises. Its burning heat dries up the plants. Their blossoms fall. Their beauty is destroyed. In the same way, a rich person will fade away even as he goes about his business.

¹²Blessed is the man who keeps on going when times are hard. After he has come through them, he will receive a crown. The crown is life itself. God has promised it to those who love him.

¹³When you are tempted, you shouldn't say, "God is tempting me." God can't be tempted by evil. And he doesn't tempt anyone.

¹⁴But your own evil longings tempt you. They lead you on and drag you away. ¹⁵When they are allowed to grow, they give birth to sin. When sin has grown up, it gives birth to death.

¹⁶My dear brothers and sisters, don't let anyone fool you. ¹⁷Every good and perfect gift is from God. It comes down from the Father. He created the heavenly lights. He does not change like shadows that move.

¹⁸God chose to give us new birth through the message of truth. He wanted us to be the first and best of everything he created.

Listen to the Word and Do What It Says

¹⁹My dear brothers and sisters, pay attention to what I say. Everyone should be quick to listen. But they should be slow to speak. They should be slow to get angry. ²⁰A man's anger doesn't produce the kind of life God wants.

²¹So get rid of everything that is dirty and sinful. Get rid of the evil that is all around us. Don't be too proud to accept the word that is planted in you. It can save you.

²²Don't just listen to the word. You fool yourselves if you do that. You must do what it says.

[23]Suppose you listen to the word but don't do what it says. Then you are like a man who looks at his face in a mirror. [24]After looking at himself, he leaves. Right away he forgets what he looks like.

[25]But suppose you take a good look at the perfect law that gives freedom. You keep looking at it. You don't forget what you've heard, but you do what the law says. Then you will be blessed in what you do.

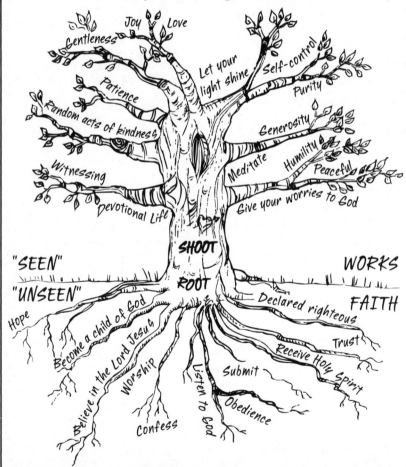

Salvation Tree
People are saved by faith alone, not by works or good deeds.

Conversion (faith) begins in our hearts – "unseen."
Genuine faith is expressed in growth and fruit – "seen."

[26]Suppose you think your beliefs are right because of how you live. But you don't control what you say. Then you are fooling yourselves. Your beliefs are not worth anything at all.

[27]Here are the kinds of beliefs that God our Father accepts as pure and without fault. When widows and children who have no parents are in trouble, take care of them. And keep yourselves from being polluted by the world.

Treat Everyone the Same

2 My brothers and sisters, you are believers in our glorious Lord Jesus Christ. So treat everyone the same.

[2]Suppose a man comes into your meeting wearing a gold ring and fine clothes. And suppose a poor man in worn-out clothes also comes in. [3]Would you show special attention to the one who is wearing fine clothes? Would you say, "Here's a good seat for you"? Would you say to the poor person, "You stand there"? Or "Sit on the floor by my feet"? [4]If you would, aren't you treating some people better than others? Aren't you like judges who have evil thoughts?

[5]My dear brothers and sisters, listen to me. Hasn't God chosen those who are poor in the world's eyes to be rich in faith? Hasn't he chosen them to receive the kingdom? Hasn't he promised it to those who love him?

[6]But you have put poor people down. Aren't rich people taking advantage of you? Aren't they dragging you into court? [7]Aren't they speaking evil things against the worthy name of Jesus? Remember, you belong to him.

[8]The royal law is found in Scripture. It says, "Love your neighbor as you love yourself." (*Leviticus 19:18*) If you really keep that law, you are doing what is right. [9]But you sin if you don't treat everyone the same. The law judges you because you have broken it.

[10]Suppose you keep the whole law but trip over just one part of it. Then you are guilty of breaking all of it. [11]God said, "Do not commit adultery." (*Exodus 20:14; Deuteronomy 5:18*) He also said, "Do not commit murder." (*Exodus 20:13; Deuteronomy 5:17*) Suppose you don't commit adultery but do commit murder. Then you have broken the Law.

[12]Speak and act like people who are going to be judged by the law that gives freedom. [13]Those who have not shown mercy will not receive mercy when they are judged. To show mercy is better than to judge.

Show Your Faith by What You Do

[14]My brothers and sisters, what good is it if people claim they have faith but don't act like it? Can that kind of faith save them?

[15]Suppose a brother or sister has no clothes or food. [16]Suppose one of you says to them, "Go. I hope everything turns out fine for you. Keep warm. Eat well." And you do nothing about what they really need. Then what good have you done?

[17]It is the same with faith. If it doesn't cause us to do something, it's dead.

[18]But someone will say, "You have faith. I do good works."

Show me your faith that doesn't do good works. And I will show you my faith by what I do. [19]You believe there is one God. Good! Even the demons believe that. And they tremble!

[20]You foolish man! Do you want proof that faith without good works is useless? [21]Our father Abraham offered his son Isaac on the altar. Wasn't he considered to be right with God because of what he did? [22]So you see that what he believed and what he did were working together. What he did made his faith complete.

[23]That is what Scripture means where it says, "Abraham believed God. God accepted Abraham because he believed. So his faith made him right with God." (*Genesis 15:6*) And that's not all. God called Abraham his friend. [24]So you see that a person is made right with God by what he does. It doesn't happen only because of what he believes.

[25]Didn't God make even Rahab the prostitute right with him? That's because of what she did. She gave the spies a place to stay. Then she sent them off in a different direction.

[26]The body without the spirit is dead. In

Control Your Tongue

Hurtful

Idiot!

Jerk-face!

Fat-head

Lying

Praise

Kindness

Blessing

Loving

Joyful

This is **not** right!
James 3:9-12

the same way, faith without good works is dead.

Control What You Say

3 My brothers and sisters, most of you shouldn't want to be teachers. You know that those of us who teach will be held more accountable.

²All of us get tripped up in many ways. Suppose someone is never wrong in what he says. Then he is a perfect man. He is able to keep his whole body under control.

³We put a bit in the mouth of a horse to make it obey us. We can control the whole animal with it. ⁴And how about ships? They are very big. They are driven along by strong winds. But they are steered by a very small rudder. It makes them go where the captain wants to go.

⁵In the same way, the tongue is a small part of the body. But it brags a lot. Think about how a small spark can set a big forest on fire.

⁶The tongue also is a fire. The tongue is the most evil part of the body. It pollutes the whole person. It sets a person's whole way of life on fire. And the tongue is set on fire by hell.

⁷People have controlled all kinds of ani-

mals, birds, reptiles and creatures of the sea. They still control them. ⁸But no one can control the tongue. It is an evil thing that never rests. It is full of deadly poison.

⁹With our tongues we praise our Lord and Father. With our tongues we call down curses on people. We do it even though they have been created to be like God. ¹⁰Praise and cursing come out of the same mouth. My brothers and sisters, it shouldn't be that way.

¹¹Can fresh water and salt water flow out of the same spring? ¹²My brothers and sisters, can a fig tree bear olives? Can a grapevine bear figs? Of course not. And a saltwater spring can't produce fresh water either.

Two Kinds of Wisdom

¹³Are any of you wise and understanding? You should show it by living a good life. Wise people aren't proud when they do good works.

¹⁴But suppose your hearts are jealous and bitter. Suppose you are concerned only about getting ahead. Don't brag about it. Don't say no to the truth. ¹⁵Wisdom like that doesn't come down from heaven. It

belongs to the earth. It doesn't come from the Holy Spirit. It comes from the devil.

[16]Are you jealous? Are you concerned only about getting ahead? Then your life will be a mess. You will be doing all kinds of evil things.

[17]But the wisdom that comes from heaven is pure. That's the most important thing about it. And that's not all. It also loves peace. It thinks about others. It obeys. It is full of mercy and good fruit. It is fair. It doesn't pretend to be what it is not.

[18]Those who make peace should plant peace like a seed. If they do, it will produce a crop of right living.

Obey God

4 Why do you fight and argue among yourselves? Isn't it because of your sinful longings? They fight inside you.

[2]You want something, but you can't get it. You kill and want what others have. But you can't have what you want. You argue and fight. You don't have what you want, because you don't ask God. [3]When you do ask for something, you don't receive it. Why? Because you ask for the wrong reason. You want to spend your money on your sinful pleasures.

[4]You are not faithful to God. Don't you know that to be a friend of the world is to hate God? Anyone who chooses to be a friend of the world becomes an enemy of God. [5]Don't you know what Scripture says? The spirit that God caused to live in us wants us to belong only to God. Don't you think Scripture has a reason for saying that? [6]God continues to give us more grace. That's why Scripture says,

> "God opposes those who are proud.
> But he gives grace to those who are
>   not." *(Proverbs 3:34)*

[7]So obey God. Stand up to the devil. He will run away from you. [8]Come near to God, and he will come near to you. Wash your hands, you sinners. Make your hearts pure, you who can't make up your minds.

[9]Be full of sorrow. Cry and sob. Change your laughter to crying. Change your joy to sadness. [10]Bow down to the Lord. He will lift you up.

[11]My brothers and sisters, don't speak

Faith Without Good Deeds is Dead

You Can't Have...

Sun w/o Light

Bird w/o Wings

Sea w/o Water

Rainbow w/o Color

Fish w/o Fins

Kitten w/o Meow

Car w/o Wheels

Rain w/o Clouds

Singer w/o Song

Flower w/o Petals

Waterfall w/o Water

Belief w/o Action

You Can't Have One Without the Other

James 2:26

against one another. Anyone who speaks against another believer speaks against the law. And anyone who judges another believer judges the law. When you judge the law, you are not keeping it. Instead, you are acting as if you were its judge.

[12]There is only one Lawgiver and Judge. He is the One who is able to save life or destroy it. But who are you to judge your neighbor?

Bragging About Tomorrow

[13]Now listen, you who say, "Today or tomorrow we will go to this or that city. We will spend a year there. We will buy and sell and make money." [14]You don't even know what will happen tomorrow. What is your life? It is a mist that appears for a little while. Then it disappears. [15]Instead, you should say, "If it pleases the Lord, we will live and do this or that."

[16]As it is, you are proud. You brag about it. That kind of bragging is evil. [17]So when you know the good things you should do and don't do them, you sin.

A Warning to Rich People

5 You rich people, listen to me. Cry and sob, because you will soon be suffering.

[2]Your riches have rotted. Moths have eaten your clothes. [3]Your gold and silver have lost their brightness. Their dullness will give witness against you. Your wanting more and more will eat your body like fire. You have stored up riches in these last days.

[4]You have even failed to pay the workers who mowed your fields. Their pay is crying out against you. The cries of those who gathered the harvest have reached the ears of the Lord who rules over all.

[5]You have lived an easy life on earth. You have given yourselves everything you wanted. You have made yourselves fat like cattle that will soon be butchered. [6]You have judged and murdered people who aren't guilty. And they weren't even opposing you.

Be Patient When You Suffer

[7]Brothers and sisters, be patient until the Lord comes. See how the farmer waits for the land to produce its rich crop. See how patient he is for the fall and spring rains. [8]You too must be patient. You must stand firm. The Lord will soon come back.

[9]Brothers and sisters, don't find fault with one another. If you do, you will be judged. And the Judge is standing at the door!

[10]Brothers and sisters, think about the prophets who spoke in the name of the Lord. They are an example of how to be patient when you suffer. [11]As you know, we think that people who don't give up are blessed. You have heard that Job was patient. And you have seen what the Lord finally did for him. The Lord is full of tender mercy and loving concern.

[12]My brothers and sisters, don't take an oath when you make a promise. Don't call on heaven or earth or anything else to back up what you say. Let your "Yes" be yes. And let your "No" be no. If you don't, you will be judged.

The Prayer of Faith

[13]Are any of you in trouble? Then you should pray. Are any of you happy? Then sing songs of praise.

[14]Are any of you sick? Then send for the elders of the church to pray over you. Ask them to anoint you with oil in the name of the Lord. [15]The prayer offered by those who have faith will make you well. The Lord will heal you. If you have sinned, you will be forgiven.

[16]So admit to one another that you have sinned. Pray for one another so that you might be healed. The prayer of a godly person is powerful. It makes things happen.

[17]Elijah was just like us. He prayed hard that it wouldn't rain. And it didn't rain on the land for three and a half years. [18]Then he prayed again. That time it rained. And the earth produced its crops.

[19]My brothers and sisters, suppose one of you wanders away from the truth and someone brings you back. [20]Then here is what I want everyone to remember. Anyone who turns a sinner from going down the wrong path will save him from death. God will erase many sins by forgiving him.

1 PETER

> - *Written by Peter from Rome to all believers*
> - *A great wave of persecution had scattered the Church from Jerusalem throughout the Roman empire*
> - *Peter shares as a fellow pastor suffering for the Gospel*
> - *Theme: " Hope and Joy in Times of Trials"*

1 I, Peter, am writing this letter. I am an apostle of Jesus Christ.

I am sending this letter to you, God's chosen people. You are strangers in the world. You are scattered all over Pontus, Galatia, Cappadocia, Asia and Bithynia. ²You have been chosen in keeping with what God the Father had planned. That happened through the Spirit's work to make you pure and holy. God chose you so that you might obey Jesus Christ. He wanted you to be made clean by the blood of Christ.

May more and more grace and peace be given to you.

Peter Praises God for a Hope That Is Alive

³Give praise to the God and Father of our Lord Jesus Christ. In his great mercy he has given us a new birth and a hope that is alive. It is alive because Jesus Christ rose from the dead. ⁴He has given us new birth so that we might share in what belongs to him. It is a gift that can never be destroyed. It can never spoil or even fade away. It is kept in heaven for you. ⁵Through faith you are kept safe by God's power. Your salvation is going to be completed. It is ready to be shown to you in the last days.

⁶Because you know this, you have great joy. You have joy even though you may have had to suffer for a little while. You may have had to suffer sadness in all kinds of trouble.

⁷Your troubles have come in order to prove that your faith is real. It is worth more than gold. Gold can pass away even though fire has made it pure. Your faith is meant to bring praise, honor and glory to God. That will happen when Jesus Christ returns.

⁸Even though you have not seen him, you love him. Though you do not see him now, you believe in him. You are filled with a glorious joy that can't be put into words. ⁹You are receiving the salvation of your souls. It is the result of your faith.

¹⁰The prophets searched very hard and with great care to find out about that salvation. They spoke about the grace that was going to come to you. ¹¹They wanted to find out when that salvation would come. The Spirit of Christ in them was telling them about the sufferings of Christ that were going to come. He was also telling them about the glory that would follow.

¹²It was made known to the prophets that they were not serving themselves. Instead, they were serving you when they spoke about the things that you have now heard. Those who have preached the good news to you have told you those things. They have done it with the help of the Holy Spirit sent from heaven. Even angels long to look into those things.

Be Holy

¹³So prepare your minds for action. Control yourselves. Put your hope completely in the grace that will be given to you when Jesus Christ returns.

¹⁴You should obey. You shouldn't give in to evil longings. They controlled your life when you didn't know any better. ¹⁵The one who chose you is holy. So you should be holy in all that you do. ¹⁶It is written, "Be

Don't allow the Old Nature to tie you up!

anger
rebellion
pride
lust
envy
trust
obey

Only with Christ can you say no to your sinful nature!

holy, because I am holy." *(Leviticus 11:44,45; 19:2)*

¹⁷You call on a Father who judges each person's work without favoring one over another. So live your lives as strangers here. Have the highest respect for God.

¹⁸The blood of Christ set you free from an empty way of life. That way of life was handed down to you by your own people long ago. You know that you were not bought with things that can pass away, like silver or gold. ¹⁹Instead, you were bought by the priceless blood of Christ. He is a perfect lamb. He doesn't have any flaws at all. ²⁰He was chosen before God created the world. But he came into the world in these last days for you.

²¹Because of what Christ has done, you believe in God. It was God who raised him from the dead. And it was God who gave him glory. So your faith and hope are in God.

²²You have made yourselves pure by obeying the truth. So you have an honest and true love for your brothers and sisters. Love each other deeply, from the heart.

²³You have been born again by means of the living word of God. His word lasts forever. You were not born again from a seed that will die. You were born from a seed that can't die. ²⁴It is written,

"All people are like grass.
    All of their glory is like the flowers
        in the field.
The grass dries up. The flowers fall
        to the ground.
²⁵   But the word of the Lord stands
        forever."   *(Isaiah 40:6–8)*

And that word was preached to you.

2 So get rid of every kind of evil. Stop telling lies. Don't pretend to be something you are not. Stop wanting what others have. Don't speak against each other.

²Like babies that were just born, you should long for the pure milk of God's word. It will help you grow up as believers. ³You can do it now that you have tasted how good the Lord is.

The Living Stone and a Chosen People

⁴Christ is the living Stone. People did not accept him. But God chose him. God places the highest value on him.

⁵You also are like living stones. As you come to him you are being built into a house for worship. There you will be holy priests. You will offer spiritual sacrifices. God will accept them because of what Jesus Christ has done.

⁶In Scripture it says,

"Look! I am placing a stone in Zion.
It is a chosen and very valuable stone.
It is the most important stone in the
building.
The one who trusts in him
will never be put to shame."

(Isaiah 28:16)

⁷The stone is very valuable to you who believe. But to people who do not believe,

"The stone the builders did not accept
has become the most important stone
of all."   *(Psalm 118:22)*

⁸And,

"It is a stone that causes people to trip.
It is a rock that makes them fall."

(Isaiah 8:14)

They trip and fall because they do not obey the message. That is also what God planned for them.

⁹But God chose you to be his people. You are royal priests. You are a holy nation. You are a people who belong to God. All of this is so that you can sing his praises. He brought you out of darkness into his wonderful light. ¹⁰Once you were not a people. But now you are the people of God. Once you had not received mercy. But now you have received mercy.

¹¹Dear friends, you are outsiders and strangers in this world. So I'm asking you not to give in to your sinful longings. They fight against your soul. ¹²People who don't believe might say you are doing wrong. But lead good lives among them. Then they will see your good works. And they will give glory to God on the day he comes to judge.

Obey Your Rulers and Masters

¹³Follow the lead of every human authority. Do it because the Lord wants you to. Obey the king. He is the highest authority. ¹⁴Obey the governors. The king sends them to punish those who do wrong. He also sends them to praise those who do right. ¹⁵By doing good you will put a stop to the talk of foolish people. They don't know what they are saying. God wants you to stop them.

¹⁶Live like free people. But don't use your freedom to cover up evil. Live like people who serve God. ¹⁷Show proper respect to everyone. Love the community of believers. Have respect for God. Honor the king.

¹⁸Slaves, obey your masters with all the respect you should give them. Obey not only those who are good and kind. Obey also those who are not kind. ¹⁹Suppose a person suffers pain unfairly because he wants to obey God. That is worthy of praise. ²⁰But suppose you receive a beating for doing wrong, and you put up with it. Will anyone honor you for that? Of course not. But suppose you suffer for doing good, and you put up with it. God will praise you for that.

²¹Christ suffered for you. He left you an example. He expects you to follow in his steps. You too were chosen to suffer. ²²Scripture says,

"He didn't commit any sin.
No lies ever came out of his mouth."

(Isaiah 53:9)

²³People shouted at him and made fun of him. But he didn't do the same back to them. He suffered. But he didn't say that bad things would happen to them. Instead, he trusted in the One who judges fairly.

²⁴He himself carried our sins in his body on the cross. He did it so that we would die as far as sins are concerned. Then we would lead godly lives. His wounds have made you whole.

²⁵You were like sheep who were wandering away. But now you have returned to the Shepherd. He is the Leader of your souls.

Wives and Husbands

3 Wives, follow the lead of your husbands. Suppose some of them don't believe God's word. Then let them be won to Christ without words by seeing how their wives behave. ²Let them see how pure you are. Let them see that your lives are full of respect for God.

³Braiding your hair doesn't make you beautiful. Wearing gold jewelry or fine clothes doesn't make you beautiful. ⁴Instead, your beauty comes from inside you. It is the beauty of a gentle and quiet spirit. Beauty like that doesn't fade away. God places great value on it.

⁵This is how the holy women of the past used to make themselves beautiful. They put their hope in God. And they followed the lead of their own husbands.

⁶Sarah was like that. She obeyed Abraham. She called him her master. Do you want to be like her? Then do what is right. And don't give in to fear.

⁷Husbands, take good care of your wives. They are weaker than you. So treat them with respect. Honor them as those who will share with you the gracious gift of life. Then nothing will stand in the way of your prayers.

Suffering for Doing Good

⁸Finally, I want all of you to live together in peace. Be understanding. Love one another like members of the same family. Be kind and tender. Don't be proud. ⁹Don't pay back evil with evil. Don't pay back unkind words with unkind words. Instead, pay them back with kind words. That's what you have been chosen to do. You can receive a blessing by doing it.

¹⁰Scripture says,

"Do you want to love life
  and see good days?
Then keep your tongues from speaking
    evil.
  Keep your lips from telling lies.
¹¹Turn away from evil, and do good.
  Look for peace, and go after it.
¹²The Lord's eyes look with favor on those
    who are godly.
  His ears are open to their prayers.
But the Lord doesn't look with favor on
    those who do evil."

  (Psalm 34:12–16)

¹³Who is going to hurt you if you really want to do good? ¹⁴But suppose you suffer for doing what is right. Then you will be blessed. Scripture also says, "Don't fear what others fear. Don't be afraid." *(Isaiah 8:12)*

¹⁵But make sure in your hearts that Christ is Lord. Always be ready to give an answer to anyone who asks you about the hope you have. Be ready to give the reason for it. But do it gently and with respect.

¹⁶Live so that you don't have to feel you've done anything wrong. Some people may say evil things about your good conduct as believers in Christ. If they do, they will be put to shame for speaking like that about you. ¹⁷It is better to suffer for doing good than for doing evil if that's what God wants.

¹⁸Christ died for sins once and for all time. The One who did what is right died for those who don't do right. He died to bring you to God. His body was put to death. But the Holy Spirit brought him back to life.

¹⁹By means of the Spirit, Christ went and preached to the spirits in prison. ²⁰Long ago they did not obey. God was patient while Noah was building the ark. He waited, but only a few people went into the ark. A total of eight were saved by means of water.

²¹The water of the flood is a picture of the baptism that now saves you also. The baptism I'm talking about has nothing to do with removing dirt from your body. Instead, it promises God that you will keep a clear sense of what is right and wrong.

Jesus Christ has saved you by rising from the dead. ²²He has gone into heaven. He is at God's right hand. Angels, authorities and powers are under his control.

Living for God

4 Christ suffered in his body. So get ready as a soldier does. Prepare yourselves to think in the same way Christ did. Do it because those who have suffered in their bodies are finished with sin. ²As a result, they don't live the rest of their lives on earth controlled by evil human longings. Instead, they live to do what God wants.

WHO WILL WIN?

Sinful Nature

New Creation

The one you feed the most!

³You have spent enough time in the past doing what ungodly people choose to do. You lived a wild life. You longed for evil things. You got drunk. You went to wild parties. You worshiped statues of gods. The Lord hates that.

⁴Ungodly people think that it's strange when you no longer join them in what they do. They want you to rush into the same flood of wasteful living. So they say bad things about you.

⁵But they will have to explain their actions to God. He is ready to judge the living and the dead. ⁶That's why the good news was preached even to people who are now dead. Human judges said they were guilty as far as their bodies were concerned. But God set their spirits free to live as he wanted them to.

⁷The end of all things is near. So keep a clear mind. Control yourselves. Then you can pray. ⁸Most of all, love one another deeply. Love erases many sins by forgiving them. ⁹Welcome others into your homes without complaining.

¹⁰God's gifts of grace come in many forms. Each of you has received a gift in order to serve others. You should use it faithfully. ¹¹If

you speak, you should do it like one speaking God's very words. If you serve, you should do it with the strength God provides. Then in all things God will be praised through Jesus Christ.

Give him the glory and the power for ever and ever. Amen.

Suffering for Being a Christian

[12]Dear friends, don't be surprised by the painful suffering you are going through. Don't feel as if something strange were happening to you. [13]Be joyful that you are taking part in Christ's sufferings. Then you will be filled with joy when Christ returns in glory.

[14]Suppose people make fun of you because you believe in Christ. Then you are blessed, because God's Spirit rests on you. He is the Spirit of glory. [15]Suppose you suffer. Then it shouldn't be because you are a murderer or a thief. It shouldn't be because you do evil things. It shouldn't be because you poke your nose into other people's business. [16]But suppose you suffer for being a Christian. Then don't be ashamed. Instead, praise God because you are known by that name.

[17]It is time for people to be judged. It will begin with the family of God. And since it begins with us, what will happen to people who don't obey God's good news? [18]Scripture says,

"Suppose it is hard for godly people
to be saved.
Then what will happen to ungodly
people and sinners?"
(Proverbs 11:31)

[19]Some people will suffer because God has planned it that way. They should commit themselves to their faithful Creator. And they should continue to do good.

To Elders and Young Men

5 I'm speaking to the elders among you. I was a witness of Christ's sufferings. And I will also share in the glory that is going to come. I'm making my appeal to you as one who is an elder together with you. [2]Be shepherds of God's flock, the believers who are under your care. Serve as their leaders. Don't serve them because you have to. Instead, do it because you want to. That's

what God wants you to do. Don't do it because you want to get more and more money. Do it because you really want to serve.

[3]Don't act as if you were a ruler over those who are under your care. Instead, be examples to the flock. [4]The Chief Shepherd will come again. Then you will receive the crown of glory. It is a crown that will never fade away.

[5]Young men, follow the lead of those who are older. All of you, put on a spirit that is free of pride toward each other as if it were your clothes. Scripture says,

"God opposes those who are proud.
But he gives grace to those who are not."
(Proverbs 3:34)

[6]So don't be proud. Put yourselves under God's mighty hand. Then he will honor you at the right time. [7]Turn all your worries over to him. He cares about you.

[8]Control yourselves. Be on your guard. Your enemy the devil is like a roaring lion. He prowls around looking for someone to chew up and swallow. [9]Stand up to him. Stand firm in what you believe. All over the world you know that your brothers and sisters are going through the same kind of suffering.

[10]God always gives you all the grace you need. So you will only have to suffer for a little while. Then God himself will build you up again. He will make you strong and steady. And he has chosen you to share in his eternal glory because you belong to Christ.

[11]Give him the power for ever and ever. Amen.

Final Greetings

[12]I consider Silas to be a faithful brother. With his help I have written you this short letter. I have written it to cheer you up. And I have written to give witness about the true grace of God. Stand firm in it.

[13]The members of the church in Babylon send you their greetings. They were chosen together with you. Mark, my son in the faith, also sends you his greetings. [14]Greet each other with a friendly kiss.

May God give peace to all of you who believe in Christ.

2 PETER

- *Written by Peter from Rome, just prior to his martyrdom*
- *Knowing his time is short, he wants to protect fellow believers from false teachers*
- *Peter reminded the believers to live godly lives since "the day of the Lord" was near*
- *Theme: "Grow in the Grace and Knowledge of Jesus"*

1 I, Simon Peter, am writing this letter. I serve Jesus Christ. I am his apostle.

I am sending this letter to you who have received a faith as valuable as ours. You received it because our God and Savior Jesus Christ does what is right and fair for everyone.

²May more and more grace and peace be given to you. May they come to you as you learn more about God and about Jesus our Lord.

Be Sure That God Has Chosen You

³God's power has given us everything we need to lead a godly life. All of that has come to us because we know the One who chose us. He chose us because of his own glory and goodness.

⁴He has also given us his very great and valuable promises. He did it so you could share in his nature. He also did it so you could escape from the evil in the world. That evil is caused by sinful longings.

⁵So you should try very hard to add goodness to your faith. To goodness, add knowledge. ⁶To knowledge, add the ability to control yourselves. To the ability to control yourselves, add the strength to keep going. To the strength to keep going, add godliness. ⁷To godliness, add kindness to believers. And to kindness to believers, add love.

⁸You should possess more and more of those good points. They will make you useful and fruitful as you get to know our Lord Jesus Christ better.

⁹But what if some of you do not have those good points? Then you can't see very well. You are blind. You have forgotten that your past sins have been washed away.

¹⁰My brothers and sisters, be very sure that God has appointed you to be saved. Be sure that he has chosen you. If you do everything I have just said, you will never trip and fall. ¹¹You will receive a rich welcome into the kingdom that lasts forever. It is the kingdom of our Lord and Savior Jesus Christ.

Prophecy Comes From God

¹²So I will always remind you of these things. I'll do it even though you know them. I'll do it even though you now have deep roots in the truth. ¹³I think it is right for me to remind you. It is right as long as I live in this tent. I'm talking about my body.

¹⁴I know my tent will soon be removed. Our Lord Jesus Christ has made that clear to me. ¹⁵I hope that you will always be able to remember these things after I'm gone. I will try very hard to see that you do.

¹⁶We told you about the time our Lord Jesus Christ came with power. But we didn't make up stories when we told you about it. With our own eyes we saw him in all his majesty. ¹⁷God the Father gave him honor and glory. The voice of the Majestic Glory came to him. It said, "This is my Son, and I love him. I am very pleased with him." *(Matthew 17:5; Mark 9:7; Luke 9:35)* ¹⁸We ourselves heard the voice that came from heaven. We were with him on the sacred mountain.

¹⁹The word of the prophets is made more certain. We have that word. You must pay attention to it. It is like a light shining in a dark place. It will shine until the day Jesus comes. Then the Morning Star will rise in your hearts.

There are so many **Heroes** of the faith...

...and there's still room **for YOU!**

[20]Above all, here is what you must understand. No prophecy in Scripture ever came from a prophet's own understanding. [21]It never came simply because a prophet wanted it to. Instead, the Holy Spirit guided the prophets as they spoke. So prophecy comes from God.

False Teachers Will Be Destroyed

2 But there were also false prophets among the people. In the same way there will be false teachers among you. In secret they will bring in teachings that will destroy you. They will even turn against the Lord and Master who died to save them. His death paid for their sins. They will quickly destroy themselves. [2]Many people will follow their shameful ways. They will give the way of truth a bad name.

[3]Those teachers are never satisfied. They want to get something out of you. So they make up stories to take advantage of you. They have been under a sentence of death for a long time. The One who will destroy them has not been sleeping.

[4]God did not spare angels when they sinned. Instead, he sent them to hell. He put them in dark prisons. He will keep them there until he judges them. [5]God did not spare the world's ungodly people long ago. He brought the flood on them. But Noah preached about the right way to live. God kept him safe. He also saved seven others. [6]God judged the cities of Sodom and Gomorrah. He burned them to ashes. He made them an example of what is going to happen to ungodly people.

[7]God saved Lot. He was a man who did what was right. He was shocked by the dirty, sinful lives of people who didn't obey God's laws. [8]That good man lived among them day after day. He saw and heard the evil things they were doing. They were breaking God's laws. And his godly spirit was deeply troubled.

[9]So the Lord knows how to keep godly people safe in times of testing. He also knows how to keep ungodly people under guard until the day they will be judged. In the meantime, he continues to punish them. [10]Most of all, this is true of people who fol-

low the evil longings of their sinful natures. They hate to be under authority.

Those false prophets are bold and proud. They aren't afraid to speak evil things against heavenly beings. [11]Angels are stronger and more powerful than those people. But even angels don't bring to the Lord evil charges against heavenly beings.

[12]Those people speak evil about things they don't understand. They are like wild animals. They do what comes naturally to them. They are born only to be caught and destroyed. Just like animals, they too will die.

[13]They will be paid back with harm for the harm they have done. Their idea of pleasure is to have wild parties in the middle of the day. They are like spots and stains. They enjoy their sinful pleasures while they eat with you. [14]They stare at women who are not their wives. They want to have sex with them. They never stop sinning. They trap those who are not firm in their faith. They have mastered the art of getting what they want. God has placed them under his curse.

[15]They have left God's way. They have wandered off. They follow the way of Balaam, son of Beor. He loved to get paid for doing his evil work. [16]But a donkey corrected him for the wrong he did. Animals don't speak. But the donkey spoke with a human voice. It tried to stop the prophet from doing a very dumb thing.

[17]Those false prophets are like springs without water. They are like mists driven by a storm. The blackest darkness is reserved for them.

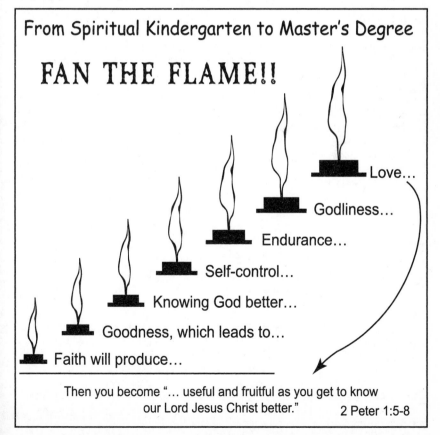

From Spiritual Kindergarten to Master's Degree

FAN THE FLAME!!

Love...

Godliness...

Endurance...

Self-control...

Knowing God better...

Goodness, which leads to...

Faith will produce...

Then you become "... useful and fruitful as you get to know our Lord Jesus Christ better."   2 Peter 1:5-8

[18]They speak empty, bragging words. They make their appeal to the earthly longings of people's sinful nature. They tempt new believers who are just escaping from the company of sinful people. [19]They promise to give freedom to the new believers. But they themselves are slaves to sinful living. A person is a slave to anything that controls him.

[20]They may have escaped the sin of the world. They may have come to know our Lord and Savior Jesus Christ. But what if they are once again caught up in sin? And what if it has become their master? Then they are worse off at the end than they were at the beginning.

[21]What if they had not known the way of godliness? That would have been better than to have known it and then to have turned their backs on it. The way of godliness is the sacred command that was passed on to them.

[22]What the proverbs say about them is true. "A dog returns to where it has thrown up." *(Proverbs 26:11)* And, "A pig that is washed goes back to rolling in the mud."

The Day of the Lord

3 Dear friends, this is now my second letter to you. I have written both of them as reminders. I want to stir you up to think in a way that is pure. [2]I want you to remember the words the holy prophets spoke in the past. Remember the command our Lord and Savior gave through your apostles.

[3]First of all, here is what you must understand. In the last days people will make fun of the truth. They will laugh at it. They will follow their own evil longings. [4]They will say, "Where is this 'return' he promised? Everything goes on in the same way it has since our people of long ago died. In fact, it has continued that way since God first created everything."

[5]Long ago, God's word brought the heavens into being. His word separated the earth from the waters. And the waters surrounded it. But those people forget things like that on purpose. [6]The waters also flooded the world of that time. It was destroyed.

[7]By God's word the heavens and earth of today are being reserved for fire. They are being kept for the day when God will judge. Then ungodly people will be destroyed.

[8]Dear friends, here is one thing you must not forget. With the Lord a day is like a thousand years. And a thousand years are like a day. [9]The Lord is not slow to keep his promise. He is not slow in the way some people understand it. He is patient with you. He doesn't want anyone to be destroyed. Instead, he wants all people to turn away from their sins.

[10]But the day of the Lord will come like a thief. The heavens will disappear with a roar. Fire will destroy everything in them. God will judge the earth and everything in it.

[11]So everything will be destroyed. And what kind of people should you be? You should lead holy and godly lives. [12]Live like that as you look forward to the day of God. It will make the day come more quickly. On that day fire will destroy the heavens. Its heat will melt everything in them.

[13]But we are looking forward to a new heaven and a new earth. Godliness will make its home there. All of this is in keeping with God's promise.

[14]Dear friends, I know you are looking forward to that. So try your best to be found pure and without blame. Be at peace with God. [15]Remember that while our Lord is waiting patiently to return, people are being saved.

Our dear brother Paul also wrote to you about that. God made him wise to write as he did. [16]He writes the same way in all his letters. He speaks about what I have just told you. His letters include some things that are hard to understand. People who don't know better and aren't firm in the faith twist what he says. They twist the other Scriptures too. So they will be destroyed.

[17]Dear friends, you already know that. So be on your guard. Then you won't be led down the wrong path by the mistakes of people who don't obey the law. You won't fall from your safe position.

[18]Grow in the grace of our Lord and Savior Jesus Christ. Get to know him better. Give him glory both now and forever. Amen.

1 JOHN

- *Written by John, the Apostle of Love*
- *John writes as an eyewitness to the historical Jesus*
- *The danger to the Church was not persecution from without, but false teachers from within*
- *Theme: "God is Light, Love, and Life"*

The Word of Life

1 Here is what we announce to everyone about the Word of life. He was already here from the beginning. We have heard him. We have seen him with our eyes. We have looked at him. Our hands have touched him. ²That life has appeared. We have seen him. We give witness about him. And we announce to you that same eternal life. He was already with the Father. He has appeared to us.

³We announce to you what we have seen and heard. We do it so you can share life together with us. And we share life with the Father and with his Son, Jesus Christ. ⁴We are writing this to make our joy complete.

Walking in the Light

⁵Here is the message we have heard from him and announce to you. God is light. There is no darkness in him at all.

⁶Suppose we say that we share life with God but still walk in the darkness. Then we are lying. We are not living by the truth. ⁷But suppose we walk in the light, just as he is in the light. Then we share life with one another. And the blood of Jesus, his Son, makes us pure from all sin.

⁸Suppose we claim we are without sin. Then we are fooling ourselves. The truth is not in us. ⁹But God is faithful and fair. If we admit that we have sinned, he will forgive us our sins. He will forgive every wrong thing we have done. He will make us pure. ¹⁰If we say we have not sinned, we are calling God a liar. His word has no place in our lives.

2 My dear children, I'm writing this to you so that you will not sin. But suppose someone does sin. Then we have one who speaks to the Father for us. He stands up for us. He is Jesus Christ, the Blameless One. ²He gave his life to pay for our sins. But he not only paid for our sins. He also paid for the sins of the whole world.

³We know that we have come to know God if we obey his commands.

⁴Suppose someone says, "I know him." But suppose that person does not do what God commands. Then that person is a liar and is not telling the truth. ⁵But if anyone obeys God's word, then God's love is truly made complete in that person. Here is how we know we belong to him. ⁶Those who claim to belong to him must live just as Jesus did.

⁷Dear friends, I'm not writing you a new command. Instead, I'm writing one you have heard before. You have had it since the beginning.

⁸But I am writing what amounts to a new command. Its truth was shown in how Jesus lived. It is also shown in how you live. The darkness is passing away. The true light is already shining.

⁹Suppose someone claims to be in the light but hates his brother or sister. Then he is still in the darkness.

¹⁰Those who love their brothers and sisters are living in the light. There is nothing in them to make them fall into sin. ¹¹But those who hate a brother or sister are in the darkness. They walk around in the darkness. They don't know where they are going. The darkness has made them blind.

12 Dear children, I'm writing to you
    because your sins have been forgiven.
    They have been forgiven because of
        what Jesus has done.
13 Fathers, I'm writing to you
    because you have known the One who
        is from the beginning.
    Young people, I'm writing to you
    because you have won the battle over
        the evil one.

Dear children, I'm writing to you
    because you have known the Father.
14 Fathers, I'm writing to you
    because you have known the One who
        is from the beginning.
    Young people, I'm writing to you
    because you are strong.
    God's word lives in you.
    You have won the battle over the evil
        one.

Do Not Love the World

15 Do not love the world or anything in it. If you love the world, love for the Father is not in you.

16 Here is what people who belong to this world do. They try to satisfy what their sinful natures want to do. They long for what their sinful eyes look at. They brag about what they have and what they do. All of this comes from the world. It doesn't come from the Father.

17 The world and its evil longings are passing away. But those who do what God wants them to do live forever.

A Warning About the Enemies of Christ

18 Dear children, we are living in the last days. You have heard that the great enemy of Christ is coming. But even now many enemies of Christ have already come. That's

---

"I'm not a Christian because ..."

"There is no hope for me."

Jesus' ministry was to reach out and give sinners hope.

"I have not come to get those who think they are right with God to follow me. I have come to get sinners to follow me." Mark 2:17

There once was a criminal who committed such evil that he was given the death penalty. He had no chance to be good or do good. He did the only thing he could:

The criminal looked to Jesus and Jesus accepted him!

The thief on the cross said: "We are getting just what our actions call for ... Jesus, remember me when you come into your Kingdom." Jesus replied: "Today you will be with me in paradise." Luke 23:41–43

"God is faithful and fair. If we admit that we have sinned, he will forgive us our sins ... He will make us pure." 1 John 1:9

how we know that these are the last days.

¹⁹The enemies left our group. They didn't really belong to us. If they had belonged to us, they would have remained with us. But by leaving they showed that none of them belonged to us.

²⁰You have received the Spirit from the Holy One. And all of you know the truth. ²¹I'm not writing to you because you don't know the truth but because you do know it. I'm writing to you because no lie comes from the truth.

²²Who is the liar? The person who says that Jesus is not the Christ. People who say that are the enemies of Christ. They say no to the Father and the Son. ²³Those who say no to the Son don't belong to the Father. But anyone who says yes to the Son belongs to the Father also.

²⁴Make sure that you don't forget what you have heard from the beginning. Then you will remain joined to the Son and to the Father. ²⁵That's what God has promised us. We have eternal life.

²⁶I'm writing these things to warn you about those who are trying to lead you down the wrong path.

²⁷But you have received the Holy Spirit from God. He continues to live in you. So you don't need anyone to teach you. God's Spirit teaches you about everything. What he says is true. He doesn't lie. Remain joined to Christ, just as you have been taught by the Spirit.

Children of God

²⁸Dear children, remain joined to Christ. Then when he comes, we can be bold. We will not be ashamed to meet him when he comes.

²⁹You know that God is right and always does what is right. And you know that everyone who does what is right has been born again because of what God has done.

3 How great is the love the Father has given us so freely! Now we can be called children of God. And that's what we really are! The world doesn't know us because it didn't know him.

²Dear friends, now we are children of God. He still hasn't let us know what we will be.

But we know that when Christ appears, we will be like him. We will see him as he really is. ³He is pure. All who hope to be like him make themselves pure.

⁴Everyone who sins breaks the law. In fact, breaking the law is sin. ⁵But you know that Christ came to take our sins away. And there is no sin in him. ⁶No one who remains joined to him keeps on sinning. No one who keeps on sinning has seen him or known him.

⁷Dear children, don't let anyone lead you down the wrong path. Those who do what is right are holy, just as Christ is holy. ⁸Those who do what is sinful belong to the devil. They are just like him. He has been sinning from the beginning. But the Son of God came to destroy the devil's work.

⁹Those who are born again because of what God has done will not keep on sinning. God's very nature remains in them. They can't go on sinning. They have been born again because of what God has done.

¹⁰Here is how you can tell the difference between the children of God and the children of the devil. Those who don't do what is right do not belong to God. Those who don't love their brothers and sisters do not belong to him either.

Love One Another

¹¹From the beginning we have heard that we should love one another. ¹²Don't be like Cain. He belonged to the evil one. He murdered his brother. And why did he murder him? Because the things Cain had done were wrong. But the things his brother had done were right.

¹³My brothers and sisters, don't be surprised if the world hates you. ¹⁴We know that we have left our old dead condition and entered into new life. We know it because we love one another. Those who do not are still living in their old condition.

¹⁵Those who hate their brothers and sisters are murderers. And you know that murderers do not have eternal life in their hearts.

¹⁶We know what love is because Jesus Christ gave his life for us. So we should give our lives for our brothers and sisters.

[17]Suppose someone sees a brother or sister in need and is able to help them. If he doesn't take pity on them, how can the love of God be in him?

[18]Dear children, don't just talk about love. Put your love into action. Then it will truly be love. [19]That's how we know that we hold to the truth. And that's how we put our hearts at rest, knowing that God is watching. [20]Our hearts may judge us. But God is greater than our hearts. He knows everything.

[21]Dear friends, if our hearts do not judge us, we can be bold with God. [22]And he will give us anything we ask. That's because we obey his commands. We do what pleases him.

[23]God has commanded us to believe in the name of his Son, Jesus Christ. He has also commanded us to love one another. [24]Those who obey his commands remain joined to him. And he remains joined to them.

How do we know that God lives in us? We know it because of the Holy Spirit he gave us.

Put the Spirits to the Test

4 Dear friends, do not believe every spirit. Put the spirits to the test to see if they belong to God. Many false prophets have gone out into the world.

[2]How can you recognize the Spirit of God? Every spirit that agrees that Jesus Christ came in a human body belongs to God. [3]But every spirit that doesn't agree with this does not belong to God. It is the spirit of the great enemy of Christ. You have heard that the enemy is coming. Even now he is already in the world.

[4]Dear children, you belong to God. You have not accepted the teachings of the false prophets. That's because the One who is in you is more powerful than the one who is in the world.

[5]False prophets belong to the world. So they speak from the world's point of view. The world listens to them. [6]We belong to God. And those who know God listen to us. But those who don't belong to God don't listen to us. That's how we can tell the difference between the Spirit of truth and the spirit of lies.

We Love Because God Loved Us

[7]Dear friends, let us love one another, because love comes from God. Everyone who loves has been born again because of what God has done. That person knows God. [8]Anyone who does not love does not know God, because God is love.

[9]How did God show his love for us? He sent his one and only Son into the world. He sent him so we could receive life through

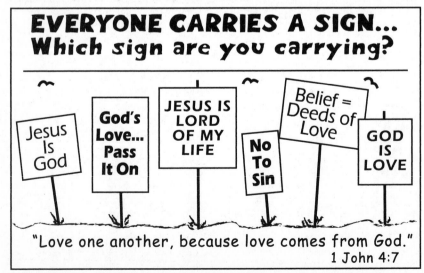

EVERYONE CARRIES A SIGN...
Which sign are you carrying?

Jesus Is God

God's Love... Pass It On

JESUS IS LORD OF MY LIFE

No To Sin

Belief = Deeds of Love

GOD IS LOVE

"Love one another, because love comes from God."
1 John 4:7

him.

[10]What is love? It is not that we loved God. It is that he loved us and sent his Son to give his life to pay for our sins.

[11]Dear friends, since God loved us that much, we should also love one another. [12]No one has ever seen God. But if we love one another, God lives in us. His love is made complete in us.

[13]We know that we belong to him and he belongs to us. He has given us his Holy Spirit.

[14]The Father has sent his Son to be the Savior of the world. We have seen it. We give witness to it. [15]God lives in anyone who agrees that Jesus is the Son of God. That kind of person remains joined to God. [16]So we know that God loves us. We depend on it.

God is love. Anyone who leads a life of love shows that he is joined to God. And God is joined to him.

[17]So love is made complete among us. We will be bold on the day God judges us. That's because in this world we love as Jesus did.

[18]There is no fear in love. Instead, perfect love drives fear away. Fear has to do with being punished. The one who fears does not have perfect love.

[19]We love because he loved us first. [20]Any-one who says he loves God but in fact hates his brother or sister is a liar. He doesn't love his brother or sister, whom he has seen. So he can't love God, whom he has not seen.

[21]Here is the command God has given us. Anyone who loves God must also love his brothers and sisters.

Faith in the Son of God

5 Everyone who believes that Jesus is the Christ is born again because of what God has done. And everyone who loves the Father loves his children as well.

[2]How do we know that we love God's children? We know it when we love God and obey his commands. [3]Here is what it means to love God. It means that we obey his commands. And his commands are not hard to obey. [4]That's because everyone who is a child of God has won the battle over the world. Our faith has won the battle for us.

[5]Who is it that has won the battle over the world? Only the person who believes that Jesus is the Son of God.

[6]Jesus Christ is the one who was baptized in water and died on the cross. He wasn't just baptized in water. He also died on the cross. The Holy Spirit has given a truthful witness about him. That's because the Spirit is the truth.

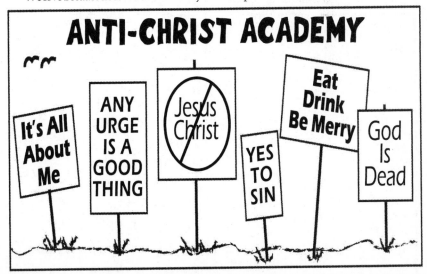

[7]There are three that give witness about Jesus. [8]They are the Holy Spirit, the baptism of Jesus and his death. And the three of them agree.

[9]We accept the witness of people. But the witness of God is more important because it is God who gives it. He has given witness about his Son.

[10]Those who believe in the Son of God have accepted that witness in their hearts. Those who do not believe God's witness are calling him a liar. That's because they have not believed his witness about his Son.

[11]Here is God's witness. He has given us eternal life. That life is found in his Son. [12]Those who belong to the Son have life. Those who do not belong to the Son of God do not have life.

Final Words

[13]I'm writing these things to you who believe in the name of the Son of God. I'm doing it so you will know that you have eternal life.

[14]There is one thing we can be sure of when we come to God in prayer. If we ask anything in keeping with what he wants, he hears us. [15]If we know that God hears what we ask for, we know that we have it.

[16]Suppose you see your brother or sister commit a sin. But that sin is not the kind that leads to death. Then you should pray for them. And God will give life to them. I'm talking about someone whose sin does not lead to death. But there is a sin that does lead to death. I'm not saying that you should pray about that. [17]Every wrong thing we do is sin. But there are sins that do not lead to death.

[18]We know that those who are children of God do not keep on sinning. The Son of God keeps them safe. The evil one can't harm them. [19]We know that we are children of God. We know that the whole world is under the control of the evil one.

[20]We also know that the Son of God has come. He has given us understanding. Now we can know the One who is true. And we belong to the One who is true. We also belong to his Son, Jesus Christ. He is the true God. He is eternal life.

[21]Dear children, keep away from statues of gods.

Overcome the World's Hurdles

"Everyone who is a child of God has won the battle over the world. Our faith has won the battle for us."

1 John 5:4

2 JOHN

- *John addresses this personal letter to a prominent woman in one of the churches*
- *John cautions her to withhold hospitality to false teachers*
- *First John emphasizes love - Second John emphasizes truth*
- *Theme: "Stand Firm in the Truth Against False Teachers"*

¹I, the elder, am writing this letter.

I am sending it to the chosen lady and her children. I love all of you because of the truth. I'm not the only one who loves you. So does everyone who knows the truth. ²I love you because of the truth that is alive in us. That truth will be with us forever.

³God the Father and Jesus Christ his Son will give you grace, mercy and peace. Those blessings will be with us because we love the truth.

⁴It has given me great joy to find some of your children living by the truth. That's just what the Father commanded us to do.

⁵Dear lady, I'm not writing you a new command. I'm writing a command we've had from the beginning. I'm asking that we love one another. ⁶The way we show our love is to obey God's commands. He commands you to lead a life of love. That's what you have heard from the beginning.

⁷Many people who try to fool others have gone out into the world. They don't agree that Jesus Christ came in a human body. People like that try to trick others. They are enemies of Christ. ⁸Watch out that you don't lose what you have worked for. Make sure that you get your complete reward.

⁹Some people run ahead of others. They don't follow the teaching of Christ. People like that don't belong to God. But those who follow the teaching of Christ belong to the Father and the Son.

¹⁰Suppose someone comes to you and doesn't teach these truths. Then don't take him into your house. Don't welcome him. ¹¹Anyone who welcomes him shares in his evil work.

¹²I have a lot to write to you. But I don't want to use paper and ink. Instead, I hope I can visit you. Then I can talk with you face to face. That will make our joy complete.

¹³The children of your chosen sister send their greetings.

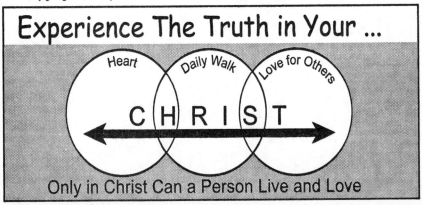

Experience The Truth in Your ...

Heart   Daily Walk   Love for Others

C H R I S T

Only in Christ Can a Person Live and Love

3 JOHN

- *Written by John to his friend Gaius, who was a prominent leader in one of the churches*
- *John encouraged Gaius to continue to show hospitality to traveling teachers as they established local churches*
- *Theme: "Practice Hospitality toward Teachers of the Truth"*

[1]I, the elder, am writing this letter.

I am sending it to you, my dear friend Gaius. I love you because of the truth.

[2]Dear friend, I know that your spiritual life is going well. I pray that you also may enjoy good health. And I pray that everything else may go well with you.

[3]Some believers came to me and told me that you are faithful to the truth. They told me that you continue to live by it. That gave me great joy. [4]I have no greater joy than to hear that my children are living by the truth.

[5]Dear friend, you are faithful in what you are doing for the believers. You are faithful even though they are strangers to you. [6]They have told the church about your love. Please help them by sending them on their way in a manner that honors God.

[7]They started on their journey to serve Jesus Christ. They didn't receive any help from those who aren't believers. [8]So we should welcome people like them. We should work together with them for the truth.

[9]I wrote to the church. But Diotrephes won't have anything to do with us. He loves to be the first in everything. [10]So if I come, I will point out what he is doing. He is saying evil things about us to others. Even that doesn't satisfy him. He refuses to welcome other believers. He also keeps others from welcoming them. In fact, he throws them out of the church.

[11]Dear friend, don't be like those who do evil. Be like those who do good. Anyone who does what is good belongs to God. Anyone who does what is evil hasn't really seen or known God.

[12]Everyone says good things about Demetrius. He lives in keeping with the truth. We also say good things about him. And you know that our witness is true.

[13]I have a lot to write to you. But I don't want to write with pen and ink. [14]I hope I can see you soon. Then we can talk face to face.

May you have peace. The friends here send their greetings. Greet the friends there by name.

"Let us keep running...looking to Jesus."
Hebrews 12:1,2

"I'm not a Christian because ..."

"I believe in evolution ... not in divine design".

How did this world and its intricate details appear?

"Just happen" or "Divine Design"

There are millions of examples of "design" in our world. Follow the path of a salmon egg inserted in a quite brook in Washington state. After the egg develops into a fish, the fish travels a journey up to 2000 miles through a stream, a river, Puget Sound, and into the Pacific Ocean. There it may spend up to seven years going as far as Japan - close to 6000 miles away. Yet the salmon returns to the EXACT brook where it began! How can this be?

Some evolutionist use the word "INSTINCT" but are unable to explain its source. INSTINCT is God's "computer chip" instilled within His creatures to equip and guide them.

In a similar way, each of us has an "inner computer chip" to guide us to the Creator. Yet we ...

- build altars to false gods
- worship things
- pursue evil
- create false religions

Are we trying to avoid the Designer of life by denying the design of life? Because of sin, our "inner computer chip" needs reprogramming so we can find our way "back home" to the Creator. And it is through Christ we truly see God's creative power.

"All things were created by Him. He created everything in heaven and on earth. He created everything that can be seen and everything that can't be seen... Before everything was created, He was already there. He holds everything together."
Colossians 1:16,17

JUDE

- *Written by Jude, a brother of Jesus*
- *He warns of the coming Apostasy and false teachers*
- *Jude paints a vivid portrait of false teachers as self-centered, immoral, "doubly dead" trees*
- *Theme: "Stand Firm Against False Teaching"*

¹I, Jude, am writing this letter. I serve Jesus Christ. I am a brother of James.

I am sending this letter to you who have been chosen by God. You are loved by God the Father. You are kept safe by Jesus Christ.

²May more and more mercy, peace, and love be given to you.

A Warning Against Ungodly Teachers

³Dear friends, I really wanted to write to you about the salvation we share. But now I feel I should write and ask you to stand up for the faith. God's people were trusted with it once and for all time.

⁴Certain people have slipped in among you in secret. Long ago it was written that they would be judged. They are godless people. They use the grace of our God as an excuse for sexual sins. They say no to Jesus Christ. He is our only Lord and King.

⁵I want to remind you about some things you already know. The Lord saved his people. He brought them out of Egypt. But later he destroyed those who did not believe. ⁶Some of the angels didn't stay where they belonged. They didn't keep their positions of authority. The Lord has kept those angels in darkness. They are held by chains that last forever. On judgment day, God will judge them.

⁷The people of Sodom and Gomorrah and the towns around them also did evil things. They gave themselves over to sexual sins. They committed sins of the worst possible kind. They are an example of those who are punished with fire. The fire never goes out.

⁸In the very same way, those dreamers pollute their own bodies. They don't accept authority. They speak evil things against heavenly beings. ⁹But not even Michael did that. He was the leader of the angels. He argued with the devil about the body of Moses. But he didn't dare to speak evil things against the devil. Instead, he said, "May the Lord stop you!"

¹⁰But those people speak evil things against what they don't understand. They are like wild animals. They can't think for themselves. They do what comes naturally to them. Those are the very things that destroy them.

¹¹How terrible it will be for them! They followed the way of Cain. They rushed ahead and made the same mistake as Balaam did. They did it because they loved money. They are like Korah. He turned against his leaders. Those people will certainly be destroyed, just as Korah was.

¹²They are like stains at the meals you share. They eat too much. They have no shame. They are shepherds who feed only themselves. They are like clouds without rain. They are blown along by the wind. They are like trees in the fall. Since they have no fruit, they are pulled up. So they die twice.

¹³They are like wild waves of the sea. Their shame rises up like foam. They are like falling stars. God has reserved a place of very black darkness for them. He will keep them there forever.

¹⁴Enoch was the seventh man in the family line of Adam. He gave a prophecy about

those people. He said, "Look! The Lord is coming with thousands and thousands of his holy ones. [15]He is coming to judge everyone. He is coming to sentence all ungodly people. He will judge them for all the ungodly acts they have done. They have done them in ungodly ways. He will sentence ungodly sinners for all the bad things they have said about him."

[16]Those people complain. They find fault with others. They follow their own evil longings. They brag about themselves. They praise others to help themselves.

Remain in God's Love

[17]Dear friends, remember what the apostles of our Lord Jesus Christ said was going to happen. [18]They told you, "In the last days, some people will make fun of the truth. They will follow their own ungodly longings." [19]They are the people who separate you from one another. They do only what comes naturally. They are not led by the Holy Spirit.

[20]Dear friends, build yourselves up in your most holy faith. Let the Holy Spirit guide and help you when you pray. [21]The mercy of our Lord Jesus Christ will bring you eternal life. As you wait for his mercy, remain in God's love.

[22]Show mercy to those who doubt. [23]Pull others out of the fire. Save them. To others, show mercy mixed with fear. Hate even the clothes that are stained by the sins of those who wear them.

Praise to God

[24]Give praise to the One who is able to keep you from falling into sin. He will bring you into his heavenly glory without any fault. He will bring you there with great joy. [25]Give praise to the only God. He is our Savior. Glory, majesty, power and authority belong to him. Give praise to him through Jesus Christ our Lord. Give praise to the One who was before all time, who now is, and who will be forever. Amen.

REVELATION

- *Written by John to the seven churches in Asia*
- *John records a vision that he had while in exile*
- *The book starts with a promise (1:3) and ends with a warning (22:18)*
- *Theme: "God Is Sovereign Over All History"*

1 This is the revelation that God gave to Jesus Christ. Jesus shows those who serve God what will happen soon. God made it known by sending his angel to his servant John. ²John gives witness to everything he saw. The things he gives witness to are God's word and what Jesus Christ has said.

³Blessed is the one who reads the words of this prophecy. Blessed are those who hear it and think everything it says is important. The time when these things will come true is near.

Greetings

⁴I, John, am writing this letter.

I am sending it to the seven churches in Asia Minor.

May grace and peace come to you from the One who is, and who was, and who will come. May grace and peace come to you from the seven spirits who are in front of God's throne. ⁵May grace and peace come to you from Jesus Christ. What Jesus gives witness to can always be trusted. He was the first to rise from the dead. He rules over the kings of the earth.

Give glory and power to the One who loves us! He has set us free from our sins by pouring out his blood for us. ⁶He has made us members of his royal family. He has made us priests who serve his God and Father. Give him glory and power for ever and ever! Amen.

⁷Look! He is coming with the clouds!
   Every eye will see him.
Even those who pierced him will see him.
   All the nations of the earth will be sad
   because of him.
      This will really happen!
      Amen.

⁸"I am the Alpha and the Omega, the First and the Last," says the Lord God. "I am the One who is, and who was, and who will come. I am the Mighty One."

One Who Looks Like a Son of Man

⁹I, John, am a believer like you. I am a friend who suffers like you. As members of Jesus' royal family, we can put up with anything that happens to us.

I was on the island of Patmos because I taught God's word and what Jesus said. ¹⁰The Holy Spirit took complete control of me on the Lord's Day. I heard a loud voice behind me that sounded like a trumpet. ¹¹The voice said, "Write on a scroll what you see. Send it to the seven churches in Asia Minor. They are Ephesus, Smyrna, Pergamum, Thyatira, Sardis, Philadelphia and Laodicea."

¹²I turned around to see who was speaking to me. When I turned, I saw seven golden lampstands. ¹³In the middle of them was someone who looked "like a son of man." *(Daniel 7:13)*

He was dressed in a long robe with a gold strip of cloth around his chest. ¹⁴The hair on his head was white like wool, as white as snow. His eyes were like a blazing fire. ¹⁵His feet were like bronze metal glowing in a furnace. His voice sounded like rushing waters. ¹⁶He held seven stars in his right hand. Out of his mouth came a sharp sword that had two edges. His face was like the sun shining in all of its brightness.

¹⁷When I saw him, I fell at his feet as if I were dead.

Then he put his right hand on me and said, "Do not be afraid. I am the First and the Last. ¹⁸I am the Living One. I was dead.

But look! I am alive for ever and ever! And I hold the keys to Death and Hell.

¹⁹"So write down what you have seen. Write about what is happening now and what will happen later. ²⁰Here is what the mystery of the seven stars you saw in my right hand means. They are the angels of the seven churches. And the seven golden lampstands you saw stand for the seven churches.

The Letter to the Church in Ephesus

2 "Here is what I command you to write to the church in Ephesus.

Here are the words of the One who holds the seven stars in his right hand. He also walks among the seven golden lampstands. He says, ²"I know what you are doing. You work long and hard. I know you can't put up with those who are evil. You have tested those who claim to be apostles but are not. You have found out that they are liars. ³You have been faithful and have put up with a lot of trouble because of me. You have not given up.

⁴"But here is something I hold against you. You don't have as much love as you had at first. ⁵Remember how far you have fallen! Turn away from your sins. Do the things you did at first. If you don't, I will come to you and remove your lampstand from its place.

⁶"But you do have this in your favor. You hate the way the Nicolaitans act. I hate it too.

⁷"Those who have ears should listen to what the Holy Spirit says to the churches. I will allow those who overcome to eat from the tree of life in God's paradise.'

The Letter to the Church in Smyrna

⁸"Here is what I command you to write to the church in Smyrna.

Here are the words of the One who is the First and the Last. He is the One who died and came to life again. He says, ⁹"I know that you suffer and are poor. But you are rich! Some people say they are Jews but are not. I know that their words are evil. Their worship is satanic.

¹⁰"Don't be afraid of what you are going to suffer. I tell you, the devil will put some of you in prison to test you. You will be treated badly for ten days. Be faithful, even if it means you must die. Then I will give you a crown. The crown is life itself.

¹¹"Those who have ears should listen to what the Holy Spirit says to the churches. Those who overcome will not be hurt at all by the second death.'

The Letter to the Church in Pergamum

¹²"Here is what I command you to write to the church in Pergamum.

Here are the words of the One with the sharp sword that has two edges. He says, ¹³"I know that you live where Satan has his throne. But you remain true to me. You did not give up your faith in me, even in the days of Antipas, my faithful witness. He was put to death in your city, where Satan lives.

¹⁴"But I have a few things against you. You have people there who follow the teaching of Balaam. He taught Balak to lead the people of Israel into sin. So they ate food that had been offered to statues of gods. And they committed sexual sins. ¹⁵You also have people who follow the teaching of the Nicolaitans.

¹⁶"So turn away from your sins! If you don't, I will come to you soon. I will fight against those people with the sword that comes out of my mouth.

¹⁷"Those who have ears should listen to what the Holy Spirit says to the churches. I will give hidden manna to those who overcome. I will also give each of them a white stone with a new name written on it. Only the one who receives that name will know what it is.'

The Seven Churches in Revelation

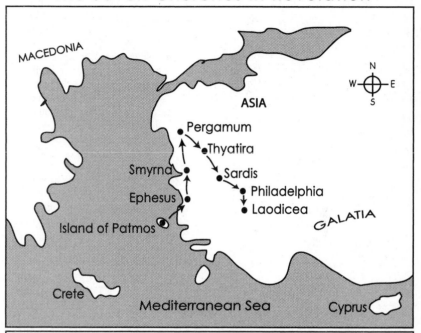

The Seven Churches in Revelation

Church	Positive	Negative	Reward
Ephesus	Patient Endurance	Left First Love	Eat from the "Tree of Life"
Smyrna	Remain Faithful	——	"Crown of Life"
Pergamum	Remain Loyal	Tolerated False Teaching	"New Name"
Thyatira	Constant Improvement	"Deeper Truth" Heresy	*"Morning Star"*
Sardis	Some Are Faithful	"Wake Up"	Clothed in White
Philadelphia	Obey My Word	——	Citizens of New Jerusalem
Laodicea	——	"I Will Spit You Out"	Share a meal with Christ

Of the seven churches, Laodicea most closely resembles our contemporary churches. Not wanting to appear dogmatic or extreme (for Christ), they seek the middle ground of compromise by "tolerance" and "political correctness." They deny the doctrines of the faith and become "world friendly." God's response: "I will spit them out from my mouth."

The Letter to the Church in Thyatira

¹⁸"Here is what I command you to write to the church in Thyatira.

Here are the words of the Son of God. He is the One whose eyes are like blazing fire. His feet are like polished bronze. He says, ¹⁹'I know what you are doing. I know your love and your faith. I know how well you have served. I know you don't give up easily. In fact, you are doing more now than you did at first.

²⁰'But here is what I have against you. You put up with that woman Jezebel. She calls herself a prophet. With her teaching, she has led my servants into sexual sin. She has tricked them into eating food offered to statues of gods.

²¹'I've given her time to turn away from her sinful ways. But she doesn't want to. ²²She sinned on a bed. So I will make her suffer on a bed. And those who commit adultery with her will suffer greatly. Their only way out is to turn away from what she taught them to do. ²³I will strike her children dead. Then all the churches will know that I am the One who searches hearts and minds. I will pay each of you back for what you have done.

²⁴'I won't bother the rest of you in Thyatira. You don't follow the teaching of Jezebel. You haven't learned what some people call Satan's deep secrets. ²⁵Just hold on to what you have until I come.

²⁶'I'll give authority over the nations to all who overcome and who carry out my plans to the end. ²⁷It is written,

' "He will rule them with an iron rod.
He will break them to pieces like clay pots." *(Psalm 2:9)*

I have received this authority from my Father. ²⁸I will also give the morning star to all who overcome.

²⁹'Those who have ears should listen to what the Holy Spirit says to the churches.'

The Letter to the Church in Sardis

3 "Here is what I command you to write to the church in Sardis.

Here are the words of the One who holds the seven spirits of God. He has the seven stars in his hand. He says, 'I know what you are doing. People think you are alive, but you are dead. ²Wake up! Strengthen what is left, or it will die. You have not done all that my God wants you to do.

³'So remember what you have been taught and have heard. Obey it. Turn away from your sins. If you don't wake up, I will come like a thief. You won't know when I will come to you.

⁴'But you have a few people in Sardis who have kept their clothes clean. They will walk with me, dressed in white, because they are worthy. ⁵Those who overcome will also be dressed in white. I will never erase their names from the Book of Life. I will speak of them by name to my Father and his angels.

⁶'Those who have ears should listen to what the Holy Spirit says to the churches.'

The Letter to the Church in Philadelphia

⁷"Here is what I command you to write to the church in Philadelphia.

Here are the words of the One who is holy and true. He holds the key of David. No one can shut what he opens. And no one can open what he shuts. He says, ⁸'I know what you are doing. Look! I have put an open door in front of you. No one can shut it. I know that you don't have much strength. But you have obeyed my word. You have not said no to me.

⁹'Some people claim they are Jews but are not. They are liars. Their worship is from Satan. I will make them come and fall down at your feet. I will

make them say in public that I love you.

[10]'You have kept my command to put up with anything that happens. So I will keep you from the time of suffering that is going to come to the whole world. It will test those who live on the earth.

[11]'I am coming soon. Hold on to what you have. Then no one will take away your crown.

[12]'I'll see to it that those who overcome will be pillars in the temple of my God. They will never leave it again. I will write the name of my God on them. I will write the name of the city of my God on them. This is the new Jerusalem, which is coming down out of heaven from my God. I will also write my new name on them.

[13]'Those who have ears should listen to what the Holy Spirit says to the churches.'

The Letter to the Church in Laodicea

[14]"Here is what I command you to write to the church in Laodicea.

Here are the words of the One who is the Amen. What he gives witness to is faithful and true. He rules over what God has created. He says, [15]'I know

"Here I am! I stand at the door and knock. If any of you hears my voice and opens the door, I will come in and eat with you. And you will eat with me." Jesus (Revelation 3:20)

Jesus is knocking at your heart's door, calling you to put aside your ego-driven way of life and invite Him in as your Lord. Although He is Almighty God, He will not force His way into an unwilling heart. Get up! Go to the door! Invite Jesus Christ to enter your life.

"Come into my life, Lord Jesus ... I accept Your peace, Your purpose and Your power into my life!"

what you are doing. I know you aren't cold or hot. I wish you were either one or the other! [16]But you are lukewarm. You aren't hot or cold. So I am going to spit you out of my mouth.

[17]You say, "I am rich. I've become wealthy and don't need anything." But you don't realize how pitiful and miserable you have become. You are poor, blind and naked.

[18]So here's my advice. Buy from me gold made pure by fire. Then you will become rich. Buy from me white clothes to wear. Then you will be able to cover your shameful nakedness. And buy from me healing lotion to put on your eyes. Then you will be able to see.

[19]I correct and train those I love. So be sincere, and turn away from your sins.

[20]Here I am! I stand at the door and knock. If any of you hears my voice and opens the door, I will come in and eat with you. And you will eat with me.

[21]I'll give those who overcome the right to sit with me on my throne. In the same way, I overcame. Then I sat down with my Father on his throne.

[22]Those who have ears should listen to what the Holy Spirit says to the churches.' "

The Throne in Heaven

4 After this I looked, and there in front of me was a door standing open in heaven. I heard the voice I had heard before. It sounded like a trumpet. The voice said, "Come up here. I will show you what must happen after this."

[2]At once the Holy Spirit took complete control of me. There in front of me was a throne in heaven with someone sitting on it. [3]The One who sat there shone like jewels. Around the throne was a rainbow that looked like an emerald.

[4]Twenty-four other thrones surrounded that throne. Twenty-four elders were sitting on them. The elders were dressed in white. They had gold crowns on their heads.

[5]From the throne came flashes of lightning, rumblings and thunder. Seven lamps were blazing in front of the throne. These stand for the seven spirits of God. [6]There was something that looked like a sea of glass in front of the throne. It was as clear as crystal.

In the inner circle, around the throne, were four living creatures. They were covered with eyes, in front and in back. [7]The first creature looked like a lion. The second looked like an ox. The third had a man's face. The fourth looked like a flying eagle. [8]Each of the four living creatures had six wings. Each creature was covered all over with eyes, even under the wings. Day and night, they never stop saying,

"Holy, holy, holy
is the Lord God who rules over all.
He was, and he is, and he will come."

[9]The living creatures give glory, honor and thanks to the One who sits on the throne and who lives for ever and ever. [10]At the same time, the 24 elders fall down and worship the One who sits on the throne and who lives for ever and ever. They lay their crowns in front of the throne. They say,

[11]"You are worthy, our Lord and God!
You are worthy to receive glory and
honor and power.
You are worthy because you created all
things.
They were created and they exist.
That is the way you planned it."

The Scroll and the Lamb

5 Then I saw a scroll in the right hand of the One sitting on the throne. The scroll had writing on both sides. It was sealed with seven seals.

**We are products of our past...
but we don't have to be prisoners of it.**

[2]I saw a mighty angel calling out in a loud voice, "Who is worthy to break the seals and open the scroll?" [3]But no one in heaven or on earth or under the earth could open the scroll. No one could even look inside it.

[4]I cried and cried because no one was found who was worthy to open the scroll or look inside.

[5]Then one of the elders said to me, "Do not cry! The Lion of the tribe of Judah has won the battle. He is the Root of David. He is able to break the seven seals and open the scroll."

[6]Then I saw a Lamb that looked as if he had been put to death. He stood in the center of the area around the throne. The Lamb was surrounded by the four living creatures and the elders. He had seven horns and seven eyes. The eyes stand for the seven spirits of God, which are sent out into all the earth.

[7]The Lamb came and took the scroll from the right hand of the One sitting on the throne. [8]Then the four living creatures and the 24 elders fell down in front of the Lamb. Each one had a harp. They were holding golden bowls full of incense, which stand for the prayers of God's people.

[9]Here is the new song they sang.

"You are worthy to take the scroll
 and break open its seals.
You are worthy because you were put to
  death.
  With your blood you bought people
   for God.
  They come from every tribe, language,
   people and nation.
[10]You have made them members of a
   royal family.
  You have made them priests to serve
   our God.
  They will rule on the earth."

[11]Then I looked and heard the voice of millions and millions of angels. They surrounded the throne. They surrounded the living creatures and the elders. [12]In a loud voice they sang,

"The Lamb, who was put to death, is
  worthy!
He is worthy to receive power and
  wealth and wisdom and strength!

He is worthy to receive honor and glory
  and praise!"

[13]All creatures in heaven, on earth, under the earth, and on the sea, and all that is in them, were singing. I heard them say,

"May praise and honor for ever and ever
  be given to the One who sits on the
   throne and to the Lamb!
Give them glory and power
  for ever and ever!"

[14]The four living creatures said, "Amen." And the elders fell down and worshiped.

The Seals

6 I watched as the Lamb broke open the first of the seven seals. Then I heard one of the four living creatures say in a voice that sounded like thunder, "Come!" [2]I looked, and there in front of me was a white horse! Its rider held a bow in his hands. He was given a crown. He rode out like a hero on his way to victory.

[3]The Lamb broke open the second seal. Then I heard the second living creature say, "Come!" [4]Another horse came out. It was flaming red. Its rider was given power to take peace from the earth and to make people kill each other. He was given a large sword.

[5]The Lamb broke open the third seal. Then I heard the third living creature say, "Come!" I looked, and there in front of me was a black horse! Its rider was holding a pair of scales in his hand. [6]Next, I heard what sounded like a voice coming from among the four living creatures. It said, "A quart of wheat for a day's pay. And three quarts of barley for a day's pay. But don't spoil the olive oil and the wine!"

[7]The Lamb broke open the fourth seal. Then I heard the voice of the fourth living creature say, "Come!" [8]I looked, and there in front of me was a pale horse! Its rider's name was Death. Following close behind him was Hell. They were given power over a fourth of the earth. They were given power to kill people with the sword, hunger and sickness. They could also use the earth's wild animals to kill.

[9]He broke open the fifth seal. I saw souls under the altar. They were the souls of peo-

ple who were killed because of God's word and their faithful witness. [10]They called out in a loud voice. "How long, Lord and King, holy and true?" they asked. "How long will you wait to judge those who live on the earth? How long will it be until you pay them back for killing us?"

[11]Then each of them was given a white robe. "Wait a little longer," they were told. "There are still more of your believing brothers and sisters who must be killed."

[12]I watched as he broke open the sixth seal. There was a powerful earthquake. The sun turned black like black clothes that were made from the hair of a goat. The whole moon turned as red as blood. [13]The stars in the sky fell to earth. They dropped like ripe figs from a tree shaken by a strong wind. [14]The sky rolled back like a scroll. Every mountain and island was moved out of its place.

[15]Everyone hid in caves and among the rocks of the mountains. This included the kings of the earth, the princes and the generals, rich people and powerful people. It also included every slave and everyone who was free. [16]They called out to the mountains and rocks, "Fall on us! Hide us from the face of the One who sits on the throne! Hide us from the anger of the Lamb! [17]The great day of their anger has come. Who can live through it?"

144,000 Are Sealed

7 After this I saw four angels. They were standing at the four corners of the earth. They were holding back the four winds of the earth. This kept the winds from blowing on the land or on the sea or on any tree.

[2]Then I saw another angel coming up from the east. He had the seal of the living God. He called out in a loud voice to the four angels who had been allowed to harm the land and the sea. [3]"Do not harm the land or the sea or the trees," he said. "Wait until we mark with a seal the foreheads of those who serve our God."

[4]Then I heard how many people were sealed. There were 144,000 from all the tribes of Israel.

[5]From the tribe of Judah, 12,000 were sealed.

From the tribe of Reuben, 12,000.
From the tribe of Gad, 12,000.
[6]From the tribe of Asher, 12,000.
From the tribe of Naphtali, 12,000.
From the tribe of Manasseh, 12,000.
[7]From the tribe of Simeon, 12,000.
From the tribe of Levi, 12,000.
From the tribe of Issachar, 12,000.
[8]From the tribe of Zebulun, 12,000.
From the tribe of Joseph, 12,000.
From the tribe of Benjamin, 12,000.

The Huge Crowd Wearing White Robes

[9]After this I looked, and there in front of me was a huge crowd of people. They stood in front of the throne and in front of the Lamb. There were so many that no one could count them. They came from every nation, tribe, people and language. They were wearing white robes. In their hands they were holding palm branches. [10]They cried out in a loud voice,

"Salvation belongs to our God,
who sits on the throne.
Salvation also belongs to the Lamb."

[11]All the angels were standing around the throne. They were standing around the elders and the four living creatures. They fell down on their faces in front of the throne and worshiped God. [12]They said,

"Amen!
May praise and glory
and wisdom be given to our God for ever and ever.
Give him thanks and honor and power and strength.
Amen!"

[13]Then one of the elders spoke to me. "Who are these people dressed in white robes?" he asked. "Where did they come from?"

[14]I answered, "Sir, you know."

He said, "They are the ones who have come out of the time of terrible suffering. They have washed their robes and made them white in the blood of the Lamb. [15]So

"they are in front of the throne of God.
They serve him day and night in his temple.
The One who sits on the throne will

POINTS TO PONDER

● GOD IS GOD -- YOU'RE NOT ● LIFE IS PREPARATION FOR ETERNITY ● GOD MADE YOU TO LOVE HIM ● WE ARE NOT SAVED <u>BY</u> WORKS BUT <u>TO</u> WORK ● ATTITUDE OF GRATITUDE ● YOU CAN'T TAKE IT WITH YOU -- BUT YOU CAN SEND IT AHEAD ● SERVICE OVER SCHEDULE ● IN THE CHRISTIAN LIFE SPEED IS NOT IMPORTANT ● WE LOOK FOR COMFORT BUT GOD LOOKS FOR CHARACTER ● IT'S ALL ABOUT GOD, NOT ME ● EVERY PROBLEM HAS A PURPOSE ● DON'T KEEP LOOKING IN THE REARVIEW MIRROR -- LEAVE THE PAST BEHIND ● FACT - FAITH - FEELING ● WHAT AM I ON THE EARTH FOR? ● CAN'T FOCUS ON TEMPTATION AND GOD AT THE SAME TIME ● YOU ONLY KEEP WHAT YOU GIVE AWAY ● GOD LOVES YOU -- HE PUT YOUR PICTURE ON HIS REFRIGERATOR ● YOU CAN'T OUTGIVE GOD ● YOU CAN'T BE A DISCIPLE IF YOU ARE NOT DISCIPLINED ● BEING ANONYMOUS DOES NOT MEAN BEING UNECESSARY ● HISTORY = <u>HIS</u> STORY ● BRUISES BECOME BLESSINGS ● LET GOD BE GOD

spread his tent over them.
16 Never again will they be hungry.
    Never again will they be thirsty.
The sun will not beat down on them.
    The heat of the desert will not harm
        them.
17 The Lamb, who is at the center of the
        area around the throne, will be
        their shepherd.
    He will lead them to springs of living water.
And God will wipe away every tear from
        their eyes."

The Seventh Seal and the Gold Cup

8 The Lamb opened the seventh seal. Then there was silence in heaven for about half an hour.

2 I saw the seven angels who stand in front of God. Seven trumpets were given to them.

3 Another angel came and stood at the altar. He had a shallow gold cup for burning incense. He was given a lot of incense to offer on the golden altar in front of the throne. With the incense he offered the prayers of all God's people. 4 The smoke of the incense together with the prayers of God's people rose up from the angel's hand. It went up in front of God.

5 Then the angel took the cup and filled it with fire from the altar. He threw it down on the earth. There were rumblings and thunder, flashes of lightning, and an earthquake.

The Trumpets

6 Then the seven angels who had the seven trumpets got ready to blow them.

7 The first angel blew his trumpet. Hail and fire mixed with blood were thrown down on the earth. A third of the earth was burned up. A third of the trees were burned up. All the green grass was burned up.

8 The second angel blew his trumpet. Something that looked like a huge mountain on fire was thrown into the sea. A third of the sea turned into blood. 9 A third of the living creatures in the sea died. A third of the ships were destroyed.

10 The third angel blew his trumpet. Then a great star fell from the sky. It looked like a blazing torch. It fell on a third of the rivers and on the springs of water. 11 The name of the star is Wormwood. A third of the water turned bitter. Many people died from it.

12 The fourth angel blew his trumpet. Then a third of the sun was struck. A third of the moon was struck. A third of the stars were struck. So a third of each of them turned dark. Then a third of the day had no light. The same thing happened to a third of the night.

13 As I watched, I heard an eagle that was flying high in the air. It called out in a loud voice, "How terrible! How terrible it will be for those living on the earth! How terrible! They will suffer as soon as the next three angels blow their trumpets!"

9 The fifth angel blew his trumpet. Then I saw a star that had fallen from the sky to the earth. The star was given the key to the tunnel leading down into the Abyss. 2 When the star opened the Abyss, smoke rose up from it like the smoke from a huge furnace. The sun and sky were darkened by the smoke from the Abyss.

3 Out of the smoke came locusts. They settled down on the earth. They were given power like the power of scorpions of the earth. 4 They were told not to harm the grass of the earth or any plant or tree. They were supposed to harm only the people who didn't have God's seal on their foreheads. 5 They were not allowed to kill them. But they could hurt them over and over for five months. The pain the people suffered was like the sting of a scorpion when it strikes a man.

6 In those days, people will look for a way to die but won't find it. They will want to die, but death will escape them.

7 The locusts looked like horses ready for battle. On their heads they wore something like crowns of gold. Their faces looked like human faces. 8 Their hair was like women's hair. Their teeth were like lions' teeth. 9 Their chests were covered with something that looked like armor made out of iron. The sound of their wings was like the thundering of many horses and chariots rushing into battle. 10 They had tails and stings like scorpions. And in their tails they had power to hurt people over and over for five months.

11 Their king was the angel of the Abyss.

In the Hebrew language his name is Abaddon. In Greek it is Apollyon.

[12]The first terrible judgment is past. Two others are still coming.

[13]The sixth angel blew his trumpet. Then I heard a voice coming from the corners of the golden altar that stands in front of God. [14]The voice spoke to the sixth angel who had the trumpet. It said, "Set the four angels free who are held at the great river Euphrates."

[15]The four angels had been ready for this very hour and day and month and year. They were set free to kill a third of all people. [16]The number of troops on horseback was 200,000,000. I heard how many there were.

[17]The horses and riders I saw in my vision had armor on their chests. It was flaming red, dark blue, and yellow like sulfur. The heads of the horses looked like lions' heads. Out of their mouths came fire, smoke and sulfur. [18]A third of all people were killed by the three plagues of fire, smoke and sulfur that came out of the horses' mouths. [19]The power of the horses was in their mouths and in their tails. The tails were like snakes whose heads could bite.

[20]The people who were not killed by these plagues still did not turn away from what they had been doing. They did not stop worshiping demons. They kept worshiping statues of gods made out of gold, silver, bronze, stone and wood, which can't see or hear or walk. [21]The people also did not turn away from their murders, witchcraft, sexual sins and stealing.

The Angel and the Little Scroll

10 Then I saw another mighty angel coming down from heaven. He was wearing a cloud like a robe. There was a rainbow above his head. His face was like the sun. His legs were like pillars of fire.

[2]He was holding a little scroll. It was lying open in his hand. The angel put his right foot on the sea and his left foot on the land. [3]Then he gave a loud shout like the roar of a lion. When he shouted, the voices of the seven thunders spoke.

[4]When they had spoken, I was getting ready to write. But I heard a voice from heaven say, "Seal up what the seven thunders have said. Do not write it down."

[5]Then the angel I had seen standing on the sea and on the land raised his right hand to heaven. [6]He made a promise in the name of the One who lives for ever and ever. He took an oath in the name of the One who created the sky, earth and sea and all that is in them. He said, "There will be no more waiting! [7]But in the days when the seventh angel is ready to blow his trumpet, the last part of God's plan will be carried out. God told all this to the prophets who served him long ago."

[8]Then the voice I had heard from heaven spoke to me again. It said, "Go and take the scroll from the angel standing on the sea and on the land. It is lying open in his hand."

[9]So I went to the angel and asked him to give me the little scroll. He said to me, "Take it and eat it. It will become sour in your stomach. But in your mouth it will taste as sweet as honey." [10]I took the little scroll from the angel's hand and ate it. In my mouth it tasted as sweet as honey. But when I had eaten it, it became sour in my stomach. [11]Then I was told, "You must prophesy again about many peoples, nations, languages and kings."

The Two Witnesses

11 I was given a long stick that looked like a measuring rod. I was told, "Go and measure the temple of God and the altar. Count the worshipers who are there. [2]But do not measure the outer courtyard. It has been given to those who aren't Jews. They will overrun the holy city for 42 months.

[3-4]"I will give power to my two witnesses. They will prophesy for 1,260 days. They will be dressed in black clothes to show how sad they are."

You never stumble when you're on your knees.

⁴The witnesses are the two olive trees and the two lampstands that stand in front of the Lord of the earth. ⁵If anyone tries to harm them, fire comes from their mouths and eats up their enemies. This is how anyone who wants to harm them must die.

⁶These witnesses have power to close up the sky. Then it will not rain while they are prophesying. They also have power to turn the waters into blood. And they can strike the earth with every kind of plague as often as they want to.

⁷When they have finished giving their witness, the beast that comes up from the Abyss will attack them. He will overpower them and kill them. ⁸Their bodies will lie in the street of the great city where their Lord was nailed to the cross. The city is sometimes pictured as Sodom, or as Egypt.

⁹For three and a half days, people from every tribe, language and nation will stare at their bodies. They will refuse to bury them. ¹⁰Those who live on the earth will be happy about this and will celebrate. They will send each other gifts, because these two prophets had made them suffer.

¹¹But after the three and a half days, a breath of life from God entered the two witnesses. They stood up. Terror struck those who saw them.

¹²Then the two witnesses heard a loud voice from heaven. It said to them, "Come up here." They went up to heaven in a cloud. Their enemies watched it happen.

¹³At that very hour there was a powerful earthquake. A tenth of the city crumbled and fell. In the earthquake, 7,000 people were killed. Those who lived through it were terrified. They gave glory to the God of heaven.

¹⁴The second terrible judgment has passed. The third is coming soon.

The Seventh Trumpet

¹⁵The seventh angel blew his trumpet. There were loud voices in heaven. They said,

"The kingdom of the world has become
    the kingdom of our Lord and of
    his Christ.
  He will rule for ever and ever."

¹⁶The 24 elders were sitting on their thrones in front of God. They fell on their faces and worshiped God. ¹⁷They said,

"Lord God who rules over all, we give
    thanks to you.
  You are the One who is and who was.
We give you thanks because you have
    taken your great power
  and have begun to rule.
¹⁸The nations were angry,
  and the time for your anger has come.
  The time has come to judge the dead.
It is time to reward your servants the
    prophets
  and your own people and those who
    honor you.
There is a reward for all your people,
  both great and small.
It is time to destroy
  those who destroy the earth."

¹⁹Then God's temple in heaven was opened. Inside it the wooden chest called the ark of his covenant could be seen. There were flashes of lightning, rumblings and thunder, an earthquake and a great hailstorm.

The Woman and the Dragon

12 A great and miraculous sign appeared in heaven. It was a woman wearing the sun like clothes. The moon was under her feet. On her head she wore a crown of 12 stars. ²She was pregnant. She cried out in pain because she was about to have a baby.

³Then another sign appeared in heaven. It was a huge red dragon. He had seven heads and ten horns. On his seven heads he wore seven crowns. ⁴His tail swept a third of the stars out of the sky. It threw them down to earth.

The dragon stood in front of the woman who was about to have a baby. He wanted to eat her child the moment it was born.

⁵She gave birth to a son. He will rule all the nations with an iron rod. Her child was taken up to God and to his throne.

⁶The woman escaped into the desert where God had a place prepared for her. There she would be taken care of for 1,260 days.

⁷There was war in heaven. Michael and his angels fought against the dragon. And the dragon and his angels fought back. ⁸But

the dragon wasn't strong enough. He and his angels lost their place in heaven.

⁹The great dragon was thrown down to the earth, and his angels with him. The dragon is that old serpent called the devil, or Satan. He leads the whole world down the wrong path.

¹⁰Then I heard a loud voice in heaven. It said,

"Now the salvation and the power and
    the kingdom of our God have
    come.
The authority of his Christ has come.
Satan, who brings charges against our
    brothers and sisters,
    has been thrown down.
He brings charges against them before
    our God day and night.
¹¹They overcame him
    because the Lamb gave his life's blood
    for them.
They overcame him
    by giving witness about Jesus to
    others.
They were willing to risk their lives,
    even if it led to death.
¹²So be joyful, you heavens!
    Be glad, all you who live there!
But how terrible it will be for the earth
    and the sea!
The devil has come down to you.
He is very angry.
He knows his time is short."

¹³The dragon saw that he had been thrown down to the earth. So he chased the woman who had given birth to the boy.

¹⁴The woman was given the two wings of a great eagle so that she could fly away. She could fly to the place prepared for her in the desert. There she would be taken care of for three and a half years. She would be out of the serpent's reach.

¹⁵Then the serpent spit water like a river out of his mouth. He wanted to catch her and sweep her away in the flood. ¹⁶But the earth helped the woman. It opened its mouth and swallowed the river that the dragon had spit out.

¹⁷The dragon was very angry with the woman. He went off to make war against the rest of her children. They obey God's commands and hold firmly to what Jesus has said. ¹³ ¹The dragon stood on the seashore.

The Beast out of the Sea

I saw a beast coming out of the sea. He had ten horns and seven heads. There were ten crowns on his horns. On each head was an evil name that was displeasing to God.

²The beast I saw looked like a leopard. But he had feet like a bear and a mouth like a lion. The dragon gave the beast his power, his throne, and great authority. ³One of the beast's heads seemed to have had a deadly wound. But the wound had been healed. The whole world was amazed and followed the beast.

⁴People worshiped the dragon, because he had given authority to the beast. They also worshiped the beast. They asked, "Who is like the beast? Who can make war against him?"

⁵The beast was given a mouth to brag and speak evil things against God. The beast was allowed to use his authority for 42 months. ⁶He opened his mouth to speak evil things against God. He told lies about God's character and about the place where God lives and about those who live in heaven with him. ⁷He was allowed to make war against God's people and to overcome them. He was given authority over every tribe, people, language and nation.

⁸All who live on earth whose names have not been written in the Book of Life will worship the beast. The Book of Life belongs to the Lamb whose death was planned before the world was created.

⁹Everyone who has ears should listen.
¹⁰Everyone who is supposed to be captured
    will be captured.
Everyone who is supposed to be killed

He is no fool to give up what he cannot keep
for what he cannot lose.

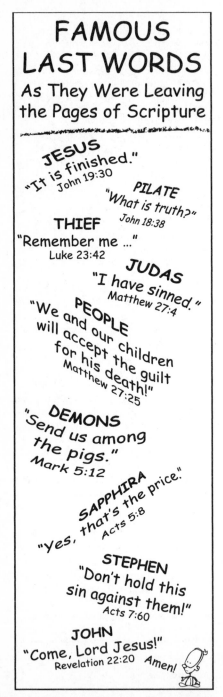

FAMOUS LAST WORDS

As They Were Leaving the Pages of Scripture

JESUS
"It is finished."
John 19:30

PILATE
"What is truth?"
John 18:38

THIEF
"Remember me ..."
Luke 23:42

JUDAS
"I have sinned."
Matthew 27:4

PEOPLE
"We and our children will accept the guilt for his death!"
Matthew 27:25

DEMONS
"Send us among the pigs."
Mark 5:12

SAPPHIRA
"Yes, that's the price."
Acts 5:8

STEPHEN
"Don't hold this sin against them!"
Acts 7:60

JOHN
"Come, Lord Jesus!"
Revelation 22:20   Amen!

with a sword
will be killed with a sword.

So God's people must be patient and faithful.

The Beast out of the Earth

[11]Then I saw another beast. This one came out of the earth. He had two horns like a lamb. But he spoke like a dragon. [12]He had all the authority of the first beast. He did what that beast wanted. He made the earth and all who live on it worship the first beast. The first beast was the one whose deadly wound had been healed.

[13]The second beast did great and miraculous signs. He even made fire come from heaven. It came down to earth where everyone could see it. [14]He did the signs the first beast wanted him to do. In that way the second beast tricked those who live on the earth. He ordered them to set up a statue to honor the first beast.

The first beast was the one who had been wounded by the sword and still lived.

[15]The second beast was allowed to give breath to the statue so it could speak. He was allowed to kill all who refused to worship the statue. [16]He also forced everyone to receive a mark on the right hand or on the forehead. People great or small, rich or poor, free or slave had to receive the mark. [17]They could not buy or sell anything unless they had the mark. The mark is the name of the beast or the number of his name.

[18]Here is a problem that you have to be wise to figure out. If you can, figure out what the beast's number means. It is man's number. His number is 666.

The Lamb and the 144,000

14 I looked, and there in front of me was the Lamb. He was standing on Mount Zion. With him were 144,000 people. Written on their foreheads were his name and his Father's name.

[2]I heard a sound from heaven. It was like the roar of rushing waters and loud thunder. The sound I heard was like the music of harps being played.

[3]Then everyone sang a new song in front of the throne. They sang it in front of the four

living creatures and the elders. No one could learn the song except the 144,000. They had been set free from the evil of the earth.

⁴They had not committed sexual sins with women. They had kept themselves pure. They follow the Lamb wherever he goes. They were purchased from among people as a first offering to God and the Lamb. ⁵Their mouths told no lies. They are without blame.

The Three Angels

⁶I saw another angel. He was flying high in the air. He came to tell everyone on earth the good news that will always be true. He told it to every nation, tribe, language and people. ⁷In a loud voice he said, "Have respect for God. Give him glory. The hour has come for God to judge. Worship him who made the heavens and the earth. Worship him who made the sea and the springs of water."

⁸A second angel followed him. He said, "Fallen! Babylon the Great has fallen! The city of Babylon made all the nations drink the strong wine of her terrible sins."

⁹A third angel followed them. He said in a loud voice, "Watch out, all you who worship the beast and his statue! Watch out, all you who have his mark on your forehead or your hand! ¹⁰You, too, will drink the wine of God's great anger. His wine has been poured full strength into the cup of his anger. You will be burned with flaming sulfur. The holy angels and the Lamb will see it happen. ¹¹The smoke of your terrible suffering will rise for ever and ever. Day and night, there is no rest for you who worship the beast and his statue. There is no rest for you who receive the mark of his name."

¹²God's people need to be very patient. They are the ones who obey God's commands. They remain faithful to Jesus.

¹³Then I heard a voice from heaven. "Write this," it said. "Blessed are the dead who die as believers in the Lord from now on."

"Yes," says the Holy Spirit. "They will rest from their labor. What they have done will not be forgotten."

The Harvest of the Earth

¹⁴I looked, and there in front of me was a white cloud. Sitting on the cloud was One who looked "like a son of man." *(Daniel 7:13)* He wore a gold crown on his head. In his hand was a sharp, curved blade for cutting grain.

¹⁵Then another angel came out of the temple. He called in a loud voice to the one sitting on the cloud. "Take your blade," he said. "Cut the grain. The time has come. The earth is ready to be harvested."

¹⁶So the one sitting on the cloud swung his blade over the earth. And the earth was harvested.

¹⁷Another angel came out of the temple in heaven. He too had a sharp, curved blade. ¹⁸Still another angel came from the altar. He was in charge of the fire on the altar. He called out in a loud voice to the angel who had the sharp blade. "Take your blade," he said, "and gather the bunches of grapes from the earth's vine. Its grapes are ripe."

¹⁹So the angel swung his blade over the earth. He gathered its grapes. Then he threw them into a huge winepress. The winepress stands for God's anger.

²⁰In the winepress outside the city, the grapes were stomped on. Blood flowed out of the pit. It spread over the land for about 180 miles. It rose as high as the horses' heads.

Seven Angels With Seven Plagues

15 I saw in heaven another great and miraculous sign. Seven angels were about to bring the seven last plagues. The plagues would complete God's anger.

²Then I saw something that looked like a sea of glass mixed with fire. Standing beside the sea were those who had won the battle over the beast. They had also overcome his statue and the number of his name. They held harps given to them by God.

³They sang the song of Moses, who served God, and the song of the Lamb. They sang,

"Lord God who rules over all,
  everything you do is great and
    wonderful.
King of the ages,
  your ways are true and fair.
⁴ Lord, who will not have respect for you?
  Who will not bring glory to your
    name?
You alone are holy.
All nations will come

and worship you.
They see that the things you do are
    right."

[5]After this I looked, and the temple was
opened in heaven. The temple is the holy tent
where the tablets of the covenant were kept.
[6]Out of the temple came the seven angels
who were bringing the seven plagues. They
were dressed in clean, shining linen. They
wore gold strips of cloth around their chests.
[7]Then one of the four living creatures gave
seven golden bowls to the seven angels. The
bowls were filled with the anger of God,
who lives for ever and ever. [8]The temple was
filled with smoke that came from the glory
and power of God. No one could enter the
temple until the seven plagues of the seven
angels were completed.

The Seven Bowls of God's Anger

16 Then I heard a loud voice from the
temple speaking to the seven angels.
"Go," it said. "Pour out the seven bowls of
God's anger on the earth."

[2]The first angel went and poured out his
bowl on the land. Ugly and painful sores
broke out on the people who had the mark
of the beast and worshiped his statue.

[3]The second angel poured out his bowl
on the sea. It turned into blood like the
blood of a dead person. Every living thing
in the sea died.

[4]The third angel poured out his bowl on
the rivers and on the springs of water. They
became blood.

[5]Then I heard the angel who was in
charge of the waters. He said,

"The way you judge is fair.
    You are the Holy One.
    You are the One who is and who was.
[6] The beast's worshipers have poured out
        the life's blood of your people and
        your prophets.
    So you have given those worshipers
        blood to drink.
    That's exactly what they should get."

[7]Then I heard the altar reply,

"Lord God who rules over all,
    the way you judge is true and fair."

[8]The fourth angel poured out his bowl on
the sun. The sun was allowed to burn people
with fire. [9]They were burned by the blazing
heat. So they spoke evil things against the
name of God, who controlled these plagues.
But they refused to turn away from their
sins. They did not give glory to God.

[10]The fifth angel poured out his bowl on
the throne of the beast. The kingdom of the
beast became very dark. People bit their
tongues because they were suffering so
much. [11]They spoke evil things against the
God of heaven because of their pains and
their sores. But they refused to turn away
from the sins they had committed.

[12]The sixth angel poured out his bowl on the
great river Euphrates. Its water dried up to prepare the way for the kings from the East.

[13]Then I saw three evil spirits that looked
like frogs. They came out of the mouths of
the dragon, the beast and the false prophet.
[14]They are spirits of demons performing
miraculous signs. They go out to gather the
kings of the whole world for battle. That
battle will take place on the great day of the
God who rules over all.

[15]"Look! I am coming like a thief! Blessed
are those who stay awake and keep their
clothes with them. They will not be caught
naked. They will not be put to shame."

[16]Then the evil spirits gathered the
kings together. The place where the kings
met is called Armageddon in the Hebrew
language.

[17]The seventh angel poured out his bowl
into the air. Out of the temple came a loud
voice from the throne. It said, "It is done!"

[18]Then there came flashes of lightning, rumblings, thunder and a powerful earthquake.
There has never been an earthquake as terrible as this since man has lived on earth. [19]The
great city split into three parts. The cities of
the nations crumbled and fell. God remembered Babylon the Great. He gave her the cup
filled with the wine of his terrible anger.

[20]Every island ran away. The mountains
could not be found. [21]Huge hailstones of
about 100 pounds each fell from the sky.
The hail crushed people. They spoke evil
things against God because the plague of
hail was so terrible.

The Woman and the Beast

17 One of the seven angels who had the seven bowls came to me. He said, "Come. I will show you how the great prostitute will be punished. She is the one who sits on many waters. ²The kings of the earth took part in her evil ways. The people living on earth were drunk with the wine of her terrible sins."

³Then the angel carried me away in a vision. The Holy Spirit took me into a desert. There I saw a woman sitting on a bright red beast. It was covered with names that say evil things that are displeasing to God. It had seven heads and ten horns.

⁴The woman was dressed in purple and bright red. She was gleaming with gold, jewels and pearls. In her hand she held a golden cup filled with things that God hates. It was filled with her terrible, dirty sins. ⁵Here is the name that was written on her forehead.

MYSTERY

THE GREAT CITY OF BABYLON

THE MOTHER OF PROSTITUTES

THE MOTHER OF EVERYTHING ON EARTH

THAT GOD HATES

⁶I saw that the woman was drunk with the blood of God's people. They are the ones who gave witness to Jesus.

When I saw her, I was very amazed. ⁷Then the angel said to me, "Why are you amazed? I will explain to you the mystery of the woman and of the beast she rides on. The beast is the one who has the seven heads and ten horns. ⁸The beast that you saw used to exist. But now he does not. He will come up out of the Abyss. He will be destroyed. Some of the people who live on the earth will be amazed when they see the beast. Their names have not been written in the Book of Life from the time the world was created. They will be amazed because even though the beast used to exist and now does not, he will come again.

⁹"Here is a problem that you have to be wise to understand. The seven heads are seven hills

that the woman sits on. ¹⁰They are also seven kings. Five have fallen, one is ruling, and the other has still not come. When he does come, he must remain for a little while.

¹¹"The beast who used to exist, and now does not, is an eighth king. He belongs to the other seven. He will be destroyed.

¹²"The ten horns you saw are ten kings. They have not yet received a kingdom. But for one hour they will receive authority to rule together with the beast. ¹³They have only one purpose. So they give their power and authority to the beast. ¹⁴They will make war against the Lamb. But the Lamb will overcome them because he is the most powerful Lord of all and the greatest King of all. His appointed, chosen and faithful followers will be with him."

¹⁵Then the angel spoke to me. "You saw the waters the prostitute sits on," he said. "They stand for all the nations of the world, no matter what their race or language is. ¹⁶The beast and the ten horns you saw will hate the prostitute. They will destroy her and leave her naked. They will eat her flesh and burn her with fire. ¹⁷God has put it into their hearts to carry out his purpose. So they agreed to give the beast their power to rule. They will give him that power until God's words come true.

¹⁸"The woman you saw stands for the great city that rules over the kings of the earth."

Babylon Falls

18 After these things I saw another angel coming down from heaven. He had great authority. His glory filled the earth with light. ²With a mighty voice he shouted,

> "Fallen! Babylon the Great has fallen!
> She has become a place where demons live.
> She has become a den for every evil spirit.
> She has become a nest for every 'unclean' and hated bird.
> ³ All the nations have drunk the strong wine of her terrible sins.

Delayed obediance is disobediance.

The kings of the earth took part in her
evil ways.
The traders of the world grew rich
from her great wealth."

⁴Then I heard another voice from heaven.
It said,

"Come out of her, my people.
Then you will not take part in her sins.
You will not suffer from any of her
plagues.
⁵Her sins are piled up to heaven.
God has remembered her crimes.
⁶Do to her as she has done to others.
Pay her back double for what she has done.
Mix her a double dose of what she has
mixed for others.
⁷Give her as much pain and suffering
as the glory and wealth she gave herself.
She brags to herself,
'I rule like a queen. I am not a widow.
I will never be sad.'
⁸But she will be plagued by death, sadness
and hunger. In a single day they will
all catch up with her.
She will be burned up by fire.
The Lord God who judges her is mighty.

⁹"The kings of the earth who committed
terrible sins with her will sob. They will be
sad because they used to share her riches.
They will see the smoke rising as she burns.
¹⁰They will be terrified by her suffering.
Standing far away, they will exclaim,

" 'How terrible! How terrible it is for you,
great city!
How terrible for you, Babylon, city
of power!
In just one hour you have been destroyed!'

¹¹"The traders of the world will cry and
be sad over her. No one buys what they sell
anymore. ¹²Here is what they had for sale.

Gold, silver, jewels, pearls.
Fine linen, purple, silk, bright red cloth.
Every kind of expensive wood.

All sorts of articles made out of ivory, valuable wood, bronze, iron and marble.
¹³Cinnamon, spice, incense, myrrh,
frankincense.
Wine, olive oil, fine flour, wheat.
Cattle, sheep, horses, carriages,
human slaves.

¹⁴"The merchants will say, 'The pleasure
you longed for has left you. All your riches
and glory have disappeared forever.' ¹⁵The
traders who sold these things and became
rich because of her will stand far away. Her
suffering will terrify them. They will cry
and be sad. ¹⁶They will cry out,

" 'How terrible! How terrible it is for you,
great city,
dressed in fine linen, purple and bright red!
How terrible for you, great city,
gleaming with gold, jewels and
pearls!
¹⁷In just one hour your great wealth has
been destroyed!'

"Every sea captain and all who travel by
ship will stand far away. So will the sailors
and all who earn their living from the sea.
¹⁸They will see the smoke rising as Babylon
burns. They will ask, 'Was there ever a city
like this great city?' ¹⁹They will throw dust
on their heads. They will cry and be sad.
They will cry out,

" 'How terrible! How terrible it is for you,
great city!
All who had ships on the sea
became rich because of her wealth!
In just one hour she has been destroyed!
²⁰Heaven, be glad for this!
God's people, be glad! Apostles and
prophets, be glad!
God has judged her for the way she
treated you.' "

²¹Then a mighty angel picked up a huge
rock. It was the size of a large millstone. He
threw it into the sea. Then he said,

No matter how low you feel...
underneath are God's everlasting arms.

"That is how
the great city of Babylon will be
thrown down.
Never again will it be found.
22 The songs of musicians will never be
heard in you again.
Gone will be the music of harp, flute
and trumpet.
No worker of any kind
will ever be found in you again.
The sound of a millstone
will never be heard in you again.
23 The light of a lamp
will never shine in you again.
The voices of brides and grooms
will never be heard in you again.
Your traders were among the world's
most important people.
By your magic spell all the nations
were led down the wrong path.
24 You were guilty of the murder of
prophets and God's people.
You were guilty of the blood of all who
have been killed on the earth."

Hallelujah!

19 After these things I heard a roar in
heaven. It sounded like a huge crowd
shouting,

"Hallelujah!
Salvation and glory and power belong to
our God.
2   The way he judges is true and fair.
He has judged the great prostitute.
She polluted the earth with her
terrible sins.
God has paid her back for killing those
who served him."

3 Again they shouted,

"Hallelujah!
The smoke from her fire goes up for ever
and ever."

4 The 24 elders and the four living creatures
bowed down. They worshiped God, who was
sitting on the throne. They cried out,

"Amen! Hallelujah!"

5 Then a voice came from the throne. It said,

"Praise our God,
all you who serve him!

Praise God, all you who have respect for
him, both great and small!"

6 Then I heard the noise of a huge crowd. It
sounded like the roar of rushing waters and
like loud thunder. The people were shouting,

"Hallelujah!
Our Lord God is the King who rules
over all.
7 Let us be joyful and glad!
Let us give him glory!
It is time for the Lamb's wedding.
His bride has made herself ready.
8 Fine linen, bright and clean,
was given to her to wear."
Fine linen stands for the right things that
God's people do.

9 Here is what the angel told me to write.
"Blessed are those who are invited to the
wedding supper of the Lamb!" Then he
added, "These are the true words of God."
10 When I heard this, I fell at his feet to
worship him.

But he said to me, "Don't do that! I serve
God, just as you do. I am God's servant, just
like other believers who hold firmly to what
Jesus has taught. Worship God! What Jesus
taught is the very heart of prophecy."

The Rider on the White Horse

11 I saw heaven standing open. There in
front of me was a white horse. Its rider is
called Faithful and True. When he judges
or makes war, he is always fair. 12 His eyes
are like blazing fire. On his head are many
crowns. A name is written on him that only
he knows. 13 He is dressed in a robe dipped
in blood. His name is The Word of God.
14 The armies of heaven were following
him, riding on white horses. They were
dressed in fine linen, white and clean.
15 Out of the rider's mouth comes a sharp
sword. He will strike down the nations
with it. Scripture says, "He will rule them
with an iron rod." *(Psalm 2:9)* He stomps on
the grapes of God's winepress. The winepress stands for the terrible anger of the
God who rules over all.
16 Here is the name that is written on the
rider's robe and on his thigh.

THE GREATEST KING OF ALL

AND THE MOST POWERFUL LORD OF ALL

[17]I saw an angel standing in the sun. He cried in a loud voice to all the birds flying high in the air, "Come! Gather together for the great supper of God. [18]Come and eat the dead bodies of kings, generals, and other mighty people. Eat the bodies of horses and their riders. Eat the bodies of all people, free and slave, great and small."

[19]Then I saw the beast and the kings of the earth with their armies. They had gathered together to make war against the rider on the horse and his army.

[20]But the beast and the false prophet were captured. The false prophet had done miraculous signs for the beast. In this way the false prophet had tricked those who had received the mark of the beast and had worshiped his statue. The beast and the false prophet were thrown alive into the lake of fire that burns with sulfur. [21]The rest of them were killed with the sword that came out of the rider's mouth. All the birds stuffed themselves with the dead bodies.

The Thousand Years

20 I saw an angel coming down out of heaven. He had the key to the Abyss. In his hand he held a heavy chain.

[2]He grabbed the dragon, that old serpent. The serpent is also called the devil, or Satan. The angel put him in chains for 1,000 years. [3]Then he threw him into the Abyss. He locked it and sealed him in. This was to keep Satan from fooling the nations anymore until the 1,000 years were ended. After that, he must be set free for a short time.

[4]I saw thrones. Those who had been given authority to judge were sitting on them. I also saw the souls of those whose heads had been cut off because they had given witness for Jesus and because of God's word. They had not worshiped the beast or his statue. They had not received his mark on their foreheads or hands. They came to life and ruled with Christ for 1,000 years.

[5]This is the first resurrection. The rest of the dead did not come to life until the 1,000 years were ended.

[6]Blessed and holy are those who take part in the first resurrection. The second death has no power over them. They will be priests of God and of Christ. They will rule with him for 1,000 years.

Satan Is Judged

[7]When the 1,000 years are over, Satan will be set free from his prison. [8]He will go out to fool the nations. He will gather them from the four corners of the earth. He will bring Gog and Magog together for battle.

Their troops are as many as the grains of sand on the seashore. [9]They marched across the whole earth. They surrounded the place where God's people were camped. It was the city he loves. But fire came down from heaven and burned them up.

[10]The devil, who fooled them, was thrown into the lake of burning sulfur. That is where the beast and the false prophet had been thrown. They will all suffer day and night for ever and ever.

The Dead Are Judged

[11]I saw a great white throne and the One who was sitting on it. When the earth and sky saw his face, they ran away. There was no place for them.

[12]I saw the dead, great and small, standing in front of the throne. Books were opened. Then another book was opened. It was the Book of Life. The dead were judged by what they had done. The things they had done were written in the books. [13]The sea gave up the dead that were in it. And Death and Hell gave up their dead. Each of the dead was judged by what he had done.

[14]Then Death and Hell were thrown into the lake of fire. The lake of fire is the second death. [15]Anyone whose name was not written in the Book of Life was thrown into the lake of fire.

The New Jerusalem

21 I saw a new heaven and a new earth. The first heaven and the first earth were completely gone. There was no longer any sea.

[2]I saw the Holy City, the new Jerusalem. It was coming down out of heaven from God. It was prepared like a bride beautifully dressed for her husband.

[3]I heard a loud voice from the throne. It said, "Now God makes his home with people. He will live with them. They will be his people. And God himself will be with them and be their God. [4]He will wipe away every tear from their eyes. There will be no more death or sadness.

There will be no more crying or pain. Things are no longer the way they used to be."

[5]He who was sitting on the throne said, "I am making everything new!" Then he said, "Write this down. You can trust these words. They are true."

[6]He said to me, "It is done. I am the Alpha and the Omega, the First and the Last. I am the Beginning and the End. Anyone who is thirsty may drink from the spring of the water of life. It doesn't cost anything! [7]Anyone who overcomes will receive all this from me. I will be his God, and he will be my child.

[8]"But others will have their place in the lake of fire that burns with sulfur. Those who are afraid and those who do not believe will be there. Murderers and those who pollute themselves will join them. Those who commit sexual sins and those who practice witchcraft will go there. Those who worship statues of gods and all who tell lies will be there too. It is the second death."

[9]One of the seven angels who had the seven bowls came and spoke to me. The bowls were filled with the seven last plagues. The angel said, "Come. I will show you the bride, the wife of the Lamb."

[10]Then he carried me away in a vision. The Spirit took me to a huge, high mountain. He showed me Jerusalem, the Holy City. It was coming down out of heaven from God. [11]It shone with the glory of God. It gleamed like a very valuable jewel. It was like a jasper, as clear as crystal.

[12]The city had a huge, high wall with 12 gates. Twelve angels were at the gates, one at each of them. On the gates were written the names of the 12 tribes of Israel. [13]There were three gates on the east and three on the north. There were three gates on the south and three on the west. [14]The wall of the city had 12 foundations. Written on them were the names of the 12 apostles of the Lamb.

[15]The angel who talked with me had a gold measuring rod. He used it to measure the city, its gates and its walls.

[16]The city was laid out like a square. It was as long as it was wide. The angel measured the city with the rod. It was 1,400 miles long. It was as wide and high as it was long.

[17]He measured the wall of the city. It was 200 feet thick. The angel did the measuring as a man would. [18]The wall was made out of jasper. The city was made out of pure gold, as pure as glass.

[19]The foundations of the city walls were decorated with every kind of jewel. The first foundation was made out of jasper. The second was made out of sapphire. The third was made out of chalcedony. The fourth was made out of emerald. [20]The fifth was made out of sardonyx. The sixth was made out of carnelian. The seventh was made out of chrysolite. The eighth was made out of beryl. The ninth was made out of topaz. The tenth was made out of chrysoprase. The eleventh was made out of jacinth. The twelfth was made out of amethyst.

[21]The 12 gates were made from 12 pearls. Each gate was made out of a single pearl. The main street of the city was made out of pure gold, as clear as glass.

[22]I didn't see a temple in the city. This was because the Lamb and the Lord God who rules over all are its temple. [23]The city does not need the sun or moon to shine on it. God's glory is its light, and the Lamb is its lamp.

[24]The nations will walk by the light of the city. The kings of the world will bring their glory into it. [25]Its gates will never be shut, because there will be no night there. [26]The glory and honor of the nations will be brought into it.

[27]Only what is pure will enter it. No one who fools others or does shameful things will enter it. Only those whose names are written in the Lamb's Book of Life will enter the city.

If you're not as close to God as you used to be...
guess who moved.

The River of Life

22 Then the angel showed me the river of the water of life. It was as clear as crystal. It flowed from the throne of God and of the Lamb. ²It flowed down the middle of the city's main street.

On each side of the river stood the tree of life, bearing 12 crops of fruit. Its fruit was ripe every month. The leaves of the tree bring healing to the nations.

³There will no longer be any curse. The throne of God and of the Lamb will be in the city. God's servants will serve him. ⁴They will see his face. His name will be on their foreheads.

⁵There will be no more night. They will not need the light of a lamp or the light of the sun. The Lord God will give them light. They will rule for ever and ever.

⁶The angel said to me, "You can trust these words. They are true. The Lord is the God of the spirits of the prophets. He sent his angel to show those who serve him the things that must soon take place."

Jesus Is Coming

⁷"Look! I am coming soon! Blessed are those who obey the words of the prophecy in this book."

⁸I, John, am the one who heard and saw these things.

After I had heard and seen them, I fell down to worship at the feet of the angel. He is the one who had been showing me these things.

⁹But he said to me, "Don't do that! I serve God, just as you do. I am God's servant, just like the other prophets and all who obey the words of this book. Worship God!"

¹⁰Then he told me, "Do not seal up the words of the prophecy in this book. These things are about to happen. ¹¹Let those who do wrong keep on doing wrong. Let those who are evil continue to be evil. Let those who do what is right keep on doing what is right. And let those who are holy continue to be holy."

¹²"Look! I am coming soon! I bring my rewards with me. I will reward each person for what he has done. ¹³I am the Alpha and the Omega. I am the First and the Last. I am the Beginning and the End.

¹⁴"Blessed are those who wash their robes. They will have the right to come to the tree of life. They will be allowed to go through the gates into the city.

¹⁵"Outside the city are the dogs and those who practice witchcraft. Outside are also those who commit sexual sins and murder. Those who worship statues of gods, and everyone who loves and does what is false, are outside too.

¹⁶"I, Jesus, have sent my angel to give you this witness for the churches. I am the Root and the Son of David. I am the bright Morning Star."

¹⁷The Holy Spirit and the bride say, "Come!" Let those who hear say, "Come!" Anyone who is thirsty should come. Anyone who wants to take the free gift of the water of life should do so.

¹⁸I am warning everyone who hears the words of the prophecy of this book. If you add anything to them, God will add to you the plagues told about in this book. ¹⁹If you take any words away from this book of prophecy, God will take away from you your share in the tree of life. He will also take away your place in the Holy City. This book tells about these things.

²⁰He who gives witness to these things says, "Yes. I am coming soon."

Amen. Come, Lord Jesus!

²¹May the grace of the Lord Jesus be with God's people. Amen.

WARNING

If you add anything to what is written here, God will add to you the plagues told about in this book.

Revelation 22:18

Psalms

The book of Psalms is one of praise, worship and joyous thanksgiving. These spiritual songs contain intense devotion, fervent feelings, and lofty emotions as well as deep despair.

Though there are calls for justice and judgment, the Psalms are filled with inspiration, encouragement, blessing, celebration and finding safety in the presence of the LORD.

The Psalms are full of prophecies of the Messiah Jesus. It is a hymn book and a HIM book.

Most of the Psalms were written by King David. Several other people wrote Psalms: Moses, Soloman, Hezekiah and Asaph. There are 116 quotations from Psalms in the New Testament.

From the 150 songs, we have selected the following to encourage you to dig deeper into the entire Book of Psalms.

Psalm 1

Blessed is the one who obeys the
law of the LORD.
He doesn't follow the advice of
evil people.
He doesn't make a habit of doing
what sinners do.
He doesn't join those who make
fun of the LORD and his law.
Instead, he takes delight in the law
of the LORD.
He thinks about his law day and
night.
He is like a tree that is planted near
a stream of water.
It always bears its fruit at the
right time.
Its leaves don't dry up.
Everything godly people do turns
out well.

Sinful people are not like that at all.
They are like straw
that the wind blows away.
When the LORD judges them, their
life will come to an end.
Sinners won't have any place
among those who are godly.

The LORD watches over the lives of
those who are godly.
But the lives of sinful people will
lead to their death.

Psalm 8

LORD, our Lord,
how majestic is your name in the
whole earth!
You have made your glory

higher than the heavens.
You have made sure that children
and infants praise you.
You have done it because of your
enemies.
You have done it to put a stop to
their talk.

I think about the heavens.
I think about what your fingers
have created.
I think about the moon and stars
that you have set in place.
What is a human being that you
think about him?
What is a son of man that you
take care of him?
You made him a little lower than
the heavenly beings.
You placed on him a crown of
glory and honor.
You made human beings the rulers
over all that your hands have
created.
You put everything under their
control.
They rule over all flocks and herds
and over the wild animals.
They rule over the birds of the air
and over the fish in the ocean.
They rule over everything that
swims in the oceans.
LORD, our Lord,
how majestic is your name in the
whole earth!

Psalm 19

The heavens tell about the glory of
God.
The skies show that his hands
created them.
Day after day they speak about it.
Night after night they make it known.
But they don't speak or use words.

No sound is heard from them.
At the same time, their voice goes
out into the whole earth.
Their words go out from one end
of the world to the other.
The law of the LORD is perfect.
It gives us new strength.
The laws of the LORD can be trusted.
They make childish people wise.
The rules of the LORD are right.
They give joy to our hearts.
The commands of the LORD shine
brightly.
They give light to our minds.
The law that brings respect for the
LORD is pure.
It lasts forever.
The directions the LORD gives are
true.
All of them are completely right.
They are more priceless than gold.
They have greater value than
huge amounts of pure gold.
They are sweeter than honey
that is taken from the honeycomb.

LORD, may the words of my mouth
and the thoughts of my heart
be pleasing in your eyes.
You are my Rock and my
Redeemer.

Psalm 23

The LORD is my shepherd. He gives
me everything I need.
He lets me lie down in fields of
green grass.
He leads me beside quiet waters.
He gives me new strength.
He guides me in the right paths
for the honor of his name.
Even though I walk
through the darkest valley,

I will not be afraid.
You are with me.
Your shepherd's rod and staff
comfort me.

You prepare a feast for me
right in front of my enemies.
You pour oil on my head.
My cup runs over.
I am sure that your goodness and
love will follow me
all the days of my life.
And I will live in the house of the
LORD forever.

Psalm 24

The earth belongs to the LORD. And
so does everything in it.
The world belongs to him. And
so do all those who live in it.
He set it firmly on the oceans.
He made it secure on the waters.

Who can go up to the temple on the
hill of the LORD?
Who can stand in his holy place?
Anyone who has clean hands and a
pure heart.
He does not worship the statue of
a god.
He doesn't use the name of that
god when he makes a
promise.
People like that will receive the
LORD's blessing.
When God their Savior hands
down his sentence, it will be
in their favor.
The people who look to God are
like that.
God of Jacob, they look to you.
Open wide, you gates.
Open up, you age-old doors.

Then the King of glory will come in.
Who is the King of glory?
The LORD, who is strong and
mighty.
The LORD, who is mighty in battle.

Psalm 37

Don't be upset because of sinful people.
Don't be jealous of those who do
wrong.
Like grass, they will soon dry up.
Like green plants, they will soon die.

Trust in the LORD and do good.
Then you will live in the land
and enjoy its food.
Find your delight in the LORD.
Then he will give you everything
your heart really wants.
Commit your life to the LORD.
Here is what he will do if you
trust in him.
He will make your godly ways
shine like the dawn.
He will make your honest life
shine like the sun at noon.
I once was young, and now I'm old.
But I've never seen godly people
deserted.
I've never seen their children
begging for bread.
The godly are always giving and
lending freely.
Their children will be blessed.

Psalm 84

LORD who rules over all,
how lovely is the place where
you live!

I long to be in the courtyards of the
LORD's temple.
I deeply long to be there.
My whole being cries out
for the living God.
LORD who rules over all,
even the sparrow has found a
home near your altar.
My King and my God,
the swallow also has a nest there,
where she may have her young.

A single day in your courtyards is
better
than a thousand anywhere else.
I would rather guard the door of
the house of my God
than live in the tents of sinful
people.
The LORD God is like the sun that
gives us light.
He is like a shield that keeps us safe.
The LORD blesses us with favor
and honor.
He doesn't hold back anything good
from those whose lives are
without blame.
LORD who rules over all,
blessed is everyone who trusts in
you.

Psalm 90

Lord, from the very beginning
you have been like a home to us.
Before you created the world and
the mountains were made,
from the beginning to the end
you are God.

You turn human beings back to
dust.
You say to them, "Return to
dust."
To you a thousand years are like a day

that has just gone by.
They are like a few hours of the night.
You sweep people away, and they die.
They are like new grass that
grows in the morning.
In the morning it springs up new,
but by evening it's all dried up.
Your anger destroys us.
Your burning anger terrifies us.
You have put our sins right in front
of you.
You have placed our secret sins
where you can see them clearly.
You have been angry with us all of
our days.
We groan as we come to the end
of our lives.
We live to be about 70.
Or we may live to be 80, if we
stay healthy.
But all that time is filled with
trouble and sorrow.
The years quickly pass, and we
are gone.

Who knows how powerful your
anger is?
It's as great as the respect we
should have for you.
Teach us to realize how short our
lives are.
Then our hearts will become wise.

Satisfy us with your faithful love
every morning.
Then we can sing with joy and be
glad all of our days.

Psalm 91

The person who rests in the shadow
of the Most High God will be
kept safe by the Mighty One.
I will say about the LORD,
"He is my place of safety.

He is like a fort to me.
He is my God. I trust in him."

He will certainly save you from
hidden traps
and from deadly sickness.
He will cover you with his wings.
Under the feathers of his wings
you will find safety.
He is faithful. He will keep you
safe like a shield or a tower.
You won't have to be afraid of the
terrors that come during the
night.
You won't have to fear the arrows that
come at you during the day.
You won't have to be afraid of the
sickness that attacks in the
darkness.
You won't have to fear the plague
that destroys at noon.
A thousand may fall dead at your
side.
Ten thousand may fall near your
right hand.
But no harm will come to you.

The LORD will command his angels
to take good care of you.
They will lift you up in their hands.
Then you won't trip over a stone.
You will walk all over lions and cobras.
You will crush mighty lions and
poisonous snakes.

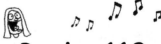

Psalm 119

How can a young person keep his
life pure?
By living in keeping with your word.
I trust in you with all my heart.
Don't let me wander away from
your commands.
I have hidden your word in my heart
so that I won't sin against you.

LORD, I give praise to you.
>Teach me your orders.
With my lips I talk about
>all of the decisions you have made.
Following your covenant laws gives
me joy
>just as great riches give joy to others.
I spend time thinking about your rules.
>I consider how you want me to live.
I take delight in your orders.
>I won't fail to obey your word.

Psalm 121

I look up to the hills.
>Where does my help come from?
My help comes from the LORD.
He is the Maker of heaven and earth.
He won't let your foot slip.
He who watches over you won't get
tired.
In fact, he who watches over Israel
won't get tired or go to sleep.

The LORD watches over you.
>The LORD is like a shade tree at
your right hand.
The sun won't harm you during the day.
The moon won't harm you during
the night.
The LORD will keep you from every
kind of harm.
>He will watch over your life.
The LORD will watch over your life
no matter where you go,
both now and forever.

Psalm 122

I was very glad when they said to me,
>"Let us go up to the house of the
LORD."

The tribes of the LORD go there to
praise his name.
>They do it in keeping with the
law he gave to Israel.
The thrones of the family line of
David are there.
>That's where the people are
judged.

Pray for the peace of Jerusalem. Say,
"May those who love you be
secure.
May there be peace inside your
walls.
>May your people be kept safe."

Psalm 139

LORD, you have seen what is in my
heart.
>You know all about me.
You know when I sit down and
when I get up.
>You know what I'm thinking
even though you are far
away.

You know when I go out to work
and when I come back home.
>You know exactly how I live.
LORD, even before I speak a word,
you know all about it.

You are all around me. You are
behind me and in front of
me.
>You hold me in your power.
I'm amazed at how well you know me.
>It's more than I can understand.
How can I get away from your
Spirit?
>Where can I go to escape from
you?
If I go up to the heavens, you are
there.

If I lie down in the deepest parts of the
earth, you are also there.
Suppose I were to rise with the sun
in the east
and then cross over to the west
where it sinks into the ocean.
Your hand would always be there
to guide me.
Your right hand would still be
holding me close.
Suppose I were to say, "I'm sure the darkness will hide me.
The light around me will become
as dark as night."
Even that darkness would not be
dark to you.
The night would shine like the day,
because darkness is like light to you.
You created the deepest parts of my
being.
You put me together inside my
mother's body.
How you made me is amazing and
wonderful.
I praise you for that.
What you have done is wonderful.
I know that very well.
None of my bones was hidden from
you
when you made me inside my
mother's body.
That place was as dark as the
deepest parts of the earth.
When you were putting me together
there,
your eyes saw my body even
before it was formed.
You planned how many days I
would live.
You wrote down the number of
them in your book before I had
lived through even one of them.
God, your thoughts about me are
priceless.
No one can possibly add them all up.
If I could count them,
they would be more than the
grains of sand.

If I were to fall asleep counting and
then wake up,
you would still be there with me.

God, see what is in my heart.
Know what is there.
Put me to the test.
Know what I'm thinking.
See if there's anything in my life
you don't like.
Help me live in the way that is
always right.

Psalm 146

Praise the LORD.

I will praise the LORD.
I will praise the LORD all my life.
I will sing praise to my God as
long as I live.

Don't put your trust in human
leaders.
Don't trust in people. They can't
save you.
When they die, they return to the
ground.
On that very day their plans are
bound to fail.

Blessed are those who depend on
the God of Jacob for help.
Blessed are those who put their
hope in the LORD their God.
He is the Maker of heaven and
earth and the ocean.
He made everything in them.
The LORD remains faithful forever.
He stands up for those who are
beaten down.
He gives food to hungry people.
The LORD sets prisoners free.
The LORD gives sight to those
who are blind.

The LORD lifts up those who feel
　　helpless.
　　The LORD loves those who do
　　　　what is right.
The LORD watches over the
　　outsiders who live in our
　　land.
　　He takes good care of children
　　　　whose fathers have died.
　　He also takes good care of
　　　　widows.
But he causes evil people to fail
　　in everything they do.

The LORD rules forever.
　　The God of Zion will rule for all
　　　　time to come.
Praise the LORD.

Psalm 147

Praise the LORD.

How good it is to sing praises to
　　our God!
　　How pleasant and right it is to
　　　　praise him!

The LORD builds up Jerusalem.
　　He gathers the scattered people of
　　　　Israel.
He heals those who have broken
　　hearts.
　　He takes care of their wounds.

He decides how many stars there
　　should be.
　　He gives each one of them a
　　　　name.
Great is our Lord. His power is
　　mighty.
　　There is no limit to his
　　　　understanding.

Psalm 148

Praise the LORD.

Praise the LORD from the heavens.
　　Praise him in the heavens above.
Praise him, all his angels.
　　Praise him, all his angels in
　　　　heaven.
Praise him, sun and moon.
　　Praise him, all you shining stars.
Praise him, you highest heavens.
　　Praise him, you waters above the
　　　　skies.
Let all of them praise the name of
　　the LORD.

Psalm 150

Praise the LORD.

Praise God in his holy temple.
　　Praise him in his mighty heavens.
Praise him for his powerful acts.
　　Praise him because he is greater
　　　　than anything else.
Praise him by blowing trumpets.
　　Praise him with harps and lyres.
Praise him with tambourines and
　　dancing.
　　Praise him with stringed
　　　　instruments and flutes.
Praise him with clashing cymbals.
　　Praise him with clanging cymbals.

Let everything that has breath
　　praise the LORD.

Praise the LORD.
Praise the LORD.

Proverbs

PROVERBS

Now Doing 2999

QUIET

SONGS

Now Doing 1004

In the Book of Proverbs we read the wisdom of King Solomon.

A proverb is a brief saying of truth and insight to guide a person in right living. These short bursts of wisdom have universal value that apply to everyone in all generations, in all lands.

Solomon gathered together 3,000 proverbs with only a few hundred in this book of wisdom. Although written over 2,700 years ago, they are as up to date as this morning's newspaper.

Solomon also wrote 1,005 songs with only the Song of Solomon included in the Bible.

Proverbs

If you really want to gain knowledge you must begin by having respect for the LORD

Post A Proverb

The LORD tears down the proud person's house. But he keeps the widow's property safe.

Wounds from a friend can be trusted. But an enemy kisses you many times.

Pride only leads to arguing. But those who take advice are wise.

Above everything else, guard your heart. It is where your life comes from.

If you churn cream, you will produce butter. If you twist a nose, you will produce blood. And if you stir up anger, you will produce a fight.

Those who make fun of others will be judged. Foolish people will be punished.

A man who is rich might have to pay to save his life. But a poor person is not in danger of that.

The lights of godly people shine brightly. But the lamps of sinners are blown out.

Proverbs

Those who erase a sin by forgiving it show love. But those who talk about it come between close friends.

Stones are heavy. Sand weighs a lot. But letting a foolish person make you angry is a heavier load than both of them.

If you don't pay attention to the law, even your prayers are hated.

Anyone who hides his sins doesn't succeed. But anyone who admits his sins and gives them up finds mercy.

Being warned openly is better than being loved in secret.

As iron sharpens iron, so one person sharpens another.

When you are full, you even hate honey. When you are hungry, even what is bitter tastes sweet.

If you don't have wood, your fire goes out. If you don't talk about others, arguing dies down.

There is a way that may seem right to a man. But in the end it leads to death.

Trust in the LORD with all your heart. Do not depend on your own understanding.

Proverbs

It is better to be poor and live without blame than to be rich and follow a crooked path.

Commit to the LORD everything you do. Then your plans will succeed.

Worry makes a man's heart heavy. But a kind word cheers him up.

it is better to have respect for the LORD and have little than to be rich and have trouble.

Coal glows. Wood burns. And a man who argues stirs up fights.

Hard times chase those who are sinful.

A man who won't share what he has wants to get rich. He doesn't know he is going to be poor.

A meal of vegetables where there is love is better than the finest meat where there is hatred.

It is better to eat a dry crust of bread in peace and quiet than to eat a big dinner in a house that is full of fighting.

Anyone who walks with wise people grows wise. But a companion of foolish people suffers harm.

Proverbs

A sinner is trapped by his own evil acts. He is held tight by the ropes of his sins. He will die because he refused to be corrected. His sins will capture him because he was very foolish.

People who refuse to work want things and get nothing. But the longings of people who work hard are completely satisfied.

A gentle answer turns anger away.

The LORD watches a man's ways. He studies all of his paths.

The teaching of wise people is like a fountain that gives life. It turns those who listen to it away from the jaws of death.

If you are afraid of people, it will trap you. But if you trust in the LORD, he will keep you safe.

Wine causes you to make fun of others, and beer causes you to start fights. Anyone who is led down the wrong path by them is not wise.

Those who trust in their riches will fall. But those who do right will be as healthy as a green leaf.

Wise people keep their knowledge to themselves. But the hearts of foolish people shout foolish things.

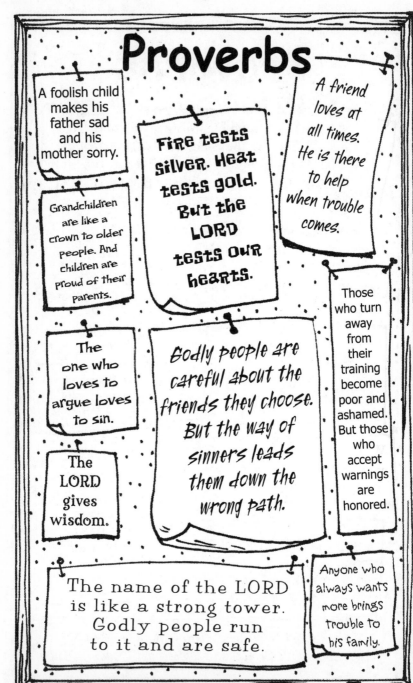

Proverbs

A foolish child makes his father sad and his mother sorry.

Grandchildren are like a crown to older people. And children are proud of their parents.

Fire tests silver. Heat tests gold. But the LORD tests our hearts.

A friend loves at all times. He is there to help when trouble comes.

The one who loves to argue loves to sin.

Godly people are careful about the friends they choose. But the way of sinners leads them down the wrong path.

Those who turn away from their training become poor and ashamed. But those who accept warnings are honored.

The LORD gives wisdom.

The name of the LORD is like a strong tower. Godly people run to it and are safe.

Anyone who always wants more brings trouble to his family.

Proverbs

A person who talks about others tells secrets. So avoid anyone who talks too much.

Everything a man does might seem right to him. But the LORD knows what he is thinking.

Don't say, "I'll get even with you for the wrong you did to me!" Wait for the LORD, and he will save you.

We think even a foolish person is wise if he keeps silent.

An evil messenger gets into trouble. But a messenger who is trusted brings healing.

Food gained by cheating tastes sweet to a man. But he will end up with a mouth full of sand.

When the storm is over, sinners are gone. But those who do right stand firm forever.

Anyone who guards what he says guards his life. But anyone who speaks without thinking will be destroyed.

Wise people act in keeping with the knowledge they have. But foolish people show how foolish they are.

To know the Holy One is to gain understanding.

Dear God:

I want a fresh start today. I would like more clarity and confidence, but most of all, I desire a new connection with you. Thank you for loving me and sending your Son - Jesus - to die so I could be forgiven. Help me understand your love and plan for my life.

Jesus, as best as I know how, I want to get to know you and learn to love and trust you. By faith, I invite you to be the Lord and Savior of my life from this day forward.

Thank you … Amen.